Where Freedom Reigns

Volume One:
A Great Thunder From The Mountain

by

R.A.R. Clouston

authorHOUSE

1663 LIBERTY DRIVE, SUITE 200
BLOOMINGTON, INDIANA 47403
(800) 839-8640
www.authorhouse.com

© 2004 R.A.R. Clouston
All Rights Reserved.

First published by AuthorHouse 08/03/04

ISBN: 1-4184-0433-0 (e)
ISBN: 1-4184-0431-4 (sc)
ISBN: 1-4184-0432-2 (dj)

Library of Congress Control Number: 2004091117

Printed in the United States of America
Bloomington, Indiana

This book is printed on acid-free paper.

To Geri—whom I shall love forever and after.

No man chooses evil because it is evil; he only mistakes it for happiness, the good he seeks.

Mary Wollstonecraft, "A Vindication of the Rights of Men"

PROLOGUE

Kingdom of the Wind Spirit

April, 1914

Who has seen the wind?
Neither you nor I:
But when the trees bow down their heads,
The wind is passing by.

Christina Georgina Rossetti

Bitterroot Mountains, Idaho

The old man moved through the forest as if he and it were one. The gracefulness of his movement made it difficult to tell whether he was part of the wilderness or it was part of him. Beside him, a dark-eyed little boy skipped along, stopping every now and then to poke at a bug, or smell a flower. Like any four year old, he was oblivious to the mystery and majesty about them. The boy was the old man's grandson, and together they climbed the trail through tall pines that had stood for centuries as sentinels on the mountain known to their people as the Kingdom of the Wind Spirit.

The old man's clothes and adornments were those of a chief of the Nimiipuu tribe, whom the Lewis & Clark expedition had named the Nez Perce over four generations earlier. His name was Gray Wolf. He had been a mighty warrior, and the scar on his face and sadness in his eyes bore silent testimony to the years of pain and privation his people had suffered at the hands of the white man. But his proud manner and quiet dignity showed that although he'd been bloodied, he had never been bowed.

Gray Wolf had been a wise and able leader of his people. He had served them well, but as he walked up the mountain that day, he knew in his heart that the life he had known was gone and would not come again, and that the age of untamed innocence was over. It had been ten years since the last of his people's great leaders, Chief Joseph, joined their ancestors, and Gray Wolf sensed that he would soon follow. Chief Joseph's eloquent and haunting speech of surrender in the Bear Paw Mountains, in which he said, "Hear me, my chiefs, my heart is sick and sad. From where the sun now stands, I will fight no more against the white man," had been etched permanently in the chief's soul. On many nights he had laid awake in the darkness and wondered about what might have been had his people not trusted the Great Father Chief in Washington. But now, as the white man's world stood poised on the brink of war, the only world that the chief had ever known was fading into the shadowbox of history. However, the betrayal and lies were all behind him now, and on that warm spring day, as the deep snow that blanketed the mountain melted and ran down the hillside in streams of liquid silver, his mind was not on the past nor the future; instead, it was focused on the present and on his grandson and their time together. It was all he had left in life, and somehow, it was enough.

Gray Wolf loved the little boy as deeply as he did his own son, the little one's father, but he was part of a generation that had begun to drift away from the legend and the legacy of his people. As much as it hurt him, the chief could not be angry at this, for the old ways were dying. A new century weighed heavily upon his shoulders, while his feet were firmly planted in the past. Now, as he journeyed to the top of the mountain with the youngest of his bloodline, he sensed that it would be for the last time. Yet he felt no bitterness nor self-pity, only the deep and abiding love that he, and the ghosts of the warriors who walked beside him, had for the land, the sky, and all things living between.

"This is a good day, little one," the chief said, drawing in a deep breath filled with the perfume of the pine needles that formed a soft carpet under their feet.

"Yes, grandfather, this is a good day," said the little boy cheerfully.

"This day we celebrate your fourth year of life by coming to the place where the spirits of our ancestors dwell."

"Will they have presents for me, grandfather?" asked the little boy expectantly, as he scurried along, taking two steps to every one of the old man.

The old man smiled gently, "Yes, my child, but they will not be like the necklace you wear."

Around his neck, the little boy wore a necklace of beads made of shell and bone, and on it hung a small amulet in the shape of an eagle with outstretched wings. The chief had made it for him out of shiny metal, and the little boy wore it constantly, even while he slept. As he bounced along the trail beside his grandfather, the eagle twisted and danced happily above the little one's heart.

"What will they be made of?"

"They will be made out of the sky and the wind and the mountains. They will fill your heart with happiness and your eyes with wonder, and when you are old like I am, they will still be with you long after the beads are gone."

"When can I see them, grandfather?"

"Be patient, little one. We are almost there."

They walked along the sun-dappled trail and soon, the trees began to thin. Suddenly, they broke out of the shadows onto a sunlit meadow perched high on the side of the mountain. Before them lay a magnificent panorama of purple peaks standing shoulder to shoulder like a parade of kings, dressed in robes of emerald and cinnamon, with their feet bathed in the crystal waters of a wild, winding river, and their heads wrapped in crowns of snow and ice. Around them, the breezes made the wildflowers dance, and the sun chased billowing clouds with flat, gray bottoms across an azure sky. It was the place the Nez Perce called the doorstep to paradise.

The old man grew silent as he surveyed all that lay before them. He closed his eyes and stretched his arms like the wings of an eagle, as if to catch the wind, and he began to dance. It was a rhythmic dance with deliberate movements of his moccasined feet to the steady beat of an unseen drummer.

TOM, tom, tom, tom. TOM, tom, tom, tom.
TOM, tom, tom, tom. TOM, tom, tom, tom.

As he danced, he recited the words of an ancient tribal chant that had been passed down by generations long gone. The little boy watched spellbound, and slowly the magic of the moment gathered him up, and the spirit of his people came upon him. He closed his eyes and began to dance beside his grandfather. The flowers and the trees danced with them, and the sun's rays streamed down from between the clouds, spotlighting them; and for one brief moment, it was as if all the energy of the universe was captured on that meadow, as the old man and the little boy made slow circles on the bosom of mother earth.

TOM, tom, tom, tom. TOM, tom, tom, tom.
TOM, tom, tom, tom. TOM, tom, tom, tom.

Then it was over. The moment had passed. The old man stopped and opened his eyes, but the little one's eyes were still closed, and he kept dancing in a tight little circle, chanting the words that he had heard the old man say, with his little arms outstretched, and the sun reflecting off his shiny black hair. The sight filled the old man with joy and he wept openly without shame. Finally, the little boy sensed that he was dancing by himself. One eye peeked open, then both, and he stopped. At first he was embarrassed, but the chief grabbed him and drew him tightly to his chest and said, "Today little one, the spirits of our fathers have come into you, and they will be with you and protect you forever." Then the chief held him high above his head and slowly turned in place so that the child could take in one last sweeping look at the wonder before them. "You see before you, grandson, the gifts that the Great Spirit gave to our people, so that we would know him and be glad."

The little boy was wide-eyed as he took in the panorama, but when his grandfather put him down on the ground he looked up at the old man and said, "I would rather have the gifts you give me, grandfather." As he said it, he grasped his eagle charm tightly as if the Great Spirit was going to take it from him.

The chief smiled and patted the little boy on the head, "It is all right my son. One day you will understand." They stood there quietly for a few more minutes, alone amidst the grandeur that surrounded them. Gray Wolf knew in his heart that it was a special moment—one that would never come again.

Suddenly the silence was shattered by a strange mixture of sounds. It was a broken scream punctuated by deep-throated croaking. Several large birds appeared in the sky, locked in aerial combat, twisting and turning as they rode the strong updrafts that gave the mountain its name. The chief could see that one was a large female bald eagle, which was being tormented by a terror of ravens. The eagle was bigger than the males of her species, as was usually the case, with a wingspan of over six feet. She had a sleek, dark brown body that contrasted sharply with the white feathers on her head and tail, along with a massive yellow beak and golden eyes that flashed angry glances like lightning bolts toward her tormentors. As the chief and his grandson watched silently, she expertly climbed and rolled and dived above the windswept landscape, slashing out with her oversized feet and deadly talons, slicing through the turbulent air, several times only narrowly missing inflicting lethal wounds upon the big black birds. But the leader of the ravens was a big male with a wingspan only a foot shorter than the eagle's. His feathers, beak, and feet were the color of midnight, and his dark brown eyes were fixed in an unrelenting stare upon her. Finally, the eagle tired of the game, and with powerful down strokes of her wings, she climbed swiftly toward the heavens, leaving her pursuers far below. Then she was gone, disappearing beyond the tree line at the top of the ridge. Deprived of their target, the ravens circled aimlessly for a moment and the little boy was certain they were looking at him. He snuggled in close beside his grandfather. Then they swooped down toward the valley, and the sky was empty once again.

"Grandfather, why did the ravens fight with the eagle?"

"Because that is their destiny."

"What is destiny?"

Gray Wolf smiled but did not answer. Instead he took a long, last look at the scene before them, grasped the little boy's hand and guided him back into the forest. As they walked, the old man began to speak in a soft and gentle way; the way he always did when he told stories passed down to him by his father, and his father before that.

"Long ago, before the time of our people, there was a tribe of mighty warriors who lived upon this mountain. It was a time of plenty, because the forest was filled with game and the rivers teemed with fish. It was a time of peace for the people, because their warriors were brave and mighty; they had defeated their only enemies who lived in the north, and their enemies were afraid of them and left them alone. So the women and the children of the tribe could walk safely on the land and tend to their crops of maize that grew tall and fat in the sun."

The little boy clutched his grandfather's hand tightly, and he listened intently as the chief began to weave the magic spell of the legend of the eagle and the raven.

"In the tribe, there lived a beautiful princess, who was the daughter of the chief. Her name was Wind Dancer, because when she walked, she seemed to dance on the wind. She was so fair that the wildflowers in the meadows leaned toward her whenever she passed by, and the trees whispered her name. She was in love with a young warrior named Runs With Thunder, and he loved her. He was big and strong and as courageous as the other warriors in the tribe, but there was something different about him; something that set him apart. It was that he did not like to fight. He was the tribe's best horseman and always fought bravely in battle, but his heart was not in it; and after it was over, a darkness came about him, a darkness that only Wind Dancer could break.

The chief liked Runs With Thunder, but he could not approve of their love. He wanted his daughter to marry Blood Moon, who was the younger brother of Runs With Thunder. Like his brother, Blood Moon was tall and strong, but unlike his brother, he was quick to anger. In battle, he never showed his enemies any mercy. When they were little boys, the brothers ran and played together through the fields and forests, but when they grew to be men and took up the ways of the warrior, Blood Moon turned away from his older brother because he was jealous of him."

"Was he jealous because the princess loved his brother?"

"No, grandson. Blood Moon believed he could take Wind Dancer away from his brother whenever he wanted. He was jealous because his brother had something he knew he could never take away from him."

"What was it, grandfather?"

"A pure heart."

The little boy looked down at his chest where the eagle amulet lay directly over his own heart. "Do I have a pure heart?"

The old man smiled and said gently, "Yes, my grandson, and no one will ever be able to take it from you."

The old man's words made the little boy happy, and he looked back up at him and said, "What happened to the brothers, grandfather?"

"Wind Dancer was afraid of Blood Moon, and she refused his efforts to win her love. The chief loved his daughter very much, but he was old, and he knew that he would not live much longer. He had no son to follow him, and he worried that after he was dead, their enemies from the north would return and attack his people. He thought that by his daughter marrying Blood Moon, their tribe would get a powerful new chief who would protect them from their enemies, so he ordered Wind Dancer to do this, and the wedding day was set.

But Wind Dancer's heart told her she could not obey her father, and on the eve of the wedding, she and Runs With Thunder decided to run away. They agreed that during the night she would leave her father's teepee and climb this mountain where she would wait for him. In the morning, he would take horses and food, and tell the tribe that he was going to hunt elk. As they whispered this plan to each other, an old woman overheard them, and she went and told Blood Moon. He became angry and during the night he came up on the mountain and hid in the forest.

The next morning, Runs With Thunder rode his great white horse up the mountain, and he came out onto this meadow where Wind Dancer was waiting for him. When he saw her, he dismounted and ran to her, and their hearts were happy. But at that moment, Blood Moon appeared at the other side of the meadow on a white horse as big and powerful as that of his brother. Blood Moon demanded that Runs With Thunder give Wind Dancer to him, but he refused. So he had his horse charge Runs With Thunder and knock him down. Then he fell upon him, and while Wind Dancer watched helplessly, a terrible fight took place. Runs With Thunder fought bravely, but it soon became clear to Wind Dancer that he could not win, for Blood Moon was bigger and stronger, and his heart was filled with evil. She called out to Blood Moon and pleaded that she would marry him if he would spare Runs With Thunder's life. But he would not listen. Instead, the two brothers fought and wrestled and rolled, nearer and nearer to the cliff, until finally, Runs With Thunder stood teetering on the edge. Hovering there between this world and the next, Runs With Thunder realized that he was about to die, and he looked his brother in the eyes and said, "I love you, my brother." In that moment, the wind died, and the trees and wildflowers stood still; it was as if the world had stopped. Blood Moon thrust his arm out toward Runs With Thunder, and he fell to the rocks far below."

The little boy's eyes grew wide, "Did he die, grandfather?"

"Yes, grandson. He died. Wind Dancer was overtaken with grief, and she wept openly. Blood Moon came up to her and cried out that he had tried to save his brother, but she did not believe him. To his horror, Wind Dancer then threw herself off the mountain."

The little boy gasped.

"But the Great Spirit had seen the fight, and he was touched by the love of Wind Dancer for Runs With Thunder. So as she fell, he turned her into a bald eagle, and she swooped down and gently took the body of Runs With Thunder into her talons. She carried him toward the heavens where she dropped his body; and as he fell, the Great Spirit changed him into an eagle, and together they soared and danced upon the wind.

Blood Moon's heart was broken, for he had not pushed his brother off the mountain. In that last second, he had tried to save him, but failed. Now seeing the sight of the two eagles, he decided to join them, and jumped off the cliff. But the Great Spirit was angry with him and turned him into a raven, a bird with great strength and power and a sharp mind and eye like the eagle, but cloaked in black from head to foot, a bird doomed forever to be a scavenger and to be known as the messenger of death. Since that day, the raven and the eagle have been mortal enemies."

The little boy thought carefully about what his grandfather had told him, and asked a question that caught the old man by surprise. "Grandfather, if ravens are evil, why did the Great Spirit make them?"

The old man paused before answering. Then he said softly, "The Great Spirit made the raven because without it, we would never know how good the eagle is."

The little boy nodded and looked down at the eagle amulet. He took it in his hands and admired it, but as he did, he didn't see the protruding root in the trail, and he tripped over it and fell. Gray Wolf reached out to him, but his hand caught the back of the necklace. It broke, throwing the beads and the eagle amulet into the air. The eagle hit the ground first, bounced once, and disappeared into a deep crack between a boulder and the hillside. The chief fell to his knees and peered into the crack, but it was too small for him to reach inside it, and it was too deep for the little boy. Sadly they stood up, and the little boy started to cry. The chief picked him up and spoke softly to him, "Do not cry, grandson. I will make you another eagle more beautiful than the one you have just lost."

"I do not want another one, grandfather. I want that one."

"That eagle is gone, my child, and you must let it go. It is the way of life that beautiful things come into our world and then pass on. We do not own them. All that we can do is to love them while they are here."

The tearful boy stared up into his grandfather's eyes and then said, "Will you pass on too, grandfather?"

"Yes, my child, but just like your eagle, my spirit will live on this mountain forever. And knowing that we are both here for you will make you happy."

Sadly the little boy replied, "Yes, grandfather, it will make me happy." He rested his head on the mighty warrior's shoulders, and the two of them melted into the shadows of the forest, on the mountain known as the Kingdom of the Wind Spirit.

September, 2017

G Day - 360

A Feather In The Wind

The day is done, and the darkness
Falls from the wings of the Night,
As a feather is wafted downward
From an eagle in his flight.

Henry Wadsworth Longfellow, "The Day Is Done"

1

Bitterroot Mountains, Idaho

If the men in the trucks knew they were about to unlock the gates of hell, they gave no sign of it. Instead, they were more intent on finishing their beers and baying out the windows at the pale moon, which slipped like a ghost rider across the empty, night sky. All of them, that is, except the men driving the trucks who were concentrating intently on steering clear of the precipice that gnawed away at the edge of the winding mountain road. They were simple and decent men, whose past crimes consisted of an occasional misdemeanor and perpetual foolishness—hardly what one might expect as the outriders of the apocalypse.

Fifty-three men of Company A of the Wolf River Militia headed up the mountain on that brisk evening in early autumn. It was an odd group consisting of a few veterans of the anti-government movement mixed with a larger and more vocal group of young idealists. For most, it would be a one-way trip. Their reason for going was difficult to define, even by the few among them who had a college education. Their reason for being was even less clear, since there no longer was a Company B, or C for that matter, and they were increasingly having difficulty recruiting new members to replace the ones who kept drifting away. Had they stayed home that night, the group might have lasted for another year or two; but they didn't, and their time together was quickly drawing to an end. And for most, their time with loved ones was already over.

They all knew they were taking a risk; some sensed it might even be dangerous, but it didn't matter, because their spirits were fortified by the false bravado created when alcohol is mixed in equal parts with passion. So

3

they put on their military fatigues, left their homes and families, and rode up the mountain in the moonlight, while no one much noticed or gave a damn. But all that was about to change. The chain of events that they would set in motion would soon put the name of the mountain on everyone's lips; and ironically, while the Nez Perce called it the Kingdom of the Wind Spirit, the world would come to know it by the name Lewis and Clark had given it, which was Mount Freedom.

Their leader, Captain Thomas Porter, thirty-four, was sitting quietly in the front passenger seat of the Humvee that led the convoy of pick-up trucks and military vehicles up the rough gravel road. He was a ruggedly handsome man with a heavy build that made him appear shorter than his six foot height, with a quick wit and a quicker smile, both of which came and went in an instant, often leaving behind a brooding darkness. Articulate and charismatic, he had an intensity about him that was captivating, and yet somehow exhausting to those with whom he dealt; but at that particular moment neither his smile nor his wit were in evidence. As he stared out the open window and felt the cool night air slip across his cheek, his mind wasn't on his mission, or his men. Rather it was on himself, which was where it had been most of his life. He didn't do it consciously; it just always seemed to end up there. No matter how hard he tried, he couldn't force himself to stay interested for very long in anyone or anything that wasn't of benefit to him. That fateful autumn night was no different. Instead of focusing upon the task that lay ahead, his mind kept drifting back to his past; and the outward calm that appeared on his face belied a restlessness within that paced back and forth in the recesses of his mind, like a lion held back by the flickering flames of a dying campfire. As much as he tried to ignore it, somewhere deep inside, a little voice kept telling him that he was about to die. And what was even more telling, was that he didn't care.

DYING HAD BEEN the last thing on Porter's mind when he left Silicon Valley three years earlier. At the time, he told everyone that he just wanted to get away; although when asked from what, he just mumbled something about idols and icons, platinum cards, and plastic people. In the beginning, as he struggled to build his company, it had all been fun, but it was a way of life he soon came to loathe. Like so many others of his kind, once he had made his fortune, he came to disavow the quest for wealth. He was too smart not to realize the hypocrisy in this, and he used to joke that those who spoke out strongly against greed had exercised their stock options the year before; but he didn't care. It all became too much, so he resigned as Chairman and CEO of Communitrex, the giant communications conglomerate he had founded, took his billions of dollars, and headed north with his wife and her seven cats.

They bought a parcel of land near Dillon, Montana, one that his wife liked to boast was bigger than half the states back East. She had grown up poor in a rich New England town. When Thomas met her, she was a stunning red-head who liked to wear tight shirts and short skirts. She was working as a secretary for a temp agency with one marriage already behind her, and if there was one person who was responsible for giving him his obsession for money, it was her. Fortunately, his lust for her had not made him blind to reason, and the one smart thing he had done was to insist upon a pre-nuptial agreement. It would later prove prescient. By the time they moved to Montana, she had acquired a circle of elitist friends along with the material possessions to match. At her insistence, Porter built a twenty-room house out of red pine, marble, and wild river rock, and settled down to get back to a quieter and simpler life. His wife put in an enormous organic vegetable garden, or at least the hired help did, and she started raising a rare breed of British chickens that had a peculiar habit of dropping over dead in response to sudden, loud noises.

Meanwhile, Porter filled his days with an eclectic mixture of intellectual and physical pursuits that included learning how to fly. In typical fashion for the chronic overachiever, he earned not only his multi-engine, fixed wing but his rotor license as well, and very few days went by when he couldn't be seen buzzing his house in one of his new multi-million dollar flying toys. He built a private airport on his land and invited all his pilot friends to hangar their planes there. With their help and his money, they bought over fifty vintage aircraft from World War One through Vietnam. He even tried to buy a damaged F22 Raptor but the Federal Government wouldn't let him. Undaunted, he learned to fly everything he could, and on any given day, he and his band of boys, who never grew up, could be seen wheeling and soaring in the skies of western Montana. Locals called them the Peter Pan Squadron and Porter loved it. He set aside a thousand acres of his ranch, and after a healthy contribution to the county and state governments, he was granted permission to bomb targets on the range. His favorite targets were Army surplus tanks, and he seemed obsessed with blowing them up. He was

5

at his happiest above the clouds, and at the end of each day's flying, the one thing that gave him particular joy was to buzz the ranch and wreak havoc among his wife's chickens.

Every night after he returned home from the squadron's mess in the W.W. II era hangar, which he had had shipped from England, he would sit down to a late dinner in the enormous dining hall he called Valhalla; and while being served dinner by an attentive staff of seven at a table that could seat forty and on china that had once belonged to a Scottish king, he would tell his disinterested wife how he planned to help those less fortunate than himself. In particular, he talked endlessly about the plight of Native Americans, whom he believed were the forgotten victims of genocide. He planned to establish a free emergency medical flight service for the Indian reservations that dotted the western landscape, and he even went so far as to order a fleet of specially equipped small jets and helicopters that would be donated to the people of the reservations. Unfortunately, his days of altruism hadn't lasted long.

His wife soon grew tired of the ranch and his increasingly long periods of absence. She became intensely jealous of the Peter Pan squadron and finally threatened to leave him if they didn't sell everything and start over. Reluctantly, he sold the ranch and his air force, and bought her seventy acres of land in Sun Valley, Idaho. There they built a house even bigger than the one in Montana and quickly became the darlings of Rocky Mountain high society. Not a day went by that a glowing article about them didn't appear in the social pages of the Idaho Statesman. Thomas Porter loved every minute of it. He couldn't seem to live life fast enough. He acted as if it would go on forever, oblivious to the fact that it wouldn't. Oblivious, that is, up until the ride up the mountain that night when the little voice began its haunting soliloquy inside his head.

At first, his involvement with the militia had been nothing more than a lark. It began when Edward Morrissey, the Governor of Idaho conferred on him a commission in the National Guard in recognition for the seven figures of soft money he had contributed to the state's Republican party—money that had guaranteed the governor's reelection. It was strictly an honorary appointment, but Porter seemed driven to make it more than that, often attending their parades and week-end bivouacs where he—and his money— were always welcome. His wife had made him promise that he wouldn't fly anymore, and his involvement with the Army Guard kept her quiet. He liked the uniform and the feeling of power that it gave him. And most of all, he soon grew to like being around guns and the men who carried them, some would say, too much.

In his youth, he had accompanied his older brother, who had done his share of reducing the earth's cottontail population with a .22 Long Rifle. But he had never shot any himself. In fact, up until being made a captain in the Guard, he never cared much about guns or the matter of gun ownership. Gradually, however, he had been drawn into the debate over gun control that burned like a wildfire across America. Applying the same skills that had made him rich, he became an outspoken and passionate leader of the pro-gun movement in the state. It didn't go unnoticed by both friend and foe alike.

One day a group of guardsmen approached him and asked him to join the militia. It was a secretive group for whom the rule of law was always open to interpretation, which was not a foreign concept to Porter, so he agreed to attend one of their secret meetings deep in the bush. From that point on, he was hooked. But there was another reason he particularly liked his new-found position of military command—something known only to himself, something even darker than the fear of dying. It traced to a jealousy that burned within him, one that all the money in the world could never satisfy.

"WE'RE HERE, SIR," said his driver, a young freckle-faced private, snapping Captain Thomas Porter back to reality. He peered through the mud-splattered windshield at the padlocked, chain-link gates that stood defiantly in the beam of the headlights. To the right of the gates hung a large metal sign with several laser burns and bullet holes in it. It proclaimed that they were standing before the Bitterroot Rod & Gun Club. A day-glow orange sticker was slapped rudely across the sign with the words, "Closed By Order of the U.S. Forest Service," printed on it in large black letters.

"Thank-you, Private Saints." He reached for the radio microphone and said into it, "Corporal, cut the lock."

"Yes, sir," came the forceful reply and, in an instant, a very large and obese man extricated himself from the truck behind the Humvee.

The man is a life-support system for a belly, thought Porter as he peered in the rear view mirror at the pick-up truck, which seemed to breathe a sigh of relief at the lessening of its load. Bolt cutters in hand, the corporal strode across the dirt road toward the gate, stumbling once over a rock but catching himself as he went.

"The corporal sure is agile for his size, isn't he, sir?" said Saints.

"What?—Oh, yes—He certainly is," lied Porter as the mountain of flesh moved by.

With a swift motion of the bolt cutters, the corporal destroyed the lock and tossed it to the ground. He also unknowingly triggered its satellite-based, remote sensing device but in the context of what they were about to do, it wouldn't matter. He swung the gates open, turned back toward the Humvee, and with a Cheshire grin on his florid face, and with a grandiose sweep of a ponderous arm, he motioned for the convoy to drive through.

I just hope he keeps his cool under pressure, thought Porter. *I hope that I do, too.*

"Well, I guess that's it, sir. Now we've really gone and done it, haven't we, sir?"

"Yes, we have," Porter answered with an air of finality. "Let's go in."

The private put the heavy vehicle in gear and headed it slowly through the gates, followed by the convoy, which stopped only long enough to pick up the winded but excited corporal. Meanwhile, sixty miles away in Missoula, Montana, an alarm went off in the regional offices of the U.S. Forest Service. It would have instantly told anyone monitoring it that the gates of the Bitterroot Rod & Gun Club had been tampered with. However, due to budget cuts in Washington, there was no one on duty and the break-in wouldn't be detected until the militia called the local media themselves later that night.

PORTER'S HUMVEE pulled up to a stop in the center of the Bitterroot Rod & Gun Club compound, right in front of the largest of the seven buildings that sliced in a lazy half circle through the tall pines. The other vehicles quickly did the same, forming a row, which then began disgorging their cargo of men, supplies, and weapons.

Notwithstanding their weapons, they looked more like kids on the first day at summer camp rather than a group of part-time soldiers about to take on the Federal Government. Many of the men hurried to the alleys between the buildings to relieve themselves, and the pungent smell of steaming hot urine added to the noise and confusion—and the darting shadows in the headlights did nothing to assuage the uneasy feeling that wouldn't leave the captain alone.

"Lieutenant Kerwood," Porter shouted at one shadow as it hurried by.

"Yeah," said the lieutenant, as he stopped short in front of the captain. A rodeo rider when he wasn't soldiering, the lieutenant was long on quiet and short on protocol.

"After you get your men and equipment squared away, I want you to assemble everyone in the dining hall. And make sure that none of them brought their NIS cards with them. If they did burn them immediately." He was referring to the mandatory national identification system card. It contained all their vital data, including the person's National Security Number, which had replaced the old Social Security Number; their physical description; retinal and thermal body scan metrics; DNA code; blood type; education; military serial number and record; criminal records, if any; and anything else that someone would ever need, or want, to know about someone else.

"You bet," he said as he turned to leave.

"And Lieutenant—"

"Yes?"

"I know none of us is regular Army but when we're on militia business, you will salute me and refer to me as, sir, or captain. Is that clear?"

With the look of a chastised puppy, the lieutenant snapped to attention and, in an obedient tone of voice, said, "Yes, sir. Sorry about that, Captain."

Softening, Porter replied, "Look, LT, things could get a bit tense up here when the government finds out what we've done. I just want us to stay sharp."

"You don't owe me an apology, Captain. We appreciate what you're doing to help us. I mean, not even being a member of the Rod & Gun Club, and all. If the Feds come up here with guns blazing, I will be mighty glad to have you leading us. That's for goddamn sure—if you'll excuse my French, sir."

"Thank-you, Lieutenant," the captain replied with a pained smile, "Let's hope calmer heads prevail. Carry on and see what's taking the men so long to get the generator started."

With that, the lieutenant wheeled and walked away across the compound. At that same instant, the floodlights snapped on, and the entire scene was immediately bathed in a harsh glare. Porter sensed it was a metaphor for what was to come.

AN HOUR LATER, the captain stood in front of Lieutenant Kerwood and the other men in the dining hall. The room was dimly lit and dank, and the dark mood it created was in stark contrast to the near euphoria that had filled the men when they began their crusade hours earlier. As Porter finished his briefing, they sat blank-faced, holding on tightly to their coffee cups, as if drawing solace from the steaming contents. He asked if there were any questions.

"Permission to speak freely, sir?" the fat corporal asked.

"Permission granted," replied Porter.

"Well, sir, a few of the men were wondering how long we'd be up here."

Porter's eyebrows arched. "We just got here, Corporal."

"I know, sir, but we were just curious."

"We'll be up here until we get the job done," replied the captain firmly, but gently.

It didn't satisfy the corporal. "Begging your pardon, sir, what exactly is our job?"

The lieutenant jumped up, "We've been through this a hundred times, Corporal!"

"I know that, LT," said the corporal defensively. "I just wanted to hear the captain's opinion."

The lieutenant flashed a look of apology at the captain, who smiled and said, "It's okay, I don't mind." Porter paused, carefully considering his reply, then he looked the corporal directly in the eye and said, "As you know, the Forest Service closed this club without any justification. They claimed it was to protect the environment—to reduce the amount of lead dust blowing in the wind. But you and I both know that's a load of cow manure."

"You can say bullshit, Captain," shouted one of the men at the back of the room. "We'll still respect you in the morning."

The room filled with laughter, which was quickly stifled when the lieutenant flashed a disapproving look at the soldier. The captain waited as the room fell silent. Then he began to speak again, in more measured tones. He carefully tailored his words and moderated his loudness, which forced the men at the back to lean forward to hear. It was one of his greatest skills as an orator. He knew his audience, and played to it without either patronizing or pandering. "The real reason for their actions is that the government of the United States of America doesn't like us or our guns. Nothing more. Nothing less." He paused to let the thought sink in. "Gentlemen, there is a growing sentiment in this country that guns, and the people who own them, are evil. That we're part of some wicked conspiracy who dance with delight every time a child finds a loaded gun left lying around, and kills himself, or even worse, someone else." The captain paused again. No one stirred. "But they are wrong." He said it firmly, and without emotion.

Several of the men nodded their heads and mumbled their agreement.

"It is the negligent gun owner who is to blame—not the gun," he continued, raising his voice slightly.

Several more expressed their support, louder this time.

"When a five year-old is left unattended and falls into a swimming pool and drowns, we don't ban pools or blame the pool manufacturer."

More joined in, "No!"

Porter ratcheted up his voice one more level and sharpened his tone, but he did so subtly, allowing the passion of the men to build of its own momentum. "When a dog mauls someone, we don't muzzle all dogs or outlaw dog ownership." It was a simplistic notion, but it served its purpose in the room full of dog owners, many more than one.

This time everyone responded, "No, sir!"

"When a drunken driver crosses the median and kills a car full of innocents, we don't prohibit alcohol or ban cars."

Like an ocean swell, the emotion of the moment began to swallow all those in its path, and the entire company now shouted together, "Hell no!"

Riding this rising tide of emotion but not allowing himself, or the men, to be carried away by it, Porter deftly pulled them back from the edge of climax, which served to prolong and intensify their feelings all the more. In a calm but no less powerful voice, he continued, "If we aren't prepared to fight, and if necessary, die for our rights, then everything our forefathers fought for, and died for, will count for nothing." He paused and stared into their young faces, many with glistening eyes. "Freedom isn't something for some of the people some of the time; freedom is for all of the people all of the time. Not freedom to ignore the law, but freedom to live by the law, and for the law, and under its protection. There can be no greater law, save that created by God himself, than that which is written in the United

States Constitution; and there can be no greater cause, save that of serving God Almighty, than to defend and protect that document. For if we allow one man to take away one right, then what is there to stop other men from taking away other rights? Until all rights are lost and the word freedom means nothing." No one stirred. Porter had always been an eloquent speaker but on that night he had outdone even himself. The silence in the room was deafening. He waited as their brains tried to quiet their pounding heartbeats lest they miss a single word. Then, he looked back at the corporal and began to speak again, slowly and forcefully.

"So, Corporal, we will stay up here on this mountain for as long as it takes to guarantee ourselves, and millions of others like us, the right to own a gun—legally, safely, and without persecution. A right which was guaranteed to us under Article II of the United States Constitution, which as you all know states that—"

At this point the men joined in and recited the quote with him, word for word: "A well-regulated Militia, being necessary to the security of a free State, the right of the people to keep and bear arms *shall not be infringed*!"

Porter stopped and looked slowly and purposefully around the room. Then, in a dead serious tone, he concluded, "Gentlemen, if we don't make a stand, here and now, on this mountain named for freedom, then the beacon of freedom that has stood for over two hundred years upon our shores, shining for all the world to see, will be extinguished forever, and we might as well all be dead." When he finished speaking, there was absolute silence. Everyone sat spellbound. To a more sophisticated audience, his speech would have been viewed as melodramatic, his logic simplistic, his analogies trite; but to that group, that night, on that mountain, it hit the mark dead center. Slowly, one man stood up and started clapping, loudly and powerfully, then another and another, until soon they were all on their feet and the room was filled to overflowing with a grand and glorious sound. It was the sound of freedom.

Finally, after they could clap and cheer no more, the meeting was over. Slowly, the men filed out of the room—all but the lieutenant. "You sure have a way with words, Captain. I wish we had a man like you running this country."

"Thank-you, LT. We did ten years ago but we don't now. However, I can assure you that we do have such a man in the Statehouse."

The lieutenant shrugged. "If you say so, sir."

His reaction surprised Porter. "I do say so. When Governor Morrissey finds out what we have done here tonight he will be sympathetic to our cause. You can trust me on that one. I am confident that he will help us make our point without any bloodshed."

The lieutenant nodded, but he seemed unconvinced. "Should I make the calls now, sir?"

"Yes. Call the Boise newspaper and television stations as discussed, and tell them what we have done."

"Yes, sir," the lieutenant answered with a nervous grin. He saluted and left.

Porter stood alone with his thoughts for a long moment. Finally, he flicked off the lights and followed the lieutenant out the door, stepping into the cold night. At that moment, somewhere in the darkness behind the dining hall, he thought he heard a horse whinny. It immediately caught his attention, not only because there were no horses within twenty miles of the mountain as far as he knew, but also because it didn't sound normal. It was sharp and harsh and deep. He heard it again and he followed the sound between the dining hall and the adjacent building. When he reached the fence at the back of the compound, where the rays of the camp's floodlights were swallowed up by the night, he paused and peered at the forest, his eyes straining to see where the animal might be. But it was useless. In the pale moonlight, the edge of the timber was a sea of dark shadows.

Suddenly, to his right he caught a faint movement in his peripheral vision. Tensing, he reached for his pistol. Slipping it out of its calf skin holster, as quietly as he could, he switched on the built-in laser targeting light beam, and began probing the darkness with its sinister red eye. Cautiously, he edged along the fence. "Who goes there?" he shouted in a voice that had more fear than authority to it.

"Captain. It's me, sir," came the startled reply from the young freckle-faced private.

"Is that you, Private Saints?" he said, pulling the red dot off the private's chest.

"Yes, sir."

The tension gone, the captain switched off the laser, and his voice regained its tough tone. "What are you doing out here?" he asked as he reholstered his side arm and walked over to the private.

"I'm sorry, sir. I thought I heard a horse."

13

The captain stepped beside the young man and together, they looked toward the tree line. "You like horses, do you?"

"Yes, sir. My dad raised quarter horses. He used to say they represented all that was good about the West. Strong and fast with an unbreakable spirit."

The captain didn't answer for a moment as he thought about the imagery. Then he said softly, "Do I take it that your father has passed on?"

"Yes, sir, he was killed in WWT," he replied, referring to the World War on Terrorism that had ended seven years earlier. Even in the shadows, the captain could see the pain on the young man's face.

"I'm sorry. What service was he in?"

"Army, sir. His Bradley was destroyed by one of our helicopters. They call it friendly fire, but my mother never could understand why."

The captain put his arm on the private's shoulder. "I'm very sorry."

The young soldier looked up at the captain and shook his head. "Thank-you, sir."

They stood there for a long moment in silence. Then the private asked, "If you don't mind me asking, sir, what are you doing here?"

"I thought I heard the horse too."

"No, I mean, why are you up here on this mountain with us?"

"I'm here because I believe all the words I said earlier tonight about freedom."

"Yes, I know you do, sir. But with all due respect, I don't think that's it. At least not all of it."

"I beg your pardon?" said the captain, obviously taken aback.

"Please don't be offended sir. I mean, I can't tell you how pleased we all are to have you here with us. But somehow I just don't get why a man like you would want to be part of a group like ours. After all, you were the CEO of a huge company that you started yourself, and you could probably buy this mountain. We're mostly a bunch of tradesmen who only get a brief glimpse into your world when you call us to fix your plumbing or build an addition on your house."

The captain looked at the younger man with a mixture of surprise and admiration. "You are a very astute young man."

"Thank-you, sir. My dad used to say that being poor was no excuse for being stupid."

"Your father was a wise man," said the captain tenderly. "What was his name?"

"Jake."

Porter looked startled. "Jake?"

"Yes."

"I have a brother named Jake. Short for Jeremiah."

"His was just Jake, sir. It wasn't short for anything."

"I see."

"Is he older or younger?" asked Saints.

"He's two years older."

"How long has it been since you saw him?"

Porter looked away and said, "Seven years."

"That's a long time. If you don't mind me asking, why so long?"

"We had a falling out. Over something that doesn't seem important now."

"It's none of my business, sir, but maybe when we get off this mountain you should call him."

"It's too late for that."

"It's never too late, sir, not as long as you are both still alive. I told my dad that I loved him before he left for the war, and I'm glad I did." The private realized that he was preaching and he quickly backed off, "I'm sorry, sir. I had no business prying into your personal affairs."

"It's okay, Private." He patted the young man on the shoulder and added, "Now I think it's time that we both got some sleep."

"Yes, sir."

They started to walk toward the buildings. Suddenly, the private stopped and said, "Captain?"

"Yes?"

The young man hesitated, then shook his head, "Never mind, sir."

"What is it?"

The private mustered his courage. "Do you think a man knows when he is about to die?" He paused, then added, "I mean, does he feel it down deep inside, like something rushing toward him in the darkness, but just not know—nor want to—what it is?

The question took Porter by surprise. At first he didn't respond, then he slowly shook his head. "I don't know; but if I had to guess, I'd say no."

The young man nodded, but it was evident that Porter's answer hadn't satisfied him. "Good night, sir." He saluted smartly, turned, and walked away.

Porter watched him disappear between the buildings. He stood there, lost in thought. *God, please don't let me be the cause of that boy's death,* he thought. And for the first time that evening, his mind wasn't on himself.

AFTER THE CAPTAIN and the private had gone, a heavy thudding noise broke the stillness of the night. It was the slow and steady sound of hoof beats, and as they drew nearer, the ground began to shake, and mourning doves that had been roosting in the pine thickets burst out as if shot by cannons, and fluttered away wildly into the darkness. Then an enormous white stallion appeared at the edge of the forest. With powerful strides it crossed the open ground separating the trees and the compound, until it came to a stop near the spot where the captain and private had been standing. On its back sat a dark rider dressed in a long, flowing, black cloak, with a hood that almost completely covered his head. His features were harsh and jagged, like broken shale, and in the moonlight, his skin was a pallid shade of gray. He had thin, bluish lips and dark eyes set back far in his head, and his black hair was thick and long and straight. In one hand, he held a mighty bow, and on his back was a quiver of arrows with silver shafts that glistened in the dim light. He sat there for a long time staring at the buildings, as one by one the lights inside were turned out, and the muted sound of voices drifted away on the night air.

Suddenly, he heard something deep within the forest. He turned his head and stared in the direction from which it came; his eyes burned through the gloom. Slowly, a knowing smile slipped across his lips as another dark rider, on another white stallion, equally large and powerful, materialized out of the forest. The second rider was also dressed in a long, black flowing cape, except that he wore a heavy bladed sword at his side, the handle of which was gold. With poise and grace and a certainty of purpose, the second horseman guided his mount across the clearing toward the first rider until they, and their mounts, came face to face. The rider threw back his hood, revealing a handsome face with smooth skin that glowed like desert sand at sunset, and eyes the color of the darkest amber. His face was framed by thick hair, the color of mahogany, with curls that cascaded down across his broad, powerful shoulders. He wore a well-trimmed beard of the same

16

color, and there was something about his features and manner that gave hint to an empyreal aristocracy.

The first rider began to speak in Aramaic, an ancient tongue, but he was quickly interrupted by the other rider who said, "Speak in English."

He stopped abruptly, stared at the second horseman for a long moment and then began again. "Very well, Michael, have it your way—you always do."

"If I did, you would no longer exist."

The first rider snorted. "Nor would you, if the same privilege were granted to me."

The rider who identified himself as Michael ignored the comment. "By what name should I address you this time?"

"Chadrian," replied the other rider with a smirk. "Stefan Chadrian."

Michael nodded but showed no emotion. "An anagram of your true name."

"Yes. Clever, is it not? But so far, these pathetic mortals have not seen through it."

"Does it matter? You will destroy all who follow you anyway."

Chadrian shook his head dismissively. "Michael, Michael, Michael. Will you never change?"

"Only the face of evil is ever changing. The face of good is constant in the Lord."

Chadrian's razor thin eyebrows formed an inverted V over his cold, gray face. "So soon the lecture? You have not even told me what surname you have taken this time. I know that you always keep your given name; the one our Father gave you."

"*Our* Father?" asked Michael sarcastically.

"Yes Michael. Whether you like it or not, we are both reflections of Him."

"Yours is but a reflection in a broken mirror."

Rage rose in Chadrian's throat but he controlled it. "Will you tell me your chosen name or must I guess?"

"It is Falconer."

"Falconer! Ah yes. Of course. I always liked Yeats." He paused and then added, "So—it begins again? The battle between good and evil in the hearts of men."

"In some men, yes, but not in all mankind."

17

Chadrian's eyes narrowed. "No, Michael, this time victory over all mankind *will* be mine. I feel it deep within me. With each war, I have brought them one step closer to the edge of the abyss."

Michael stared back with equal intensity. "But they have always turned away from you before it was too late."

"This time there will be no turning back. Evil has grown strong in America. Their leaders are weaklings in body and soul; prone to the sins of power and place and possessions. They are even more stupid than when we last walked among them."

"Not all."

"Enough for my purpose."

"Blind hatred knows no purpose!"

Chadrian finally lost control of his anger and began to speak in Aramaic again. He quoted verse from The Revelation of St. John The Divine, which translated as follows:

> *And they worshipped the dragon which gave*
> *power unto the beast, saying Who is like unto*
> *the beast? Who is able to make war with him?*

Falconer was quick and resolute in his response. He too spoke in the ancient tongue, quoting Revelation:

> *If any man have an ear, let him hear.*
> *He that leadeth into captivity shall go into*
> *captivity: he that killeth with the sword must*
> *be killed with the sword. Here is the patience*
> *and the faith of the Saints.*

Chadrian replied:

> *And it was given unto him to make war*
> *with the Saints, and to overcome them:*
> *and power was given him over all kindreds,*
> *and tongues and nations.*

Falconer persevered:

And I heard a voice from heaven, as the voice
of many waters, and as the voice of a great thunder—

Chadrian snickered, switched back to English and broke out of verse. "You shall have your great thunder, Michael—a great thunder from the mountain! But it will not bring the hour of judgment you seek; instead, it will cause a great darkness to fall upon the land—one that will last forever."

Falconer steeled himself for the battle that he knew was now inevitable. "Yes. And no. There will come a great darkness, and that darkness will lead to a great battle. It will begin 360 days from now, on the day these mortals will call G-Day, as kindred armies march against each other across common ground. But the darkness will be fleeting." He paused, then began to quote Revelation again in Aramaic:

And there shall be no night there; and they
need no candle, neither light of the sun; for
the Lord God giveth them light; and they shall
reign for ever and ever.

With a toss of his head, Chadrian shook off the words and quoted another passage that served his purpose:

For they are the spirits of devils, working miracles,
which go forth unto the kings of the earth and of
the whole world, to gather them to the battle—

Falconer interrupted him and finished the passage:

—of that great day of God Almighty.

Chadrian retorted:

And he gathered them together into a place
called—

They both said the word together, and it echoed through the blackness of the night.

—Armageddon!

Chadrian fell silent, convinced that his point had been made, and that the end of mankind had been foretold.

Falconer was undeterred, but his voice was now lower, tinged with melancholy, and wrapped more in faith than certainty. Again he spoke the words of St. John in the ancient tongue:

> *Behold, the tabernacle of God is with men*
> *and he will dwell with them, and they shall*
> *be his people, and God himself shall be*
> *with them, and be their God.*

When he stopped speaking, a deafening silence fell upon them, punctuated only by the staccato breathing of their horses.

Finally, Chadrian shook his head, and replied, in English, with a sigh, "We shall see, Michael. We shall see." He gathered up his reins and started to leave but then stopped and looked back at his adversary. "Answer this, Michael. If good in the world is pre-ordained, then why is it that God chooses to let me live?—If heaven will reign forever and ever, what need is there for hell?"

Falconer paused before answering, then said softly, "That is not for us to know."

Chadrian shook his head slowly in frustration. "Oh Michael. How predictable. And how empty." He gave a smile that was more sad than sinister, bowed his head in a gesture that bordered on respect, and with a haunting loneliness in his voice, said, "So be it. Let us get on with our destiny." He pulled his hood down over his brow, spurred his horse hard, prompting it to rear up and paw the darkness, and then they melted into the forest. Falconer watched him go, and then with a light tug on the reins, he guided his magnificent horse into the shadows and disappeared.

And the mountain known as the Kingdom of the Wind Spirit surrendered once more to the silence of the night—a silence before the great thunder to come.

2

Lewis & Clark Elementary School, Boise, Idaho

Governor Edward Morrissey, sixty-one, was a successful rancher turned politician. Lanky and laconic, with a face bronzed by the sun and etched by the wind, and with the fierce independence born of riding the range alone, he stood in front of a large group of citizens at a town hall meeting in the school gymnasium. He had used such meetings often when he first ran for governor, and after he was elected, he continued to hold them despite the objections of his staff. They felt they were a zero-sum game, in which the governor could gain very little but lose a lot. However, in addition to being a charming and handsome man with a disarming cowboy way about him, he was also bull-headed, and the meetings continued. Despite the concerns of his staff, on that particular autumn night, the governor was winning as evidenced by the smile on his face and the friendly banter of the crowd.

The governor was a survivor. He had been orphaned at seven, when his father was killed in Vietnam and his mother died of cancer, and he had been raised on a cattle ranch by an uncle who was quick to anger, and even quicker with his belt. At the age of sixteen, Morrissey ran away and got a job on an oil rig. Never one to back down from a fight, regardless of the size and strength of his opponent, he earned the respect of those around him during the day, and his high school diploma at night. He saved enough money to finance his way through college, and after graduation he agreed to help his aunt run the struggling cattle ranch, following the untimely death of his uncle. Upon his beloved aunt's death several years later, he inherited the ranch, which by then he had turned into a thriving operation. Along the way he acquired a taste for politics and when the opportunity presented itself, he successfully ran for governor, financing his multi-million dollar campaign largely out of his own pocket. Morrissey was a true loner who was quick to bridle at the demands of others. It was a trait that had served him well. At least up until that moment in his life. But all that was about to change.

"Yes ma'am, what can I do for you?" he asked, as he pointed at a rosy-cheeked, chubby woman in a plain dress.

"Well, Governor, for starters you could come home with me," she said, punctuating her statement with a giggle, setting off a wave of laughter in the room.

The governor's wife had passed away from cancer three years before he ran for office, and although he had occasionally been seen out in the company of beautiful women, he had never gotten serious about any of them. This fact gave great comfort to the single women of Idaho, and to many of the married ones as well, as each harbored their own personal fantasy about riding off into the sunset with this tall and tanned son of the West.

As soon as the crowd quieted, the governor put on his most charming face and said, "What's your name, darling?"

Her eyes brightened as she replied, "Betty."

"Well, Betty, at present I'm not looking to start a serious relationship, but if and when I do, I'll give you a call, and we'll see where it goes from there. If you're still available, that is," he added with a twinkle in his eye.

The smile on Betty's face was bright enough to light the entire room, and the governor's staff began to count the votes for his second term.

Immediately, several women raised their hands, desperately seeking the chance to flirt with the governor, but he pointed at a man sitting at the back of the room.

"Yes, sir, what's your question?"

The man said loudly, "Governor, when we elected you, you promised that you wouldn't allow the Federal Government to interfere with our state."

The governor's face tightened, "Yes, sir. That's true. And I haven't so far."

The man nodded without expression and then continued, "What do you propose to do when they try to take our guns away from us?"

A murmur spread through the audience. The governor waited for the noise to die down, then said, "There are three parts to my answer. First, to my knowledge there is no gun-control legislation currently before the United States Congress. Second, our representatives feel as you and

I do, that gun ownership is a right protected under the Constitution. And third, if Washington tries to enact such legislation, which would require a Constitutional Amendment, I would do everything within my power to see that the rights of the citizens of this state are protected, no matter the cost."

The governor's chief of staff winced, but the man smiled and said, "Thank-you, Governor. We'll hold you to your word."

More hands shot up, but before he could point at any of them, one of the governor's senior aides entered the room and walked over to the chief of staff. They spoke for a moment and then the chief of staff gave the governor a signal.

"Ladies and gentlemen, I'm afraid I must go," said the governor, which drew groans. "But I assure you we'll do this again. Real soon," which turned the groans into applause. With a wave to the crowd, the governor, his chief of staff and aide, plus his State Police bodyguards, who had maintained a discreet presence throughout the meeting, left the room together.

The governor and his staff walked out into the hall until they were well away from the people who were already starting to depart. He turned to the senior aide, "What is it?"

"Chief Swank just called, sir," he said, referring to the chief of the Idaho State Patrol. "A group of men has taken over that gun club up on Mount Freedom, and the media is already on it."

"How many men?"

"At least fifty," replied the aide.

"Why have they done it?"

"Apparently, they are protesting the closing of the club by the Forest Service."

Morrissey shook his head angrily. "I knew Washington was asking for trouble when they did that."

"There was nothing you could do, sir, the club is on Federal land," said the chief of staff. "It's their problem."

"Yes, but it's quickly going to become our problem."

"You're right, Governor," said the chief of staff.

"And there's more sir," said the aide.

"Go on."

"Their leader is Thomas Porter."

"What?" exclaimed the governor.

"I'm afraid so, sir. The man who called the media said they were under his command."

"What the hell is Porter doing?"

"Their message to the press was that they intend to stay up there until you personally guarantee them that the State of Idaho will refuse to ratify any Federal ban on guns."

The governor and his chief of staff quickly exchanged a knowing look.

"We've just been had," said the governor.

Without responding, the chief of staff ran back to the auditorium.

The aide looked at the governor, "What happened in there, sir?"

"Someone just asked me a question about guns."

The chief of staff returned, slightly out of breath, "He's gone."

"Terrific," Morrissey said sarcastically. "I played right into their hands. Porter knows I can't make any guarantees like that. But now, they've got me on the record saying I will."

The three men just stood there for a few moments and then the chief of staff said, "Actually, we can use this to our advantage, Governor."

"How?" asked the governor.

"This action will quickly gain national attention and if anyone is skilled at managing the media to his advantage, it is Thomas Porter."

The governor thought about it for a moment and then said, "You're right. Let's get back to the State House."

The governor, his chief of staff, and the State Police bodyguards walked out the door of the school. As he left, the governor tried to put on a smiling face for the crowd, who waited patiently for the man they idolized. They cheered as soon as he appeared.

"The people love you, sir," said his chief of staff as they got into the waiting SUV.

One of the State Police bodyguards closed the door behind the governor and tapped twice on the vehicle's roof. The driver put it in gear, pulled out of the parking lot, and they drove away under the cold bright moonlit sky.

"Let's hope they still do when this is all over."

"Another five miles to the East and it would have been Montana's problem, not ours."

"It wouldn't have mattered; the entire West will be painted with the same brush."

The chief of staff replied plaintively, "Let's hope it's not covered in red paint."

Morrissey nodded solemnly and said, "Get Swale on the telcom. I want to see him the minute we get back." He was referring to the device that combined a telephone, television and computer into one unit and it had replaced the other three machines in virtually all homes and offices around the country. It was available in a base unit, or BTC, that came in various sizes and capabilities, and a hand-held or portable unit, referred to as a PTC.

"Yes, sir."

"And tell him, for God's sake, not to let his men do anything stupid, like shooting someone."

"Got it."

The governor sat back, stared out the window, and muttered, "It's going to be a long night."

He was right. For Edward Morrissey, the Governor of Idaho, the night would last forever.

3

The White House, Washington, D.C.

Alexander Webster, the forty-fifth President of the United States of America, looked younger than his forty-nine years, and he was every bit as Hollywood handsome as he had appeared to be in the glossy posters from his first campaign for President—perhaps even more so because of the touch of gray that appeared on his temples by his second campaign. At least that was what the young women in the West Wing thought. He had a truly brilliant mind, thanks to the genes his parents had bequeathed him, one of whom had been a Ph.D. in psychology, and the other a neurosurgeon. Moreover, his fertile intellect had been further nurtured at the best schools, culminating in his graduating magna cum laude with a joint Doctor of Laws and Master of Business Administration degree from Stanford University. However, as rich and stimulating as his upbringing had been intellectually, it had been emotionally barren, as neither parent particularly loved each other, much less their only child. As a result, Webster was an eternal loner, even when surrounded by friends, whom he kept to a bare minimum, and admirers and hangers-on, who were legion.

That night, as was often the case, he sat alone in the Oval Office, on one of two pastel yellow loveseats that his former wife had chosen when he and his band of intellectuals, idealists, and dreamers were swept into office on the wings of change six years earlier. Those had been heady days for the handsome and idealistic Democratic governor from Los Angeles. Both he and the nation had been filled with high energy and great expectations. Back then, Webster and his Vice President, Richard Knox, a proud and aloof intellectual from Vermont, were still getting along despite their dramatically

26

different styles. Knox was an agnostic, but he could have easily passed for a Presbyterian elder, while Webster, a lapsed Catholic, believed morality was a purely subjective term. What was more, Knox hadn't been Webster's first choice as a running mate, a fact that the Vice President had never really gotten over but kept it to himself.

The two men implemented a brilliant campaign, targeted slightly left of political center, during which Webster promised, among other things, to bring the remaining troops home from their post-war peacekeeping missions in seven countries on two continents. They won a sweeping mandate, which critics scoffed was due to Webster's charisma and Knox's brains. Neither man cared. They had won, and the White House was theirs. Unfortunately, the love affair between America and its handsome young President began to unravel three months after the inauguration, when the President's wife became the first First Lady in the history of the Republic to divorce a sitting President. It had been a long time coming, and the former governor's extra-marital dalliances had been well documented by the media. But the public had always been willing to forgive him, if for no other reason, because his wife, whom they absolutely adored, never seemed to particularly care.

All that changed, however, when, after apparently having fulfilled her self-imposed duty to get him elected, the First Lady left him and headed back to Los Angeles, taking with her the crowd of Hollywood sycophants who had followed the two to the Capitol. There, she rejoined the successful entertainment law practice she had started and began dating the head of a large movie studio. Outwardly, Webster had taken the rejection and the public humiliation quite well, but behind closed doors it had infuriated him. To add insult to injury, his critics joked publicly that what probably hurt him even more than his wife's rejection was that there were no more nubile starlets lounging around the White House for him to seduce.

The divorce also drove a wedge between Webster and Knox, whose wife of twenty-five years was disgusted by the sexual encounters that occurred regularly in the bedrooms of the White House. Even after the President's divorce, Knox's wife protested to her husband that his behavior demeaned the aura of the people's house. This created a state of constant tension between the Vice President and the President, the net effect of which had been to create a subtext of mistrust, anxiety, and deep frustration in the West Wing. The fact that Knox's wife harbored a not-so-subtle sexual attraction to Webster had done nothing to help.

But on that stormy night, neither his ex-wife nor his Vice President occupied his mind. Instead, he was deeply absorbed in a thick, briefing document that had been compiled by Constitutional scholars. The central issue that this brain trust had spent hundreds of hours, and thousands of words, exploring could be summed up in a four-letter word: guns. Ironically, despite the billions that had been spent by the Department of Homeland Security on Granite Shield, the government's gigantic online database, powered by the world's first quantum computer, and referred to by its acronym, GOD, America was being torn apart by simple mechanical devices forged in steel, filled with lead, and fired in passion. During Webster's first term in office, Granite Shield's potential for law enforcement had only just begun to be explored. But the government's attention had been drawn away from fully developing this functionality, to what politicians perceived to be a greater danger—the spread of firearm-related crime across the land. And so Granite Shield's as yet untapped nor fully understood functionality had been refocused on registering every single firearm in America. Congress was afraid that the rule of law was giving way to the rule of the gun, and that the measure of a man was not his character, but simply at which end of the barrel he stood. Guns were now found everywhere one looked. Guns in the hands of professionals and ordinary citizens alike. Guns in the hands of the guilty and the innocent. Guns, guns, and more guns: loaded, lethal, and uncaring. At once, the salvation and the scourge of a nation.

Guns had been part of the very fabric of America ever since Columbus landed and the first hapless native American was felled by a bullet, thereby sealing the destiny of the new world forever. But at no time since the Founding Fathers signed the Declaration of Independence had the gun so deeply inflicted itself upon the American psyche, or upon its way of life, as it had following the first horrific attacks on America by terrorists in the early part of the new century—attacks which ultimately led to a bloody world war, known to the American-led coalition as the World War on Terrorism, or WWT. To America's global critics, which were legion, it had a far more sinister name—the War of the New Imperium. By either name, it lasted for over ten years, beginning with protracted, yet ultimately successful campaigns in the Middle East; it ended appallingly when it shifted to the Pacific Rim. It was there, on the desolate battlefields of North Korea, that the U.S. military's doctrine of lightning advances with lightly armored forces had failed, and failed miserably. Were it not for the fact that the North Korean dictator made a fatal error in judgment when he unleashed tactical nuclear weapons against the allies, his more heavily armored cavalry regiments might have prevailed. Retribution was swift and decisive as a single strategic nuclear bomb wiped the city of Pyongyang from the face of the earth, instantly vaporizing the dictator, his government, and nearly three million civilians. When the mushroom cloud and its attendant global paroxysm died away, a great silence fell upon the earth. Out of the ashes of the right war fought for the wrong reasons, America and her allies proclaimed victory over the forces of evil, and the weary warriors of the modern-day crusade returned home, with the legacy of the enemies of freedom consigned to the trash heap of history.

Unfortunately, the sword of liberty that America had wielded against its enemies was double edged. During the war years, and in the years of restless peace that followed, the incidence of gun ownership increased exponentially, to the point that by the time President Webster took office, there were more guns in America than there were citizens; and one out of every two American households owned at least one firearm. Some saw gun ownership as a necessary evil, some saw it as a God-given right. Others simply didn't care, and by their apathy they unwittingly abdicated their rights as surely as if they had placed them at the curbside with the recycling. Inevitably, politicians on both sides of the aisle in Congress became paralyzed; and while the nation's political leaders debated ad nauseum, deaths by gunfire had become the leading cause of death for all adults.

Late in his first term in office, President Webster nationalized state and local law enforcement agencies across the land and created the National Police Force, or NPF. Over the objections of the Federal Bureau of Investigation, he placed the NPF under the control of the Department of Homeland Security. Generally, it was a success and the national crime rate gradually began to drop, but it did nothing to reduce the steady increase in legal gun ownership. In fact, it only served to stimulate it, as it now became possible for American citizens to get a national gun license, which usurped individual states' rights to license and control gun ownership. This created a flood of lawsuits, as numerous municipalities sued the Federal Government to regain local control over guns. Finally, in the second year of the second term of Webster's presidency, he began to consider the introduction of a sweeping gun-control bill into Congress—a bill that would virtually eliminate personal gun ownership. He couldn't possibly know it at that moment, but that simple piece of paper would symbolically weigh more than the land itself, and by its very weight, would crush the Republic it was intended to preserve.

On that night, as the President sat alone in the office that reeked of power and purpose, there was an air of pathos about him, a sense of silent desperation as he sought to understand the meaning of words written over two hundred and forty years earlier—words crafted by men who set a standard of leadership that he could never keep. He knew it. His staff knew it. What was worse, he knew they knew. As a result, he increasingly craved solitude, for it was only in his aloneness that he could be certain of not feeling alone.

A loud clap of thunder echoed through the room as he reached for the dark blue coffee mug that bore the Presidential Seal. It was empty. He put down the document, stood up, and started to walk over to his desk, but before he could press the intercom button on his BTC, there was a sharp knock at the door, and two men stepped in. The first was Maddun Gordon, his chief of staff, followed closely behind by Patrick Fitzgerald, his national security adviser. Neither man was smiling.

Fitzgerald, thirty-seven, an effeminate, yet appealing man who looked like he had just come from a fashion magazine shoot, spoke first. "There has been an incident in Idaho, Mr. President that we think you need to be aware of."

"What kind of incident?" asked Webster.

"The wrong kind," answered Gordon who had a slickness about him that was vaguely alarming. At sixty-three, he was relatively fit but his habit of slouching, and the dark circles under his eyes made him look much older. "Some soldier wannabes have taken over that gun club the Secretary of the Interior closed last fall."

"Who?"

"It's a group of militia, Mr. President," replied Fitzgerald.

"Militia? Damn, that's all I need—right wing extremists with rifles. Do we know who they are?"

Fitzgerald responded, "With the exception of their leader, who chose to be identified, we don't have any names, Mr. President. Granite Shield scanned the mountaintop but none of them had NIS cards on their person, nor were there any implanted NIS chips, indicating none of them are regular military."

Gordon interjected, "But get this," — he had a way of speaking with the President that fell short of decorum, but Webster never called him to task over it — "their leader is Thomas Porter."

The President's expression widened. "You mean…"

Gordon interrupted him. "Exactly. Morrissey's reclusive billionaire buddy."

Fitzgerald corrected him, "Buddy may be overstating it just a tad."

"Whatever. We know Porter's money is in Morrissey's pockets and they're big pockets."

Webster shook his head. "I should have overruled the secretary when she closed the club."

Gordon nodded his agreement but Fitzgerald said, "You did the right thing at the time, sir."

"Has the press got it yet?"

"I'm afraid so, sir," said Fitzgerald. "They got it directly from the men themselves."

The President picked up his coffee mug and went to take a sip but remembered that it was empty, so he put it down and pressed his intercom.

A woman's voice instantly replied, "Yes, Mr. President?"

"I need some coffee, Marva, and make it strong."

"Yes, Mr. President."

He turned to Fitzgerald. "Have you spoken with Governor Morrissey?"

"Not yet, sir. His staff said he was at a town hall meeting and that he's on his way back to the State House right now."

"Do you want me to get him on the telcom?" Gordon asked.

"In a minute," he replied. "First I want to know what the implications of this action are for my bill."

Gordon and Fitzgerald looked at each other to see who wanted to stick his neck out first. Gordon hesitated, forcing Fitzgerald to go first. "Well, sir, the timing is obviously inopportune."

Inopportune! Gordon thought to himself, *Why couldn't this little Harvard twerp just once say the timing sucks.* Gordon had never been comfortable with the President's selection of Fitzgerald as his national security adviser. In his opinion, Fitzgerald was an "I-cubed" — inexperienced, intellectual, and ideological. Everything he was not. Then again, the President hadn't asked him for his opinion on the matter; and therein lay the biggest single reason why he didn't like him, even though he would never admit it to anyone, especially himself.

Fitzgerald continued. "It will certainly draw media attention away from you just as you issue your executive communication to the Speaker of the House containing the draft of your bill. And it may serve to solidify the pro-gun movement by giving their cause a focal point, especially if it were to end in an inimical and potentially climactic way."

Inimical. Christ, if he uses just one more fairy word I think I'm going to puke, thought Gordon.

The President replied, "True. But we have some control over that. After all, they have occupied Federal property."

"Yes, sir. However, it is still located in Idaho, and we will have to walk gently with Morrissey since his views are antithetical to yours, sir, especially on the issue of guns."

"I can handle Morrissey. At least with him I always know where I stand. He detests me and makes no effort to conceal it. I don't worry about my enemies; it's my friends that I don't trust." Without missing a beat, Webster looked at Gordon and asked, "What do you think, old friend?" The President said it with a sly grin, but Gordon didn't get it.

"I think we might be able to use this to our advantage," said Gordon.

"Go on."

Gordon flashed a look at Fitzgerald and back at the President. "There's no need to keep Fitz waiting. May I suggest, Mr. President, that he makes the first contact with Morrissey."

The President thought about it and then turned to Fitzgerald. "Maddun's right, Patrick. You should talk with him first. See what he proposes to do about it, and have him call me when he's ready to discuss his plan."

"Yes, sir," said Fitzgerald. "What would you like me to do with your letter? Should I send it to the Speaker?"

"Okay, send it, and let's begin the most important initiative of my presidency."

"Right away, sir," said Fitzgerald and he started to leave.

"Oh, and Patrick?"

"Yes sir?"

"Find out where my damned coffee is, will you? And fill this." The President handed Fitzgerald his coffee mug.

Fitzgerald took the mug. "Of course, Mr. President," he answered firmly, but the look on his face couldn't hide the frustration of being asked to do such a menial job. He wondered what his fellow classmates at Yale Law School would have thought had they seen him fetching coffee like some production assistant on a movie set. *Oh well,* he thought. *At least I'm a gopher to the most powerful man on the face of the earth.* With Presidential mug in hand, he exited the oval office. As he passed Marva's desk, she was just returning with the freshly brewed pot. Fitzgerald handed her the mug without saying anything and kept on walking.

Now alone with the President, Gordon proceeded to lay out his plan. It was a simple one. Most of his ideas were. It was a trait that had served him well in business before he joined the Webster team, and he had no intention of abandoning it now. When he finished describing his plan, he said, "As my mother used to say, Mr. President, it is better to light one candle than to curse the darkness."

"Yes, I'm familiar with the expression. It's the motto of the Saint Christopher Society."

"That's exactly how your actions will be seen, Mr. President. Soon, every American will follow your lead and pick up a candle, and the dark tyranny of guns will be chased from the land forever." But Gordon's plan would not light a candle. Rather, it would put fire to a fuse. And once lit, nothing would be able to put it out.

4

Rayburn Congressional Office Building, Washington, D.C.

The Speaker of the U.S. House of Representatives, Jeremiah S. Kincaid, Sr., was the very image of what Americans wanted their leaders to be, but seldom got. At fifty-nine, he was tall and handsome, with thick, but closely cropped brown hair, tinged with gray, and a kind but stern face, with deep blue, probing eyes and a strong jaw. Despite his height, he carried himself with the poise and grace of an aristocrat; but he had never lost touch with his middle-class roots, which made him approachable to all. This personality trait had also been enhanced by his education, which, unlike many of his peers in Washington, Kincaid received at public schools; and although both his undergraduate and law degrees were from respectable universities in his home state of Wisconsin, they were what national rating services would classify as second-tier schools, which barely drew a polite smile from Washington's elite at the mention of their names—a fact which did not bother the Speaker in the least.

Kincaid was a morning person, and at 6:00 a.m. on most days, he could be found hard at work in his office located on the top floor of the Rayburn House office building directly across from the Capitol. That particular autumn morning was no exception; as the first rays of sunlight crept up the Capitol Dome, he was sitting at his desk surrounded by the adornments and memorabilia he had gathered over twenty years in the Congress. The walls were covered with photographs of him, with a virtual who's who of American and world leaders, and an original oil painting of Abraham Lincoln hung in one corner. On the credenza behind him were family photographs of his wife, his children and grandchild. The Speaker was looking out the window at the sunrise when there was a knock at the door.

"Come in," he said, turning toward the door.

His chief of staff, George Ross, entered. At forty-one, he was brilliant, bookish, and intensely loyal. He wasn't smiling, but that wasn't unusual at that time of day; unlike his boss, he was definitely not a morning person. But it wasn't the early hour that prevented his smile that morning.

"I love this city, George." said Kincaid, "Especially at sunrise when the first light bathes the top of the Capitol in a gentle glow."

Ross acknowledged the comment with a polite but impatient nod and said, "I'm afraid we have a problem, sir."

"Yes, I know. The President is sending us his letter with the draft of his anti-gun legislation. Patrick Fitzgerald called yesterday to tell me it would be here this morning."

"Yes, sir. But that isn't it."

"What then?"

"Last night a group of militia took over a gun club in the Bitterroot Mountains."

"In Idaho?"

"Yes, sir."

"Was anyone hurt?" said Kincaid.

"No, sir. The Club had been closed by the Forest Service several months ago."

"Why did they do it?"

"Apparently they feel that the closure was a trumped up excuse by the government to restrict their right to own a gun."

The answer obviously exasperated the Speaker, "What is it with these people and their paranoia about gun ownership? They seem to think everyone in Washington is out to overturn the Constitution."

Ross did not want to be drawn into the argument. He knew the Speaker loved to debate any issue, and he was very good at it. He could eloquently defend or attack the same position, and there were few issues in Washington for which there was only one right answer. Gun control was a perfect example. The Speaker was neither pro- nor anti-gun ownership, and he was frustrated by the irrationality that permeated the issue. "It's not that, sir." Ross sat down, leaned across the desk, and spoke in a low voice as if to prevent anyone in the outer office from hearing, which was unnecessary because the door was closed. "The leader of the militia group is T.J." The words hung in the stillness of the room like frost in a winter forest.

"What?"

"The group is under the command of Captain Thomas Porter of the Idaho National Guard."

The Speaker's body sagged and the blood drained from his face. "Oh my God."

Ross took a sheet of paper out of the leather portfolio that he carried everywhere. "Here's their press release. They're protesting the closing of the club, which they say is an attempt by the Federal Government to obstruct their lawful right to own and shoot their guns."

Both men sat there quietly. Only the ticking of the large grandfather clock standing against one wall filled the silence. Finally, the Speaker said, "He was always a foolish and impulsive boy, but this—" The Speaker shook his head in sad disbelief, "What was he thinking?"

Ross waited for the Speaker to absorb what he had just heard and then asked, "What do you want me to do, sir?"

The Speaker didn't answer. He was looking at Ross, but his mind had drifted to another time and place. Back to the moment when the bedrock under the Kincaid clan had been shattered.

"Excuse me, sir." Ross's words brought the Speaker back to the present.

"I'm sorry, George. What did you say?"

"What do you want me to do, sir?"

"There is nothing we can do, other than tell the world that he's my son, I suppose," added the Speaker wistfully.

"With all due respect, I don't think you should, Mr. Speaker. The fact that he is your son is no one's business but yours."

The Speaker said, "Legally true, ethically murky."

"The last thing you need right now, either professionally or personally, is to be drawn up into this mess."

Kincaid thought about it for a moment longer and then said, "Okay, I'll hold—for now. Find out everything you can for me will you?"

"Of course." He left the Speaker alone.

Kincaid reached down, opened a drawer in his desk, and took out an old copy of Fortune Magazine. On the cover was a photograph of Thomas Porter, beaming from ear-to-ear. In the world of big business, Porter was a superstar who had the golden touch; but to Jeremiah Kincaid, Thomas Porter was simply Thomas Johnston Kincaid, or T.J., the prodigal son whose departure had left a gaping hole in his father's heart—one that would never heal.

<u>5</u>

The Streets Of Washington, D.C.

Sarah McGill disliked the rain. Most beautiful women did. But most beautiful women could avoid having to go out into it—or at least they could choose how and when they did. McGill couldn't; she was a network television reporter who went where the story was, and in her business, time was an enemy. On that cold and stormy autumn night in the nation's capital, the story had taken her up to the Hill, which was what Washington insiders called the Capitol Building. It was a journey she had made many times before, but that time would nearly be her last.

A true American beauty, Sarah McGill possessed charm and wit and intellect, combined with a certain impertinence that spoke to the land she was born in. She made men rise above their baser instincts and immediately want to love her; but she had none of the pretentiousness that would have driven other women away. In sum, McGill was what every little girl dreamt she'd be when she grew up, and what every little boy dreamt he'd marry; and the fact that most never would achieve that dream did not spoil its existence. She was one of the most admired and respected correspondents on television, and it was clear to everyone, both critics and supporters alike, that she was destined for greatness; clear to everyone, that is, except McGill herself. She was a talented but driven young woman to whom success was a fickle friend, and for whom today's achievements were as irrelevant as yesterday's news. She had grown up as the only child of an automobile industry chieftain in a wealthy suburb of Detroit, but for all its affluence and amenities, her home had been devoid of love, at least as far as her parents were concerned. They divorced when McGill was seven, and her father had been granted custody of the pretty and precocious little girl. Two other marriages followed in quick succession. Both failed, but through it all, he had managed to raise a talented and well-adjusted human being. He had been a demanding, but loving father, and she was completely devoted to him, right up until one night when she was a senior at the University of Michigan, and a drunk driver removed him from her life forever.

She went on to graduate near the top of her class, and the pattern of high achievement continued through her graduate studies at Northwestern's Medill School of Journalism, and at the series of increasingly important jobs she had held at progressively bigger television stations around the country. Eventually, a senior executive at GNBC had spotted her, and before you could say superstar, McGill was the most respected young news correspondent in Washington. Everyone in the capital knew her name and even those who didn't certainly knew her face. Without seeking it nor really wanting it, she had become America's sweetheart. She was bright and beautiful and never made mistakes. Never, that is, until that stormy night when she declined the offer of a Capitol policeman to walk her to her car.

Normally, McGill would have parked in the area reserved for the media in the Capitol parking lot, but earlier that afternoon she had visited a girlfriend, who clerked for one of the Supreme Court Justices, and she had parked on a side street nearer to the Supreme Court building. It had started out as a crisp and golden day in Washington, and instead of moving her car, she had decided to walk over to the Capitol. It was a mistake, and she knew it. As the dark rain clouds closed in on the city, McGill sensed that danger was closing in on her. It wasn't just the normal feeling of apprehension that might be expected from any woman in a situation like that; it was much more. All her life, Sarah McGill had known she possessed certain special cognitive abilities that others did not. Her awareness of these mental skills had started in grade school when she always seemed to know the right answer to her teacher's question, even before the teacher had asked it.

Gradually, she discovered she had other talents that she could neither explain nor understand, from the practical to the almost laughable, such as being able to flip open a book to exactly the page she was seeking and the strange habit of extinguishing street lights just by looking at them. In her early years, these talents had been a silly little game, but as she got older, she became aware of their scope and potential—and it sometimes frightened her. She found herself capable of not only predicting the outcome of events, but affecting their outcome as well, even those in which she was not directly involved. Even more unsettling was that people whom she disliked often had bad things happen to them, in direct proportion to the magnitude of her feelings about them. And so it was, that as she walked along that dark street on that stormy night, McGill's inner sense told her something bad was about to happen, but by then, there was nothing she could do about it.

McGill reached her car, placed her big leather bag and computer on the ground, and started to place her thumb on the biometrics ID lock pad when the man came upon her from the rear. He grabbed her harshly, and instinctively she reached for her bag which held her PTC. In addition to being a cell phone, computer, wireless internet link, digital camera and mini-video receiver/player/recorder, it could also administer a fifty thousand volt charge to her attacker. The admonition of the Capitol public safety officer about holding the PTC in hand at all times when walking the streets alone flashed through her mind, but in her bag on the ground, it might as well have been a rock.

"Don't scream, bitch, or I'll blow your fucking brains out." He was dirty and unkempt, with an ugly black gun, which he jammed against her cheek. The gun was a .38 caliber double-action revolver that had been mass produced in Eastern Europe, using the cheapest of materials and slip-shod manufacturing processes. It had been illegally imported by an international arms dealer, and sold to him over the Internet for twenty-nine dollars. It was cheap, unreliable, but at close range, deadly.

The suddenness of the attack took her breath away and literally overwhelmed her nervous system. As the man half dragged her into a nearby alley way, she wet her pants and was embarrassed by the utter humiliation of it all—but her embarrassment quickly turned to terror. Once inside the shadows, the man spun her around and threw her backwards against a brick wall, smashing her side into a concrete ledge. She heard a dull cracking sound as her rib fractured, but it seemed distant and there was no pain, only a strange sensation of not being able to catch her breath.

"Please," McGill begged, "take my money and laptop, but don't hurt me."

"Shut up." He slapped her hard across her face with the back of the hand that held the gun. It stunned her, and through the haze, she felt him press his thighs against her. Then she felt his hand slip between the lapels of her suit jacket, past the silk blouse underneath it. Roughly he thrust his hand down, cupping her breast. He started to rub his pelvis against her, moaning like some primal beast in the night.

As she stood there in the darkness, smelling his foul breath, her mind cleared of its haze, and began to function again with the rapid fire precision that it had been trained to do. Her terror became anger, and her anger turned into a fierce determination to survive. As the adrenaline flooded through her veins, she knew that she would escape this evil beast or she would die trying. Either way, she resolved to take a hand in her own destiny. Although she didn't know it, at that moment her abduction was being recorded on the thermal sensing devices in one of the unmanned aerial vehicles circling overhead, as well as on the automated high throughput screening devices located on two Homeland Security towers in the park directly behind her. Instantly, the data was being fed through the Granite Shield civilian protection subsystem, and on to the nearest police station. Help was on its way. The only issue was, would it be too late? For the one thing that GOD could not do was to expand or contract time.

As Sarah McGill stood there against the stone wall, she realized that in this pig's brain, all that mattered at that moment was sex. So instead of trying to divert him to her money or computer, she decided she would use his lust to her advantage. "Wait, I'll do whatever you want if you'll just let me go afterwards," she said, knowing that he never would. "Here, let me help you," she added as she pulled her arms up and unbuttoned what was left of her torn blouse. "I've always wanted to do it with a real man," she said, desperately trying to mask her fear with seductiveness. "I bet you have a huge dick, don't you? Well, come on, let me see it," she demanded as she reached down toward his groin.

"What the fuck are you doing?" he said in consternation. Her tone and manner had caught him off guard and he stepped back ever so slightly taking the gun away from her cheek. It was all the space that she needed.

He started to say, "If you think this will…"

Her knee caught him squarely in the testicles, sending a blinding flash of pain to his brain and cutting him off in mid-sentence.

"Uuuugh." He groaned, doubled over, and vomited.

The smell of it was overpowering, as it gushed in a steaming flood onto the sidewalk. But Sarah wasn't there to smell it. Instead, she was already running blindly toward the lights of the street, screaming at the top of her lungs and gasping for air as she ran. She stumbled once as the heel of one of her shoes broke. She kicked them both off and kept running, out into the street, right into the path of an oncoming taxi that screeched to a halt. Quickly she ran around the side of the cab and pulled on the passenger door handle. It was locked and she yanked on it violently as she yelled for the driver to let her inside, all the while looking over the roof of the cab toward the alley. But the frightened cabby shook his head and stomped on the accelerator. He might have acted less cowardly were it not for the fact that only days before, the mayor of the District of Columbia had succeeded in overturning a bylaw, allowing taxi drivers to carry weapons. And so, unarmed and afraid, he sped away at the exact moment that the man staggered out into the muted glow of the streetlights. He stopped and raised the ugly black gun and pointed it directly at her face. McGill looked left and right, down the deserted street. Then she glanced over her shoulder into the shadows of the park behind her. Nowhere offered safety or solace. Convinced that there was no escape, no hope, she turned back to face her fate.

"I'm going to enjoy watching you die, you fucking bitch," he said, spitting out some chunks of a partially digested taco.

Sarah McGill closed her eyes and prepared to die. A calmness came over her, and the face of her father passed before her eyes. At least she would soon join him, and the thought gave her comfort. She waited for the shot and found herself wondering if she would hear it before it tore into her body. But it never came. Instead, she heard something strangely out of place; it was the sound of hoof beats rising in a steady, throbbing rhythm from somewhere behind her in the park. She opened her eyes and saw a look of terror in the eyes of her tormentor. He stood there frozen, staring over her shoulder, as the sound grew louder and louder. The pounding noise was now unmistakable, as heavy hooves met concrete instead of grass. She turned her head just in time to see the onrushing shape of a giant white horse with fiery red eyes and a dark rider dressed in a black cape, the flowing folds of which rose and fell in cadence with the animal's gallop. The sight was overwhelming, and the she felt herself growing faint. And the last thing she saw just before the darkness overtook her was a terrible, swift sword held high in the rider's hand. Then everything went black.

"SARAH. IT'S OVER." The deep tones of a man's voice permeated the fog that filled her mind. Gradually regaining her senses, she opened her eyes and found herself lying on soft grass with a big and powerful

42

man kneeling beside her. He was dressed in the black leather uniform of a mounted policeman, and under one arm he held a shiny white helmet; but despite his appearance, there was something about him that seemed out of place. His face was tanned, he wore a close-cropped beard, and his long, dark-brown hair was pulled back into a tight pony tail. He repeated his calming words, "You are safe now, Sarah."

From somewhere deep in her soul, she knew she was, and had never been more so.

"Can you stand up?"

She nodded but still could not quite find her voice. With his help, she regained her feet and remembering what had transpired, she looked down at the street in front of her. There she saw the body of the man.

"Do not worry. He will harm no one ever again."

She paused and then asked, "How did you know my name, Officer?"

A pure white smile flashed across the golden smoothness of his face. "Everyone knows you."

"Who did you say you were?"

"I did not. My name is Michael," he said extending his hand. "Michael Falconer."

She smiled and put out her hand. He shook it very gently, but she still winced slightly. "I think my rib is broken."

"Yes, it is, but you'll be fine."

"If you hadn't come along," she looked down at the dead man whose hand still clutched that little ugly gun, "I'd be dead."

"Yes. You would be. But I did, and you are very much alive."

"Where did you come from? Just before he took aim at me I was certain that I was all alone," she asked.

He smiled at her and said, "You are never alone."

McGill glanced at his crisp black uniform, which was without any identifying badge or shoulder patches. As she did, her mind raced back to the vision that she had seen just before passing out.

He seemed to know what she was thinking. "Do not worry, Sarah. In time, all will become clear." He put his helmet on and started to leave.

"Wait! Please. I don't understand."

Before he could answer, the wailing of a siren filled the night air. She looked toward the sound and saw the fast-approaching flashing lights of an ambulance. She turned back to where the officer had been only a second before, but both he and his horse were gone. Instead she was alone with the lifeless body of the man who would never harm another. Feeling suddenly alone again, she felt her knees growing weak. All her life, she had fainted easily, and she knew the signs of an approaching loss of consciousness. Her vision narrowed into a tunnel and just as the tiny pinpricks of light began to fill the onrushing darkness, she found herself standing in a sun-filled meadow high on the side of a mountain. She was staring at the dark rider, astride his white stallion, standing at the edge a dark pine forest. Gone was his uniform; in its place, he was wearing a long, flowing cape of white linen with fine, gold embroidery. He smiled at her and there was a radiance about him that filled her with joy and peace. Then everything faded to black again.

WHEN SARAH McGILL awoke for the second time, she found herself lying on a stretcher, and two paramedics were loading her into an ambulance. Beyond them, she could see several policemen milling about. Any shooting in Washington, particularly so near to the Capitol, always brought out legions of law enforcement personnel. This one was no different.

"Don't worry miss, you are going to be fine," one of the medics said softly. "We're just taking you to the hospital as a precaution. Now lie back, and relax."

At first, she was distracted and simply did what he said. She nodded and leaned back against the crisp cool pillow. But suddenly, she remembered. "No. Wait!" she said, trying to sit up, but the pain of her broken rib prevented her from doing so.

The medics stopped what they were doing. "What is it, miss?"

She glanced around, but neither the officer nor his white horse were anywhere to be seen. Just policemen and a growing crowd of onlookers, held back by a fluttering yellow, plastic ribbon, and the now-blanketed body of her assailant. She looked back up into the medic's eyes. "Where did he go?"

"Who, miss?"

"Officer Michael Falconer."

The medic stared at her with a look of puzzlement. "I don't know. I'm afraid I didn't see him."

As they rolled her stretcher past the body of her assailant, she tried to look down at him.

The medic flashed a glance at his colleague and then back at her. "You don't need to trouble yourself with him, miss. He will harm no one ever again."

She looked at him with questioning eyes. "Did you say that before?"

It was his turn to be puzzled. "No."

She laid her head down slowly on the pillow.

"That's it. Now close your eyes and rest." They loaded her into the ambulance, and she closed her eyes and surrendered to its sanctuary that smelled of linen, latex, and alcohol. There was no point in trying to explain to them what had happened. They wouldn't believe her. She wasn't sure she believed it herself. A tall, dark, and handsome rider on horseback with a mighty sword raised high above his head. It was the stuff of fairy tales, or Bible stories, in a world that had long since abandoned both.

THE EMERGENCY ROOM resident at George Washington Hospital had been gentle and considerate with his examination of Sarah McGill. He spent a disproportionate amount of time with her, especially given the heavy patient load that night in the ER. Not because she was a television personality but because he was captivated by the quiet strength she seemed to possess. He marveled at how calm and collected she was.

"Your whole-body scan showed that you *did* break a rib, Ms. McGill, but not tonight. It's already healed, but I can still see the old line of fracture."

She was puzzled, "I never broke a rib before, I'm sure of it."

He smiled patiently. "Sometimes you can crack a rib and not realize it. Perhaps you fell or…"

"No. I didn't," she interrupted. "I would know whether or not I had broken my rib and I had not up until tonight when that man threw me against the building. That was when I felt it break."

The doctor didn't know what to say. He was certain that she couldn't have broken it that night; the fracture line was too well healed for it to be so. However, he chose not to argue with her. "The good news is that there is nothing wrong with you. In fact you are in excellent health," he said with a smile.

"Thank-you, doctor," she said, looking up at him through tired eyes.

He continued, "Since none of the man's blood hit you in the face, we don't have to worry about the possibility of infection. But I'd like to give you a series BS Triple A shot, anyway. It's a broad-spectrum, anti-microbial, viral, and prion inoculation, just as a precaution, if that's all right. Just as a precaution."

"All right," she said, glancing over at her stained clothing.

He opened a drawer and took out a small plastic device which had no point on it. He unwrapped it carefully and simply touched her upper arm. Then he pushed a small button at the back end of the device, and there was a pop from a sharp, short burst of air. She didn't even flinch. He disposed of it in a plastic drum.

"There. Now you'll be safe from every microscopic killer known to man. I wish I could give you one to protect you from the macroscopic variety." His pager went off. He flipped it off his belt and looked at it. "Another GSW. You'd think it was Saturday night."

"How many gunshot victims do you get in here on a Saturday?" she asked.

"More than I can count, but every day brings in its grisly share."

She shook her head sadly, "What an incredible waste. Can't it be stopped?"

"Yes. It can. By removing guns from the streets. But somehow, the people who run our country seem to have other matters on their minds."

She nodded and said, "You'd better go. Head wounds are serious."

"I didn't say it was a head wound," he replied with a puzzled look.

"Really? I guess I just assumed that it was."

"I see," he said, staring at her. "Well, I'll write up these discharge papers and we'll get you out of here."

She nodded and stood up with a slightly unsteady movement.

He helped her and said, "Is there someone I can call to come pick you up?" She shook her head no. The doctor couldn't believe that someone that beautiful didn't have a significant other to come and get her. "Surely, there is someone?"

She knew his concern was genuine. She could tell when a man was hitting on her. It happened all the time. But she also could sense that this wasn't one of those occasions. "Thank-you, but I'll be fine."

"Are you sure?" he asked, unable to let it go. He couldn't explain it, but it was everything he could do not to put his arms around her and hold her tightly. Not out of any prurient interest but simply because he felt something drawing him to her. Some unseen force that destroyed the

46

normally dispassionate attitude he displayed to the hundreds of patients he treated everyday.

"I'm sure," said McGill, smiling at his tenderness and concern.

The doctor smiled and said, "You can get dressed. I'll send a nurse back in a minute with a prescription." He stood there for another moment then said, "Well, I guess I'd better get to that GSW."

She nodded, but by then she sensed that he need not hurry. The doctor went out into the busy hallway, making sure to pull the door to the examining room closed behind him. Several police detectives stood waiting patiently to talk with Sarah McGill, and he spoke with them briefly before continuing on his way. He reached the treatment room just as the senior resident pulled a sheet across the bloodied head of a young man.

"He's gone. Large caliber through the skull," said the resident, who checked his pager and walked away. The doctor stood there for a moment, contemplating what had just happened. He looked back toward McGill's examining room and then, shaking his head, he walked toward the nursing station. As he did, he saw a bear of a man coming into the emergency room. He was dressed in a rumpled suit and a shirt to match, with a tie that fell short in its efforts to meet his belt. The man spoke with the detectives who seemed to know him. Then he headed over to the doctor.

"Excuse me, doc, where can I find Sarah McGill?"

"Are you a policeman?" asked the doctor, as he eyed the man suspiciously.

"No, I'm Keene Lange, Washington Bureau Chief for the Global News Broadcasting Network. I'm Ms. McGill's boss."

The doctor's expression changed immediately, and he thrust out his hand to shake that of Mr. Lange. "Nice to meet you, sir. I'm glad someone has come to take her home. She didn't seem to want any help."

"That's Sarah." Keene said with an understanding look.

"She's getting changed. She should be out in a minute. I was just about to write her a prescription for pain."

"Is she all right?"

"Yes, sir, she's emotionally distraught, which is of course understandable, but other than that, she'll be fine."

"Thank God," said Keene, although he didn't believe in a supreme being.

"Yes, she's a very lucky young lady." The doctor's pager beeped. He looked down at it, then back at Keene. "If you'll excuse me. I've got another gunshot victim coming in. Seventh one tonight."

"Busy night?"

"No, not really," he said matter-of-factly.

"I hear you," Keene said with a knowing smile.

The young doctor started to walk away, then he turned back to face Keene. "Excuse me, Mr. Lange."

"Yes."

"I hope you won't think this question improper or strange, but have you ever noticed something different about Ms. McGill?"

"Different in what way?" responded Lange.

The doctor thought about it for a moment and then said, "I don't know. Something almost" —the doctor looked around to see if any of the medical staff were within hearing distance, which they weren't, and then he continued — "something almost magical?"

Lange didn't react at first. "Why do you ask?"

"Well, you probably think I'm nuts, which is certainly not a good thing for someone entrusted with the lives of others, but I could swear that the hematoma, that is the bruising on her side, was much bigger when they brought her in here a few hours ago than it was just now when I examined her again."

The expression on Lange's face indicated that he did not think the doctor nuts. Far from it. "Go on."

The doctor glanced down at the floor as if embarrassed to say what he wanted. "Never mind."

"And you found yourself captivated by her?" said Lange with a smile.

The doctor said, "Yes."

Lange smiled a soft smile and said, "You aren't the first person who has felt that about her. It happens all the time. It's called being star struck."

The doctor looked at Lange without answering. That wasn't it at all, but there was no use in pursuing it any further. He was exhausted, and he had already given McGill ten times the amount of attention that she needed. "If you'll excuse me." He headed off to attend to the dozens of others who needed him. As he did, he knew he wouldn't forget this particular patient. Ever.

At that moment, Sarah McGill exited the examining room. Lange smiled at her. "How are you doing, kiddo? You've had quite an adventure this evening," he said, intentionally trying to not dwell on the darkness that had passed over her only hours ago.

She stood there looking more defiant than wounded, but still obviously happy to see him. "How did you know I was here?"

"The police called us," replied Lange.

She nodded, but didn't reply. They both just stood there for a few seconds, staring at each other. Then slowly he walked over to her and carefully placed his hands on her upper arms.

"I'd hug you, but I'm afraid your sore side wouldn't appreciate it," he said, sounding more like a father than a boss.

"Actually, it doesn't hurt at all."

"Good. Sarah, there are some detectives here who need to ask you a few questions. Are you up to it?" Lange asked gently.

"Yes," she said, still not wanting to show any signs of weakness, even though inside, her will to keep talking was fading fast.

"All right. If you're sure, I'll go get them. I'll tell them to keep it as brief as possible," he said.

She took a deep sigh and sat down in a wheelchair that sat empty in the hallway to wait for the questions she wasn't sure she would be able to answer. Especially the part about how her attacker died.

KEENE LANGE was normally a careful driver, in fact, too careful for McGill's tastes, and she often criticized him for driving too slow. As he cautiously navigated his way through the heavy traffic around Dupont Circle on his way to her apartment, she sat there quietly, without complaint.

Suddenly, she remembered something, "Oh dear. What about my car?"

"It's all right, Sarah. Your buddy Latrel already took it back to your place and parked it safely in your garage."

"But how did you know where it was?"

"The police found your key card on the ground where you dropped them. They gave them to me when Latrel and I arrived at the scene. We got there five minutes after they took you away in the ambulance. It didn't take us long to locate your car. After all, how many purple Mustangs do you find parked near the Supreme Court?"

"It's fuchsia," she replied.

"Okay—How many *fuchsia* Mustangs are there in D.C? Or in the whole country for that matter?" he added with a smile.

She let it pass.

"I called my friends at Granite Shield, and they guided me right to it. They even unlocked it for me from the satellite just to show off. Then Latrel took it home while I came here to the hospital. He said he wanted to come too, but he really didn't. You know that he's not very good around blood and that peculiar smell. So I sent him home. I didn't think it would help you to have him fainting all over the place."

She smiled but didn't say anything.

They drove a few blocks in silence and then Lange asked, "Do you want to talk about it?"

"No," she said firmly.

"Very well." Lange knew better than to push it. Sarah McGill never said or did anything unless she wanted to and obviously, this was not one of those occasions.

They sat quietly for a few more blocks, then she asked, "Do you know how many guns there are in this country?"

"I thought you didn't want to talk about it."

"I don't want to talk about me. I want to talk about the country as a whole."

"All right. I think it's about three hundred million," he said.

"Actually, it's closer to three hundred and fifty," she replied, "But until tonight, those were all just ugly statistics."

"They don't mean much until you're looking at the wrong end of a barrel," he said gently.

"I never felt so completely helpless."

"You wouldn't have felt helpless if you had had a weapon yourself."

"That won't solve the problem," she replied sharply. "If we armed everyone, it would just turn our streets into shooting galleries, and our children into targets." She shook her head in obvious frustration. "Why can't America be more civilized, like the British?"

He glanced at her and then back at the road. "I hate to tell you this, Sarah, but ever since Great Britain adopted the most restrictive gun laws in the world, their rate of violent crime has continually risen, while here in America, it has steadily fallen. And the only people who have guns over there are the criminals."

"Statistics don't tell the whole story. Even one death by gunfire is too many and you know it."

"I'm sorry. You're right. I'm supposed to be comforting you, and instead, all I'm doing is getting you all riled up."

But she wouldn't let it go. "Regardless of the crime rate, during the past ten years, while there has been a steady rise in gun ownership, there has been an equal drop in the number of Americans who claim to believe in God. More people today go to gun shows than to church, and last year gun sales outnumbered Bible sales a hundred to one."

He nodded and added, "But which is the cause and which is the effect?"

"Does it matter?"

"Yes, it does. Are people turning away from religion because they are buying guns, or are they buying guns because they feel that America has become a godless land?"

"The end result is still the same, with children dying in the streets," she said, as emotion rose in her voice.

"A land without God is a land living in fear. Evil thrives on the faithless and the good guys feel the need to protect themselves."

"We can't force people to turn back to God, but we can take away their weapons," she snapped angrily.

"Sarah. I'm not the one who tried to kill you remember?"

She fell silent and looked out the windshield. They didn't say anything for several blocks, and then she looked at him and said, "I want to go out to Idaho."

"What? What for?"

"I want to interview that militia captain who took over that rod & gun club."

"Sarah, you cover the Hill remember?"

"And what's the hottest topic in Congress these days?" she asked, setting him up the way only she could.

He sighed, "Gun control."

"Exactly. What better way to get the story than to go out to where it's happening?"

He knew that once Sarah made up her mind, it was no use to argue with her. "New York won't like it. They've already got one of their guys out there."

51

"Who?"

"Perry Waters."

She didn't react to the mention of his name. But they both knew what she thought of Waters, and it wasn't good. In truth, Lange felt the same way. "I promise I won't get in his way. As soon as I've interviewed the captain, I'll come right back here."

"What makes you think he'll meet with you? So far he's refused to grant one-on-one interviews with anyone, including Waters."

"I just have a feeling that he will."

"Okay, you win—as usual."

She smiled for the first time that evening.

The car reached her apartment and he pulled up in front of the large glass double doors. Her uniformed doorman stepped over and opened her door. She greeted him and then turned back to her boss. "Thank-you, Keene. Tell Tanner thanks, too."

"I will. Get some rest. I'll cover it off with the network."

"You're a doll, Keene."

"Yes, I am."

She leaned over and kissed him on the cheek and then got out of the car and headed toward the door.

"Sarah."

She turned. As she did, she was backlit by the bright lights in the lobby and they cast a glow about her. The sight caught Keene off guard and he hesitated.

"What?" she asked with a angelic smile.

"I'm glad you're all right."

"Thanks. Me too." Then without thinking, she added, "I wouldn't be if it weren't for Officer Falconer."

"Who?"

She hesitated, but it was too late to retract it now. "The mounted policeman who saved my life. He said his name was Michael Falconer, but he didn't stay around long enough for me to thank him."

Lange looked at her with probing eyes and then added softly, "Well then, just look him up and send him a thank-you card or something."

"I will."

"Good night, Sarah. I'll see you tomorrow."

"Good night, Keene."

52

He watched her go all the way to the elevator, and then he hit a speed dial button on his PTC. After a few rings, the voice of his assistant came over the Speaker. He waited until her message finished and then said, "Hi there. It's me. Check out a Michael Falconer. That's F-A-L-C-O-N-E-R. See if he's a park policeman or any other kind of mounted cop. He paused and then added, "And get me all the latest statistics on national gun ownership and all deaths by gunfire over the past twelve months. Thanks. See you tomorrow." He hung up and headed his car out into the late evening traffic.

SARAH McGILL'S BUILDING had not yet converted to biometrics recognition scanners so she still had to use the old key card system to open the door to her apartment. As she did, she dropped her key cards, which the doorman had given back to her after Spence returned them. *Damn it all,* she thought, as she bent down to pick them up. She noticed that her rib didn't hurt as she did so, but when she stood back up she hit her forehead on the door handle. It startled her and she stepped back, rubbing her head with one hand and closing the door with the other. She placed her keycard in a brass bowl on a table in the hall and walked into the kitchen. She flicked on the light over the center island, walked over to the refrigerator, opened the freezer, and reached in to get some ice. As she pulled out the tray, it caught on the arm of the ice-making machine and slipped. She grabbed it, but not before it flipped over on its side, dumping its entire contents on the stone tile floor. For a moment, she just stood there holding her forehead in one hand and the empty ice tray in the other. Then slowly she sat down at the kitchen table, lowered her head and started to cry. The events of that horrible evening finally caught up with her, and she could hold her emotions back no longer. The sobs welled up from deep within and through her tears she whispered the words, "Angels Nine."

AT THAT SAME MOMENT the corpse of her attacker was being slid into the cooler at the medical examiner's office. In the morning, his body would become the eleven hundredth autopsy performed that year on the victim of a gun-related death in the city. It was a new record and there were still three months to go.

6

Fort Carson, Colorado

The coyote was small for its age, but otherwise healthy. This, in itself, was not particularly noteworthy. However, the fact that he lived right in the middle of the Fort Carson military reservation, where every day, seventy-ton mechanical monsters maneuvered at high speed, trying to kill each other in war games, made it downright remarkable. He had been part of a big litter whose mother was blasted to pieces by a .50 caliber machine gun twelve months earlier. His litter mates were long since dead but this tough little guy had learned to survive on pure wits alone, dodging in and out of the heavy armor that regularly raced across the dusty plains. He was a strong runner, capable of galloping at nearly forty miles an hour, which, when combined with his keen eyes and cunning brain, kept him out of harm's way from even the most deadly of the Army's armored vehicles—the main battle tanks.

Despite this hostile environment, he had learned to survive, and the pot belly that hung between his gangly legs like a softball in a fur sack was kept full on a diet of field mice, lizards, and an occasional snake that fled before the tanks. He had become so brazen and nimble at doing this that the men of the 3rd Armored Cavalry had adopted him as their unofficial squadron mascot. Not surprisingly, they named him Wiley and the word quickly spread through the squadrons that he was not to be harmed. This put added pressure on the tank drivers, for now, not only did they have to avoid "enemy tanks" during their war games, but Wiley as well.

However, the tank crews participating in the exercises on that particular day need not have worried, because Wiley was sitting safely up on a hill, watching units of the 3rd Armored Cavalry and the 49th Armored Division of the Texas National Guard attempt to out-maneuver and destroy each other. Even though his little brain could not comprehend the significance of humans playing at war, the sight of so many killing machines all moving at once told him that on that Colorado autumn day, he was better off going hungry.

As Wiley watched intently from afar, the front of an M1A2 Abrams Main Battle Tank smashed into a ditch filled with water, sending mud and spray flying everywhere. The tank easily cleared the ditch and continued on its way, followed by two others, crossing Phase Line Debbie as they went, which was the code name the squadron gave to imaginary lines on the map used to mark progress along their line of advance. The little coyote shifted uncomfortably as the ground literally shook, and the air was filled with mechanical thunder and the pungent smell of diesel fumes. He watched intently as the three tanks raced across the desert floor, placing a thousand yards between them and himself.

In the open commander's hatch of the lead tank of Company B of the 49th, Captain Larry Stirritt, thirty-four, sat staring intently out across the plains through binoculars. "Do you have him?" he shouted into the microphone on his headset. Not getting a reply, Stirritt dropped into his command seat, pulling the lid of the hatch closed above him. Directly in front of him, the tank's gunner was anxiously typing coordinates into the computer console, as the tank jolted and jostled its way down the arroyo. "Do you have him or don't you?" shouted Stirritt again, his voice filled with a mixture of impatience and apprehension.

"I think so, sir," came the young gunner's reply.

Sitting beside the captain, the loader got a shell ready.

"I've got him!" the gunner suddenly said with relief.

With that, the loader put down the shell instead of loading it, but closed the breach exactly as if he had and yelled, "Up!"

In quick succession, the gunner then yelled, "On the way!"

The captain looked through his thermal imaging scope at the target fast approaching them, and then at his digital video display. Then he looked away, disgusted.

"Shit, we missed him."

Suddenly, a loud electronic buzzer blared through the claustrophobic confines of the tank and the captain tore off his headset and slammed it down on the metal console beside him.

"What do we do now, sir?" asked the young gunner who was experiencing his first war games.

"It doesn't matter, Sergeant, because we're all dead."

"It's pretty tough to beat Granite Fist, sir," said his gunner, referring to the latest iteration of the Army's command and control function built into their opponent's newer M1A3 tanks. It was the military's version of Granite Shield, run on the same quantum computer platform, and it took control of the weapon system during battle and relegated the crew to driving the tank and loading the gun.

The captain looked at his crewman and said, "A machine, no matter how complex, will never replace good soldiering, Sergeant."

"Yes, sir," the crewman answered, but he didn't really believe it.

FIFTEEN HUNDRED YARDS AWAY, an Abrams Main Battle Tank similar, but not identical, to the captain's, roared up the slight rise directly across from Wiley and lurched to a stop. The commander's hatch opened and Lieutenant Colonel Jeremiah S. Kincaid Jr., the commanding officer of 1st Squadron, of the 3rd Armored Cavalry Regiment, stood up and peered out across the valley through his binoculars. Jake, as he was known to his family and friends, lowered them and said with a deep sigh, "God, I love this," as he watched another tank roll up beside his and stop.

During the latter part of the twentieth century, the Army had gradually disbanded all of its remaining armored cavalry regiments but one, the 3rd or "Brave Rifles." And had it not been for the outbreak of WWT, the 3rd ACR might also have been dismantled. However, with the war looming on the horizon, the regiment survived and went on to distinguish itself in action.

The commander of the other tank, a lieutenant, opened his hatch and gave the colonel a big grin.

"Well done, Lieutenant," said Kincaid.

"Thank-you, sir."

The two men looked back out across the plain in silence, savoring their victory, which despite being only a simulated one, still tasted as sweet. As more tanks began to appear, Kincaid looked back at the other man and said, "You know, if the Book of Revelation had been written two thousand years later, death would have ridden a tank rather than a pale horse."

"With all due respect, sir, I think a better analogy would be the Second Horseman."

Kincaid nodded. "The red horse."

Over the noise of the arriving tanks, the lieutenant loudly began quoting Revelation.

And there went out another horse that was red:
and power was given to him that sat thereon to take
peace from the earth, and that they should kill one
another and there was given to him a great sword.

Kincaid was obviously impressed. "I didn't know you were religious, Lieutenant."

"Yes, sir. I am. And this is my church." He smiled and patted the side of the hatch. One thing that could be said about tankers, they loved the machines in which they rode into battle, in the way that few other warriors could appreciate, with the exception of fighter pilots. For the tank was as close to the perfect killing machine as mankind had yet invented. Magnificent, maleficent, and absolutely mesmerizing. Squat and sinister, with perfect simplicity of design, functionality of form, and singularity of purpose. It was built to do one thing, which was to kill others of its kind and the fragile beings hidden deep inside. And it did it extremely well. Each day with endless repetitiveness, squadrons of these beasts maneuvered on the practice plains at Fort Carson Army base and pretended to destroy each other. As they did so, high overhead, their every move was closely scrutinized by the watchful eye of Granite Fist, and digitally recorded for all to see. After the battle, each commander would relive in either excruciating or exquisite detail, the errors of his ways or the excellence of his actions. But on that particular morning, under a clear desert sky, these predators of steel were also being watched by one of God's smallest and wiliest of predators. And his eyes were no less attentive than the eyes in the sky, for his life literally depended upon it.

Normally Lieutenant Colonel Kincaid would have ridden in an M879 command vehicle, but the tank that he was commanding that day was one of the newest and most awesome pieces of military hardware that the Army, or the world for that matter, had ever known. Designated the M1A3, along with nine others exactly like it, they comprised Cavalry Troop A of the 1st or "Tiger" Squadron of the 3rd Armored Cavalry. As they engaged in war games against the older M1A2 Abrams Tanks of the visiting unit of the

Texas Guard, the Lieutenant Colonel was doing what the cavalry termed a "ride along," and he was thoroughly enjoying every minute of it.

Jake Kincaid was the son of Jeremiah Kincaid, the Speaker of the House of Representatives, a fact that hadn't helped his military career but it certainly hadn't hurt it either. At thirty-six, he was big and strong, with deep blue eyes and an easy smile. He looked like what every man would see himself as were it not for mirrors. Even without the uniform and the aura of power it conveyed, he was the kind of person who instantly commanded respect and attention wherever he went. He was at once proud and self-confident, yet with a certain vulnerability about him that was bathed in loneliness. In a day and age when the term "hero" was thrown around too freely, during the last days of WWT, Jake Kincaid had proven himself to be truly a man of distinguished and rare valor. A hero in every sense of the word. However, as with all the heroes who had come before and who would follow, he was not without his faults, the most unfortunate of which was contained in a bottle. Thankfully, for those who served with him, Jake kept a safe distance between the bottle and the battlefield. As a result, the only person he dragged down into his personal hell was himself.

Several more M1A3 tanks roared up to a stop beside him. The forceful rumble of their diesel engines provided a dramatic counterpoint to the silence of the desert morning. Through his binoculars, Kincaid could see numerous other tanks sitting immobile on the plains stretching before him, each with a flashing yellow beacon on top of it, indicating that the tank and its occupants had been destroyed, theoretically at least. He smiled as he put down the binoculars and spoke into the microphone on his headset. "Well done, Tiger Squadron! Blue Force is history. We really whipped their asses." Then something in his peripheral vision caught his attention. He looked down into the eyes of Wiley who seemed to sense that the mock battle was over and hurried to get his share of the "spoils of war."

"Hey there Wiley, did you like the show today?"

The animal loped over to within ten yards of the tank and sat down expectantly.

Jake looked down inside his tank and yelled, "Wiley's here."

The gunner handed something up through the hatch, which Kincaid carefully unwrapped. Inside was a large steak bone which he held up so that the coyote could see it. "Come on, what do you say, little fella?" Jake teased, as he climbed up out of the turret, down across the tank, and slowly eased himself onto the ground.

Wiley scurried back several yards, then turned back to face the colonel who made no move to follow the little animal. Seeing this, the coyote seemed reassured and put his little head back and let out a sharp, short series of yaps and half-howls.

By now the other members of the tank's crew had climbed up on top and along with the crews of the nearby tanks, they began to place bets on whether the colonel would succeed in what he had apparently failed to do on numerous previous occasions.

"I'll give five to one that the colonel doesn't get within ten yards," said the colonel's gunner, a staff sergeant and the tank's usual commander. He and Kincaid went back a long way together and had survived real shooting wars in which other men, good men, had not.

"He doesn't need to get any closer; even I could shoot that mangy critter from up here," replied a soldier on another tank who was obviously new to this unfolding drama.

One of his crew mates immediately whacked him on the side of the head, "Try it, and we'll be using you for live fire target practice."

"What?" he asked them sheepishly. They all just stared at him.

"Didn't anybody tell you about Wiley?" asked another more sympathetic soldier.

The now very embarrassed soldier answered sheepishly, "You mean, *that's* our mascot?" he asked.

"Yes, Private shit-for-brains," replied the first crew mate.

"Okay, I'll take your bet for fifty," answered the soldier, as he tried to redeem himself.

"You're on," said the sergeant, already counting his money.

"How close has the colonel gotten before?" asked the soldier as an afterthought.

"Never closer than he is right now," one of them answered.

"How many times has he tried?" the soldier continued.

"About a hundred," another replied.

"Shit," said the soldier under his breath, who then sat back quietly, wishing he'd kept his mouth closed in the first place.

"Begging the colonel's pardon, sir, but are you sure you grew up on a farm?" shouted the staff sergeant.

"You know I did, Sergeant," said Kincaid as he inched closer to the coyote, who never took his eyes off the man with the big juicy bone, despite all the attention that the activity was getting.

"That wouldn't have been one of those fancy hobby farms that big-time politicians like your daddy go to on weekends, would it, sir? You know, where they get manure on their pant cuffs and feel close to the earth."

Kincaid ignored the teasing and continued on his stealth mission. "Here you go, boy. Come on, I'm not going to hurt you. Now, let's try it again, shall we? Say I love you," said the colonel, making the statement very deliberately as if he was talking to a two-year-old child. The more the colonel tried to get the little creature to say "I love you," the more amusing the men found it. "Come on, Wiley. Say it just for me."

Everybody was laughing and hollering but then a remarkable thing happened. The crowd began to notice that Colonel Kincaid was actually closing the distance. First ten yards, then five, then only two yards separated the little animal and the soldier. They stood there facing each other—a warrior and a wild animal—not as enemies, but simply fellow passengers on spaceship earth.

Finally, Wiley formed his mouth into an oval shape and half howled half barked a sound that seemed to all present to sound like "I love you," in a coyote sort of way.

"Yes!" Thrilled, Kincaid handed Wiley the bone, which he grabbed and raced away, leaving a beaming colonel and eleven stunned soldiers staring at him go.

"I love you, too, Wiley," shouted the colonel. No one laughed. They never would again.

Kincaid climbed back up onto his tank and took a deep bow towards his men who cheered, "Way to go, sir."

"The coyote has given us his blessing, men. We can go back to the base now," said Kincaid triumphantly.

Still not quite sure that they believed what they had just seen, the men climbed back into their tanks. These were brave young warriors, trained to kill without hesitation; yet each one of them was touched by the encounter between man and beast.

Kincaid was the last one in, pulling the hatch closed behind him. As he settled down into the tank commander's seat, his crew was still murmuring about what they had just seen.

"How did you do that sir?" asked the sergeant, swiveling around in his seat to face the colonel directly behind him.

"Do what?"

"Get that little critter to talk to you like that? You been taking ventriloquism lessons, Colonel?"

The colonel gave the staff sergeant a big smile and said, "I don't know how I did it. I guess it's because he really does love me."

"What's not to love?" said the loader.

"Thank-you, Private," Kincaid said, flashing a smile at the soldier who sat immediately to his left.

"But I'd be careful though, sir, if I were you," said the sergeant with a cheeky smile.

"Why is that?"

"Because next thing you know, Wiley is going to invite you home to meet the parents."

"Is it just me, or has anyone else noticed that Wiley is a he?" asked the loader.

The sound of laughter filled the tank and the colonel laughed the loudest. He had the ability to walk a fine line between commanding his men and being their friend. It was a skill that had served him well in both peace time and in war. Nowhere had this been proven more true than when the 3rd Armored Cavalry had taken part in the successful invasion of Syria during WWT. There, Kincaid had led his men to a rapid and decisive victory against a rebel force of Russian tanks. In the first twenty minutes of the fight, Kincaid and his troop destroyed twenty-eight of the enemy tanks, while only losing one tank, which they had had to destroy themselves after it broke down.

Three days later his own tank had been destroyed by a suicide bomber driving a car loaded with plastic explosives and children. The colonel had placed himself directly in the line of fire of snipers to drag his wounded men, including the staff sergeant, out of the burning tank, saving their lives while risking his own. It was a feat that made him a true hero within the ranks of the men who served under his command, and others who wished they did. It also earned him the nation's highest military award, the Congressional Medal of Honor.

"Okay, men, let's go home."

The powerful turbo-diesel engine roared to life and the tank lurched forward, as its eighteen hundred horsepower engine, three hundred more than its predecessor, transferred its tremendous torque to the steel wheels and treads. Right on cue, the diesel engines of the other tanks started up with their throaty roars, and one by one, the giant machines rumbled off into the midday light, leaving Wiley alone with his meal.

As they departed the colonel sat back and smiled. The laughter was a fitting ending to the war games. After all they were driving the newest and most powerful land weapon that the world had ever known; they were in the greatest Army of the greatest country in the history of mankind; and on top of it all, they had wiped out the "enemy." *What could be better?* He thought. Little did he realize that the land that he loved, with all its power and pride and glory, was about to change forever.

JAKE KINCAID was still feeling good as he parked his classic 1978 Indy Pace Car Corvette coupe in front of the officer's mess, got out, and closed the door. He stood there for a moment admiring the two-tone black and silver car. It was a beautiful afternoon in early Fall, and the sky was filled with crisp white clouds brushed onto a pastel blue canvas sky. Everything seemed right with the world. Apart from the weather and his precious car, Kincaid had reason to feel good. Earlier that day, his squadron had decisively won their war games, and that afternoon he had been advised by his commanding officer that he was being promoted to full Colonel. To make the day complete, his CO told him that General McWilliams, Chief of Staff of the Army, had requested that he be temporarily assigned to the Pentagon to work on a team that was assessing the readiness of the new M1A3 Main Battle Tank. The promotion in itself was enough cause for him to be excited, but the assignment to the Pentagon was more than he could have hoped for. He knew it was an ideal opportunity to fill out a resume that might one day lead the Chairmanship of the Joint Chiefs of Staff. It was a dream that he had had since his days in Beast Barracks at West Point, and so far his career had been a steady progression of victories in a profession where the pyramid of command narrows rapidly near the top and the path grows ever more slippery.

Jake also knew that he was fully qualified for his new assignment, but also the fact that he was the son of the Speaker of the House had probably not gone unnoticed by the Army brass. Moreover, his father's steadfast support for the military over his years in Washington certainly helped. He also realized that there would be some resentment among more senior officers over his being promoted to Colonel at his age and chosen for this assignment. But that didn't bother him. Throughout his rapid rise in the Army, he had had to deal with the jealousy of others many times. He didn't care what they thought. He would often say to himself, *There are only two types of officers in the military—the quick and the dead—literally or figuratively.* And Jake Kincaid was at the head of the line for the former group. The only thing that did trouble him, at least a little, was the fact that he had some doubts about the readiness of the M1A3 tank for active service. But he told himself that if they didn't want to hear what he had to say, then they wouldn't have offered him the assignment. One thing was for certain: he was never shy about saying what he believed. It was a trait that had stood him well in his professional life but hurt him in his personal life. However, on that day, he was feeling good and the ghosts of his failed relationships with a fiancée and a long-lost brother were merely muted shadows, lurking in the recesses of his mind. Shadows that faded a little more with each passing year—and each glass of scotch that he downed. And lately, the shadows had been getting a lot shorter.

As he strolled along the sidewalk toward the Club's front door, he saw another soldier walking toward him. The soldier was wearing the uniform of the Texas National Guard that bore the rank of Captain. Jake could see that he wasn't paying attention as he walked with his head down, obviously deep in thought. He was sure the man would look up, but by the time he realized that he wouldn't, it was too late to get out of his way, and the other officer bumped into him.

"I'm sorry, sir," the captain said, as he backed off and snapped to attention.

Kincaid smiled and saluted him back. "No harm done."

"Are you sure? That was careless of me, sir."

He could see that the man's eyes were red and swollen. It was not a sight that Jake was used to seeing on a soldier's face, especially an officer.

"Excuse me for prying, Captain, but are you all right?" he asked.

The other officer looked at the colonel and smiled gamely. "Yes, sir. I'm fine." With that, he nodded politely and started to walk away. Most other regular Army officers would have let the matter go but Jake wasn't like most other officers. He said, "Can I buy you a drink?"

The captain looked at his watch and said, "It's a little early for that, isn't it, sir?"

"It's past five o'clock in Chicago, and I have always loved that city," answered Kincaid with a broad smile.

The captain hesitated. "Actually, that sounds pretty good right about now, sir. I think I'll take you up on that."

"Good." He held out his hand, "I'm Jake Kincaid, 3rd Armored Cavalry."

The captain took a closer look at the insignia on the colonel's shoulder and then a smile cracked the sadness on his face. "I'll be damned. You're the man who blasted my troop to hell this morning." He thrust out his hand and said, "I'm Larry Stirritt. It's an honor to meet you, sir."

A big grin flashed across Kincaid's face as he shook the other man's hand warmly. "Nice to meet you, Captain. I'd be pleased to give you and your part-time soldier boys another whipping anytime you'd like."

"With all due respect, Colonel, not if I have anything to say about it."

With that, the colonel put his arm around the captain's shoulder and said, "Well, come on, let's go do some real damage to a bottle of scotch and swap war stories. Any man that rides into hell in a main battle tank is okay in my books, Captain Larry Stirritt."

Stirritt smiled at the colonel, but Jake noticed that it was tinged with sadness, and as they walked into the officer's club, he wondered what was troubling the other soldier. He was about to find out, and it had nothing to do with their encounter on the battlefield.

KINCAID AND STIRRITT sat in a quiet corner of the officers' club bar. The walls were covered with an eclectic assortment of military paraphernalia and photographs. In the corner, tattered battle flags of the 3rd Armored Cavalry stood proudly in a lighted glass case, which protected them from the dust and humidity that would have otherwise done what bullets and bombs had been unable to do—that is, to destroy the proud and honorable colors under which many men had bravely served and died.

Kincaid had two glasses of scotch on the table before him, one empty and the other half full, while Stirritt was nursing a beer. Judging by their tone and demeanor, they looked more like brothers than new acquaintances.

"With all due respect, Colonel, you'd have had a bit more trouble beating us if the Guard had the M1A3s instead of the older M1A2s."

"I hear you. And why don't we drop the formalities. Call me Jake," said Kincaid.

64

Stirrett looked at Kincaid and smiled. "It's a deal, Jake. Now tell me how do those babies handle? Sweet I bet."

"Very sweet, Larry. Very sweet."

"Better than that Stryker the Pentagon tried to impose on you boys a few years ago?" asked Stirritt, referring to the eight-wheeled light armored vehicle that was supposed to be the Army's replacement to the aging, sixty-ton M1A2 Main Battle Tank.

"The Stryker still serves a purpose but against heavy armor it's a rolling coffin. We learned that lesson the hard way in WWT," added Kincaid sadly.

"So talk to me, Colonel, about the M1A3. How significant are the improvements versus the M1A2?"

"It's faster, lighter, with twenty percent more horses under the hood, and carries a deadly arsenal that is unmatched by anything that rolls upon the face of the earth" replied Kincaid, sounding more like a proud father than a soldier.

"Jeeze, eighteen hundred horsepower?" asked Stirritt.

"Yes, more power in a lighter vehicle."

"I suppose that new composite plastic armor saved all the weight?"

"Yes, plus it added an entire new dimension of crew protection against long rod penetrating rounds."

"What about the new digital electronics?"

"The advancements in the Command Independent Thermal Viewer and the Position Navigation Sensor Unit are incredible, Larry. They provide a far superior seek and destroy capability over the M1A2, not to mention anything in NATO or Chinese armor."

"And?" said Stirritt.

"And what?" answered Kincaid.

"And what about Granite Fist?"

"I don't know what you're talking about."

"Aw, come on, Jake. Everyone knows about the Granite Fist command and control capability."

The colonel studied the other officer for a moment and then said, "You tell me."

Stirritt didn't hesitate, "Well, sir, the way I hear it, the techtronics are infallible and the tank crew are simply along for the ride. And a sweet ride at that."

The colonel smiled and said, "I'm not at liberty to discuss that, Larry, and now I'm afraid that I'm going to have to kill you," he added with a smile.

"What! Again?" laughed Stirritt.

"Let's just say that the M1A3 uses sophisticated global tracking and weaponry response electronics that are light years ahead of the airborne Q-STAR system, and let's leave it at that."

"I knew it! So the M1A3 is one helluva killing machine."

The colonel hesitated before answering. He threw back another swallow of his scotch. "Yes. I suppose it is. Relative to everything else that rolls or crawls anyway."

"But —" said Stirritt. By Kincaid's tone, Stirritt sensed that there was a "but" coming.

Kincaid stared at Stirrett for a moment and then said, "No. Now I really am going to stop talking and you're going to change the subject."

Stirrett nodded and said softly, "Sorry, Colonel. I shouldn't have pushed, but before I shut up, I just want to say one more thing. You don't have to say anything. Just listen. The way that I hear it, there's a glitch somewhere in the servo system that under certain circumstances delays the firing control. And even a few seconds can be lethal. So if you don't know about this, I suggest that you keep yourself and your men out of the M1A3 until those dickheads in the Pentagon figure this one out."

Kincaid was stunned. "How did you know about that?"

"I surf the net a lot. Purely legal, I assure you. You'd be surprised how much stuff is out there on the Internet for anyone to see. Especially on matters of weapons and the military. It's called freedom of information."

Kincaid shook his head. "It's called freedom of stupidity, if you ask me."

"I hear you. And if I know about it, who else does?"

Kincaid nodded, "I'm very familiar with it, Larry. That's because I'm the one who first reported it."

Now it was the Captain's turn to be startled. "Oh man. Well, now that I've got my foot in my mouth, please excuse me while I go swallow it and die."

"It's all right. Actually, you've done me a favor. I've been assigned to the Pentagon to help work out the bugs. And the fact that their top secret isn't a secret will help me get their attention."

"I hope they listen to you, Colonel, before we get in a shooting war. Any delay, even a few seconds, and that baby is nothing more than four dead men rolling."

"You're right," said Kincaid, looking away.

Stirritt sensed immediately that he had touched a nerve. "Did I say something wrong, Jake?"

"It's nothing," said Kincaid, obviously not wanting to talk about it.

There was a pregnant pause, and Kincaid took another deep drink from his scotch. Then he broke the silence. "So tell me about your family."

A fleeting smile crossed Stirritt's face, and he pulled out his wallet. He opened it and took out a photo of him, his wife, and daughter. The girl was wearing a soft, brightly colored hat, even though it appeared to be a hot summer day. It didn't seem out of the ordinary and Kincaid, who had been engaged once but never married, didn't pick up on its significance. He examined the picture carefully and said, "Your wife and daughter are very beautiful."

"Thank-you."

"How old is your daughter?"

"Eight. Her name's Shiloh."

"What a beautiful name. She must be the light of your life." Then he added, "That's a pretty hat," he added.

Stirritt nodded but didn't say anything at first. Then he spoke softly, "I shouldn't lay this on you Jake, but my daughter has leukemia."

A look of dismay flooded Kincaid's face. "I'm sorry."

"You obviously didn't know. She has good doctors, and they say that she is responding well to the chemo. But I have to tell you I'm scared to death."

Kincaid didn't say anything for a few seconds. He finished his drink and waved at the bartender to bring him another, his third. He motioned to Stirritt to see if he was ready for another beer, but he shook his head no.

"I certainly won't pretend that I know exactly what you're going through," said Kincaid in a calm and soothing tone, "But anyone can appreciate the pain of having a child who is struggling with a life-threatening disease, and there is no shame in being afraid, my friend. None whatsoever."

Stirritt nodded but didn't look up as he swirled the remaining beer around inside his glass. "She's a nut about basketball and you should see her shoot hoops. That is, when she isn't so weak that…" The words caught in his throat.

"From what you've told me, she is getting proper medical treatment," Kincaid said gently. "I'm sure she'll have plenty of time for basketball and all the rest of the wonderful things that life has in store for her. You'll see."

"Yes, sir." He cleared his throat as his words seemed to get stuck there. "But the one thing my wife and I have learned through this experience is that medicine is as much of an art as it is a science, and that doctors are not infallible."

"I hear you. But she has a mother and a father who obviously love her very much and love is a powerful force."

"God, we do love her," said Stirritt trying to be brave.

Kincaid reached over and gently patted the captain on the shoulder. "So just hold on to her very tightly and put your faith in God, and everything will turn out all right.

The two men sat there quietly for a few more minutes, then the captain looked at his watch and said, "I've got to go. We're shipping out at 0500 tomorrow morning to return to Fort Bliss." He stood up and extended his hand to Kincaid. "I can't tell you how much I appreciate your taking this time with me, Jake. I wish there was something I could do to repay you."

"That isn't necessary."

"Thank-you. Perhaps we'll meet again someday."

"Actually, I'd like to stay in touch. Who knows, to maybe shoot a few hoops with your daughter when she's fully recovered."

A smile spread across the captain's face, "Yes, I think she'd like that."

"Good," said Kincaid, taking a business card out of his pocket, handing it to Stirritt.

Stirritt took it and then fumbled for a pen in his pocket. "I don't have my cards." He grabbed a napkin off the table, wrote his name and number on it, and handed it to the colonel. "If you'd like, Jake, I'll send you a picture of Shiloh."

"I'd like that very much."

"I'll get it off to you right away."

"Good." Then something caught his eye. It was the BTC screen behind the bar. On it was the image of Thomas Porter, sitting in front of a faded clapboard building at the Bitterroot Rod and Gun Club. Were it not for the young men standing nearby with automatic rifles, it might have been an

68

interview with a ball player after a winning game. Kincaid watched the screen intently for a few moments and Stirritt noticed.

"What is it?" Stirritt looked over his shoulder and saw the BTC. Then he looked back at Kincaid, "That militia captain and his men sure are getting a lot of airtime."

"Yes."

"What's his name again?"

"Porter. Thomas Porter," replied Kincaid.

"Yeah, that's it." Stirritt looked back at the screen.

The bartender asked, "You want me to turn it up, Colonel?"

"No thanks." He stood up and said to Stirritt. "Let's go."

Stirritt chuckled, "The guy's a gazillionaire, he's good looking, and he's wearing a uniform. Some guys get all the luck."

Kincaid shrugged. "Yeah. Don't they?" With that, he tossed back the rest of his drink and headed for the door, followed by Stirritt.

When they got outside Stirritt looked at him quizzically. "Are you all right?"

"Yes. Thanks." His smile returned, and he put out his hand. "Take care of yourself, Larry, and your family. This is a lonely world without the love of a family. Believe me, I know."

"Thank-you, Colonel. You take care of yourself, too. Who knows? Maybe we'll get a chance to play war games again sometime?"

"Suits me. And just in case we do, I'd practice if I were you," said Kincaid with a smile.

"I hear you, Colonel. You don't have tell me twice."

Then the two men headed off in separate directions. As they did, neither one knew that they would indeed face each other again across a battlefield; but the next time the ammunition would be live and the killing would be for real.

7

Bitterroot Rod & Gun Club, Idaho

It was a beautiful early autumn afternoon as a solid line of law enforcement officers made up of U.S. Marshals, Idaho State Troopers, and sheriff's deputies kept an unruly crowd of anti-gun protesters away from the gates leading up to the Bitterroot Rod & Gun Club. They had been gathering for days to provide a counterpoint to the heavy television coverage that the militia had been getting. In the middle of the crowd of protesters stood the Reverend Ezekial Freeman: pastor of the Church of the Revelation; champion of the poor and downtrodden, although enormously wealthy himself; self-appointed magistrate of the court of public inquisition; and a national thought leader on everything that affected people of color. With him was Congressman Rodwell Crane, an overdressed but physically underwhelming man who had never been known to stay silent on an issue put before the Congress, whether or not he knew anything about it. He was a fervent opponent of gun rights, and his disdain for firearms and all those who used them carried over to a general mistrust and lack of support for the military, the police, and anyone else who might have occasion to pull a trigger.

Right in the middle of it all, where she always seemed to be, was Sarah McGill, with microphone in hand and cameraman in tow. Standing by her side was Perry Waters, who had just celebrated his fifty-ninth birthday for the third time. He was a veteran reporter for GNBC with a reputation for showboating and shaving the truth. Waters' glory days were long past, but his dyed hair and Botox smile showed he didn't know it yet.

"The white men illegally occupying this Federal property claim to be doing so in the name of freedom; but the real reason they, and others like them, refuse to give up their weapons, is to keep men of color under their control," said the reverend to the cameras.

McGill pushed closer to the reverend and asked, "Reverend Freeman, are you saying that gun ownership is synonymous with racial bigotry?"

"Yes I am, Ms. McGill," he replied without hesitation. This was not the first time that he and Sarah McGill had spoken on camera, as he was a frequent visitor to the Hill. "The gun has been the oppressor's tool for over five hundred years in this land, ever since white Europeans began slaughtering the red-skinned man with it. And the white man's dominance over people of color has continued right up to today, thanks to the Republican members of Congress, who continue to allow uncontrolled gun ownership."

McGill turned the microphone to Crane and asked, "Representative Crane, do you agree with Reverend Freeman?"

Crane smiled generously at McGill, and in his most patronizing tone said, "Ms. McGill, the issue is not whether I support the Reverend's views. It is whether or not a majority of Americans do. And in my humble opinion, they do."

Just then, three young, heavily armed enlisted men appeared from around a bend in the dirt road on the other side of the fence. As they walked in the shadows of the tall trees toward the gate, an officer could be seen following them. It was Captain Thomas Porter. Immediately all attention turned their way, as reporters and protesters alike jockeyed to get as close to the gates as the police officers would allow.

"Killed anything today?" yelled one of the protesters as the soldiers neared the gate.

The soldiers smiled and refused to take the bait. With automatic rifles at the ready but fingers off the triggers, the enlisted men took up defensive positions near the gate. Then Captain Porter stepped out of the shadows into a shaft of golden sunlight; and for Sarah McGill, the noise of the crowd was suddenly silenced, leaving only the whisper of the wind in the tops of the tall pines that surrounded them, and the creaking of their ancient trunks. For a second, her eyes locked with Porter's, and she felt as if something passed between them; something intangible, and yet as profound as if it had substance and form. In the back of her mind, she was sure that somewhere in the distance she heard an eagle cry. But the crowd would not allow them to remain in each other's silent gaze for long.

"Captain Porter," shouted out Perry Waters.

Others instantly joined in and the din of reality broke the magic spell.

Porter's eyes abruptly shifted off her, leaving a chill behind that made her shiver. She felt like a school girl at a rock concert who was certain that the star was only interested in her alone, among the crowd of thousands, only to realize that he was not. As irrational as she knew it was, jealousy swept over her, which only served to make her feel even more foolish. It took her a moment to regain her poise and by the time she did, he was already charming the crowd of reporters, as they surged forward against the fence. Fearing trouble, the reverend's bodyguards quickly moved him away from the gate, and from the young men with guns, leaving Representative Crane on his own among the crowd, along with McGill and Waters.

Porter stepped closer to the fence and flashed a mischievous smile at the reporters. He held up his hand to quiet them and said, "Ladies and gentlemen. I'll be glad to answer your questions, but please, one at time."

One of the protesters shouted, "Why the armed guard, Captain? What are you afraid of?"

Porter smiled at the man and said, "They're not here to protect me." He paused and then added with a wry smile. "They're here to protect you."

Some in the crowd chuckled.

"After all, if I really am as dangerous as the White House would have you believe, it's the least I can do."

Laughter now rippled through the crowd, easing the tension. For most in the audience, it was easy to see why this rebel warrior had developed a national following of almost movie-star like proportions. But not everyone on the mountain that day was falling under his spell.

"Do you and your men think breaking the law is a joke, Captain?" shouted Waters, injecting a note of harsh reality into the love fest.

Porter's eyes narrowed and his smile vanished. He didn't reply at first. Instead he just stared at Waters, making him squirm. Then with calm deliberation he replied simply, "No."

"Then why are you doing it?" Waters demanded with the smugness of a debater who had not yet realized he was out of his league.

"You asked me, Mr. Waters, if I thought breaking the law was a joke, which I do not. Had you asked me if I thought there have come times in the history of our nation when the law had to be broken, then I would tell you that I do. Times when the law took away from the people the very freedoms upon which this nation was founded. This is one of those times." Few noticed that Porter knew the reporter's name, other than Waters himself, and of course, Sarah McGill. Porter always made a point of knowing both his critics and his supporters, and he responded accordingly.

Before Waters could pursue the matter further, Crane loudly interjected, "You mean the freedom to shoot people, Captain?"

In a calm and commanding tone of voice, Porter replied, "No, Mr. Crane, I mean freedom itself. You are a student of world history, Congressman, and therefore you should know that outlawing the private ownership of guns is the first step on the road to tyranny."

Porter was right. Crane did consider himself to be somewhat of a historian, and he was impressed that Porter knew it, but he was unwilling to concede the point. "Come now, Captain, where do the history books give credence to your argument?"

"Nazi Germany, 1939," said Porter without missing a beat.

"Really, now, you can't blame the rise of Hitler on a disarmed Germany."

Porter continued, "Russia, 1917."

The second statement slowed Crane down slightly, but he kept at it. "Those were overseas. This is America, Captain."

"The Thirteen Colonies, 1776," said Porter with a friendly smile, seeming to enjoy the debate.

Porter's disarming manner visibly flustered Crane. "Those examples all occurred in the past. This is the twenty-first century." But no matter how hard he tried to trip up the captain, Crane was simply his straight man feeding him lines.

"Really, Mr. Crane? Tell that to our neighbors to the north. They were promised that mandatory gun registration would not jeopardize their rights, and they believed it, right up until the day that the RCMP knocked on their doors and seized their guns, all of which had been duly registered."

Crane had no response, because nothing is more difficult to debate than the truth.

Seeing that Sarah McGill's cameraman, along with the news crews of the other television stations, were focused on the captain and the congressman, and no longer on himself, Reverend Freeman pushed himself back closer to the gate. His bodyguards tried to stop him but he waved them off and took a few more steps. "Captain Porter, my name is Reverend Freeman."

Porter flashed the same disarming smile at the reverend that he had just been using on the congressman and said, "Yes, Reverend, your reputation precedes you. Welcome to Mount Freedom. It's a rather apt name, don't you agree, given the circumstances?"

The question momentarily disarmed the minister. "Yes. Well, whatever you call it, Captain, I would like to talk about the 'why' and not the 'where' of your occupation."

"Certainly, Reverend, but the two are related."

Again the minister paused. He assumed that Porter was alluding to their presence at the Bitterroot Rod & Gun Club and didn't pursue it. Instead, re-tracking his train of thought, he rolled forward, "Captain, do you think it's a coincidence that people of all colors, including native peoples, are safer walking the streets of Toronto, or Vancouver, day or night, than they are in any American city?"

"Actually, if you check the facts, Reverend, you'll find that violent crime has steadily been on the increase in Canada ever since private gun ownership was banned, exactly as was the case in Great Britain earlier. That's why the British Parliament has recently been loosening their restrictions on gun ownership. However, since these facts do not support President Webster's position, it's not surprising that the liberal leaning media hasn't publicized them."

All eyes focused upon the minister to see his response, which brought several cameras swinging his way, which of course was exactly what he wanted. But before he could reply, Perry Waters, still smarting from his earlier rebuke, but too arrogant to have learned anything from it, thrust his microphone toward the fence, and said in an accusatory tone, "Captain Porter, as a former CEO, you should know that statistics can be manipulated to support any argument, or to use the vernacular of your former trade, 'Bullshit baffles brains.' But cutting through all your altruism and rousing talk of freedom, isn't this occupation really all about one thing, and one thing alone—namely, money? The money that the NRA gives to politicians like your friend Governor Morrissey? Or indeed the millions that you, sir, have also contributed?"

Porter's eyes narrowed on Waters, like a bird of prey just before it kills a lesser creature, and then without any expression said, "No, Mr. Waters, it isn't, but that won't stop men like you from trying to make it seem so." The reply caught Waters flat-footed. He was not used to interviewees attacking him personally, but he had brought it on himself. Before he could respond, Porter continued, "And with regard to your vulgar quote, it is not a strategy with which I am familiar, but it would seem to be a rather futile one to employ where there are no brains to be baffled—don't you think, Mr. Waters?"

Sarah McGill, who had reflexively widened the distance between herself and her GNBC colleague, held her microphone toward Representative Crane who was whispering something to her while Waters made a fool out of himself. The two of them both looked at Porter who directed his attention to them. He was done with Waters, even though the latter didn't know it.

Crane asked, "Captain Porter, may we get back to the issue at hand?"

"I was hoping someone would." As he said it, he flashed a puckish grin at McGill.

Crane continued, "Regardless of who is right or wrong, Captain Porter, why did you feel it necessary to register your complaint by force of gun rather than the force of reason? Surely, someone with your intellect and skills could have found a more peaceful and civilized way to get your point across."

"You mean like your colleagues do on the floor of the House?"

Crane knew exactly what Porter meant. The debate over gun control had brought out the worst in people all over America, and nowhere was this more evident than in the Congress itself, where decorum had given way to disorder on more than one occasion of late. Even the normally unflappable congressman had been guilty of it, and although he would not admit it, his own sense of reason had begun to sour into rage—a rage deep inside his soul that one day soon would lead to tragedy.

But there was no sign of the impending tragedy present at that moment, either for the congressman or the captain. With a little boy grin, Porter replied, "With all due respect, Congressman, if I was standing on a street corner in downtown Boise, or Washington, for that matter, would you be talking with me? Would any of you?"

Crane had no comeback. He knew Porter was right. Before he could think of something, Reverend Freeman brought the conversation back to his own agenda. "The Reverend Martin Luther King led our people to victory through peaceful debate, Captain, and not by taking up arms against the government."

"Reverend Freeman." Porter began his answer with the same tone of controlled passion; with the same empowering sense of purpose; and the same irresistible roguish smile that had endeared him to virtually all of the women in America, and many of the men. He was an unabashed bad boy and he knew it: disrespectful of fools, damning of tyrants, and disobedient to would-be kings. He was exactly like the rebels of long ago, called "saucy boys" by John Adams, who had stood defiantly on a hill in Boston in the face of withering gunfire from men in long red coats, and built a new nation. As he spoke, there was no mistaking that his audience was not the reverend, nor the congressman standing there before him; it was the millions of Americans sitting at home, watching him, hanging on his every word, completely captivated by him. At once, it was his greatest strength, and yet his greatest vulnerability, for as the vast army of his admirers grew, so did the number of his enemies. And the latter group included those few angry and jealous men who had the power to bring an army against him—an event that Sarah McGill, and others like her, knew one day would surely come.

Oblivious to his fate or perhaps driven by it, Porter continued, "I have the greatest respect for Martin Luther King and all that he stood for. But he, more than anyone, knew that you can never place your absolute trust in government. A government that for over two hundred years denied your people the equality promised to them in the Declaration of Independence, guaranteed to them by the Constitution, and affirmed to all the world in the Emancipation Proclamation." Porter paused and then closed with, "I respectfully submit, Reverend, that before you dismiss the rights of the millions of law abiding, gun-owning Americans, ask yourself this one, simple question. How many times have politicians made promises to people of color, including the savage innocents whose spirits now walk upon this mountain that they could not, would not, nor ever intended to keep?"

For the first time that anyone in the media could remember, Reverend Freeman was speechless. As much as he tried to resist, like millions of other Americans all across the land, he had fallen under the spell of the charismatic, and unapologetically defiant captain, who along with his little band of rebels was holding the entire might of the United States Government at bay.

Having vanquished the reverend and the congressman, Porter looked at the television cameras. "My fellow citizens of this great land, who among you thinks we can believe everything that politicians promise us? Who among you is willing to accept with blind faith everything President Webster is saying?" He paused for effect. "Being an American does not mean giving up the right to disagree, to question, and to challenge. It does not mean resigning the responsibility to think for ourselves on matters of the gravest importance. And it certainly does not mean changing the Constitution because someone in a place of privilege and power chooses to disagree with it. To make such a change is the singular act of a tyrant or a king, not the responsible act of a government elected by the people, of the people, and for the people."

Neither Freeman nor Crane said anything further. Porter's invocation of the words of Abraham Lincoln made it hard to do so. They both knew when to cut their losses and move on. Before the protesters could re-muster their opposition, Porter nodded to one of his men who immediately produced a key and stepped over to the gate and unlocked the heavy padlock and chain. Then Porter looked at Sarah McGill and motioned for her to join them. "Ms. McGill."

For a second, the articulate reporter was caught speechless. Then, she snapped out of the trance and said, "Yes, Captain?"

Porter smiled at her and said, "Would you come with me, please? You may bring your cameraman."

The line of police separating the crowd from the fence stepped aside and allowed Sarah and her cameraman to pass through the cordon. But when Perry Waters started to follow them, the soldier with the keys blocked his path and closed the gate.

"Hey! I'm with her," he barked at the soldier. But the young man ignored him and snapped the gate shut.

"Captain Porter!" Waters cried out.

Both Porter and McGill stopped and looked back at the gate.

"McGill and I are on the same team."

Porter shook his head and said, "No, Mr. Waters. You aren't even in the same league." Then he looked at Sarah and said, "Let's go." He started up the road.

McGill gave Waters an embarrassed and apologetic look. As much as she didn't like the man, she wasn't about to be mean to him, either. That wasn't her style. Then she turned and quickly followed Porter with her cameraman and the three soldiers trailing behind at a discrete distance.

"Bitch!" said Waters, a little more loudly than even he might have wished.

But no one paid him any attention, least of all Sarah McGill and Thomas Porter, both of whom heard the comment. As they walked up the dirt road in the fading autumn afternoon light, Sarah looked over at the captain and said, "You should have been a politician yourself, Captain Porter."

He laughed, "Not a chance."

"You could have worked to change the system from the inside."

His smile disappeared. "I've never been an insider, Ms. McGill."

"Why not?"

The smile returned but only slightly. "Did you come all the way out here to talk about me—or my cause?"

"Aren't they one and the same?"

They rounded a bend in the road where the crowd could no longer see them. Porter stopped walking and faced her, with the fading afternoon sun at his back, and the mountain looming above them in all its grandeur. "Not necessarily. How do you know that I'm not just some rich dilettante out for glory?"

She heard the words and saw his lips moving but it was all that she could do to get her brain to assimilate the data that it was being fed. *Come on Sarah, snap out of it. Talk, Sarah. Say something. Anything.* She fell back on the one trait that she detested most in others. It was a technique used by people whom she characterized as "the stupid or the guilty" when they were buying time to think or to lie as the case might be. She repeated the question word for word.

He smiled patiently and said, "Yes. I believe that was what I asked."

Now her cheeks betrayed her as they flushed hot pink. *Traitors! I'll buy the cheap moisturizer next time.* She shielded her eyes from the sun, a simple and innocent act that joined the conspiracy of her mouth and cheeks. Finally, her mind clicked back into gear and she said, "Because, Captain, you're an intelligent man and you know that by your actions you have placed yourself and your men in harm's way. Any man who would risk his life, and the lives of those who depend upon him, for a cause, can be called many things, but a dilettante is not one of them."

He reached out and grasped her by arms and the suddenness of the act combined with the gentle firmness of his grip sent a shiver up and down her spine. For an instant she thought he was going to pull her to him and kiss her, but he didn't; and somewhere deep inside, she felt a tiny twinge of disappointment. Instead he stepped slowly to his right, guiding her with him in a slow arc, until she was no longer looking into the sun. He let go of her arms and stood there for a long, lingering moment staring deeply into her pretty eyes. Finally he said, "Sarah, I think this is the beginning of a beautiful friendship."

"I beg your pardon?" she said as a mixture of emotions flooded into her. Casablanca was her favorite movie, and she knew every line. That he used one of the most well known lines from it momentarily flustered her.

"Come now, Sarah, surely you are familiar with the line?"

"Yes, I am," she said, as she regained her composure. "Casablanca is my favorite movie."

"Really! What a coincidence?" he said with an impetuous grin. "I guess that means that no matter what happens, we'll always have Paris, or in our case, this mountain." His words and manner flustered the normally unflappable news reporter and she didn't know what to say. Moreover, she didn't know what bothered her more—the fact that this irresistible desperado was flirting with her, or that she liked it. For a moment, just a moment, she let herself forget the setting, the circumstances, and one other important fact: Thomas Porter was a married man. Together they started up the dirt road. The feel of the soft, sandy gravel under her feet; the gentle rustling of the wind through the treetops; and the pungent smell of the pinewoods all about them momentarily overpowered her senses, and she found herself being caught up in the majesty of the mountain. After a few steps, she asked, "Captain, you said to Reverend Freeman that the reason you are here is related to the location. Somehow I sensed that you were referring not just to the gun club but to the mountain itself. Was I right?"

Porter smiled broadly and said, "Yes." He put his arm around her and said, "Come with me, Sarah, and I will tell you about this place where the spirits of a people dwell who were betrayed by the Great Father Chief in Washington. I will also tell you about my band of patriots, and why we, too, must make a stand here, on this mountain where freedom reigns."

Together they walked up the dusty road in the pale light of a high-mountain autumn afternoon, followed by her cameraman, toward the Bitterroot Rod & Gun Club, where Sarah McGill would get her story—a story like that of the first people to walk upon that mountain, one that she knew could not possibly have a happy ending.

8

GNBC Studios, Washington, D.C.

As usual, Sarah McGill was late for her meeting with Keene Lange. Keene was a tough newsman with a very low tolerance for arrogance or incompetence on either side of the camera. He saw neither of those traits in Sarah McGill. Quite the opposite. As a result, he had promoted her several times over older and more seasoned peers. On that particular day, he was about to do it again despite her chronic tardiness.

McGill reached his open door and hesitated when she saw that he was on the telcom. He beckoned her in and motioned for her to sit down, which she hated to do and rarely ever did. In fact the only time she ever really stayed still was when she was on camera.

"Okay, I agree. She's here now. I've got to go," he said making no effort to conceal the fact that he was obviously talking about her.

"You're late, as usual," he snapped in mock anger as he hung up the telcom receiver.

"I know. I was watching our coverage of the Bitterroots."

Lange nodded. The moment McGill returned from that mountain with her penetrating and poignant interview with Thomas Porter, he sensed that her interest was more than simply professional. However, since it had not gotten in the way of her story, he had stayed away from the subject. Besides, he realized that her feelings made her coverage even more impactful. It was one of the reasons that America loved her. She was wonderfully, willfully human.

"What's the status out there?"

"No change," she replied, but the worried look in her eyes spoke to the harsh reality that they both knew was yet to come. "Who was that?"

He stared at her over the top of his glasses, which she told him made him look like Benjamin Franklin. It was a comparison he did not find unwelcome.

"The chairman," he answered with a sly smile, referring to the head of the network.

"Don't tell me," she said with the look of a person who knows what's coming and isn't happy about it.

"What? I haven't said anything yet," he replied as his smile got even bigger.

McGill closed his door and walked up to the desk and stood there defiantly. "Damn it all, Keene, did Senator Niles call the chairman to complain about my coverage of the gun issue?"

Lange smiled. "No. Quite the opposite. He called the chairman to compliment you on your coverage of the issue, especially the way you presented Captain Porter and his cause."

She shrugged in her own little appealing way, like she did everything else. "The Captain did the talking. I just reported it."

Lange flexed an eyebrow. "That's not the way I saw it."

"What does that mean?"

"Relax, Sarah. Don't get defensive. I just meant that on film there was— well, let's just call it a certain connection between the two of you. Nothing inappropriate, mind you, but a connection nevertheless."

"He's married." It was a simple statement of fact, but her delivery belied her true feelings.

"Not happily, from what I hear."

"Really?" She caught herself. "I mean, that's too bad."

She didn't mean it and Keene knew it, but he sensed he was stepping too close to the line, and he backed off. "What's even more amazing is that the White House likes what you've been saying as well. You seem to have woven your magic again, Sarah, making everyone on both sides of an issue believe you are a friend of their cause."

"Thank-you." With that, she headed toward the door. She never felt comfortable being given praise. "Now, if you don't mind, the gun story is far from over, and I have to get back up to the Hill."

"No. You don't."

81

She spun around. "Why not?"

He smiled tauntingly. "Because you don't work there anymore."

She was stunned and didn't realize that what was coming was good news. "Where do I work now?"

"1600 Pennsylvania Avenue," he grinned.

For a moment she didn't say anything. Then she got it. "Are you saying what I think you are?"

"Yup. You're GNBC's new Chief White House Correspondent."

She flopped down into the chair across from him with her mouth open. Lange sat there smiling like a Cheshire cat. "Well, say something."

"When?"

"Now."

Her smile vanished. "I can't."

"Why not?"

"My gun story."

"Sarah, where do you think ground zero is in the gun issue?"

She nodded thoughtfully. "The White House."

"Bullseye!"

For a moment, she didn't seem to know what to do. Then with a vixen's smile, she got up and started to walk around his desk.

"What are you doing?" he said, flexing his bushy eyebrows.

"I'm going to give you a kiss."

"The hell you are," he said, jumping up and spilling his coffee. It didn't matter; the pile of old newspapers that were always present on his desk soon absorbed it.

"Why not?" she teased.

"Because you'll threaten me with sexual harassment charges every time I say no."

She laughed and continued her pursuit. "I would never do that."

"Right. Now get over to 1600 Pennsylvania Avenue and do your job."

"My new job can wait," she said, as the two of them circled the desk slowly.

"No, it can't," he said firmly. "You need to get on the President's anti-gun bill. It's already been approved by the House Subcommittee on the Constitution, and it has been sent back up to the full Judiciary Committee. I want to know when it will get to the chamber floor."

She stopped her pursuit. "I know the answer to that one. It's never."

"I think you're wrong. This one may just go all the way," said Lange, as he slipped into his chair, obviously relieved that the chase was over.

"No. It will never make it. The President caught a lucky break with the subcommittee because the Republican representatives from New York and California voted against party lines, but you can be sure that won't happen with the full Judiciary Committee."

"I don't know about that. Besides this is as much an issue of the heart as it is the head, and all it's going to take is a few impassioned testimonies by relatives of gun victims to shift the balance."

McGill shook her head, "That may be true, but even if it does squeak through committee, there is no way that the full House will approve it. The Speaker will see to that. And Alex Webster has neither the will nor the way to take on Jeremiah Kincaid."

"I wouldn't be so sure about that. Regardless of what you may think of the man, the office he occupies has virtually unlimited power."

"The measure of power is the ability to wield it," McGill replied.

"We'll see."

"I'd better get over to my new assignment," she said, heading for the door.

"Sarah." His change in tone told her something serious was coming.

"Yes."

"I'm stopping the investigation to find that cop who saved you. There's no officer named Michael Falconer in any law enforcement agency in D.C., mounted or otherwise."

"Maybe he was visiting from out of state?"

"With his horse? Moreover, there isn't any record of any officer of the law by the name of Michael Falconer in the entire Granite Shield database."

McGill's eyebrows knitted and she said, "I don't understand it."

"You were pretty shook up that night. You must have gotten his name wrong."

She thought about it for a minute, then shrugged. "Maybe."

"There's one more thing that's strange about the incident," he added.

"What?"

"The medical examiner couldn't find any cause of death for your attacker."

"Really?" The image of the horseman with his sword raised high flashed through her mind. She shrugged. "Maybe I just dreamt it."

Lange nodded sympathetically. "It was a traumatic moment."

She nodded. "Well, it's over now."

He nodded. "I guess you'd better get going to your new assignment."

"Yes." She started to leave.

"And Sarah—"

"Yes?"

"No more going into dangerous situations. Okay?"

"Okay."

She turned and was gone. Despite her answer he knew otherwise. Sarah McGill would go wherever the story was, and damn the consequences.

November, 2017

G Day - 300

So Dies Freedom

Hail, Columbia! happy land!
Hail, ye heroes heaven-born band!
Who fought and bled in Freedom's cause.

Joseph Hopkinson, "Hail Columbia"

9

Smythe Estate, Tysons Corner, Virginia

Major Anthony Conlan Gardener Smythe, fifty-nine, stood stiffly on one side of the room, in front of a large brick fireplace with a rough-hewn wooden mantle, above which hung a large painting of a black stallion. The room was dark and foreboding, like a forest at sundown, with mahogany paneling, burgundy leather chairs, and dark green wool carpeting. Six other men sat around a huge coffee table facing the fireplace, and above them hung a thick cloud of cigar smoke. They were deep in conversation and the heavy tones of their voices were in stark contrast to the tinkling of ice in crystal glasses that contained single malt Scotch. The focus of their attention was the major. He was a muscular and tightly wound man, of above-average height, although he looked shorter because of his disproportionately short legs and long body. He was a former officer in the British Army with a murky pedigree and an even murkier profession.

"We are growing increasingly uncomfortable with your activities, Major Smythe," said an aging man with a deep Southern accent. His name was Harridan Niles, seventy-nine, a former United States Senator from Mississippi, who was the very essence of poise and dignity, even though it had been many years since his face had been seen in and around the Capitol. In his day, he had been one of the most powerful men in Washington, or on earth for that matter.

"We?" queried the major.

"Yes," Niles replied, obviously unwilling to explain further.

The other men in the room sat quietly. Three were approaching the senator in years and had the look of self-confidence that comes with a life time of power and money. The other two were younger but equally impressive in dress, manner, and poise.

"What exactly is it that troubles you, Senator?"

Perturbed at having to explain, the senator cleared his throat and said, "I don't feel it necessary to explain myself. Suffice to say that our organization must not be associated with your gun-running activities."

The major sized the old man up before answering. "I assure you that it won't. But equally, may I remind you, that my 'gun-running' as you call it, provides a significant amount of lobbying money in support of our mutual cause."

"All the money in the world will serve no purpose if we lose the support of our members, sir. Up until now the New Sons of Liberty have done nothing illegal or immoral in the cause of freedom, and as long as I am the Chairman of this committee, that will not change. Do I make myself clear?"

The major took a long sip of his scotch, all the while staring at the senator over the upper rim of his glass. He finished it, and in his most deferential tone said, "Perfectly. I apologize for any ill will that the recent actions of my company may have caused you, and I assure you that I will do nothing to destroy what you have created. Although I am a British citizen, I am committed to the cause of freedom in this great land and I deeply admire the passion and sense of purpose of the New Sons of Liberty." The major was a charming man with all the mystery and panache of a soldier of fortune. The irony of a Brit helping the modern-day New Sons of Liberty against tyranny was not lost on any of the members of the group. However, the major's rapidly expanding gun importing activities had greatly strained their relationship.

"Good. Now let's turn to another pressing matter. I believe you said you had some information regarding the continuing standoff in Idaho?"

"Yes. My sources tell me that at present, the militia seems to have the upper hand. Their leader, Thomas Porter, happens to be an acquaintance of mine. He is a multi-billionaire businessman turned patriot, who has done a superb job making a fool out of the President and the Federal Government."

A few of the men nodded.

"His articulate and passionate pleas are being eaten up by the public like word candy, and he has brought national attention to the Federal Government's attempts to disarm America. We couldn't have asked for a better spokesperson for the pro-gun movement if we had picked him ourselves."

"That may well be, but sooner or later the governor is going to send in the police, and it will be bloody," said the senator.

The major smiled and said, "That won't happen, Senator. Thomas Porter is the single largest supporter of the governor's reelection fund, and I am certain that the governor will seek to negotiate a peaceful end to this affair. In fact, my sources have informed me that he is reaching out to someone right now who can do just that."

"Who might that be?" asked the senator.

"His name is General Jesse Latrobe. He is an old friend of the governor's and a retired military man."

The senator seemed miffed that Smythe was on the inside in this matter and that *he* was not. "Regardless of what the governor does or does not do, there is another factor that we must not dismiss. That is the President. He is unpredictable and very dangerous. I doubt that he will give the governor much latitude on the matter."

"Regrettably, you may be right, Senator," replied Smythe. "But for all of our sakes, let us hope not."

"Yes, indeed. Thank-you for that update, Major. Now if you would please give us a few minutes alone?" said the senator.

The major smiled and said, "Yes. Of course. Take all the time you need and feel free to help yourself to my Cuban cigars and single malt scotch. After all, you paid for it." With that, he left the room.

Senator Niles stood up, walked over to the bar beside the fireplace, and poured himself another drink. After asking the others if they wanted any, which they did not, he sat down. "Gentlemen, I don't need to restate my position. You all know how concerned I am that the Major is becoming a liability for our organization."

One of the older men interjected, "Excuse me, Harridan, but do you think it's appropriate to have this conversation here? I mean this is the Major's house." He glanced around the room, as if expecting to see microphones everywhere.

The senator paused briefly and then said, "That's an excellent question, Lamar, and one that I might have expected from you." He was referring to the fact that Lamar Wacker, seventy-six, was a five-term senator from Georgia, and the current Chairman of the Senate Committee on Armed

89

Services. "My people had this room swept for listening devices this morning before we arrived. The major was quite accommodating in allowing this. The room is perfectly clean, I assure you." Unfortunately for the senator, the experts his staff had used to check the room for electronic bugs were one step behind the technology curve. One of the pieces of glass covering the wooden shelves in the bookcase was different from the others. Although it looked the same to the naked eye, it was embedded with a tiny micro-transmitter that was, at that moment, sending everything they were saying to the major's men located in the basement of the mansion.

Having satisfied Wacker's concern, Niles continued, "As you know, the New Sons of Liberty was formed to take a stand against the egregious actions of the present administration and to protect our Constitutional rights. Over the past six months, we have grown in number and stature, as men and women from all stations of power and influence have placed their money and moral support behind our cause. We have come too far, and our mission is too important to risk it all by continuing to allow the major to be affiliated with us, despite his financial support. This is especially true, now given the tinder box situation in the Bitterroot Mountains. President Webster will stop at nothing to gain complete victory in his war on guns. Intervention by the authorities is inevitable and we simply cannot afford to risk being drawn into the maelstrom by our association with the major's group. Therefore, I propose to you, the Executive Committee of the New Sons of Liberty, that we disassociate ourselves from the major immediately."

The others indicated their support, except for one of the younger men, who did not seem comfortable with what the senator was proposing. His name was Franklin Latham, and he was Chairman and Chief Executive Officer of Heartland Foods, Inc., the world's largest consumer products company that sold everything from candy to coffee to cigarettes. After taking a slow drink from his glass, during which time the senator became increasingly annoyed, Latham spoke. "With all due respect senator, if the original Sons of Liberty had disassociated themselves from the shady side of human nature, we would still be part of the British Commonwealth. Although I have the deepest respect for you, I must disagree and urge this committee to keep the major and his organization closely affiliated with ours. If this situation turns violent we will be glad to have his money—and guns—with us."

"We can live without his money, and his guns do nothing to support our cause," snapped the senator.

"We may need both if America goes to war over this matter," persisted Latham.

"That's preposterous!" The senator was incensed at being challenged. He was a founding member of the New Sons of Liberty, and this impertinent young man, despite being well-connected and a heavy benefactor of their cause, was still a relative newcomer. However, through his long years in Congress, he had learned that passion was a raging river that could more easily be directed than dammed. He looked the other man directly in the eyes and said, "My dear, Mr. Latham, you are obviously a man of considerable intelligence, charisma, and passion. Three admirable traits. Moreover, it is quite clear to me that after we are through with this odious matter, and once this administration has been thrown out of power, there will be a place in the new world order for a man such as yourself. However, for the moment, I submit to you that our cause would be better served if you were to direct your talents toward defeating the President though legal and peaceful means. The major is a stick of dynamite looking for a match, and at this moment, we are standing far too close to him."

Latham was not convinced, but he was flattered which was exactly what Niles had expected. "Very well, Senator Niles. I will support your proposal."

There was an audible sigh of relief in the room.

"Gentlemen, now is the time to put this to a formal vote. All those in favor of disassociating ourselves with the major, say aye."

The senator and the other men all said "Aye."

"The vote being unanimous, the motion is carried," said the senator. "I will tell the major myself, but I see no need to involve you in this discussion." The senator took a finely crafted pocket watch out of his vest. It had been left to him by his grandfather, and he thought that wearing it gave him an air of dignity. In fact, to most people it was simply another indication of the senator's reluctance to let go of the past. "This meeting is adjourned. Have a safe trip home."

The men all stood up to go.

Latham extended his hand toward the senator. "I trust that there are no hard feelings, Senator Niles."

The senator shook his hand and smiled in the patronizing way that had annoyed his opponents throughout his long career. "No, of course not, Franklin. Open and honest debate is what this country is all about. It is precisely because of the President's unwillingness to accept any such debate that we are all here."

Latham smiled, but it was shallow. "Of course, you're right. Good night, Senator. Sleep tight."

"I always do," the senator boasted, sticking his chest out and flexing his shoulder muscles. "I'm in better shape at seventy-nine than many men your age."

Latham was clearly uncomfortable with where the conversation was headed. "Yes. I'm sure you are," he replied politely.

The senator held up one arm and bent it at the elbow, "Go ahead. Feel my bicep."

The last thing that Latham wanted to do was feel the old man's bicep but he indulged the senator. He knew that if he didn't, the senator would keep him there talking about how good a shape he was in all night.

"As solid as a rock," said Latham.

The senator said, "Clean living and exercise, son. That's the secret."

"Yes, sir. Thank-you for the tip. Now good night."

The meeting was over. After the others had all left the mansion, the senator met privately with Smythe and told him that the New Sons of Liberty no longer wanted him to be a member. The major listened politely and graciously accepted the decision. Then the senator got into his sleek black limousine and headed back to Georgetown, satisfied that he had eliminated a threat to his larger organization. He was quite pleased with himself and the way he had handled the major. He should not have been because the issue of the major's participation with the New Sons of Liberty was not dead. Far from it.

AFTER SAYING goodbye to Niles, Smythe headed back to the den. The lights were off and he didn't bother to switch them on as he entered and closed the door. He walked over to the coffee table, opened the humidor and took out a large cigar. He expertly prepared it for lighting, clipping the end and smelling it with obvious pleasure. Then he placed it in his mouth. As he reached for a long wooden match on the mantel an arm was suddenly thrust out of the shadows. Smythe flinched. In the hand was a match which burst into flame without being struck.

"Jesus Christ! You startled me." He exclaimed, but he obviously knew that he should not have said what he did. Quickly recovering he said, "I'm sorry. That was rather tasteless of me."

"You are forgiven. This once," said a deep and rumbling voice. The speaker stepped into the light of his own match. It was Stefan Chadrian. His face seemed translucent in the flickering light, and his long black hair was draped back over his bony ears like the curtains in a hearse. Smythe seemed uncomfortable in his presence. Chadrian added, "You handled that well."

Smythe nodded. "Yes, I did." He held the other man's hand as he lit his cigar and then with a puzzled look on his face said, "Your hands are ice cold, Stefan."

The match continued to burn, but the flame did not move down the wooden shaft.

"Cold hands, warm heart," replied Chadrian, with obvious sarcasm.

"You mean cold hands and an even colder heart, don't you?" parried the major.

"Warmth is a relative term, Major," he replied with a bemused smile. "Now let us talk about the future and the role that you will play in it."

The major walked over to a heavy brass lamp that was sitting on a table near the window and started to turn it on.

"No. Leave it dark. That way your brain will be totally focused upon my words." The match abruptly went out.

The major smiled uneasily. "Very well."

Both men sat down in two of the heavy leather chairs and Chadrian began speaking in a slow and measured pace. And Smythe listened as if his life depended upon it.

It did.

10

The White House, Washington, D.C.

President Alexander Webster was an outrageous flirt, as one of his visitors was discovering. He sat in a wing-backed chair in the Oval Office, with Patrick Fitzgerald sitting immediately to his right on one of the two yellow sofas, and Maddun Gordon standing off to the side behind him. But the focus of his attention was Mary Lou Pritchard, forty-two, the Deputy Attorney General, a shapely woman with auburn hair, pouting lips and full, earnest breasts, who was sitting to the President's left on the other sofa. Beside her was her boss, Arnold Greenberg, seventy-three, the Attorney General, a frail and thin man with mottled skin and a hawk-like nose.

"Go ahead, Mary Lou," said Greenberg.

"The leader of the group is a man named Thomas Porter, Mr. President. He was formerly the CEO of Communitrex, Inc., a Silicon Valley broadband communications company he founded. He subsequently joined the—"

"Yes, Ms. Pritchard," the President interrupted, "I'm well aware of Mr. Porter's recent past, but it's his life before that that's at issue here. Wouldn't you agree?" he said, flashing a charming smile. "Mr. Fitzgerald tells me that the FBI has been unsuccessful in figuring out just exactly who this mysterious Mr. Porter is. Is that right?"

"Yes, sir, I'm afraid so," she replied with a slight blush. "And it's Mrs. Pritchard, sir," she added, "My husband is Colonel Mitchell Pritchard. He works at the Pentagon in General McWilliams'—"

"The President doesn't care where your husband works, Mrs. Pritchard," interrupted Maddun Gordon.

The President flashed an annoyed look at Gordon and turned back toward Pritchard. "You'll have to excuse Mr. Gordon, Ms. Pritchard, he's not much on charm. Now please continue."

Slightly flustered, Pritchard looked at her boss, who gently touched her arm, a move that did not go unnoticed by the President. He urged her to continue, "Go ahead, Mary Lou."

Reassured, she did just that. "Mr. President, in trying to trace Mr. Porter's background we have hit a dead end, but I can assure you that it is only a temporary setback."

Obviously disinterested in what she was telling him, the President once again interrupted her, "No, no, no—I meant please continue telling me about your husband." The President stared at her with a sly smile that completely unnerved her. She looked at her boss once more, but even he was now becoming unsettled by the President's blatant flirting.

Finally, Patrick Fitzgerald stepped in and eased the awkwardness of the situation. It was a role that he had become quite accustomed to filling. "Colonel Pritchard works on General McWilliams' staff. He personally spearheaded the development of the Army's new M1A3 Abrams Main Battle Tank."

The look on Mary Lou's face indicated her delight that the President's national security adviser knew about her husband's accomplishments.

"Is that right, Mary Lou? I hope you don't mind me calling you that, now, do you?"

"Yes sir—no sir—I mean, I don't mind you..."

"I understand what you mean, Mary Lou," the President replied, his personal charm now in overdrive.

"Perhaps we should get back to the situation in the Bitterroots, sir," interjected the Attorney General.

"Why yes, why don't we do just that." The smile disappeared from his face. "Go ahead, Arnold, let's see if you know more about Captain Porter than your deputy does."

"I wasn't trying to..."

"Look, Arnold," interrupted the President, but the tone and inflection of his voice changed: it was softer, gentler. Even his enemies admired his ability to change his demeanor in an instant, like a chameleon changes color. "I apologize for being a little testy. But this incident has taken attention away from my proposed legislation and I am getting tired of it." He finished his apology and turned back to face Pritchard, glancing at her breasts before looking into her eyes, sending her as clear a message as he could, without actually coming right out and saying that he wanted her.

Arnold relaxed only slightly. He knew better than to ever completely let his guard down with the President, for as quickly as the storm abated, it could return again with a fury. "I understand, Mr. President. I was pleased to hear that your bill had been approved by the House Constitutional Subcommittee and forwarded to the full Judiciary Committee for review. The speed with which it is moving is really quite remarkable. A testament to the gravity of the matter and the import of your bill."

The President reluctantly took his eyes off Pritchard and looked at Greenberg. "Yes, Arnold. It's proceeding well and I think we have a chance of getting an affirmative vote on it before the summer recess."

"Really?" asked Pritchard, immediately regretting her forwardness.

Webster smiled. "You say that as if you have some doubts, Ms. Pritchard."

"Please don't misunderstand me, Mr. President. I believe your bill has significant merit. It's just that the Speaker has made it clear that the Republicans intend to add some amendments to the bill, which will dilute its impact before it gets to the full House."

Pritchard's comment had made Greenberg wince and his body language indicated that he desperately wanted to get himself and Pritchard out of there.

The President clearly wanted just the opposite and he would have had his way were it not for a knock on the door. It opened to reveal a tall black woman dressed in a crisp suit.

"Excuse me, Mr. President."

"What is it, darling?" the President asked.

"I have Governor Morrissey on the telephone, sir." His assistant still used the old term out of habit but the large, wireless communications console, or BTC, on the President's desk, bore only a slight resemblance to the hard wired telephone of the past. At the flick of a switch, incoming calls could be transferred to the wall-mounted video screen hidden behind a panel in Oval Office. However, at Webster's request, this feature had been disabled in the White House.

"Very well. I'll be right with him." The President glanced back at Mary Lou and said, "I'm afraid we'll have to continue this discussion later, Ms. Pritchard."

"Of course, Mr. President," Greenberg said, cutting off Pritchard before she could reply. As he stood up, he looked over at her and said firmly, "Let's go, Mary Lou." Both of them got up and left the room.

After they were gone, the President turned to Patrick Fitzgerald and said, "Find out everything you can about Colonel and Mary Lou Pritchard, will you? You know the usual drill."

Fitzgerald gave him a questioning look, then nodded and said, "Yes sir," with an unmistakable tone of 'I'd rather not.'

As the younger man turned to leave the President called him back, "Patrick."

"Yes, sir," Fitzgerald answered like a child who knew his father was about to give him a lecture.

"Do you have something you want to say?" asked the President with a sly smile.

"No, sir," came the half-hearted response.

"Patrick, you are one of the most intelligent and politically savvy people who has ever worked in the West Wing, but you are a lousy poker player."

"Yes, sir. It's just that I don't think it would be wise for you…"

"For me to get involved with a married woman?"

"Yes, sir."

"First of all, Patrick, let me remind you that I am single now and best friends with my former wife."

"Yes, sir."

"Second, if it turns out that the Pritchards are happily married, the matter will end there. But, there was something in the way she looked at me that told me that they aren't. Now let's go back to the part where I'm the President and you're my adviser."

"Yes, sir," Fitzgerald answered, barely hiding the frustration in his voice as he headed out of the office.

Gordon sat down heavily on one of the sofas. "I didn't know you had made up with your ex-wife?"

"I haven't—I still hate the bitch," the President said as he walked over, took a cigar out of a humidor on his desk, and slowly lit it, all the while staring at the blinking light on his desk-based telcom unit. "But best friends plays better with the public."

Changing back to the subject at hand, Gordon asked, "What are you going to say to Governor Morrissey, Mr. President?" Even as he asked it, he already knew the answer.

"I'm going to tell that pompous little asshole, who's had his balls handed to him by a ragtag band of mountain men, that if he can't handle the situation, I will." The President picked up the telcom handset, clicked his charm into high gear and said, "Eddy, what's the good word in the Bitterroots, old buddy?" His use of "Eddy," which what was not the governor's nickname, made it clear that they were anything but buddies.

Puffing deeply on his cigar, Webster listened as the governor obviously launched into a long and detailed answer. He let him ramble on, only occasionally interjecting a "Yes," or an "I understand." Finally, after several minutes, he said, "Governor, I appreciate the spot you're in and I want you to know that like you, I seek a peaceful solution to the problem. However— and Eddy, I want you to hear me loud and clear—this situation is like having a dead whale on the beach; it doesn't get any better with time. Sooner or later you are going to have to deal with it."

The President listened again as the governor said something. Then he replied, "Quite frankly Governor, I don't give a rat's ass for what your Supreme Court Justices say or do. Native American claims to Federal lands is old news. So tell those old farts to rule against the petition and move on." The President paused and then lowered his voice, "Please understand that what I am about to say is not meant as a threat, simply a heartfelt desire to try to help you. But that band of toy soldiers has illegally occupied Federal property for eight weeks now and if you can't, or won't deal with it, I assure you, I can, and I will. Do I make myself clear?" He paused and said, "Good. Keep me posted. Good-bye."

He hung up the receiver, walked over to the window behind his desk, and stood there staring out across the lawn. "The Idaho Supreme Court has agreed to rule on a petition filed by a Boise law firm on behalf of the Nez Perce, claiming they own all the lands around and including that bloody mountain that the Bitterroot Rod & Gun Club sits on. Until they do, they have issued an injunction prohibiting any actions on the part of law enforcement to retake the club."

"Where in the hell did the Nez Perce get the money for that?"

"I wonder," Webster replied sarcastically.

Gordon thought about it for a minute. His eyes widened. "Porter?"

The President nodded. "You got it."

Both men fell silent as they contemplated the situation. Finally, Gordon said, "How much more time should we give him, sir?"

The President gave him a cold stare and replied, "None."

Gordon nodded. "I understand, sir. I'll take care of it right away."

The President thought about it for another minute and then shook his head. "No. Before we resort to that, there's something else I'd like to do."

"What?"

Webster took a deep puff on his cigar. "I think I'll go to the Bitterroots and talk with that young captain myself."

Gordon was stunned. "I don't think that would be a good idea, sir."

The President ignored him. "Yes. That's exactly what I'll do."

Gordon knew better than to argue with the President when he had made up his mind. "Very well, sir, I will arrange it. When do you want to go?"

"Immediately." His eyes narrowed. "But just in case I can't talk some sense into Porter, have the other plan ready to go."

"Of course," said Gordon with a knowing smile. The *other* plan as the President referred to it, involved sending the Army in to take back the club, and Gordon looked forward to giving General Halston Pace, the Chairman of the Joint Chiefs that order. He knew Pace didn't like him, and especially wouldn't like the order, which made it an even more pleasurable task.

"One more thing," said the President. "Find out more about Porter. I think there's something going on between him and the governor."

"If the FBI and DHS haven't succeeded at that, I'm not sure I can, Mr. President."

"Just do it!"

"Yes, sir." With that, he excused himself and left. The President's tone and manner didn't phase Gordon at all. It was a style that he knew all too well and was fond of using, himself. He had met Webster twelve years earlier when he was the governor of California and Gordon was a rich and bored CEO. Their friendship grew when Gordon left his company to help Webster's struggling Presidential campaign during the Democratic primaries five years later. He succeeded in turning around the campaign, and it was widely accepted that he was the main reason that Webster now occupied the White House. But it had evolved into a rocky friendship as both men had huge egos, and only one of them was President. However, Gordon was willing to take a lot of grief, not for any altruistic reason, such as shaping the course of history, but simply because of the raw, unadulterated power that someone who sits beside the President of the United States enjoys.

Webster looked at a framed black-and-white photo of President Kennedy standing in the same spot. Keeping his eyes glued on the photo, he shifted his position several times, trying to mimic JFK's pose. Finally, satisfied that he stood exactly where his hero had before him, the President took another drag on his cigar and closed his eyes. Then he said softly to himself, "A nation totally free from guns. That's every bit as bold as putting a man on the moon, don't you think, Jack?" He paused and then added, "Just think of what it might have meant for you."

MARY LOU PRITCHARD and the Attorney General sat in the back of his government limousine as it pulled out of the White House back gate and headed north on East Executive Avenue. Pritchard was visibly upset, and she barely noticed the small group of protesters dressed in camouflage fatigues who were walking back and forth in front of the White House. They carried signs that indicated their support for the militiamen who occupied the Bitterroot Rod and Gun Club two thousand miles away. While Pritchard didn't notice the protesters, her boss did.

"Those foolish young men up on that mountaintop are gaining the sympathy of a growing percentage of the population," said Greenberg.

Pritchard acknowledged his statement with a hollow, "Yes. They are."

"I just hope our boys at the Bureau keep their guns holstered until we have exhausted all options. The last thing we need right now is another Ruby Ridge or Waco."

Pritchard came out of her trance and looked at her boss. "Sooner or later, that egomaniac in the big white house we just left is going to get jealous of all the attention the militia captain is getting. Then it won't matter what the Bureau does or doesn't do. Alexander the Not-So Great will likely charge up the mountain himself."

"Just a minute, Mary Lou." With that, he leaned over and pressed the button that raised the smokey-gray, sound proof glass between them and their driver. He motioned for her to wait until it was all the way up. Then he said, "Mary Lou. He is the President." Greenberg was a lifelong Democrat but he had hand picked Pritchard to be his deputy, despite the fact that she was a Republican. To him, talent and brains were all that mattered, not political affiliation but as much as he would never admit it to Pritchard, he knew that it was her other ample physical assets that got her the most attention, particularly from the President.

"He's a jerk, and you know it," she replied sharply.

"Don't let him get to you. You're better than that."

"Don't let him get to me. He practically raped me right in front of you. Doesn't the man ever get laid?"

"All the time," he answered with a sad shake of his head.

"By anyone who doesn't do it for a living?"

"Obviously you need to vent, Mary Lou. So go ahead. I'm listening."

"You're dammed right, I will. I am the Deputy Attorney General of the United States of America. I graduated Magna Cum Laude from Simmons College and third in my class at Harvard Law School. I have clerked in the Supreme Court and I was the youngest partner in the history of the most prestigious law firm on Wall Street. I have earned the right to be treated with respect. I don't care if he's the most powerful man on the face of the earth. I object to him undressing me in public."

"Are you finished?" he asked her with the gentle fatherly tone he often used on his associates.

"No—yes. Oh hell, what does it matter anyway, he's the President. And he holds all the cards."

"Look, Mary Lou, you are all that you said you are and much more. But, if you will allow me to overstep the bounds of political correctness just for one moment, women like you, who possess both raw, sensual beauty and mensa level I.Q.'s are magnets to all men, not just to those who never learned to keep their libido in their pants. I know how much of a burden it is to be brilliant and a babe—but you are, so build a bridge and get over it. Besides me thinks thou dost protest too much," he added with a teasing smile.

She stared at him in disbelief. "You think that I'm attracted to that sophomoric cock-for-brains who believes he's God's gift to womankind?"

"Most women are."

"Arnold, I'm happily married, for God's sake." With that, she slumped back into her seat. She sat there quietly for a minute, staring out the window, then without looking at her boss she said quietly, "You think I have raw sensual beauty?"

"I knew I'd regret that the moment I said it."

With an impetuous grin she asked, "Does your wife know you think that I have raw sensual beauty?"

Feigning his most stern demeanor he stared at her and said, "No. And if you ever tell her I will see to it that you are appointed as our first Ambassador to Antarctica."

She giggled and said, "Well, you have succeeded in diffusing my temper, like you always do, but I swear if that lecher ever tries to undress me with his eyes again, I will tell him exactly what I think he is, career be damned."

"Understood."

Her anger having been alleviated, at least for the moment, Mary Lou stared idly out the car window as it eased into the driveway to the underground garage at the Department of Justice. She looked at her boss, "What do we do about the Bitterroots?"

"Nothing for now."

"Understood."

The limousine came to a stop inside the garage, and the driver knocked once and opened the door.

They got out and headed across the basement toward the elevators. "Thank-you. You always know what to say, boss, and when to say it."

"You're welcome. Now let's get back to work. I want you to forget about the man at 1600 Pennsylvania Avenue and simply remember the office he occupies."

"I will, but don't ever send me over there alone."

"I won't. I promise."

They got into the elevator and the doors closed.

FOUR STAR Army General Halston Pace, sixty-four, Chairman of the Joint Chiefs of Staff was a proud man who suffered fools lightly. Whenever he found himself in the presence of someone who neither understood, nor appreciated, the military he always flexed his jaws so strongly that the veins in his forehead bulged. That was the case as he stood beside the long table in the Situation Room of the White House. Across from him sat Maddun Gordon, who by his laid-back posture and smug look, obviously had very little respect for the man across from him.

"Say that again, Mr. Gordon," said the general with a look that could melt glass.

"You heard me the first time," said Gordon.

"With all due respect to your boss, Mr. Gordon, humor me."

Gordon leaned forward and said very deliberately, "I said that the President wants you to be ready to send the Army into Bitterroot Rod & Gun Club pending his final orders."

"That's what I thought you said, and it sounded just as stupid the second time."

"What did you say?" said Gordon.

The general leaned across the table toward Gordon, who reflexively pulled back a bit. "Listen to me sonny boy, I was watching men die and wiping their brains off my sleeve while your boss was still having his nose wiped by his mama." There was no mistaking the anger in the general's voice. "The Army is not a civilian police force and it will not be used as such as long as I hold this post. Moreover, even if I were to go along with this stupid idea, I think the Congress might just remind your boss that the Posse Commitatus Act prevents me from doing so. Or did your boss sleep through that lecture at law school?"

"My boss doesn't need you to teach him the law, General, and the White House Counsel feels that there is ample precedent for using the Army in domestic matters, just as we did during WWT, or did you sleep through that little war?"

"Go to hell," said the general, and he meant it.

Gordon was unfazed. Summoning all his bravado, he stood up and said, "May I remind you, sir, that the President is your commander in chief, and he has given you an order. If you choose not to obey it, the President will get someone who will. Do I make myself clear, sir?"

The general glared at Gordon for a long moment. Then he said, "I'll carry out his order, Mr. Gordon, but so help me God, if this goes as badly as I think it will, you and your boss will have to face the consequences—all of them. I shit you not."

"Are you threatening the President, General?"

The general walked around the table, got right into Gordon's face, and said, "Listen to me, you slimy little sycophant. If this goes badly, I will be the least of your worries. And you can quote me." Then he stormed out of the room.

Gordon collected himself, took a deep breath and then picked up his PTC. He punched a key and said softly, "It's done." He listened for a moment and then said, "Yes, but he'll calm down. He always does." He paused again and then said, "Don't worry, sir, the Bitterroots are about to become yesterday's headlines. Good night, sir." Then he hung up the telcom receiver, walked over to the door, flicked out the lights, and left. He was wrong—on both counts.

11

Bitterroot Rod & Gun Club, Idaho

The front gates of the Bitterroot Rod & Gun Club were closed and locked as they had been for two months. During that time, they had gradually been barricaded by a jumbled pile of fallen trees, rusty bed springs, and old truck tires. Up until the day before, it had been an ugly sight in keeping with the national mood, but during the night the first snowfall of what would prove be a long and cold winter had covered everything in a light dusting of white, including the tall pines that framed the scene, giving it an almost fairy tale look. Outside the gates, a mixture of paper trash and aspen leaves danced on a chill breeze across the well-trodden ground, while a muzzled German shepherd tried to tongue a bit of chocolate from a candy bar wrapper. Behind a fleet of squad cars and other official vehicles, a large and heterogeneous group of law enforcement officers milled about, some dressed in heavy SWAT gear but most simply wearing their various local or state patrol uniforms. Intermingled among them, but clearly not of them, were numerous Federal agents with their respective agencies marked in large yellow letters on the backs of their navy windbreakers, prompting some of the local cops to refer to them as hard targets walking.

Off to one side, a group of reporters and cameramen were gathered in a semi-circle and over the sound of a departing helicopter, they strained to hear the FBI Special Agent in Charge, as he wrapped up his daily morning news briefing. The reporters all clamored for his attention, and he seemed annoyed by their raucous shouting.

"You!" he said, pointing at one reporter. As he spoke, his breath hung in the cold mountain air. It was Perry Waters, looking more tired than he had when Sarah McGill had stolen the interview that he felt he had deserved.

"We are entering the ninth week of this standoff with no apparent end in sight. During that time, Captain Porter, with the cooperation of the governor, has given the media wide access to his camp and, as a result, the American people have gotten to know him and his men on an almost personal basis."

"Is this a question or soliloquy?" the agent sharply interjected.

"My question is this, sir: given Porter's impassioned and some have said, eloquent pleas to the country, aren't you concerned that the FBI, and not the militia, are in jeopardy of becoming the bad guys in this standoff?"

The agent answered sharply. "The only bad guys in this situation are those criminals posing as patriots up that dirt road, but if this situation goes on long enough, you in the media will have the American people believing that this is Concord and we are the British redcoats. Nothing could be further from the truth."

"Then why have you let it go on so long, sir?" asked Waters.

"That's a question you'll have to take up with Governor Morrissey and the State Supreme Court."

"Are you prepared to stay up here all winter, officer?" shouted another reporter who had been jumping in place and hugging himself, trying to shake off the morning chill.

"If necessary, but apparently, you aren't," replied the agent.

Waters wouldn't let it go, "Don't you think that the chances for a non-violent solution slip away with each passing day?"

"I'm not paid to think," the agent snapped back, regretting his words the moment they left his mouth, "Now, if you'll excuse me."

The agent walked quickly away, ignoring the numerous shouts for him to answer more questions. Standing beside the podium were several Idaho state troopers, including their chief, Chank Swale. Throughout the crisis it had become quite evident to all those covering the story that there was no love lost between the State Police and the FBI, and after the agent left the podium, the reporters shouted to the chief to take the microphone. At first he shook his head no, but after only a little prodding he stepped up to the mike and said with a wry smile, "Ladies and gentlemen, I believe the SAC told you that the press conference was over."

"Aw, come on, Chief Swale," shouted one of the newspaper reporters, a curmudgeonly old character with a large following, "The Feds are all dickheads, and you know it."

Laughter rumbled through the crowd.

"I take the Fifth on that one," replied Swale with a broad smile on his face. "As for the press conference, I think it's best that we follow the SAC's lead and call it a day." With that, he started to leave the podium.

"Is it true that Captain Porter is a personal friend of the governor's?" shouted Waters.

The question froze the chief in his tracks. He stopped and turned around. "Who asked that?" he asked, the smile now gone from his face. The reporter from GNBC raised his hand. The chief studied the reporter for a moment.

"Captain Thomas Porter is the former CEO of Communitrex, Inc., who presently resides outside Sun Valley. While he has been a strong supporter of the Republican Party, the governor only recalls meeting Mr. Porter on one occasion."

Waters persisted. "Yes, we know that, Chief, but according to the Associated Press, the FBI has been unable to trace Mr. Porter's background any further back than seven years ago, when he started his company, and apparently the governor's office has refused to cooperate with the investigation. Can you comment on this?"

"No."

"No, you *cannot* or no, you *will* not?"

"Take it any way you want to. Now, ladies and gentlemen, this press conference really is over." He joined several of his senior officers, and as they walked away, none of them were smiling.

Waters looked toward his cameraman, held the microphone up to his mouth, and began speaking in the quasi-solemn tones that reporters use when they are searching for a story that doesn't want to be found.

"As you just heard, ladies and gentlemen, the situation here in the Bitterroots remains tense as a company of militia, led by the charming but enigmatic Captain Thomas Porter, holds the entire nation spellbound and the law enforcement establishment at bay. Meanwhile, the state's leading law firm, acting on behalf of the Nez Perce Indian Tribe, and paid for by the wealthy Mr. Porter, has filed a petition with the State Supreme Court seeking to nullify the Federal Government's ownership of the land upon which the gun club is built. The basis of the claim is that the land was taken illegally from its rightful owners, the Nez Perce, over one hundred years ago, and as such, only they have the right to evict the militia from the club. So far, the Nez Perce have had no public comment on the matter; however, our sources tell us that the elders of the tribe are strong supporters of Captain Porter. Meanwhile, the high court has agreed to hear the case, and has issued an injunction preventing the Federal Government from taking any action pending their decision. And no one has any idea when that will be, apparently including the justices themselves. For GNBC, this is Perry Waters on a mountain that the Nez Perce people call the Kingdom of the Wind Spirit. Now, back to our studios in New York."

The reporter turned to his cameraman, made a cutting motion at his throat and lowered his microphone. "Well, that was much ado about nothing. When are they going to tell us something that we don't know?"

"If you ask me," said the cameraman, "They should take lessons on how to win friends and influence people from Captain Porter and his boys."

"You're right. He's making them look pretty foolish."

"And stupid," added the cameraman.

The reporter nodded and said in somber tones, "And it isn't going to help the militia one bit when the day of reckoning finally comes."

The cameraman thought about it for a moment and added, "I hate this place. It has the look and the feel of death."

"Come on, let's go get a cup of coffee," said Waters. "You're buying."

The cameraman shrugged, "Don't I always?"

IN THE GNBC studios in New York, Allistair Blevis, forty-nine, a glib man with a slight overbite and a swept-back pompadour that made him look like he was in a constant state of acceleration, swiveled away from the screen to face the camera. He sat behind a large, horseshoe-shaped table, and to his left sat a man and a woman, both of whom were obviously eager to speak. But for the moment, he ignored his panel and stared directly at the camera.

"For those of you who just joined us, I am Allistair Blevis and this is *Speak Up America*. We have just had an update from our reporter on the scene up in the Bitterroot Mountains of Idaho, where the situation remains uncertain. As you know if you have been watching our continuing coverage of this situation, the FBI and half the policemen in Idaho have been held at bay for two months by a ragtag band of mountain men under the command of a charming billionaire. A man with a mysterious past and a purported friendship with the governor that his office denies."

Blevis gradually shifted his position to face his panelists. "Joining me here this afternoon are my regular guests, Mr. Cresswell Saunders Peabody, former editor of the National Republic and founding partner of the Polaris Enterprise Institute, a prestigious Washington think tank, representing the right. And Ms. Jarlene Martisse, President of the Democratic People's Foundation of America and who previously served as an adviser to President Webster, from the left. Let me start with you, Jarlene." Peabody, a dapper and trim man in his early sixties had thick white hair and piercing brown eyes, while Martisse was an attractive and classy African American woman in her late thirties.

"What do you make of the Idaho State Police chief's reaction to the question about the governor's relationship to Porter? After all, wasn't it the governor who gave him an honorary commission in the National Guard in the first place?"

"Your absolutely right, Allistair," said Martisse, as she held a piece of paper toward the camera. "I have here a photocopy of three canceled checks totaling over ten million dollars that Mr. Porter gave the Republican Party, most of which went directly into television commercials supporting the reelection campaign of Governor Morrissey—in direct violation of Federal election laws, I might add."

Blevis turned to Peabody and said, "Cresswell, what do you think about that?"

Peabody completely ignored Martisse and spoke directly to Allistair in the way that he knew would irritate her. "As usual, Jarlene seems to have contracted a convenient case of amnesia with respect to the seventy-five million dollars which the Democratic National Committee spent in television ads to get President Webster elected."

She stared coldly back at him but without rising to the bait, "That money was strictly issue-related and had nothing to do with the President's campaign, and you know it Cresswell."

He looked over his glasses at her and replied. "I suppose, Ms. Martisse, that you really believe the President was giving all those starlets a history lesson in the Lincoln bedroom."

"Come now, Cresswell, is that the best you've got? Resorting to old news about the President's indiscretions. I think you can do better than that."

Blevis jumped in. "I don't know about you, Cresswell, but if someone gave me over ten million dollars, I think I would remember meeting him."

"Do you have any idea how many people a governor meets in an average week? And every single one of them either wants to give him something or get something from him," replied Cresswell, oblivious to Martisse's snorting and huffing. "My esteemed colleague's protestations aside, the Democratic party was the one who wrote the book on soft money. For them now to complain about the fundraising for the Idaho Republican Party is disingenuous at best."

"So what's the deal with the Feds? Why don't they just trace Porter's past through the data on his NIS card?" continued Allistair, trying to get his panel back on the subject at hand.

Martisse ignored Blevis's question. "As usual, Mr. Peabody is attempting to deflect our attention from the real issue. It is his party's chronic insensitivity to the downtrodden and disenfranchised. And nowhere is this more evident than when a rich white man can stand on a mountain top with an automatic weapon in his hand and flaunt the law while a decent black man gets thrown in jail just for driving his car through a white neighborhood."

"Oh, come on, Jarlene. You make Captain Porter sound like a ruthless plantation owner threatening his slaves with a whip in one hand and a smoking gun in the other."

"Why don't we let our audience take a look at the man and judge for themselves?" interjected Blevis. He looked off camera at his producer and asked, "Do we have that clip?" The producer nodded. "Good," said Blevis. "Let's take a look at an excerpt from an interview that Captain Thomas Porter gave earlier today." He looked back at the producer and nodded. Then he and his two panelists faced a large flat-screen monitor that rose up from behind the console.

THOMAS PORTER'S IMAGE appeared on the screen. He was standing in front of a bank of microphones. His mood was subdued and he looked tired but there was still a hint of the charm and grace that had been so clearly evident in the first national television interview that he had done with Sarah McGill.

"Captain, how much longer can you and your men hold out?" asked one of the reporters.

"As long as we have to, and until we achieve what we came up here for in the first place," he replied.

"Other than seeking to extend your fifteen minutes of fame, Captain, what exactly is your mission?" asked another reporter with a heavy French accent in an adversarial tone of voice.

Porter did not respond in kind. Instead, with a boyish grin, he replied softly, "Who do you work for?"

The question caught the reporter off guard. "I represent the largest television network in France."

"Ah, you're from France," said Porter.

"Yes, but why do you ask?" said the man, growing more suspicious.

"You seem like an educated man. Have you ever read any American literature?"

"Yes of course, but—"

Porter cut him off. "Then you must be a fan of Washington Irving."

The reporter hesitated, then said, "I am familiar with his work, but I'm afraid that I don't understand…"

"Well, judging by the stupidity of your question, I thought perhaps that Rip Van Winkle might be a personal hero of yours, because you have obviously been asleep on the mountain for the past eight weeks."

The other reporters laughed. The Frenchman didn't. "You find this situation amusing, Captain?"

Porter's smile disappeared in a flash. "No. Quite the contrary, sir. I take my mission very seriously, and I have little time for people such as yourself, who do not. My men and I are here for one purpose and one purpose alone. To bring national and global attention to the Federal Government's slow but inexorable movement to deny us our rights. Rights that were guaranteed by the Constitution. And if you had paid any attention to what has been going on here instead of seeking your own fifteen minutes of fame by insulting me and the brave young men who stand with me, then you would have known that."

BACK IN THE STUDIO, Blevis said, "That's good. Let's stop it there." He turned to his panelists and said, "So what do you think?"

"Well, it's obvious that Porter doesn't like the French," said Martisse.

"Who does?" asked Peabody. "They are an odious people."

"I object to that. My ancestors are French," snapped Martisse.

111

"My case rests," said Peabody with a smile.

"Can we get back on point, please?" asked Blevis. "Notwithstanding Porter's dislike for the French, is the captain a dilettante, like some have called him, or a freedom fighter, as he would have us believe?"

"I'm not sure either descriptor applies," replied Peabody. "I believe he is just a man alone in a crowd. Passionate. Principled. Naive. And doomed."

"Whoa there, big guy," said Blevis. "Do you mean doomed as in failure or doomed as in dead?"

"Yes," said Peabody. "For Captain Thomas Porter, the two are mutually inclusive."

Blevis flashed a look to Martisse. "What say you, Mademoiselle Martisse?"

"I would have to agree with my colleague, with one notable difference. Behind Cresswell's words, there lies sympathy. Behind mine there is none."

"Very interesting. Of course, you both realize that neither of you answered my question, but why am I not surprised?" With that, he turned to the camera and said, "Ladies and gentlemen, we'll take a commercial break and after we return, we'll let you decide. Our subject tonight on *Speak Up America* is "Standoff in the Bitterroots: Malignant Militia or Boys Will Be Boys?" Call us at 1-777-BAD-BOYS.

BACK ON THE MOUNTAIN, Perry Waters and his cameraman stood watching the Allistair Blevis show on a small BTC that was propped up on a fruit crate. It stood in front of the concessions tent which had been set up by an enterprising Vietnamese grocer, named Ho Ming, from Missoula, Montana. During the eight weeks since the occupation began, he and his wife had made more money selling coffee, snack food, and girlie magazines to the army of policemen and Federal agents than they usually made in an entire year.

"Boys Will Be Boys, my ass," said the cameraman, "These poor bastards are going to have their friggin' heads blown off, and Allistair Big Hair Blevis treats it like a schoolboy prank."

Waters just shook his head in quiet agreement. "The rating point is king, my friend. Long live the king." He paused and then said quietly, "To hell with it. Let's go back to town and get some warm food. Nothing more is going to happen here today."

"You're right. I'm friggin freezing," said his cameraman, eager to get off the mountain where they had spent almost every waking moment for two months.

Waters and his colleague started to pack up their video equipment.

As they did, the cameraman said, "Doesn't matter whether the public has grown enamored with Captain Thomas Porter and his baby-faced soldiers; sooner or later the Feds will pressure Governor Morrissey to do something."

"He's in a lose-lose situation. If he doesn't go in, they'll say he's soft on the militia. If he does, it will be bloody."

"Why the hell did the Forest Service close the Club in the first place?" asked the cameraman, as he snapped the lid shut on the sturdy aluminum box holding his equipment.

"Something about it being a threat to the environment, with all the lead dust from their firing range blowing in the wind, contaminating bald eagle nests or some such thing."

The cameraman finished packing the camera away and stood up. "Man, I'm so sick of hearing about the environment, I think I'll shoot the first spotted owl I see."

"Everybody's got a cause these days, but I think this time the Forest Service should have stuck to preventing forest fires instead of provoking gunfire."

The cameraman's expression darkened. "Those boys up the road are in for some serious shit, aren't they?"

At first, Waters didn't answer. Instead he stared through the barricade toward the two militia point men standing fifty yards up the dirt road, both barely visible in the shadows. He watched them silently for a moment and then slowly raised his hand and waved at them. "God, I hope not."

His comment surprised the cameraman. "Whatever happened to mister hard ass who was one-upped by the prom queen?"

"Nothing," answered Waters defensively.

The cameraman smiled and teased, "Could it be that under that hard exterior, there beats the heart of an old softy?"

Waters nodded. "Yeah. So what?"

The cameraman grinned. "Well, I'll be damned. That piece McGill did about passion and principle and untamed innocence got to you after all."

"Maybe it did. But if you tell anyone, especially her, I'll throw your ass over the fence when the shooting starts."

"Don't worry, my lips are sealed. She'd have to beat me to get anything out of me. And beat me and beat me."

"In your dreams," added Waters.

"How'd you know?" laughed the cameraman. Then he caught himself and cocked his head. "What's that?"

"What?" said Waters.

"Listen! Do you hear it? Choppers." They both listened and in the distance, but growing louder by the second, the sound of helicopters could be heard. "Lots of them. After WWT, I'd recognize that sound anywhere."

The sounds got louder and louder and both Waters and the cameraman noticed that the law enforcement personnel were all looking up as well. No one seemed to know what was going on. Suddenly, three large Marine helicopters roared overhead. They were so low, that their downdrafts blew a cloud of dust and snow into the eyes of everyone on the ground.

"Holy shit! The whole damned Army is invading the mountain!" yelled Waters, grabbing his microphone.

But his cameraman, who had been in combat, stood there without moving, staring up at the sky. "I'll be damned!" he said, calmly as yet another helicopter appeared overhead.

"What?" asked Waters.

"It's the President."

Waters' eyes snapped upward just in time to see Marine One disappear over the trees. "My God, you're right. It is him. Come on!" he exclaimed as he started to head toward the gate, but he stopped abruptly as he saw the militia guards standing non-plussed on the road with their weapons at the ready. "Shit. Shit. Shit. We can't go in there."

By now, a large crowd of law enforcement personnel, including Chief Swale, were milling about in front of the gates, and several were shouting into PTC's. Swale just stood there looking stunned by what was happening. But there was nothing that any of them could do. The President's helicopter could be heard landing while his escort gun-ships circled overhead, keeping their weapons trained on the ground.

Disgusted, Waters threw his microphone into their equipment case and flopped down on a folding chair. He looked at his cameraman and back up the road and said, "Fuck!"

IN THE LARGE CLEARING in front of the main building of the gun club, Marine One sat on the grass while its big heavy rotors slowed to a stop. The forward door opened and swung down slowly to the ground, revealing the steps on the other side. Without any delay, out stepped the President of the United States of America. Tanned and fit and wearing sunglasses, a leather flight jacket, pressed blue jeans and cowboy boots, he looked like he had just stepped out of a movie. Captain Porter, who, in stark contrast to the President, looked weary and bedraggled, walked over to greet him.

"Mr. President," said Porter, giving the commander in chief a crisp salute.

"Captain," replied Webster, with a controlled smile and a perfunctory wave of his hand that was as close to a salute as he ever gave anyone in uniform.

"Thank-you for coming, sir."

"Glad to be here." He shook Porter's hand warmly and placed his other hand on the captain's shoulder. "Can we talk? Somewhere private ."

"Of course, Mr. President." Porter motioned toward a trail that led further up the hill though tall pines.

The two men started walking together up it, followed closely by the President's Secret Service detail, who carefully scrutinized the location, the gun emplacements, and the heavily armed men. Meanwhile, another helicopter landed and disgorged a select group of reporters from the White House press corps and first among them, looking her usual beautiful self, was Sarah McGill. She glanced up the trail at the President and captain, then she walked over and introduced herself to Lieutenant Kerwood. She began taking notes as he gladly gave her his opinion on their mission and the two months on the mountain.

FIFTY YARDS FURTHER up the mountain, the President and Porter were deeply absorbed in a passionate conversation. They looked more like old friends than enemies, and from the expressions of their faces, they might have been discussing professional football rather than guns, protests, and the law.

"Tell me, Captain, what's it going to take to end this thing peacefully?" asked Webster.

115

Porter thought about it carefully as they walked beneath the overhanging bows of pine and spruce. "Mr. President, it would be presumptuous of me to give you the obvious answer, which is to withdraw your bill from Congress. I've found that in any negotiation, it's wise to consider the other person's position as carefully as you do your own."

The President was clearly impressed. "Smart policy. There are many in Congress who could take a lesson from you, Captain."

"Yes. And from you too, sir."

The President eyed him carefully. At first he wasn't sure whether or not Porter was sincere.

Porter quickly added, "By that, I mean I admire someone with the courage of their convictions like you. While I disagree with your politics, Mr. President, it took courage to take on the National Rifle Association."

The President realized that Porter was being sincere. He smiled, "Yes. Some would call it courage. Others call it a death wish."

It was Porter's turn to smile, but it was a melancholy one. "Yes, sir, well, let's hope it never comes to that. However, back to your question. In return for us stopping this occupation, I would ask that you amend your bill to guarantee certain rights to lawful gun owners."

"Such as?"

"Such as grandfathering the current ownership of all rifles and handguns, provided they were properly licensed, of course."

"It would have to exclude assault weapons."

"Understood."

"What else?"

Porter took a piece of paper out of his pocket and handed it to the President. "I have taken the liberty of listing the key issues on this page, Mr. President."

Webster stopped walking and took the paper. He glanced at it, then looked at Porter. "If I agree to these points, will you leave the mountain?"

"Yes, sir."

"And support my bill?"

"Yes, Mr. President. I will."

The President tucked the paper into his pocket. "Okay, Captain. Let me sleep on it, and I'll get back to you tomorrow. Is that acceptable?"

Porter was obviously uncomfortable with the most powerful man on earth asking him if something was acceptable. "Of course, Mr. President."

They shook hands and started back down the trail. On the way, neither man said much. To Porter it had all seemed too easy, too simple; and a little voice inside his head reminded him that when something seemed too good to be true, it probably was. At the same time, the President was clearly troubled, but not by the prospect of changing his bill—something that he had no intention of doing. Rather, he was troubled by the fact that he actually found himself liking this young man. But one thing he had learned long ago was that in the world of politics, the strong never let their emotions guide their actions. It would be no different here. And as he boarded the helicopter, he turned to one of the men dressed in civilian clothes, and asked him, "Did you get what you needed?"

The man, who was not the Secret Service agent he appeared to be, smiled coldly and replied. "Yes, sir."

The President nodded somberly, climbed into the helicopter, and never looked back.

Marine One took off and headed toward Mountain Home Air Force Base, fifty miles southeast of Boise, where Air Force One waited to whisk the President away from Idaho, before the governor could react. After it was gone, Porter walked over to McGill and politely asked the other members of the press corps standing with her to excuse them for a moment, which they did. Jane Kimberly, the White House press secretary, reminded Sarah that their helicopter had to leave in a few minutes. Then Porter and McGill walked over to a spot that overlooked the valley.

"You look terrific."

She replied teasingly. "I wish I could say the same about you." Two months of growth had turned his thick hair into a birds nest, and that, combined with the stubble on his face, made him look more like a mountain man than simply a man on a mountain.

He pretended to be wounded, until she laughed gently. He rubbed his hand over his head. "If I had known you were coming, I wouldn't have canceled my hair appointment."

She smiled, and for a moment, they stood there lost in each other's eyes. It was clear to both that something was happening between them, something neither was ready to embrace, but equally, something neither could deny.

Abruptly, the mood was broken by the voice of the helicopter pilot, who shouted, "Ms. McGill, we've got to go, or you'll miss Air Force One."

117

"Thank-you. I'll be right there." She looked back at him and with worried eyes, asked, "Do you think this will be over soon?"

Without either fear or self-pity, he replied, "Yes. One way or the other."

"Don't say that."

"I'm simply being a realist, Sarah. My men and I are prepared for both outcomes."

She hesitated, then said, "Your wife must be worried about you." It was calculating of her, but she had a way of doing it that didn't seem offensive.

His expression darkened. "I doubt it."

"I'm sorry," she replied, but she wasn't.

"Don't be."

They stood in awkward silence for a moment longer. She couldn't help but feel that he was like a little boy lost, who desperately needed to be held, and it was all that she could do not to lean forward and kiss him, hug him, and love him. But she didn't. Instead, she simply whispered, "Is there anything that I can do for you back in the world?"

He smiled at her use of an expression that soldiers in a war zone often used to describe home. "No thank-you." He thought about it for a moment more and then said, "Just take care of yourself."

She smiled sadly and whispered, "Goodbye, Thomas."

"Goodbye, Sarah."

"I will pray for you and your men."

"Thank-you." Free of the constraints of professional correctness that dictated her behavior, he stepped forward and gave her a kiss on the cheek. The move caught her by surprise and brought a flush of pink to her cheeks. A photographer in the press corps snapped a picture of it, but one of the militia immediately walked over, grabbed the camera, extracted the video disk and placed it in his pocket. The photographer grumbled as he was handed back the camera, but he knew better than to protest.

Oblivious to the confrontation, McGill hurried over to the helicopter and climbed in. She didn't look back. She knew if she did, she would have broken into tears, and she was not going to let the others see that. Once the doors were closed, the drooping rotor blades began to spin slowly and then faster, until they were a blur; and with a slight hesitation, the aircraft lifted off the ground and leapt up into the clear mountain air. Porter and his men moved away from the downdraft, and watched until it disappeared in the clouds. After it was gone, the soldier who had confiscated the disk handed it to Porter and said a few words. Porter smiled and thanked him, and together they walked back toward the main building. As they did, an overwhelming feeling of loneliness came over him, more powerful than he had felt at any time during the previous two months. The feeling was not foreign to him, but that did not make it any easier to bear.

TWELVE HOURS LATER, the eastern sky was just beginning to turn from black to shades of gray and pink when the lead Humvee of the Army convoy pulled out of the frost-covered meadow onto the highway ten miles from the Bitterroot Rod & Gun Club. Immediately behind the Humvee were two Bradley armored personnel carriers, three Stryker wheeled armored vehicles, each fitted with a .50 caliber machine gun, and a flatbed carrying an M1A2 Abrams Main Battle Tank. The heavy steam rising off the grass gave the entire setting an eerie and vaguely threatening look. At the back edge of the meadow, four large helicopters sat with their turbines humming at idle, while inside, stern-faced warriors checked and rechecked their automatic weapons. The scene looked like a group of dragonflies watching a parade of caterpillars hurrying to a picnic in the woods. It would be anything but.

SHIVERING in their foxholes fifty yards inside the barricades that blocked the only road leading up to the club were four young sentries, all of whom were completely unprepared for what was about to happen. This was understandable given the two months of inactivity and boredom and their lack of training and combat experience. All that was about to change.

In one foxhole the two sentries were sound asleep, while on the opposite side of the road, the two men were smoking and talking quietly about the things that young men do. Suddenly, three things happened simultaneously. First, both foxholes were swarmed by men wearing grease paint on their faces and tree branches in the webbing of their helmets. Looking like forest monsters, the Army Rangers quickly and silently subdued the sentries without inflicting any mortal injuries. Second: four Army helicopters burst overhead and roared across the treetops, so low that the wash from their rotors bent the tall pines over like ferns, snapping several of them like matchsticks. Third: from around the corner behind a dense thicket of trees a hundred yards away, an M1A2 Abrams Main Battle Tank roared into view.

119

The forest floor literally began to shake as it thundered up the road and plowed through the barricade as if it weren't there at all. As it did, the tank threw brush and debris onto the four sentries who were now being led quietly down the mountain by two Rangers. Their captors had made it clear to the sentries that they had two choices—be led quietly away or die—and that either scenario was just fine with the Rangers.

12

Big Lost Ranch, Ketchum, Idaho

A hundred miles west of the Bitterroot Rod & Gun Club, the cry of a female bald eagle pierced the silence of the forest. The eagle sat in her nest high in the top of a tall pine tree that stood on the hill overlooking a valley. As was usual for her kind, the nest was large, the largest of any bird in North America, nearly seven feet across and three feet tall. But what was unusual was that this eagle was weak and malnourished. Several days earlier, her mate had been killed by an elk hunter who had missed his quarry and decided to take out his frustration on the male eagle, who would otherwise have shared the incubation with his mate. As a result, she had been forced to choose between her mothering instinct and her need to eat. Up until that moment, the latter had lost out. So she sat there, forlornly guarding her unborn brood, and calling in vain for her mate who would never return, all the while growing weaker and weaker.

Suddenly, an Idaho State Police helicopter swooped overhead, the pounding of its rotors an unwelcome intrusion in the wilderness. As it began its descent toward the two-thousand-acre ranch that abutted the Sawtooth National Forest, the noise and smell of the aircraft was more than the eagle could take. What hunger and thirst had not been able to do, the helicopter did. She stood up, spread her wings, and flew away. Her departure went unnoticed by the people in the aircraft. Unfortunately, the same was not true for the large, black birds sitting in the branches of nearby trees.

THE HELICOPTER landed noisily in front of a sprawling ranch house with a well-tended rose garden out front. Two State Police officers jumped

121

out and ducked reflexively as they headed away from the aircraft toward the large green metal door. One stepped up on the porch and knocked heavily, while the other stood back. Both were wearing black T-shirts under their shirts.

The door swung open, revealing Jesse Latrobe, the ranch's owner, who had a reputation for shooting uninvited guests. At sixty-six, he was a hard man in both body and soul, with piercing black eyes and stiff, bristly white hair cropped closely against his imposing head. He looked like someone who had been to hell and back many times, which he had.

"Mr. Jesse Latrobe?" the officer asked.

The tall man smiled as he detected the hesitancy in the young officer's voice, "Yes, I'm Latrobe."

"I'm sorry, sir, but I'm afraid I'll have to ask to see your NIS card."

Latrobe studied the young man's face for a long moment and then he reached back inside the door. Both officers visibly tensed, though neither of them drew their weapons. They were soon glad they hadn't, as Latrobe's hand came back with just his jacket in it.

"Kind of jumpy, aren't you, son?" Latrobe asked patiently.

"These are jumpy times, sir."

Latrobe took his wallet out of his jacket and produced the card which the first officer quickly placed under a small black scanner. Then he looked up sheepishly at Latrobe and asked, "May I?" Latrobe nodded and leaned forward slightly to allow the officer to let the scanner read his retinas. Instantly, the machine flashed a green light.

"Now that we've established unequivocally who I am, what can I do for you boys?"

"The governor would like to see you," the policeman replied. His voice grew stronger at the mention of the governor's name. As if invoking it gave him some measure of protection from this man who had once killed an entire platoon of North Vietnamese Regulars with a twelve gauge in one hand and a knife in the other.

"What if I don't want to see him?" came the reply.

The officer hesitated, gathering up his courage and said, "I'm afraid that's not an option…sir," adding the, sir, as a hopeful afterthought.

"Good answer. Well then, let's not keep the governor waiting."

With that, Latrobe pulled the heavy door closed and joined the two officers as they walked back toward the helicopter. The three of them got inside. Immediately, the powerful turbine engines began their wind up and the heavy rotors started to rotate, slowly at first, then faster and faster. Finally, the aircraft lifted off the ground and, dipping its nose, it climbed quickly into the clear mountain sky.

As it swooped up over the eagle's nest, none of the men inside noticed the terror of ravens who were busily tearing open the three large dull white eggs.

THE AMERICAN AND IDAHO flags flapped noisily in the stiff breeze in front of the Capitol building in Boise as Latrobe and the two officers strode purposefully up the steps. Latrobe took the stairs two at a time, forcing the policemen to hurry along like school boys following their teacher to the principal's office.

Once inside, the little parade continued past the guard station, where Latrobe paused briefly for a biometrics scan, then through a backscatter x-ray machine that provided an anatomically correct picture of what was underneath his clothes. In fact, the x-ray picture was so detailed that the machine had to have both a female and a male officer present at all times so that only a same-sex officer viewed what was on the screen. Finally, after the officers checked their weapons, they were allowed to walk down a hallway, up the elevator, and into the outer office of the governor. There they were greeted by Maude, a striking woman in her mid-sixties, who served as the governor's personal assistant.

"Maude, you look more beautiful every year," said Latrobe.

"And you just get more sexy, you old silver fox," she beamed back.

"Damn, Maudey, have you been peeking at my backscatter x-rays again?" he teased.

"You wish," she giggled girlishly and then said, "Go on in, he's expecting you."

"Thanks, darling," said Latrobe, and he walked over to the door and knocked lightly.

Inside the office, Edward Morrissey stood talking with his chief of staff when Latrobe's knock interrupted them. Before he could reply, the door swung open and in strode Latrobe. A broad smile spread across the governor's face as he immediately thrust out his hand. "Jesse."

"Governor Morrissey," Latrobe said with a dead pan face.

Morrissey turned to his chief of staff, "Would you give us a minute?" His assistant nodded and left, closing the door behind him.

"Thanks for coming, Jesse," the governor replied. More formally this time.

"It's been a while, Teddy," Latrobe said, with a hint of melancholy in his voice.

"Yes, I'm afraid it has been, old friend. I could ramble on about how busy I've been, but that would be lame, so I'll just say I'm truly sorry. Please forgive me." With that, the governor held open his arms.

The two men stood looking at each other for a moment, then Latrobe's expression melted and he grabbed the governor and gave him a big hug. After he released him, he asked, "What in the hell did you tell those two kiddy cops? They acted like I was going to skin them alive."

"Just trying to maintain your image as the last of the mountain men," the governor chuckled as he motioned toward two leather chairs that faced a coffee table, and suggested they sit down, which they both did. Then with a deep sigh, the governor continued, "It really is good to see you, Jesse. It's been too long."

"The feeling's mutual, Teddy."

"We had some great times together, didn't we?"

"Yes, we did. But you didn't fly me in here to talk about the old days, now, did you?"

"No. You're right," said Morrissey, relieved that Latrobe gave him the opening he needed. "And I think you already know why I called you."

"The Bitterroots."

"Yes."

Latrobe studied his friend's face for a moment before responding. "That was quite the show yesterday by the President."

"The bastard never told me he was coming."

"That's what I figured. So what happens now?"

"He's threatening to send in Federal troops."

Latrobe's eyebrows arched. "One of these days he is going to push things too far."

The governor looked directly into Latrobe's eyes and spoke the words that he knew were coming but didn't want to hear, "I need you to go in there, Jesse."

"I was afraid you were going to ask that."

"You have to, Jesse. You're my last best hope."

Latrobe got up and walked over to the cabinet above the credenza and picked up a large bronze eagle that sat in a lighted alcove. It was a beautiful work of art in which the eagle stood with wings outspread on a bare and twisted tree trunk. He carefully examined it as he thought about the governor's request. Without turning around, he said, "I could have told you that something like this would happen when you gave Porter that commission in the Guard."

"Don't go there—please," pleaded the governor.

Latrobe carefully put the eagle back down and looked at the other man. "What makes you think he'll listen to me?" He walked back to the chair and sat down.

"He's in way over his head and he's smart enough to know it. If you go in there as my representative, he'll do whatever you say. I guarantee it."

"What about the men?"

"My God, Jesse. You're a legend to everybody in this state."

"The Nam was a lifetime ago, Governor. Besides, I've got flannel shirts older than half those men."

"Those boys will die if you don't go in there."

Conflicting emotions raced through Latrobe's mind as he stared at the lonely figure seated before him; not the tough and proud leader of the Gem state; simply a human being in desperate need of help. But as much as he loved his friend, Latrobe hated the Federal Government even more, and the last thing he needed right now was to put himself in a position where bureaucrats could second guess his every move.

Realizing the appeal was failing, the governor switched tactics. "You remember that time when we were up on the Middle Fork of the Salmon? The sky was powder blue, the wind smelled of fresh clover, and the trout were biting. But I couldn't enjoy it, because I had a feeling in the pit of my stomach that something bad was about to happen."

Latrobe nodded.

The governor continued, "If you hadn't of listened to me and reached for your rifle, that grizzly would have killed both of us." He paused for effect. "I've got that feeling again. Only this time it's much worse."

"It wasn't our turn to die."

Like a buck-tailed fly being laid in front of a rising trout, the governor immediately jumped on his friend's comment. "Then, as God is our witness, Jesse, don't let it be those boys' turn, either."

The room fell silent. Finally, Latrobe gave in. "When do I leave?"

Before the governor could react, there was a frantic knock on the door and it flew open. His chief of staff rushed in and walked straight to the BTC, and turned it on. The look on his face said it all. "Governor! They've gone in."

"What?"

"Federal troops have attacked the Rod & Gun Club."

It took a moment for the BTC to come on. Given the situation, it seemed like an eternity and the chief of staff tapped it sharply on top, as if that would hurry it up. Finally, an overhead camera shot of the Bitterroot Rod & Gun Club filled the big screen. A reporter's voice could barely be heard over the thumping of the rotors and the unmistakable sound of heavy weapons fire below.

"We're flying over the Bitterroot Rod & Gun Club, where only moments ago, Army troops moved in force against the militia who have illegally occupied the premises for over two months now..."

The governor muted the sound as soldiers could clearly be seen jumping out of armored personnel carriers in the compound, with their weapons blazing. Thick smoke began to curl up out of the main building, and young militia men were being cut down in a withering crossfire as they tried to escape the noxious fumes.

Suddenly, through the smoke, the obese corporal ran out of the building with a thirty caliber machine gun in his hands. With a crazed look on his face, he ran a zigzag pattern, more befitting a wide receiver than an offensive guard. As Latrobe and the governor looked on in anguish, the corporal's body shuddered as an unrelenting stream of bullets ripped into his body, and transformed this mountain of a man into a quivering pile of blood and soft tissues.

"Enough!" the governor turned to his chief of staff, "Get me the President. Now!"

"Yes, sir," the ashen-faced man responded, as he hurried out of the office.

"My God. What has he done?" the governor whispered as he walked slowly over to the BTC, transfixed by what he saw before him. He reached out toward the screen as if to try to protect the young men on both sides who were fighting and dying on daytime television. "That fool—that vain and stupid fool."

Finally, the Rod and Gun Club's main building exploded into flames and with that, Jesse picked up the remote and switched off the BTC. The governor continued to stare at the screen for another few seconds.

The chief of staff returned, "I'm sorry, sir, but the President wasn't available to take your call."

The governor pulled himself away from the BTC and walked over to his desk, falling heavily in the chair. "Doesn't he realize that some things can never be undone?"

Latrobe stood frozen for a moment, lost in thought, and then he said quietly, "So dies freedom."

13

GNBC Studios, Washington, D.C.

Sarah McGill strode in her usual imperious way across the television studio. For a beautiful and unquestionably feminine woman, she sometimes walked like a man, at least when she was off camera. It was nearly 6:00 p.m. on a day that had been even more hectic than normal, and her pace matched the tempo of the day. She was late for a meeting with her boss, which was nothing new, but she had promised him during her last performance review that she would try to correct this habit. Of course, both of them knew that it was a hopeless task, but the network's review form had an obligatory section titled "Opportunities For Performance Enhancement," and he felt compelled to at least find some development need for her, so that head office in New York would get off his back about being too soft on McGill.

"Ms. McGill," said a handsome young man from across the studio as he hurried to catch up with her. Over his shoulder, he was carrying a thin black case, the kind that usually held a laptop computer, except that this one was much thinner than would normally have been expected. Catching up to McGill was not an easy task, because once she had a full head of steam, she could walk faster than most men. This prompted some to speculate that her fast walking was the cause of her not being married, while others said it was the other way around.

"Ms. McGill," he said again, more urgently. "Could I please have a word with you?" This time, she heard him and stopped.

"Yes?" she said, giving him a quick once-over that told her he was too young to be important but too cute to be ignored.

He smiled as he closed the distance between them. "Ms. McGill. My name is Tanner Spence. I work for the Department of Homeland Security, and I would appreciate a few minutes of your time." As he said it, he showed her his NIS card, which had his photograph on it.

"How do you do, Mr. Spence," she said with a friendly smile. She looked at his ID and then back at his face. "What do you do at DHS?"

"I'm the CCO."

"The what?"

"Sorry. It stands for the Chief Compliance Officer. I make sure that everybody and everything that has anything to do with Granite Shield operate precisely as they should. I assume you're familiar with Granite Shield?"

"Yes. Quite." McGill knew all about the Federal Government's quantum computer and its gigantic online database, commonly referred to by its acronym, GOD. She was certain that in its virtually infinite databanks, there was a file concerning her. When it was under construction, she had written an editorial damning it and had even signed a petition to stop it. But all that was history now. Clearly impressed with the boy-genius standing before her, she asked, "How old were you when you joined DHS? Twelve?"

Without missing a beat he replied, "No, thirteen."

"Really?"

He chuckled. "No. Not really. I joined DHS when I was twenty-six. That was seven years ago."

"Where were you before that?"

"In a doctoral program at M.I.T."

"In what field?"

His eyebrows arched and he pulled back slightly. "Do you always ask everyone you meet twenty questions before you talk with them?"

"Sorry. My big reporter's nose gets the best of me sometimes."

He glanced at her nose. "Your nose is perfect."

She smiled. "Thank-you." He had a way about him that put her at ease.

"You're welcome. My field of study was nanotechnology."

"What's that?"

"It's the study of the manipulation of matter at its most fundamental level—the atom. But I dropped out after a year."

"Why?"

"Because I knew more than my professors did." Normally that would have sounded arrogant, but for some reason, it didn't. She sensed that it was the truth.

"Where did you do your undergrad work?"

"I got both my masters and bachelors degrees in computer science at the University of Michigan at Ann Arbor."

Her face lit up. "I graduated from there as well."

"How about that—a Wolverine!" He stepped over and gave her a big hug. It momentarily flustered her.

She collected herself and added, "I graduated with a Bachelor of Arts degree, with a double major in English Literature and American History. After that, I got my Masters in Journalism from Medill."

"At Northwestern," he added with feigned disgust.

"Yes."

"Lousy football team."

"Compared to Michigan, everything is," she replied.

He grinned again. "I think I like you, Ms. Sarah McGill."

"I like you too, Mr. Tanner Spence. And any fellow Michigan grad can call me Sarah."

With a serious look he replied, "Actually, I would prefer it if you would call me Mr. Spence." Then he laughed. "Just kidding."

Before he could misinterpret where their brand new relationship might be heading, she quickly added, "But you still look twelve to me."

He shrugged. "I get the 'How old are you' question all the time. It's hard to be taken seriously when you have a baby face."

"Don't complain about looking younger than your age. Plastic surgeons get wealthy off people trying to achieve that." Sarah McGill was nice to everyone she met until they did something to spoil it. With some people that didn't take very long, but her instincts told her Tanner Spence would not soon do that. To the contrary, he was about to offer her something that would quickly endear him to her, although not in the way that he might have hoped. "So what can I do for you and the DHS, Tanner?"

"Nothing. I think I can do something for you."

His comment piqued her interest. "Which is?"

He looked around the office bullpen and said, "Can we go somewhere private?"

She glanced up at a wall clock and said, "I'm late for a meeting with my boss and I really should be—"

Spence interrupted her. "It's all right. I just left his office. I'm the reason that Keene wanted to see you, and he said we should go ahead without him."

McGill wasn't sure what surprised her more, the fact that Tanner had called her boss by his given name, which absolutely no one inside the beltway did, other than her, or that he apparently felt whatever it was that Tanner wanted was worthy of her time. One of the things she liked most about working for Keene was that he was very protective of his staff's time. "In that case, let's go to my office."

Her offer instantly produced a broad grin across the young man's face. "Great."

She headed off in the direction from which she had come, followed by Spence, who looked more like a puppy than the world-class computer scientist and genius that he was. Sarah McGill had that effect on people. The bad news was that she knew it. The good news was that she never took advantage of it.

In addition to being very handsome in a boyish way, Tanner Spence was what many people wished they were or claimed to be, but weren't—simply brilliant. He had been among the last group of high school students to take the long-since abandoned SAT's tests, and he had scored a perfect 1600. Moreover, he had accomplished this and still had time to draw pictures of his favorite super heroes on the margins of the test paper, while his fellow students furiously tried to finish each section within the allotted time. He skipped his senior year in high school and it took him only four years to earn both his bachelors and a masters degrees. At the time, nanotechnology was an emerging branch of computer science, and he quickly became an expert in the field.

After dropping out of M.I.T., he took a job that would change his young life forever. He was hired by the National Security Agency, or NSA, to work on Project Columbus, which was the code name for the commercialization of the world's first quantum computer. The project was finished ahead of schedule and under budget, a first for a Federally-funded project of that size and scope; and it was largely as a result of Spence's hard work and profound genius. He supervised the building of the machine and personally created the software that ran it, which he called qubitware, and for which he obtained a trademark and a patent, forcing the entire world to pay the U.S. a royalty every time they used it. But after the quantum computer was fully operational, Spence suddenly dropped out of view. Some said it was because he was burned out; others said he was simply bored and had gone home to read his comic book collection. Finally, a year later, he showed up at the Department of Homeland Security one day, which by that point encompassed the NSA, as well as several other Federal agencies, and asked for a job. He was hired on the spot.

Sarah ushered Spence into her spacious and immaculate office and suggested that they sit down, which they both did, across from each other at her desk.

"Now, Tanner, what is it that you and the DHS can do for me?"

His expression grew serious. "Actually, I'm not here on official business for the DHS. In point of fact, I probably shouldn't be here at all. But, Mr. Lange is a friend of my father's and he suggested that I speak with you. "

McGill's thin eyebrows arched in perfect symmetry. "Speak with me about what, Tanner?"

Spence took a deep breath and then said, "I've uncovered something that might be helpful to that story you're developing about that group of politicians. You know, the ones who rumor has it, are conspiring against the government."

His statement startled her. "How did you know about that?"

"It doesn't matter," he answered. "What *does* matter is that I think I have found them."

"Where?" she asked, with all her senses suddenly going to full alert.

"On the Internet."

"I don't understand?"

"Here, I'll show you." He unzipped the black case and took out a slim and obviously very light laptop. He opened it, placed it on her desk in front of him, and motioned for her to come around the desk so that she could see it.

"Why can't you use my computer?"

He smiled patiently, "I'm sure it's good enough for what you do, Sarah, but relatively speaking, it's a biplane compared to a spaceship. Besides, you can't get to where I want to go on your system." He booted it up and began a typing a series of quick key strokes. At first the screen was black, then the word "WARNING" appeared on it in red type, and underneath, in smaller white type, was a paragraph that said the viewer had reached a restricted site. In the left corner of the screen a small window opened up with numbers that began counting down quickly from thirty. Simultaneously, a digital voice began to speak in a threatening tone, "You have reached a restricted private user network. Unauthorized access will be intercepted, and intruders will be punished to the full extent of the law."

As McGill watched in rapt silence, Spence expertly typed in a complex series of letters and numbers. Instantly, the screen changed to brilliant color, with the image of a bald eagle soaring over a rugged mountain range set against a backdrop of the Stars and Stripes. It was both beautiful and captivating in its color, graphics, and layout, and it was completely unlike anything McGill had ever seen on a computer screen.

"Oh my," she whispered, "That's beautiful."

Then, above the eagle, the words, "The New Sons of Liberty" slowly materialized on the screen, and the soft sound of "America the Beautiful" began to play over the laptop's micro-speakers.

Spence turned to McGill, and with a smile as broad and proud as that of a child who has just won a science project, he said, "Welcome to the New Sons of Liberty extranet."

"Is that a private network?"

"Exactly." He typed another few keystrokes, and instantly, the screen filled with a highly detailed menu. "Actually it's a very private computer network, or VPCN, for a group that calls itself the New Sons of Liberty."

"As in Samuel Adams?" McGill asked, referring to the Sons of Liberty from the American Revolution.

"Yes. Apparently, they are the modern-day version."

"What do the Sons of Liberty have to do with the twenty-first century?"

"I don't know," replied Tanner. "But I will, soon enough. For now, what I can tell you is that it's a private, wide area network of computers, both individual and those linked internally by intranets, all of which are tied together on the internet through exterior screening routers, bastion hosts, and proxy servers protected by five one two bit encryption."

"In English, please."

"It's a group of people who communicate with each other electronically, similar to your company's e-mail system, except that this one links different people in different parts of both the public and private sector. It's very well protected by leading edge cryptography."

"But we're connected to it right now?" said McGill.

Spence grinned again, "Yes, at least to the server that links them together." He looked up at her with a devilish smile on his boyishly handsome face.

"Are we being monitored right now?"

"No."

"So we can see them, but they can't see us?"

"In essence, but the 'they' is a computer that interacts with the other computers linked to the network. I have tricked it into thinking I am one of the authorized users, so it isn't monitoring our access."

"How did you do it?"

"It's very complicated. I am one of a very small number of what are called cyber lords in the world today. There are three of us at DHS and I trained the other two. There are four others in different parts of the Federal Government and seven in academia. Outside the U.S., there are ten others known to the National Security Agency; two in Britain, two in Japan, and six in China. Of course, with the way kids are these days, it won't be long before the number doubles or triples."

"Twenty-four cyber lords around the globe. That sounds rather omnipotent."

Without a trace of arrogance, he replied, "It should. In the world of quantum computing, the qubit is king, and people like me are the lords of the realm."

She stared at him thoughtfully and then said, "You've got my attention, Lord Spence. Lead on."

He smiled and continued, "During my day job I spend a lot of time making sure unlawful users are kept out of Granite Shield and during my off hours, I try to find unauthorized ways to get in. Ironic, isn't it? The skills that allow me to go anywhere in cyberspace, including the military platform in Granite Shield called Granite Fist, make me invaluable to uncle Sam. A cyber lord is a kind of hunter-killer in cyberspace. There's no system in the world linked into the Internet where I cannot gain access, including those of foreign governments, the global military establishment and large corporations." He paused and then added with a smile, "The personal computers of people like you, Sarah, are no more private than a book left open on a park bench."

As soon as he said it, she wished that she hadn't gone to that porn Web site on a dare by her girlfriend while in college. "But isn't that illegal?" she asked, trying not to look guilty.

"No, not since WWT. However, I didn't say I went into these sites, only that I could if I wanted to—anytime and from anywhere in a nanosecond," he replied, with mock innocence.

"Okay, now tell me why I should be interested in all this?"

"You should be interested, Sarah, because I think the people who are part of this extranet might be the ones you have been looking for."

"Tanner, thinking that they are is a far cry from being certain."

"I'm still working on it. As I said before, I have penetrated the server that links their network together but so far I haven't been able to drill down farther to the actual users. But I will."

"If you don't know who they are, then why did you come to see me?"

"It's what they are saying to each other that I thought you'd find interesting. Watch and listen." He placed the cursor on the "TALK" icon, and the screen changed to a rolling page of dialogue. Simultaneously, she could hear the voices of unknown persons, somewhere in cyberspace, actually talking to each other, but what they were saying didn't immediately make any sense to her:

> *"What's the latest count?"*
> *"Not good. Raven is running ahead right now."*

"Who's Raven?" she whispered in Tanner's ear.

"You don't need to whisper, they can't hear us," he answered with a smile. "I don't know who these people are or who they're talking about, but I'm on their trail."

She focused her attention back on the screen and resumed listening to what sounded like three different people carrying on an intense conversation.

> *"Raven's going to win."*
> *"No doubt about it."*
> *"That's impossible."*
> *"Oh it's possible all right. And likely."*
> *"Are you sure?"*
> *"Yes. Eagle had better do a deal soon, or it's all over."*

> *"You can't make a deal with a pathological liar."*
> *"That's a bit strong."*
> *"No. He's right. Raven is a chronic liar. He doesn't know what truth is."*
> *"Yes, he does. To Raven, telling a lie in a good cause is the same as telling the truth."*
> *"Who defines 'good?'"*
> *"He does."*

The sound of muted laughing could be heard. Then there was a pause in the exchange.

McGill kept her eyes fixed on the screen but said, "How do we know this isn't just one of those internet football leagues talking about a trade? I mean, aren't the Eagles and the Ravens two NFL teams?"

"Yes," said Spence, "But based on my past monitoring of their conversations, these people are definitely not talking about football."

The onscreen dialogue started again.

> *"I've got a question for you."*
> *"What?"*
> *"What do you think is stronger, a flight of eagles or a terror of ravens?"*
> *"What the hell is a terror of ravens?"*
> *"That's what a group of ravens is called."*
> *"No kidding."*
> *"Yes."*
> *"So which is it?"*
> *"I'd put my money on eagles every time."*
> *"Yeah. Me too."*
> *"I agree. But what if the eagle is alone?"*
> *"Then he's dead."*

There was a pause, and then one of them said very softly:

> *"No. We all are."*

"I think you get the idea," said Spence, disconnecting from the site.

"That's all very interesting, Tanner, but I still don't understand why I should care about people discussing ravens and eagles?"

"You should care, Sarah, because I believe they are discussing the anti-gun legislation. And I think Raven is the President."

"Really!"

"Yes."

"That would make Governor Morrissey, the Eagle?"

"No."

"Why not?"

"Because they were talking about the Eagle needing to make a deal, and Morrissey has been adamant that he will not consider any deals with the President. Period."

McGill thought about it for a minute and then asked, "So who is the Eagle?"

"I think it's Jeremiah Kincaid."

"The Speaker of the House?"

"Yes."

"And you think that the people linked into this extranet are the group of dissident politicians whose trail I've been chasing for weeks now?"

Spence smiled. "Absolutely. Now do you see why I thought this might interest you?"

McGill looked back at the screen, then turned back to Tanner and said, "It depends on who they actually are. As interesting as your little cyber eavesdropping is, I can't use it in my story until you can get me their names."

"I will," he answered without hesitation.

"There's one important thing that you haven't told me."

"What?"

"Why did you come to me rather than to your supervisor, or someone else at the DHS?"

"I did. I went to my boss, the Deputy Director."

"And?"

"At first he seemed really interested, and he said he would discuss it with his boss, the Secretary of DHS. But then a week later, he came back to me and said that I should let the whole matter drop. That it was probably just some group of cranks."

"Some what?"

"Cranks. It's a term we use at DHS to describe hackers, crackpots, and other cyber vermin. He said that I shouldn't waste my time monitoring the site any further. That really bothered me, but what they did next, or at least tried to do, told me that I was onto something big."

"What did they do?"

"They secretly installed a T Rex Carnivore, or TRC, on my computer."

"What's that?"

"It's a sophisticated software tracking program, that keeps an electronic record of every keystroke that you make, so that later someone can tell what you have typed. They obviously wanted to make sure that I was following their orders."

"Something tells me that you didn't," she said, with a smile.

"Of course not. They forgot that I was the person who wrote the code for T Rex. So I immediately deactivated it and went back to monitoring the site. Then I told my dad, who is a retired FBI agent. He called Mr. Lange, and here I am."

She didn't say anything for a long moment as she digested the implications of what he had just told her.

"So Ms. Soon-To-Be-Pulitzer-Prize-Winner McGill, do we have deal?"

"What do you mean?"

"I'll keep tracking this group and you'll decide what to do with it."

"Of course. How could I not agree? But I still don't get what's in this for you, Mr. Chief-Compliance-Officer Spence.

He shrugged. "I get to save the planet from the forces of evil."

Spence said it with such sincerity that she could tell he wasn't joking. "Okay. Let's do it!"

"Great," he said with a big grin. He stood up and packed up his computer.

"Wait, how can I get in touch with you?" she asked.

"You can't. I'll get in touch with you."

As he headed for the door, she called after him, "Tanner."

"Yes, Sarah?"

"If you can get on their extranet, it means that you can get on anyone's computer, right?"

"Yes," he said, knowing where she was going.

She sat there staring at him and said, "I see."

He smiled at her and added, "Don't worry. I won't read your E-mails, unless of course they're sent to me."

Suddenly, Keene Lange appeared in the open doorway. The ashen color in his cheeks told them that something was terribly wrong.

"Hello, Mr. Lange," said Spence hesitantly.

Other than a nod in acknowledgment, he didn't respond.

"What's the matter, Keene? You look like you've seen a ghost."

"It's the Bitterroots," he replied with a grim look.

McGill froze. "Did the police go in?"

"No. It was the Army."

"The Army?" said McGill, as she grabbed the remote and pointed it toward the large screen built into one wall.

"We've got the camera feed on now."

Instantly, the horrible images of men killing other men filled the screen.

"Oh my God!" she exclaimed.

Spence just stared coldly at the screen.

"What about Captain Porter? Do you know if he's all right?" asked McGill anxiously.

"I don't know," replied Lange.

The three of them stood there in silence watching men die. Finally, Spence said, "Looks like the President just found a way to get his gun bill through Congress."

14

Bitterroot Rod & Gun Club, Idaho

Captain Porter was holding Private Saints when he died. Just before the end came, a strange look of peace spread across the young man's face. "I'm dying, aren't I, Captain?" he asked.

"No, son," the captain lied, as tears filled his eyes.

"It's all right sir—I'm not afraid. I'm going to see my daddy, and I think he'll be…" He never finished the sentence. His young body, torn wide open by the hot piece of shrapnel, tensed and became still. Tenderly, the captain closed the boy's eyes and laid him gently on the floor of the bombed-out building. "He'll be proud of you, soldier. Very proud," said Porter, finishing the young man's sentence. Then, slowly, the captain stood up and looked at the circle of Rangers who stood quietly watching the scene before them. "Someday when you are old and gray, you men remember this young boy and the others like him who died here today, and you ask yourself— was any of this worth it?"

None of them moved or made any sound. Finally, the captain walked out of the building into the sunlight, followed by his captors. All around them, bodies lay where they fell, as medics worked on the dying and a chaplain prayed for those already dead.

Porter saw Lieutenant Kerwood lying on a stretcher being attended to by an Army medic. He hurried over and knelt down beside him.

"How are you, LT?"

"Good, sir," he answered.

Porter looked at the medic, who nodded his agreement. Then he smiled back down at Kerwood. "I want to thank-you for saving my life."

Kerwood looked embarrassed. "It wasn't anything, sir."

"Yes, it was."

During the first few minutes of the fight, when mass confusion had taken over and bullets had started cutting his men to pieces, Porter ran out of the command post to see what was happening. One minute he and his men had been discussing what the President had told him, and the next minute, the world was caving in. As Porter stood there out in the open, a stream of fifty-caliber bullets started to walk their way over to him like a giant zipper being opened in the earth. Lieutenant Kerwood saw what was about to happen and threw himself into Porter, knocking him safely out of the way and taking one of the heavy slugs in his lower leg. Luckily, it had only nicked the bone, and he would probably keep his leg, unless, of course, there were complications.

"The doc here told me there's a good chance I'll keep my leg," said Kerwood.

"That's good. That's real good." Porter patted Kerwood on the arm and then stood up. "Take care of yourself, LT."

"You too, sir." Then he raised his arm and gave Porter as smart a salute as he could from his prone position.

Porter smiled and turned away just in time to see three soldiers trying unsuccessfully to get the fat corporal's bloody remains into a body bag.

An Army first lieutenant approached the captain and saluted. "Captain Porter?"

"Yes, lieutenant."

"I'm afraid I have to place you under arrest, sir."

"Where's your commanding officer?"

"Dead, sir," answered the young lieutenant, with an emotionless face that Porter figured traced more to shock than a lack of caring. "He was hit as soon as the assault began."

"I'm sorry," replied Porter, staring off into the dark woods. "Could you tell me how many KIA's there are in all?"

"Yours or ours, sir?"

Porter's head snapped around and he stared the lieutenant in the face, "Does it make a difference?"

The soldier shook his head slowly. "Forty nine, sir, including seven of my men and the rest, yours. Plus twice that, wounded."

Porter shook his head and said, "Why did your guys open up on us like that?"

The lieutenant gave Porter a puzzled look. "You mean, you don't know?"

"Know what?"

The lieutenant stared at the other man for a minute and then said, "One of your men shot my C.O. right between the eyes as he entered the compound with a white flag in his hand."

"What?" asked Porter incredulously. "That's impossible. I had given my men orders not to resist."

"Tell that to the captain. I still have some of his brain matter on my webbing."

"Where is he?" asked Porter.

"Over there," said the lieutenant, pointing toward one of the bodies lying under green ponchos.

Porter walked over to where the captain's body lay. He was followed by the lieutenant and several of his men. He knelt down and lifted the poncho. There, lying on his back with his eyes open was the dead captain. His face was puffy and a single, small-entry wound could barely be seen right above his nose. Porter shook his head sadly. Just then, a helicopter came in for a landing. The wash from its rotors blew the ponchos off several of the bodies lying in a row beside the dead captain. The dust and noise caused everyone to shield their eyes, and as Porter looked down, he saw the captain's military NIS card lying half out of his pocket. It was a violation of military code for him to have carried his NIS card into action. Of course, it didn't matter now, because the card would be of no use to him ever again. It might, however, be of use to Porter, and without really thinking about it, he scooped it up and hid it inside his jacket. After the rotor wash had diminished, he stood up and turned to the lieutenant. "Let's get this over with."

The two officers walked back across the compound toward a waiting Humvee. Neither looked back at the body bags that were now being loaded onto the helicopter.

Just as he was about to get into the Humvee, the captain spotted something lying in the dirt over beside the tall pines.

"Just a minute! What's that? Over there." Without another word, Porter headed toward the shadows.

A soldier immediately raised his weapon and shouted, "Halt, or I'll shoot."

"No!" barked the lieutenant, "Haven't enough men died already today?" he said as he followed Porter.

When he got to the trees, Porter was already stooping over the pathetic heap of blood and feathers that lay on the forest floor. It was a bald eagle.

"Probably cut down by one of the choppers," the lieutenant said sadly.

Captain Porter didn't respond. Instead, he carefully picked up the dead bird and turned to face the lieutenant. By now, the other soldiers had arrived, and they seemed more upset by the pathetic sight than they had by the bodies of the fallen men.

"Get me a shovel," Porter said in a tone that made it clear he would not accept no for an answer.

The soldiers hesitated and looked at their lieutenant for direction.

"Do it," he said to one of the men.

The man ran off to get the tool.

"Let me help you," the lieutenant said softly.

"No," said Porter, looking the lieutenant directly in his eyes, "I don't think so."

The lieutenant nodded, took the shovel from the returning soldier, handed it to the captain and said, "We'll wait for you by the Humvee, Captain."

Porter walked slowly into the shadows to bury the fallen eagle.

PORTER WAS HALFWAY down the other side of the mountain when the Army lieutenant realized something was amiss.

"Come on," he shouted at his men, as he raced over to the edge of the forest and plunged into the dense undergrowth. It didn't take them long to find the hastily dug grave and the shovel standing over it.

"Shit, shit, shit," cried the lieutenant, as the two soldiers smirked at him behind his back.

"Do you want us to follow him, sir?" one of them said, trying to suppress his bemusement.

The lieutenant didn't answer. He just stared at the eagle's grave and shook his head. Finally, he turned around and without even looking at his men, he said curtly, "Fuck it. It's over. Let's get off this godforsaken mountain." He was wrong. It had only just begun.

SEVERAL HOURS LATER and a few miles away, Porter tripped over a root that was hidden in the shadows and fell heavily, scraping his chin on a rock and knocking the wind out of his lungs. He lay there for a minute, trying to suppress his gasps so that he could hear if anyone was following him down the steep mountainside. He heard nothing. Reassured, he stayed down a little longer and then slowly started to get up. The emotional trauma of the day and the extreme physical exertion of running downhill had taken their toll on his mind, body, and spirit. He stood up in a stooped posture, like someone twice his age, placing both hands on the small of his back and arching back and forth a few times to try to relieve the stiffness in his body. Then he straightened up and surveyed his surroundings.

It was getting darker and colder as the last rays of sunlight raced up the side of the mountain directly across the valley from where Porter stood. He knew that he had to find shelter from the cold night air and he set about doing that. He walked along between the pines, which surrounded him on every side, stooping over to peek under the heavy branches. He studied the terrain and kicked at the thick pile of pine needles that carpeted the forest floor. For a few moments, he thought about simply burying himself in the carpet, but he dismissed the idea and kept walking.

Then he saw it. An enormous boulder had split away from the side of the hill, and a tree had fallen over the top of the gap, creating a cave. Cautiously, he peered inside the small dark space. He wasn't much for camping and nature but he was too tired to be fussy, so he crawled inside, pushed some hanging roots out of the way, and curled up on his side, facing the opening of the shelter with his head resting on his forearm. It had been months since he had slept in his own bed, and even though this was clearly another step down from the Army cot that he had been sleeping on recently, it would have to do.

As his eyes slowly closed, his thoughts drifted away, far from the mountain top and the sound of gun fire and the flash of tracer bullets. Far from the limp body of the freckle-faced private and the screams of dying men. Back to a different time and place. It was a memory that he had effectively been able to suppress in his waking life but one that often visited him after dark, and that night would be no different. It was the memory of the night when love died.

15

Kettle Moraine, Wisconsin

The beaten-up pick-up truck towing a horse trailer threw up a cloud of dust into the early evening light as it turned off the county highway and headed down a long dirt road. Sitting behind the wheel was Jeremiah Kincaid, and tucked safely under a child's seat belt on the rear seat was his five-year-old granddaughter, Madison. Kincaid was returning to the family farm with a horse that he had bought for his wife, Kathleen, for her fifty-seventh birthday. It was an Andalusian that she had wanted for a long time, and it would be a surprise. His daughter Joanna had been in on it and had sent Madison along to keep her grandfather company, while he went to get the pale gray horse.

"Grandpa?" she asked, as she stared out the window at the huge red ball that was sinking slowly toward the golden cornfields.

"Yes, Maddy?" he replied glancing in the rear view mirror.

"Why does your rooster crow every morning?"

"What do you think, honey?"

"I think he crows to wake up the sun," she replied, with the simple logic of a child.

Kincaid smiled. "But if that's true, then who wakes up the rooster?"

She looked up at him and said, "You do, grandpa. When you get up to go potty."

He shook his head and laughed. *Out of the mouths of babes,* he thought. His increasingly frequent trips to the bathroom in the middle of the night were just one of the things he hated about growing old. But as Kathleen reminded him whenever he complained, the alternative was worse. Although he would never admit it to her, there had been times during the past several years when he wasn't so sure.

Kincaid pulled the truck and trailer up beside the large farmhouse, in front of which the Stars and Stripes hung limply against the tall, white flagpole. He hopped out, walked around the truck and helped Madison climb down. While she stood excitedly beside the trailer, he opened the tailgate, got in, and carefully led the beautiful animal out into the soft evening light. He led it to a split rail fence near the large barn behind the house and tied it up; then he walked around to the front of the house, with his granddaughter skipping along beside him. They reached the front steps and he was just about to send Maddy up to the door to get her grandmother when she and Joanna stepped out onto the broad verandah. The look on both their faces told him immediately that something was wrong. Madison could sense it, too, and she ran to her mother, who took her by the hand and pulled her close.

"What's wrong, Kathleen?" asked Jeremiah.

"It's the gun club, Jeremiah," she replied with a mixture of fear and pain in her voice.

His face went as pale as the animal he left standing behind the farmhouse. "Did the police go in?" he asked.

"No. It was the Army."

"What! That's impossible."

"It was Army Rangers, dad," added Joanna.

"It's horrible," added Kathleen.

The Speaker braced himself for the worst and asked softly, "Is T.J. dead?"

Kathleen couldn't answer. It was too much for her.

"No, he got away, Daddy," Joanna answered, with a grim look.

Jeremiah stood there for a moment, staring out across the front lawn toward the distant tree line.

Finally, Kathleen asked, "Jeremiah. Are you all right?"

He looked at her and said sadly, "Your birthday present is out back. It's the horse you wanted." But there was no joy in his voice and with a deep weariness, he walked up the stairs and headed toward the door. "I'm sorry, but I can't do this right now." As he passed his wife, he gave her a soft peck on the cheek, then he opened the screen door and disappeared into the house.

The two women looked at each other. Joanna said, "Go to him, Mother. I'll put the horse in the barn."

Kathleen nodded and followed Jeremiah into the house. She found her husband upstairs in their bedroom, packing. "Where are you going?" she asked, already knowing the answer.

"Back to Washington."

"Now?"

He stopped what he was doing and said, "I know it's your birthday, darling, but this can't wait. I'm sorry."

"Do you really have to?"

He stared at her. "Kathleen, the President ordered in Federal troops without even giving me the courtesy of a telcom call."

She nodded sadly, took some shirts out of the closet, and began folding them.

He took one of the shirts and noticed that a button was missing on it. He grabbed it and said, "I wish you could find us a new dry cleaner. Ever since that damn national chain bought the cleaner in town I have had to walk around looking like I slept in my damn shirts," he said, the anger rising in his voice. He threw the shirt with the missing button down on the floor.

Kathleen picked it up and laid it on the bed. Then she walked over to him and softy said, "T.J. will be all right, Jeremiah."

He stopped what he was doing and slowly put his arms around her. He nodded and hugged her, even though they both knew that their youngest son very likely would not be all right ever again.

"Where did we go wrong, Jeremiah, where did we go so wrong?"

He stood there for a moment before answering, holding her safely in his deep embrace. "We didn't, Kathleen. We are the same parents who raised Joanna and Jake. He has their blood and their background. We gave him everything we gave them, nothing more, nothing less." He released his hug and sat down on the bed, motioning for her to do the same. "We lost him somewhere along the way." His voice cracked and the last few words choked in his throat.

Wiping her eyes with the little white handkerchief that she never went anywhere without, she asked, "I just don't understand how such a good boy could drift so far away from his family."

"These are troubled times, Kathleen. An entire generation has been blinded by the pursuit of wealth, and power, and possessions. And the

147

saddest part of all, is that the leadership of this country seems incapable of providing the guidance and sense of purpose that this lost generation so desperately needs."

Regaining her composure, she looked up at him. "Why is there so much bitter partisanship in Washington, Jeremiah? Why can't you in the Congress and the President work together to help the lost generation?"

"If I knew, Kathleen, I would fix it."

"Maybe it's because, as a nation, we have lost faith in God," she replied.

They sat there silently for a few moments. Then he stood up and started packing again.

"What are we going to do about T.J?" she asked.

"Nothing."

"Jeremiah. He's in serious trouble and needs us."

He gazed lovingly at her. "There's nothing we can do to help him now. He's made his choices and now he has got to live with them."

"But Jeremiah, he's our son."

"No, Kathleen. We have only one son."

"Please don't talk like that. God will hear you."

"God stopped listening to me a long time ago, Kathleen, a long time ago."

"I think it's the other way around, Jeremiah."

He looked at her and then closed his suitcase. He picked it up, walked over, and gave her a kiss on her cheek; then he left the room. She listened as he walked down the stairs and out the front door. She didn't move. She sat there staring vacantly at the pictures on her dresser of her and Jeremiah with their three children in happier times that seemed so long ago and so far away.

16

Bitterroot Mountains, Idaho

It wasn't the first warm rays of the sun poking their way through the pine bows in front of the cave that woke Porter. Nor was it the tiny red spider that raced across his cheek causing him to swipe it away with eyes still closed. Instead, it was the sudden shrill cry of the Blue Jay that pierced the stillness of the forest. Instantly, Porter's eyes snapped open. He was lying with his back to the mouth of the cave, and the alarm sounded by the Jay instantly brought him to full awareness. Somewhere behind him a twig snapped, and for an instant, Porter froze, afraid to roll over—afraid to see the guns and the soldiers who almost certainly were standing there. *Damn,* he thought, *I should have kept running last night.* But it was too late now. With a deep sigh of resignation, he rolled over to face his captors.

What he saw took the breath out of his lungs. At the mouth of the cave was a full-grown timber wolf. The animal was a large male in his prime with a sleek gray coat and the tips of its long hairs the color of midnight. One hundred and twenty five pounds of coiled muscle wrapped tightly around a steel-like frame, with amber-colored eyes and long white incisors, set like scimitars in jaws capable of cracking a moose skull. It stood there, unmoving and unmoved in the crisp, cool morning air, a gray ghost silhouetted against the dawn's early light. Alone. Unafraid. Completely at one with the forest.

The pleading words of animal rights supporters raced through his mind: *There has never been a documented case of a wolf attacking a human in the history of North America.* Then, he thought, *That's because dead men don't file reports.* Porter tried to remember what he supposed to do. *Do I play dead or fight back? No, that was for grizzlies and black bears. Damn*

149

it, why didn't I watch the Discovery channel more? All the while this little dialogue was transpiring in his head, Porter didn't take his eyes off the wolf. Nor it off him. Their eyes were locked in a timeless frozen stare. The more they stared into each others eyes, the more Porter's field of vision began to narrow and blur, until finally it was as if he was looking down a long, bright tunnel that led directly into the animal's soul.

Then it happened. The wolf looked away. Just for an instant. Not with his head, just his eyes, and only with the slightest of movements. But Porter saw it and the spell was broken. The tunnel evaporated into the reality of the cave and the forest. Before Porter realized what was happening, the wolf vanished without a trace, as silently as a shadow becomes part of the shade.

It took a few moments for Porter to get his lungs and heart working again. His mind raced back over the past few moments, trying to relive every terrifying and yet exquisite second of it. *God, how exciting,* he thought. There had been no baring of fangs. No threatening posture. No hairs standing up on the back of his powerful neck. Instead, only curiosity and wonder. *Maybe he knew that I was the hunted, not the hunter. Just like him. Maybe he was trying to tell me something. Or maybe he was looking for me to tell him?* Porter had been deeply affected. But soon, reality and the events of the past twenty-four hours seeped into his consciousness. *All right. Enough of this.* The rational side of his brain brought him back to reality. It was time for him to go.

He sat up slowly and rubbed his neck, which was stiff from the damp cold night beside the boulder. He started to get up when something caught his eye. On the ground beside him, lying half buried in the dark and damp soil, was a shiny object. He picked it up and brushed off the dirt. It was a tiny eagle amulet with outstretched wings. He stared at it for several moments, turning it over in his hands, looking for any writing or symbols on it, but there were none. *Probably Nez Perce,* he thought. *If I ever get out of this mess, I'll return it to its rightful owners.* He stared at it for a few more seconds, then put it into his pocket and crawled out of the cave. He stood up stiffly and cautiously looked around to see if the wolf had come back. But it had not. Then he took one last look up the mountain and listened carefully. He heard nothing except a few chickadees squabbling over some seeds. Satisfied that he was alone, he continued his downhill journey.

Within a few minutes, he broke out onto a logging road. He stood there for a moment, first looking up the road and then down it. He listened again carefully to make sure he was alone, then he headed down the road toward the highway. The fact that he didn't have a clue how he would get back to civilization without being caught or what he would do when he got there, didn't bother him. After all, he had spent his entire life running away from something: first it was college, then his family, followed by his company, and now this. It was just one more in a long series of failures. *Why not?* he thought, *Dad never thought I'd amount to much, and I'm going to prove him right if it's the last thing that I do.* He stood there for a few more moments, all alone and abandoned in the wilderness. And then he started off down the road to his date with destiny.

THE DINER was located on the outskirts of Salmon, Idaho, and it was a welcome sight to Porter as he approached it. It had been over eighteen hours since he had run down the back side of the mountain and four hours since he had been awoken by the gray wolf. He was tired, cold, and hungry. During that time, he had changed out of his uniform into some clothes he had liberated off a clothesline on a ranch near Gibbonsville and hitched a ride with a trucker from Missoula.

The trucker hadn't recognized him, or if he did, he had kept it to himself. Porter had learned that the people in his adopted home state tended to mind their own business. It was a characteristic that he greatly appreciated, especially on that particular morning when he was in no mood to make idle talk. As they drove down Highway 93 and crossed back from Montana into Idaho, all he could think about was the freckle-faced private, the fat corporal, and the others whom he had lost forever up on that mountain. Later, without anything more than a simple exchange of "Here you are," and "Thank-you," Porter got out of the truck at the junction of Highway 23 and walked the rest of the way into town. It wouldn't be until several hours later when the trucker got to Boise that he would discover the thousand dollar bill left tucked into the passenger seat, with "Thank-you" written on it.

Perhaps it was because he was tired or perhaps he just didn't care. Either way, Porter let his guard down. As he rounded the side of the diner, he walked smack into two state troopers who were just getting back into their patrol car. Even if it hadn't been for the look of resignation and defeat written on Porter's face, the troopers would have recognized him, since they had been part of the contingent assigned to the Bitterroot Rod & Gun Club throughout the ordeal. Porter made no fuss as one of the troopers approached him.

One of them said, "I'm afraid you'll have to come with us, Captain Porter."

He just nodded quietly.

The trooper looked at the tired and beaten man and said, "How long has it been since you've eaten?"

Porter replied in a soft voice, "I'm not sure. I think it was the day before yesterday." As he spoke, there was a far-away look in his eyes.

The trooper looked at his partner, who nodded. Then he turned back to Porter, closed the back door of the patrol car and said, "Come on, let's go inside, and get you some hot food."

Thomas looked at him, genuinely appreciative of the courtesy and kindness he was being shown. Without making too much out of it, he made a mental note of the man's name on his uniform. *Officer Seaton Horner.* He would not forget the kindness.

THE IDAHO STATE POLICE cruiser was parked in a small clearing beside the road, twenty five miles south of where its occupants had captured Thomas Porter two hours earlier. Porter sat comfortably in the back seat of the car, playing with the small eagle amulet. His captors stood twenty feet away. One of them spoke into a PTC and then flipped it closed. He looked back at his partner.

"The governor's chopper's two miles out."

The other officer nodded and said, "You have any idea what the hell is going on?"

"All I know is that the Chief told us to bring Porter here, and that's all I want to know."

"I guess you're right."

As they finished speaking, the sound of rotor blades slapping the air could be heard. They grew louder until finally the sleek aircraft appeared overhead, and the pilot skillfully brought it to a smooth landing fifty yards away. As it settled, the rotor wash blew a cloud of sand and dust in every direction with such force that when the officers got home later that night, they would find sand inside their shoes.

The whine of the turbine engines wound down, and the co-pilot jumped out of his seat on the left side of the cockpit and opened the passenger compartment door. As Porter watched, Governor Morrissey stepped out, followed by Jesse Latrobe. They walked over to the two police officers and the governor acknowledged their salutes with a short nod. He then started speaking with them and as he did, they looked over at the car a few times.

When the governor finished speaking, one of the officers walked over to the car, opened the door, and motioned for Porter to get out. Together they walked over to where the governor was standing.

"Thomas," said the governor with a curt nod.

"Governor," replied Porter.

"Walk with us, Thomas," said Morrissey.

Thomas followed the governor and Jesse as they walked away.

As they did, the governor said, "Thomas, this is Jesse Latrobe."

Porter looked at the tall man and said, "It's an honor to meet you, sir. I've heard a lot about you."

The serious demeanor on the older man's face remained unchanged, and he replied, "And I, you."

"Yes, sir. I guess you have." With that, Porter looked back at the governor and said, "Governor, I want to assure you that I never meant for it to turn out this way."

"Just exactly what did you expect to happen?" asked Latrobe.

"Easy, Jesse," interjected the governor.

When they reached a discreet distance from the state troopers and the helicopter, the governor stopped as did the other two men.

"What in the name of God were you thinking, Thomas?" asked the governor.

"I just wanted to make our case, Governor," answered Porter.

"By killing people?" asked Latrobe.

Porter ignored Latrobe's comment and looked at the governor. "Governor, I know that I am solely responsible for what happened. But I also want you to know that I had ordered my men not to fire unless fired upon, and that I personally did not shoot anyone."

The governor looked at Porter and said in a quiet tone, "It doesn't matter now, does it?"

"With all due respect, Governor, it matters to me," said Porter.

The governor nodded.

"What happens to me now?" asked Porter.

"I don't know," said the governor.

"Are you going to turn me over to the FBI?"

The governor looked Porter straight in the eye and said, "No."

"May I ask, why not?"

The governor looked at Jesse, who then turned to Porter. The harsh expression on his face softened slightly and he said, "There are some of us who believe that while your actions were ill-advised, your intentions were good. So while we haven't decided exactly what to do with you, turning you over to the Federal authorities is not an option."

Porter acknowledged what Latrobe said with a sad nod. Then he turned to the governor and said, "May I ask another question, sir?"

"Of course."

"Why did you order the takeover?"

The governor just stared at him for a minute and then said, "I didn't."

"Then who did?" asked Porter.

"The President," answered Latrobe sharply.

Porter looked at him incredulously. "The President? But that can't be! He said he would think about my demands and get back to me."

Latrobe shook his head. "Apparently he did. Now let's get out of here."

"That lying bastard," mumbled Thomas.

Latrobe flashed a glance at the governor, who said nothing.

Together, they headed to the helicopter. Almost as an afterthought, Porter asked, "I suppose I should get word to my wife that I'm all right."

Latrobe stopped abruptly and gave the governor a knowing glance.

"What is it?" asked Porter.

"Do you want the truth?" replied Latrobe.

"Of course I do," said Porter, with a puzzled look on his face.

Latrobe looked at the governor, who nodded silently. Then Latrobe pulled a manila envelope out of his pocket and handed it to Porter.

At first, Porter didn't catch on to what they were saying. But then the governor explained it in all its unpleasantness. "As you might expect, as a result of your occupation of the gun club, we set up a 24/7 surveillance of your house in Sun Valley." He motioned toward the envelope with his head. "I assure you that these were an unintended consequence of that surveillance." He paused and then said gently, "We'll wait for you by the chopper."

With that, the governor and Latrobe walked away and left Porter alone. He watched them go and then looked down at the envelope. He opened it slowly and looked inside. It was filled with several large black and white photographs, which he slid out of the envelope. The first photograph had been taken through the window of the great room of their house, and it showed his scantily clad wife in the arms of a tall and muscular man at least ten years her junior. The rest of the pictures were even more graphic. Without any emotion, he flipped through the rest of them, then looked up and stood there staring at the tree line for a few moments. Finally, a smile spread across his face and with a few short, sharp movements of his hands, he tore the pictures into many pieces and threw into the dirt, stepping on them as if extinguishing a cigarette. Then he walked over to the governor and Latrobe and said, "Gentlemen, I'm all yours."

The governor waved to the pilots and immediately the turbine engines started to whine and the heavy rotors began to slowly turn. The co-pilot hopped out and held the door. The governor got in first and sat in one of the two high-backed swivel chairs that had its back to the cockpit. Latrobe took the other.

Porter settled himself onto the bench seat facing them, and over the now-thundering sound of the rotors, he said to no one in particular, "I always hated those goddamned cats."

The co-pilot closed and locked the passenger compartment door and took his seat back in the cockpit. As the two state troopers watched, the beautiful mechanical bird lifted up ever so slightly off the ground, hesitated for a second, then leapt up into the sky and disappeared over the tall, dark pines.

January, 2018

G Day - 240

River Of No Return

The flow of the river is ceaseless
and its waters never the same. The
bubbles that float in the pools, now
vanishing, now forming, are not of
long duration: so in the world are
man and his dwellings.

Kamo no Chomei, "Hojoki"

17

River of No Return Wilderness, Idaho

The members-only Wolf River Club sat overlooking the river that gave
the club its name, deep in the heart of the River of No Return Wilderness
Area. There were only three ways to reach the rambling log building and
its collection of outbuildings. The first was via a half-mile path from a non-
descript parking lot, hidden in the forest ten miles off Highway 93. The path
was covered with wood chips, and it wandered through deep, dark woods.
During the day, it was an uninviting trail at best, while at night, the dim light
of gas lanterns, intentionally kept low, made it appear downright threatening.
The second way in was via a rough dirt road that wound for twenty miles
through the mountains from Highway 75, fifty miles north of Ketchum.
This latter way in was reserved for deliveries and the handicapped. Most
club members used the dirt path, since there were no handicapped members,
nor were there ever likely to be. The third way in was via helicopter to the
well-maintained landing pad a hundred yards in front of the club. The pad
was big enough to accommodate two helicopters. The most affluent of the
members used this form of transportation, although there was an unwritten
law among the club membership that aircraft never arrived or departed
between eight and eleven p.m., so as not to disturb the evening meal.

In addition to a large and modern kitchen and a well-stocked wine
cellar, the club encompassed a great room, a cigar bar, a billiards room,
and five dining rooms, two of which could accommodate a banquet, while
the other three were smaller and more intimate. It was the kind of club
where you had to be male, and rich or famous, or both, to join, but even that
didn't guarantee membership, as some of the nation's most powerful men

had discovered much to their chagrin. It was an inner sanctum where the talk slipped effortlessly back and forth between big business and big game, but rarely ever politics. This was because in its seventy-five year history, the club had never had a member who wasn't a Republican, and they rarely wasted their time complaining about Democrats, who held a place in the members' minds only slightly above the vermin that lurked in the woods just beyond the verandah lights.

However, on that night, the first one of the new year, politics was the only thing that was being discussed by a somber group of men gathered around the fieldstone fireplace in the great room. Specifically, they were discussing the politics of Alex Webster and his increasingly more strident efforts to ban the ownership of guns. That politics was being discussed was, in itself, unusual, but what was even more noteworthy was the presence that night of one of the most powerful and charismatic of the club's members, Edward Morrissey, the Governor of the State of Idaho. Sitting beside him, actively leading the discussion, was Jesse Latrobe.

"That goddamned son of a bitch," said Latrobe, making no effort to hide his disgust. "He murdered nearly fifty innocent young men, and now he has the nerve to try to blame it on the decent God-fearing citizens of this state."

"He is blaming it on me, Jesse, not the entire State of Idaho," said the governor calmly.

"They are one and the same, Governor," replied Latrobe.

"Here, here," said several of the other men gathered around the fire.

"It's a shame that Webster doesn't like to hunt or we could invite him up here and arrange for an unfortunate accident," said one of the men with a wry smile.

"Gentlemen, I'm not sure I like the direction that this conversation is heading and given my position I think I had better excuse myself and go have a cigar."

With that, the governor stood up, as did Latrobe. They excused themselves and walked down the hall to the cigar bar where they found a quiet booth tucked back in the corner. As they passed by the bar, the governor said a few words to the two state troopers who served as his bodyguards and the two pilots of his helicopter. The four of them always liked it when the governor came up to the club because they didn't have to worry about their boss's safety, and because even though they couldn't drink while on duty, they got to sample some of the finest cuisine and best contraband cigars in the country.

Latrobe and the governor sat down and ordered drinks from the bartender. Latrobe also asked him to get a Cuban cigar from his private stock in the temperature and humidity-controlled room behind the bar, where members had there private humidors. These were stacked row on row from floor to ceiling, and each had a tasteful brass plate engraved with the member's name. The wall was a veritable who's who of the rich and famous, including several A-list Hollywood actors and directors, as well as numerous CEO's from the Fortune 100.

The bartender returned with their drinks and Latrobe's cigar, and the governor settled back into the deep leather seat, obviously more relaxed now that he and Latrobe were alone.

"Are you sure I can't offer you one, Governor," Latrobe said, as he savored the pungent aroma of the long, dark cigar.

The governor shook his head no as he took a sip of his scotch. "How is our guest doing?"

"Other than getting a little restless, he's fine."

The governor nodded. "I suppose having nothing to do all day is hard on a man of his accomplishments."

Latrobe nodded and then added, "He hasn't exactly been idle. He had his lawyers start divorce proceedings against he wife. Apparently, there was an adultery clause in her pre-nuptial agreement, and with the photos we provided, he will get off lightly, at least as far as money is concerned."

"As if Thomas Porter has to worry about money," added Morrissey, with a hint of jealousy.

"He is indeed one of the super rich, but I will give him this, Governor, he isn't greedy. He's paid out nearly fifty million dollars to the families of the men who died on that mountain, and get this, including the dead from the Army."

"Really?" said the governor, obviously impressed.

"And he paid another huge sum to the wounded on both sides of the battle, including five million to that lieutenant who saved his life."

"Five million?"

Latrobe nodded. "Not bad for taking a bullet in the leg."

The governor smiled, "I can't pay you even one million, Jesse, but I hope if the time comes, you'd take one for me."

Latrobe laughed and said, "As long as it's only in the leg. And not too high up, either. I've still got a heap of loving to do before they turn me into spud fertilizer."

"In your dreams, mister spud stud," said the governor with a broad smile. Then his expression grew serious. "Does he know that we know who he really is?" the governor continued.

"No, sir."

"Good. Let's keep it that way."

"Do you intend to tell his father?"

The governor paused before answering. "I don't know, Jesse. I just don't know."

"It's a tricky situation at best," said Latrobe. "Based on the way he handled himself up on that mountain, if this whole matter leads to armed conflict, I would be glad to serve with him. But I'm worried that he has another agenda that he hasn't shared with us."

"His agenda right now is to stay out of Federal jail. And aren't you getting a little ahead of yourself, Jesse, when you talk of armed conflict?"

"I don't think so, sir. This nation is being led by a man without honor, and in my book, there is nothing lower, or more dangerous."

"Jesse, I know you mean well, but you should be a little more circumspect about what you say, even here at the club."

"Message received," said Latrobe between puffs as he re-lit the big Cuban. "But that doesn't change the way I feel. I assure you that I am not alone."

"I don't deny that these are trying times, but it is up to men of reason to stop fights, not to start them."

"You are a thoughtful and patient man, Governor, but you have to admit that the talk coming out of the White House is disconcerting to say the least. The President plans to use the Constitution as a stepping stone for his own ambition."

"I agree, but the Democrats have been trying to get anti-gun legislation passed for years with no success. And with the exception of California and New York, every single member of Congress has almost as many constituents who are pro-gun as against. Besides, the President doesn't have the balls to stand up to the Republicans in Congress under the leadership of Jeremiah Kincaid."

"Perhaps. However, Webster is an ambitious man, and he's desperate to leave a legacy. Ambition mixed with amorality is a dangerous brew."

"If he tries to force his hand, he will certainly leave a mark on history—although not the one he wants," said the governor with concern on his tired face. "But I think the legislation he's proposing is simply for gun registration, not prohibition."

"One is the precursor of the other, sir, and you've seen what's happened in Canada. I've heard the Mounties are arresting people up there for simply hiding their rifles and shotguns in the barn."

"That's different, and you know it. Canadians, and the Brits for that matter, are willing to accept government control in every aspect of their lives. It's the tradeoff they tolerate for socialized education and medical care."

"That's not what I hear from my friends north of the border. But what can they do about it now that they have let the government disarm them?"

"Well, it won't happen here, Jesse."

"With all due respect, you're damn right it won't, because millions of men like me will die before we let it."

The governor said softly, "Let's pray that it won't come to that."

"I'm afraid that prayer isn't going to be enough, Governor."

"What would you propose that we do, Jesse?"

"It's time to seek out men of like minds. To build a coalition of leaders such as yourself. Men of vision and men of courage. Men who see what is in store for this country if we continue on our present course, and who don't like what they see."

"Such as?"

"Such as the men in the governor's mansions and in the Congress who are our friends and potential future allies."

"Allies? You sound like we're going to war."

"I'm afraid that we just might be, sir. There are rumors about growing dissent in the ranks of senior military officers at the Pentagon, between those who are loyal to the President and those who are now beginning to talk openly about disobeying him."

"Talk is cheap, Jesse. Reason will prevail."

"With all due respect, Governor, the first bullet fired in anger puts an end to reason. It happened in 1776, and again in 1861; and it could happen now."

"I don't dispute that the issue of gun control is as serious to some as the issues that started those wars, Jesse, but this is the twenty first century, and we are a civilized nation."

"Unfortunately, Governor, the dogs of war take no notice of time and achievement. As history has shown, progress does not eliminate the need for weapons. On the contrary, it only makes them bigger and more deadly.

The two men sat quietly for a few moments in the room that smelled of fine cigars, old leather, and even older whisky, each mulling the matter around inside their heads. The muted sound of a helicopter taking off from the club's helipad broke the silence. The governor glanced at his watch and then looked back at Latrobe. He had to raise his voice over the sound. "You realize that this talk has the earmarks of treason written all over it?"

"So, too, did the secret meetings among those brave men in Philadelphia over two hundred years ago."

The governor nodded sadly and said, "Perhaps."

"Governor, treason is sometimes the other edge of the sword of freedom—the sharper edge."

"Do you think this is one of those times, Jesse?"

"Yes, sir, as God is my witness, I do."

The governor thought long and hard about what his trusted friend had just said. Then he nodded and said, "I'll give it further thought, Jesse."

"That's all I can ask," replied Latrobe.

Just then, a state trooper walked up to their booth and interrupted the two men. "I'm afraid we have a problem, sir." The look on his face was a mixture of anger and embarrassment.

"What is it?" the governor asked.

"It's Captain Porter, sir."

"What about him?"

"I'm afraid he's gone, sir."

"What!" said the governor. "How?"

"He took your helicopter, sir."

"He did what?"

The trooper lowered his head like a puppy that had just soiled the living room rug, "Your pilots were doing their preflight check when Captain Porter stole it."

"How?"

"Apparently, he got in and locked the doors, started the motors, and took off, while they just stood there not knowing what to do."

Despite his sense of concern, Latrobe had to suppress a smile. The audacity of the young man had to be admired, and the image of the two pilots caught with their thumbs up their bums was quite amusing. "All right, officer, there is no need to panic. Call Boise and alert them. And get us another helicopter right away."

"Yes, sir." He left.

"Perfect! That's all we need right now," said Morrissey as he slumped back into his chair. He thought about it for a few moments and said, "He's too smart to have done this on impulse. I'm sure he's got someone waiting for him in the nearest place he can safely put the aircraft down."

Latrobe stared darkly at the governor and said, "I think I know where he's going."

"Where?"

"To kill the President."

"What! No. Porter is many things, but he isn't a killer."

"Every soldier is a killer, Governor. That's what we pay them to do. And Porter's been brooding about the President's lying to him ever since he got here."

The governor shook his head. "No, Porter's not a soldier like his brother. He's just in love with the idea of being a soldier. There's a big difference."

"Maybe. But whatever he does, if he's captured, it will threaten our cause and destroy your career," said Latrobe ominously.

"Let me worry about my career, Jesse. Meanwhile, I want you to go find him."

"I'm a retired soldier, not a bloodhound."

The governor looked directly into his friend's eyes and said softly, "Jesse, just do it."

Latrobe hesitated for only an instant and then nodded. "Yes, sir." He knew there was no other choice. "Should we notify the FBI?"

Morrissey thought about it and replied, "No." Then he stood up and, as he did, something on the table caught his eye. It was a book of matches with the name of the club on it. He picked it up, stared at it for a few seconds, and just shook his head. "How ironic."

"What?" asked Latrobe.

The governor looked at him and then tossed him the matchbook.

R.A.R. Clouston

Latrobe stared down at the words written on it. It said "River of No Return." He looked up at the governor and said, "So be it."

18

1600 Pennsylvania Avenue, Washington, D.C.

The joy and good fellowship of the Christmas holidays in the nation's capital ended abruptly on the second day of the new year when a large and boisterous group of protesters began their march in front of the White House. The group was mostly made up of middle-aged white men and women. By their dress and manner, it was apparent that most had only climbed the first few rungs on the ladder of society. But unlike those higher up the ladder, these were the kind of people who were quite happy with their lot in life. They didn't spend their time dreaming of what it would be like to be rich. In fact, whenever one of their numbers won a lottery, they usually didn't quit their jobs, although they might come in late a little more often.

They were first-line supervisors in manufacturing plants, over-the-road truck drivers, auto mechanics, and various tradesmen. The very bedrock of America. They shopped at Wal*Mart, ate at Applebee's, bought their cars second hand, and went to church every Sunday, as long as it didn't interfere with the broadcast of the big game. They were the kind of people that the classes above them would never think of inviting to dinner but equally wouldn't think twice about calling them on Christmas night to fix a plugged drain. They asked little from society and they gave little back to it. For the most part, they were simple, peaceful citizens, living out their lives on the other side of town. They were cheerful in their ignorance of the finer things that money and higher education could offer. Completely willing to live and let live. Until that is, someone tried to take something away from them.

Then, unlike those higher up the ladder who were constrained by decorum and the rule of law, these people took whatever steps they felt were appropriate to protect their families, their friends, and their possessions. These were not the kind of people who would allow a murderer of one of their own to go free because of police ineptness or a legal technicality. Such a person would soon be found floating face down in a river, and the police would never in a million years break the code of silence in the victim's community. It was crude and simple justice. And it worked.

On that particular morning, several hundred of these people, many of whom had driven all night to be there, were marching outside the seat of American power to protest the most serious of all thefts, that of their freedom. The theft of liberty had taken place two months earlier and two thousand miles away in the Bitterroot Mountains of Idaho, farther away than most of them had ever traveled in their lives, but to them it was every bit as serious and threatening as if a convicted pedophile had moved next door to their local elementary school. And they were simply not going to stand for it. Period.

They chanted, "Freedom. Freedom. Freedom," as they paraded up and down on the sidewalk directly in front of the house they had always been told belonged to the people. However, the concrete street barricades, spiked iron fences, and armed guards that stood between them and the man who supposedly served at their pleasure, somehow didn't support that notion. As they marched back and forth, their faces were being scanned by automated high throughput screening cameras perched on poles high overhead, and the telltale characteristics of their faces were being converted into algorithms and compared to the database of known criminals on the Federal Government's Granite Shield quantum computer.

"What do we want? Freedom! When do we want it? Now! What do we want? Freedom! When do we want it? Now!" they shouted, but their efforts were largely wasted, since the President was away on a fundraising trip to the west coast, and the television networks would likely have very little interest in another peaceful protest outside the White House. However, as they chanted it over and over again on loud bullhorns, it did have the effect of making the job of the tour guides inside the White House extremely difficult as they tried to talk to the tourists, most of whom didn't understand English anyway.

For the most part, the other people walking along the sidewalk on that brisk but sunny January morning in the nation's capital weren't particularly upset by the demonstration. Many were civil servants hurrying to their jobs after the Christmas break, and they were accustomed to that stretch of heavily fortified real estate being used as a platform for peaceful civil disobedience. Unfortunately, on that particular morning, the demonstration was about to become anything but peaceful.

As the protesters continued their march back and forth on Pennsylvania Avenue, they couldn't see another crowd of people gathering at the far side of Lafayette Park. This group was more eclectic in its make up. It was comprised of a mixture of young, pseudo-impoverished, upper-middle-class college kids, who felt that life owed them something but weren't exactly sure what it was. They were accompanied by a potpourri of older, better-dressed intellectuals, including those who actually were, as well as those who only thought they were. Also present were numerous state and Federal politicians from the liberal side of the aisle and a coterie of celebrities, both real and imagined. Finally, there was the usual contingent of hangers-on that always seem to populate liberal causes. However, as polyglot as the crowd appeared to be, they all shared one common fear and belief, namely the fear of guns and the belief that the country would never be safe until all guns were outlawed.

Marching along at the front of the crowd were none other than the perennial gun-hating twins, the Reverend Ezekial Freeman and Congressman Rodwell Crane. As this terrible twosome led their group across the park to meet the pro-gun crowd, they seemed less concerned with making their own views known, and more determined to stop the other group from making theirs. Clearly it was a recipe for disaster, and anyone could see that there was but one likely outcome from these two groups coming together in front of the White House.

SARAH McGILL was in her car three blocks away from the White House when her PTC rang. She pushed the hands-free button and said, "McGill."

Over the tiny speaker came the loud sound of Lange's voice. "Sarah, where are you?"

She glanced out the window and said, "Seventeenth and M. Why?"

"Because we just heard on the police scanners that there is trouble brewing in front of the White House," he replied.

"I'm on it. I'll be there in thirty seconds," she answered excitedly.

"No. That's the last thing I want you to do. Someone just called the station and said they saw several people with guns in the crowd. I want you to get the hell out of there. Now!"

"Okay, relax, boss. I'll turn off on L and head back to the station."

"Good. See that you do. I'll be waiting for you," he said, with obvious relief in his voice.

"Understood." With that, she hung up and drove the car straight through the intersection of L and Seventeenth.

By the time McGill neared Pennsylvania Avenue, the two crowds had converged and they were exchanging the first round of verbal salvos. However, in the noise and confusion, Messrs. Freeman and Crane were nowhere to be seen. The reverend's bodyguards had determined that the situation was too dangerous, and the two of them were at that moment safely tucked inside a stretch black SUV that was taking them to Representative Crane's sumptuous townhouse in Georgetown. There, a select group of Washington's elite, drawn from both sexes but only one party, would pontificate on the sad state of affairs in America and commiserate over the difficult job that President Alex Webster now faced.

Back at the White House, Sarah McGill's Mustang screeched to a stop on Jackson Place beside the park, and she jumped out and ran across the grass toward the commotion. At the same time, the sounds of sirens filled the air and police cars began converging on the scene from every direction. Among them was the unmistakable battlewagon of the D.C. SWAT team. It stopped within sight of the West Wing and out of it's back door poured six heavily armed officers. Meanwhile, a uniformed detail of the Secret Service had taken a defensive position on the lawn of the White House directly behind the metal fence, from where the two groups of protesters were standing face to face across an imaginary no-man's land.

As McGill ran toward the crowd, she hastily pressed a number on her PTC. "Hello. Harry, where's my camera crew?" She listened to his reply and then said, "I know what Lange said, and now I'm saying this. Get them here now. Got it? Good." She flipped the device closed and then waded into the crowd of anti-government protesters who were now closing their ranks against the threats and taunts of the students and hecklers.

"Murderer!" screamed one of the co-eds at a red-faced white man who was holding a Freedom poster.

"Go to hell," replied the man.

"Moron," shouted her companion, who then turned to the students around him and shouted, "How many red necks does it take to kill a deer?" Another young man shouted, "Ten. One to shoot the gun and nine to do a circle jerk while he does it." The girls in their group laughed and one of them screamed, "Perverts."

"Fuck you, bitch," shouted one of the opposite group.

All up and down the line of convergence of the two groups, similar heated exchanges were taking place, and the police, who at that moment were still in the minority, were doing their best to keep the sparring verbal. And right there in the thick of it all was Sarah McGill. As more sirens filled the air, at several points along the line, the two groups were coming dangerously close to each other, and some rough shoving had started. By now, Pennsylvania Avenue was in complete disarray, with hundreds of screaming protesters, overtaxed police officers, morbid onlookers, and some roving bands of punks who had been drawn to the scene like sharks circling drowning sailors. Then, just when it looked as if the police, whose numbers were increasing with each passing minute, were gaining the upper hand, the sound of a gunshot boomed like thunder over everyone's heads.

Instantly, McGill tried to work her way through the crowd in the direction from which she thought the shot had come. But the deeper that she got into the roiling sea of humanity, the more she began to doubt the wisdom of her actions. Instead of scattering the crowd, the gunshot had stirred it up like a sharp stick thrust into a hornet's nest. Now the entire street in front of the White House was a boiling mass of screaming, punching, and wild-eyed humanity. The situation was now totally out of control, and people were starting to be trampled as the combatants fought with the police and with each other.

Mob hysteria began to weave its deadly hand, and several punks started smashing the windows of the police cars that were parked just outside the concrete barricades that blocked off the ends of the street. Instead of serving their purpose of keeping danger off the street directly in front of the White House, the barricades were now having exactly the opposite effect, as they prevented the people who wanted to get away from easily doing so. The crowd started to rock one of the police cars, while others hammered on the SWAT truck trying to get to the arsenal of weapons inside. Meanwhile, the officers were spread out among the crowd trying to help their less well-protected colleagues, many of whom had lost their helmets and some of whom were literally fighting for their lives as hooligans pulled at their holsters trying to get at their weapons. It would later be recorded as one of the worst riots that the nation's capitol had seen since the riots of the sixties. And it wasn't over yet.

Up until that point, McGill was doing relatively well. Apart from being jostled, she was in no real danger, but as the situation escalated, she knew that once again she had placed herself in harm's way. Slowly and methodically, she worked her way in the direction of Seventeenth Street, where she could see police reinforcements arriving in numbers. She thought that if she could get within shouting distance of the growing cordon of officers, she would make it all the way. But that was still fifteen or twenty yards away. So she pressed on, trying to not stand out in the crowd. She almost made it when suddenly one of the rioters noticed her upscale clothes and began closing in on her with several of his accomplices. She saw them coming out of the corner of her eye and tried to push through the wall of people blocking her path. But it was too little, too late. In an instant, they were upon her. They formed a circle around her like a tiny eye of a hurricane and began to taunt her.

"What's the matter, bitch? A little out of your league, are you?" taunted the scruffy leader with a tuft of dirty hair under his lower lip and a pin through his nostril.

McGill avoided direct eye contact with him and said, "Excuse me, please."

"What's your hurry?" he asked with an evil sneer. "Why don't you and I party a bit?" Then he looked at his buddies and said, "I don't know about you guys, but I for one would like to see this woman's tits. What do you think, guys?" They were quick to agree.

"I don't think you want to do that," she said in as firm a tone of voice as she could muster.

The leader laughed. "Why? What are you going to do about it, bitch?"

As she talked to him, she searched the crowd for someone who could help her. She sensed that there was help nearby, but she didn't know where or from whom. At that point, no one nearby was paying any attention to the unfolding drama. She took a few steps in the direction of the police line, which seemed to be growing farther away, but the man reached out and grabbed her purse. McGill knew better than to resist, and she immediately let him have it. Then someone seized the lapel of her suit jacket, and with a

172

strong jerk ripped it open, tearing with it a piece of her blouse. This exposed McGill's lacy bra, which drew an instant reaction from several others in the perimeter of the circle. As their hands reached out and tore at McGill's suit, she tried to defend herself, but it was of little use. Very quickly she was being groped, fondled, and disrobed in public.

The image of the man in the alley with the ugly black gun flashed before her eyes. She couldn't believe this was happening to her again. But it was. She was alone in a crowd of madmen without hope or help nearby—or so she thought. But she would not give in without a fight, and as the leader of her attackers took a step toward her, she swung her right fist with all her might and caught him full force in the nose, right where the pin pierced it. The force of the blow sent him staggering back a few steps and blood began to spurt out of his broken nose. Instead of rushing to his assistance, his cohorts stood there laughing at the sight of their fearless leader who had been bested by a slim blond in a slip.

For a moment, he stood there glaring at McGill, and then he reached inside his jacket and pulled out a gun. It was a .45 caliber autoloader pistol with enough killing power to drop a bull in a barnyard. A direct hit virtually anywhere on a human body would be lethal. He raised it and pointed it at McGill, but before he could squeeze the trigger, the crowd suddenly began to part behind him like tall grass before an onrushing beast. He felt the movement and turned just in time to see an enormous white stallion and dark rider bearing down on him. McGill saw them too and knew at once that it was Michael Falconer. "Michael!" she cried out. The man raised the weapon, but it was too late; the stallion reared up, pawing the air with its enormous black hooves and fell forward, striking the man in the forehead with one of them. His eyes rolled back in his head, and he collapsed to the pavement. As he did, his finger reflexively squeezed the trigger, and the heavy bullet smashed harmlessly into the snow-covered ground, but the noise of the shot was deafening, and the crowd panicked. People started running in every direction at once, and the wall of humanity quickly closed in on McGill, squeezing the breath out of her. The last image her brain registered before darkness swallowed her was the face of Michael Falconer thrusting his strong hand down to lift her out of harm's way.

WHEN SHE CAME TO, she was lying on a stretcher, covered in a bright red blanket beside an ambulance, behind the police lines.

"Is she all right?" said a female police officer.

"Yes. She'll be fine," replied a paramedic, who then hurried off to assist some of the other victims of the riot.

McGill sat up and pushed the blanket off her. She looked at the policewoman and asked, "What happened?"

"You fainted dear, that's all. You'll be fine."

She looked at the confused scene before her. "Did you see him?"

"Who, dear?"

"Officer Falconer."

"Who?"

McGill sighed. "Never mind." She looked around, but her dark rider and his white stallion weren't anywhere to be seen. She shook her head and whispered, "Can I go now?"

The officer studied McGill's face. "Yes, but before you do I need to ask you a question."

"Yes?"

"A man died in the crowd and witnesses said he was talking to you just before he collapsed. Did you see anything that could help our investigation of his death?"

McGill shook her head and looked away. "No."

The policewoman didn't believe her, but there was nothing she could do about it. She took down her name and address, said, "Very well, Ms. McGill. You take care of yourself, now, you hear?" Then she walked away, leaving Sarah sitting on the stretcher feeling confused, frustrated, and alone. But in fact, she was not alone. Ten yards away, beside the high steel fence that separated the street from the snow-covered lawn of the White House, a tall, dark and handsome figure stood with the hood of his black duffel coat shrouding his bearded face. It was Thomas Porter, and for a long while, he studied her, making sure that she was all right. And when he was satisfied that she was, he turned and melted into the crowd.

TWO HOURS later, Sarah walked into the studios after having gone home and changed out of the remnants of the suit that the mob tore from her. She was still shaken, and the air of self-confidence that she usually radiated was nowhere in evidence. She gave the receptionist the barest hint of a smile and headed to the elevator. When she reached the floor where her office was located, she hurried down the plushly carpeted hallway, trying to avoid eye

174

contact with her fellow workers. As she passed each office and desk, she could feel the stares of her colleagues and hear their whispers. She almost made it to her office, the door of which stood wide open and beckoned to her like a port in a storm, when the voice of Keene Lange boomed out from across the office.

"Damn it, all Sarah, this time you went too far!"

She faced him as he rumbled up to meet her. "Can we discuss this in private, please?" she asked in as calm a voice as she could manage, given the fact that she was on the verge of an emotional breakdown.

He stopped abruptly and stared at her. Then, in a more moderate, but no less angry tone of voice he said, "Inside." He motioned with his head toward her office. They entered, and he closed the door behind them. Outside the office, darting eyes and shaking heads gave a hint of what was to come.

McGill sat down behind her desk in a heap, and he stood directly in front of it. Without looking up at her boss she said, "I don't think I can deal with this right now, Keene."

"You don't think you can deal with this right now! How the hell do you think I feel?"

She looked up at him with hurt in her eyes. The hurt of knowing that she had done something stupid for which there would be no smart-ass answer or cute little word game.

"Sarah, what in the name of God were you thinking? First the Supreme Court, then the mountain, and now this! If I didn't know better, I'd think you had a death wish."

She didn't answer. She just sat there with a sad look in her jade green eyes. Finally, she said, "I thought I could get the story, but instead I just made a fool of myself on national television."

Gradually, his anger melted. "Sarah, Sarah, Sarah. When will you ever learn that you are not indestructible?"

She didn't answer. She also didn't tell him about Officer Falconer. She didn't see any point to it.

"Will you please promise me that you will stay away from guns, at least until I retire?"

She nodded, but said nothing.

"That means I want you either here or *inside* the White House. Is that understood?"

"Yes," she answered softly.

"Good. Then that's that." In all the years that he had known her, he had never seen anything penetrate her facade of toughness and self-confidence. Not even that dreadful night when she was almost raped and murdered. But now, finally, he thought he detected a crack in her armor. And it unnerved him. "I need a drink," he said softly. "Come on, I hate to drink alone."

She looked over at the clock on her credenza and back at him. "It's only eleven thirty in the morning."

He reached over and turned the clock upside down. Then he said, "No. It's precisely five o'clock." He headed for the door. "Are you coming, or are you going to sit there and feel sorry for yourself?"

To an outside observer, the comment might have seemed insensitive. But it was just what Sarah needed. Slowly, a smile slipped across her lips. She stood up and followed him.

As they walked out of the office together, he reached into his pocket and pulled out a thick wad of money. He counted out seven hundred-dollar bills and handed them to McGill. "Here."

"What's that for?" she asked.

He smiled and said, "Remember the other day, when I said that I was hoping the Eagles would win their playoff game against the Ravens, and you blurted out that they would? You even correctly predicted the final score."

"Yes. So?"

They continued down the hall and across the spacious lobby of the building.

"Because of you, I bet on them. Heavily. This is your share of the winnings." He held the door open for her and they walked toward the parking lot.

"You don't owe me any money."

"Sarah. You know less about football than I know about quantum computing. And yet you predicted their victory and their exact margin of victory. I don't know how you did it, but you are certainly going to share in the proceeds, even if it was because of that spooky sixth sense of yours again."

She walked along beside Lange and glanced at the money that he held in his hand. Then a smile broke across her face and she said, "Okay, I'll take it—thanks." She reached over, took the seven bills, and stuffed them in her jacket pocket.

"Good. Now, about the Superbowl…"

"Sorry, I can't turn on that spooky sixth sense you talk about. It just happens. Like when I am thinking about a specific page in a book, and I reach over and flip it open to that exact page. If I try to repeat it, it never works."

They reached his car, and he opened the door. "Well, I just happen to have the racing form lying there on the passenger seat. And when you get a moment, could you please just flip it open and put your finger on a horse's name? Any horse. I don't care."

She smiled and slid into the seat. "I can't do that."

"Why not?"

"Because if I do, every politician in this city is going to ask me to predict the outcome of his or her next election."

"What's wrong with that? You might even be able to affect the outcome!"

"That's exactly my point. Does this country need a government selected by me?"

Lange laughed and said, "It couldn't possibly be any worse than what we've got now."

She smiled and said, "Just drive."

19

The Pentagon, Arlington, Virginia

General Halston Pace, Chairman of the Joint Chiefs of staff, sat at his desk in the impressive office filled with the military memorabilia of nearly forty years of war and peace. In front of the desk stood Lieutenant General Pete Corcoran, Commander of the U.S. Army Special Operations Command. Rangers Wings hung proudly on the taut and immaculate uniform, and his three stars shone brightly on his heavily starched collar.

"At ease, General," said Pace.

The soldier relaxed, but did not sit down.

"What can I do for you, Pete?"

General Corcoran looked uncomfortable as he replied, "It's about the Bitterroots." He hesitated. "Permission to speak frankly, sir?"

"Permission granted," said Pace.

"Sir, we made a terrible mistake sending troops to take over that gun club. The Army should have never gone up that damned mountain. Period."

"I appreciate your position, General."

"No, sir. With all due respect, I don't think you do."

Halston Pace studied the other soldier carefully. He knew that General Corcoran had had a long and distinguished career. He was well respected and liked by the Congress, his peers, and subordinates alike, and up to that point, his record was unblemished. As commanding officer of the U.S. Army Special Operations Command based in Fort Bragg, North Carolina, Corcoran was responsible for some of the most lethal fighting units of all the armed forces. But Halston knew that the general had taken the disaster in the Bitterroots as a personal failure, and even though he had reassured

Corcoran that it would not reflect badly on his record, he knew the general didn't believe him. And if the truth be told, he had every reason not to. Despite all assurances to the contrary, the incident had likely killed any chance Corcoran had for a fourth star. And what made the whole tragic situation even worse was that Corcoran was a native Idahoan who had been put in the position of sending young men up that mountain to kill other young men from his home state.

"Go on," said Pace.

"The fiasco on that mountain has completely demoralized my staff officers. It has given the Army a black eye and made us look like incompetent fools at best, or morons at worst. It has undermined all the good that we accomplished in WWT. In short, it was an unmitigated disaster from the moment we gave the order to take over the gun club, until the last soldier was buried, and I am not sure if the damage that has been done to my command can ever be erased."

"General, you know how sad I am that so many young men died, both those in your command and those from your home state, but whether or not I agree with you, what would you have me do about it now?"

The general reached inside his tunic and pulled out an envelope which he held out toward Pace. "Nothing, sir. It's too late for anyone to do anything, including you. That is why I am asking you to accept my letter of resignation from the Army."

General Pace did not take the envelope. Instead, he stood up, walked around his desk, and motioned with his hand toward two embroidered chairs that faced a mahogany coffee table. "Let's sit down and talk."

The other man looked for a moment like he was not going to accept Pace's offer. Then he nodded and did as he was told. Before Pace joined him, he pushed a button on his intercom. A man's voice instantly replied, "Yes, sir?"

"I don't want to be interrupted."

"Understood, sir."

Then Pace sat down beside Corcoran.

"Pete, how long have we known each other?"

"Since Beast Barracks," replied Corcoran, referring to the summer before their freshman year at West Point.

"A lifetime ago," added Pace with a wistful smile.

"Yes, sir, it was."

179

"Since then, have I ever done anything to destroy the bond of trust and friendship that exists between us?"

"No," said Corcoran softly.

"You did not give that order Pete, I did. You did what you had to do."

"It was a bad order, sir, and I shouldn't have followed it."

Pace pounded his fist on the arm of the chair. "Damn it all, Pete, we are soldiers. We follow orders. That's what we do. The first time that we allow any soldier, regardless of his or her rank, to choose whether or not to follow an order is the beginning of the march to anarchy." The general paused to allow his words to sink in. "You know that as well as I do."

Corcoran looked Pace in the eyes and said, "With all due respect, General, that doesn't ease my conscience, nor bring those men back." He paused, and with a slow shaking of his head, like a water buffalo before oncoming lions, he added, "I'm not sure I will ever be able to look anyone from my home state in the eyes again."

Pace softened. "Listen to me, I understand. I really do. But your men knew that you were following orders that came from the commander in chief and so should your friends and family in Boise. There was absolutely nothing that you could have done to avoid the tragedy on that mountain. The militia wrote their own epitaphs the moment they opened fire on soldiers of the United States government."

"Soldiers who are paid to defend this land from enemies abroad, not from within," replied Corcoran.

"No. You're wrong. They're sworn to defend America from all enemies, foreign or domestic. But be that as it may, if you resign now, you will be abandoning all those who look up to you, and some will see this as a betrayal of faith. That is not the legacy that you should leave in this man's Army."

Corcoran looked down at his hands, which were trembling. Then he looked back up at Pace and said, "You have no idea what this has done to me, to the Army, or to America."

"Yes. I do. But time heals everything, General—even this."

The two men sat there quietly for a moment. Then General Corcoran said, "Please tell me, General, that you won't let the President involve the Army in his crusade against guns."

"You know I can't speak for the commander in chief, General."

Corcoran shook his head. "Isn't it ironic? He's going to destroy us while trying to save us, and there is no one who can stop him."

"Pete, as your boss, I can't accept you talking like that in my presence. As your friend, I will pretend I never heard it."

Corcoran knew he had pushed the matter to the limits of the other man's friendship, and it was time to go. "I understand, General."

"Now, go back to your command and continue to provide the leadership that I, and your troops, have come to expect from you."

Both men stood up. For an instant, they just stood there staring at each other. Then, spontaneously and without embarrassment, they embraced.

"Good luck, General," said Pace after they stepped apart.

"Thank-you, sir. But it's not me that needs the luck. It's our country."

General Pace smiled sadly and watched his friend walk out the door. He would never see him again.

20

The Capitol, Washington, D.C.

The House Committee On The Judiciary, under the leadership of Representative Snede from Arkansas, sat listening attentively to Chief Justin Law, head of the National Police Force's Chicago Division and former President of the now defunct National Association of Chiefs of Police, as he finished his presentation on the need for more police, and by definition, more guns on the streets of the nation. When he was first introduced, there had been a few derisive smiles among several Democrats on the committee and some snickering around the room at his improbable name. However, by the time the poised and polished professional was done, the room was silent and the audience was captive, for the picture he painted of a society where criminals outnumbered the police was grim and foreboding and harkened back to a time in America where the rule of law was the rule of the gun, and justice was left to a few beleaguered men wearing shiny tin stars.

Chief Law was followed to the microphone by Senator Harridan Niles, who exchanged a knowing smile and a warm handshake with the chief as he stepped aside.

"Mr. Chairman, honorable Members of the Committee, ladies and gentlemen. Chief Law has spoken eloquently on the issue before you, and I can think of no more fitting punctuation to his presentation than to add fourteen words. Just fourteen words. Words written by men of great wisdom, men of great vision, men upon whose shoulders fell the burden of creating all that we here today embody—a great democracy with liberty and justice for all. And I quote, 'the right of the people to keep and bear arms,'" he paused.

His voice became deeper and more resonant as he carefully and slowly enunciated each of the last four words "'shall—not—be—infringed!'"

As he said the last word, his fist slammed down onto the table, causing many in the audience to jump in their seats. The room fell silent. The chairman should have cautioned the senator to avoid such drama, but whether he would have or not soon became moot, as the senator looked him directly in the eyes and continued, "We in the National Rifle Association are not, as some would have you believe, a self-righteous group of zealots." His eyes then slowly worked their way down the length of the committee table.

"We are your neighbors, your friends, and fellow worshippers in your church or synagogue. We have the same fears, hopes, and dreams as every other citizen of this great land—and the same rights that our founding fathers gave us when they wrote the mightiest piece of paper that has ever existed upon the face of this earth: the Constitution of the United States of America. We respectfully submit that those fourteen words are no less important than the thousands of other words written in our Constitution. To dismiss them is to dismiss the entire document itself. To take away some rights from some of the people is to take away all rights from all of the people." He paused one last time. Then with the power and portent of distant thunder, he added fourteen more words. Just fourteen, "And if the government chooses to do so, then it must suffer the consequences."

When he was finished, he sat there for a long moment. No one spoke. No one moved. Then slowly, he stood up. He did not thank the committee, for he did not approve of their mission on this matter, and he knew not what their ultimate findings would be. However, he did nod respectfully. Then he walked away, wincing as he went, as if the years or the issue, or both, had taken a heavy toll on him. It did not go unnoticed by the Democrats on the committee, who were quick to whisper to each other that this man had made a career out of winning listeners over to his side through a pinch of reason on a plateful of drama.

After the old gentleman had returned to his seat, Chairman Snede leaned over to the microphone and called out the name of a woman who then stood up at the back of the room and approached the witness table with obvious trepidation. Another woman, apparently a close friend or relative, accompanied her to the front of the room. She carried a large black portfolio.

They both sat down and the younger woman fiddled with the microphone until a congressional aide walked over and adjusted it for her.

"Go ahead, madam," said the chairman patiently.

"Thank, you, Mr. Chairman. My name is Mrs. Beverly Brooks. I would like to thank this committee for allowing me to speak to you this morning." She glanced back at the senator. "I also have the utmost respect for Senator Niles and his record of service to our nation. When I was a little girl, I used to listen to my father talk in glowing terms about the senator and how his views help shape America."

The senator smiled politely at the woman.

She acknowledged his smile with a sad one of her own. Then she turned back to face the committee. "Unlike you, Mr. Chairman, or Senator Niles, or the members of your committee, I am no one of importance in the grand scheme of life. I hold no office, I have no constituency, and I carry no mandate. I am just an ordinary housewife from Omaha who has lost her child to a senseless school shooting." She paused, not for effect as a professional speaker might have done, but simply because the magnitude of her loss was overwhelming to her. And her loss was not lost upon anyone in the room, most of whom were immediately drawn to her because of the heavy burden she carried and the graceful way she did it. "However, I believe that gives me the right to speak out on behalf of the parents who have lost a child to gunfire and those who will." The statement cast a chill in the room. Had she been coached before her appearance by the anti-gun movement, she might have cited the fact that the group of parents who would bury children with bullet holes in their bodies that year would number in the thousands. But Mrs. Brooks spoke from the heart, not the head, and in so doing, the power of her message was magnified to a far greater degree than any statistics could have done.

Her voice wavered for just a moment, but then her friend patted her gently on the arm and whispered something in her ear. She nodded and began again, "I am certain that this committee and the Congress that you represent are honorable and learned men and women who feel only too heavily the onerous burden that this issue has placed upon your shoulders. But before you debate the moral, ethical, and legal aspects of this issue; before you become locked in a partisan debate that will be driven by those who shout the loudest among your respective constituencies; and before you decide whether or not the Congress should support the President's legislation, I want to introduce you to my daughter, Meagan."

With that, she paused as the other woman placed a tripod directly in front of the committee on which she set up a three foot by two foot blow-up photograph of a beautiful, blonde-haired, seventeen-year-old girl in a cheerleader's outfit. The committee chairman squirmed a little uncomfortably in his chair but said nothing. The woman continued, "I want to describe for you the last few moments of Meagan's life."

"Mr. Chairman," said another Republican on the committee, "this is highly unusual and I must protest."

The gavel slammed down on the hard wood plate. The chairman, himself a Republican, but one with a slightly less hard heart, glared at his colleague and said, "Excuse me, congressman, this woman has the floor, and we will hear her out." He looked back at the woman, smiled gently and said, "Go ahead, Mrs. Brooks."

She nodded, took a deep breath, and continued, "Meagan and I had a fight on her last morning on earth. I don't remember exactly what it was about. It wasn't particularly serious. Just the kind that a mother and a daughter have all the time. But I will carry the memory of it with me until the day I die. For you see, because of the argument, I let her go to school that morning without giving her a hug or telling her that I loved her." Again, the woman paused.

The other woman with her poured her a glass of water, but she refused it. "The school bus dropped Meagan and her friends at school at 7:35 a.m. that day, five minutes earlier than normal. Five minutes. Just five minutes. Insignificant, really, when measured against the fourteen hundred and forty minutes in a day. How many of you keep track of every five-minute period in your day?" She looked at several of the committee members' faces. No one moved or said anything.

"In my daughter's case, those five minutes made all the difference between living and dying. For, you see, because of those five minutes, Meagan walked down the hallway toward her locker at exactly the same moment that a tormented young classmate, only three months older than my daughter, rounded the corner carrying a handgun." The woman stopped and her friend took another large photograph out of the black case and leaned it against the tripod below the photograph of Meagan. On it was a photo of a 9 millimeter autoloader pistol lying near a pool of blood on what appeared to be a schoolroom floor.

185

"By the time Meagan came face-to-face with him, he had already shot two other students outside the back of the school, and he was on his way to the principal's office, where he would later shoot and kill three more students and the assistant principal and wound four others, before turning the gun on himself." Her mouth went dry and she took a sip of the glass of water, which she held in unsteady hands.

"I will never know what went through my daughter's mind when she watched that boy as he raised his gun—the same gun as you see here before you in the photograph—then pointed it directly at her chest and pulled the trigger. I don't know if her eyes met his. I don't know if she knew she was about to die. I will never know what her final fleeting glimpse of the world was. I can only pray that the Lord was with her in those final moments of her life—that he comforted her, and carried her in his arms into paradise. Because I wasn't there to hold her or to tell her that I loved her, as her life slipped away on that cold, hard tile floor."

At this point, Mrs. Brooks, who had maintained her composure throughout her address, lowered her head and began to sob silently. No one stirred except her friend, who put her arm around her and held her tightly. After only a few moments, she regained her composure and looked back up at the committee. There was not a dry eye among them, even the man who had only moments before objected.

The woman then gathered her last bit of emotional strength and began to speak again. "Ladies and gentlemen of this venerable committee, I must ask you, what kind of a land is this, and what kind of people have we become, when I have to bury my daughter, while you sit here and debate what was in the minds of our founding fathers when they wrote those fourteen words over two hundred years ago. Do you really believe they would have traded the life of even one innocent child for someone's right to carry this lethal piece of steel? Do you think they would have agreed that the rights of the man whose son took this weapon to school are more important than my child's right to live or the rights of the other children? Do you believe they would say that the boy who stole my daughter's life, and that of seven others, including his own, was to blame for this tragedy?" She stopped and stared directly into the eyes of the chairman and said softly, "Ladies and gentlemen, you don't owe me an answer. Your answer is strictly between you and God." She paused to let her final words sink in. Then she added, "Thank-you for hearing me." With that, she and her friend stood up, gathered their things, and turned away from the microphone.

They took a few steps, and then the mother faced the committee and said, "Do you want to hear the final irony of this tragedy? The police said that it only took that boy five minutes to break open his father's gun case. Five minutes. Just five minutes. Think about that when you go home tonight to your loved ones. Be sure to hold them and tell them you love them. Because in five minutes they could be taken away from you—forever." Then she turned and walked away, and the only sounds that broke the silence of the room were the soft footsteps of the two women who left without looking back. As they passed the row where Senator Niles was sitting, he averted his eyes. He knew that while he and those who supported him might still win the war, on that day in that room, they had lost the battle. And it had been a decisive defeat.

ACROSS THE STREET from the Capitol, in the Rayburn Congressional Building, Jeremiah Kincaid walked quickly along down the corridor with George Ross toward his office. Under his arm he carried a large stack of papers. The two men were deep in conversation when they rounded a corner and came face to face with a large crowd of reporters standing outside his office.

One of them immediately shouted, "Mr. Speaker. Would you care to comment on the President's proposed gun legislation?"

"No," answered the Speaker and kept on walking.

The reporter persisted, "Why are you so strongly against the President's bill?"

"I already said I have no comment."

"Are you a gun lover, Mr. Speaker?" another reporter asked.

The Speaker stopped abruptly and turned to the reporter.

"I am neither a gun lover nor a gun hater."

"Do you own any guns?" asked the man, refusing to let it go.

"No, I do not. But my father did. In fact, he owned many." The Speaker paused, as the reporters furiously scribbled on their note pads. "But he never threatened anyone nor robbed a bank nor shot his neighbor. He was a normal, well-adjusted and law-abiding citizen." The Speaker started to walk away. Then he turned back to face the reporters. "But he did die with a gun in hand."

The reporters all looked up from their pads. One asked, "How?"

"In Vietnam, along with fifty eight thousand other selfless Americans."

The reporter had no comeback.

"Now, if you'll excuse me." With that, Ross and the Speaker walked into his office. Waiting for them there was Jake. He was in his dress uniform and he looked every bit the hero warrior that he was.

"Hello, son, what brings you up to the Hill?" he asked.

"I just wanted to see how you were doing, dad."

"Hello, Jake," said Ross.

"Hello, George," replied Jake with a friendly smile.

"I'm doing fine son," replied Jeremiah, placing his papers down on his desk.

"Any word on T.J?"

The expression immediately darkened on the Speaker's face. "No." He walked over to the window and looked out across the lawn toward the Capitol. "I wonder if they know?"

"If who knows?" asked Jake.

"Everyone," said the Speaker, turning back to look at his son.

"I'm sure they don't," replied Ross. "If they did, it would be all over the front page of the Post right now."

With resignation in his voice, the Speaker replied, "I suppose you're right. But sooner or later, they will."

"Ever since your brother was captured by the Idaho State Patrol and then escaped, we haven't heard a thing," said Ross.

Jake nodded and said, "The President must have loved that."

"Yes," said Ross. "That was strike two for Governor Morrissey with the White House."

The Speaker added, "With the entire FBI looking for T.J., I'm sure his freedom will be short-lived."

"I don't know, dad, T.J.'s rich and resourceful. And he made a lot of friends among the general population by the way he handled both the situation on that mountain and the media's coverage of it."

"Sort of like a modern-day Jesse James," said Ross, with obvious admiration in his voice.

"I suppose that analogy applies. Except let's hope that he doesn't suffer the same fate," said Jake.

There was a long pause in the conversation, during which the Speaker walked over to a painting of George Washington sitting on horseback at Valley Forge in the deep and dark of winter. He stood there for a moment, staring at it, and then said softly, "I think it's time I told the truth."

"About T.J?" asked Jake.

"Yes."

"With all due respect, sir, I strongly disagree!" said Ross.

"You say that with such certainty George. Since when didn't the truth matter?"

"When it has absolutely no bearing upon the situation, Mr. Speaker. In this situation, the fact that Thomas Porter is your youngest son, T.J. is irrelevant. In effect, he disowned you and your family seven years ago, and you had no knowledge of his involvement in the militia. That is, until you saw him being interviewed up on that Idaho mountain."

The Speaker walked back to his desk and sat down heavily. "Legally and technically correct, but ethically wrong. And Americans have grown weary of men who do not understand the difference."

"What can it hurt, George?" asked Jake.

"If your father tells everyone now, the Democrats, led by the White House, will crucify him. It's that simple. He risks losing all credibility within our party and ultimately, the gun vote in the House." Ross looked back at the Speaker. "Mr. Speaker, which is more important, the truth, or defeating legislation that might destroy America?"

"Why must it be either-or?" asked the Speaker with heaviness in his voice that echoed the pain in his heart.

"Because, Mr. Speaker, sometimes circumstances must trump the truth, and this is one of those times."

The look on the Speaker's face showed that he reluctantly agreed. There would be no public admission that Thomas Porter, one of the wealthiest men in America and now a fugitive from the law, was in fact Thomas Johnston Kincaid, or T.J., as his family knew him. Where the name Porter came from, the Speaker had no idea. But then again, it didn't matter now. All that did matter was to hope that the press or the FBI didn't discover the connection. But somewhere down deep inside, he knew it was a foolish hope. And he was right.

<u>21</u>

The White House, Washington, D.C.

President Webster sat silently, watching a replay of Mrs. Brook's eloquent speech on the evening news. With him in the room were Patrick Fitzgerald, who was talking quietly into his PTC, and Vice President Richard Knox, who was standing stiffly behind the President. It was evident that the woman's words had had a deep affect upon both the President and the Vice President. When it was over, Webster switched off the BTC and turned to face the Vice President.

"That woman and her dead daughter are what this is all about, Richard."

"Yes, Mr. President, and she was no ordinary housewife from Omaha. Whether she realized it or not, today that gentle woman who holds no office captured a constituency of millions and added immeasurably to the momentum of the mandate that you, Mr. President, will carry on to victory. May I be the first to congratulate you, sir, on the committee's vote."

The President smiled, "Score one for the good guys."

The Vice President continued, "Now that they have approved your bill and referred it to the Rules Committee, I expect a speedy and successful debate on the House floor, followed by—"

"Did you get them?" the President asked, interrupting the Vice President and looking at Fitzgerald as he hung up the telcom.

"Yes," answered Patrick.

"Well?" asked the President.

"Your favorable rating has climbed back another three points from its low, following the Bitterroots incident."

"What is it now?"

"Fifty-two percent."

The President smiled, "You see, I told you that the public would grow tired of that story. What about the gun bill?"

"Forty-two percent against, thirty-five for, and the rest undecided."

The answer clearly did not please the President. "Forty two against? Isn't that five points higher than last week?"

"Seven, actually."

"Goddamn it. What the hell did that?"

"The amendments proposed by the Speaker are gaining support among the uncommitted, Mr. President," said Fitzgerald.

The President looked at Knox and then turned back to Patrick. "How are his approval ratings?"

You're ahead of him with women under thirty-five, but he's higher, overall."

"Damn it," said the President.

"The Bitterroots is still hurting us, Mr. President, regardless of what the polls show," said the Vice President.

"I wish the networks would stop referring to it as a massacre." He looked at Patrick and asked, "How many soldiers died that night, anyway?"

"Seven, sir, including the commanding officer, but among the militia there were—"

The President interrupted him, "Maybe we should arrange another photo op with the wives of those men?"

The Vice President and chief of staff clearly did not like the idea, but the President did.

"Your speech at the memorial service gave us a lift of five points in the polls already, sir, and I doubt that—"

The President cut Fitzgerald off again. "Let's award a medal to that officer who died."

Fitzgerald and Knox looked at each other. Fitzgerald spoke first. "I think your intentions might be misinterpreted, sir."

The President snapped back, "Patrick, we have to do whatever it takes in order to get this legislation passed into law. I do mean *whatever*."

The Vice President joined in, "I have to agree with Patrick, Mr. President. I think our efforts would be better directed elsewhere."

Patrick continued to plead his case, "I don't think it's a good idea, Mr. President."

The President looked directly at Fitzgerald, and said in a quiet but tense tone that belied a coming storm, "If I want to give a medal to the widow of some poor soldier who got his brains blown out on that godforsaken mountain in Idaho, then I will. Do you understand me?"

There was absolute silence in the room. Fitzgerald said softly, "Yes, sir."

"Good, now go make it happen," said the President. "While you're at it, see what General Pace wants. That old stiff's been trying to see me for days. Probably to cry on my shoulder about slipping morale in the military again. God, I'm sick of hearing it."

"Yes, Mr. President," said Fitzgerald. By his expression, it was clear that he wasn't pleased with the President's curt manner. But as usual, he chose not to say anything about it. Instead, he walked out of the Oval Office.

After he departed, the Vice President spoke in his normal patronizing way to Webster. "You know, Mr. President, Patrick has been your most loyal supporter and defender through all of the rough times that you have experienced during the past five and a half years. He is also one of the brightest people in Washington, present company excluded, of course."

The President slowly looked over at Knox with an icy stare, and for just a moment, it made the Vice President regret that he had spoken up.

There was a knock at the door of the Oval Office. Marva opened it and said, "Excuse me, Mr. President, Messrs. Gordon and Dunn are here."

"Thank-you, Marva. Send them in." The President turned back to the Vice President and in a much softer tone said, "You're right, Richard. You're right. I'll make it up to him. You'll see. Now go help Patrick set up the medal ceremony, will you? Make sure there are plenty of scrambled eggheads in attendance." It was a term he liked to use when describing high-ranking military personnel. Outside their presence of course. It aptly reflected his discomfort with the military, and he realized that the feeling was mutual. He had not served in the armed forces, and now he believed that without having done so, he could never command their respect. He was right about their lack of respect for him, but not about the reason. It wouldn't have mattered had he known, because he really didn't care. The truth was that they didn't like or respect him for one simple reason: they didn't trust him. And in the military, where trust was inextricably linked to survival, it was the most grievous and unforgivable of sins.

The Vice President left just as Maddun Gordon stepped into the office with his usual look of disdain that he saved for everywhere except the mirror. With him was Richard Dunn, the President's General Counsel, a tall man whose slightly stooped posture made him look much shorter than he was, and whose yellowed fingers and red blotches on the side of his neck bore evidence of his three-pack-a-day habit.

The President immediately turned to Dunn and asked, "Well. Who is he?"

"We don't know, Mr. President."

It was not the answer that the President wanted to hear, and Dunn knew it. He seemed to stoop even lower as his angry boss stared him down. "I thought you said you knew who Porter was."

Dunn hunched his shoulders slightly the way a dog does when he thinks his master is going to cuff him. "Actually, what I told Mr. Gordon was that we knew who he wasn't. That is to say, Mr. Porter is definitely not Mr. Porter."

"And that's it?" asked the incredulous chief executive. "You go away for three weeks, spend fifty thousand dollars, and all you can tell me is that the man isn't who he says he is?"

The lawyer had no comeback. He was so rattled by the cross examination of the President that he was having trouble speaking.

"A lot of good that Harvard Law diploma has done for you, Dunn. I've known night-school lawyers who could do better." The President turned to Gordon. "Is that all you've got?"

"Mr. President, the National Security Number that the man we know as Porter has been using was issued to a Thomas Jules Porter thirty years ago in Sacramento, California. He was a student at Berkeley who died of AIDS seven years ago, at about the same time as the captain first started his communications company. The captain must have met Mr. Porter, and either with or without his cooperation, taken his identity."

"So go find someone who knew the real Porter, and ask them why he gave up his identity."

"We tried to do that," said Dunn sheepishly.

"And?" asked Webster coldly.

"The real Thomas Porter's parents are both deceased. And as far as we can tell, he had no other relatives."

"Great work, guys. Just fucking great," said the President, lapsing into language that he himself knew was beneath his office. But at that moment, he really could care less.

Dunn said quietly, "Mr. President, while the FBI hasn't found Porter yet, they are getting closer."

"So's Y3K," said the President.

Dunn hesitated, and then continued, "The FBI has at least been able to determine what happened to Porter, or whoever he really is, after the Bitterroots massacre." As soon as he said the word, he knew that he shouldn't have said it. "I mean— the Bitterroots incident."

The President didn't answer. He just glared at Dunn until Gordon stepped in.

"He was seen the morning after the Rod & Gun Club incident at a diner in Salmon Idaho, which is about seventy miles south of there. The FBI have a positive ID on our man from several patrons of the diner who saw him in the company of two Idaho State Troopers."

"Judging from the fact that he is still on the loose, I suppose the bad news is that the State Police lost their prisoner sometime thereafter."

"Yes, sir. He got away a few hours later, when he asked to use the bathroom at a gas station outside a place called Lowman. According to the police, he shinnied out a bathroom window and jumped into the Payette River. They claim he must have drowned."

"But the FBI doesn't buy it?" asked Webster.

"They're not sure."

"I think the whole thing strains credulity," said Dunn.

The President looked at him and answered sarcastically, "You think?"

Gordon continued, "Any man that can win over the national television audience while defying the entire Federal Government for eight weeks can surely charm a couple of county Mounties, sir."

The President nodded and said to Dunn, "That's all for now."

The lawyer hurried out of the Oval Office, thankful to have survived the encounter, more or less intact.

"Idiots. I'm surrounded by idiots—present company excluded," said the President.

Gordon smiled and said, "Do you want me to handle the matter of the mysterious Captain Porter?"

The President's expression tightened, "Frankly, Maddun, I don't give a flying fuck about Mr. Porter any longer. Let those dicks at the Bureau chase his shadow. Thanks to the mother of that murdered girl, we won our battle with the Judiciary Committee. And just to be safe, I'm going to make some calls to put the fear of God into a few representatives."

Gordon said smugly, "They fear the wrath of the White House more than they fear the wrath of God, Mr. President."

"I'm not so sure. I think a few of them are actually starting to believe that altruistic pabulum the Speaker has been spouting so eloquently," answered the President, "But I'm going to remind them where their loyalties lie."

"How can I help?" asked Gordon.

"As added insurance, I want you to turn your attention to the matter we discussed this morning."

Gordon looked at the President knowingly and said, "How far can I go to achieving that objective?"

"Use your own judgment. But I want some dirt on Jeremiah Kincaid—and I don't mean the soft and woody designer dirt that yuppies spread on their tomatoes. I mean the smelly, hard black clay that rots around the edges of a swamp. Do you read me?"

"Perfectly."

With that, Gordon turned and left the President standing there all alone in the mightiest office that the world has ever known. Yet for all its power and might, it was an office that had been stymied by fifty-three men on a mountain in the Bitterroots, most of whom were now dead. But all that was about to change. And when it would, many more would die.

22

The Mall, Washington, D.C.

Thirty minutes after getting his telcom call, Sarah McGill and Thomas Porter were walking together on the slippery sidewalk in front of the National Museum of Natural History. It had been a warm and wet winter in Washington with brief periods of heavy snowfall, followed by quick thaws that turned the streets into rivers of slush and covered the sidewalks with speed bumps of ice. McGill had left her office in such a hurry that she didn't have time to change into the sneakers she wore to and from work, and the pumps she was now wearing made her unsteady on her feet, forcing her to hold on tightly to Porter's arm. It was not an unpleasant necessity for either of them, and when he confirmed to her what she had read in the papers about his divorce, she held on even tighter.

Halfway across the Mall, with the Washington Monument looming on their right and the Capitol perched high on the hill to their left, both of which were bathed in the milky light of a mid-winter sun, they stopped at a wooden bench and sat down. She wore a long black coat over her pantsuit, but before they sat down, he brushed the bench to remove the last few granules of corn snow. He was dressed in the same duffel coat he had been wearing on the day he watched her in front of the White House, but the hood now lay softly on his broad shoulders. His hair was long like it had been when last they met on the mountain, but unlike then, it was soft and clean, and wisps of it danced on the wind. His beard was full but well-trimmed, such that the totality of his being was that of a long-lost mariner home from the sea.

"You look so different than when we last met," she said, reaching up to brush a few wayward strands of hair out of his eyes. It was not what someone would do to another person unless they were close friends or lovers, and in the unconscious act, Sarah had unwittingly declared her intentions.

He smiled. "I should hope so. I'm a wanted felon." As he said it, his eyes glanced over her shoulder at the approaching figure of two park policemen, who passed by without even noticing them.

Her face darkened. "Yes. I know. Is there anything that I can do to help?"

"Not unless you can get the President to pardon me," he said jokingly.

She didn't take it that way. "I could ask him."

"I was teasing, Sarah."

"I wasn't. I work at the White House now."

"I know. I saw you there."

"When?"

"Last week. During the riots. When that mounted policeman pulled you out of harm's way."

Her face tightened and her eyes grew wide. "You saw that?"

"Yes. I was just about to throw myself into the crowd to save you when your knight on that white stallion came charging over and rescued you. It was all very gallant." He could tell by her vacant stare and pained expression that something was wrong. "What is it, Sarah?"

She didn't answer at first. Then, hesitantly, she told him the story of Michael Falconer and how they first met, as well as how her boss had been unable to find a record of a policeman by that name anywhere. When she was finished, he sat there for a long moment without saying anything; and just when she was convinced that he was going to say something patronizing like Keene Lange had, he surprised her. "Perhaps he's your guardian angel."

If there had been any doubt in Sarah's mind that she had fallen in love with the man sitting before her, his words dispelled it. Tiny tears welled up in the corners of her eyes, and for a moment she was speechless, like she had been when they first met.

"Now I've gone and made you cry." He reached into the pocket of his coat, pulled out a wrinkled but clean handkerchief, and handed it to her. "It's clean, Sarah—I'm just not very good at ironing. I never was—but I'm a great cook."

She laughed through her tears. "You didn't make me cry, Thomas," she blurted out, carefully wiping her eyes so as not to smear her mascara. "What you said about my having a guardian angel was the nicest thing anyone has ever said to me."

"Then what is it?"

She grasped his handkerchief tightly in her fist and pressed both her hands into her lap. Then she looked up into his blue eyes and said, "Thomas"—she caught herself, because what she was about to say was something that she had never said to any man, except her father, and for obvious reasons that was different—"I've fallen in love with you." There it was; she had put her heart out on her sleeve—something she vowed she'd never do, at least not without someone saying it first. But with the handsome fugitive sitting there before her, she couldn't help herself. And she didn't care. She knew she was in love with him, and deep inside, that little voice that never lied told her she always would be; but even in that knowledge, she couldn't help but feel a certain sadness—the kind that comes with a love not returned, or even worse, one that is returned, but can never *be*.

If eyes could talk, his shouted, *I love you too*, but the words did not spill from his lips. Reflexively, she began to pull back, both emotionally and physically, like a shadow retreats before the dawn. He sensed at once that he had hurt her, which was the last thing he'd intended. He reached over and took her hand gently, firmly, and lovingly. "Sarah."

She shook her head and looked down. "No. Don't. You needn't say anything."

"Sarah. Listen to me—please." There was an urgency in his voice that drew her eyes back to his. "Ever since we first met on that mountain, I've been unable to get you out of my mind. Thoughts of you fill my every waking hour, and dreams of you rule my sleep. That's why I had to see you." The tenderness and depth of emotion behind his words brightened her face, but it was only fleeting, because then he added, "But our love can never be."

She struggled to understand. "Why?"

He paused. "Because there is something that I must do—something I have to do. Please don't ask me what it is. After it is done, you will understand."

She was crushed. She knew he loved her; she could feel it with every fiber of her being. But this thing he seemed obsessed with doing; this thing he was not proud of; this evil thing, stood between them like a specter blocking the sun, and she felt helpless to stop it from happening. They sat there in silence for a few, painful moments, each alone in the other's presence, each wanting to reach out and hold onto the other, each wishing they could push back the onrushing darkness. But it was not to be. Finally, he stood up, and while still holding her hand in his, he leaned over and kissed her softly on the forehead and whispered, "Goodbye, Sarah. I hope your guardian angel never leaves you."

As he turned to leave, she grasped his hand tightly and held him back, just for a moment. Their eyes met and she said, "Please be careful Thomas."

He nodded but said nothing. Then he walked away.

She watched him go until he disappeared in the stream of people, all going about their daily lives, oblivious to the tiny human drama that had just unfolded before them. Deep inside, she wasn't sorry that she had told him she loved him. But she sensed she would never say those words to him again, and she was right. The same would not be true for him, and therein would lie the great tragedy of their love.

23

Potomac Park, Washington, D.C.

Maddun Gordon walked slowly around the pathway that circled the Jefferson Memorial. Warm air passing over the cold waters of the Potomac had formed a mist that hung over the deserted memorial like a gray shroud. He was wearing a rumpled coat that was too big for his trim frame, and it would have flapped as he walked were it not for the thick black camera strap that he wore across his chest. He looked every bit the tourist he was pretending to be, and to complete the disguise, he was deeply absorbed in the map as he meandered beside the monument.

A tall, thin man in a long, black overcoat approached Gordon from the rear. It was Stefan Chadrian. "Excuse me, sir. Are you lost?" he asked Gordon.

Gordon flashed a subtle smile of recognition and answered, "Aren't we all?"

"Perhaps I can help you find your way?"

Gordon pretended to struggle with the open map he held in his hands. "Thank-you, sir. That would be most appreciated."

The two men stepped closer together.

Two tourists approached them, and Gordon continued the polite exchange, "Do you know Washington at all, sir?"

"Yes, I know the city quite well."

"Good. Then I wonder if you wouldn't mind directing me to the Franklin Roosevelt Memorial," continued Gordon.

"I can take you there. It is not far."

"That would be very kind of you."

"Follow me."

The two men walked off together, and the tourists paid them no attention, which was exactly what they intended. As soon as they were clear of anyone who might have been watching them, the expression on their faces changed to all business.

"What the hell have you done to your hair, Chadrian?" asked Gordon, staring at the close-cropped buzz of black that covered the man's large head.

Chadrian grinned through perfectly symmetrical, but sharply edged teeth as he rubbed a black leather glove over his head. "It is my new look. I am into a military mindset these days."

"Whatever," said Gordon with an apathetic shrug. "I have a job for you."

"What! Three years without so much as a Christmas card, and now this? Whatever happened to foreplay?"

"I've been busy. Besides, since when do you celebrate Christmas?"

Chadrian shrugged. "When in Rome."

Some more tourists approached, and the tone of the conversation abruptly changed again.

Chadrian stopped and pointed, "If you follow that path, the Roosevelt Memorial is just up ahead on your right." The tourists passed by, and the tone of Chadrian's voice suddenly took on a dead serious tone. "All right, Gordon, what can I do for you?"

"I need your help to do a smear job."

"On whom?"

"The Speaker of the House of Representatives."

Chadrian grinned. "My, my, Jeremiah Sinclair Kincaid, Sr. When did you and your boss take up big-game hunting?"

"That's no concern of yours."

"It will be good to be back in the Oval Office. It has been a while."

"You will never be back in the Oval Office."

"I was speaking metaphorically."

"Frame it in whatever terms you want, but you must have no direct contact with the President, do you understand me?"

Chadrian smiled, "Direct. Indirect. It matters not to me. Both serve my purpose."

201

"Just stay away from him. He is not your concern. Kincaid is your fucking target."

"Everything the President does is my concern," he replied harshly. "Everything! Including what he thinks, and does, and dreams of doing. His past actions granted me that right—and it is an irrevocable trust."

The thought troubled Gordon greatly.

Chadrian's eyes narrowed and he took a step closer to Gordon, adding harshly, "Do not swear in my presence. You have not earned that privilege."

Gordon's tone and manner softened, "I'm sorry. I need your help to get Kincaid off the President's back on the matter of gun control."

Chadrian smiled, "Guns. My favorite subject. But it will cost you."

"How much?"

"The usual times two."

"That's too much."

"Come now, money is never a problem for your kind of people."

"You mean *your* kind of people, don't you?"

"I suppose they are all my kind of people. Corrupt CEOs and politicians, conceited movie stars and big-mouthed preachers, and all others driven by blind ambition and the lust for fame and fortune. It is what makes my world go around."

"Yeah, well, you should know that I'm not rich—even though I admit that I would like to be."

"Desire provides the bricks of achievement, Gordon. Opportunity is the mortar." Chadrian paused then added, "The price stands as stated."

Gordon sighed. "All right. Done!" Several tourists approached. "Oops!" Gordon said, dropping his maps as they walked by.

Chadrian stooped over and picked them up. As he handed them back to Gordon, he expertly slipped the envelope that was hidden among them into his breast pocket.

Gordon added, "The money in there will get you started. Remember, it comes from me, and no one else. Just like this assignment. Got it?"

Chadrian muttered, "It was ever thus. The servant pays while the master plays." Then in a much louder voice, he added, "I hope you enjoy your visit, mister. This is a magical city. Purely magical." With that, Chadrian walked off into the gathering gloom, as a thick fog rolled in off the Potomac.

For a moment Gordon stood there pretending to look for the Memorial, all the while trying to hide the sense of unease that always gripped him whenever he dealt with this man. A man whom he considered to be as dangerous as tightly coiled razor wire. Gathering himself, he started to walk away when he heard a loud and annoying sound above his head. He looked up and saw a large black bird sitting in the bare branches of a tree staring down at him. Its raucous croaking seemed directed at him, and it added nothing to the sense of unease that held him in its grip.

"Now, *that* is interesting, eh?" said a voice with a heavy Canadian accent from behind him. Gordon spun around, nearly knocking over a man wearing a University of Toronto jacket.

"Excuse me?" Gordon asked.

"I'm very sorry, mister, I didn't mean to startle you," said the man. "It's just that I didn't know that you had them down here, eh?"

"Had what?" asked Gordon, wishing he wasn't having the conversation.

"Why ravens, of course."

"It's just a crow," snapped Gordon, barely hiding his growing annoyance.

The man looked back up at the tree. But the branch where the black bird had been sitting was now empty. He just shrugged. "Well, he's gone now, anyway. But I know a raven when I see one, and that was a raven. Crows are smaller, and they have tiny little feet, you know, like this." He motioned with his index finger and thumb.

"Whatever," said Gordon. "You come all the way from the North Pole just to look for birds?"

"Me? No. I'm not into that, but I know a raven when I see one. For whatever reason, he did not like you, mister. That's for sure. Where are you from anyway, Texas? I heard they shoot ravens for target practice down there."

Gordon had had enough of North American diplomacy. "No, I'm not from Texas. Now, if you will excuse me—"

"Okay then. I hope I didn't bother you; it is just that this is the first time I have ever been in these here United States and I—"

Gordon cut him off, "Yes well, say hello to the boys back on the hockey team for me." With that, he walked away.

The man turned to a Japanese couple who happened upon the scene and said, "Boy, he sure was not very friendly, was he? So typically American, eh?"

The couple smiled and bowed. The man from Toronto smiled back at them and then walked in the opposite direction from Gordon. As soon as he was a safe distance from the couple, he stopped and looked back to make sure no one was looking at him. Gordon was long gone, and the Japanese couple was standing fifty yards away, deeply absorbed in a tourist brochure. He then reached into his jacket and pulled out a tiny earphone. He placed it in his right ear and started talking softly without any accent whatsoever, "Alpha One to Omega base."

"Omega base. Go ahead, Alpha One," came a muted voice in his earphone.

"We've got a positive ID on Red Dragon and the Oracle," he said.

"Are you sure?" came the reply.

"Affirmative. I'm transmitting the pictures now." He put the earpiece back into his coat and headed quickly down the path into the lengthening shadows. He was looking down at the camera and at first did not see the dark shadow standing behind a stonewall fifty feet ahead. After he'd passed by the wall, suddenly something made him stop and turn around. What he saw sent a chill through his body; standing barely ten yards away was an enormous white stallion. On its back sat a dark rider, dressed in a long, black, flowing robe, and in one hand he held a mighty bow, while the other hand gripped a silver arrow with a razor tip. As he watched in horror, the rider placed the arrow in the bow and drew it back, pointing it directly at his chest.

"No! Please don't!" cried the agent. But it was of no use. The dark rider released the bowstring. There was a sudden ripping sound, as if the air itself were being torn, followed by complete and absolute silence. For a second the agent stood there with eyes wide open, gasping for breath. With a disbelieving look, he stared down at his chest and crumpled to the ground, twitched twice, and then lay still.

The dark rider slipped silently off the horse, glided over to the fallen man, and popped open the camera. He removed the disk, which he placed inside his robe, and stood up. Suddenly there was a scream behind him, and he turned around sharply to face the Japanese couple who had approached unnoticed.

"Damn. Why must you people walk so quietly!" he muttered to himself. Then raising his arms under his robe like a giant black bird preparing for flight, he snarled, "Be gone!"

The woman began screaming even louder, despite her husband's frantic efforts to quiet her and pull her away from the scene. Chadrian stood there for a moment, then walked over, remounted his horse, and disappeared into the mist.

February, 2018

G Day - 210

Winter Lasts Forever

O but we dreamed to mend
Whatever mischief seemed
To afflict mankind, but now
That winds of winter blow
Learn that we were crack-pated when
we dreamed.

W. B. Yeats, "Nineteen Hundred and Nineteen"

24

Smythe Estate, Tysons Corner, Virginia

The limousine pulled up in front of the Georgian brick mansion that sat well back in the woods of the sprawling estate. Even in the darkness, the limo's lone passenger, Thomas Porter, could tell that the house was worthy of its reported twenty-four million dollar price tag. If anyone could appreciate what money could buy and how best to spend it, it was Porter.

"Wait for me," said Porter to the uniformed driver who opened the door for him.

"Very good, sir."

Porter walked up to the front door, pushed the doorbell, and turned to face the overhead security camera.

"May I help you?" came the disembodied voice of a man.

"My name is Thomas Porter. Major Smythe is expecting me."

A moment later, the heavy wooden door swung open, revealing a tall, muscular young man with blonde hair and a strong jaw, who was wearing a shoulder holster with a heavy caliber sidearm. "Please come in, Mr. Porter. The major is waiting for you in his study."

Porter stepped into the foyer that had a sweeping, curved staircase that looked like it was suspended in mid-air.

"Follow me," said the man, as he closed the door behind Porter. Together they walked down a long hallway that was paneled in dark cherry. At every ten feet on each side of the hall, there were original oil paintings of American soldiers in combat from the two World Wars, Korea, Vietnam, and WWT. They were lit by tiny recessed spotlights hidden in the ceiling, and the triumph and tragedy they represented were not lost on Porter as he passed by.

Soon they reached two imposing doors that were open, revealing an enormous two-story high library. Standing inside the room in front of a brick fireplace that contained a roaring wood fire was Major Smythe. He was holding a crystal shot glass with what appeared to be whisky in it. As Porter entered the room, a broad smile spread across the man's slightly pock-marked face, and he extended his right hand toward him.

"Thomas! Thank-you for coming, old chum."

"Hello, Tony. It's been a while." Porter liked the heavy British accent in Smythe's voice. When they first met, he couldn't help but think that a black eye patch would have been a perfect complement to this man of mystery.

They shook hands warmly and the major patted Porter on the shoulder. "Yes it has, Thomas. A lot of water has slipped beneath the keel since you and I sailed together. Much of it rough."

"Yes. Indeed," replied Porter with an empty stare.

"Will that be all, Major Smythe?" asked the young man with the strong jaw.

Smythe flashed a look at him and held up his hand. He turned back to Porter. "Can I offer you something to eat or drink, Thomas?"

"No, Thank-you."

Smythe nodded at the young man, who immediately excused himself and pulled the doors closed behind him. When the major turned back to his guest, he saw that Porter was admiring the painting that hung over the fireplace.

"Isn't he a beauty?"

"I'm not into horses, but even I can see that there is something special about that one."

"He's an Arabian. I bought him from a Saudi prince, but etiquette prevents me from telling you I paid ten million dollars for him.

Porter laughed. "That's good, because then I don't have to tell you I spent more than that on three WW II Spitfires that were recovered in nearly perfect condition under the ice in Greenland."

Smythe smiled. "That's what I like about you, old chap. You are one of the few people in the world who has more money than I do. Come and sit down, and let's chat, shall we?"

They both sat down in overstuffed leather chairs, and the major put his feet up on the wrought iron and glass table. Just then, there was a soft, musical chiming sound. The major reached into his pocket and pulled out a beautiful pocket watch. He opened it and admired it, as it played its gentle little tune announcing the hour.

"That's beautiful," said Porter.

The major nodded appreciatively. "Yes, it is, isn't it? It belonged to my good friend, Senator Harridan Niles. He gave it to me just before his untimely passing last month. It's all that I have left to remind me of him."

"What a shame it was that the senator died so unexpectedly. After all, he had become quite a strident spokesperson for the rights of the gun owner."

"Indeed. It was a deep loss for both the nation and for those of us who knew and loved him," answered Smythe.

"And what a bizarre way to die—drowning in your own bathtub."

"Yes. Quite."

There was something in the look in Smythe's eyes that told Porter there was more to the story but he chose not to pursue it. Smythe quickly changed the subject.

"I must say, Thomas, I still get a chuckle at the thought of you stealing the governor's helicopter right out from under his nose."

"He didn't find it very funny."

"Don't worry about Edward Morrissey. He's just happy that the Feds haven't captured you."

"It's amazing how easily one can hide behind a few billion dollars."

"Closer to six or seven isn't it?" asked Smythe with a smirk.

"As you Brits would say, Tony, that's none of your bloody business."

The major was amused. "You never were one to flaunt your wealth were you Thomas? No flamboyance in this farm boy."

"It has served me well. And I am certainly not a farm boy."

"No offense. Tell me, are you this way with women, too? Do you bother to chitchat at all before you boff them, or do you approach lovemaking like a business problem? 'Excuse me miss, but my objective is orgasm, and my strategy is to wage sex.'"

Just the hint of a smile cracked Porter's hard expression, but there was a wistfulness about it.

Smythe broke out into a broad grin. "There it is. There's the Porter that I knew. For a minute there, I was afraid that I'd lost him."

"I'm sorry, Tony. Lately, I haven't had much to smile about."

The major nodded, and his grin disappeared. "It must have been bloody awful watching your men die."

"They wouldn't have had to but for that egomaniac who lives across the river in the big white house."

Smythe became deadly serious. "I hear you. Which brings me to why I asked you here. I'd like to discuss a proposition."

"What kind of a proposition?"

"An extremely—shall we say—sensitive one."

Porter tensed, "Is it safe to talk?"

"Of course," replied Smythe. "I have the most sophisticated anti-bugging device that money can buy. It's made in Germany, and it's called a Wolfhound—what else? It is capable of sniffing out even the micro-transmitters embedded in clear glass, or T-glass, which your government likes to spread all over everywhere. You know, in my line of work, it doesn't pay to be careless."

Porter glanced around the magnificent room, "Your line of work pays very well."

"I wasn't able to cash in on the broadband surge like you did, my friend, but selling surplus armaments to foreign buyers does indeed provide a certain standard of living that I have grown accustomed to."

"Some not so surplus, as well," said Porter with a knowing look.

Smythe shrugged his shoulders. "If the ponderous bureaucracy of the American military can't control its own inventories of weapons and equipment, who am I to tell them how?"

"The country gets the kind of military that its President deserves," said Porter with a disgusted shake of his head.

"Of course, I'm not complaining. During the past five years, I've been able to profit handsomely from the creeping decay of the military establishment."

"A decay brought about by a Democratic administration," added Porter. "If the White House had spent half the money on national defense that they spent going after big corporations, the Pentagon would be a happier place these days."

"I can assure you that it's not," Smythe paused. "President Webster had almost no allies inside that fortress before the Bitterroots massacre. He has even less now."

Porter's expression darkened. "A tyrant has no allies, only varying degrees of enemies."

Smythe studied the other man carefully. "Quite so. And now that the President is pushing his gun bill through the Congress, the legion of his enemies grows by the day."

"I'd have thought that a ban on guns would be good for you. Prohibition made the rum-runners wealthy."

"They only had to deal with Elliot Ness. Do you have any idea how big a law enforcement bureaucracy the proposed new law would create? The new search and seizure laws don't require a warrant; they will make Nazi Germany look like a game of hide and seek in kindergarten. Just imagine how difficult it will be for me to smuggle weapons in and out of the country if there were armies of customs agents swarming all over every port of entry looking for guns instead of dope."

"That's what it would take," concurred Porter. "Armies and billions of dollars."

"But somehow the liberals in Congress have overlooked that aspect of their proposed new world order. In addition to wiping me out, it will be a financial disaster of monumental proportions for the country."

"You may be right, Tony."

"I know I am. Which brings me to my proposition."

"Yes?"

Smythe looked Porter directly in the eyes and said, "I'm affiliated with a group of true patriots who don't want to see America become a socialistic state. We'd like you to join us."

"With all due respect, Major, I have no interest in joining another protest group. I think I've already played that role badly."

Smythe's jaw flexed. "Oh no, my dear boy, you misunderstood me. This is not one of those million moron marches. We don't intend to protest to the President. We plan to kill him."

Porter didn't bat an eyelash. He sat there quietly for a moment, and then he said very slowly, "It's something that I have thought about doing myself, but the Secret Service might have other ideas."

Smythe smiled and said, "Come with me. I want to show you something."

THOMAS PORTER stood behind the heavy sound-proof glass of an indoor firing range in a secret section of the mansion's enormous basement. Inside the range were twelve, blonde-haired young men dressed in black military utilities, and apart from their uniforms, Porter could tell that they were not civilians from the accuracy of their shooting. Although exactly who they were and where they came from was as mysterious as the major himself. During the years they had known each other, Smythe had never volunteered which branch of the military he had served in, or for what country for that matter, although rumor had it that he had been with the British Special Air Services. They first met at an executive retreat for the rich and powerful, held on a windjammer in the Caribbean. Despite their immediate liking of each other, Porter hadn't asked Smythe about his past. He didn't seem to be the type that one could, or should, ask something like that. At the time, Porter didn't even know the major's first name, since he preferred to be referred to by his military rank.

"Excellent shots, aren't they?" said Smythe as he entered the viewing room.

Porter said, "Yes, they certainly are. Who are they?"

The major smiled and said simply, "Let's just say that they're friends of mine from overseas."

Porter let it go.

Smythe continued, "Come over here, and let me show you something." With that, he walked over to a large cabinet marked with a distinct sign that read "Danger-Explosives." Reaching into his pocket, he took out a key card and inserted it into the lock on the door of the cabinet. He swung the heavy, steel-reinforced door open and carefully pulled out a wood box, which he placed on the workbench. He opened the lid and pushed it toward Porter. Inside were several tightly wrapped, cellophane packets of what appeared to be white powder.

"Plastic explosives?"

Smythe nodded. "Yes and no. It's a new compound called Cepox. It has a hundred times the explosive power per gram of T.N.T., and—here comes the best part—it is odorless, tasteless, and extremely stable. It can be combined with virtually any inert material into a shaped charge."

Porter thought about it for a minute and then said, "I don't know, Major, any would-be Presidential assassin wearing a bulging belly pack of explosives might as well have a sign on his forehead saying 'Shoot me.'"

"Quite so. But how about an arm cast that looked and smelled just like plaster?" asked Smythe, showing almost too much glee for the somber subject at hand.

Porter thought about it for a moment and then said, "Where would someone with a cast get close enough…" He caught himself. He thought about it for another minute, and then he said, "Of course. In a hospital."

"Indeed. In the Walter Reed Military Hospital, to be exact. My contacts in the Pentagon tell me that within a fortnight, POTUS will visit the hospital."

"You mean in two weeks?" asked Porter.

"Yes. And you'll never guess for what? He's going to award a posthumous medal to the widow of the man who led the raid on your mountain fortress— an Army captain by the name of Jackson."

Porter gave no sign of recognizing the name. "He is probably using it to build support for his gun bill."

"Which is all the more reason why my associates and I feel it is time to act."

"I assume you know that whoever you get to do this will also die?"

"Of course. The one thing that the Secret Service fears most is an assassin who is willing to die along with the President. It's an attack against which they have their weakest defense. And my Middle-Eastern associates have no shortage of volunteers. Even men of Caucasian descent. But we have designed the bomb so that it has a very tight-kill radius. It will only kill the wearer and the President. The last thing we want is to murder innocent soldiers and civilians standing near by."

"Sooner or later evil catches up with itself," said Porter, slowly digesting the plot in his mind. "But what do you need from me? Is it money?"

Smythe smiled, "Hardly. We have all the money we need. The pro-gun lobby is well funded, I assure you. No, I need something else. Something that I can get from no one but you."

"What?" asked Porter, still pretending he didn't know.

"Captain Jackson's NIS card. Apparently he broke military regulations and took the card with him into battle. In addition to dying, the poor bugger lost the bloody thing—or more accurately, someone took it." He paused and stared directly at Porter. "I think you know who."

Porter's eyes narrowed. For a moment he didn't say anything. Finally, in a subdued voice, he asked, "How did you know?"

"I have assets inside the Pentagon. One works in the Granite Fist personnel control and deployment section. He discovered that the captain's card was missing shortly after the gun club was captured. Instead of immediately reporting it to his superiors, who naturally would have traced it and arrested the thief, he got word to me. And ever since, he has been keeping tabs on the card for us, and the person carrying it." He paused and then added with a smile, "Which, my good man, is none other than you."

"So you knew that I had it all along?"

"Actually, at first we couldn't be sure if it was you who had it. Even when we traced the card to the Wolf River Club, we still couldn't ascertain who had it. But when we heard the news reports that you had stolen the Governor of Idaho's helicopter, which my contact confirmed also had the card on board, we knew it had to be you."

Porter didn't say anything. He reached in his pocket and pulled it out.

Smythe's eyes focused tightly upon it. "Thomas, you hold in your hand the one thing that we need to complete this mission. With that card, our man can kill the President, and the Secret Service won't be able to stop him."

Porter sat there turning the card over and over in his hands. "Remarkable, isn't it? The government spent literally tens of billions of dollars developing the Granite Shield national database and created a little card that's virtually impossible to counterfeit. But all of their efforts can be subverted by one mole buried deep in the underground vault where they keep GOD."

Smythe shrugged, "Machines will never take over the earth as long as they have to depend on the human factor."

Porter laughed and looked up. "Then you must have figured out a way to get around the biometrics scanning?"

"Yes. You said the operative word a moment ago."

"Which is?"

"You said it was *virtually* impossible to counterfeit. Actually, thanks to our friends in China, we have obtained the technology that enables us to digitally alter the data micro-warehouse contained inside the card to make it compatible with whomever's biometric readings we so desire. But the one thing that no amount of money or technology can create or copy is the person's National Security Number, or NSN."

"Of course," said Porter.

"As you know, that's the number your government has adopted in place of the old social security number. It's comprised of a complex sequence of letters and numbers that are derived from the person's genotype, something unique to every citizen on earth; and it exists in only two places other than in the person's cells themselves, encrypted in the NIS card, and inside Granite Shield's quantum computer. Without it, an impostor is doomed. With it, he is unstoppable." His expression grew dark and merciless. "With the card you have in your possession, Thomas, our impostor will be able to get close enough to the President to kill him. Ironically, he will appear to have been so severely wounded on that mountain in Idaho, that the Secret Service will probably help the poor son of a bitch walk right up to the President." He paused to let the message sink in, then added, "So, old chap, would you be willing to donate it to our cause?"

Porter stared through Smythe rather than at him, and then he said firmly, "No."

An evil smile slipped across Smythe's lips. "No, of course not. You didn't get to be a billionaire by giving things away. We are prepared to buy it."

Porter shook his head again. "It's not for sale."

Smythe was taken aback. "But I thought…that is to say, I was hoping… you'd be willing to cooperate."

Porter's mind slowly drifted away from that room, back over time and distance to the mountain, and the men and the words that he had said to them on the first day they began their occupation: *Because if we don't make a stand, here and now, on this mountain named for freedom, then the beacon of freedom that has stood for over two hundred years upon our shores, shining for all the world to see, will be extinguished forever, and we might as well all be dead.*

"Thomas?" said Smythe. "Are you all right?"

Porter snapped back to the present. "I won't give it or sell it to you, because I will use it myself."

"What? For God's sake, man, do you know what you are saying?"

"Yes," he replied coldly.

"Why would you want to do such a thing?"

"Because the President looked me in the eye and lied to me. And in that cold-blooded lie, he knew he was condemning my men to death."

Smythe stared at him for a long, lingering moment. Then a big grin spread across his face and he exclaimed, "You're a better man than I am, Gunga Din!" The quote was from Kipling's poem of the same name, and it was fitting, as Porter had just committed himself to die for a cause. That the cause was of questionable virtue was left unsaid.

PORTER WAS already in the back seat of the limo heading down the driveway when the young man with the strong jaw entered the library. "You sent for me, sir?" he asked.

Smythe was sitting, staring at the fire. He looked up and said, "Yes. I have an assignment for you."

"Yes sir. What is it?"

"A clean up detail."

"Of course. Where and when?"

"The gentleman who just left intends to get rid of our problem."

The young man smiled, "The President?"

"Yes," replied Smythe.

"With Cepox?"

"Yes. When Webster goes to Walter Reed Hospital."

The young man nodded and then asked, "Do you think he can do it?"

"Yes. My only doubt is whether or not he will."

"Why?"

"I'm not sure he has it in him."

"Doesn't sound like the man who held the whole government at bay for two months up on that mountain."

"He talked a good story on the evening news, but when the shooting started, the word is that the captain was no where to be found."

The young man nodded and then asked, "If he doesn't go through with it, do you want me to terminate him?"

"Yes. If he bolts, follow him and kill him. Either way, Thomas Porter is a dead man."

"Understood," said the young man. Then he nodded and left the room.

Smythe looked back at the roaring fire, took a sip out of his shot glass, and said, "Sorry about that, old chap. But business is business, and loyalty is a luxury that I cannot afford."

25

The Capitol Building, Boise, Idaho

It was an unusually cold winter's day, even for Boise. A front had swept in the night before from the Canadian Rockies, and at sun-up, the thermometer hovered barely above zero. The local television weathermen were making their usual complaints about the cold air that always blows down from Canada, while on the other side of the border, their colleagues were snickering about the hot air that always blows up from the States.

However, the temperature was not on the mind of Governor Morrissey, as he sat on one side of a long table in a large conference room filled with politicians, their staff administrative assistants, as well as members of the media. The room, located on the second floor of the Capitol Building, was noisy as everyone talked at the same time, and the politicians in the room were doing what politicians do. To Morrissey's left sat Governor Ted Sanderson of Montana, and to his right, Bodey Butler of Arizona and Toby Diamond of Wyoming. Across the table sat Governors Wynn Taylor, Sam McCabe and Luis Lopez of Utah, Colorado, and New Mexico, respectively.

The official reason for the conference was to discuss the recent edicts issued by the White House, declaring huge portions of their respective states as wilderness preserves. It was no secret that the majority of the governors' constituents had been infuriated by the President's unilateral actions, which closed off millions of acres to any further exploration, commercial development, or even recreational use. To the press and public, it was not at all unusual that these men would meet to discuss these matters.

However, there was another agenda to the meeting, a hidden one known only to those seven men and a highly select group of people who could be trusted implicitly. For they had gathered not only to talk about wild rivers, rugged canyons, and old-growth forests. They had also gathered to talk about guns.

Governor Morrissey's chief of staff tapped on the microphone at the podium at one end of the room. "Ladies and gentlemen, may I please have your attention."

Only a few in the room paid him any attention at first, but he persisted. "The governors have asked for a closed door session this morning, and I would appreciate it if you would all join me down the hall where breakfast is being served." The mention of food got the media's attention, as it always did. They knew that Governor Morrissey put on quite a spread, and it took only a few minutes for the room to empty of everyone but Morrissey's chief of staff and the governors themselves. As the last of the press left, the chief of staff walked over and whispered something to the governor. They both nodded, and then the chief of staff left the room, pulling the heavy double doors closed behind him.

A few of the governors were still talking quietly to each other when Morrissey began to speak. "Gentlemen, I think you all know why I asked you here."

Rubbing his arms briskly, Governor Lopez of New Mexico said, "I sure do, Edward, you wanted to freeze our balls off."

The others laughed.

Lopez continued, "When does spring start in your state, anyway? July?"

Sanderson interjected, "Winter lasts forever up this high, Governor."

A few of the other men chuckled.

Morrissey smiled, but his expression soon turned serious. "Sorry, Governor, but we've set all the thermostats at sixty-five, as an energy savings measure. Now, if we can get back to business, you know what we are here to talk about."

"Excuse me, Edward," interjected Governor McCabe. "Can we speak freely?" he asked. "I mean without anybody with long ears listening, if you catch my drift."

"Yes, Sam, I had the room swept this morning," he answered.

"But couldn't one of the reporters have slipped something under the table?" asked McCabe.

Diamond leaned over and scanned the underside of the table. After satisfying himself that there was nothing there, he straightened up and rested his elbows on the smooth dark glass that covered the entire surface of the table. "It's clean Sam."

"All right, gentlemen," said Morrissey, "I assure you that we are not being recorded or monitored. Now, let's get to the matter at hand, shall we?"

The other men nodded, and McCabe sat back in his chair, obviously unconvinced.

"As you know, the President's bill is currently being debated on the House floor, and the DNC's anti-gun ad campaign is gaining purchase with the general public.

"Those hypocrites. I'd love to be there with my Smith & Wesson when some freaked-out coke head breaks into their condo at three in the morning. Then I'd ask them if they'd rather talk or shoot," said Diamond.

"That notwithstanding, there's growing concern among our people in Washington that the President's bill just might have enough support to pass."

"Ah, come on, Governor, there's no way that pompous piece of cow shit will ever get enough votes to pass such an overreaching bill, and we all know it," said McCabe.

"No, we don't know it, Sam," said Morrissey.

"What about Kincaid?" asked Diamond, "I thought you said the Speaker would be able to hold the party together?"

"I did say that, Toby, and he may. But there are still about fifty or sixty in his party who are uncommitted, and we can't afford to take any chances."

"So what are you proposing we do?" asked Lopez.

"I'm glad you asked that, Luis. I am proposing a three-pronged plan of action. First, I want you each to contribute five million dollars to fund a media and public relations campaign."

"I don't know about you, but my MasterCard is maxed out," said McCabe loudly.

"I'm serious, Sam," said Morrissey coldly.

"So am I," snapped back McCabe. Several of the other governors squirmed uncomfortably in their chairs.

Morrissey stayed calm. "I'm not talking about you or your state treasuries contributing to this funding. I am talking about seeking money from corporations and from the public themselves."

Taylor said, "With the obvious exception of the gun manufacturers, I doubt that the Fortune 500 would have any interest in supporting a pro-gun campaign, Edward."

Governor Morrissey leaned forward in his chair. "Gentlemen, why in the hell are we here this week? At least, why does the media think we are here? Come on, use your heads for more than a photo op," he said, with clearly waning patience.

There was a pregnant pause in the room. Taylor got it. "Brilliant, Edward. Simply brilliant."

"What?" said Diamond. "Tell us."

Taylor turned to the others and said, "We'll tell the corporations that we need money, big money, to put a stop to Webster's great land grab. We'll tell them that if we don't take a stand, then all future mining, logging, and oil exploration is in jeopardy." Heads began to nod around the table as the thought took hold.

"Exactly," added Morrissey. "With the initial seed money from the corporations, we'll put an advertising campaign on air that talks about freedom in all its meanings and applications."

"Freedom to explore the wilderness," said Sanderson.

"Freedom to build a cabin on your own land and to have a wood-burning fireplace without some bleeding-heart Liberal from the East lecturing us on the ozone layer," added Taylor.

"Freedom from the worry that their company will lay them off," said Lopez. "Because Washington has created so many regulations and restrictions, that it can't make a profit."

"Freedom to own a gun," said McCabe. "Hell, a whole locker full of them."

"Yes, Sam, that too. Because freedom isn't something that Washington can divvy out wherever and whenever it so chooses. It isn't subject to the laws of supply and demand. We either all have it or none of us do. Period." Morrissey let the idea sink in for a few more moments, then continued, "So we will develop an advertising and PR campaign that will talk about freedom. Nothing more. Nothing less. Freedom and our inalienable right to live peaceably without interference from afar. Just like the thirteen colonies did, over two hundred years ago. And if we do it right, gentlemen, we will build a groundswell among the general population that will send a clear message to Washington. One far louder and more impactful than simply dumping a few bales of tea into Boston harbor. You can count on it."

Once again, the room fell silent. Then Sanderson said, "Edward, you said there were three things you wanted us to do?"

"Yes, I did. The second one is that I want you to contact the members of Congress from each of your states. I want you to meet with them and sound them out on their position."

"You know that's a given, Governor," said Taylor.

"With all due respect, Governor, nothing is a given right now. Nothing!" The look in Morrissey's eyes and his tone made it clear that he was serious. Dead serious.

The other men nodded quietly.

"In addition, I want you to discreetly begin to talk with your friends in the governors' mansions in states where you think you might find a receptive audience. Be careful what you say and how you say it, but make sure they know that we do not intend to stand by while Washington eats away at our state's rights one at a time. Tell them that we want them to pledge us their support."

"You can forget California and the entire Northeast. They think Webster is the second coming," said Taylor.

"Webster thinks Webster is the second coming," added Lopez.

"That's because all those Hollywood starlets are terrific actors, 'Oh Alex, don't stop…don't ever stop. You are a god, do you hear me, a god!'" said Taylor, doing his best impersonation of a young woman in climax.

Several of the governors chuckled. Morrissey did not, and as soon as they noticed they stopped.

"We can do it," said Taylor. "What's the third thing?"

At first, Morrissey didn't answer. Instead he looked slowly around the room at each and every face. Later, long after the events that began up on that mountain in the Bitterroots had run their terrible and bloody course, some of the governors who were present that day would say that an aura came over him; that his voice had a resonance and power that they could feel in their chests; and that his green eyes seemed to shine with a radiance that reached out and touched their very souls.

"Gentlemen, the final thing that each of you must do is prepare for the possibility that the President may be successful in getting his bill through the Congress."

"And do what?" said McCabe, "Secede from the Union?" he added, with a snarky little laugh.

Morrissey looked at him without any expression and said quietly, "Yes. If necessary."

The room fell silent. After a minute, Diamond spoke up. "With all due respect, Governor, don't you think you are being a little dramatic?"

Morrissey reached into a portfolio that was lying on the table in front of him. He took out a stack of large color photographs and passed them across the table to Diamond, who took them and began to slowly flip through them. The muscles in his face tensed. He looked up at Morrissey, who nodded with an icy stare. Diamond spread them out on the table with a deep sigh. One by one, the other governors stood up and gathered around him, their eyes trying to take in what their minds found difficult to accept.

The photographs had been taken at the Bitterroot Rod & Gun Club immediately after the attack. On them, the battered and bloodied bodies of forty-nine young men could be seen lying where they fell, both Army Rangers and Wolf River Militia alike. Death had made no distinction between the uniforms.

"How did you get these, Governor? I thought the Army PAO didn't let any press up on the mountain that day," asked McCabe, referring to their Public Affairs Office.

"The photographer who took them made copies and sent them to me just before the video disk disappeared." The governor paused to let the full horror of the photographs sink in. Then he said softly, "Gentlemen, this is no longer a philosophical debate where we all seek to get our sound-bite on the six o'clock news. This is a matter of life and death. Our lives and their deaths." He pointed at the photographs. "Those young men were not terrorists. They were not a mortal threat to the safety of our nation. Simplistic, yes. Foolish and idealistic, yes. But threats to our national security? No. They did not deserve to die any more than did the other men who were sent to fight them. They could have been your sons or mine. Do you really believe that a man who went golfing after giving the order to send these young men to their pointless deaths would stop at anything to achieve his ends?"

The governors stood there, silently looking, absorbing the enormity of the moment. No one said anything. There was a long and powerful pregnant pause.

Finally, Diamond spoke up, more respectful now, and more somber. "Edward, let's suppose that the President's bill somehow manages to squeak out a two-thirds majority in both Houses of the Congress; it would still require a Constitutional Amendment to become law, and there's no way that three quarters of the states will ratify it."

"I have two answers to that. First, Webster has impaneled a group of Constitutional scholars who are working right now to find a way to circumvent the need for a state vote."

"On what basis?" asked McCabe.

"On the basis that the Second Amendment never guaranteed the rights of the individual to own firearms, only that there should be a well-armed militia—which of course they say means a regular Army in today's terminology. And second, even if it does go all the way to ratification, are you really willing to bet your freedom and that of generations yet unborn on that vote? If we allow this right to be taken away without a fight, at what point do we draw the line? On the next one. Or the one after that?"

McCabe didn't answer. His eyes said it all.

Governor Lopez asked, "Governor Morrissey, what do you want us to do?"

"Nothing right now, Luis. But if and when the time comes, I am asking you to follow my lead, to do what I do, and say what I say. I pray that it never comes to this, but if it does, you will either be my friend or my enemy. There will be no middle ground." He paused and then continued, "To that end, I strongly urge you to take a personal interest in the growing numbers of young men and women who are swelling the ranks of the militia units in each of your states."

Several of the governors nodded, while others sat stone-faced, indicating they knew very little about what was going on right under their noses back home.

The governor continued, "As you know, here in Idaho we have brought together several different militia groups under one central command, and my close and trusted friend General Jesse Latrobe has assumed command of this overall unit. As we speak, they are being trained at a facility that we have built in the Bitterroots at a place called Wolf River."

225

"What about the Army, Air National Guard units, and state defense forces in your state?" asked Taylor.

"For now, they will continue to operate under the command of the state adjutant general. However, at some appropriate time in the near future, I can see bringing these forces together under one commander," replied Morrissey.

"Not if he can help it," said McCabe with a snort.

Morrissey's eyes flashed at McCabe, "What do you mean?"

"Easy, Edward. No offense intended. It's just that from what I hear, the adjutant general doesn't support your views and has confided in some of his officers that if you try to separate the state from the Union, the Guard will not support you."

Morrissey was stunned. That the general didn't agree with him was problematic; that he talked about it openly was blatant insubordination. "Quite frankly, Sam, I think you have enough issues in your own state without trying to create some in mine." He turned to the other governors and said, "Gentlemen, back to the issue at hand. If and when force is needed to preserve and protect freedom, I will expect your support. Whether you choose to give it is of course up to you."

"You mean, it's up to the people of our respective states?" asked McCabe.

Morrissey looked at McCabe without saying anything for a long, awkward moment. Finally, he said, "Sam, one of these days you will realize that the secret to being a good leader is to get the people to do what you want them to, and make them think it's their idea. That is, if you survive long enough." He paused for effect and then added, "I meant in office, of course."

The look that passed between the two men said far more than their words ever could. McCabe was clearly going to be a problem for Morrissey.

Morrissey looked back at the others and said, "Gentlemen, my position is very simple. When the time comes, you will either be an ally or an enemy. So choose carefully, because there will be no second chance."

Around the table, each man was lost in his own thoughts, wondering what he would do and knowing that there really wasn't a choice.

After a few minutes of silence, Governor Lopez spoke up. "Governor Morrissey, there is one other matter that you haven't addressed."

"Which is?" asked Morrissey.

"Thomas Porter," said Lopez.

"What about him?"

"If the government catches him, doesn't that put you, and therefore us, at risk?"

"Thomas Porter is one of the richest men in the world, and one of the shrewdest. Based on what my sources in Washington tell me, the President has lost interest in finding him, and the FBI is getting nowhere with their search. With all his money and power, they won't find him unless he wants them too."

Lopez nodded and let it lie. Once again the room fell silent. Finally, Morrissey looked around the room and then said, "Well, gentlemen, unless there is anything else…"

Governor Butler, who up until that moment had not said anything, spoke up. "My fellow governors, I have been silent up until now, because quite frankly, I wasn't sure where your collective sympathies lay. But now I feel reassured of your intentions. I am therefore obligated to tell you that we are not alone. For the past several months, I have been privy to a growing movement in Washington. It is a group of men and women from both the public and private sector, people who share our concerns and are determined not to let the obsessions of the few destroy the rights of the many. I was made aware of this group through my father-in-law, whom you all know is Senator Lamar Wacker from Georgia. After hearing what they are doing, I think it may be time that we all joined this group. They are called the New Sons of Liberty."

Governor Morrissey looked around the table and back at Butler and said, "Thank-you for your candor, Bodey. And thank-you for trusting us enough to talk about the group and Senator Wacker's involvement with it. However, I believe that for us to align ourselves with the New Sons of Liberty will distract us from our cause, which is the preservation of the Constitutional rights of the citizens of the West."

"But Governor—" Butler tried to interrupt, but Morrissey wouldn't let him.

"Therefore Bodey, while you certainly may convey our best wishes to the Senator from Georgia and his band of patriots, we in the Group of Seven will not align ourselves with them." He paused and then looked Butler directly in the eyes. "Is that clear, Governor?"

"Perfectly," said Butler, who slumped back in his seat.

"Excellent." Then Morrissey got up, walked over to a large closet, and opened the door. "Ted, give me a hand, will you?" Governor Sanderson stood up and joined him. Morrissey began taking small black fiberglass cases out of the closet. "Give one to everybody. You'll find names on the side of the cases." Sanderson did as he was told. Then Morrissey looked over at the others and said, "Don't open them until I say."

When each of the governors had his case, Morrissey stood in front of them and said, "Gentlemen. Today is an historic moment for our cause. Accordingly, I thought it would be appropriate to mark this occasion with a gift. Now go ahead, and open the cases."

They did as they were told. Inside each was a chrome-plated, .44 caliber, single-action revolver. The craftsmanship of the weapons was obvious and the governors nodded their approval as they carefully handled the heavy gun. Morrissey continued, "On the frame you will see that I have engraved your name along with the words 'Group of Seven.' Together we seven men have become the last best hope for the salvation of freedom in America." He paused and then added with deep conviction in his voice, "'Men and brethren, to you is the word of this salvation sent.' Acts chapter thirteen, verse twenty six."

MEANWHILE, in a non-descript tradesman van parked in a deserted alley ten blocks from the governor's mansion, two men sat in front of a bank of electronic equipment. One of them was wearing earphones, which he took off. "Well, that's it. The conference is over."

"Did we get it?" asked the other.

"We got it," his associate said, with consternation in his voice.

"What's the problem?" asked his partner.

"It won't transmit."

"What's wrong?"

"The satellite uplink isn't working."

"It doesn't matter. We've got it all on a disk. Let's get out of here," he said, as he opened the partition between them and the front seat and slid behind the wheel. He started the ignition, looked in the outside mirror, and then slumped back into the seat. "Oh shit."

"What?" asked his partner, as he was climbing into the passenger seat.

"It's the State Patrol," he said, shaking his head.

His buddy looked at him and said, "Have they made us?" he asked.

"I don't know. Be cool. Let me handle this." He put on his dumb, friendly face and turned to come face to face with the business end of a 9 mm semi-automatic.

"Step out of the vehicle," said the trooper, who wore a black T-shirt under his standard issue dress shirt, in a 'Don't fuck with me' tone.

The man behind the wheel looked back at his associate and for just an instant, they both considered reaching for their weapons. Then they decided not to. There were things worth dying for, but this wasn't one of them.

"Anything you say, Officer. Anything you say."

As they were being helped into the back seat of the patrol car, a large truck backed down the alley toward them. While they watched through the windshield of the patrol car, two men got out of the truck, opened the back doors, and pulled out a honeycombed metal ramp. Then one of them hopped into the van and drove it up into the larger truck. As it disappeared inside the truck, one of the captured men looked at his associate and said softly, "I think we're fucked."

26

The Department of Justice, Washington, D.C.

Attorney General Arnold Greenberg, the most powerful law enforcement officer of the most powerful country on earth, felt totally helpless, and it made him furious. He paced back and forth behind his desk in the corner office on the top floor of the Justice building, holding a stiletto-like letter opener in one hand and waving it around in the air like a sword. To his two top assistants, it looked as if at any moment he was going to take it and stick it somewhere unpleasant. The person sitting directly across the desk was Mary Lou Pritchard. The other person was Harry Erickson, an athletic-looking man in his early forties who was wearing a heavily starched white shirt, a navy bowtie with tiny white polka dots, and a shoulder holster with a very large handgun.

"Damn it all, Mary Lou, we can't subpoena the chief of staff to the President of the United States of America just because he might have been in Potomac Park on the same day our agent was murdered." Now he was pointing the opener toward her and piercing the air with it. "Or because he might have talked with a professional killer named Chadrian who might have committed the murder. Three mights don't make a right, no matter how much you wish they would."

"I know that, Arnold," said Pritchard, remaining her usual calm and collected self. "But with all due respect, I never said to subpoena him."

"Then what did you say?"

"If you will stop shouting and put away that sword and sit down, I will tell you."

He stood there for a moment just staring at Pritchard. Erickson was sure he was about to take her head off, figuratively if not literally, but he was wrong. Instead, Greenberg just nodded, put the opener down on his massive desk, and then sat down quietly behind it. "Go ahead, Mary Lou."

"I simply suggested that we meet with Gordon, tell him about the palm print, and see what his reaction is," said Pritchard.

Seeing that the storm had passed, Erickson jumped back into the discussion. "Exactly, chief. We tell him what we know and see what he says."

The Attorney General sat there for a moment, eyeing the opener as if tempted by its shiny, smooth presence. Then he looked back up at his colleagues. "Give it to me again. But save the speculation. Just tell me what we know as fact."

"Fact," Pritchard began, "We have been investigating a possible link between Maddun Gordon and the persons who broke into the headquarters of the National Rifle Association three years ago. You will recall that they killed a night watchman, who interrupted the break-in before the burglars could get whatever it was they were looking for."

"Fact," continued Erickson, "Before he died, the watchman managed to shoot one of the burglars, and radio his command center. He said there had been two intruders wearing black ski masks. Fact, one of them left a partial palm print smudge in his own blood on the glass door before he left."

"Evidently, he either wasn't wearing any gloves, or more likely, he took them off to try to stop the bleeding," added Pritchard.

Greenberg said, "Go on."

"Fact," continued Pritchard, "The palm print turned out to belong to a man named Timo Latola, a Finnish-born mercenary who served as a field operative for the CIA in the Middle East during WWT. He died suddenly, shortly after the break in."

"You remember, Arnold, they found him floating in the Potomac," added Erickson. "The cause of death was drowning, which was strange because he was a former triathlete on the Finnish team."

Greenberg didn't remember and didn't particularly care to. "Does this tale have an ending?" he asked.

"Yes, sir," said Erickson. "During WWT, Latola worked closely with one of the Agency's most proficient and cold-blooded contract killers. Apparently they used him to terminate several high government officials of

231

friendly nations who had done decidedly unfriendly things. The killer goes by the name of Chadrian."

"It seems that whenever the Agency has been accused of spilling sovereign blood anywhere in the world over the past decade, Chadrian's name keeps popping up."

Greenberg's interest seemed to have been whetted. "What do we know about Chadrian?"

"His full name is Stefan Chadrian," said Pritchard, taking a folder out of the leather case by her feet and handing it to her boss. He put on his reading glasses and started looking through it. He kept flipping back and forth through the relatively small number of papers in it. "If you're looking for his photograph, it's not in there."

"Why not?"

"Apparently no one has ever been able to get a clear photo of him. We checked with Interpol and Britain's MI-5. No one has one."

Greenberg sat up a little straighter and started listening a little more attentively. "Go on."

Erickson added, "We think he was born in one of the former USSR countries, you know, like 'Wherethefuckistan' or something like that, but there is no actual birth certificate. Virtually nothing is known about his early life."

Pritchard joined in. "The then Soviet Union's record keeping was primitive at best. Evidently there is no hard copy on Chadrian until he shows up in the mid-eighties as one of the KGB's most ruthless agents. He subsequently defected to the West and became a contractor for the CIA, doing wet work in the Middle East, where he teamed up with Latola."

"What's the connection with Gordon?" asked Greenberg.

"Maddun's third wife was a Finnish woman named Reeta Latola. She was Timo's sister," replied Pritchard.

"Was?" asked Greenberg.

"She drowned in a boating accident at their country house in Finland. According to the CIA, both Gordon and Chadrian were there at the time," said Erickson.

"And Reeta, like her brother, was a world class athlete who had medaled in several triathlons," added Pritchard.

"So?" asked Greenberg.

"So, tri-athletes are strong swimmers," said Pritchard.

Greenberg sat staring at them over the top of his glasses. Finally he said, "And that's it? That's all you've got? Some convoluted coincidence involving a sister and a brother who both drowned?"

"It's too much of a coincidence, if you ask me," said Pritchard. *Damn*, she thought to herself. She knew better than to say that, but she had, so now she readied herself for the cross-examination.

"Coincidence is a distant cousin to proof, Mary Lou. You know that as well as I do. You simply don't have enough to justify approaching Gordon. Besides, even if we suppose that he is somehow implicated in the NRA break-in, we have no proof that the killing at Potomac Park is related, or that Gordon was even there that day."

"The agent said it was him just before he died."

"His last words were that he photographed Gordon with Chadrian."

"May I see the photos?" asked Greenberg already knowing the answer.

Pritchard shrugged. "You know there aren't any."

"Oh, really. What a coincidence!" chirped her boss, with gentle sarcasm.

"The agent was killed just as he was starting his wireless uplink and before he could transmit anything. Then the killer took his video disk. The only thing we have is a blurry photo from a Homeland Security UAV that was flying at altitude overhead. Unfortunately, there were some clouds that day and we didn't get a clear photo."

Pritchard added, "But we are reasonably certain that it was Chadrian and Gordon talking together."

"Reasonable certainty—I see." He nodded his head and smiled. "That's sort of like conceivable doubt, isn't it?"

"I suppose it is. We can't tell for certain. Even the computer can't tell us anything," replied Erickson.

"Look, it's bad enough that the agent's backup was so far away, they couldn't protect him. And on top of that, if the agent had used the simultaneous transmission function on his camera like the manual says, we might have something. But he didn't, and we don't."

"Apparently he forgot."

"And now he's dead, and so are we. At least as far as this investigation. Going public with our suspicions about Gordon will only do two things. First, it will incur the wrath of the President, who already feels this department is disloyal. And second, if Gordon is guilty of conspiracy, or possibly worse, we will have tipped our hands and he will dive for deep cover. Then the White House will throw up an iron wall of legal obfuscation that we couldn't even drive a tank through. So the answer is an unequivocal no! Now go get me some hard evidence that the President's chief of staff is guilty of a high crime, or let it alone. Got it?"

"Yes, sir," said Pritchard as she stood up, revealing her long, beautiful legs, which were covered in black tights under a short charcoal suit skirt.

"Loud and clear, chief," added Erickson as he too stood up and headed for the door.

"Now let me get back to being the Attorney General."

Erickson opened the door and walked out. Pritchard was about to follow him when Greenberg called out, "Mary Lou."

"Yes, sir."

"A moment please. Close the door," he said, as he motioned for her to come back in and sit down.

Pritchard said, "I'm really sorry if I was out of line back—"

He interrupted her, "You were, but that's not why I called you back," he said with a sad smile.

"Then what?" she asked, her curiosity aroused by his strange tone of voice.

At first he didn't answer. Then his eyes began to water.

"Arnold, are you all right?" she asked, with growing concern in her voice.

He looked at her with a dead serious expression and slowly shook his head no. "I've got cancer."

She let out a gasp, "Oh no… no."

"Yes. I'm afraid it's true. I skipped my annual physical for about four, maybe five years, and finally my wife made me go. They found a lump on my prostate which turned out to be malignant."

"Oh, Arnold. Are they going to operate?"

Again, he shook his head no. "The bone scan showed that it has spread." He paused and took a long deep breath. "It's everywhere in my abdomen and they said it has now moved into my liver. They've given me only a fifty-fifty chance of living another six months."

Pritchard's eyes too began to fill with tears. "Oh, Arnold." She slowly stood up and walked around his desk. She leaned over, put her arms around her boss and hugged him tightly as her eyes began to well up.

He patted her on her shoulder like a father consoling a distraught daughter. He took a handkerchief out of his desk and handed it to her. She took it and dabbed her eyes carefully, "I'm so sorry; here you are the one who's ill and you're comforting me."

She walked back in front of his desk and sat down.

"I am going to submit my letter of resignation to the President tonight and recommend that he appoint you as my successor."

She wiped her eyes again. "I don't want to be Attorney General, Arnold; I'm only here because of you. When you go—" she caught herself. "When you step down, I will too."

The tone in his voice switched from loving father to stern teacher, "No, you will not. You are the most qualified person in this entire country for this job. A fact which you have made very clear to me on more than one occasion, I might add," he said with a tender smile. "While this President has many faults, stupidity isn't one of them. He would be very stupid not to recommend you to the Congress as my successor. Moreover, Mary Lou, nothing would give me greater joy, as I take on the most serious battle of my life, than to know that my best student and dearest friend has stepped into my shoes."

Pritchard nodded and lowered her head. "Thank-you, Arnold. You are my hero. I hope you know it."

He stood up. "Enough of this maudlin crap. Let's get back to being the good guys in a world filled with evil."

She stood up and adjusted her short skirt. He noticed.

"Damn, I am going to miss those legs, and if that's sexual harassment, sue me." Then he added with a mischievous smile, "But you had better hurry."

There was a knock at the door and his administrative assistant entered. "I have Springer White on the telcom. He said it's urgent."

"Very well, I'll speak with him."

His assistant nodded and left the room, closing the door behind her.

"Do you want me to leave?" Pritchard asked.

"No." Then he walked over to his desk and picked up the telcom. "Hello, Springer. What's up?" Greenberg then listened intently as Springer White, the head of the CIA, spoke to him without pause for several minutes. Finally Greenberg said, "I see. Yes. I agree. Thank-you for telling me." He hung up and looked out the window. He sighed deeply.

"What is it, Arnold?"

Slowly he turned around and said to her, "As my replacement, even if it's only temporary, you'll need to know this. Two outside contract agents working for the NSTF disappeared this morning in Boise, Idaho." He was referring to the joint National Security Task Force that was comprised of agents from the CIA, FBI, and DHS. It had been established during WWT to ensure better cooperation and coordination of anti-terrorist activities on American soil. Some civil libertarians likened it to the Nazi SS but most Americans were happy to have the protection it provided.

"What were they doing there?"

"They were on a covert mission monitoring Governor Morrissey's meeting with the other governors in the Group of Seven when they simply disappeared. Along with the truck full of a million dollars worth of electronic surveillance equipment."

"You mean to tell me we bugged the Governor of Idaho's office?"

"Yes. As authorized by the second amendment to the Patriot's Act."

"How?"

"Micro transmitters."

"You put T-glass in the State House?"

"Yes," he said, with a big smile. "Although he doesn't realize it, the governor got a completely new glass top on his conference table. The Department of Homeland Security ordered it."

"I don't believe it." She paused and collected her thoughts. "Has NSTF contacted the local authorities?"

"Yes. They claim they don't know anything about it."

That fact didn't sit well with Pritchard at all. "Why were they there in the first place?"

"We had reason to believe that Morrissey was a co-conspirator with those men who occupied the gun club on that mountain in the Bitterroots. And if not a conspirator, at least an accomplice after the fact. We think that he aided and assisted the leader of the group to escape."

"That mysterious billionaire. Thomas Porter?"

Greenberg stared at her and then said softly, "That's his alias." He paused and then said, "But his real name is T.J. Kincaid. He's the youngest son of Jeremiah Kincaid."

Mary Lou Pritchard's jaw literally dropped. "What!" She shook her head in disbelief. "I don't understand."

"Sit down and I'll tell you all that I know about it." Then the Attorney General and his likely replacement sat back down together, and he started to tell her the tale that began five months earlier on a mountain top in Idaho.

HALF AN HOUR LATER Arnold Greenberg stood with his back to Mary Lou, staring out the window of his office. Night had fallen on Washington, and everything inside the Beltway, including the government buildings, and the monuments stood out against the darkness in washes of pale white light.

"This is my favorite time of day in this city, Mary Lou. The beautiful parts are all visible and the ugly parts are hidden in the darkness."

She nodded but didn't say anything for a few moments. Finally, she asked, "Does the President know what you've just told me, Arnold?"

"No," he said returning to his desk.

"Sooner or later he'll find out, and it would be better if he did from us."

Arnold nodded his head affirmatively but added, "Jeremiah Kincaid is a good and decent man. He has been a personal friend of mine for over twenty years, despite our disagreements on politics and policy. When their youngest son walked out of their lives seven years ago, it nearly killed Kathleen, and it broke Jeremiah's heart. So you can just imagine the pain they must have felt when they realized who it was on top of that mountain. When the FBI came to me several days ago with the truth about Thomas Porter and his potential involvement with Governor Morrissey, I knew full well what my duty was. But I just couldn't bring myself to do it. I am certain that Jeremiah is going through the very same agony right now, and quite honestly, I wasn't prepared to give the President the satisfaction of rubbing Jeremiah's face in the blood of the Bitterroots."

They sat silently for a few moments, and then Mary Lou asked, "Did the President know about the covert operation?"

"No. And other than Harry Erickson and two of his guys at NSTF, no one else knows about T.J. Kincaid, not even Springer White. All anyone else knows is that we suspect a link between the Idaho State House and the man named Thomas Porter."

"Do you think the Governor is involved in the agent's disappearance?"

Greenberg sighed, "I don't know. And notwithstanding my own comments earlier to the contrary, it is a rather pointed coincidence."

"What about the Speaker's son? Is he involved?"

"No. Not according to the Bureau." He paused. "But I'm going to have to tell the President everything, including Porter's real identity. You know Jeremiah Kincaid is a good friend of mine, and Webster will certainly use this against him."

"Why do you have to tell him?"

"What do you mean?"

"I mean other than destroy the Speaker, what use does the President have for that piece of information right now?"

Greenberg's face tightened. "Mary Lou, what you're asking me to do is unethical, if not illegal."

With a straight face she replied. "I know. But I firmly believe that the Speaker is a voice of reason in the current madness over gun control, and at present, he is the only thing keeping Governor Morrissey and the President from elevating the matter beyond the boiling point."

Slowly, Greenberg's expression softened. "Okay. As long as the young Mr. Kincaid stays lost, I'll say nothing. But if and when we find him, or if he finds us, then I will have no choice but to tell the President."

"And if that happens, let me alert the Speaker first. That way he won't be caught by surprise."

He nodded. "Thank-you Mary Lou."

"No need to thank me. I owe you more than you will ever know." She got up and walked over to him and put her arms around his head and shoulders. She hugged him tightly for a moment and then said softly, "Life isn't fair."

He reached up and patted her and said, "Don't worry my little raw sensual beauty. I will be fine."

But they both knew that he wouldn't be.

27

Walter Reed Army Hospital, Washington, D.C.

Outside the casement windows of the hospital cafeteria, a pale sun bathed the manicured grounds in a pastel yellow wash. It was a mild, midwinter day and ordinarily the sidewalks around the building would have been filled with patients enjoying a few moments of escape from the ever-present pain and fading memories that filled its dreary hallways. But not that day. The reason was that the commander in chief was coming to the hospital for a medal presentation ceremony, and throughout the facility, everything was shipshape. The well-worn marble floors were polished, the radiators were dusted, and the smell of touch-up paint was everywhere. And the medical staff and patients who could usually be found populating the outside walkways and the inside passageways were now jammed into the cafeteria. They were joined by a large group of civilians and military personnel and a contingent of Secret Service agents, all of whom stood or sat patiently waiting for the President to arrive.

In typical fashion, President Webster was late. Not just fashionably late, but annoyingly so. There was nothing anyone could do about it, least of all the wounded men from the Bitterroots, some of whom were in their dress uniforms, but most in hospital gowns. They were seated in wheelchairs or perched uncomfortably on stiff metal chairs at the front of the cafeteria near a wooden podium with the Presidential Seal affixed to it. One soldier was lying in a hospital bed that had been wheeled into the room for the occasion, and sitting beside him with his arm and shoulder in a cast that extended from his neck to his waist was Thomas Porter. A bandage partially covered Porter's face, and it would have been virtually impossible for anyone to recognize this fugitive from justice had they been looking. But this was hardly the place or the time that anyone was expecting to see the man who, indirectly at least, had been the cause of all the pain and suffering about him.

Immediately behind the soldiers who were to be honored sat a large group of senior military officers, including General Pace. The ribbons and medals lying against their stiffly starched tunics gave the television cameramen headaches, as they tried to prevent the glare from their lights from reflecting off the shiny metal into their lenses. Noticeably absent was General Pete Corcoran. He had still not gotten over the President sending his troops up that mountain, and he never would.

Seated behind the military were the friends and families of the men who came down from that mountain in the Bitterroots and those who never would. The White House press corps, including Sarah McGill, came next in the seating order and finally, at the very back of the room was a large contingent of the hospital's medical staff. And standing off to one side, dressed inconspicuously in surgical scrubs under a white lab coat was the young man with the strong jaw sent by Major Smythe. No one took particular notice of the fact that his hospital identification card was pinned on backwards. If they had, they would have immediately seen that the man in the photograph wasn't him. The body of the doctor to whom the card belonged would be found that night at the bottom of an elevator shaft. But for now, no one looked at him, and the only place he looked was at the back of Thomas Porter's head.

Suddenly, the soldier standing near the door of the cafeteria came to attention and shouted "Ten hut!" From somewhere just out of sight, a small ensemble from the Army's brass band began to play Hail to the Chief. Everyone in the room who could, stood up, and into the room strode President Alex Webster. He marched quickly up to the podium and faced the audience, giving a compassionate smile and a nod of his head to the men in the front row.

Following the President into the room was a young woman dressed tastefully in dull gray tones and her two small children, a seven-year-old girl and a four-year-old boy. The latter didn't understand what was going on, nor did he care, as he tugged persistently on his mother's skirt. Finally, Maddun Gordon and Patrick Fitzgerald entered the room and stood beside the woman and her children.

"Ladies and gentlemen, the medal we are awarding posthumously today to Captain Jackson recognizes his courage above and beyond the call of duty." The President paused and smiled at the young widow who looked like she would never smile again. As he did so, the little boy stuck out his tongue at the President. Smiling benevolently, the President turned back to the microphone. He had learned long ago to always talk directly into it, and today was no exception. "It will also stand as a beacon in the darkness to guide our collective efforts to free this land of the tyranny of guns."

The President looked at the press corps, focused briefly on Sarah McGill, and continued, "I believe deeply in my heart that if our founding fathers were standing here beside me today, they would say, 'Mr. President, we did not intend the Second Amendment to be a license to kill. We did not intend it to be a permit for our poor and uneducated to slaughter themselves on the dark streets of the ghetto.'"

He clenched his jaw. "'We did not intend it to be the means by which an innocent child,'"—he looked back at the woman and her children—"'like this brave young woman's little boy, could snuff out the life of a sibling or classmate, and then have to live with that burden for the rest of his life. And we certainly did not intend this amendment to be the first cobblestone on a boulevard of bloodshed that would be perpetuated for all eternity.'"

The President paused for effect, looked directly at the television cameras, and raised his hand with one finger pointing at some imaginary bad man and continued, "My fellow Americans, if I accomplish nothing else during my Presidency, I promise you that I will rid this land of the plague of locusts made of lead that tear apart our bodies and destroy our souls. This I pledge to you so that the valiant officer we are honoring today, and the brave young soldiers who died with him on that mountaintop in Idaho, will not have died in vain. So help me God!"

After he finished, there was not a dry eye in the audience. Even several of the hardened Secret Service agents had to gulp to clear the lumps in their throats. The young widow wiped several tears from her eyes with a pretty little handkerchief and stiffly accepted the medal and the subsequent embrace from the President. To many of the people in the audience, he seemed to hold her just a bit too tightly and too long. As he did, the little boy took a big whack with his tiny fist against the President's knee, which prompted Webster to break his embrace and attempt without success to shake the boy's hand.

After giving up on it, the President leaned over and kissed the little girl tenderly on her cheek, said a few more words to the widow, and then walked around the podium. There he began slowly working his way down the long line of wounded soldiers, shaking their hands and listening intently to the answers to his questions. He started at the opposite end from where the heavily bandaged Thomas Porter sat, patiently waiting with his right arm in a large protruding cast. It would be a little while until Webster worked his way down that far, but Porter was in no hurry. After all, he wanted to savor this moment. Soon he would terminate the life of the man who he had hated for so long. He only wished that he could say something to Webster before he detonated the shaped charge. Something that would tell him why he was being sent to hell. But helping him depart on his eternal journey would have to suffice. For the moment, he could only sit there and avoid making eye contact with Sarah McGill, who was sitting several rows behind him. The fact that she apparently had not recognized him gave him confidence that no one else had. However, having her so close at such a traumatic moment in his life, and the fact that she would soon be a witness to his death, began to bother him more and more with each passing second, fanning the tiny spark of morality that smoldered in his troubled soul.

DOWNSTAIRS, two members of the Military Police detachment guarding the main entrance to the hospital were discussing the event that was occurring upstairs.

"So who's he giving the posthumous medal to, anyway?" said one of the MP's.

"Some Ranger Captain named Jackson. The one who led the Special Forces Group who took back that gun club in Idaho."

The other policeman looked puzzled. "What was his first name?"

The first one thought for a minute and then said, "Randall, I think. Yes, that was it. Randall Jackson."

"No way!"

"What are you talking about? Of course it was him," said the first MP.

"Man, I'm telling you it couldn't be. Captain Randall Jackson is here today. He's one of the honorees who returned as an outpatient for the ceremony. I know, because I checked him in through security myself."

The expression on the other MP's face darkened. "Are you sure?"

"Yes, I'm sure. I remember because he was wearing a heavy cast on his arm. The Secret Service and I checked him out carefully, because the cast set off the metal detector. They even used those high-tech scanners that checks for explosive particles in the air."

"Didn't you check his NIS card?" asked the second MP.

"Hell, yes. His NIS card scanned perfectly and confirmed his biometrics, including iris, facial thermography and fingerprints. According to that card, there is no doubt that he is a Special Forces Captain by the name of Jackson. Randall Jackson."

The second MP looked at his partner with a mixture of concern and disbelief, "Listen to me," he said very slowly and deliberately, "Captain Jackson of the 10th Special Forces Group from Fort Carson, Colorado died up on that fucking mountain. Do you understand me? I know, because I escorted his widow and children upstairs to meet the President myself."

The two MP's looked at each other with wide eyes.

"Oh shit!"

"I'll call upstairs. Get up there. Stat!"

"I'm on my way," he said, as he sprinted toward the elevators.

THE PRESIDENT was speaking to the man lying in the bed beside Thomas Porter. The young private had been grievously wounded in both the chest and head and could barely speak.

"Where are you from, son?" asked the President.

With great effort and in obvious pain, the young man whispered, "Min…" He winced and then continued, "Minot, North Dakota, sir." He took another deep breath and then whispered to the President again. "Mr. President?"

The President leaned over so that he could hear better, "Yes, son?"

"Could you tell my mother that I'm going to be okay?" He struggled to get the sentence out. "My dad died last year, and my mother didn't have enough money to travel here to see me, what with the medical bills and all."

The President looked puzzled and asked, "You mean that you haven't seen your mother since you came here, son?"

"No, sir."

The President turned to Maddun Gordon and said "See to it that this boy's mother is flown here at government expense."

243

Gordon nodded. The President patted the man gently on the shoulder and then turned his attention to the next man in line, which was Thomas Porter.

Seeing that he couldn't talk because of the burn bandages wrapped around his face, the President just looked deeply into Porter's eyes and said, "Thank-you for your bravery, soldier."

Porter nodded, and for an instant that seemed to last forever, he stood there on the edge of the abyss, facing the man that he had hated for so long. But nothing happened. There was no explosion, no blinding flash of light followed by eternal darkness. No blissful end to the torment that had plagued him from the moment that he escaped from the mountain. Nothing save the pounding of his own heart. Porter hadn't squeezed the trigger. Nor would he. At the last second, something happened. Something that made the difference between life and death, between hatred and forgiveness, between yesterday and tomorrow. A tear, a tiny drop of water and salt that formed in the corner of the President's eye, rolled across his cheek and fell in slow motion, bursting like a translucent liquid flower on the chalk-white cast. The cast that contained enough explosives to obliterate the man whose tear it was.

Suddenly it all became clear to Porter. It was not the President of the United States of America standing there before him. It was simply another human being, frail and fragile, alone in a crowd, mere inches away from eternity. At that instant, Porter knew it was over. He could no longer do what he had come to do. He been given a peek behind the facade of power and there, like the little man behind the curtain in the Land of Oz, he found neither wizard nor devil, only a man. Just another lonely sojourner on the dark side of happiness; not evil itself, but rather, just another victim of it.

"Take care of yourself, soldier. God bless you," said the President as he stepped closer, pressing the cast deeply against his chest, giving Porter a hug. Then he stepped back and moved on down the line. The moment was over. All Porter could do was nod politely and mumble, "Thank-you, Mr. President," through the heavy bandages.

McGill and the other reporters stood quietly watching the incident. It was a touching moment for all who were standing nearby.

One reporter whispered to McGill, "Pretty powerful stuff."

Another added, "He's hard to resist when he gets going."

McGill nodded and said, "Yes, indeed. But this time, charisma may not be enough."

The other two reporters nodded solemnly.

As soon as the President had moved past Porter to the next few soldiers, he squeezed himself between the several rows of chairs behind his. He was looking back at the President and the men guarding him when he nearly bumped into McGill. Without saying anything, he stepped to his left to move around her at the exact moment she moved to her right. They now found themselves blocking each other again. She said, "Excuse me, Captain," and moved aside to let him pass. As she did, their bodies brushed against each other, separated only by the stiff white cast on his arm. For an instant their eyes met; he quickly looked away, but not quickly enough. Suddenly she felt the tiny hairs on the back of her neck stand up and goosebumps rise on her arms. She recognized him at once. It was Thomas Porter. She gasped, but before she could say or do anything, he pushed by her. Blindly, without reason, she followed him to the back of the room.

Just ahead of her, Porter said something to the two agents guarding the door. They allowed him to exit. Her mind was racing as she reached the door, and when she held up her White House press credentials, they stepped aside and let her exit the room. Looking back through the open door, McGill saw the Secret Service agents standing beside the President suddenly react as if they had been given an electric shock through the miniature earphones they wore in one ear. Instantaneously, other agents burst through the main doorway with their weapons at the ready, and went to work doing what they had been trained to do. The two agents guarding the door where Sarah had just exited pushed it closed and as they did, she caught a glimpse of the agents nearest the President grab him and hustle him toward the door at the front of the cafeteria. Simultaneously, the other agents and several MPs quickly covered the doors and shouted for everyone to stay calm and not to move. But by that time, Sarah McGill was already heading down the hallway. She came to a corner and quickly rounded it, where she caught a fleeting glimpse of Porter heading into a stairway. As fast as she could without running and drawing undue attention to herself among the hospital staff in the hallway, she followed him.

Back inside the cafeteria, the young man with the strong jaw had watched both Porter and McGill leave. He immediately started to follow, but his timing had been just a few seconds too slow, and he had been caught by the sudden lock down of the room. Frustrated, he stood impatiently among the crowd of medical and military personnel and other guests under the watchful eye of MPs who were blocking the doors until the President was safely out of the building. That only took a few minutes, and then the agents and MPs allowed everyone in the room to exit. The man they were looking for was the heavily bandaged soldier, so the two agents at the back door of the cafeteria did not scrutinize the credentials of the people filing out as closely as they should. Had they done so, they would have noticed that the photo ID of the young man dressed in surgical scrubs did not match his face.

Their lack of attentiveness was a serious lapse of vigilance given the situation. But then again, in addition to being well-trained and heavily armed professional bodyguards for the President, they were also human beings. A fact that no amount of training and discipline could ever change. Human beings who worked under a constant state of tension and danger, with long hours and low pay. Men and women who regularly missed important family events, such as birthdays and soccer games and anniversaries. Their job was one of those few in society that could be categorized as a zero-sum game. Because like other men and women who wore badges and carried a gun, or airline pilots, or surgeons, the best these professionals could do was break even. If they did their jobs well, it was taken for granted by the public at large. But there was plenty of opportunity on the down side, for if they made a mistake, they were immediately castigated. It was the life that they had chosen, and they did it to the best of their ability. Sometimes, however, their best was simply not good enough. Tragically, this would be one of those occasions.

Freed of his confinement, the young man hurried down the hall, taking with him his concealed weapon. Two other agents walking toward the cafeteria were more vigilant. And they would pay for it with their lives.

"Hello, doctor," said the thinner of the two agents, as he scrutinized the doctor.

The young man nodded, but said nothing. As he walked past the agents, the other agent noticed the identification card lying backwards on the young man's lab coat. It sent an alarm signal to his brain. But it was too little, too late. In their line of work, vigilance delayed is vigilance forsaken.

"Excuse me, doctor," he said in a firm tone.

What happened next seemed to the agents to be happening in slow motion, although it took only a matter of seconds. It doesn't take very long for men to die. Not when guns are involved. The young man started to spin around, and both agents watched his arm make a sudden movement as he thrust his right hand under his lab coat. The man finished his turn and dropped into a shooting stance. As he did, his hands came up in an expert movement, and in their grip was a gun. It was a .22 caliber auto-loader handgun fitted with a silencer, both of which were made out of a special new material that was virtually undetectable by metal screeners.

The second agent instantly shouted, "Gun!" and stepped between his partner and the killer, while slipping his own weapon out of his coat. The thinner agent reached for his gun but a fraction slower. In less than a blink of an eye the first two bullets from the young man's gun sliced neatly between the taller agent's third and fourth ribs, staggering him back against the hard plaster walls as the air was sucked right out of his left lung. For an instant, the dying man stood there with eyes wide open, thinking his last mortal thoughts about his wife and children, wondering how his wife was going to pay for college tuition. Then he slid down the wall, leaving a trail of bright red blood and collapsed on the cold marble floor.

During his partner's death slide, the thinner agent finally managed to squeeze the trigger of his weapon, but the only thing that happened was a hollow click. The weapon had jammed. With incredible courage and poise in the face of death, he tried to unjam it, but it was no use. The young man seeing that his opponent was helpless slowly raised his weapon and pointed it directly at the agent's head.

"Do you have any last words?" asked the young man.

"Yes," replied the agent. Then without any fear or emotion whatsoever, he said, "Go to hell."

The young man's weapon spit out two shots in rapid sequence and the thinner agent slumped heavily down on top of his partner. The young man methodically pumped another shot into each of the agent's heads. Then he sprinted down the hallway. Within seconds, three other agents came around the corner with weapons drawn. They were completely unprepared for what they saw before them—the two lifeless bodies of men who only moments earlier had been their friends and colleagues, oblivious to what fate had in store for them. Now they were gone. It had been a very bad day for the Secret Service. One that would not soon be forgotten.

The cast and bandages Porter had been wearing were found in the lower basement behind a boiler where he had discarded them. Although it would take specialized tests to confirm that the innocuous plaster contained a deadly explosive, the small detonator they found inside the metal brace told them all they needed to know. Namely, that the President had very nearly become the fifth President to die at the hands of an assassin. And, what made it even worse, there had been another would-be assassin carrying a concealed weapon in the same room as the President. A fact for which two Secret Service agents had paid the ultimate price. Because of these events, the full force of military and Federal law enforcement was now rapidly spreading out through the nation's capital, intent on finding the man who had worn the body cast and the gunman who was assumed to be his accomplice.

It would be in vain. For at that moment Thomas Porter was several miles away, sitting in the back seat of a limousine, heading to Dulles International Airport, where a chartered jet would carry him west, back to the mountains and safety; and sitting beside him was a distraught Sarah McGill. She had followed him into the basement and found him as he was taking off the cast and bandages. There followed an awkward and painful, but silent confrontation. When she started to ask him why, he cut her off with a sharp, short command, "We must get out of here. Now!" To which she obeyed willingly, even as her heart was breaking.

As the limousine inched its way through heavy traffic westward along Constitution Avenue toward the river, neither of them could know that while they had safely eluded the Secret Service and MPs, the young man with a strong jaw was sitting behind the wheel of a sedan just three-car lengths behind them. As they neared the Vietnam Veterans Memorial, the traffic came to a dead stop. It was the opportunity that the young man needed. Instantly he jumped out of his car and began to run toward the limousine, being careful to stay out of the line of sight of its mirrors. When he got within twenty paces, he stopped and assumed a firing position, pointing his weapon directly at the back of the driver's head. By killing him first, he would immobilize the car and be able to easily finish off its passenger. At the last instant, he realized that Porter was not alone in the back seat, but it didn't bother him. He steadied his arm and started to squeeze the trigger. Suddenly something distracted him. It was the sound of heavy hooves pounding on the grass. He jumped up and turned to look, just as an enormous white horse with a dark rider dressed in a flowing black robe thundered down upon him.

248

In the rider's hand, raised high over his head was a huge sword, the blade of which glistened in the sunlight. For a fraction of a second, the man stood there transfixed, staring at the onrushing angel of death. Then, as suddenly as they had appeared, horse and rider passed by him and were gone, leaving the man alone, arms limp at his sides and sightless eyes pointed at the war memorial. At first nothing happened, then seemingly in slow motion, he dropped his gun, his knees buckled, and he collapsed face forward to the ground. At that exact moment, the log jam of traffic broke, and the limousine with Porter and McGill in the back seat pulled away. They and their driver remained unaware of how close they had come to death.

THE LIMOUSINE was far from the city when McGill finally got up the courage to break the silence. "Why, Thomas? Why?"

He turned away from the window and looked at her, "You wouldn't understand."

"Try me."

He thought about it for a minute, and then with great depth of feeling, said, "That day when you and the President came to my mountain, he promised me he would consider my demands. He looked me in the eyes, Sarah, and lied—a cold-blooded, cruel lie. And then he left, and ordered the death of my men. From that moment on, I knew I had to kill him."

Sarah nodded, but didn't reply. His choice of the word "my" when describing the mountain, didn't go unnoticed by her. He had personalized the tragedy, placing himself at the center of it, like some terrible wheel of misfortune, with everyone else, including his men, the soldiers, and the President, being nothing more than spokes radiating away from him—rather than seeing himself for what he was: simply another victim of it. It troubled her deeply, but it also explained, at least in part, his irrational desire to kill the President. She looked down at her hands, which were folded tightly in her lap the way they always were when she was sad or frightened. "Now, I understand," she said softly, thinking back to the day on the Mall, and what he had said.

"I couldn't let my feelings for you stop me from what I had to do."

"But you didn't do it!"

He looked back out the window. "No—I didn't."

"Why not?"

He faced her. "I don't know. Maybe because I knew you were there."

249

"No. That's not it. It was because you are not a killer."

"What difference does it make? I still wanted to kill him."

"In God's eyes, it makes all the difference."

"God!" he snorted. "There's a joke."

"You don't mean that."

"How would you know?"

"I just do." She reached over and took his hand. "Please, Thomas, let me help you."

"You can't help me now. No one can."

"Where will you go?"

He tensed but didn't answer.

"Never mind. That was a stupid question. It's better that I don't know."

They sat there in deafening silence. Finally, she collected her wits and began to act like the disciplined professional that she was. "Listen to me, Thomas. We can go to the authorities together. We'll get you the best legal counsel money can buy, and we'll plead diminished mental capacity, due to post-traumatic stress syndrome produced by your experience on the mountain. With your background, and all the good that you have done for society, I'm certain that you'll only be remanded to a mental care facility, or one of those country club prisons, or possibly even released in my recognizance."

He smiled sadly. "Sarah, Sarah, Sarah. You are a world-class reporter, but you are not a Federal prosecutor. I will be lucky not to get life in prison. And the Federal Government closed all those country-club prisons, as you call them. White collar criminals do hard time now—and even if they don't, would-be assassins certainly do." He paused and then added, "The driver is going to drop me at the airport, where I will get on a plane and disappear. After he drops me off, he will take you back to the city, where you will tell the police that I kidnapped you. Then you will forget about me."

She shook her head no and turned away, pulling her hand from his, and clutching the other one tightly. Her heart began to pound, and a mixture of fear and anger and determination boiled within her. Desperately, she tried to find the words that would convince him not to go, not to leave her, not now, just when she had finally found true love. But for the first time in her life, her intellect failed her; it had been overwhelmed by the pain of unrequited love.

The limousine reached the airport, and the voice of the driver came over the intercom. "What airline are you on, sir?"

Thomas looked at McGill and said, "Drop me at Nationwest."

"Very good, sir."

Within a few minutes, they pulled up to the departure level outside the Nationwest terminal, and the driver got out and came around to the curbside door. He opened it and stood waiting patiently for Porter to exit the vehicle. Porter sat there unmoving for a long, lonely minute, staring deeply into Sarah's eyes. "Perhaps our paths will cross again someday—who knows, maybe it will be back on our mountain. But for now, I must go." He leaned over and kissed her on the lips. In that brief second when their mouths touched, all the happiness that she had known in her life, or would ever know, collapsed upon itself, like a Supernova of the heart, leaving a giant nothingness behind. "Goodbye, Sarah." He slid across the seat and got out. He handed the driver a thousand dollar bill. "Take Ms. McGill back to the city," then without looking back, he disappeared into the crowd in front of the terminal.

The driver closed the door and got back into the front seat. With eyes still wide with appreciation, he looked at her in the rear-view mirror and asked, "Where to, Ms. McGill?"

Fighting back the tears, she said, "GNBC studios."

"Right you are."

Within ten minutes, they were back on the highway heading for the city. Sarah was now sitting where Thomas had sat, leaning back against the soft leather headrest, with her eyes closed, thinking about the handsome young captain with sad and lonely eyes, and the mountain in the Bitterroots that he called his own—a mountain known to the people who had once reigned over it with savage innocence, as the Kingdom of the Wind Spirit.

28

Kincaid Farm, Kettle Moraine, Wisconsin

Kathleen Kincaid sat in the hearth room of the farm house, knitting and watching the evening news broadcast as the talking heads continued with their analysis of the failed assassination attempt on the President the day before. A few feet away, her daughter Joanna stood behind an ironing board, and in the corner of the hearth room sat her granddaughter, Madison, playing with her doll.

Kathleen shook her head and marveled at how supposedly well-educated and intelligent reporters could spend so much time analyzing and re-analyzing every word in the White House's official press release.

"They just keep saying the same thing over and over," said Kathleen. "Even though the White House hasn't released anything new since last night."

"They have got to fill the airwaves, even if it is just with the sound of their own voices," added Joanna.

"They're all empty suits, just like Jeremiah said. All except that cute young blond. What's her name?"

"Who?" asked Joanna.

"You know, the one on GNBC who Jeremiah likes. He says she's the only one with any brains."

Joanna thought about it for a minute and then said, "Oh, I know the one you mean. McGill is her name."

"Yes, that's the one. Sarah McGill."

"Well she's certainly not any empty suit. In fact, she fills the jacket out pretty well. Of course, her chest was probably given to her by a surgeon rather than God." As she said it, she glanced down at her flat chest. "Perhaps if I had done the same, I wouldn't be divorced now."

"Joanna. Not in front of Maddy," said Kathleen. "Besides, any man whose love is due to sub dermal saline sacks isn't worth having."

Suddenly, there was a light cracking sound as a pebble hit the glass door that led to the back porch of the house.

"What was that?" said Joanna.

Kathleen got up and walked over to the door, flicked on the floodlights, and peered out into the yard.

"Oh my God!" she said and flicked the lights off.

"What is it, mother?" asked Joanna.

But Kathleen didn't answer. She reached for the door handle, unlocked it, and slid the heavy door open, letting a sudden rush of Wisconsin winter air into the room. The dress that Joanna was ironing caught the breeze and fluttered, causing her to grab it. "Mother, what are you doing?" Before Kathleen could answer, the dark shadow of a man slipped into the room and quickly closed the door behind him.

"Oh my God!" exclaimed Joanna.

"No. Far from it, sis. It's just me," said the figure. Standing there, looking for all the world like a little boy lost, was T.J., whom the world knew as Thomas Porter. A wanted man and a tormented soul. He smiled at his sister and then turned toward his mother, who stood there in shock. "Hi, mom," he said softly. For an instant she stood there frozen in place; then she burst into tears and threw her arms around him.

T.J. KINCAID sat at the big kitchen table wolfing down a second piece of apple pie and a third glass of milk. Joanna sat across from him with a stare that was as cold as the liquid he was drinking. In the life of the Kincaid family, the seven years that had passed since T.J. stormed out of that kitchen, and out of their lives, had seemed like an eternity.

Kathleen put the pie back into the refrigerator in the understated, but high-end kitchen. Then she walked over to the table, touched her son lightly on the back of his neck, as if to see if he was really sitting there, and then sat down beside him.

"We have all been so worried about you."

"All of you?" he questioned.

"Yes. Your father, too."

"You mean, he's been worried that the world will discover that I'm his son."

Her expression clouded up, "Please, T.J., don't."

He nodded gently, "Okay, Mother, I won't."

She looked at him with a mixture of love and worry and said, "The FBI is looking for you."

"They aren't the only ones."

"What do you mean?"

"Don't worry, my pursuers think I'm Thomas Porter. They won't be looking for me here. Besides, I was very careful. I parked the rental car two miles from here in the woods by the creek, and I walked through the forest all the way here. I'm sure no one saw me."

"Who else is looking for you?" Kathleen asked again.

T.J. looked at his mother with a far-away look in his dark eyes and said softly, "Never mind, mother. I'll be fine."

"Regardless," Joanna said firmly, "you simply can't stay here."

"I know. I just had to come to see mom. But I won't stay long," he replied.

"Oh no, no. You must stay. At least for a while," said his mother, flashing a pained look at her daughter.

"I'll stay for a little while," he replied, which calmed her down.

"Good," said Kathleen, as she refilled his glass with milk.

"Does your wife know where you are?" asked Joanna.

"No, and she's not my wife anymore."

"What happened?" asked Kathleen.

"Let's just say that while I was up on the mountain, she wasn't alone."

"Oh my darling little boy, what have you gotten yourself into?"

"A world of trouble, that's what," said Joanna, with very little sympathy in her voice.

"Joanna," said her mother, "Please stop it."

But Joanna couldn't stop. She slid her chair back and stood up, "I'm sorry, mother, but I can't. T.J. walked out of our lives seven years ago and never once tried to contact any of us: not when you had your surgery, not when I had Maddy nor when I got divorced, and not when Jake won the Medal of Honor—not once. And now that he's a fugitive, he waltzes in here and expects us to welcome him back with open arms." She looked directly at her little brother. "I'm sorry, T.J., I love you, but I don't like you; and as far as I'm concerned, by your coming here, you have shown me that you are every bit as selfish as you were the night you left. If you have even the tiniest bit of love and concern for us, you will leave and never come back again." She finished talking and stormed out of the kitchen.

"She doesn't mean that, T.J. She's still hurting from her husband deserting her and her daughter," said Kathleen.

"No, mother. She's right. I've made a mess of my life, and on top of the pain I caused all of you, I led a group of innocent men to their deaths."

Kathleen reached over and held his hand, rubbing it and gently the way she always used to do when he was a little boy frightened of the dark. "God will forgive you, my child."

"Maybe God will. But my father won't."

"No. You're wrong, darling. Very wrong."

He sat there with a forlorn look on his face and said, "I am so very tired."

She stood up and walked over behind him. "Come, my precious little boy, and I will tuck you into bed. Tomorrow, when you are rested, we will talk some more."

He looked up at her through sorrowful eyes. He nodded and got up, and the two of them walked out of the kitchen.

THE NEXT MORNING, T.J. walked into the great room and sat down in a deep armchair. He had slept for eleven hours, which was something he had never done before. His hair was twisted in a knot the way it always would when he was a little boy, and his eyes were puffy. "Hi Mom," he said in a loving tone that ignored the fact of the seven years they had been apart.

"Did you have a good sleep, honey?"

"Yes. I did. Where's Joanna?" he asked, looking around the great room and into the adjacent kitchen.

"She took Maddy to school, and then she said she had some errands to run. She should be back in a couple of hours."

T.J. nodded sadly, and looked out the window. "Will you tell her goodbye for me?"

The thought of him leaving brought an instant look of horror to his mother's face and she said, "No. You can't leave so soon."

"I can't stay, mother. It will place dad in a very difficult position."

"He doesn't need to know that you're here. At least not right now. Please stay, T.J. I just can't say goodbye again right now," she pleaded.

"All right. I'll stay, but just for a little while," he answered reluctantly.

They sat there in silence for a few moments, each lost deeply in their own thoughts, neither knowing how to bridge the distance that separated the lost boy from his family. Finally, Kathleen said, "Do you want to talk about it?"

He wasn't sure whether he did or not. Then slowly, he started to talk. "I met the governor after having made a significant contribution to the state Republican Party. After that, we saw each other again at several fundraising dinners and the like. During that period, he and I had several conversations about the issue of gun control. And gradually, I just became caught up in the matter."

"But why did you lead the militia up to that gun club?" asked his mother.

"I know what you are thinking. But not everyone who disagrees with the Federal Government is a neo-Nazi. If George Washington hadn't rebelled against the government, America would be part of Canada right now."

"There is a big difference between the Continental Army of 1776 and the militia of today," replied Kathleen.

"Maybe in your eyes, but not in theirs."

She said softly, "Tell me about it, son."

T.J. leaned back in the deep comfort of the chair and began to recount the events of that final, fateful day on the mountain. As he spoke, his eyes glazed over, and he was no longer sitting in the safety of his parents' home. Instead, he was back up on the mountain with his men, where a part of him would forever be. "The first few weeks went well. We had become the darlings of the media, and I actually thought my plan was going to work. But on the day that the President came to the mountain and met with me, I made the fatal error of believing him when he said that he would consider changing his bill in return for a peaceful resolution of our protest. It wasn't even twelve hours later when he sent in the soldiers." He stopped talking.

"Why didn't you just put down your arms and surrender?"

His eyes glazed over as he retraced the memories that would haunt him forever. "I had given my men specific orders not to fire unless fired upon. When the tank broke through the barricade, no shots were fired. Instead, the men on picket duty just put down their weapons and were led quietly away.

256

We could hear the tank coming up the road long before we saw it. It was a sound that I will never forget. The sound of rolling thunder. A deep and frightening rumble that shook the earth and sent adrenaline rushing through our bodies." Again he stopped, but his mother didn't say anything. She, too, was now up there on the mountain with him.

"Just before the tank rounded the corner and came into view, helicopters appeared overhead. We could see that the doors were open and that the soldiers were getting ready to do a fast rappel down upon us. I knew then that my foolish dream of helping America resolve this painful issue had been just that. A naive and stupid dream. I was just about to order my men to surrender when the shooting started."

"The news media said that your men fired first," said his mother in a compassionate and non-challenging way. "That the captain of the Rangers was holding a white flag of truce when he entered the compound at the front of his column."

Her son nodded. "Whether anyone chooses to believe it, it was an accident. One of my men, an overweight corporal, tripped and fell as he was taking cover behind one of our trucks. He was carrying a light machine gun and it went off, killing three of our men who were standing nearby. A sergeant standing in another part of the compound assumed that the shots were theirs and put a round between the eyes of the Ranger captain." T.J. paused and then continued. "You pretty much know the rest."

"Did you kill anyone, son?" asked Kathleen.

T.J. looked at her and said without hesitation, "No. I didn't. The firefight lasted only minutes, although the government would have you believe otherwise. I ran into the compound to try to stop my men from firing, but then a soldier took aim on me with a heavy machine gun, and one of my officers pushed me down and saved my life."

His mother gasped. "Did he die?"

"No. It was all over almost before it began, and when the firing stopped, forty-two of my men were dead or dying, along with seven Army soldiers. Nearly a hundred were wounded. I was the only one of the militia left standing. It was a bloody massacre in every sense of the word." T.J. looked directly into his mother's eyes and said, "And while I didn't actually kill anyone, for all intents and purposes, I am responsible for every one of their deaths."

Kathleen said firmly, "No you aren't."

R.A.R. Clouston

"Yes, mother. I am. Although at the time I didn't think so. I believed the guilt lay elsewhere and I tried to do something about it."

"What do you mean?" his mother asked.

"I'm afraid there is more," he said softly, knowing that he had to get everything off his chest. He took a deep breath and began talking. "After it was over, I became blinded by rage, and all I could think about was revenge against the man who ordered the military action; against a country who would condone such a horrible overreaction to our protest; and against everyone and anyone other than the real guilty party which was me. As a result, I almost did something else that neither you nor God could have ever forgiven."

Kathleen looked at him with the unconditional forgiveness that only a mother can dispense, "I know. The man in the cast at Walter Reed Army hospital was you. I saw it on the news this morning."

"Was it Sarah McGill who announced it?"

"No. I haven't seen her make any public statement at all, including on her own network. But GNBC did report that she was with you when you fled, or at least that she was with a man named Thomas Porter. Apparently, neither she nor they knows who you really are."

"That's right. She doesn't. I just couldn't put her through that. I've caused her enough pain." The look in his eyes as he spoke told Kathleen far more than his words could about her son, the beautiful young blonde reporter, and what had transpired between them. But she decided not to pursue it, at least not then. "Thank God, T.J., that you didn't go through with your plan."

"When the President stood there in front of me looking me in the eyes, thinking I was one of the Army's wounded, and thanking me for my bravery and courage on the mountain, I realized I couldn't do it. I knew then that it wasn't him who was responsible for the deaths of my men. It was I. And that all the hatred I had directed at him was simply what I felt about myself, but was too blind to see. But nothing I can ever do or say will change the fact that I went to that hospital with murder on my mind."

Silence fell upon the great room. Neither T.J. nor his mother said anything, for there was nothing more to say. Perhaps time would heal the wounds that he had created in his family, in the lives of the families of the dead men, and in the country as a whole; but at that moment, only pain, fear, and sadness filled the hearts of T.J. Kincaid and his mother. Pain and the unspoken concern for another man, the Speaker of the House of Representatives, who was about to have his heart broken again by the son whom he had lost so very long ago.

29

GNBC Studios, Washington, D.C.

Ever since she returned from her ride to the airport with Thomas Porter, Sarah McGill had not been the same; and nothing that Keene Lange said or did seemed capable of dispersing the cloud of sadness that had settled upon her soul. That day was no different as she sat in stony silence across from Lange in his office. Their eyes were fixed on one of three large, flat-screen BTC monitors built into one wall of the cluttered room. The monitor was tuned to C-SPAN, and they watched the Speaker of the House, Jeremiah Kincaid, presiding over a session of the House, with both the floor of the House and the visitor galleries filled to capacity.

Without taking his eyes off the screen, he asked, "Sarah, what really happened inside that hospital?"

She glanced at him. "What do you mean?" The tone of her voice told him it was dangerous ground upon which he was about to tread.

He looked over at her. "Whatever possessed you to follow him into the basement?"

She shrugged—body language for either *I don't know* or *I'm not going to tell you.*

Either way, he read the signal and retreated. He looked back at the screen and added as a throw-away, "Well, at least he didn't hurt you."

She frowned. "Thomas Porter is not a killer, Keene. If he were, President Webster would be dead."

He let it go. "What about that other guy? The one they found dead near the Vietnam Memorial?"

"What about him?"

"The police think he was chasing Porter, since his car was found on Constitution Avenue, only yards from where your limo had been moments earlier."

"Along with a hundred other cars," she replied. She paused and added, "Thomas said nothing about an accomplice, and I don't believe that he had one."

"All I know is that my best reporter—in fact, the best reporter in the entire country—keeps putting herself in harm's way. And I, for one, am tired of worrying about her safety."

"Did you ever stop to think that the two might just be related?" she snapped back.

The battle over, with neither side achieving victory, both looked back at the screen and fell silent. At that moment, Tanner Spence knocked and entered the office. "Hi guys."

Neither acknowledged him at all. Tanner stood there for a moment and then said, "All right. I guess I'll see you two later."

Sarah said, "It's all right, Tanner. Come in. Keene is just in one of his grumpy moods. He'll get over it."

"*I'm* in a grumpy mood!" he protested. "This from the queen of broken hearts."

She flashed a glance at him filled with pain and anger.

He melted. "I'm sorry, Sarah. I didn't mean that."

Tanner studied the other man's face, and seeing no sign of further outbreaks, he plunked himself down on the sofa beside Sarah and looked at the BTC screen. "Looks like a full house."

"Gun control is a hot topic," said Lange.

"Especially now that the Secret Service has linked the attempted assassination to the pro-gun movement," said Spence.

McGill shook her head in frustration, but said nothing.

"One thing is for sure; it has made it more difficult for the Speaker to get his amendments added to the President's bill," added Lange.

"Sssh," said Sarah, as Jeremiah Kincaid appeared on the screen. "I want to hear this."

"Yes, boss," said Lange. By the gentle way he said it, Sarah knew that his temper tantrum was over.

JEREMIAH KINCAID stood behind the podium at his customary spot and rapped his gavel several times. "The Chair recognizes the Honorable Member from Pennsylvania."

A woman in her late forties approached the podium in front of the Speaker's chair. She appeared nervous, and it took her a few moments to arrange some papers in front of her. As she began her address, most of the members were paying attention, but many were not.

"Thank-you, Mr. Speaker." She had a slight accent, but she spoke crisply and clearly. "I was not born in this country. I chose to be an American, but I love this land as if it had chosen me." Her opening statement grabbed everyone's attention, including those few members who were still whispering to each other as she took the podium. The chamber gradually fell silent.

"For many days now, I have sat here patiently listening to the honorable members who oppose the President's bill. I have listened as they argued that if we allow the government to take away one right, it will only be a matter of time before we lose another. And another after that. But with all due respect, these men and women speak of things they can not know and do not understand." The woman continued to speak in measured and gentle tones, but with such conviction, that even at that point in her speech, she had captured the attention of everyone in the room.

"For they were not born in a country where freedom is a foreign language. They did not grow up knowing terror and indignity as the currency of daily life. They did not have to wonder each night, as they lay awake in the darkness if that would be their last night on this earth—or worse, if it would be the last night of a loved one. They did not see the effects of a corrupt government and a corrupted society, where the rule of law meant simply who had the most weapons, and where the police were either part of the problem or incapable of dealing with it."

She paused and took a sip of water from a glass hidden on a shelf behind the podium. No one moved. Not a sound could be heard. The look of deep emotion on the Speaker's face behind her was a mirror to the hundreds of faces before her.

"For some of you to state that giving up your guns is giving up your freedom is an affront to the millions of oppressed people around the world to whom happiness is simply surviving another day." She paused again. "And please, do not insult my intelligence by saying that without weapons we will be a deprived people; because, with all due respect, you have absolutely no understanding of what that term means."

The audience was spellbound. All eyes were fixed upon her and all ears strained lest they miss a single word.

"In closing, I would like to ask my colleagues who oppose this legislation one simple question. Is the single freedom you seek to preserve more important than freedom itself?" Her question hung in the silence of the room and echoed through the hallways of their minds and the chambers of their hearts. "Thank-you. And God bless America." She gathered her notes and stepped away from the podium, and a great silence fell upon the chamber—one that would last long after voices once again filled the air.

"WOW," SAID SPENCE, muting the BTC monitor. "She should run for President."

"She can't," said Lange. "She wasn't born here."

"Pity," added McGill. "Let's see what Allistair Blevis and the dynamic duo have to say." She picked up the remote, muted C-SPAN, and turned on one of the other two monitors, revealing Allistair Blevis and his usual panel, just as the station cut away to a commercial.

Lange got up and headed toward the door. "I've got a meeting, but you two kids just snuggle down and relax." He looked at Sarah, "After all, I'm paying you good money, and I wouldn't want you to actually earn it." Then he looked at Spence, "And as for you, when I first told your father that I would meet with you, I didn't realize it meant you were going to move in permanently."

Spence jumped up, but McGill looked over at him, "Sit down, Tanner," which he did. She looked back at her boss. "You've got to stop scaring him, Keene, the poor boy never knows when you're kidding."

He just shook his head and said, "Apparently, neither of you do." Then he walked out of the office.

Spence looked over at McGill and said, "Ouch, that hurt."

"Don't worry about him; he's still mad at me for chasing Thomas Porter. He'll get over it by tonight. Now, be quiet so I can watch *Enemies and Other Lovers*."

Spence laughed. "What?"

"Don't you ever watch Martisse and Peabody savage each other?" asked McGill.

"Not usually."

"You ought to. It's very entertaining, and it's even more delicious watching them when you know that off camera they are lovers."

"You're kidding?" asked Spence with wide eyes.

"No. I'm not."

"How do you know?"

"Everybody knows it. It's in all the magazines," said McGill.

"You mean to tell me, that stiff white shirt and that black satin blouse, who attack each other verbally on the air, run home afterwards and jump into the sack together?"

"Yes," said McGill, "Isn't that hot?"

Spence looked at her through excited eyes and answered, "Yes, it's really hot." As he spoke, she could almost hear the hormones rushing through his bloodstream.

She smiled benevolently and said, "Down boy. It isn't going to happen here."

His face flushed with embarrassment, and then he said softly, "You can't blame a guy for dreaming."

"You're a sweet kid, Tanner, and I do love you, but like a brother; and it's going to stay that way. Got it?"

He slumped back into his chair and said, "Okay. Got it." Then with a smirk he added, "By the way, sis, what are your thoughts on incest?"

She picked up a cushion and hit him. "Is this the way you act at DHS?"

He laughed and ducked as she swung it again. "Always."

"Which reminds me, you haven't told me how your cyber tracking is going?"

"It's going," said Spence, his expression turning serious. "The people who set up the New Sons of Liberty extranet knew what they were doing. The encryption system is more sophisticated than I originally thought, and I'm going to have to use the quantum computer to help me decipher it."

"How soon can you do it?"

"Soon."

"Is there any danger that they will know you are doing it?"

"Who is 'they'?"

"I don't know. Secretary Bouchard," she said, referring to the Secretary of Homeland Security.

"No. Remember I'm the one who built the quantum computer and wrote the qubitware in the first place. Don't worry, I'll crack this one. It's only a matter of time."

"I believe you." She looked at her watch and said, "I've got a meeting with my producer. After that I'll be in my office if you need me." She got up, walked over, and gave him a tender kiss on his cheek. "You're one of the good guys, Tanner Spence." Then she left the room.

Spence sat there staring at the monitor for a few seconds, and then he un-muted the sound and waited for *Speak Up America* to return from the break. Something was bothering him. He hadn't been completely truthful with McGill. Contrary to what he had told her, he wasn't certain he could use the quantum computer to trace the NSOL sites without detection. But he had to try. Without the use of the computer, it would take weeks if not months to decipher the NSOL encryption codes. And he knew that time was not on their side.

ALLISTAIR BLEVIS sat quietly reading his notes as he waited for the commercial break to end. Sitting across from him were Peabody and Martisse, and between them was another man who was not a regular on the show.

The producer counted him down, using his fingers, "Five, four, three…" The last two counts were silent, and then they were back live.

Allistair came alive as he turned to camera, "Ladies and gentlemen, what do you think about that? Who was that congresswoman we just saw in that clip from the House floor, and how many hearts and minds do you think she just won over to her cause?"

"You mean, other than the one in the Oval Office," said Peabody.

"Come on, Cresswell, she was terrific and you know it," said Blevis.

"She was indeed, but the last time I checked, C-SPAN had a Nielsen rating in single digits."

"That's exactly what's wrong with this country," interjected Martisse. "If more people would watch their government in action, instead of the nightly murder tallies, we would all be better off."

"I think there are a lot more serious problems with this nation than the poor ratings of C-SPAN," said Peabody to Blevis, completely ignoring her, as was his usual practice.

"You ought to watch it, Cresswell, you might learn something," she snapped.

Peabody continued, "Allistair, I think that congresswoman was eloquent in her speech. She spoke from the heart with grace, and passion, and sincerity. But this is not some third world country with criminals running loose in the streets, raping and pillaging as they go. And the reason it isn't is because we have a Constitution. One that can't be changed every time someone decides that they don't like certain parts of it."

"You're absolutely right, Cresswell. Instead of trying to change the law through a Constitutional amendment, they just make a bomb and try to blow the President's head off, like Thomas Porter did," said Martisse.

"Well, for whatever reason, Captain Porter didn't go through with it," replied Peabody.

"The bomb probably was a dud," said Martisse.

Blevis jumped in. "According to our sources at the FBI, the bomb worked quite effectively when they blew it up later."

"Whatever the reason, this has served to show just how bloodthirsty the pro-gun movement is and how far they will go."

"It has certainly put the Speaker's attempt to get amendments added to the President's bill in jeopardy," said Blevis.

"What a shame," said Martisse. "Just think of all those madmen out there who might have to turn in their steel penises that ejaculate lead upon the innocents."

"With that pleasant image, I think it's time to introduce our special guest today."

The camera focused on the man sitting between Peabody and Martisse. He was a chubby man with a fulsome beard and a bald pate, which gave the impression that his head was upside down.

"Ladies and gentlemen, joining us today is Dr. Melvin Horrowitz, who is an adjunct professor of statistics at Georgetown University and the President and CEO of Stat Trax, a national polling service that is regularly used by the Democratic National Committee."

"And by the White House," Horrowitz added with a self-satisfied smile.

"Come now, Doctor Horrowitz, you are being far too modest," interjected Peabody. "We should also make note that your services are in great demand, both here and abroad." Horrowitz began to smile. "Your counsel is eagerly sought by every left-wing group from Boston to Beijing." The smile quickly vanished.

"Now, now, Cresswell, you promised me that you'd behave today," said Blevis.

Peabody smiled benevolently at Horrowitz, "Don't worry, Allistair, Melvin and I go way back to our undergraduate days at Columbia, don't we, old sport?" He looked back at Blevis, "While I strenuously disagree with his political views, I have the highest regard for his integrity and the veracity of his work." To the viewing audience, Peabody's attitude appeared genuine. It was not.

"Yes, we're old friends," said Horrowitz awkwardly, not wanting to appear petty in front of the viewing audience.

"I too can attest to the value that Doctor Horrowitz and his staff add to the political milieu," added Martisse gratuitously.

"Great. Great. Well, let's hear what you have to say, Doc, and perhaps we can add a touch of controversy and debate to this love fest," said Blevis.

Horrowitz obviously did not appreciate being referred to as "doc" but he let it go. "Thank-you, Mr. Blevis. I'm here today to report on the results of the latest Stat Trax and New York Times poll on the matter most pressing to our nation these days—gun control."

"What do your polls say, Doc? Are the majority of the people for or against guns?"

"It's not quite that simple, Mr. Blevis, but if you force me to phrase it in those terms, I'd have to say that a slight majority are now in favor of the President's bill."

"So you're saying that the President is going to pull this one off?" asked Blevis.

Professor Horrowitz squirmed uncomfortably in his chair. Like all men of statistics, he knew that numbers could be interpreted in many ways and that polls were not infallible. "Yes, I suppose that if the House vote were to be taken today, and if every member voted exactly as the majority of his or her constituents wanted him or her to, then the bill would narrowly pass. A similar outcome is possible in the Senate, where the Republicans have only a two-vote margin, and many of their members are uncomfortable with the current state of uncontrolled gun ownership. Should it pass the Senate, the Constitutional amendment would then move to the states for ratification."

"It will never get that far," said Peabody with a sly smile.

"Do you know something we don't know, Cresswell?" asked Blevis.

"Yes," said Peabody. The power and conviction of his response caught Blevis and the others by surprise.

"Really. What do you know, pray tell?" asked Blevis.

"Yes, tell us Cresswell. Are you finally going to admit that there really is a vast right-wing conspiracy in this town whose current mission is to thwart the wishes of the President and the people?" added Martisse.

Peabody, breaking his normal pattern, looked directly into Martisse's eyes. His stare appeared to unnerve her. "I think you should be very careful about where and how you use the word conspiracy, Ms. Martisse, lest you find yourself in a multi-million-dollar libel suit."

By her expression, it was clear that Martisse realized that she had overstepped the bounds of propriety, and it was now her turn to act out of character. "You're quite right, Cresswell." She turned to the program's host, "Sorry, Allistair."

"No worries, love. Let all those high-priced lawyers in the network worry about it. We're here to get ratings, and I don't know about you, Cresswell, but conspiracy sounds like a ratings magnet to me."

"Cresswell, you know as well as I do that this town is rife with rumors about a secret group of politicians who are planning ways to thwart the President's bill."

"Yes, Jarlene, I'm aware of the rumors, but I seriously doubt that anyone in high office would be party to such activity. After all, treason is a capital offense," replied Peabody.

"So is murdering a President," shot back Martisse.

"On that pleasant note, it's time for us to take a break," interjected Blevis. He turned to the camera and continued, "When we come back, we'll take some calls, and if you'd like to ask the good doctor here, or either of my regular panelists, a question, then give us a call. Our subject for today is, 'The President's Gun Bill: Powerful Stuff Or A Power Trip?' Our toll-free number is 1-777-GUN VOTE."

30

The Capitol Building, Washington, D.C.

Senator Lamar Wacker, Chairman of the Senate Committee on Armed Services, brought the committee hearing to order. Seated around the room were twelve Republican senators and twelve Democratic colleagues. Wacker was a staunch conservative who had earned the respect, if not the amity, of his colleagues on the committee and in both Houses of Congress. He was a plain-spoken, hard-working man, with clear and consistent views on all matters of import that came before the Congress. He was willing to listen to opposing viewpoints if they were well-prepared and presented. However, he suffered fools lightly and made no apologies for dismissing those who shirked their responsibilities or played strictly for the camera, regardless of their political affiliation. With this latter group, he was blunt to the point of being brutal, and with those whom he perceived to be deceitful, dull-witted, or deficient in some way, he was unmerciful. As a result, other than among hawks and hard-line right wingers, he had few friends and many enemies inside the Beltway. Most prominent among the latter group was President Webster himself. The rancor that existed between the two men would have been far worse had the President known of Wacker's membership on the Executive Committee of the New Sons of Liberty.

On that particular day in committee, Senator Ronald Zion from New York was feeling the chairman's wrath. "Mr. Chairman," whined Zion, "I would like to draw the committee's attention once more to the Congressional Budget Office report, titled, 'Restructuring the Army for the Future,' issued in December of last year, which, as you know, was conducted at the request of the Subcommittee on Personnel of the Senate Committee on Armed Forces.

Parenthetically, I would like to state that the CBO did an outstanding job of capturing the enormity of this issue along with its attendant complexities, and of course, I would be remiss if I didn't mention that they were ably assisted in this matter by a consulting firm on Long Island that has a long history of providing well-thought-out countervailing views on the matter of military funding and staffing—"

"Excuse me, Mr. Zion," interrupted the chairman. Anyone who used the term 'parenthetically' in his or her speech was already placing themselves in harm's way with Chairman Wacker. Zion had not only done so once, but he was at that very moment digressing from his own digression. "With all due respect to the honorable member from the great state of New York, I would like to conclude this hearing before my granddaughter graduates from college." There were a few snickers around the room from those who knew that the chairman's grandchild was five years old. "Now, if you please, make your point."

Zion was obviously not pleased at being chided, but he knew better than to take on the chairman. "Yes, of course, Mr. Chairman. My point was…" He hesitated as he struggled to remember exactly what his point had been, "My point is simply that I believe the CBO provided a compelling rebuttal to the Army's contention that it needs three quarters of a million troops in deployable units to fight two simultaneous major regional conflicts. Many of my colleagues both in the House of Representatives and Senate believe that the probability of America having to fight two major regional conflicts at the same time is nominal. And as support for this view, I need not remind the committee that during the protracted and difficult World War on Terrorism, the military did just fine with its present deployment of five hundred thousand soldiers. Therefore, the Army's projected budget of fifty-five billion dollars for the pay, operations, and maintenance of active duty forces could be significantly reduced were we to adopt alternative five as presented in the CBO's proposal."

The heads of most but not all of the Democratic members of the committee nodded in agreement.

"Mr. Zion, we are well aware of the details of the CBO report in general, and with alternative five in particular. However, as you know, the CBO's proposal would entail a significantly increased reliance on the reserves to provide additional combat troops in times of crisis, and on civilian contractors to provide logistical support. And although I cannot dispute that our brave fighting men and women performed admirably during WWT, it is no secret that the reserves were stretched almost beyond the breaking point. Moreover, it took an unacceptably long period of time at the beginning of the war to fully mobilize the reserves and National Guard, and an even longer period after it was over to bring them home."

"I respectfully disagree, Mr. Chairman. The Commission on Roles and Missions felt that the Army Guard was able to bring its enhanced readiness brigades up to combat status within an acceptably short period of time. And if they did it once, they can do it again. Moreover, in my state alone, there are numerous contractors who are mission capable. In conclusion, Mr. Chairman, I would like to propose that we impanel a subcommittee to reopen the matter of whether or not the Army should receive the funding it requires to maintain sufficient active duty forces to conduct two simultaneous major regional conflicts."

The chairman was growing impatient, and it was fortunate for the senator that he concluded his remarks when he did, because the chairman was about to conclude them for him. Wacker had not intended to revisit the CBO's report during that committee hearing and was loathe to having it rehashed by Zion, whose motives were suspect.

"Thank-you, Mr. Zion. The chair will take under advisement your request for a subcommittee to review this matter. However, I must point out to you that what we are dealing with here is the need to respond to two simultaneous regional conflicts, and you know as well as I do that this was not the case in WWT, where we targeted our attacks sequentially rather than concurrently against nations that harbored terrorists." Everyone in the room, including Zion, knew that the chairman had absolutely no intention of impaneling another committee. In fact, he had spent his early years in Washington trying to avoid serving on committees and subcommittees and commissions and advisory panels, most of which, he felt, were nothing more than venues for pomposity. However, he had soon discovered that this was akin to stomping on Jell-O; it simply squirted out from underfoot. As a result, he had decided to join them rather than fight them, but he had done so sparingly and wisely, and his current role was one of power and command. And he had no intention of allowing the vainglorious Mr. Zion to take over his committee or set its agenda.

Wacker continued, "Before we move on to other matters, I would, however, like to make a comment on the CBO's recommendation, which you have resurfaced before this committee. I hope that the honorable senator from New York will not take this personally, for I assure you that that is not my intent. Shakespeare once said that 'He jests at scars who never felt a wound.' Before this committee, or any group so empowered, should deem to reduce the funding and the manpower of our fighting forces, we would be well-advised to remember that war has many faces; that it rarely comes at times of convenience or with sufficient warning to permit an orderly and effective transition from peace time to a war footing. Before we place the youth of our great nation once again in harm's way, and before we ask them to risk their lives, we had better make certain that their ranks are full; that they have the world's best training, weaponry, and logistical support; and that their faith in themselves and the country they serve is strong and unyielding. Before I relinquish the chairmanship of this committee, I intend to put before the Congress legislation that will ensure that we never, ever, again ask our young men and women to die for a cause, which the people do not support. We did that in Vietnam. We did not do that in WWT. And it does not take a military mind to compare the outcomes. As long as I chair this committee, we will not break faith with that long thin line that stands between the abyss and us. This is our mission, this is our obligation, this is our promise."

By their reaction to the chairman's words, it was clear that everyone on the committee and in the room, whether or not they shared his views, was still moved by his passion. What none of them could realize was that the probability of two major regional conflicts was growing with each passing minute. And even those who *could* foresee the possibility of such an event occurring at some point in the future would never have dreamt that both battlefronts would be on American soil.

March, 2018

G Day - 180

But For Honor

De toutes choses ne m'est demeure que l'honeur
et la vie qui est sauve.

(All is lost save honor).

Francis I

<u>31</u>

Inter Mountain University, Boise, Idaho

The auditorium on the campus of IMU was filled to overflowing. The audience was an eclectic mixture of men and women from every walk of life. There were students, faculty, politicians, professionals of every type, and most important of all, there were ordinary citizens. Ordinary citizens of the West who, by the contemptuous standards of New York and Los Angeles, would be considered hicks and rubes. But it was precisely the presence of these citizens in such large numbers that gave what was about to happen its far-reaching significance. An imposing podium had been constructed on the broad stage, and the enormous hall looked like a venue for a national political convention, which in essence, was what it was, with one critical difference—this convention would not entail a reaffirmation of allegiance to either the Republican nor Democratic Party. On the contrary, all these people, drawn from all over the Heartland of America, were there to participate in, and witness the birth of, a new political party. This party, both by its name and platform, would soon send shudders down the spines of American nationalists everywhere. For that day would be the birthday of the Western Freedom Party.

The hall was filled with the noisy exuberance that might be expected in such a situation, and as Ms. Lacey Garland, a svelte and dark-haired socialite, approached the podium, the noise level in the room had reached permanent hearing damage proportions. Garland stood at the bank of microphones for a moment, smiling her snow-white smile at the audience and occasionally pointing or nodding at faces she recognized in the teeming throng before her. After a few minutes, she picked up the gavel and smacked it loudly on its hardwood base, even startling herself. "Ladies and gentlemen," she said. The noise level dropped only a few decibels, and she hit it again, this time louder and with a greater sense of purpose, "Ladies and gentlemen, please, may I have your attention." Finally, the clamor subsided, and as she began to speak, the hall fell quiet, or at least as quiet as any hall with over twenty thousand exuberant people in it could ever be. "Thank-you. My name is Lacey Garland, and it gives me great pleasure to welcome you to the opening session of the inaugural convention of the Western Freedom Party." The audience erupted in a roar that literally shook the building and which could be felt in the breastbones of the people at acoustical ground zero in the middle of the audience.

"I hope y'all didn't mind having to check your guns at the door," she smiled. "But you never know what kind of dangerous element might be in the audience, be it criminal, or maniacal, or even Federal." The audience roared its approval. She laughed with them, but she wasn't kidding. Anyone who had brought their weapons to the hall, whether licensed or not, had been required to check them at the entrance. There were no questions asked but neither were there any exceptions. There were also high-powered cameras discreetly hidden throughout the hall that were at that very moment conducting automated high-throughput screenings of the audience. The entire safety and security operation was being run by a special unit of the Idaho State Police that the governor had created after he took office. Within the department, they were called the Black Shirts in recognition of the special black T-shirts that only they were allowed to wear under their uniforms. Their mission was never really explained to anyone outside the department, but it was very simple. It was to keep enemies of the governor away from him, whether their grievance with him was political, public, or personal. It didn't matter. The truth was that the governor of the State of Idaho was as well protected as the President of the United States, and he liked it that way.

Garland gave them a few minutes to revel in the exquisite joy of rebelliousness, and then she brought her gavel down hard three times and said, "Now, if you will please rise, we will begin this convention with a special video and audio presentation." With that, she stepped away from the podium as the auditorium darkened. The curtains drew back, and the audience gasped as the giant screen filled with a sweeping shot of the prairie, obviously taken from an aircraft racing along at less than a hundred feet above the ground. While some in the audience instinctively leaned back against their seats and others closed their eyes, most were captivated as a colorful patchwork quilt of the landscape sped by below them, revealing a complex kaleidoscope of shapes and sights and shades of resplendent color. As their eyes were dazzled by this visual medley, their ears were filled with the powerful strains of inspirational music, the kind that chills the body and stirs the soul.

The music gradually built, and as it did, the scenes on the screen became even bigger and more awe-inspiring, as the camera soared and raced across the land that they all knew and loved so well. Then, as the emotional crescendo neared its climax, the camera turned skyward, and a bald eagle appeared, soaring on windswept heights. She had a sleek, dark brown body that contrasted sharply with the snow-white feathers on her head and tail, with a massive yellow beak and golden yellow eyes that flashed angry glances like lightning bolts toward the camera. And as the mighty bird climbed and rolled and dived above the windswept landscape, the music changed from instrumental to choral, and the voices of a hundred men and women could be heard singing, "America the Beautiful."

Suddenly, in a spectacular move, the eagle banked and flew directly toward the camera and just when the audience thought that it would collide with whomever it was who was filming this mighty warrior of the skies, the screen went absolutely dark and laser beams sliced through the air over the audience's heads. Without them noticing, the room had been filled with vapor, and the lasers formed the perfect, three-dimensional image of the eagle; and as everyone stared in raptured silence, the laser-generated bird swooped and dived and soared through the air of the hall. The effect was totally overwhelming: not a single neck didn't have its tiny hairs standing straight up, and twenty thousand hearts were beating as one.

The eagle made one last circle of the auditorium and appeared to fly back into the screen where it disappeared into the most spectacular sunset that any of them had ever seen. Then the giant screen faded to black. No one moved. There was absolute silence in the auditorium, except for the clearing of a thousand throats and the soft brushing of tissues against tingling cheeks.

Suddenly, a spotlight hit the podium and standing there was a tall, silver-haired man dressed in buckskin and beads, looking like a mountain man, which in another time is exactly what he would have been. A booming voice over the sound system said, "Ladies and Gentlemen, the Chairman of the Western Freedom Party and our native son, Mr. Jesse Latrobe." This time the applause would have broken sound meters if there had been any. Not only because of the love and pride that people had for this war hero, elder statesman, and true son of the West, but also because of the experience that they had just collectively been through, which had created such a pent-up level of passion and emotion within, that had it not been given vent, it would have surely consumed their very beings.

Latrobe was deeply touched as he stood there before the cheering crowd, humbled and validated at the same time. The noise continued unabated for nearly three minutes, but neither Latrobe nor the organizers of the convention cared because, after all, this was exactly the kind of reaction that they had prayed for. It would serve as a permanent foundation for the weeks and months to come. And the leaders of this new party knew it. "Thank-you. Thank-you," said Latrobe, holding his arms outstretched like the laser eagle that only moments earlier had swooped around the room. "Thank-you and good evening, my fellow citizens of the West." He made a sweeping gesture toward the screen. "Wasn't that spectacular?"

Again, applause, whistles, and shouts filled the furthermost reaches of the auditorium. He smiled and then raised his arms again. As if they were some enormous orchestra and he was their maestro, the audience immediately quieted. "We are gathered here tonight to join together in the most important cause of our lives. We stand at a crossroads in the American journey. And like that traveler in the poem by the great American poet Robert Frost, we now must take the path less traveled, and in so doing, it will make all the difference for the rest of our lives. Ladies and gentlemen, you are the modern-day sons and daughters of liberty. Upon your shoulders has fallen the mantle of responsibility to once again rise up against tyranny. Not the tyranny of a king from a far-off foreign land, but something far more evil— the tyranny of our own Federal Government and a President who would be king. A man who dwells in what was once our house. The people's house. A house that has now become an armed fortress with battlements, anti-aircraft batteries, and concrete barricades; with legions of soldiers and Secret Service agents whose sole purpose is to distance him from you. A man who would have you believe that God-fearing, law-abiding citizens who keep guns are children of the devil. A man who would have you believe that it is *our* failing and not that of the Federal Government, that has allowed criminals to roam the streets of our nation, kept there by liberal judges who have been blinded by their own reflection in the mirror of hypocrisy."

He paused to let their hearts and minds catch up with his words. Eagerly they watched him, loved him, and wanted to just be with him. Not just the thousands who stood under the same roof, but the millions who sat watching him on their BTC screens across the Heartland of America and even outside it. When he was certain that he had them where he wanted them, he lifted his arms up and placed the palms of his hands toward the audience on either side of his head.

"Ladies and gentlemen, listen." The crowd was already quiet, but many in it now even held their breath so as not to miss what he was about to say. "Listen," he said once more, and absolute silence filled the giant hall. "Do you hear it? It is the battle cry of freedom. And it says to us, 'Rise Up! Rise up and take a stand against the oppressor.' And if you do, my fellow patriots, as God is our witness, twelve months from now, and twelve times twelve months from now, you will look back and remember this minute, this hour, this night, as the defining moment in your lives. Where each of you drew a line in the sands of time and said, 'This will not stand'." He spoke the last four words slowly and with increasing intensity. The audience wanted to explode, but he wouldn't let them. By his gestures he held back the applause. He wanted them to experience an emotional orgasm, the likes of which they had never known. One that would cement their commitment to the cause and seal the fate of their enemies. And the longer he could hold it back, he knew the greater it would be. And so he continued.

"Throughout history, man has had one sacred birthright that no other man can legally, morally, or ethically take away from him. It is as fundamental to life as the food that provides sustenance to our bodies and the words of the Almighty that nourish our souls. It is more precious than gold or diamonds, and it can neither be hoarded nor traded nor spent. It was the impetus for our forefathers to set out in fragile wooden ships powered only by fickle winds across foreboding waters toward a distant land. A land of hope and promise and freedom. And generations later, for their descendants to set out again across the broad prairie in wagons powered by oxen.

"It is the most noble of causes for which one man can lay down his life for another. It is the reason brave men fought and died at places like Bunker Hill, Gettysburg, Vimy Ridge, Omaha Beach, the Chosin Reservoir, Hue, and the streets of Baghdad." As he pronounced each symbolic battle, a montage of artist's renderings and actual photographs from each war marched across the giant screen behind him, and all the while the muted sounds of the Battle Hymn of the Republic played over the auditorium's loudspeakers. "My fellow citizens, make no mistake. The enemy that we face today is no less evil and no less committed to taking away the liberties that our Founding Fathers guaranteed us in our Constitution—a noble document that those brave men crafted for all the world to see, and a document that Washington now seeks to change at the whim of a man without honor. This, my brothers and sisters, is the reason why we are gathered here tonight. It was once, is now and forever shall be, the cause of freedom. And as long as I have breath in me, and as long as these hands can hold a weapon in self-defense, then under God, with the grace of God, and by the terrible swift sword of God, we—shall—be—free!"

The audience exploded out of their seats. This time there would be no quieting them before they were ready to be quiet. Latrobe stepped away from the podium and let the audience vent their emotion. He knew exactly how long to let them go and when to cut them off—too soon would stifle the building emotion and too late would allow them to tire. Just before their hands became sore from clapping and their voices hoarse from shouting, he stepped back up at the podium, raised his arms, and signaled for their attention.

"Ladies and gentlemen. The die has been cast, and the molten metal of our souls has been poured into the new bell of liberty. All that remains now is for someone to sound it. And it is my honor, my duty, and my greatest privilege to introduce to you the man who will let the sweet sound of liberty ring out anew across the land. He is my friend. He is freedom's savior. He is your governor—Edward Morrissey!"

It took seven minutes for the auditorium to quiet down. By the time it did, there was not a dry eye in the House. Even those who were not prone to public outbursts of emotion could not help themselves. The reason was that when Morrissey stepped up to the podium, and the cameras closed in for a tight shot that was projected onto the giant screen behind the podium, for just an instant, the tall, handsome cowboy who had waited his whole life for this moment, lost control. There on the screen for all the world to see, one tiny tear streamed down across his cheek. It was a seminal moment for not only the people in that auditorium, but for the millions of Americans watching the event in their homes all across the West. And during the speech that followed, with the image of that single tear etched deeply into their hearts and souls, his audience became as one, completely in awe of the man who would lead them to glory. In simplest terms, his speech was magnificent. The perfect statement of all that was right and good about America dramatically juxtaposed against the picture that Latrobe had painted of an evil empire that now loomed on the eastern horizon. To the adulation of friend and aversion of foes, the governor that night became the very embodiment of an American icon. A modern-day Moses sent from God to save them.

Of course, it was a preposterous premise. There was no evil empire in the east. There was no Army poised to invade the west. There was only a Federal Government that was doing its best to deal with the issue of gun control, the overwhelming majority of whom wanted simply to stop the death of innocents by bullets. Nothing more. Nothing less. However, none of that mattered to the believers inside the hall and outside it. For the President of the United States had foolishly worn his pride and arrogance on his sleeve for all the world to see. In so doing, he had played the perfect foil to Morrissey. It was a tragedy in the making on a national scale.

The governor's speech started slowly, with the subtle understatement of distant thunder rumbling just over a prairie horizon. Gradually he skillfully built its tempo and theme like a farmer hurrying to finish his plowing while keeping a watchful eye toward the gathering storm clouds on the horizon. Finally, as he reached the very sum and substance of his message, his words struck the audience with the full force of the summer thunderstorm as it raced across the fertile fields of their collective imaginations. It was at once terrifying in its untamed power, exhilarating in its call to heavenly glory, and yet somehow strangely calming as its warm rain of proverbs and platitudes flooded the freshly plowed fields of their minds.

Then, with a perfect sense of timing, he finished and stepped down off the stage. As he walked through the surging crowd, they cried out his name and tried to touch him, and he knew that he had far exceeded his expectations of simply not appearing foolish. Quite the contrary, he was certain that he had scored a decisive and stunning victory for both his new party and for himself. He had elevated the matter of gun control to a whole new plateau. Instead of it being an issue of gun ownership, it was now a matter of freedom. Pure and simple. Take my gun—take my freedom. Take my freedom—take my life. Period. It was as clear as that. It was a cause for which men would willingly die. Indeed, thousands now would. And so the fuse was lit.

<u>32</u>

The Fiddler's Green Pub, Georgetown, D.C.

Mary Lou Pritchard and Jeremiah Kincaid sat in a private booth tucked in a corner of the swank Washington eatery. It was not at all unusual for senior government officials, lobbyists, and politicians to meet there for lunch, and this particular meeting drew no more attention than any other. But this was not an ordinary encounter, and the topic of conversation was far from the usual mixture of lobbying, ogling, and imbibing that was being carried on elsewhere in the restaurant. At this table, none of those activities was present, as the dead-serious expressions on their faces would have indicated to anyone who chose to look. No one did look, however, as staring at other patrons was strictly frowned upon, and the out-of-the-way location and minimal outdoor signage of the restaurant precluded patronage by few people other than Beltway insiders.

"Thank-you for coming, Mr. Speaker."

"Please call me Jeremiah."

She smiled warmly. "Thank-you. And I much prefer Mary Lou over Madam Deputy Attorney General. It's such an unwieldy title that people are already tired of me after saying it."

They both chuckled and the tension between them began to lessen. But not completely.

"How is the Attorney General doing?" asked Kincaid in a gentle tone that reflected his awareness of Greenberg's illness and Pritchard's deep feelings for her boss.

"As well as can be expected," she added, trying not to tear up. "His spirits are good."

The Speaker nodded. "Good. Please give him my best, Mary Lou."

"I will."

Then he added with equal sensitivity, "How are *you* doing?"

She shrugged, "I've been better, Jeremiah."

"For what it's worth, I think you and the Department of Justice are doing an excellent job."

She smiled weakly. "Thank-you. That means a lot coming from you. But judging by your colleagues across the aisle, and their outspoken supporters in the entertainment industry, the Department of Justice is single-handedly the cause of the rising tide of violence in America."

"I make it a practice never to listen to criticism that emanates from ignorance, and both the groups you mention, especially the latter, have their fair share of that."

She nodded and said, "You know what really bothers me about actors, or at least a radical, outspoken few among them? It's that I graduated at the top of my class from Harvard Law School, and yet the media gives greater credit to the opinions of someone who never even graduated from high school, and who makes their living by mouthing the words of others. It's as if society values the thoughts of a ventriloquist's dummy more highly than those of an educated man."

Kincaid listened patiently and then asked, "More to the point, what does the President think? About the job you and the department are doing, that is?"

"Apparently he's satisfied." She added, "With both."

"Good. Very good." He paused then said, "But somehow, Mary Lou, I don't think you asked to see me to discuss the gun bill."

"No. You're right. I want to talk about the attempted assassination of the President at Walter Reed Hospital."

The Speaker's eyes narrowed and his jaw muscle flexed. "I see." He paused and then asked, "Have you had any luck tracking Thomas Porter?"

Pritchard paused before answering, as if deciding exactly what to say. "No. He got away cleanly. The jet he chartered landed in Chicago, and the crew said they didn't know who he was or where he went—and we believe them."

Without saying another word, the Speaker reached into his jacket and pulled out a letter addressed to the Attorney General. "Here." As he handed it to her, he said softly, "In it I confirm what I think you already know; namely, that Thomas Porter, the man you are pursuing, is actually my youngest son, T.J. Kincaid."

She was visibly relieved that he told her before she confronted him with it. She took the envelope and nodded sadly.

The Speaker continued. "For your information, I plan to address the nation on this matter. My chief of staff has arranged for air time on national television tomorrow night."

"I'm so sorry, Jeremiah."

"I want to assure you that I don't know where my son is right now," he added. "I have not talked with him in nearly seven years."

"We know."

He sat there in silence for a few moments and then asked, "How did you find out?"

As diplomatically as possible, and with great empathy, she told him what the Department of Justice knew about T.J.'s involvement with the tragedy in the Bitterroot Mountains of Idaho, and his actions at the hospital. When she finished, the waiter came to clear the table. They both sat there quietly as he did.

After he took their orders for coffee and left, the Speaker looked at her and said, "I appreciate the sensitivity that you and the Attorney General have shown my family by coming to me in this manner," said Kincaid in a solemn tone of voice.

"And I appreciate your honesty and candor, Mr. Speaker."

He shook his head. "I should have come to you long ago and for that I am embarrassed and contrite. Ever since we first saw the pictures of T.J. standing on that mountain, my wife and I have been heartsick."

Pritchard nodded and said softly, "Of course, I understand. And since you had no contact with him, you were under no legal obligation to come forward."

"Perhaps not. However, I was under a *moral* obligation to do so, and as such, you should know that in my television address to the nation, I will resign my position as Speaker and my seat in the House."

"Oh no," she gasped. "Are you sure that's the right thing to do?"

"Yes. It is the *only* thing to do."

She hesitated. She had to say what came next, but it obviously troubled her to do so. "Jeremiah, now that I have met with you, I will have to tell the President about your son."

"Yes. Of course."

"I doubt that he will keep it a secret for very long. He may even announce it before your television address tomorrow night."

"I understand."

She thought about it for a moment and then said, "What time is your address?"

"9:00 p.m."

She thought about it for a moment and then said resolutely, "All right. The President will learn about it at precisely 8:45 p.m."

"Won't that get you and the Attorney General in trouble?"

"Perhaps, but even if it does, a President gets the respect he deserves."

"Mary Lou, if I can ever return the courtesy and the kindness that you have shown me, please let me know."

"I will. I promise."

They fell silent again as their waiter returned with the bill, which Kincaid took.

After the waiter left, Pritchard asked, "Did you watch the coverage of the Western Freedom Party's convention last night?"

"No. Did you?"

She smiled, "Of course."

He nodded knowingly. "That was a silly question."

"We're taking them very seriously."

"I know Ed Morrissey well, and he should never be taken any other way."

"How far do you think he'll go with this?"

"It depends on how far the President goes."

Pritchard nodded. "That's not good."

"I know."

She looked at her watch and said, "I must go."

"Me too."

They stood up.

"I have truly enjoyed meeting you, Jeremiah," she said, extending her hand. Mary Lou Pritchard had a firm handshake, the kind that men never expect from a woman but find strangely appealing.

"The feeling is mutual."

She smiled, but it quickly vanished. "Jeremiah."

"Yes?"

"Please be careful. These are dangerous times."

"I hear you. You do the same."

"I will. Goodbye. And good luck tomorrow night."

"Thank-you. Goodbye, Mary Lou."

The meeting was over. The Speaker of the House of Representatives and the Deputy Attorney General of the United States of America went back to doing what they were paid to do—serving the people of their great land. But on that day, a friendship had been formed that would prove to be a beacon in the darkness to come.

33

The Capitol, Washington, D.C.

The Speaker of the House, Jeremiah Kincaid, sat in his chair in the overheated and overcharged House chamber. Despite the bitter cold of a March wind that howled outside the Capitol, not one of the seats was empty in the House nor in the visitor's gallery. The Speaker brought down his gavel loudly and said, "The Chair recognizes the honorable member from Texas, Mr. Pundy Parsons."

A heavy man with a large head and eyebrows that had been permanently joined at birth, wearing a two thousand dollar suit and equally expensive cowboy boots, strode down the aisle and stood behind the podium. He was perspiring profusely, and he repeatedly wiped his brow with a large, red-white-and-blue bandanna. He politely acknowledged the Speaker with a genuine smile, "Thank-you, Mr. Speaker," and then turned to face his colleagues.

"Honorable members, my colleague from the great state of California has just made a passionate plea to you all in favor of the President's proposed gun ban. It is a shame that his logic was not as strong as the emotion in his voice. But, then again, a lack of reason seems to be a common characteristic among those who support this unconstitutional bill. But decibels do not make up for substance. And bravado is no substitute for brains."

There was a murmuring across the Democratic side of the aisle.

"My esteemed colleague told you that eighty percent of the students who take guns to school and murder their classmates or teachers have played video games involving guns. He made this statement in an authoritative fashion, despite the fact that he has absolutely no credentials in the field of child psychology, nor has he had any children, nor is he ever likely to have any."

A loud voice rang out from the Democratic side of the House, "How dare you!" It was that of Representative Crane of California.

Speaker Kincaid was also obviously displeased with Parsons' comment, and he rapped his gavel harshly on the desk, "The honorable member would be well-advised to stay within the bounds of decorum."

Parsons looked at the Speaker with a look of feigned innocence, "It was a simple statement of fact, Mr. Speaker. The member himself has made no secret of his sexual orientation."

There was a tittering in the visitor's gallery.

"Mr. Speaker, I demand to have the floor!" shouted Crane.

"Sit down, Mr. Crane." Kincaid stared at Parsons and spoke with measured anger, "Mr. Parsons. I will not warn you again."

"Very well, Mr. Speaker," said Parsons. He looked toward the back of the chamber, and said, "I was simply going to say that my opponent would have the American people believe that there is a direct causal relationship between some harmless arcade game and cold-blooded murder. However, using the same flawed logic, I would submit that because eighty percent of all murderers nursed as infants, we should pass a Constitutional amendment banning breast feeding."

The gavel slammed down hard as the Speaker's patience ran out. "Mr. Parsons, that is enough!"

Parsons shrugged and stepped down. "I yield the remainder of my time to the Chair." He gathered up his papers and walked back down the aisle. As he passed the row where Crane was sitting, he muttered loud enough for all those nearby to hear, "Of course, a woman's breast is a foreign and frightening land to some men."

It was more than Crane could take. He literally launched himself out of his seat and stumbled past his fellow members into the aisle, where he took a wild swing at Parsons, screaming, "You bastard!"

Parsons reached out and grabbed Crane's fist in one hand and the member's lapel in his other hand, and the two of them began what the talking heads would later refer to as the summo shuffle.

"Order—I will have order!" shouted Kincaid.

Finally, Crane was able to pull one arm free, and he managed to land a glancing blow on Parsons' nose, much to the horror of the other members and the amusement of the gallery. Before Parsons could retaliate, the sergeant at arms assisted by several others pulled the two men apart.

By then, the Speaker had left his dais and walked down onto the floor. He strode purposefully up to the tight knot of men who were gathered around the two combatants. As the members saw him coming, the crowd quickly parted and Kincaid took a few more steps forward, placing himself right in the face of the two men.

"You are both a disgrace to this House."

"I'm sorry, Mr. Speaker," said Crane, "But I demand satisfaction."

"This is not two hundred years ago, Mr. Crane, and you are not Aaron Burr. Now, calm down." Kincaid then looked directly at Parsons and said, "You will apologize to Mr. Crane, and you will do it now." By his tone and manner, Kincaid made it clear that Parsons had no other choice but to comply.

Parsons, still holding his bloody nose, nodded. He then turned to Crane and said without any attempt at sincerity, "I'm sorry."

Crane stared at him coldly.

"Mr. Crane," said the Speaker.

Crane nodded grudgingly. "Apology accepted."

Parsons then looked at the Speaker and said, "Mr. Speaker, if we allow the President's bill to pass, then what we have seen here today is only a tiny portend of things to come."

"It needn't be," replied Crane, his voice trembling. "Not if men of reason and common decency prevail."

"And they will, if I have anything to do with it," said Kincaid. "Now, both of you, sit down and conduct yourselves in a manner befitting this House, or you will suffer the consequences."

The two men nodded, and the Speaker walked back to the podium. As he went, every pair of eyes in the chamber was upon him. No one spoke. There would be time for talk later. For now, there was only a haunting silence and a palpable sadness in that hallowed hall.

JEREMIAH KINCAID sat with his oldest son, Colonel Jake Kincaid, in the House dining room. The father's weariness was matched only by the tension on the son's face. Jake was dressed in his uniform with ribbons that bore silent testimony to his bravery on the field of battle. But nothing on the crisp olive jacket could capture the conflict within.

The Speaker was eating a bowl of soup. Jake wasn't eating at all.

"I understand that you had to break up a fight on the House floor today," said the younger Kincaid, trying to make conversation.

"The President's proposed legislation is bringing out the worst in all of us."

"Are you going to be all right through all of this?"

"I'll be fine, Jake, but can we please change the subject?"

"Yes, sir."

There was an awkward pause. When he was a little boy, Jake had always had difficulty talking with his father. It hadn't gotten any easier with the passing years. Jake knew his father didn't intend to be so curt and so tough. It was just the way he was. He had learned to accept it long ago, unlike his brother, who never could.

The Speaker studied his son's face. "What's the matter?"

"Nothing."

"Are you sure?"

"I'm sure."

"Why aren't you eating?"

"I'm not hungry."

"You look like you've lost weight—"

"I'm fine dad."

"Suit yourself." He went back to eating his soup.

To anyone watching a replay of the scene without the benefit of sound, it would have seemed like an interview between strangers. It was hard being the son of a great man. Very hard. And what made it all the harder was that most great men don't know it.

"Thank-you for letting me stay at your apartment."

"Glad I could help save you some money."

Jake hesitated. "Dad, I want you to know that I haven't had a drink in weeks." To a more approachable father, the statement would have prompted a loving and sympathetic statement of support for a son who had struggled with alcohol throughout his adult life. But it was not to be.

His father looked up from his meal, "It's one battle that you are going to have to fight alone, son." Jeremiah Kincaid loved Jake deeply, but he had never been able to show it. At least not in ways that his son could understand and accept.

A few minutes passed, and finally Jeremiah asked, "How are things at the Pentagon?"

"Fine. I'm almost finished the first draft of my report."

"On the readiness of new Abrams M1A3 Main Battle Tank?"

Jake shook his head in amazement. "How did you know that? It's top secret."

Jeremiah smiled for the first time during lunch. "I have a friend on the Armed Services Committee whose idea of keeping a secret is to tell only one person at a time."

Jake laughed. "I guess he figures you're a safe risk."

"I believe that's an oxymoron."

"You mean like an honest politician?"

"Or a peacetime soldier?"

"Touché," replied Jake.

Both men chuckled. It seemed to break the tension at the table.

Jake continued, "Well, for whatever reason, the Army brass seems interested in my viewpoint, and I'm grateful for that, because I believe there is a potentially fatal flaw hidden in the tank's target recognition software."

"Is it fixable?"

"Yes, sir. But first I've got to convince them it needs fixing."

"Since the M1A3 program is hundreds of millions over budget already, that's not going to be easy."

"I've already discovered that, sir. There's a colonel on the general's staff by the name of Pritchard, who doesn't seem to like what I've got to say."

"I recently met his wife."

"The Deputy Attorney General?"

"Yes. From what I understand, the M1A3's been Pritchard's baby ever since it was on the drawing boards, so what did you expect?"

"I don't know. I think I'd rather face the enemy without rather than within."

"The mantel of leadership is a heavy one. You simply have to deal with it or pass it to someone who can."

Jake nodded and went back to fiddling with his food. He looked up and asked, "Has there been any word on T.J?"

A wave of sadness passed across the older man's face, like a cloud across a furrowed field. "No."

"Are you going to be all right, dad?"

"I'll be a lot better when your mother can rejoin me here in Washington."

"When will that be?"

"Soon. Joanna is almost back on her feet. The divorce took a lot out of her."

"I know."

"Is there anyone new in your life?"

"No," said Jake looking down at the table.

His father studied his son. "Well, I'm sure one day you'll find the right person to share your life, like I did."

Jake brought the subject back to his brother. "Do you think anyone knows about T.J?"

"Yes, but it doesn't matter. After tonight, the whole world will know."

Jake was shocked. "Tonight! What's happening tonight?"

"I am going to go on national television and admit that Thomas Porter is my son—and your brother." It was clear to the Speaker that this news upset his son. "What's wrong, son?"

"I guess I'm a little surprised that you didn't tell me this sooner."

His father nodded and said, "You're right. I didn't decide to do it until after the incident at Walter Reed. And since then, I have changed my mind at least a dozen times."

Jake softened, "I just wish that you had included me in your deliberations."

It was at that point that the Speaker realized he had made a mistake in not doing so. It was a mistake that he had made often in his life, and each time only served to widen the emotional gap between them. He was about to apologize when Governor Edward Morrissey walked up to the table and politely interrupted father and son. "Excuse me, Mr. Speaker."

Jeremiah looked up and smiled at the governor, but like most such smiles inside the Beltway, it was forced, and it showed. "Hello, Edward. I believe you know my son, Jake?"

The governor reciprocated the smile in like fashion, and said, "Yes, of course. Everyone knows Colonel Kincaid. A war hero and patriot."

Jake stood up and shook the governor's hand. "Thank-you, sir," he said, obviously wanting to change the subject.

The governor turned to the Speaker, "My office told me you were looking for me."

"Yes. I called Boise this morning and was surprised to learn that you were in town."

"I flew here right after our convention ended. Did you watch it?"

Clearly uncomfortable with the question, the Speaker replied, "I'm afraid I missed it."

"Too bad. I think you would have been impressed. We have tremendous support and it's growing every day."

"I know you do. Actually, that's what I wanted to discuss with you, Edward."

"I expected as much," said the governor without emotion. "And there is something that I need to discuss with you, as well."

"Won't you sit down?" said the elder Kincaid.

The governor looked at Jake and then back at the Speaker. "Perhaps now would not be an opportune time."

"Nonsense. Sit down. There are no secrets at this table."

Jake ignored his father's comment. He was bitterly disappointed by how his father had handled the decision to go public with T.J., and at that moment, all he wanted to do was put some distance between himself and his father. The appearance of the governor provided just such an opportunity. Before the governor could say anything further, Jake stood up and said to his father, "I have to be getting back to the Pentagon. I'll call you later." With that, he left.

The Speaker knew he had hurt his eldest son's feelings, but he would have to deal with it later. He turned back to Morrissey and said, "Please, Edward, sit down."

The governor hesitated, then did. "Very well, Mr. Speaker, what did you want to talk about?"

The Speaker's face became serious. "I need your help, Edward, in building support for my amendment to the President's bill in the Heartland."

"You know I can't do that."

"Why not?"

"Because the bill does not deserve to survive, with or without amendment. I will not compromise my principles."

"Compromise is the way of Washington, Edward, and you know that."

"Yes, Jeremiah, but with this President, give and take means you give and they take."

"As much as you and I may disagree with his policies, I believe that he is sincere in his efforts to save our country from any more blood being spilled by gunfire."

"Just like he did in the Bitterroots?" asked the governor.

"The President has accepted full responsibility for that tragic mistake, Edward."

"With all due respect, Jeremiah, the man doesn't know the meaning of the word."

"He is still the President," said Jeremiah, "and as such, he deserves respect."

"Respect has to be earned."

"I agree, and if I have earned even a modicum of your respect over the past twenty years that we have known each other, then I'm asking for your help to hold this country together."

The governor didn't answer at first. Then he said softly, "I'm afraid there is nothing I can do. The matter is out of my hands, and whether or not you chose to accept it Jeremiah, it's out of yours as well."

The Speaker shook his head sadly, "Perhaps. But I'm not prepared to give up yet." The governor smiled weakly. The Speaker continued, "But there is one thing you can do."

"Yes?"

"Please tell Jesse Latrobe to tone down his rhetoric."

"Jesse is his own man."

"He is also his own worst enemy."

"How so?"

"If Jesse truly wants to be heard, then he should stop throwing gasoline on the President's campaign fire."

"He would say that it's too late for talk."

"No, it's not—but it soon will be."

The governor sighed. "With all due respect, Jeremiah, you're wrong. And even if the gun bill passes, it will never make it to a ratification vote by the states."

"What do you mean?"

The governor shook his head. "I have already said too much. Suffice to say that the actions of the many will overshadow the words of the few."

"If you are referring to your colleagues who are threatening to act in defiance of the Congress, they're so full of wind that their ears must whistle."

The governor stared the Speaker directly in the eyes and said, "That wind just might be a gathering storm, Jeremiah."

The Speaker paused and then said, "I take it then that you will not help me."

"I'm sorry, Jeremiah. As God is my witness, I wish you—I wish *all* of us well. But I am afraid we are indeed heading into darkness." The governor fell silent.

"I thought you said there was something you wished to discuss with me?" asked Jeremiah.

The governor hesitated.

"Please go ahead."

The governor looked around the room to be certain that no one was within ear shot. Then he looked directly at the Speaker and said, "It's about your son."

"Jake?"

"No—T.J."

The Speaker's face clouded over. "What about him?"

The governor then described how he had discovered Thomas Porter's real identity; how T.J. had been hiding at the Wolf River Club until recently, with his knowledge and approval; and how he had escaped and disappeared until the incident at Walter Reed. After he was finished, Jeremiah looked him straight in the eyes and asked, "Do you know where he is now?"

"No. But I can tell you this, Jeremiah, if he comes to me for help again, I will provide it."

"He is a wanted felon."

"To my people he is as much of a hero as his brother, Jeremiah."

"He is anything but and quite frankly, I'm not pleased that you have helped him."

Morrissey couldn't believe what he was hearing. "My God, Jeremiah, he is your flesh and blood."

The Speaker looked down at the table and then back up at the governor. "He stopped being my son seven years ago, and everything that he has done during the past six months has only served to separate us further."

296

The governor paused and then added, "You are wrong, Jeremiah. Dead wrong. But for what it's worth, I have no intention of going public with this matter."

"That's very gracious of you, Edward, but it's academic, as I intend to address the nation on television tonight and reveal the truth."

"As you choose. I only hope that one day, you will see the error of your ways."

To which Kincaid quickly replied, "And I you."

With that, the governor stood up and walked away without saying goodbye.

FIFTEEN MINUTES LATER, Jeremiah Kincaid ambled back to his office in the Rayburn Building. As he entered the outer office, he was met by one of his administrative assistants, who were herding a group of eager and excited constituents from his home district. It was the last thing he wanted to do at that moment, but true to the form that had gotten him reelected ten times, he smiled politely and graciously posed for the obligatory photographs. After it was done, he entered the sanctuary of his inner office and closed the door behind him. He walked over to a large cherry credenza, stooped down, and opened a drawer. He reached inside and pulled out a framed photograph. Then he closed the drawer, walked to his desk, and sat down heavily in his chair. He placed the photo on the desk, in front of him and leaned back with his eyes fixed firmly upon it. The photograph was a picture of himself, T.J., and Jake in happier times that seemed so very long ago.

ACROSS THE STREET from where the Speaker sat alone in his office, Representative Pundy Parsons walked briskly out of the Capitol, into the bright spring sunshine, and down the front steps. He was accompanied by two of his fellow right-wing members of the House.

"You're going to have quite a shiner there, Pundy, my boy," laughed one of the colleagues, a red-headed man.

"Yeah, well that fag from the land of fruits and nuts is just lucky that the Speaker stepped in when he did," groused Parsons, as he lightly touched his bruised and swollen nose.

297

"I'd be careful not to get on the wrong side of Jeremiah Kincaid if I were you, Pundy," cautioned the taller of the two men, following Parsons down the steps.

"Jeremiah Kincaid's power and influence is greatly overrated, my friend," said Parsons.

"Pundy is right," added the red-headed man. "If Kincaid doesn't stop trying to please everyone, he will end up pleasing no one."

"Somehow I doubt that the Speaker spends much time worrying about pleasing anyone," answered the tall man.

Just as the three men neared the bottom of the steps, Representative Crane stepped out from around the side of the sweeping staircase and approached the group.

"Oh brother, here comes your boyfriend, Pundy," snickered the red-headed man.

Parsons stopped abruptly as did the other two men. Crane walked up to them without speaking. He was wearing his overcoat and had his left hand buried deeply in the side pocket.

"What can we do for you, Mr. Crane?" asked Parsons with a smug self-satisfied look on his portly face.

Crane didn't answer. He simply pulled his hand out of his pocket. To everyone's horror, in it was a gun—a .38 special, double action revolver. Without hesitation, Crane leveled the weapon directly at Parson's head. As he did, the sun glinted off the shiny barrel and temporarily blinded the doomed man.

"Oh my God!" said his tall colleague.

"In the name of God, please don't!" screamed Parsons.

But it was too late. Crane's finger squeezed the trigger twice in rapid succession, and both of the bullets found their mark. The back of Parson's head erupted in a shower of fine red mist and scrambled gray matter. As the others watched in silent horror, the portly man from Texas crumbled to the sidewalk and lay completely still. Immediately, a dark red pool spread out across the dry, dusty sidewalk.

For an instant, nobody did anything. They remained motionless in various stages of stoop and cringe, as if they were marionettes under the control of some giant puppeteer who had simply drifted off to sleep in mid-performance. However, the sound of gunfire on the steps of the Capitol had not gone unnoticed, and soon three uniformed police officers raced up to the scene with their weapons drawn.

"Drop it!" one of them shouted to Crane, who stood there staring down at his victim.

"I said drop, it now!" screamed the officer, pointing his weapon at Crane. The others followed suit, and Parsons' two friends slowly edged away from the gunman.

But the third-term congressman from San Francisco didn't do as he was told. Instead, he slowly lifted his hand and placed the gun barrel into his mouth.

"Oh no!" gasped the tall man. But too late.

The weapon fired for the third and last time. This time the sound was muffled, but the effect was the same. More red spray. More gray matter. And another body crumbled onto the well-worn steps of that magnificent white building that stood as a testimonial to the rule of reason and preservation of the Republic.

<u>34</u>

Bluewater Wildlife Refuge, Maryland

The great blue heron stood patiently in the shallows near the old wooden dock, watching for the tiny flashes of silver that would trigger the sudden unbending of its neck and the plunging of its head and spear-like beak into the water. It was the luminescence of the light bulb in the rusty metal bracket on the end of the dock that was luring tiny fish to their doom inside the bill of the stately bird. The heron was a full-grown male, standing nearly three and a half feet high, with a white head and a black stripe that extended back from its yellow eyes to slender black plumes. Its back was a pale blue and its breast was white with streaks of black, but in the flickering light on the dock, the bird appeared to be a ghost in several shades of gray. It was hungry after having watched over its young all day, and now that its mate had taken over that duty, the male methodically went about fulfilling his role as a link in the middle of the food chain. As it stood there in the semi-darkness, it paid no attention to the two dark shapes, one human, the other canine, sitting motionless on a bench in the shadows where the dock met the shore.

Suddenly the headlights of a car pierced the night and swung out across the waters of the bay, as the vehicle pulled into the dirt driveway beside the cottage that squatted fifty yards up a slight incline from the dock. Its high beams hesitantly probed the darkness, as if reaching for something—something that lay just beyond the margins of the light—something frightening and mysterious. Then, as abruptly as they appeared, the lights went out, plunging the entire scene into darkness once more. Instantly, the great bird spread its wings and issued a dull, guttural cry; then it leapt into the night air and was gone.

The figure sitting at the end of the dock stood up. The dog jumped off the bench onto the ground, and together they headed up the path toward the car, whose lone occupant had just stepped out of it. The dog yelped excitedly, and he reached the car first.

"Chadrian. Is that you?" asked Gordon, as he reached down and patted the dog. He then squinted toward the figure silently approaching him. There was no answer and Gordon called out again, this time with rising tension in his voice, "Chadrian?—quit fucking around!"

Again there was no answer, and just as Gordon was about to slide back into the car, Chadrian stepped into the glow of the car's inside dome light. In one hand was a rugged compound bow, and on his back lay a quiver of long, silver arrows with serrated, razor heads. Attached to the bow was a spool with fishing line, and in the other hand he held a huge Striped Bass.

"You scared the shit out of me," exclaimed Gordon when he saw that it was Chadrian.

"Be quiet. You will disturb the heronry," said Chadrian harshly.

"Who are you talking to? Me or the dog?"

"Both," growled Chadrian.

The puppy quieted down immediately.

"Where did you get the puppy?" asked Gordon in a softer voice.

"From a friend," said Chadrian coldly.

"What's his name?"

"Danny Boy."

"I didn't know you were Irish," said Gordon with a smirk.

"I am everything and nothing," replied Chadrian, staring into Gordon's eyes, which made him squirm.

Gordon's smile vanished. "It was just a little joke. What's got you so uptight?"

"You," answered Chadrian. "Now let us go into the house and get this over with."

Together the three of them headed toward the cottage.

"What the hell is a heronry anyway?" asked Gordon, looking over his shoulder into the darkness.

"Look it up," said Chadrian, as he stepped up onto the wooden verandah.

"I thought you couldn't own land in a national wildlife refuge?"

"You can not. The boundary of the refuge is a hundred yards over that way." He pointed off to the right into the darkness. Getting back to business, he asked, "Did you bring the money?"

"Of course."

"Lucky you."

"What if I hadn't?"

"How long can you hold your breath?" said Chadrian, matter-of-factly. He opened the front door and disappeared into the house.

Gordon had no comeback. He knew when to be quiet. He followed Chadrian into the cottage. When he got inside, he looked around the great room and was surprised to see how tastefully it was furnished and decorated.

Chadrian noticed, "Not what you expected?"

Gordon looked at him with a new appreciation and said, "No. Not exactly."

"It never is," said Chadrian with an sly smile. He strode across the room into the adjoining kitchen and tossed the fish into the black porcelain sink, where it began to flop around.

Gordon followed him. "Aren't you going to put it out of its misery?"

Chadrian gave him a cold stare, and then to Gordon's horror, he picked it up, placed the fish in his mouth, and with his teeth clamped right behind the head, he crushed the spine with a sharp, short bite. The animal quivered violently once and became still.

"Jesus saves."

Gordon jumped. "What in the hell was that?" He looked around the room but saw nothing to explain the sound.

"Well said." Chadrian smiled and walked over to a large domed shape, off which he pulled a quilted cover revealing a parrot in an ornamental cage.

"The Lord is my shepherd," the bird squawked.

"This is Gideon. He belonged to a preacher, which explains his rather limited vocabulary. I am trying to teach him to stop saying that odious name."

The expression darkened on Gordon's face. "Don't tell me you delivered a package to a preacher?" asked Gordon using the vernacular for murder.

"No. I delivered one *for* him."

"You murdered someone for a preacher?" Gordon asked incredulously.

Chadrian smiled, "Yes. I terminated a fifty-six-year-old congressman who was sleeping with the preacher's twenty-one-year-old daughter. She had been an intern in his Washington office before I converted him into fish food," he added with a smile.

A look of recognition spread over Gordon's face. "You mean that was you when they found that Representative from California floating face down in the Chesapeake last summer?"

"Yes."

"Jesus saves," added the parrot to the conversation.

Chadrian frowned.

"But I thought they ruled it an accidental drowning."

"It was. I accidentally held him under water too long."

"You are too much," Gordon chuckled. "But tell me, how could the preacher afford your delivery charge?"

"He could not. I did it pro bono. He gave me the parrot to thank me."

"The Lord is my shepherd," the bird squawked again.

Gordon shook his head and sat down.

CHADRIAN STOKED THE FIRE in the pot-bellied wood stove that sat in one corner of the kitchen and threw in another log. The fire crackled as he closed the door. "I love a fire on a cool night. In fact I love a fire on any night." He returned to his chair and sat down with the dog at his feet.

Gordon took a sip out of a mason jar filled with bourbon and kept reading a report that he held in his other hand. Finally, he finished and looked up, "This is fucking terrific. Absolutely fucking terrific! Thomas Porter, that filthy-fucking-rich traitor, who led all those men up onto that mountain, is none other than the Speaker of the House of Representative's son. What a hypocrite Jeremiah Kincaid is. A fucking hypocrite."

"That word does not improve with use, Mr. Gordon."

"What word?"

Chadrian did not answer.

"You mean fucking?"

Chadrian still did not answer.

Gordon shrugged. "Whatever. How did you ever find all this out? I mean, I asked you to get dirt on the Speaker, but this is fuck...I mean, *frigging* terrific. In one fell swoop, you not only got me what I needed, but you solved the mystery of Porter's identity. It's amazing."

Chadrian eyed him coldly. "Yes. It is."

"But how did you do it?"

A wry smile appeared on Chadrian's face. "Simple. To get the father, I went after his prodigal son, T.J., who, as you know, mysteriously disappeared over seven years ago. I obtained his prep-school graduation photograph off the internet and took it to Berkeley, which was one of the many universities that he attended. There, I found someone who recognized the picture but knew him not as T.J. Kincaid, rather as Thomas Porter. From there it was a simple matter to search the university records and discover that there had been a student named Thomas Porter enrolled at the same time as T.J. Kincaid. Apparently he died of AIDS during his first year and after that, Kincaid became Porter."

"So the little son of a bitch stole some poor dead kid's identity?"

"No. He bought it from the parents of the real Thomas Porter, who were struggling with medical bills after the death of their son. Both parents died several years ago, but I tracked down the doctor who had treated the boy, and he told me everything I needed to know."

Gordon's face tensed. "Don't tell me that you killed him afterwards—"

"All right, I will not."

"Fuck," said Gordon. "I mean shit."

Chadrian glared at him.

"You are too much, Stefan. A professional killer who doesn't swear." He reached inside his pocket and handed Chadrian a fat envelope.

Chadrian took it and laid it on a table beside his chair. "Are we done?"

Gordon stood up and said, "Yes. We are."

"Good," said Chadrian, also getting up out of his chair.

"Aren't you going to count the money?"

Chadrian looked at him with a cold smile and said, "There is no need. The first time you cheat me will be your last. You can tell that to your boss, too."

"The Secret Service would have something to say about that. At least as far as my boss is concerned."

"Just like they did with Thomas Porter at Walter Reed?" Chadrian said with a chuckle.

"They stopped him."

"No, Mr. Gordon, they did not. Porter aborted the mission himself. If he had not, everyone in that room would have been wearing a little memento of the President. Of course, it would have started to smell after a few days."

Gordon paused before answering. "Do you know something about the hospital incident that you're not telling me? If you do, you had better not fuck with me."

Chadrian stood up, took a step toward Gordon and then looked him directly in the eyes and said, "What did you say?"

"Jesus saves. Jesus saves," said the parrot, obviously getting agitated by the tension in the room. Chadrian flashed an angry look at the parrot and the animal instantly was silenced.

Gordon backed away and said, "Relax. I simply wanted to know if you knew anything about it, that's all. No need to get all hot and bothered."

Chadrian stood there for a moment and then slowly, a smile slipped across his lips like a tear in a silk dress. "No. I do not know any more than you do. But I will tell you this. He had professional help."

"What are you talking about?" asked Gordon.

"I am talking about the explosive that was used in the cast Porter wore. It employed leading-edge technology developed by the Chinese, and it is only by pure luck that the head of the country still has his head. You can be sure whoever provided Mr. Porter that cast are not the kind of people who will miss the next time."

Gordon thought about it for a moment and then answered, "Are you telling me that there's a conspiracy to assassinate President Webster?"

Chadrian shrugged. "I would not stand too close to him in a crowd, if I were you. Now go away before I get tired of you. I do not think Danny Boy likes you."

Gordon shook his head slowly and said sarcastically, "So this is what our friendship has come to?"

Chadrian looked at him and said, "We were never friends, Mr. Gordon. We just killed people together, and only a sick human like you would consider that friendship."

"I wasn't the one who killed that watchman."

"Yes, you were. Because if it had not been for you, he would still be alive."

"Whatever," said Gordon with an uncaring shrug. It was time to leave, and Gordon knew it. He started for the door when the sound of his PTC pierced the silence.

"Maddun, could you please pick me up a woman on your way back to the White House?" said Chadrian mockingly. "Make sure she is pretty and preferably an aspiring starlet."

Gordon reached for the telcom and muttered to himself, "Fuck you." He flipped it open and said, "Yes, Mr. President." He paused, and his eyes widened. "When?" He listened intently for a few minutes and then said, "Yes, sir." He hung up and said, "Do you have a BTC?"

Chadrian pointed toward a small monitor sitting on a bookcase.

"Does it work?"

"No. I use it as a paperweight."

"You know what I meant," said Gordon, hurrying over to turn it on. "What kind of reception do you get way out here?"

"Every channel there is."

"Of course."

"Did you and your boss get a sudden urge to watch reruns of his latest speech?"

Gordon switched on the set, and the picture of the pressroom at the Capitol appeared on the screen. "The Speaker of the House is about to address the nation."

Chadrian sneered and said, "And you did not know about it?"

Gordon shook his head no and sat down.

"You guys really are amateurs." He laughed out loud, which made Danny Boy nervous, and the little dog tried in vain to climb up on the chair with his master. Chadrian reached down and picked the animal up gently. "Come on, Danny Boy. We are going to see what a real leader looks like."

"The Lord is my shepherd. Awwk. Jesus saves," shouted the parrot.

"Be quiet, Gideon," said Chadrian, and the bird did as he was told.

Gordon glanced at the bird and then back at the screen. He knew there would be hell to pay later, but for now all he could do was hope that what the Speaker was about to say wouldn't be bad for the President's legislation.

JEREMIAH KINCAID strode into the House of Representatives' press-briefing room and stood ramrod straight behind the podium. Against the backdrop of navy blue curtains, he appeared drawn and pale. He took a deep breath, straightened his shoulders, and began to talk. "My fellow Americans. Six months ago, a group of men who called themselves the Wolf River Militia illegally occupied a private gun club in the Bitterroot Mountains of Idaho—a club that had been closed by order of the Federal Government. As most of you know by now, that occupation ended tragically two months later, in a battle during which forty-nine men died." The Speaker paused and took a sip of water. By his demeanor, he was clearly nervous, which to those who knew him was unusual, for if ever there was an eloquent speaker in front of the television cameras, it was Jeremiah Kincaid.

He continued, "The leader of that group was a man known to you as Thomas Porter. During the occupation, his face was frequently seen on your BTC screens as he used the media to plead his case against gun legislation. And then, less than a week ago, that same young man was implicated in an assassination attempt on the life of the President. Mercifully, it failed." He paused and took another sip of water, then looked directly into the cameras. "It is my sad duty to confess to you tonight that Thomas Porter is not that man's real name. His name is Thomas Johnston Kincaid, or T.J., as his family knows him. He is my youngest son." There was a gasp in the briefing room. He paused again and then continued, "Seven years ago, T.J. and I had a terrible fight. One that no man should ever have with his son. As a result, T.J. turned his back on his family and literally disappeared from our world. For years, we had no idea of where he was, or even if he was alive. And then one night, several years later, we read about a successful Silicon Valley business man named Thomas Porter, a self-made, secretive billionaire, who avoided publicity. But then, we caught a fleeting glimpse of Mr. Porter on a BTC business report, and we knew what had become of our long-lost son."

The Speaker reached down and picked up the glass of water once again. But his hands were shaking so badly, he couldn't get it up to his lips, so he placed it back down. "For years we followed his career from afar, hoping against hope that one day he would reappear at our door so that we could hold him and tell him we loved him. Unfortunately that day never came." The Speaker paused and cleared his throat. "All we knew was that he had sold his company, and again dropped out of sight. Later, we learned, as did you, that Thomas Porter was the leader of those young men up at that mountain in Idaho. Then, of course, came the appalling incident last week. First, let me assure you that I do not know the whereabouts of my son, nor have I aided him in any way in his flight from justice. But that is not the issue.

"The issue, ladies and gentlemen, is honor. There is no question that I should have told the authorities who Thomas Porter really was the moment I saw him being interviewed up on that mountain. But I did not. I wish I could give you a good reason why I did not do this. But I cannot. Given the position of trust I enjoyed over my career, it would have been the honorable thing to do. However, the sad truth is that up until this moment, I have not acted with honor. Ladies and gentlemen, make no mistake, but for honor, this would not be the great land that it is, and the great land that it will always be. Therefore, it is with a heavy heart that I am submitting my letter of resignation as Speaker of the House, and announcing that I will not seek reelection this fall." There was another gasp—this time loud enough to be heard on camera.

"I hope that one day you will forgive me and understand that my judgment was clouded by emotion. It was never my intention to deceive you, the American people. My actions were guided by my heart and not my head. And the heart can be a foolish master." He paused one last time, and then summoning his last bit of strength, he said with a noticeable quiver in his voice, "As I said before, I don't know where my son is tonight. I don't know if I shall ever see him again. But to all those of you who are suffering from the anguish of fighting with a loved one, I ask you not to make the same mistake that I did. Reach out and hold onto that person very tightly, lest one night he or she walks out of your life forever." Slowly he wiped a tear from his eye and as he did, millions of others in households all across America did the same thing. He looked straight into the camera and said, "Now it is time for me to do the honorable thing and step aside. I thank-you for your support, and I pray for your forgiveness. Good night, ladies and gentlemen, and goodbye. And God bless America."

The Speaker stepped away from the podium and quickly left the room. He had walked into the room third in line for the most powerful office on the face of the earth. He walked out as just an ordinary man with extraordinary courage. Everyone who watched him go shared his pain, drew strength from his courage, and loved him all the more because of it. While neither the Speaker nor his fellow citizens could possibly know it, this would not be the end of their relationship. It was only the end of the beginning. And what a powerful beginning it had been.

STEFAN CHADRIAN sat for a moment staring at the BTC and slowly began to clap. "Now that was presidential." He got up and turned off the BTC.

Gordon, who was as pale as a ghost, said nothing.

Chadrian continued, "If you are thinking of asking for your money back, do not."

Gordon looked up at him with a vacant stare and said, "The money is the least of my worries now."

"What worries? I thought you wanted the Speaker out of the way?"

Gordon shook his head and said softly, "You don't get it, do you? He isn't going anywhere. The fucking telcoms are probably ringing off the hook right now in every congressional office. Whether he realizes it or not, the Speaker just slam-dunked the President, and everybody inside the Beltway knows it."

"I guess you had better run back up to the White House and help your boss change his boxer shorts."

Gordon momentarily lost his cool and his senses. He got out of his chair and took a step toward Chadrian. "Listen to me, asshole. I've been taking shit from you all night, and I've had it up to here. Now back off."

Chadrian stood there expressionless for an instant, and then a thin smile spread across his lips. "What do you know? The man has balls after all. The way you have been acting, I thought the President had had you castrated, but it seems not." Chadrian motioned for him to sit down. "Sit down, Maddun, and I will tell how I can help you and your boss get your bill through Congress. And all it will take is a few pounds of gold and a few ounces of lead."

Gordon didn't understand at first, but then he got it. His face contorted, "Oh no. Don't even go there."

Chadrian's eyes narrowed, "How many children were shot this year at school?"

Gordon sighed. "How the hell should I know?"

"288. Oops! I mean 289. No, make that 290."

"All right. I get your point."

"Good. And for the record, I was not proposing to do anything permanent. There are shootings and then there are shootings. Some kill, others merely cause an attitude adjustment."

"What are you talking about?"

"I am saying that a well-placed bullet will lay him low for quite a while. And by the time he is back on his feet, the anti-gun bill will have sailed through the Congress."

"But you must not kill him."

"First, Gordon, I will not do anything. You should know that by now. I only work through others. And second, your concern for his survival would be charming were it not disingenuous."

"I could care less about his survival. Wounding him will bring sympathy for our cause. Killing him just might help *his* cause."

Chadrian was amused by the other's man's logic, but then he couldn't disagree. Martyrs attract supporters; victims drive them away. "Trust me, Gordon, the Speaker will live—and wish that he had not." He added with a slick smile. "Besides, what choice do you have?"

"All right, all right. Arrange it."

Chadrian smiled but didn't answer.

"But make it look like random violence," added Gordon.

Chadrian stared at him. "Random violence?"

"Yes. I don't want the Bureau getting involved. This has got to look like your typical run-of-the-mill street crime. Period."

"You know, it is people like you who keep me in business."

"Are we done?"

"No. Not quite. We did not discuss my fee."

"A half of a million, like always."

"No. This one will cost you a million."

"What? I only asked you to shoot him, not sleep with him."

"How much are the lives of children worth to you and the President?"

Gordon shook his head. "This is turning into a fucking cottage industry with you."

"You are right—two million," said Chadrian with a smile.

"All right! All right! One million, but that's all."

"It is now up to three."

"Jesus-fucking-Christ. Two million then, and that's that."

Chadrian's expression went stone cold. He stepped over to Gordon and got in his face. "If you ever say that in my presence again, I will rip out your throat. Do you understand?"

Gordon sheepishly nodded. "You don't have to freak out over every swear word."

In a flash, Chadrian reached out with one hand, grabbed Gordon by the throat, and lifted him effortlessly off the floor, choking the breath out of him.

"Jesus saves," said the parrot. "Jesus saves."

Gordon panicked and grabbed Chadrian's hand with both of his own hands, while his feet struggled in vain to reach the floor. Just as he was about to pass out, Chadrian put him back down. Gordon made a sucking sound and then doubled over and vomited onto the floor. The dog ran over and started eating it while Chadrian stood there, watching the scene without any emotion. Finally, Gordon regained a modicum of composure and straightened up. At that point, Chadrian took a white handkerchief out of his pocket and handed it to Gordon, who took it and wiped his mouth.

When it seemed that Gordon was able to talk again, Chadrian said, "It was not the swear word that offended me."

"Then what?" whimpered Gordon.

"It was the name you used."

Gordon thought about it and then glanced at the bird and back at Chadrian. "But…"

Chadrian interrupted him. "He can say it. You cannot. Understand?"

Gordon nodded. Finished with the handkerchief, he started to hand it back to Chadrian, who wouldn't take it. Instead, Gordon stuffed it into his pocket.

"And one more thing. Do not ever come here again unless I invite you to. Ever. Do you understand?"

Gordon nodded and struggled to talk. "Next time I'll call."

"No."

Gordon looked at Chadrian with questioning eyes. "Then how can I contact you?"

Chadrian thought about it for a minute. "The White House uses 1024-bit cryptography on your extranet, is that not so?"

"Yes."

"Good. Leave me a message there."

"But to use that, I'd have to give you the codes and passphrases."

"Your point is?"

"That would give you access to the entire government's internal computer system, including Granite Shield."

"Maddun," he said, using Gordon's first name for the first time that evening, and seeming to soften his attitude toward the man he had nearly killed only moment before. "In case you have forgotten, you just hired me to arrange the shooting of the Speaker of the House of Representatives. That alone could get you fifty years in prison. And you are worried about giving me access to government electronic files?"

Gordon nodded, took out his wallet, and pulled out a small card with a hole in the center of it. "Where's you're computer?"

Chadrian got up and went into the bedroom. He returned with a very slim laptop. He booted it up and handed it to Gordon, who immediately saw that it was different from any available to the public. "Where did you get this? I thought only DHS had these," he said, referring to the equipment that was specially designed to interface with Granite Shield's quantum computer.

Chadrian slowly shook his head as if to say, "Do not ask."

"Sorry," replied Gordon. He had had enough pain for one night, and he decided not to push his luck. He placed the card into the CD-ROM drive and pressed it closed. The computer made a soft whirring sound and then stopped. Then he extracted the card and handed the computer back to Chadrian. "There. Now you and I can communicate in complete secrecy."

Chadrian took the laptop. "I understand that the Department of Homeland Security insists that these codes and pass phrases be changed frequently."

"How did you know that?"

"I know everything, Maddun," he said with a sly smile.

"But you didn't know these codes," he replied without the usual attitude in his voice.

"I do now, is that not so? Now, what about the changes?"

"I'll get you the new ones each day."

"Excellent. And I will get you your gun-control bill." Chadrian walked over and picked up the cover to the birdcage and covered it. As he did, the parrot squawked, "Jesus saves. Awwk. Jesus saves."

With that, the meeting was over. Gordon gathered himself together and headed toward the door, still rubbing his throat.

Chadrian followed him, placed his hand on Gordon's back, and said softly, "I am sorry, Maddun, that I hurt you."

Gordon looked at Chadrian and said, "Thank-you." But he knew that Chadrian didn't mean it. And he was right.

35

The White House, Washington, D.C.

Two hours after the Speaker's televised address, Arnold Greenberg stood unsteadily in the Oval Office in front of its furious occupant. The terminally ill man should have been home in bed, but he had been summoned to the White House, and it was an invitation that he couldn't ignore despite his deteriorating health. As agreed with Mary Lou Pritchard, Greenberg had intended to personally advise the President about what Jeremiah Kincaid was going to say, fifteen minutes before the Speaker went on camera. Unfortunately, on his way to the White House, he became violently ill in his limousine, and his driver had taken him directly to the hospital. Immediately upon being notified of his collapse, Pritchard called the White House and briefed the President, literally seconds before the speech began. By the time Greenberg had recovered from the incident, the Speaker had long since finished, and all that was left for him to do was go to the Oval Office and take the heat. Also present in the room were Patrick Fitzgerald and the Vice President, both of whom were seated on the yellow sofas.

"What do you mean, the Bureau hasn't gone to the Kincaid farm yet?" demanded the President of Greenberg.

Greenberg started to reply, but the President pressed on without giving him a chance. "What the hell are they waiting for? It's been two hours since the Speaker told the whole goddamned world that Thomas Porter is his son, so don't you think we might just want to go there and see if that's where he's hiding?" The President shook his head in frustration and looked at the other two men. "Jesus Christ. Am I the only one who wants this man captured?"

The Attorney General maintained his composure despite the intense verbal assault. "No, Mr. President, but we're having trouble getting a search warrant for the Kincaid farm."

"Why? He's on the FBI's most-wanted list, for God sake."

"We can't find a judge to issue the warrant, Mr. President. As a result of the Governor of Idaho's pardon of Mr. Porter, and the fact that he is a native son of Wisconsin, we've lost the cooperation of the state and local authorities."

Webster exploded again, "That's no excuse, Arnold, and you know it! Porter—damn it—I mean, Kincaid is wanted on Federal felony charges. The governor's pardon isn't worth the paper it's printed on and if the Bureau is going to let some cheese heads stonewall them, then I'll send in the goddamned Army."

The very thought of that made Fitzgerald flinch.

Greenberg continued, "Mr. President, I assure you that we're doing the best job we can. We hope to have the warrant issued within a few hours."

"Hope? Listen to me, Greenberg," the President interjected, pointing his index finger at the Attorney General and pounding the air with it. "If I wanted an Attorney General with no balls, I would fire your ass and appoint Mary Lou Pritchard as you're replacement."

Greenberg didn't say anything for a long, awkward moment. The others present could not help but feel sympathy for the beleaguered man. Finally, he spoke, and what came out of his mouth startled everyone, most especially the President. "That won't be necessary, Mr. President, because I intend to resign."

At first, the President didn't respond. He just stood there staring at Greenberg, as if trying to determine if it was a bluff. He was about to discover that it was anything but. Finally he said, "What are you talking about?"

Greenberg, summoning every vestige of the grace that had characterized his long and distinguished career, replied softly, "I have terminal prostate cancer, Mr. President, and I have been given only a few months to live." He paused and added, "However, if it meets with your approval, I would like to remain at my post until my health prohibits me from ably doing so."

The room fell deathly silent, and it was clear that the disclosure had deeply affected the President. He was not above feeling compassion. He just did it sparingly; and this was one of those occasions. His entire demeanor changed. "Arnold, I am so terribly sorry."

"That's all right, Mr. President. You had every right to be angry with me."

The President shook his head apologetically. "I would be honored to have you remain in office until you tell me you cannot."

"Thank-you, Mr. President. And may I add, sir, that when that time comes, I strongly recommend that you appoint Mary Lou Pritchard as my replacement. She is eminently qualified for the role, and you would gain broad bi-partisan support by nominating a Republican."

The President said gently, "Let's cross that bridge when the time comes, Arnold."

Greenberg started to look unsteady on his feet. Instantly the President sprang to him and placed his arm around him.

"If you will excuse me, Mr. President, I think I'd better go."

The President nodded. "Of course. Shall I get someone to assist you to your car?"

"No, thank-you, sir. I can make it on my own." Greenberg smiled weakly at him and the other men and then left the office. As he did, he held his head high, both literally and figuratively.

The President said to no one in particular, "He stood there politely taking my diatribe, while the angel of death hovers over him."

"You didn't know, Mr. President," said the Vice President.

The President sat down behind his desk. He was visibly shaken. "I am letting the Kincaid family get the better of me."

"Apparently the governor's pardon is tantamount to a cloak of invisibility, at least inside the state of Idaho's borders," said Fitzgerald.

"Inside Wisconsin also, based on what we just heard," added the Vice President.

"And probably every state in between."

"Of course the pardon's worthless."

"We know that, and you can be damned sure Morrissey and Kincaid know it, but the American people don't. From now on, anything I do to pursue the young Kincaid will be seen as being vindictive," answered Webster, shaking his head in frustration.

"Or worse," added Fitzgerald.

For a few moments, none of them spoke. Then Webster asked, "So now what, Mr. National Security adviser?"

"That depends on how we handle Governor Morrissey."

"And T.J. Kincaid," added the Vice President.

"All the more reason for you to appoint a replacement for Greenberg, sir, as quickly as possible," said Fitzgerald.

"Perhaps we should start vetting the Deputy Attorney General, Mr. President," said Knox.

Webster replied, "Is she any good?"

"Yes, sir," added Fitzgerald. "Her views on most major policy issues are only slightly to the right of yours, plus I think she can help us in other ways."

"How?"

"Well, first, she's a woman," said Fitzgerald. "Adding her voice to our call for gun control will reach out to the distaff side of the pro-gun movement and talk directly to their mothering instinct."

"That's a stretch," said the President.

"Perhaps the feminine appeal might not work, but beyond that, I have reason to believe that Pritchard has some connection with Jeremiah Kincaid."

"Sexual?" asked the President, leaning forward in his chair.

"No. It's nothing like that. The Speaker has been married for over thirty years, and there's never been even a hint of impropriety in his behavior throughout his career. I meant that Kincaid and Greenberg go back a long way, and Pritchard is extremely devoted to her boss. I think that's where the connection probably started."

The President thought about it and then said, "Okay. Begin the process of checking her out."

"Yes, sir. What do you want us to do about the search warrant for the Kincaid farm?"

"Call Pritchard and tell her to get the local FBI office out to that farm now, with or without a search warrant."

"Yes, sir."

"It will be a good test of her ability to make things happen," added the President.

The meeting was over, but the President's problems with the Kincaid clan were just beginning.

36

Rayburn Congressional Office Building, Washington, D.C.

The soon-to-be former Speaker of the House sat behind the desk in his office. He had just given the most difficult speech of his career, and he looked like it. There was a soft knock on the door, and George Ross entered the office. "I think you should see this, sir," he said. He grabbed the remote that was lying on the coffee table, pointed it at the wall-mounted BTC monitor, and tuned it to GNBC. The screen was immediately filled with the image of Sarah McGill. As soon as the Speaker saw who it was, he told George to turn up the volume.

SARAH McGILL was standing on the East lawn of the White House in a light, misting rain. She had an umbrella in one hand and a microphone in the other. Despite the gloomy and damp night, she looked her usual poised and professional self.

"What impact the Speaker's surprise announcement this evening will have upon the gun legislation is of course unclear at this point. However, despite the White House's continued outward expressions of optimism, unnamed sources inside the West Wing say that prospects for passage of the bill are about as gloomy as the weather. Apparently the intense lobbying by the President's staff and Cabinet has so far had little effect upon opponents of the bill." She paused to shift the umbrella slightly and then continued. "The question now is, will this President, who has never bothered to cultivate a rapport with the Congress, be able to use the resignation of the Speaker to help his own cause? Or will it have no impact whatsoever on how the President acts? Regardless of the course he chooses, there is no question that the political landscape has just undergone the equivalent of an earthquake registering 10.0 on the Richter scale." She paused once more for effect, the way only she could do, and then she continued in a voice as plaintive as the weather, "Tonight, ladies and gentlemen, this nation has lost one of its greatest leaders. And because of that, the course the Congress must now chart across the storm-tossed seascape of debate is a little less certain and a lot more discomforting." She hesitated then regained her composure, and closed with, "For GNBC, this is Sarah McGill reporting from the White House."

THE SPEAKER'S CHIEF OF STAFF switched off the monitor and sat down in front of the Speaker's desk. "We've got the White House on the run."

"Yes. We do. The only problem is they're running right at us."

"Even more reason for you not to step down, Mr. Speaker."

"It's a little late for that, George."

Ross got up and opened the office door. Outside the office, the sound of many ringing telcoms could be heard, and every light on the Speaker's communication's console was blinking.

"America doesn't think so, Mr. Speaker. Just listen to that." He paused to let the sound of the telcoms fill the air. "They haven't stopped ringing since you finished speaking." He closed the door and sat back down.

"No, George. It's over. I'm only sorry that it had to end like this."

"With all due respect, sir, it isn't over yet. Not for you, nor for our party, nor for the millions of Americans who believe in you," said Ross. "Truthfully, I don't think you really believe it is either."

The Speaker didn't answer. Instead he looked at his watch and asked, "What time is it? My watch seems to have stopped running."

"It's ten after ten," answered Ross.

"Damn. I was going to call home right after my speech and I completely forgot."

"Shall I get your wife for you, sir?"

"No thank-you, George. Go home. We'll talk again in the morning."

"I've got some things to finish up first, so if you need me after your call, I'll be here."

319

The Speaker nodded as his trusted colleague left the room. He pressed a key on the BTC. Within seconds, the soothing sound of Kathleen's voice filled his office. "Hello, Jeremiah," she said, obviously reading the caller ID on her end. She was talking on a telcom wall unit, but at his end, the feature was disabled as it was in all Federal buildings.

"Hi, honey," he said, with a weariness in his voice that seemed to weigh down even the telcom receiver.

"Are you all right, Jeremiah?" she asked.

"Yes. Did you see my speech?"

There was a long pause on the other end of the line.

"Kathleen?"

"Yes, Jeremiah?"

"What's the matter?"

"I wish you had talked to me about what you were going to say."

"What do you mean? You knew I was going to disclose that Thomas Porter was our son."

Again there was a pause.

"Kathleen, what's wrong?" He paused and then suddenly realized what was going on. "Oh my God! T.J.'s there, isn't he?"

Again there was silence, and finally she answered, "Yes."

The answer hit him like a body blow taking the wind right out of his lungs. He lowered the receiver for a minute and stared out the window into the darkness beyond. Then he put it back to his mouth and said, "Kathleen, what were you thinking?" Before she could answer, he added, "Don't you realize what you've done? You have made me look like a liar on national television!"

In an unsteady voice, she replied, "I am so sorry, Jeremiah. I thought that you were simply going to say that he was our son and then resign. I didn't think you would go as far as you did."

"You didn't think? Kathleen, do you know what you have done?"

There was a long pause and then she said, "Please forgive me."

He ignored her apology and instead said in a cold and angry tone, "Put him on."

"Jeremiah, I don't think you should do this over the telcom."

"Put him on right now," said Kincaid in a tone that he usually saved for his political opponents.

"Just a minute," she snapped back, more angry at herself than her husband. She knew that she had failed her husband while trying to save her son, and in the process, she had risked losing both.

There was a pause and then Jeremiah heard his youngest son say, "Hello father."

At the sound of his son's voice the Speaker's soul became a cauldron of mixed emotion. He wanted to cry out in joy and in pain; to reach through the telcom, grab his son and shake sense into him, but at the same time press him close to his chest; to scream at him but also tell him that everything was going to be all right, the way he had done so many times when he was a little boy; to thank God that the prodigal son had come home and to curse God for having given them this son in the first place. He wanted to do all these things, and he wanted to do none of them. A tiny voice deep inside told him to tell his son that he loved him. But he could not. And he did not. It would be yet another time that he pushed his son away, and it would be the last. As he had done so many times in his life, Jeremiah Kincaid spoke not from the heart but from the head, and he would regret it forever. "T.J. What have you done to us?"

"Dad. I am so very, very sorry—"

Jeremiah interrupted him, "How could you put your mother in that situation? Don't you realize how hard it would be for her to see the FBI storm into our home and to watch them cuff you and drag you out."

"Dad, please—"

"Don't you ever think about anyone except yourself?"

"Dad, I need your help."

"I will help you, but first you must get out of the house. Right away. Go to a hotel and call me. Then I will arrange to have you brought safely into custody."

"Please listen to me. No one knows that I am here. Until your speech tonight, no one even knew that I was your son."

"Damn it all, T.J., the Governor of Idaho knew. The Attorney General knew. And God only knows how many others."

There was a pause, then his son asked, "They knew before tonight?"

"Yes."

"But how could they?"

321

"It doesn't matter. Listen to me. All that matters now is for you to get out of that house and turn yourself in, and accept whatever punishment the law dictates."

There was a long silence at the other end of the telcom, and finally T.J. said, "I can't do that."

"You have no choice. You must do it, now." He waited for a response but none came. "T.J?" Still no reply. "T.J? Answer me!"

Finally, Joanna came on the line. Her voice was shallow and thready. "Daddy. It's me."

"Joanna. Where's T.J?"

"He's gone."

"What do you mean?"

"I mean he just walked out the front door."

Jeremiah sighed deeply. "Where's your mother?"

"She's upstairs crying."

"Go get her."

"No." Joanna was the only one of Jeremiah's three children who had ever been able to say that word to her father and get away with it. "Mommy said she doesn't want to talk to you right now. She'll call you in the morning."

He didn't say anything.

"Daddy..."

Finally he replied, "What?"

"I love you."

"I've got to go."

"I understand," she whispered softly, but she *didn't* understand. She had never been able to understand why it was that her father had so much difficulty with expressing emotion. It was a trait that he had used to his advantage in Congress, but it was one that had hurt him beyond measure at home.

"Goodbye, Joanna.

"Goodbye, Daddy."

He hung up and sat alone in silence. His expression was frozen, showing no emotion, in exactly the same way that his father before him had shown none at times like that. Kincaid men didn't cry. It was as simple as that—and yet so complicated that it could fill an entire chapter in a psychology book.

A half an hour later, the Speaker finally came out of his office. When he did, his staff were still there, pretending to be working, but in reality, simply waiting anxiously to see if they could help the man they cared about so deeply. It had been an emotionally wrenching night, not only for the Speaker but for his entire staff, and when he emerged from his inner sanctum and told them all that he would be all right, there was a noticeable release of tension in the room.

"Can I walk you to your car, Mr. Speaker?" George Ross asked.

"Yes, George. But have it meet me over at the Capitol."

George understood immediately. The Speaker always liked to walk through the Capitol after a particularly trying day. It seemed to calm him and give him strength. "Of course, sir. That's a good idea. I'll call downstairs and tell your driver to meet us over there."

The Speaker nodded, and together they left the office and headed for the underground subway that would whisk them back up to the Hill.

FOR OVER TWENTY YEARS, Jeremiah Kincaid loved to be in the Capitol at night, after the members had departed for their nocturnal fundraising rounds, and the last of the tourists were tucked safely back in their hotel beds. It always seemed to rejuvenate him no matter how difficult the day had been. He loved the subdued sound of footsteps down distant marbled corridors, the long shadows created by deferential lighting in the Great Rotunda, and most of all, the palpable sense of history. All of this combined to create an atmosphere more in keeping with a great cathedral than a place of government. To Jeremiah Kincaid, that was exactly what the building was—a holy sepulcher, a shrine to the dignity, the honor, and legacy of the men and women who had gone before. And just being there, being a part of the unfolding history of America, in whatever role that fate had in store for him, filled him with an inner peace and an unwavering sense of duty.

It was what made Jeremiah what he was, with all his strengths, which were many, and all his flaws, which were few. Unfortunately, it was the country that benefited from the former and his family that had taken the brunt of the latter. As powerful as the love he felt for his country was, it paled by comparison with the love he felt for his wife and children; yet, sadly, he had never learned how to show it. Perhaps it was his strict Presbyterian upbringing, or his fear of failure, or his aversion to weakness. More likely it was a blend of all three. Regardless of the cause, at the age of fifty-nine, he had achieved what, by any standard, would be considered an unparalleled measure of greatness in his professional life, and yet, at least with his two sons, he had managed to be a failure as a father: cold, unyielding, unforgiving. And what made it all the harder to bear was that he had no idea how to fix it before time and opportunity ran out. And so, as the man who many called the Lion of Congress walked down the hall, his heart was heavy, his mood was disconsolate, and the lion's roar was now stilled.

"Sir, it's none of my business, but I think you should forgive T.J." said Ross, struggling to keep up with his boss.

"No, it's too late."

"Beg your pardon, sir, but it is never too late, until one of you is dead." His words were harsh, but his intentions were good and the Speaker knew it.

"George, you know that I love you like a son, but please stay out of this."

Ross was undeterred. "Mr. Speaker, I am not saying you should do this for only personal reasons. I am saying it in the interests of the country as well. Now that Governor Morrissey has pardoned him, I'm afraid that T.J. will return to Idaho and publicly align himself with the Western Freedom Party. That will embolden them even more, perhaps to the point of doing something stupid."

Kincaid glanced over at his chief of staff, "Like what?"

"You know, sir, I'm not one to give credence to rumors, but there is a lot of talk around this town that the Western Freedom Party has a much larger and far more powerful group of supporters in the halls of government, both here and at the state level, than the White House believes it has."

Kincaid stopped in his tracks. "If you are referring to the New Sons of Liberty, I wouldn't lose any sleep over it."

"I hope that you're right, sir, but consider the consequences if you're wrong."

The Speaker started walking again, stepping up his pace as if to escape the discussion that his assistant wanted to pursue, both literally as well as figuratively. As he walked, he said firmly, "George, I don't doubt that there are a large group of disgruntled members of Congress who don't share the President's views. Even some among his own party. But this isn't 1776 or 1861. This is the twenty-first century, and we are a nation of law and order. The thought that a renegade group of elected officials could try to hold the

Congress hostage as a means of subverting the Constitution is quite simply preposterous."

The two men came to the entrance reserved for members, and the Speaker smiled at the two Capitol policemen standing by the doorway. They returned the smiles, as he and Ross walked out into the beautifully clear night and headed toward the Speaker's limousine that sat nearby with its engine running.

"Yes, sir, but—"

"But nothing, George," interrupted the Speaker, "We will have no more talk about bogeymen hiding in the shadows of these halls, waiting for their chance to seize power."

Ross was obviously upset, and he made one more attempt at pursuing the matter, "Mr. Speaker, you know how much I respect and admire you. But I believe that you and your colleagues in the Congress haven't grasped the gravity of the situation."

The Speaker eyed his assistant carefully and said, "Go on."

Ross nodded. "I'm not talking about anyone attempting to vote the government out of office. I'm talking about something far worse. I'm talking about the people turning away from the government itself. And when they do, what's left? A group of powerless men and women in a large, white building with pretty statues and marble floors. Nothing more."

Kincaid's eyes narrowed. He paused for a moment and then said, "The issue of gun control is a grave one. But despite all the rhetoric and posturing that is going on here in this city and in places like Boise and elsewhere, we are still a country of law and order. And in this instance, I am confident that reason will prevail."

Ross listened respectfully, and then with a quiet strength that he drew from deep within, he said softly, "With reasonable men I will reason. With humane men I will plead. But to tyrants, I will give no quarter nor waste arguments where they will certainly be lost."

The words hung in the silence of the night. A sad smile slowly spread across the Speaker's lips, and he replied, "William Lloyd Garrison on the subject of abolition."

Ross nodded.

"Do you feel that gun control rises to the level of slavery?" asked the Speaker.

"No, sir. But to many, it does. Whether you choose to believe it or not, there is a growing and significant number of Americans who view the President as a tyrant. Tyranny, whether real or perceived, is the precursor to rebellion. And rebellion is the jackboot to war."

"War?"

Ross had been uncomfortable saying it, but there it was in all its ugliness. The ultimate consequence of tyranny. "Yes sir. War."

The Speaker looked directly into Ross eyes and said harshly, "There will be no more such talk between us. For the Speaker of the House of Representatives of the United States of America and his chief of staff to even be discussing this idea gives it credence and momentum." He paused then added, "We will not speak of it again. Is that clear?"

Crestfallen, Ross murmured, "Yes, sir."

Seeing the hurt look on the young man's face, the Speaker softened his tone. "Look, George. Talk of war is like a tumor. It starts with just a few aberrant cells that can easily be destroyed. But if it is not stopped at an early stage, those cells soon become hundreds, then thousands and so on, until it has grown into a monster that devours the very being that gave it sustenance."

"Yes, sir," said his assistant softly.

The Speaker stood there quietly for a few moments, lost in thought. "I know that your intentions are good, and that your love of this nation runs deep. I also realize that you raise these issues with me in a sincere desire to help me lead this nation through these perilous times. But if you value our relationship as deeply as I think you do, then you will spend less time worrying about the New Sons of Liberty and the Western Freedom Party, and more time planning how we can deal constructively with the White House. Because I believe that under the President's facade of arrogance, there is a tiny flicker of goodness. And it is my job to reach out to the man, to find common ground, and to put the good of the people above all else."

At first, Ross said nothing. And then he looked the Speaker directly in the eyes and said, "I hear you, sir."

"Good," said the Speaker, gently touching the younger man on the back and then stepping over to where his uniformed chauffeur was holding the back door of the limousine open. "Now, if you'll excuse me, George, I am suddenly very tired."

"Yes, sir."

The Speaker glanced at the starry night sky and drew in a deep breath. Then he looked with tenderness at his chief of staff. "A man cannot lead by looking over his shoulder, George. Forget the rumors, the rhetoric, and the radicals. My mission, and by association yours, is to unite the nation behind a voice of reason. And we simply must not rest until we have brought the issue of gun control to a peaceable and mutually agreeable resolution."

Ross nodded, but said nothing.

"Now, go home, and get some rest. There will be no more talk of guns and war."

"Good night, Mr. Speaker."

"Good night, son." With that, the Speaker got into the limousine and it drove away.

Ross couldn't help but notice that it was the second time that night the Speaker had used the word son in connection with him. Years later after Jeremiah Kincaid's death, when Ross wrote a book about him, he would think back on that night and the pain that was etched across the older man's face—pain that would haunt the elder Kincaid all the rest of his life.

THE SPEAKER sat wearily in the plush seat of the limousine as his driver, Payton, skillfully navigated it through the late-night traffic on Constitution Avenue. He had silenced Ross's concerns about the direction the country was heading, and effectively cut off any further discussion about his youngest son. But the tiny little voice that dwelt deep inside the Speaker could not be so easily deterred, and now as he sat there alone, watching the streetlights on Constitution Avenue slip by, it gnawed at him like a hungry lion on a weathered bone.

Looking up in the rear-view mirror, the driver could see the look of fatigue on the Speaker's face. "Tough day, Mr. Speaker?"

Kincaid looked into the mirror and said, "Aren't they all, Payton?"

"You got that right, sir," said the driver with a polite chuckle. He paused, as if reluctant to intrude any further upon the Speaker's quiet moments, but then added, "If I may say so, sir, I thought your speech tonight took real guts."

"Thank-you, Payton. That means a lot."

There were a few moments of quiet as the limousine passed the Ellipse and took a soft right on Virginia Avenue. Then Payton said, "May I ask you a question, sir?"

"Of course."

"Do you think this country is ready to give up its guns?"

Ever the politician, the Speaker replied, "Do you?"

"No, sir. Not without a fight."

"Why not? Other civilized countries have."

"It took the English over a thousand years to give up their weapons. And during that time, there were many changes of policy and practice. Why should we be any different?"

The Speaker knew his driver to be a history buff, and he could always count on him to have an informed opinion. "Hopefully we have learned by their example."

"I hope that you're right, Mr. Speaker, but in my heart I'm afraid that the guys with guns in their closets and bedside tables, and in the gun racks on the back windows of their pick-up trucks, will never let you take them away. Never."

Kincaid nodded and said, "I don't want to take them away. I just want them to be registered and controlled in the same way that automobiles are."

The driver shook his head and said, "No disrespect, Mr. Speaker, but they will never believe that the one doesn't lead to the other. Look at what happened in Canada."

The Speaker nodded and said, "I don't disagree with you, Payton. But that's what leaders are for. To lead both by reason and by example."

"Yes, sir, but if I may say so, sir, not all of our leaders are like you."

The Speaker smiled and said softly, "Thank-you, Payton."

The limousine pulled up in front of the Watergate apartments and stopped. Payton quickly got out, walked around to the Speaker's door, and opened it.

"Good night, Mr. Speaker."

"Good night, Payton."

The Speaker stepped slowly toward the building's door, which was being held open by a uniformed doorman. Neither the Speaker nor the doorman saw the figure in the black, hooded sweatshirt, who appeared suddenly out of the shadows near the street. As he scurried like a rat up the sidewalk toward the Speaker, he pulled a handgun out from under his shirt and pointed it in the direction of the Speaker. However, Payton saw him the instant he cleared the shadows, and he was already stepping toward the Speaker while reaching inside his coat. "Get down!" he screamed.

His shout grabbed Kincaid's attention, and he looked at his attacker. His eyes were drawn to the small black gun, with its cold black eye pointing right at his chest. Then inexplicably, at the last second, the attacker froze. His eyes became wide with fear as he stared past the Speaker at something across the street from the hotel. By that point, Payton had pulled his weapon out and fired two quick shots. The first ripped through the sleeve of the attacker's sweatshirt but missed his body and smashed one of the building's plate glass windows. The second bullet missed the attacker completely and hit a concrete column on the building's facade. Simultaneously, the attacker flinched and squeezed the trigger of his weapon. The bullet punched into the Speaker's shoulder, knocking him to the pavement. The attacker ran in a panic across the street, narrowly missing being run over by several speeding cars.

"Mr. Speaker!" shouted Payton in anguish. After feeling for a pulse at the side of the Speaker's neck and being relieved to find one, Payton shouted at the terrified doorman to call 911. He then carefully opened the Speaker's coat jacket, looking for the wound. He found it high on the Speaker's left shoulder, and he was relieved to find that it hadn't punctured his chest cavity.

The door man returned and stood there staring at the scene.

"Did you call it in?" shouted the driver.

The man nodded but didn't say anything. The sight of the Speaker's blood-soaked coat was too much for him, and he fainted dead away.

Payton shook his head in disgust and turned back to the Speaker. "Hold on, sir. Hold on," he whispered. "Help is on the way."

Kincaid tried to say something but he couldn't get it out.

"You can't die on us now, Mr. Speaker," said Payton. "A thousand years isn't up yet."

Jeremiah Kincaid looked up at the driver through glassy eyes and smiled feebly. As he lay there staring up at the night sky, fifty yards away, the lifeless body of the attacker lay crumpled on the ground, and standing over it was a magnificent white stallion upon whose back sat a dark rider. Satisfied that all was as it should be, the dark rider slowly pulled on the enormous beast's reins, and together, they disappeared into the night.

A THOUSAND MILES to the West, an FBI SWAT team was descending on the Kincaid farm, just as Kathleen was on the telcom with George Ross learning about her husband's shooting. At that same moment, T.J. Kincaid, alias Thomas Porter, was boarding a chartered jet at the Milwaukee airport, while his older brother sat all alone in their father's apartment in Washington, staring at a bottle of scotch that sat unopened on the table in front of him. And so it was that the Kincaid men were once again plunged into the depths of despair. Their dysfunction and disorder were an apt metaphor for the current state of the nation—a nation that they loved so very deeply, each in his own way. Lesser people would have given up and surrendered to the onrushing darkness. But the Kincaid clan was made of sterner stuff. They were not lesser people, and just like the land that they lived in, the clan would survive; but sadly, exactly like their fellow citizens, not all of them would be there to celebrate the victory.

37

GNBC Studios, Washington, D.C.

It was nearly 11:00 p.m. and Sarah McGill was sitting alone in her office, deeply absorbed in some work that she was preparing for the following day's newscast, when suddenly, Tanner Spence burst in. Barreling through the door, he exclaimed, "I did it!"

McGill flinched but quickly relaxed when she saw who it was. "Tanner! You scared the 'you-know-what' right out of me."

"Sorry, Sarah, but I had to see you right away."

McGill's thin eyebrows arched. "How did you get in here?"

"Through the front door."

"But your NIS card isn't programmed for this building."

He flashed a mischievous grin at her. "My card is programmed for every building, everywhere."

She shook her head, "Is there anything in cyberspace you can't do?"

"Let me think," he said. "Ummm, that would be a no."

"I'm glad you're on the side of the angels."

The comment obviously pleased him. "Wait 'till I show you what I just did."

"What?"

"I broke through the NSOL firewalls and bastion hosts."

"You did!" she said, feigning excitement, then added, "I have absolutely no idea what that means."

"It means I now know the IP addresses of the computers linked into the New Sons of Liberty extranet."

McGill's expression lit up. "You do?" This time her excitement was real. "Who are they?"

"I think you'd better see this for yourself." He opened his little black bag and took out his computer, which he quickly booted up. After tying a few keystrokes, a list of names began scrolling down the screen.

Sarah McGill couldn't believe her eyes as the names of some of the most powerful politicians and public servants in the nation appeared before her. "Oh my," she whispered. "Congressmen, senators, governors, judges, and CEOs. The list reads like a who's who of American society."

"Exactly. But there's a catch," he added.

"What?" she asked, looking away from the screen at his face.

"I have identified the specific Internet Protocol addresses of computers that are located in the offices of the men and women whose names you see before you."

"Go on," she said, not getting it at first.

"However, just because someone using those specific computers is linked into the NSOL extranet doesn't mean it's the actual person whose office the computer is located in."

She nodded, letting the thought sink in. "So we can't be sure who's really on line?"

"No," he replied. "Not without a Granite Shield satellite scan of their NIS cards which would tip my hand to my superiors right now. Besides, that wouldn't be conclusive evidence, given that most of these people refuse to carry them half the time anyway."

"But you're absolutely sure that the computers are located in the offices of the names you showed me?"

"Yes. Offices and in some cases private residences."

"Private homes?" she asked.

"Yes."

"But doesn't that make it more likely it's the person who you think it is?"

"Yes. But it wouldn't stand up in a court of law."

"Court of law?" she said, with a startled look on her face. "Aren't you being a little dramatic?"

"I don't think so. Treason makes a pretty powerful screenplay."

"Treason!"

"Yes. Treason. Lately, their talk has been treasonous. It remains to be seen, of course, whether their actions will be."

"What have they been saying?"

"Over the past few days, they've been using the 's' word, and I don't mean you-know-what."

"The 's' word?"

He looked up at her with a serious expression, the likes of which she had never seen on his face before, and said almost matter-of-factly, "Secession."

"Really?" Just then her PTC began playing the love theme from Romeo and Juliet. She looked down at it, "It's Keene. I was supposed to meet with him when I got back to the studio."

Spence was obviously impressed with her choice of music for the PTC. "Romeo and Juliet?"

She blushed. "I like it." She then answered it. "I'll be right there, Keene," and then clicked off.

Spence chuckled. "Once a romantic, always a romantic."

"You're one to talk," she teased back. "Now, come with me, Mr. Cyber Lord. You've got some talking to do." She grabbed his arm and pulled him up out of his chair. "The boss man has got to hear this—and right away."

SARAH McGILL and Tanner Spence stood in Lange's office in front of his cluttered desk. Lange was leaning back in his chair with his elbows on the chair's wooden arms and his chin resting on his hands. For a few moments he sat there, silently digesting what Spence had just told him. Then he looked up at McGill and said, "Cyber space is full of wackos, Sarah, or cranks, as young Tanner here calls them. What makes you think this group is legitimate?"

She glanced at Spence and back at her boss. "Because Tanner says it is, and his I.Q. is higher than both of ours combined."

Spence grinned at McGill until he saw Lange looking at him sternly, which quickly wiped the smile off his face.

Lange thought about it for a few more moments and then said to McGill, "Okay, go ahead and pursue it. But I still don't think there's a story there."

"Since when isn't treason a story?" she replied.

"Now hold on. Before we start throwing that word around, I think we had better get corroboration from at least one, and preferably two, other sources that there really is a group called the New Sons of Liberty, and these are not just some teenagers who have found a way to hack into the computers of all the people on Tanner's list.

McGill nodded, "Of course."

Lange added, "And if my memory serves me, the original Sons of Liberty were a pretty scruffy lot. I'm certain they had nothing in common with the names on that list."

"Nothing perhaps—except freedom," added Spence.

Lange frowned at Spence, but it was a gentle one, filled with admiration for a mind far brighter than Lange had ever known in all his years of covering the beat in a city populated with the best and the brightest. "You always were an annoying little boy."

"Yes, sir." Spence replied with his irresistible, boyish grin. But it quickly vanished as he added, "If these people are who I think they are, and they are going to do what they say they will, then they deserve to be annoyed with extreme prejudice."

"Point made, Tanner. Now go find out if your new patriots are for real."

"Yes, sir," said Spence.

There was an urgent knock on Lange's door.

"Enter," he yelled.

The door swung wide open, and a young woman entered with a look of anguish on her face. "The Speaker's been shot."

"What?" said Lange.

"Oh no!" McGill exclaimed.

"Is he dead?" asked Lange.

"No."

"Thank God," said McGill.

"Do they know who did it?" asked Spence.

"The police said it was an attempted mugging in front of his apartment this evening. Apparently, the Speaker's driver shot and killed the attacker."

"A mugging?" Spence's eyes narrowed. "Someone tried to mug the Speaker of the House in front of his apartment with an armed driver standing beside him?" It was clear from the way he said it that he didn't believe it.

McGill looked at Spence. "I didn't know congressional drivers were armed."

"Apparently neither did the attacker," added Lange.

The woman shrugged. "They've taken the Speaker to George Washington Hospital, and so far all they've released is that he is in serious, but stable condition."

"Thank-you, dear," Lange said to the woman, who took no offense to his male chauvinistic way. She nodded and left.

McGill looked at Lange, "I have to go there."

"The Hill isn't your beat anymore, remember?" replied Lange.

"No. But gun control is; and the shooting of the leader of the opposition to the President's bill in Congress is certainly my beat."

Spence added, "She's right. And I don't buy the mugging story. There's more to this shooting than just a bad guy with a gun."

He stared at Spence and then looked back at McGill. "Go."

"If I can get to see the Speaker, should I mention the New Sons of Liberty?"

Lange thought about it and asked Spence, "Was his URL on your list?"

Spence said, "No, sir."

"Use your own judgment."

She smiled and headed for the door. He shouted after her, "What if I had said no?"

She turned back and said in the special way she saved for people she loved, "I don't know. You never have." Then she left.

Lange shrugged his shoulders and looked at Spence. "What is it about that woman that I can't say no to?"

"Nobody can," answered Spence.

"I think you had better get back to DHS, son. Just in case this is the start of something bigger than a simple mugging."

"Yes, sir. You're right." With that, Tanner got up and headed for the door. As he was about to leave, he looked back at Lange. "I can tell you one thing. If this was something more sinister than a simple street crime, it wasn't anyone from the NSOL who was behind it."

"Why do you say that?"

"Because whoever they are, they see Jeremiah Kincaid as their last, best hope to prevent the President's gun bill from becoming law. As they would say, he's their eagle in a sky full of ravens." Then Tanner turned and was gone, leaving a haunting image in Lange's mind and a sinking feeling deep inside.

38

George Washington Hospital, Washington, D.C.

Jeremiah Kincaid sat up in bed looking annoyed and uncomfortable. But his discomfort had little to do with the large bandage on his left shoulder or with the intravenous line in his right arm. Nor was it a result of all the attention he was receiving from his son Jake, his chief of staff George Ross, two nurses and a doctor who were in the spacious private room, or the two Secret Service agents who stood just outside the door checking the ID's of everyone who came near. Rather, the Speaker's discomfort traced to the telcom conversation that he was having.

"I don't want you to come to Washington, Kathleen. Jake's here with me and George's got half of the Congress worrying about me." He paused while she said something. Then he continued, "I'm fine. The bullet passed right through my shoulder without hitting anything vital. Promise me you'll stay home." Again he paused. "Good. Thank-you, darling. Here's Jake." He passed the telcom receiver to his son. "Here. You tell your mother not to come." As he did, the medical staff excused themselves and left the room.

"Hi mother. Don't worry, he'll be fine." Jake listened silently to something his mother was saying. Then he said softly, "Yes, I know. I know." He listened again and then finished with, "I love you, too. Bye." He hung up and looked at his father.

"What did she say?" asked the elder Kincaid.

"She said her flight gets into Reagan at noon."

"Damn." The Speaker gave a deep sigh. "And what else?"

"It was nothing. She said she could handle it."

336

The Speaker's tone made the room turn cold. "I asked you what else your mother said?" It was the same tone he had used when Jake was a little boy and he knew Jake or T.J. were not telling the truth.

And it brought back the same reaction from Jake as in his youth. He grew sullen and retreated into himself. "She just said that the FBI had been to the house."

The Speaker grimaced but said nothing.

Jake sighed and added, "She said they were very polite."

"But T.J. wasn't there?" It was a rhetorical question, because the Speaker never doubted for one instant that his son would have dared to return after their telcom conversation earlier that evening.

"No."

"Good." But there was nothing good about it or the way the Speaker said it. Then he turned to Ross and said, "I don't understand why I need Secret Service protection. Can't we get rid of them?"

"No, sir. At least not until we find out who the shooter was."

"Why?" snapped the Speaker. "People get shot every day in this city. Why should I be any different?"

Jake frowned at his father and said, "Dad. Nobody is looking to make this bigger than it already is. But someone tried to kill you, and we need to find out who and why."

The elder Kincaid gave his son a stern look. "I don't want to discuss this any further. I mean it." He turned back to Ross and said, "Now get me out of here."

"I don't think that would be a good idea, sir," said Ross. He loved the man, but it saddened him when the dark side of the otherwise great man reared its ugly head. As charming and gracious as the Speaker could be with people who didn't matter to him, he was always hard, terribly so, on those close to him, sometimes bordering on being harsh.

"You were almost killed tonight," added Jake.

"But I wasn't," said the Speaker. "Now can we please change the subject?" he added, with growing anger in his voice.

Jake gave up. His father was the only person in the world who could make him do so. No friend or foe, nor words or weapons could get the defiant warrior prince inside Jake to back off. No one except the king, that is. He looked at Ross, who nodded knowingly. The chief of staff had always been able to handle the Speaker better than his own family could. And that night was no exception.

"I think you should rest here tonight, Mr. Speaker," said Ross. "Nothing is going to happen on the gun bill before tomorrow."

At that moment, one of the Secret Service agents stepped inside the room and said, "Excuse me, Mr. Ross, there's a reporter here who wants to speak with Mr. Kincaid."

"Now?" said Ross, obviously perturbed.

"Who is it?" asked the Speaker.

"The last thing you need right now is to be questioned by some pushy reporter who doesn't have the decency to wait until your blood has dried," said Jake.

Ross said to the agent, "Tell him to call my office in the—"

"It's not a 'he' sir. It's Sarah McGill from GNBC."

At the mention of her name, the atmosphere of the room changed instantly. Ross knew all too well of how much the Speaker liked McGill. It was hard not to like her. During his long tenure in the Congress, both as a representative and now the Speaker of the House, Jeremiah Kincaid had always treated reporters with courtesy and respect, even though he felt many of them didn't deserve it. But Sarah McGill was different; he held her in the highest regard.

"Show her in," said the Speaker to the agent who then left.

A minute later Sarah McGill stepped through the door and came face to face with Jake Kincaid. Their eyes locked, and for an instant, neither of them moved nor spoke. Instantly the younger Kincaid's displeasure with the "pushy reporter" evaporated. Finally, just when their silent interface was becoming awkward, she said, "You must be Jake Kincaid." She extended her hand. "I've heard so much about you." As soon as she said it, she wished she hadn't. The person she had heard it from was his younger brother; and it was neither the time nor the place to bring up T.J.'s name. Thankfully, he didn't pursue it.

"It's a pleasure to meet you, Ms. McGill." He wanted to say more; something charming or debonair; something, anything; but he couldn't get his mind to focus on speech. It was too busy processing the image before him.

She could sense his discomfort immediately. One thing a truly beautiful woman with a high intellect gets used to is the effect she has on men; and each woman deals with it in a different way. Some are embarrassed by it, some take advantage of it, but a few, like McGill, just accept it and handle it gracefully and without production. "The feeling is mutual," she replied, putting him at ease. She looked at Ross and said, "Good evening, George."

Ross smiled a polite but controlled smile and said, "Hello, Sarah." Then he said to the Speaker, "Mr. Speaker, you know Sarah McGill."

"Yes, of course. Good evening Sarah. Congratulations on your promotion to chief White House correspondent for GNBC."

"Thank-you, Mr. Speaker."

"I'm afraid we miss you on the Hill."

"I miss you too, sir."

She took a few steps closer to the bed and said, "Mr. Speaker. I'm sorry to intrude upon you under such dreadful circumstances, but some information has come to my attention that I think you need to know."

Her comment got everyone's attention. The Speaker spoke first, "What does this information pertain to?"

She hesitated before answering and looked at Ross and Jake Kincaid. The Speaker immediately picked up her body language and said, "Anything that you want to say to me can be said in front of these two men."

"Of course, Mr. Speaker." She then asked, "Have you ever heard of the New Sons of Liberty?"

Ross and the Speaker exchanged a knowing glance. Jake noticed but had no idea what was going on.

"Yes. As a matter of fact, we have," answered Ross.

"I have just learned some things about this group that I think the Speaker should hear. Assuming, that is, that you haven't already heard this, sir."

The Speaker's eyes, focused intently upon the young woman before him, the way they did when something caught his attention and interest. When they were little boys, Jake and T.J. knew that look all too well. T.J. called it eagle eyes, like a bird of prey preparing to strike. And it always frightened them. "Please sit down, Sarah, and tell us everything you know," as he motioned to her to take a seat in one of the large comfortable chairs in the sumptuous suite.

She did. Ross also sat down, but Jake remained standing.

McGill gathered her thoughts and started talking. She told them about her friend Tanner Spence, and encryption and firewalls, and treasonous talk and the long, imposing list of names—names that the Speaker knew and would somehow never mean the same to him again.

FIFTEEN MINUTES LATER, Sarah McGill finished her story. For a moment no one spoke. Finally, the Speaker said, "I'm not surprised about Morrissey and a few of the others." He shook his head sadly. "But as for the rest of the list, it's just incredible."

"Maybe I shouldn't have come here tonight," said McGill.

"No, Sarah. You did the right thing. Now I must ask a big favor of you."

"What is it, Mr. Speaker?" McGill asked.

"I need some time before your network reports the story."

"Without any corroboration, there isn't any story yet, sir."

"She's right, Mr. Speaker. At this point, there is no hard evidence linking all these people to the conspiracy, if that is indeed what it is," added Ross.

"No. Not yet, perhaps. But there will be," said the Speaker.

McGill thought about the Speaker's request for a moment and then said, "I think my boss will agree to give you a head's up before we break the story. Assuming that you give us the first call on anything that you uncover."

"Deal."

As he said it, Ross winced. He hated it when the Speaker made "deals" with the press. But it was too late now.

Jeremiah turned to his son and said, "Jake, forget about what you have just heard here tonight." He said it more like a general giving a colonel an order than a father talking to a son. "I probably should not have involved you in this."

"Done," was Jake's terse reply. He thought about saying, "Involved in what?" but didn't. He was in no mood for cute word games.

"Good." The Speaker looked back at McGill, "Now, Sarah, if you will excuse us."

"Certainly, Mr. Speaker. Once again, thank-you for seeing me. I'm sure America will rest easier tonight knowing that you are all right."

"Thank-you."

McGill started for the door.

Jake quickly asked, "May I walk you out?"

She smiled, "Of course."

He looked back at his father and with an absence of emotion given the situation said, "Good night father."

"Good night, son. Don't worry about picking up your mother at the airport tomorrow. After George and I are done here, I will call her and tell her not to come."

"Yes, sir."

Jake stood there for a moment looking back at his father, but the elder Kincaid was already talking with Ross. He frowned and looked away and walked out. Sarah saw it all, and it told her more than words ever could. She quickly followed him.

"Should I call the Attorney General?" Ross asked.

"Not yet," answered Kincaid.

"But as she said, this could constitute a conspiracy for treason."

"Yes. And it could also be some administrative assistants playing games."

"What would you like me to do, sir?"

"Get a jet."

"To go where?"

"Boise."

"Good idea. When do we leave?" asked Ross.

"I'm going alone."

"But—"

"It's non-negotiable," said the Speaker firmly. "I want to leave at first light."

"It may take hours to discharge you in the morning."

The Speaker swung his legs over the edge of the bed, pressed the call button and said, "No it won't, because they are going to do it right now. Get me my clothes, will you?"

Almost immediately, a nurse appeared in the doorway. "May I help you, Mr. Speaker?"

"Yes. Please remove this," he said, pointing to the intravenous line in his arm.

The nurse was taken aback and said, "I can't do that, sir."

"If you don't miss, then I will yank it out myself."

The nurse hesitated. She didn't want to argue with the Speaker, but her sense of duty told her she shouldn't let him go.

The Speaker said in a gentle but firm way, "Trust me, miss, this is a matter of national security."

She did what she was told.

"Thank-you, nurse. Don't worry. I will see to it that you don't get into trouble."

She smiled weakly and left the room as the Speaker stood up and started to get dressed.

Ross helped him, but he was not happy about it.

After he was dressed, the Speaker said, "Now George, go downstairs and bring your car to the front door, I've got a telcom call to Wisconsin to make…" The Speaker stopped talking in mid-sentence and staggered over toward the bed.

"Are you all right, Mr. Speaker?" asked his alarmed chief of staff. But before the Speaker could reply, he passed out and slumped to the floor. Immediately Ross hit the call button on the wall. Then he knelt down and cradled the Speaker's head in his lap.

Within seconds the room was filled with medical personnel, and much to the relief of everyone, especially the nurse who had removed the IV, the Speaker had only fainted. But when he regained consciousness, he did not resist when the doctors demanded that he get back into bed. The only thing he asked for was that the nurse who had taken out the IV not be punished. The doctors agreed, but a few days later, after the Speaker had been discharged, the nurse was unceremoniously fired. Months later, when Jeremiah Kincaid visited the hospital to thank them for their treatment that night and found out about the nurse's dismissal, the hospital administrator and nursing supervisor were summarily fired, and the nurse was re-hired with back pay. Such was the way of power in a city where title and position meant everything.

OBLIVIOUS to what was transpiring seven floors above them, Jake Kincaid and Sarah McGill walked slowly across the parking lot.

"That was a class act, Ms. McGill, if I may say so," said the colonel.

"What?"

"Telling my father about that group instead of having him learn about it on the evening news."

"Thank-you. Not all reporters are unscrupulous,"

"Nor all politicians."

McGill nodded. "Touché. Your father is a good man."

"Yeah."

She glanced over at him. The edge in his voice cut the night air like broken glass. "I guess he can be pretty tough on people sometimes."

"On 'people' no. Just on his family."

She nodded sympathetically. "It must have been tough growing up with such a powerful man as a father."

"More than you can know."

She could read the pain of a difficult childhood in his face. It wasn't the first time she had seen it in one of the Speaker's sons. It had been evident in T.J.'s face as well. She wanted to say something to comfort him, but she decided not to. He looked and sounded so much like his younger brother that it created strong feelings of ambivalence in her; on the one hand, the similarity instantly attracted her to him, but in that attraction she felt she was being disloyal, and the totality of these feelings made her uncomfortable. They reached her car. "Here's my car, Colonel. It doesn't weigh seventy tons, and it gets twenty-five miles to the gallon instead of one, but it gets the job done."

He laughed. "I'm impressed. It's not the kind of fact about tanks that I would have expected from…"

"From a woman?" she interrupted.

He flushed red. "No. That's not what I was going to say."

"Sorry. Force of habit."

"What I was going to say was *from a civilian*."

"I did a news feature on the armored cavalry during WWT. I was a rookie reporter and my local television station sent me to Fort Irwin, Texas, which was then the home of the…"

He finished her sentence, "The Third Armored Cavalry Regiment."

"Yes."

"That's my unit," he said with pride.

She stopped and looked at him. "I also know that you served with them in the Middle East and that it was there you earned the Medal of Honor."

He obviously didn't want to talk about the circumstances that earned him the nation's highest military honor. "Now, tell me, what else did you learn about tanks?"

With the look of a schoolgirl reading her essay to the class, she rattled off a brief but thorough listing of the specifications and raw killing power of the M1A2 Abrams Main Battle Tank. He was delighted. When she finished, he said, "You left out one thing."

"What?"

"It's nickname."

"I was being polite. I think it's called a Mud Belly."

He chuckled. "There are those who dare to use that term—then we kill them."

"What do *you* call it?"

"Tankers call it the Whispering Death."

"Oooh. Very impressive. So are you going to have to kill me now?"

He laughed. "No. Not tonight."

They stood there for a few moments, neither knowing how to end their brief encounter, nor wanting to. Finally she asked, "Where are you parked?"

"I'm not. I came with George Ross."

"Can I offer you a ride somewhere?"

He hesitated, staring at the purple Mustang with questioning eyes.

"It's not one of your precious tanks, but then again, we'd look pretty strange driving down the streets of D.C. in Whispering Death now, wouldn't we?"

"That would be very kind of you. I'm staying at my father's apartment in the Watergate."

"Perfect. It's right on my way."

"Are you sure?"

"Absolutely."

"Terrific."

They got inside and she started the powerful engine, put it in gear, and steered the nimble car expertly out of the lot.

As she did, he mused, "Tanks on the street of the nation's capital. Now that would get everyone's attention pretty quick. But that will never happen."

"Why not?"

"Because the only circumstances under which that would occur would be if we were under attack, and since the end of WWT, there's no country on the face of this earth that's a danger to America. Fifty years from now, maybe after China finally catches up with the twenty-first century, but not now."

"I pray that you're right."

But he was wrong. He forgot about the one country that America had to fear. The only one—itself. Months later, as main battle tanks did roll down Pennsylvania Avenue, he would remember that night in the hospital parking lot and what he had said; and his own words would haunt him as he got into one of those tanks and rode off to war.

<u>39</u>

Boise, Idaho

It was nearly three in the morning when Thomas Porter got off the jet he had chartered using an alias, and walked into the terminal at the Boise Municipal Airport. It had taken him seven hours to get back to Boise from Wisconsin after he stormed out of his parents' house. Waiting to greet him was Idaho State Police officer, Seaton Horner, dressed in plain clothes.

"Welcome back to Boise, Captain Porter."

"Thank-you, Seaton. It's good to be back."

The officer quickly looked around the terminal and said to Porter, "Let's get out of here, sir." With that, he pointed toward a door marked "Authorized Personnel Only." But before he could say another word, both men heard the announcer on a nearby BTC monitor say T.J.'s father's name and something about a shooting.

Porter hurried over to the monitor.

"I was going to tell you in the car, sir," said the officer, hurrying alongside. They reached the BTC just as the program cut away to a commercial.

"Tell me what?" said Porter, looking at the officer with obvious concern.

"Your father was shot tonight."

Without any expression or emotion, Porter asked, "Is he—"

"No," interrupted the officer. "He'll be all right."

Porter gave a barely perceptible sigh of relief. "Who did it?"

"Your father's driver shot and killed the assailant, but so far they don't know who he was."

"Where?"

"Outside his apartment building, apparently in an attempted robbery."

Porter's shoulders sagged, and he looked back up at the screen. "I just spoke to him several hours ago."

Just then the programming returned from the commercial break, and the two men looked up at the screen. On it the faces of Allistair Blevis, Cresswell Peabody, and Jarlene Martisse appeared. The two men stopped talking and listened to what they were saying.

"WELCOME BACK to this special late night edition of *Speak Up America*, ladies and gentlemen. I'm Allistair Blevis, and I'm here with my usual guests." After introducing Peabody and Martisse, Blevis got to the point, "So what do you think, was it just a botched mugging or an assassination attempt?"

Peabody stared at Blevis and said, "It will serve no purpose to speculate on that, Allistair. However, I will say that regardless of the cause, it was fortunate for the nation that the Speaker's bodyguard was armed. And that he obviously knew how to use his weapon. It spared us a protracted trial that would likely have become a public spectacle."

Martisse rolled her eyes, and added, "I, like my colleague, am certainly grateful that the Speaker of House was not seriously wounded. But I hardly think it appropriate to express pleasure at the death of another human being, regardless of his actions. And if the President has his way, men like that assailant will not have access to guns, and therefore, attacks like this one tonight won't happen."

Peabody snapped back, "On the contrary Ms. Martisse, if the President's bill were already law, government chauffeurs would likely not be permitted to carry weapons, and the Speaker would be dead instead of some slimy creature that is at this moment on its way back to hell from whence it came."

Blevis interjected, "I think we're missing the point here; namely, was this shooting part of some evil conspiracy to eliminate one barrier to the anti-gun legislation?"

Martisse looked aghast. "Are you insinuating that the President is somehow involved in this heinous act?"

Blevis squirmed in his chair and quickly added, "Of course not! I am simply asking a question. One which I am sure is on the minds of many of our viewers." Then without pausing to allow either of his guests to respond, he looked at the camera and said, "What do *you* think, ladies and gentlemen?" Was this just another crack head looking to rob a well-healed Washingtonian? Or was it something darker and more evil? Call us and let us know. The number is 1-777-C-NO-EVIL."

THE STATION CUT AWAY to a commercial break, and Porter turned away from the monitor.

"Would you like me to arrange a flight to Washington, sir?"

Porter looked at the officer and didn't answer at first. *What good would I be to him from a Federal jail cell?* he thought to himself. "No thank-you, Seaton. Please just take me to the governor."

"Yes, sir. I know he's looking forward to seeing you." With that, he and Porter walked through the deserted terminal and got into the limo waiting at the curbside. As the car headed off into the night, memories of his boyhood flooded into Porter's mind—a boyhood long since lost and never to be found again.

GOVERNOR MORRISSEY and Jesse Latrobe sat in the governor's office. It was late at night, and the governor was on the telcom. The expression on his face was deadly serious.

"Yes. Of course, Mr. Ross. Thank-you for taking my call, and please give the Speaker my best. Tell him I look forward to meeting with him as soon as he is fit to travel." With that, the governor hung up.

"How is he doing?" asked Latrobe.

"Ross said the bullet didn't hit anything vital."

Latrobe glanced at the governor's gun collection displayed in a lighted case standing against one wall of the richly furnished office. "Do you think this will change anything?"

"In what way?"

"I don't know. Do you think being shot will push the Speaker toward the President's position? Especially following the deaths of those two congressmen on the Capitol steps."

"I doubt it. I'll give him this: Kincaid is a man of principle. Bullets might kill the man, but they could never kill his principles," said the governor with an obvious admiration in his voice. "Besides, I don't think he would have asked to meet with me if he had joined Webster's camp."

"I still don't trust him. Even with his youngest son on our side," said Latrobe.

"Thomas is not on our side yet, Jesse."

"Why else would he have returned to Idaho and asked to see you tonight?"

"Let's wait and see, shall we?"

"Regardless of his son's allegiance, I still have my doubts about his father's intentions," said Latrobe.

"Don't give up yet on winning the Speaker over to our cause."

"Well, he'll be out of action for a while, anyway. A heavy slug in the shoulder would slow a man half his age."

"The timing of these shootings couldn't have been worse. At least as far as building public support against Webster's spin machine," said Morrissey.

"Is there ever a good time to be shot?" asked Latrobe. "Kincaid's just damn lucky that the shooter was an amateur."

A troubled look clouded over the governor's face. Latrobe noticed it. "What's bothering you, Edward? I mean other than the fact that those bastards in the White House may win this battle yet."

Morrissey paused before replying. Then with a frigid expression on his face, he asked, "Tell me that your people had nothing to do with the shooting, Jesse."

The question shocked Latrobe. "I resent that you would even think that, Edward."

The governor's expression changed to embarrassment. "You're right. I'm sorry, Jesse."

"Apology accepted."

The two men sat there for a few moments, each lost in his own thoughts.

Finally Latrobe said, "This whole matter may come to a shooting war, but if it does, it will be the kind where two enemies face each other in broad daylight. Not a cowardly act like an assassin in the dark of the night."

"There you go again, Jesse. Couldn't you at least ease up on the war rhetoric?"

Latrobe stood up and walked over to the window. "Edward. You're the reason that I'm in this, remember?"

"I didn't ask you to start a war. I simply wanted you to help those foolish and frightened young men up on that mountaintop."

"But I never got the chance, did I?" shot back Latrobe.

"No. You didn't," said the governor softly.

"The President saw to that."

"Just promise me there'll be no more violence, Jesse. We can't win the hearts and minds of the American people with bullets."

"Violence, if it comes, Governor, will not be of my doing."

"Good."

"But as much as I care about our friendship, if the President or anyone else tries to take my guns away, there will be nothing but gunfire until there is only one of us left standing."

"That's not going to happen, Jesse."

"You always were the one to avoid conflict, Edward. But when that wild-eyed grizzly came tearing out of the bush up on the Salmon, I don't recall you objecting to my use of a gun."

"Webster isn't a grizzly, Jesse, and Washington isn't the wilderness."

"We'll see, Governor. We'll see." Then he added, "Now if you will excuse me, sir, I have got to meet with my brigade commanders."

"Of course. How is the recruiting going?"

"We can't sign them up fast enough."

"What about in the other states?" he asked, referring to the six other western states who had aligned themselves with Idaho.

"They're growing as fast as we are."

The governor nodded thoughtfully.

"Soon, there will be over a hundred thousand men ready to follow your orders, Governor."

"We will prepare for the worst but pray for the best, Jesse."

"Yes, sir. I hear you." With that, he saluted the governor and left.

As he did, his chief of staff poked his head in and said, "Governor, Captain Porter is here."

"Send him in."

The chief of staff nodded and stepped aside. The door swung open wide and in stepped Porter, or as America now knew him, T.J. Kincaid. "Hello, Governor. Thank-you for seeing me."

The governor strode across the room and threw his arms around the younger man. "I am very glad to see you, son."

The two men warmly embraced, and then Kincaid looked the older man in the eyes and said, "Governor, I apologize for my past actions, and I ask you to let me join you in your crusade."

"You are most welcome here, Thomas. I mean T.J."

"No, Governor, even though the whole nation now knows who I am, or at least who I was, I would prefer it if you still called me Thomas Porter."

"Suit yourself, son. It's who you are deep down inside, and what you stand for, that matters. A name in and of itself means nothing," Morrissey said.

It was a lie and both of them knew it, but for different reasons they were comfortable with it. As Kincaid shook the governor's hand and felt his arms around him, he knew all too well that the governor's welcome was one part sincerity and two parts pragmatism. This was because Kincaid's father, as a result of an overwhelming outcry from both the public and Congress alike, had rescinded his letter of resignation from his hospital bed and agreed to remain as Speaker of the House. Accordingly, there could be no better way to ensure the success of their mission than for the governor to gain Jeremiah Kincaid's endorsement of their cause. What the governor had no way of knowing was that it would take a miracle for T.J Kincaid and his father to ever come together again, in either a common cause or in love. But Kincaid played along with the lie, because without it, he knew that he would not have been welcomed back into the governor's inner circle. To him, it was a fair trade. The governor needed his link to the Speaker and the credibility that it could provide. And T.J. Kincaid, in turn, needed a place to belong, because the sad truth was that for all his wealth and notoriety, he had no friends, no family, and simply no where else to go.

The son of the lion of Congress had ironically become a lone wolf, exactly like the one he had faced on the mountain on that morning four months earlier. The parallel had preoccupied him in his lonely westward journey from his parent's home. It was an apt analogy and he knew it, for a wolf without a pack soon becomes a hide on a hunter's wall. However, there was one ominous aspect to the analogy that Kincaid didn't know, which was that there can only be one alpha male in every pack, and when another wolf seeks to gain this role, one of them must die.

April, 2018

G Day - 150

Pilgrims In A Barren Land

Guide me O Thou great Jehovah; Pilgrim through
this barren land; I am weak but Thou art mighty;
Hold me with Thy Powerful hand…

William Williams

40

River Of No Return Wilderness, Idaho

The black and green grease paint on the young soldier's face hid his bronze skin, but the look in his eyes could not hide the fear contained within. Nor could the first lieutenant's bar hide the fact that he wasn't sure about what he was doing. He proceeded slowly and cautiously, in a partially bent-over position, through the forest of the night, stopping every now and then to raise his fist and stare into the darkness ahead through his night vision goggles. Whenever he did so, the platoon of men strung out behind him instantly froze. Some squeezed ever more tightly the automatic rifles they held in their arms while others shifted their weight silently from one leg to the other. The heavy packs on their backs and the bits of brush and leaves tucked into the webbing on their helmets made them look like white-eyed, hunched-back swamp creatures. They were anything but; in fact, they were highly trained but woefully inexperienced young warriors. Exactly the kind of fodder that the gristmill of war had ground to dust for thousands and thousands of years.

They were twenty-eight men from the Third Platoon, Bravo Company, Second Infantry Battalion of the Wolf River Militia, a large, quasi-military unit that with each day grew stronger and more deadly. They were being led by First Lieutenant Billy Lightfoot, and his platoon was made up of just a few of the literally thousands of young men from all over the West who had joined the militia during the five months since the Bitterroot massacre. They were being trained at the new military base that had been literally carved out of a wilderness valley thirty miles northeast of the Wolf River Club. Despite the natural nervousness of young men about to be put in harm's way, they were as committed to their cause as any men who had ever fought for home and country; because freedom was the most powerful calling that had ever driven men into battle from the dawn of history.

Suddenly the woods in front of the platoon leader exploded with the sound and fury of machine gun fire. "Take cover," screamed Lightfoot but it was unnecessary, as his men had already dropped to their bellies alongside the trail and were now hugging the ground as tightly as a child hugs his pillow after a nightmare.

The firing continued unabated for a few more moments. Then it stopped. After a few moments of silence in which the smell of cordite filled the nostrils of each man, Lightfoot got up on one knee and looked over his shoulder toward the dark lumps on the ground behind him. Then, doing his best to mask his fear he shouted, "Corporal!"

"Yes, sir," came the disembodied reply.

"Take your squad around the left flank. Now."

"Got it, LT. Second squad, move out." The sound of men moving quickly through the darkness could be heard. Lightfoot repeated the command to another corporal, whose squad headed off in the opposite direction. Again there were the sounds of muffled shouts and rustling undergrowth. Satisfied that his platoon now had the enemy machine gun nest outflanked, the lieutenant motioned for the men beside him to get up and follow him. Just as they started forward, a flare shot up into the sky over their heads and suddenly, Lightfoot and the eight men standing right behind him were backlit against the sky. Dead men standing in the night.

"Third Platoon. That's it. Stand down," a voice boomed over a loud speaker. Out of the gloom, a group of men appeared, wearing the uniforms of the Idaho Army National Guard, including several senior non-commissioned officers, a lieutenant colonel and a tall man with a shock of white hair visible under his chrome helmet with four stars on it. It was Jesse Latrobe.

Latrobe and the others walked over to where the chagrined platoon leader was reassembling his men and shouted, "Lieutenant!" Lightfoot ran over to him and saluted smartly.

"Yes, sir."

"At ease, soldier."

The lieutenant did as he was told.

"You did fine, Lieutenant Lightfoot," said the general, glancing at the lieutenant's name patch.

"Thank-you, sir," said Lightfoot with the beginnings of a smile.

"Right up until the point when you and your men were cut to ribbons by the fifty caliber gun," continued the General.

The lieutenant's smile swiftly disappeared. "Yes, sir. I'm sorry, sir."

"Sorry doesn't count for squat when you're dead, Lieutenant."

"No, sir."

"Remember that next time. Dismissed."

"Yes, sir. Thank-you, sir," he said and returned to his platoon.

Latrobe turned to the lieutenant colonel who was standing with him and said, "The men are green, Colonel. So young and so green."

The colonel was Joseph Snow Eagle, tall and proud, with broad shoulders, powerful arms, and big, strong hands. He was a full-blooded Native American Indian from the Nez Perce tribe, as was Lightfoot. But there were two important differences: first, in addition to being a senior officer in the Army Guard, Snow Eagle was a seasoned veteran of combat who had distinguished himself during WWT; and second, he was a chief of the Nez Perce nation, who through his words and deeds had brought much honor and pride to his people. Snow Eagle had been assigned to help train the militia, but neither he nor Latrobe had any allusions of how big a challenge that would be, especially given the sense of urgency which everyone now felt given the governor's increasingly strident opposition to the President's anti-gun legislation. "Don't worry, General, we'll be ready, if and when we're needed."

"Not if, Colonel, just when."

"Understood, sir."

The general rolled his head and rubbed his neck. "I could use a cup of coffee."

"Yes, sir. Follow me, General," said a master sergeant standing with them.

"If it's okay with you, sir, I'd like to talk with the lieutenant," said Snow Eagle.

"Of course." Then the general and the sergeant disappeared into the darkness.

After they left, Snow Eagle walked down the trail to where Lightfoot's platoon sat on some fallen logs, listening to their lieutenant brief them on their performance. When they saw the colonel coming, a sergeant jumped up and shouted "Ten hut!"

Lightfoot saluted the colonel, who replied, "As you were, men."

"I was just briefing the men, sir," said the lieutenant.

"Carry on, Lieutenant," replied Snow Eagle.

The lieutenant turned back to face his men.

"What did the general say, LT?" asked one of them.

"He said that I got us all killed," replied Lightfoot.

One of the men looked down at his body and said mockingly, "Ah hell, I hate being dead. It's so—friggin' permanent."

"If you don't like the idea of dying, man, then why did you join the militia?" asked one of his buddies with a big grin.

The jokester snapped his head around and looked at him with wide eyes and said, "The militia! I thought this was the training camp for the Minnesota Vikings."

The men laughed but for most, it was a nervous laugh.

However, the lieutenant did not find it amusing. "Unless you boys take this training seriously, you will die."

There was a pause and then one of the corporals said, "Yes, but with all due respect, LT, there's no way Americans are going to kill other Americans. Despite what the General's been saying."

The lieutenant's expression changed from anger to pain. He looked directly at the corporal and said softly, "Tell that to the men who died up on Mount Freedom."

The corporal shook his head slowly in embarrassment and chastised himself under his breath. "I'm sorry, Colonel. I forgot about your brother, sir." The colonel's younger brother had been a soldier with the Army Rangers who had retaken the Bitterroot Rod & Gun Club, and he had been one of the men who died that day.

Snow Eagle nodded and said, "It's all right, Corporal. My brother's death means no more than any of the other forty-nine who died that day—or than any of yours will, if this turns into war."

The men standing in a circle around the two officers nodded quietly, each lost in his own thoughts about the possibility of dying in battle. Somehow that thought seemed more frightening than being killed in a car crash, which was the only way that most of them had witnessed death at their young ages.

"Okay, listen up," said Lightfoot. "Gather your gear, and let's get back to camp. We've had enough dying for one night."

They did what they were told, and Lightfoot and Snow Eagle followed a short distance behind.

"Colonel, do you think this will turn into a real shooting war, the kind of war my dad experienced in Vietnam?"

"It looks like it might, Lieutenant, which is all the more reason for you and your men to be ready."

"Sir, if you don't mind me asking, what is combat like? I mean, like when you were there in the invasion of Syria. Were you scared?"

The colonel answered slowly, with a depth of feeling that only soldiers who have been in battle can know. "Before the bullets started flying, hell yes, I was scared. Real scared. But when it began, there was no time to be brave or scared. No time to spout Hollywood lines or act nobly. No time to think. No time to do anything at all except kill or be killed. And the only thing that kept going through my mind was, 'Jesus Lord, don't let me screw up; don't let me fail my buddies. Anything, but that.'"

The lieutenant nodded. "I guess that's what worries me the most, sir. The fear of failure and the fear that others will die because of me."

They reached the edge of the camp near the platoon's barracks. The colonel stopped and looked Lightfoot directly in the eyes and said, "Lieutenant, you have warrior blood in your veins. Your ancestors and mine faced the same enemy that we now face. An enemy that threatens our lands from the east. They fought where we will now fight, and they died where we too may die. But when you are fighting for your freedom, there can be no failure, except the failure to fight in the first place."

"Yes, sir. Thank-you." He saluted and walked away.

Lieutenant Colonel Joseph Snow Eagle, thirty-eight, had grown up on a reservation outside of Lewiston, Idaho, and in his early youth he had seen what the depth of despair and self-doubt had done to his once proud people—despair that had led his father to kill himself slowly with alcohol, when he and his brother were little boys. But they were lucky. Thanks to their industrious and loving mother, they had risen above their humble circumstances and had grown up strong and straight and true. True to their ancestry but also true to their country, for all its history of mistreatment of their people. True, that is, up until the Bitterroot massacre. All that changed with the death of his brother.

Snow Eagle had never been so proud and so happy as he was on the day his brother graduated from Army Ranger school, exactly seven weeks to the day before he died. And now, all that Joseph had left of his brother was a faded photograph of the two of them as children playing in a high windswept meadow on the mountain known to their ancestors as the Kingdom of the Wind Spirits.

41

Department Of Justice, Washington, D.C.

Acting Attorney General, Mary Lou Pritchard, and her associate, Harry Erickson, sat across from each other in her office. Outside her window, the flat light of a raw spring morning painted the Department of Justice building in a dull gray wash. Her former boss, Arnold Greenberg, had urged Pritchard to use his old office, which was on the other side of the building facing the National Mall, but she wouldn't do that unless and until the President decided to recommend her to the Senate as Greenberg's replacement.

"How is he doing?" asked Erickson. As usual, he was wearing a heavily starched white shirt, a bowtie, and a shoulder holster with a large handgun.

Pritchard looked away and said, "Not good."

Erickson nodded sadly.

"When I saw him yesterday, he recognized me but couldn't speak," she added with tiny tears welling up in the corner of her eyes, which she quickly wiped away with the tissue she always held tightly in the palm of one hand.

They sat quietly for a few moments. Then Pritchard said, "What do we have on the man who attacked the Speaker?"

Erickson opened a folder that he had in his hand and spread a photograph of a Hispanic man plus a few typed sheets on her desk. "He wasn't carrying any identification, and his finger prints had been previously removed with acid. Unfortunately, he was already dead by the time the first response unit got to the scene, so a retinal or thermal scan were not possible. But the DNA scantrack was successful, and we identified him as Emilio Coriagra, a native of Nicaragua who was naturalized three years ago and lived in Miami."

"What about a record?"

"Mostly petty stuff. Three drug-trafficking arrests but no convictions. Just another small-time hood with big time dreams."

"Toxicology?"

"Clean. His blood tested negative for anything except ibuprofen."

"Ibuprofen?" asked the startled Pritchard. "A drug addict with Advil in his veins."

Erickson shook his head and said, "I know. There's more."

"Go on," said Pritchard.

"The chauffeur's gunfire didn't kill Coriagra. In fact he wasn't even hit."

"Really! What killed him?"

"The M.E. said it was Sudden Adult Death Syndrome," replied Erickson.

"SADS?"

"Yes."

"That's the last thing I would have expected to have killed this guy."

"Me too. I checked and there have been two other cases of SADS recently in the District."

"Two?" Pritchard was surprised. She had never heard of an actual case of SADS in all her years at the Department of Justice, and now suddenly there were three.

"Yes. I had the computer run a factor analysis looking for any connection between those two cases and this one."

"And?"

"I didn't find any link but get this, both those other cases involved that television newswoman, Sarah McGill."

"What?"

"Apparently the guy who attacked her near the Supreme Court last September, and the other one who assaulted her in that riot in front of the White House in January, both died from SADS."

"Really! You'd better dig into this deeper."

"Of course. I knew that you'd want me to." He paused. "But honestly, I wasn't exactly sure where to begin. I got a C in forensics at the academy, and besides, I never did like being around dead people."

"I don't know what to tell you, Harry. But suddenly we've got an mini-epidemic of people dropping dead for no reason in the District, and I want to know why."

"Understood."

"Start by trying to find a link between Mr. Coriagra and Ms. McGill."

"That's highly unlikely, but okay."

"Do a thorough background check on him," she added. "Somehow I don't think he was a drug addict. I've never heard of a crack head who takes Advil. "

"You got it."

Pritchard's expression darkened. "And look for a possible connection with the CIA."

He paused and his eyes narrowed. "Can I ask why?"

She shrugged. "Just a hunch. See if you can link him to Stefan Chadrian."

Erickson smiled knowingly. "And Maddun Gordon?"

"Exactly," Mary Lou nodded and then added, "This could get messy, so be careful."

"I hear you." He stood up to go and then turned back to his boss and asked, "I almost forgot. They found those two CIA outside contractors who disappeared in Boise a few weeks ago."

By the way he said it, Pritchard sensed what their fate was. "Dead?"

Erickson nodded. "Yeah. I'm afraid so."

"Don't tell me…"

"No. Not SADS this time. There was no mistaking what killed these guys. They were found in their van at the bottom of a thousand foot gorge."

Pritchard stared at her associate and then said, "Are we on it?"

"Yes, but the Bureau's not getting much cooperation from the State Police."

"I'm not surprised. Idaho is one of the few states who refused to join the NPF."

"Yeah. The President should never have allowed that to happen. Maybe things would be different today if he had."

Pritchard nodded, "Maybe. Keep me posted."

Just then, there was a knock on Pritchard's door.

"Come in."

R.A.R. Clouston

Pritchard's administrative assistant stepped in. The tears streaming down her cheeks said it all.

The blood drained from Pritchard's face. "Is it Arnold?" she asked.

The assistant nodded. "Yes. He's gone." Then she completely broke down.

"When?" asked Pritchard.

"A half an hour ago," the assistant sputtered through her tears.

Erickson looked at Mary Lou and said, "We're on our own, now."

Pritchard nodded and said softly, "Let's make him proud."

42

The White House, Washington, D.C.

"Will there never be an end to gun violence?" Vice President Richard Knox asked rhetorically. "What kind of a country is this, where even the Speaker of the House can be gunned down on a busy street?" The Vice President was sitting on one of the two pastel yellow sofas.

"It's not a happy time for Jeremiah Kincaid," added the President, who was sitting on a high-backed chair between the sofas. He was smoking a cigar.

With them in the Oval Office were Maddun Gordon and Patrick Fitzgerald. Fitzgerald was sitting across from Knox, while Gordon paced as he usually did.

"If Kincaid's driver hadn't been armed, the Speaker wouldn't be unhappy. He'd be dead," said Gordon with a smirk.

"I didn't know that congressional drivers were armed," said the President.

"Once your bill passes, there won't be any need for them to be," replied Fitzgerald.

"Maybe we won't even need armed protection," said the Vice President.

"Don't be ridiculous," quipped Webster. "There will always be some nut out there who wants to kill me."

No one in the room wanted to touch that line. Finally, Knox said, "Mr. President, you mean, who wants to kill the President, whomever he or she may be."

"Yeah, right," muttered Gordon.

The President nodded but didn't say anything. He just took another puff on his cigar.

Fitzgerald brought the conversation back to the central issue, as he often did. "Perhaps we should suggest to the Speaker that he delay the House debate."

"Absolutely not," snapped Gordon. "This plays right into our hands. How many of his own party are going to vote pro-gun after the man they revere was nearly shot to death?"

"Maddun's right, Mr. President," added the Vice President. "This is a telling example of what the merchants of death are doing to our country."

Gordon looked at Knox and asked facetiously, "The Speaker was shot by a merchant? I thought we killed all those foreign camel jockeys."

The Vice President was not pleased with such a serious matter being treated flippantly, but he kept his cool, "The gun that was used by the man who shot the Speaker was typical of the kind that anyone can buy at a gun show. Cheap, but deadly."

There was a pregnant pause that was broken by Fitzgerald. "I can't see how it would hurt to delay the floor debate for a few days. However, Maddun's right about this helping us, Mr. President. Our preliminary assessment is that we will pick up ten Republican votes, possibly more, because of this incident."

"Then let's not delay anything, gentlemen," said the President.

Fitzgerald looked like there was something else he wanted to say. The President noticed, "Let's have it, Patrick. I can tell by the look on your face that there's something else eating at you."

"Yes, sir. There is. I would like to re-open the possibility of you meeting with the Speaker."

Gordon abruptly stopped pacing and said emphatically, "No! The President already told you that he won't. Besides, now with this shooting, we don't need to."

"It's precisely because of the shooting that I think we should," said Fitzgerald, making his case directly to the President and ignoring Gordon.

"Oh, for shit's sake," muttered Gordon in a huff, resuming his prowling.

The Vice President flashed an annoyed look toward Gordon. He did not approve of such language at any time in the White House, especially not in the presence of the President. But for whatever reason, Webster tolerated

Gordon's foul mouth, and there was little anyone else could do. Looking back at the President, he said, "I agree with Patrick, Mr. President."

The President thought about it for a moment and then asked Fitzgerald, "Do you really think we can gain ground in the House by reaching out to Kincaid?"

"Yes, sir," said Fitzgerald. "In several ways. First, it will appear to be a genuine expression of your respect and concern for him, which will sit well with both the Congress and the public. And second, he might be more willing to listen to your ideas now that he has looked down the killing end of a barrel and felt its leaded bite."

"Bullshit," snapped Gordon, clearly overstepping the bounds of Oval Office decorum. Both Fitzgerald and Knox glared at him this time. He just gave them a slight shrug.

The President thought about it some more and then said, "I'll give it serious consideration."

Fitzgerald and Knox were pleased. It wasn't the answer they had hoped for, but at least it wasn't an outright rejection.

"I strongly disagree, Mr. President," said Gordon, as he tried to restrain himself from any further obscenities.

"Your point has been duly noted, Maddun," answered the President. Turning back to the others, he said, "What's next, gentlemen?"

"We should discuss replacing the Attorney General, sir," replied Knox. "Now that Arnold Greenberg has passed on—may God rest his soul—the Senate will expect to get your recommendation on a permanent replacement soon."

"How is the vetting going on Pritchard?" he asked Fitzgerald.

"It's done, Mr. President. She's as clean as the driven snow," he replied, handing the President a file folder that he took out of his briefcase. "I agree with the Vice President, sir. I think you need to act decisively on this matter."

The President took the folder. Without opening it, he looked at Gordon, "Do you agree?"

Gordon nodded his agreement, but not for any altruistic reasons. He was simply delighted at the prospect of having her hot body around the White House more often.

"I'll think about it," replied the President. He stood up, prompting Knox and Fitzgerald to do the same. "Now, if you will excuse me, gentlemen, I need some time to prepare for my meeting with the party leadership this afternoon."

They left, and Webster walked back to his desk with the folder in one hand and a cigar in the other. He put the cigar down in a large, crystal ashtray that bore the Presidential Seal, flipped open the folder, and pulled out a glossy photograph of Pritchard. It looked more like a model's headshot than a government ID. He smiled and said out loud, "Mary Lou Pritchard, I think you and I are going to become close friends." He propped up the photograph against the lamp on his desk and sat down. Then he re-lit the cigar and leaned back in his chair. "Very close, indeed." The fact that the object of his affection was a married woman didn't trouble Alex Webster in the least. After all, what was power and privilege for? If stealing another man's wife was good enough for CEOs, movie stars and kings, it was certainly good enough for the most powerful man on the face of the earth. Besides, no woman can be stolen who doesn't want to be.

TWO HOURS LATER, the President sat in the taller chair at the center of the east side of the oval mahogany conference table in the Cabinet Room, which was his customary place whenever he met with his Cabinet. However, on that afternoon, there were no Cabinet members present. Instead, the President was meeting with the Democratic leaders of the House and the Senate, including Douglas Martin, the House Minority Leader, and Sydney Fairfax, the Senate Minority Leader. Also present were Maddun Gordon, Patrick Fitzgerald, and Jefferson Brewster, the President's chief congressional liaison.

The President looked like his patience was wearing thin, which was not a good thing, and everyone in the room knew it. "Gentlemen, if I can cut through all the 'tell him what he needs to hear but do it diplomatically' bullshit, your consensus is that the bill would have had an easier passage through the Congress if I had introduced it into the Senate first."

The room fell silent as eyes darted to and fro. Finally Brewster spoke up. "Mr. President, given what we knew at the time, I think our plan was a good one."

"Then why do we now feel this strategy was in error?" asked the President.

Again silence. And again the burden fell to Brewster to take the heat. But he hit the issue head-on, which spared him from the wrath that the President reserved for people who tried to dance around issues. "Mr. President, I underestimated the negative impact that the Bitterroots incident had upon the general population and, in turn, the House members."

Fairfax added, "We all did, Mr. President—that is, all of us in the leadership who advised you on the matter. Instead of turning the public against guns, the way those young men and their leader Thomas Porter—"

"You mean, T.J. Kincaid," interjected Maddun Gordon as if he was spitting out a hair from his mouth.

"Yes, thank-you, Mr. Gordon," said Fairfax, not really meaning it. "I stand corrected." He turned back to the President. "The way those young men and their leader, T.J. Kincaid, handled themselves, combined with the fact that almost all of them later died, created sympathy for them and their cause that we could not possibly have predicted."

Everyone in the room held their breath, expecting the President to explode the way he usually did whenever the Bitterroots or T.J. Kincaid were mentioned. But he didn't. Instead he just nodded and remained silent.

Sensing that the storm had been averted, Martin jumped in. Never one to stick his neck out first until he saw which way the wind was blowing, the minority leader had been given the nickname, "Turtleman" by those who sat across the aisle. It was an apt descriptor, and more recently during the gun debate, he had done it so relentlessly, even some among his own party had begun using the nickname, behind his back of course. Once again, in that room on that day, he was about to prove it so. "Mr. President, I think a series of events outside your control have clouded the issue and made it seem that those who oppose gun control are the victims in this national crisis, rather than the thousands of real victims who die by the gun each and every day." When he finished speaking, Martin flashed an inane little grin that only served to make him look even more like a turtle, and he sat back down, contented with himself. It would last but a nanosecond.

"Thank-you, Douglas," said the President, lighting up Martin's face even further, "for that blinding flash of the obvious." The smile vanished, and Turtleman retreated into his metaphorical shell. The President looked around the room at the others and said, "All right, gentlemen. You have spent over an hour telling me what the problem is, but so far, I haven't heard any solutions."

Brewster started to speak, but Fairfax beat him to it. Unlike his colleague from the House, Fairfax was a man of sweeping vision but verbal restraint, and when he spoke, members on both sides of the aisle paid attention. It was no secret that he had great respect for the Speaker of the House despite their political differences, so what he was about to say surprised no one. "Mr. President. The solution lies in two words." He paused. Everyone in the room waited to hear the answer. They knew that whatever Sydney Fairfax believed would get them through this difficult situation would be the best solution out of the many choices facing them.

"Go ahead Syd," said the President.

"Jeremiah Kincaid," he replied without either hesitation or apprehension.

Gordon gagged quietly while a smile slipped across Fitzgerald's lips.

Fairfax continued. "Even with the recent horrible events on the steps of the Congress and the Speaker's own near brush with death, public opinion is still widely split. And whether or not we like it, the hard reality is that the Speaker's continued calm and steady voice of reason in favor of a compromise, even in the face of his own shooting, has prevented us from building the necessary majority that we require in the House."

For a moment the President didn't say anything. Then slowly he nodded and asked, "So you think I should meet with him?"

"Yes, Mr. President."

"And work with him to find a mutually acceptable solution to the impasse?"

"Yes, sir. I know the two of you can, Mr. President. I'm sure of it."

The President paused before replying. The others were certain that he would reject the idea as he had done so many times before. But this time was different. "All right, I'll do it." And with those words, the President showed that despite all the inappropriate behavior regarding women, the hair-trigger temper, and the anti-gun crusade that had its roots more deeply embedded in narcissism than altruism, the man, like many of those who preceded him, had inexplicably begun to rise to the higher standards of the office rather than bring the standards down.

43

Municipal Airport, Boise, Idaho

As the U.S. Air Force passenger jet began its initial descent into Boise, Jeremiah Kincaid peered out the oval window toward the snow-capped peaks of the Sawtooth Range off in the distance. They brought back happy memories of Christmases that he and his family had spent in Sun Valley. The thought that they would never be together again depressed him deeply. He turned away from the window and winced slightly as his left arm, which was in a sling, bumped the armrest of the captain's chair. *Now is not the time for personal matters. I must concentrate on my mission,* he thought. But it was of no use; he couldn't get T.J. out of his mind.

It had been nearly two weeks since he had been shot, and at least physically, he was feeling stronger. Enough so that he had convinced his wife Kathleen to return to their farm in Wisconsin. He would have liked to have had more time to prepare for his meeting with Morrissey as he hadn't been able to get much done in Washington while his wife was there. But time wasn't on his side, and he knew it. Within a few days, the Congress would resume the floor debate of the President's bill, and he hoped that he could convince Edward Morrissey to join with him in a compromise proposal. It was a long shot but at least Morrissey had agreed to meet with him. Throughout his long career, he had learned one lesson well, which was that the best outcome to a disagreement was usually obtained in face-to-face contact. Usually, but not always. The words of William Lloyd Garrison that George Ross had recently quoted to him, kept sounding in his head: *With reasonable men I will reason. With humane men I will plead. But to tyrants, I will give no quarter nor waste arguments where they will certainly be lost.* Which would it be with Morrissey, he wondered. Humanity, reason, or tyranny? He was about to find out.

A gentle bell tone went off inside the cabin and the co-pilot's voice came over the intercom, "We've begun our descent into Boise, Mr. Speaker. Please make sure that your seatbelt is fastened."

It was fastened, but the Speaker gave it another tug anyway. Then he settled back in his seat. He heard the flaps being lowered and then a short while later the sound of the landing gear being locked into position. Then, as smoothly as a Teflon zipper closes, the jet's wheels touched down onto the runway, and the thrust reversers slowed the plane, pushing the Speaker forward slightly against his belt. As the sleek jet with its proud Air Force marking slowly taxied toward the corporate aviation terminal, the Speaker was surprised to see several Idaho Air National Guard jet transports being unloaded by a large contingent of soldiers and airman. There seemed to be a significant amount of military supplies and equipment positioned all across the tarmac. He wondered if they were conducting a major training exercise that weekend. He made a mental note to check on it later.

What the Speaker also didn't know was that one hundred yards away, his youngest son, T.J. Kincaid, known to the locals as Thomas Porter, was sitting inside an Idaho Army National Guard helicopter waiting to take off. It was going to take him high up into the mountains to the Wolf River Militia training site in the River of No Return Wilderness. Although the militia was obviously not a legitimate government military unit, ever since the Bitterroots incident, the line between the Idaho Guard and the militia had become blurred.

The air force jet slowly rolled to a stop, and the door opened and lowered itself to the ground, becoming steps as it did. The co-pilot was first out of the aircraft. He stopped at the bottom of the stairs and assisted the Speaker. When the Speaker reached the bottom of the stairs, the two men exchanged a few words. It was obvious that the air force officer had the deepest respect for the Speaker, whom he knew to be a graduate of West Point; who had served honorably in the Army during several years of peace following the Vietnam War and before the First Gulf War; and who had shown steadfast support for the military throughout his political career.

"When you're ready to depart, just call us at this number, sir," said the co-pilot, handing the Speaker a slip of paper with the number on it. The co-pilot stepped back and saluted the Speaker, who gracefully acknowledged it with a nod.

The Speaker headed over to the limousine that the Governor of Idaho had sent to pick him up. Just as Kincaid slipped into the back seat of the stretch vehicle, the Army Guard helicopter, with his son on board, lifted off the tarmac and swooped overhead. For just the briefest of moments, father and son were only a few hundred feet apart. But it might as well have been a few million miles.

JEREMIAH KINCAID and Edward Morrissey were seated across from each other in the governor's office. One on each side of the governor's enormous Brazilian mahogany desk. Neither man was smiling. The frustration on the Speaker's face was matched only by the growing fatigue. "Edward. What is it about this issue that makes you so unwilling to listen to reason?"

The governor got up and walked over to a large gun cabinet made of glass and wood that matched his desk. Inside was only a small part of his vast collection of rare and expensive guns. He opened the glass door, reached inside, and carefully took out a Purdy double-barreled twelve gauge shotgun. He opened the breach to make sure that it wasn't loaded, and then he walked over to where the Speaker was sitting. "Look at this, Jeremiah." He held it out for the Speaker to see. "Just look at the craftsmanship, the polished British walnut stock, the hand engraving." The governor's eyes were filled with pride bordering on obsession.

"It *is* beautiful, Edward. Just like the other fine possessions in this office. But unlike them, this one can kill. And that makes all the difference. Which is why it should be registered."

The governor snapped the breach shut and returned the gun to its case. "So, too, can a knife, Jeremiah. Would you have the Federal Government register all knives? Or would we just require anything with a blade longer than three inches to be licensed. Oops! Wait a minute. I forgot about scalpels. The blade on them is only an inch long but maybe we had better include scalpels on the list and case cutters too, since we *know* what they can do. And come to think of it, a mirror can be broken. Perhaps we should register all mirrors while we're at it, or why not anything made out of glass, or metal, or…"

Kincaid interrupted him, "Edward, a gun is different, and you know it."

The governor sat down behind his desk and pointed his finger at Jeremiah, "Exactly! It *is* different. It is a part of our history. It is as American as a coonskin hat and a bowie knife. And to take guns away from Americans is to pull just one thread from the quilt of our heritage. Do you really want to pull that one thread, Jeremiah? Are you willing to take the risk that it might unravel the entire quilt itself?"

The Speaker remained cool and calm and spoke with slow deliberation. "With all due respect, Edward, you are mistaken in your presumption that the gun is a thread in the American quilt, as you describe it. It is not. The fact is that only one in seven of the citizens in the thirteen colonies owned a weapon, and less than half of those could even be fired. They were unwieldy and inaccurate implements, which rusted easily and often killed the shooter instead of his target. After the American Revolution, the government couldn't even give the heavy muskets away. And surely you don't believe the carnage of the Civil War endeared guns to the people. My God, Edward, just look at the photographs of the aftermath of any of those battles, and tell me that the survivors of that bloody war wanted to run right out and buy themselves a gun. Tell me that they wanted to proudly own and keep close to them one of the implements of death that had stolen life and limb away from hundreds of thousands of their fathers, brothers, and sons."

Morrissey said nothing. He just sat there staring at Kincaid across the gaping chasm of dissent.

Jeremiah continued, "It wasn't until some pandering Eastern novelists sensationalized the six gun in gory fairy tales about the American West that anyone even thought about weapons as other than an instrument of war." He paused and shook his head. "No, Edward, the gun is not a thread woven into the fabric of American history. Far from it. It is a bottle of indelible ink perched precariously upon it. And if you and the Western Freedom Party persist in your mission, the bottle will tip, and the quilt will be destroyed. Forever."

The governor's eyes narrowed. "If it does, Jeremiah, it will have been your President who is responsible. Not me."

"*Our* President," replied the Speaker, emphasizing the first word.

"No, Jeremiah. He is no more *our* President than King George was *our* monarch."

"Your analogy is weak. The Federal Government does not seek to tax your weapons nor take them away from you. All we want is for you to register them and obtain a license just as you do with cars. There is nothing more threatening or oppressive to it than that."

"An oppressor knows not oppression, Jeremiah."

The Speaker shook his head sadly, "What has Washington done, Edward, to deserve your animosity and distrust and that of the thousands of people who follow you?"

"Millions, Jeremiah. Millions who follow me," the governor corrected him ominously. "I am surprised that you would even ask that question after what happened five months ago on that mountaintop northeast of here."

"That was an unfortunate incident," snapped the Speaker, who was obviously growing tired of the debate.

"No, Mr. Speaker, it was not! It was only the most recent example in a long history of the Federal Government crushing those who disagree with it."

"I will not dispute that the government was inept and even heavy handed in the way that it handled the Bitterroots Rod & Gun Club incident. But those men had broken the law, Edward. They occupied government property and murdered the Army Ranger captain, who had been sent as the duly authorized representative of the government and the people who elected it."

"Now it is you who have distorted history, Jeremiah. That club belonged to the men who occupied it. They still had thirty years remaining on the ninety-nine year lease on the land that it sat upon, and they had done nothing to violate the terms and conditions of that lease. And if you had listened to your son before condemning him, you would know that the death of the Ranger captain was precipitated by a tragic accident and not a murderous act." The governor instantly realized that he had stepped over the line with his comment about T.J. Sadness clouded the Speaker's face and an invisible weight made his shoulders sag. It was apparent to the governor that the person sitting across from him was not just the Speaker of the House of Representatives of the United States of America but also a human being. Flawed and vulnerable and no less precious than any one of the over three hundred million Americans just like him. "I'm sorry, Jeremiah. That was completely uncalled for," said the governor, with compassion in his voice.

The Speaker didn't answer. It was obvious that he was having difficulty maintaining his composure.

There was a long silence, then the governor said softly, "Your youngest son is safe and well, Jeremiah. I have seen to that."

The Speaker looked up at the governor and nodded sadly. "Thank-you, Edward."

"I promise that I won't let any harm come to him."

The Speaker gathered himself and said, "Perhaps you might..." he paused.

"Yes, Jeremiah?"

"Perhaps you might give him a message for me?"

"Of course."

The Speaker took a deep breath and then said the words that he had wished he had spoken that night on the telcom. "Tell him—tell him that I love him."

The governor stared at the other man and then slowly nodded. "Of course." Then he summoned compassion from beneath the anger of his position and said softly, "Jeremiah, for the sake of your sons, both of them, and the millions of others just like them, you must prevent the President from succeeding on his mission. He is the rider on a pale horse, and hell follows with him. You must believe me." The governor was obviously playing to the emotion of the moment. He knew that Jeremiah often quoted from the Bible and he was certain that the reference to Revelation chapter six, verse eight, would touch a resonant chord with the Speaker.

But by then Jeremiah Kincaid had regained his composure and was now the Speaker of the House again, not the father of his long-lost son. "This is a nation that was built upon the rule of law, Edward. You know that as well as I do. We, as a people, will only survive if our citizens continue to honor that premise. The process of crafting, debating, approving, and enacting laws is the thin line that separates us from the land of perpetual shadows. And the most fundamental precept of this entire system is that when there is a dispute over the interpretation of those laws, we use the courts to decide. What the Federal Government did up on that mountain was inexcusable, and there are many of us in Washington who have publicly condemned President Webster for what he did.

"However, that does not change the central issue here, which is that my son, and those men who followed him, broke the law. They did not seek the help of our system of justice by going to the courts to get an injunction against the closure of the club. They did not march peaceably in front of the Department of the Interior. They did not circulate a petition among the people of this state demanding their rights to use that property. Instead, they took a convoy of trucks, loaded with guns and ammunition and supplies, up to the top of that mountain, and they waited for the inevitable to happen. And forty-two of them, along with seven young Army soldiers, paid for this act of defiance with their lives. I feel nothing but the deepest of sorrow for the loss of these young lives, but the brutal fact remains that if my son, T.J. Kincaid, had not led those men up that road, they would all be alive today."

Morrissey shook his head slowly and sighed deeply. "It is not my place, Jeremiah, to tell you how to deal with the boy who is made from your own flesh and blood, but the fact is that those men would have gone up that mountain with or without him. And I categorically reject your premise that those young men did not seek justice. That is exactly what they sought. But what happened to them was not justice—it was vengeance. And no man, or group of men, has the right to wreak vengeance upon another." The governor paused and then quoted one last Biblical reference. "'For it is written, Vengeance is mine; I will repay, saith the Lord.' And although the man who currently occupies the office apparently does not read the Bible, nor would he grasp the difference, the President of the United States of America is not God."

"Romans twelve, nineteen," said Kincaid. "But Edward, you didn't finish the chapter. Romans twelve, twenty-one says, 'Be not overcome of evil, but overcome evil with good.'"

Again the room fell silent. The governor should have known better than to quote the Bible to Jeremiah Kincaid. They sat there in stony silence. Each man wrestling with the issue that would have profound consequences not only for the two of them but for the divided nation, which they represented. The mantel clock sitting in his bookcase sounded it's steady beat. Tick. Tock. Tick. Tock. And as it did, the last chance for a covenant of peace, and the contract for the salvation of the American way, slipped slowly, inexorably away.

"Edward, is there nothing that I can say to gain your support to my compromise?"

The governor's initial reaction was to say no and be done with it. For he was certain that compromise would only delay the inevitable. He was about to say so when a strange feeling came over him. It was one of overwhelming apprehension. As if something bad was about to happen, right then and there. His vision narrowed into a tunnel and suddenly, he felt as if he was being transported through time and space, on silent wings of a giant bird. When his vision cleared, he and the Speaker were facing each other, in a great hall, and standing behind the Speaker, directly in his line of vision, was a dark rider sitting on a pale horse, backlit by a blinding light. And a voice sounded in his head and it said to him, *And his name was Death and hell followed with him.* And in that horrible, frightening moment, Morrissey knew with stone-cold certainty that the angel of death was coming for him. Then, as abruptly as it had seized his mind, the vision was gone, and he was back in the safety of his office; but the terrible memory of it wouldn't leave him. His pulse was pounding and he struggled to regain his breath. He felt a cold sweat run down his back.

"Edward, are you all right?"

At first, the governor didn't answer. Gradually, he came out of his trance. He shook his head sharply from side to side to clear his muddled mind. He looked at the Speaker and slowly nodded. "Yes, thank-you. It was just an anxiety attack. My doctor says I'm getting them, because I am working too hard."

Kincaid looked upon the other man with genuine empathy. "I understand, Edward. Perhaps you should follow his advice and slow down."

Morrissey stared at the Speaker and then said softly, "I cannot."

The Speaker nodded and let it go. He repeated his question. "How can I get your support to my compromise bill?"

Morrissey spoke slowly. His haughtiness seemed gone. "If I could believe that your compromise bill would be approved by the Congress and signed by the President, then, and only then, I might be willing to put it before my party."

"Not just put it before them, Edward, but give it your full and unconditional support," added the Speaker passionately.

The governor leaned back into his leather chair seeking solace in its deep embrace. He desperately tried to reconstruct the image that only moments ago had so vividly engrossed his mind. As if by bringing it back, he could prove to himself that there was nothing to fear; that he had not been troubled by it at all, and that thereby he would retrieve his self-assurance. But he could not get it back. Finally, without even realizing what he was saying, he uttered the words that Kincaid so desperately needed to hear, "Yes, Jeremiah, I will support it."

The Speaker was overjoyed. "Thank-you, Edward. You are truly a wise and brave leader."

The governor quickly added in a monotone, "I have agreed to do this only upon the condition that the bill contains your amendments to safeguard the people's rights. Under no circumstances can their privilege to own guns be abrogated. Period. Even then, I cannot promise that the people who follow me will endorse it."

"If you add your voice to the call for compromise, Edward, and commit yourself to overcome evil with good, there will be peace," said the Speaker.

The terrifying vision that had overwhelmed the governor only moments earlier seemed to be fading, and with it, his willingness to compromise. "It is not my voice that is the issue here, Jeremiah. It is the voice of freedom." He gazed out the window of his office toward the dry foothills and pale mountains beyond. "Less than two hundred miles from here, a militia is being formed deep in the wilderness. Like a giant bear that has just awoken from a long winter's sleep, they sit in a remote valley, flexing their muscles, sharpening their claws and feeling an insatiable hunger deep inside. Moreover, other groups just like it are springing up all across the western landscape. They are not made up of some motley rabble of fanatics and fascists who lurk on the fringes of society. They are young men and women who have heard the call of freedom no less faintly than did our nation's first patriots over two centuries ago."

The governor's statement obviously troubled the Speaker. "I hope you are not telling me that you, or men who work for you, are inciting these young people to take arms against their own country, Edward. Because any such act is treason and would be punishable by death."

"There is nothing illegal about what they are doing, Jeremiah. You, better than anyone, should know that the First and Second Amendments to the Constitution grant them the right to assemble and to bear arms. It was true two hundred years ago, and unless we allow Webster to burn that hallowed document, it is still true today."

The Speaker shook his head. "Edward, Edward, Edward. What propaganda are you putting into their young heads?"

"One man's propaganda is another man's truth, Jeremiah. What do you suppose the British called it when John Adams began his crusade? And like those armies of long ago, these young patriots of the new West look to the East and see a tyrant rising with the morning sun. And they will not stand for it."

The Speaker was visibly angry. "Please, Edward, cut the bombast and the bravado, will you? Neither the White House nor the Congress will tolerate ultimatums from any enemy, foreign or domestic. If you have any vestige of concern for these young people's lives, then you must tell them to go home and trust their elected representatives in Washington to protect their rights."

The governor shook his head angrily. "They will not go home, Jeremiah. Not until they are certain that the tyrant is either defused or defeated." He paused and calmed himself slightly. "However, you can be assured that neither I, nor they, will take any unilateral action against anyone." He got up, walked over to his credenza, and picked up a bronze plaque. On it were inscribed the names of the Wolf River Militia who died at the Bitterroot Rod & Gun Club. "These young men climbed a mountain that is known to the native people as the Kingdom of the Wind Spirit. They went there to raise their voices against a Federal Government that had betrayed them. And just like the Native American warriors over a hundred years before them, they were slaughtered in the name of law and order. But whose law, Jeremiah? And whose order?" The governor put the plaque down and returned to his chair. He looked the Speaker directly in the eyes and said, "We will never again stand idly by and allow Federal troops to march into the West and murder our people."

The Speaker stared coldly at Morrissey. "No good can come of words like those, Edward. And the louder you speak them, the greater the chance that what you fear will happen. The purple mountains, the green foothills, and the golden prairies will run red with the blood of our children. And you will have your American quilt, but it will bring no comfort and no glory. It will be a shroud of death."

The governor paused before answering. "You speak eloquently, Jeremiah. You always have. But your passion for peace has blinded you to the timbre of our times. In the history of mankind, whenever a government has tried to stifle the voice of its people, they have simply learned to speak in whispers and walk in shadows, until the day they could rise up and shake off the shackles of oppression—that glorious day when they could once again be free to stand up on the rooftops and shout out the one word that men have fought and died for through all eternity. Liberty. Liberty. Liberty!" His words hung in the silence of the room. He paused for a moment and seemed to be wrestling with whether or not he should tell the Speaker something else. Then he decided to do so. "Jeremiah, we in the Western Freedom Party are not alone. There is another group of far greater influence than the party or our young patriots in the mountains."

The Speaker's eyes narrowed. He knew what was coming, but he wanted to hear the governor say it.

"It is a group of men and women who walk in the highest circles of power, in both the private and public sectors. Its membership is a veritable who's who of the best and the brightest in our land, and they are strongly opposed to what the President is attempting to do. They call themselves the New Sons of Liberty. And while my young men and women will be the teeth and claws of the bear, the New Sons of Liberty will be its roar."

The Speaker nodded. "Which is all the more reason that you must place your full support behind my proposed amendments, Edward. Before this goes any further. Before the New Sons of Liberty act foolishly. Before any one dies."

The governor stared at Kincaid with an intensity that the Speaker had never seen in all the years they had known each other; and then he added something that sent a cold chill down the Speaker's back, "Jeremiah, I will support your compromise, but remember this, the only thing standing between the bear and the tyrant is you."

The Speaker nodded solemnly and stood up. The governor did also.

"Edward, you also have a way with words. Why don't you run for President and change the government from the inside, instead of shouting your dissatisfaction from afar?"

The governor thought about it for a moment and then answered with a sly smile, "Because, Jeremiah, I might lose."

The Speaker had no comeback. They stepped toward each other and for just the briefest of moments, it looked as if they might embrace. But they did not. Instead they simply shook hands, but neither man indulged himself in any overt display of emotion. The meeting had drained all the emotion out of each man.

"Thank-you, Edward, for your support. As God is my witness, I will not fail," said the Speaker bravely.

"I pray that you don't, Jeremiah," answered the governor, but his heart was not in it.

"For now, all I ask is that you hold back the bear," added the Speaker.

The governor nodded with a slow deliberate movement. "I will do what I can, Jeremiah. For the sake of freedom, for the sake of America, and for the sake of the young men who will be called upon to defend both."

The governor's meaning was not lost on Kincaid. The Speaker started to leave the office. As he did, he noticed the large bronze eagle sculpture sitting in an alcove of the bookcase. It was the same one that Jesse Latrobe had handled the day the men died on the mountain. He walked over and looked at it closely.

"Beautiful, isn't it?" said Morrissey.

"Yes. It is," said the Speaker. "Where did you get it?"

"It was a gift from a wealthy supporter. I don't know where he got it or who made it."

"May I?" asked the Speaker, motioning with his hands that he wanted to pick it up.

"Of course."

The Speaker carefully lifted it up and looked at the bottom of it. There he spied a small symbol. As soon as he saw it, he smiled. "This is truly a treasure, Edward. It was created by a Nez Perce chief who lived over one hundred years ago, by the name of Gray Wolf."

"Really! How do you know that?"

"The study of native American art is a hobby of mine."

Morrissey shook his head in admiration and amazement. "You are truly a renaissance man, Mr. Speaker."

The Speaker became demure. "Thank-you, Edward. It's not only a beautiful work of art, it is a symbol of all that is beautiful about the land that we both love."

In a magnanimous gesture, Morrissey said, "Take it. Please. As a gift from me."

The Speaker's smile vanished. "No. I cannot. But thank-you. It is a most generous offer. Now I must go."

"Very well. Goodbye, Mr. Speaker."

"Goodbye, Governor." Then he walked out of the office.

All that remained now was to make the compromise work. In his heart, Jeremiah Kincaid knew that he must not fail. In his mind, Edward Morrissey believed that the Speaker could not possibly succeed. Only time would tell which would prevail, the hearts or minds of America. And time was running out.

44

River of No Return, Idaho

The helicopter carrying T.J. Kincaid flared like a fat goose and settled down gently on the helipad of the training camp of the Wolf River Militia. This group now numbered over ten thousand men, or the equivalent of a regular Army division. And it was growing every day, along with similar groups located in the other western states, in direct parallel with the war of rhetoric between Boise and Washington. Increasingly, the American population was beginning to believe that the angry words and warnings might indeed turn into mindless bombs and bullets.

The entire population, that is, with the exception of those living in New York and Los Angeles. In New York, the only thing that was on the minds of the people was the fact that the Red Sox, who had won the World Series the year before, were already seven games ahead of the Yankees, and there was talk of lynching the Yankee's coach, figuratively and even literally. In fact, there had been so many threats made against his life, serious or otherwise, that with the help of the captain of his local police precinct, he had obtained a concealed weapon permit, and now carried a .357 magnum revolver with a snub nose barrel everywhere with him, including into the dug out, where he hid it in a case of sunflower seeds. While on the other coast, Los Angelinos viewed the growing tensions in the Rockies as simply a potential made-for-TV movie; it was the way they tended to view all of life's dramatic events, whether they were good or bad.

Nevertheless, despite this bicoastal indifference, the Group of Seven governors who had met in Boise two months earlier were now busily following through with their plan to blitz the airwaves with anti-big-government advertising. And at least in the Heartland, it was working.

As soon as the helicopter's rotors began to slow down, the Idaho National Guard co-pilot hopped out and opened the passenger door. Immediately Kincaid stepped out.

"I hope the flight wasn't too rough for you, Captain Porter," said the attractive young woman whose firm figure could still be seen even under the baggy flight suit.

Kincaid had been so preoccupied when he got on board the helicopter in Boise that he hadn't noticed that the co-pilot was a woman. But now he couldn't help but notice her as she stood there smiling, holding the door. "No. It was fine, Lieutenant," he hesitated, as his eyes found the name tag on the top of her right breast and lingered there.

"It's Wright, sir," she answered brightly. She couldn't help but notice.

"What?" he said, obviously embarrassed, his eyes regaining her face.

"I said Wright, sir. That's my name, Kelly Wright."

"Oh yes. Well, it's nice to meet you, Lieutenant Kelly Wright."

"Thank-you, sir. Have a great day." With that, she closed the passenger door and climbed back into the left cockpit seat.

Kincaid watched her intently through the side window for a moment and then turned and walked at right angles away from the helicopter toward the road where a Humvee and driver sat waiting for him. He had had another successful fundraising trip to Boise, and now all he wanted to do was get out of his suit and tie, into his blue jeans and sweat shirt, and relax. Since rejoining the governor's team, Kincaid had personally raised over fifty million dollars for their cause, and more was pouring in every day. The message of the Western Freedom Party had struck a resonant chord with people all across the nation as well as around the world, and cash donations were being received faster than the auditors, who had been appointed by the governor, could count it. Much of it was being channeled into advertising and legislative programs in support of the Western Freedom Party's platform. However, a large portion of it was being used to purchase weapons and military supplies, and to fund the training of the militia. In fact, so much material was being procured that Governor Morrissey was growing concerned that the enormous stockpile of armaments and ammunition accumulating in Boise and several other western cities was becoming increasingly difficult to hide from the prying eyes of the media and Federal authorities. Not that what they were doing was illegal. But if it got wide coverage in the national media, it would be awkward to explain at the very least. As a result, he was becoming paranoid about spies who he was certain were everywhere.

While the governor worried about the presence of spies, Kincaid constantly worried about the possibility of being captured by the FBI. Up until that point, he had managed to stay just outside their grasp with the protection of the governor and his far-reaching powers. Most significant of these was the Idaho State Police, who viewed Kincaid as a hero rather than a felon, as did virtually the entire population of the West. Moreover, ever since his ex-wife had been forcibly removed from their estate in Sun Valley by the local sheriff, complete with her cats and chickens, Kincaid had converted the property into a halfway house for underprivileged and troubled Native American teenagers.

This was only one of the many altruistic acts that his fortune had enabled him to do. Among them was also the establishment of a scholarship fund for the children of all policemen and firemen killed in the line of duty in Idaho and her six sister states. It was certainly not why Kincaid had done it, but the highly publicized act had served to guarantee that Kincaid would be treated royally wherever he went in the state, and shielded from all outsiders including Federal authorities. In effect, Kincaid had become a modern-day Robin Hood, and he enjoyed every minute of it.

Ironically, while the father of the man named T. J. Kincaid had visited the governor in Boise trying to prevent the coming confrontation, the man known as Thomas Porter was working diligently to fund it. But at that moment, neither fundraising for guns nor being captured were on Kincaid's mind as he hurried across the helipad toward the waiting vehicle.

"Welcome to Camp Freedom," said the corporal.

"Thank-you, Corporal," replied Kincaid, as he threw his duffel bag in the back of the Humvee and climbed in.

Immediately, the powerful vehicle headed down the dirt road that led to the main barracks and base command center. Along the way, the Humvee had to pull over several times to allow main battle tanks pass. The noise of their engines, the enormity of their physical presence, and the sinister capability of their guns was both exhilarating and intimidating. General Latrobe had suggested that it might be a good idea for Kincaid to spend some time at the camp and see how the money that he had been raising was being spent. He had immediately agreed. Besides, he was looking forward to being around guns and the men who knew how to use them again. It had been five months since the Army Rangers stormed the Bitterroot Rod & Gun Club and Kincaid had not held a gun in his hands since. As he witnessed the hectic activity of a full-scale military build up, Kincaid was filled with an unmistakable sense of excitement mixed with dread.

"What's going on, Corporal?"

"We're having a live fire exercise today, sir."

"Is that a big deal?"

"Yes, sir. Thanks to the money you've raised, the camp has enough tank simulators to train an entire squadron; but the truth is, sir, that there is nothing like the real thing to get your heart pumping."

As he spoke, they had to pull off to the side of the road to allow another tank platoon rumble by. After they had passed, Kincaid asked, "Where are they going to do this?"

"In Grizzly Flats, sir," he replied, referring to a broad valley five miles wide and ten miles long that was a twenty-minute ride from the main camp.

"I sure would like to see that," he said, as he watched the latest iteration of what the armored cavalry called a command track growl along the dirt road toward them, followed by several Stryker wheeled armored vehicles, fitted with wire cages to defend against rocket propelled grenade attack.

"I think that can be arranged. There's the squadron commander's Bradley now, sir." With that, the corporal jumped out of the Humvee and waved his arms at the oncoming vehicle. It slowed down and lurched to a stop. The hydraulically powered rear door slowly lowered to the ground, and two men got out. One was a lieutenant colonel and the other was a command sergeant major. They walked over to the Humvee and the corporal came to attention and saluted. As they did, Kincaid climbed out of the Humvee to greet them.

"At ease, Corporal," said the lieutenant colonel, who then walked a few more steps and extended his hand to Kincaid. "You must be Captain Porter."

The colonel addressed Kincaid by his name and rank from his days in the Idaho National Guard, but since he was not in uniform, protocol did not dictate that Porter salute the more senior officer. "Yes, Colonel, I am."

"My name is Snow Eagle, Captain, and this is CSM Jones." The CSM saluted Kincaid.

R.A.R. Clouston

"Nice to meet you, Sergeant Major," said Kincaid with a smile.

"The pleasure's all mine, Captain."

"So what can we do for you, Corporal?" asked Snow Eagle.

"Mr. Porter—that is—Captain Porter said he would like to see the live fire exercises, sir."

The colonel looked at Kincaid and said, "We'd be glad to have you. Why don't you climb on board and come along?"

A broad smile flashed across Kincaid's face, "Thank-you, Colonel. I will."

The CSM looked at the corporal and said, "Take the captain's kit to the VIP quarters, Corporal."

"Yes, Sergeant Major."

The three men climbed back inside the Bradley; the door then closed, and with a lurch and a puff of black diesel smoke, it rumbled away.

A HALF AN HOUR LATER, Kincaid found himself standing beside two Bradley command tracks, six other command vehicles, and several Humvees on a ridge overlooking a broad, flat expanse of a high mountain valley. Beside him were Snow Eagle, Jones, and the men of the Headquarters & Headquarters Troop, or HHT, of the 1st Cavalry Squadron, 1st Cavalry Brigade of the Idaho National Guard.

"My God, it's incredible!" exclaimed Kincaid, watching through binoculars the impressive display of firepower below them on the valley floor, as three cavalry troops encompassing nearly a hundred war machines moved with precision against an imaginary enemy.

Snow Eagle looked at Jones. "We'll make a tanker out of him yet, Sergeant Major."

Jones smiled at Kincaid. "It gets in your blood, sir."

"The sights and sounds and smells are almost overpowering, Sergeant Major!" he exclaimed, as successive waves of M1A2 tanks fired their 120 mm guns with precision at targets barely visible to the naked eye. What was even more incredible to Kincaid was that the tanks were firing as they raced at forty miles an hour across the bumpy ground, and not necessarily in the direction that the tank was heading.

"During WWT, our squadron killed over seventy enemy tanks, Captain," said the CSM proudly.

"How many tanks did your squadron lose?" asked Kincaid.

His expression clouded, "We lost five tanks, sir. Unfortunately, two of those were to friendly fire. In total, fourteen soldiers were killed."

"That was before we had Granite Fist," added Snow Eagle.

"I'm sorry to hear that."

"Thank-you, sir. They were good men."

"They're all good men," replied Kincaid, as his mind drifted back to that day on the mountain that loomed above them at the far end of the valley.

"Yes, sir. You're right about that," added Jones.

Another senior NCO approached and said he needed the sergeant major's help with something. Jones saluted Snow Eagle and Kincaid and left with the other man.

Kincaid looked at the colonel and said, "I'm sorry that the money we are raising can't buy that level of technology for us, Colonel Snow Eagle."

Snow Eagle nodded and said, "All the technology in the world is useless if the men in the tanks don't have the will to win in their hearts. And I assure you that the threat of losing our freedom fills their hearts to overflowing."

"Well said, Colonel. Believe me, I know what that means."

Snow Eagle smiled sadly, "Yes. I expect that you do." He studied Kincaid for a moment and asked, "Do you mind if we dispense with the formalities? At least when we're alone."

"Not at all."

"Good. My name's Joseph, but my friends just call me Joseph."

Kincaid laughed. "As you know, the governor calls me Thomas, but actually, I'd like it if you called me T.J."

"You got it, T.J." Snow Eagle paused and then added, "For what its worth, I think you did as well as anyone could up on that mountain."

Kincaid returned the smile. "Thanks." He liked the colonel, and he could tell the feeling was mutual. He turned back to the action below them and raised his binoculars, just as nine main battle tanks lined up along a ridge line three hundred yards off to their right and fired their guns at the same time, obliterating a row of targets in the distance. "Now I understand what Jake must feel," he said, more to himself than to the other man.

Snow Eagle heard him and said, "Your brother is one of the best tank commanders in the Army—possibly the best."

Kincaid nodded and changed the subject. "Joseph, tell me, how big is the squadron?"

"We're configured pretty much the same way as you would find if you went to Fort Carson and saw the Army's 3rd Armored Cavalry. My squadron is one of three that are a part of the 1st Cavalry Brigade. In addition to the HHT, which you've been with this morning, each cavalry squadron is comprised of three cavalry troops, a pure tank company and an artillery battery. The cavalry troops, in turn, have a total of nine M1A2 Abrams Main Battle Tanks, thirteen M3A3 Bradleys, eight M577 command vehicles, four mortar carriers and twelve support vehicles, both tracked and wheeled."

"Sounds impressive."

"Believe me, it is, but not because of the fighting machines; rather, it's because of the well-trained and highly dedicated tankers inside each tank." He looked at his watch. "Oh, damn. I'm afraid that you're going to have to excuse me. I need to meet with my troop commanders. If you don't mind, I'll have one of my NCOs drive you back to base."

"Not at all, Joseph. You've been most generous with your time this morning."

"It was my pleasure. Once again, I want to thank-you for all that you've done for us. Without your fundraising, we would not be at anywhere near the level of combat readiness that we are."

"Let's hope that we won't need to go into battle."

"Yes. But if we do, we'll be ready."

The colonel walked over to one of his non-commissioned officers and said a few words. Within minutes, Kincaid was back in a Humvee heading away from the valley and the legion of warriors who were ready to ride their mechanical monsters into harm's way. But as much as the events of the morning had impressed him, he knew that elsewhere in America, there were other soldiers, in other tanks, who were training just as hard, with equipment just as deadly or even more so, and with the same degree of commitment and conviction. And if the two forces ever faced each other across fields of fire in another civil war, the results would make even the bloodiest day in the first Civil War pale by comparison. The thought was worrisome enough in and of itself, but what troubled Kincaid even more was that in one of those armored vehicles on one of those battlefields would be Jake Kincaid, and knowing his older brother, he would be up at the front, where the fighting was the most terrible.

THE HUMVEE stopped in front of the cabin where VIP's were housed during their visits to the base, and Kincaid thanked the driver and walked inside. In addition to wanting to see the men and machines of war that his fundraising had been supporting, he had another reason for coming to the camp; he wanted to become proficient with firearms. The reason was simple; it was to protect himself. Ever since the incident at Walter Reed Army Hospital, Kincaid had wondered whether or not Major Smythe had sent the young man with the strong jaw to back him up, or to kill him. Ironically, much of the armaments that the Wolf River Militia had bought recently had come from Major Smythe, and although they hadn't met in person, Kincaid had talked with Smythe several times on the telcom since the incident. During those conversations, the major had expressed his full support for Kincaid and had sworn that his man had been at the hospital to try to help him escape in case something went wrong. Kincaid didn't believe him, and the thought had occurred to him that he should probably get some shooting practice in while he was up at the training camp, both with sidearms and long guns. He had learned in business that only the strong survive. But that was then—when the threats were only figurative. And this was now—when the threats were literal and the danger could be mortal. Over the past five months, Kincaid had amply demonstrated that he was a survivor. And he was determined to remain so. So for the next few days, he intended to put fundraising out of his mind and focus on the visceral world of learning not only how to shoot, but to shoot to kill.

45

Arlington National Cemetery, Arlington, Virginia

Arlington National Cemetery is spread over two hundred acres of gently rolling Virginia hills, overlooking the Potomac River, directly across from the nation's capital. Over a quarter of a million men and women lie in repose for eternity under its sacred soil. Each year, over four million visitors get out of tour buses or private vehicles, and walk up the hill toward the Kennedy gravesite. Another fifty-five hundred come in feet first and take their place among the honored dead. On that beautiful spring day, as the country moved inexorably toward a deadly confrontation over guns, the sound of gunfire echoed once more over those hallowed hills. After the honor guards finished their salute, the last earthly remains of Arnold Peter Greenberg, Attorney General of the United States of America, a former Major in the U.S. Army and a veteran of the Vietnam War, were lowered into the ground under the soil of the land that he had loved and served nobly for so long.

The gravesite was crowded with the elite of Washington, including those who loved Greenberg and those who feared him. President Alex Webster was part of neither group, but still he was there to show his respect. With him was Patrick Fitzgerald, along with several Cabinet members; but Maddun Gordon was noticeably, and as far as Mary Lou Pritchard was concerned, thankfully absent. The presence of the President elevated the level of security at the graveside far beyond what would normally have been expected given the nature of the audience. Armed agents were everywhere, and overhead unmanned drones made lazy circles in the cloudless sky, looking like hawks and serving a similar purpose, except the prey they sought were two legged. The usual contingent of White House press corps, including Sarah McGill,

392

were also in attendance, dutifully following the President wherever he went.

Pritchard stood next to the Greenberg family, and standing beside her was Harry Erickson. She tried to concentrate on what the rabbi was saying, but she couldn't. It was simply too difficult for her to accept that her mentor and best friend was gone forever. Finally, it was over. She discreetly wiped a tear from her eye as she watched the President offer his condolences to the grieving family. After the President departed, Mary Lou stepped over to Arnold's wife and exchanged a long embrace. Then she looked back at Erickson.

"Shall we go?"

"Yes."

The Speaker of the House approached and greeted them, and then paused in that awkward silence that occurs when two people want to say something but another's presence prevents them from doing so. But Erickson was a quick study and said "I'll wait for you at the limo, Mary Lou," and discreetly left them alone.

"Thank-you, Harry," she called out after him. She looked at Kincaid.

"Are you okay?" Kincaid asked gently.

"No," she said, fighting back more tears.

He placed his hand on her shoulder. "He was a good man, Mary Lou. One of a diminishing number."

She nodded and smiled. Then they headed down the hill together, surrounded by the Speaker's Secret Service protection and the acting Attorney General's security detail comprised of FBI special agents.

"Your father is buried here, isn't he, Jeremiah?" she asked, trying to focus on something else.

"Yes. Up over the hill there."

Part way down the hill, a soldier approached them. It was the Speaker's son, Jake, dressed in his uniform.

"Hello, son," said the Speaker.

"Dad," he replied with a nod.

The Speaker introduced Jake to Pritchard, and they exchanged friendly greetings.

"I didn't know you knew Arnold, Colonel," said Pritchard.

"Actually, I didn't, ma'am," he replied, making her feel like his mother, despite the less than ten years that separated them in age. "I came here with

General McWilliams, who knew the Attorney General during his Army days."

She smiled and nodded. "Yes. He often spoke fondly of his days in uniform."

"My son and I are going to have lunch together, Mary Lou. Would you care to join us?"

Pritchard smiled and said, "No, I don't think I'm up to it. I hope you understand."

"Of course," said the Speaker.

Pritchard excused herself as they neared her limo. As she did, the Speaker spied Sarah McGill walking nearby. He waved to her and she approached them.

"Hello, Mr. Speaker," said Sarah, with a subdued smile appropriate to the setting and occasion.

"Ms. McGill," he gestured with his head toward Jake. "I believe you know my son."

She exchanged a warm smile with Jake. "Yes, sir. We met that night at the hospital."

"Yes, of course."

"Jake and I were just about to go to lunch. Can you join us?"

McGill's first instinct was to refuse; she had much work to do. But then she saw the look of rejection in Jake's eyes, and she accepted.

"Excellent!" said the Speaker. "I know just the place. They serve the best Omaha steaks that money can buy."

"You mean there's other meat in this town besides pork?" said Jake.

The Speaker ignored the gentle jab and focused his attention on McGill. "Did you know, Sarah, that Omaha steaks don't come from Omaha?"

Jake shook his head vehemently no at McGill, but she ignored him. "No, I didn't, Mr. Speaker. Where *do* they come from?"

The Speaker was delighted with her answer. "It just so happens that I am exactly the man to tell you."

"Great!" mumbled Jake to himself, now feeling like a third wheel on a motorcycle. "Here comes the entire history of meat packing in America."

"Go ahead, Mr. Speaker," said McGill. "Please tell me all about it."

Jake grimaced, "Can I take a rain check on lunch? I just remembered I have to go for a root canal." It was too late; the Speaker of the House of Representatives, among his many other traits, was a trivia master, and in particular, historical trivia. Jake knew that they were about to get a complete description of something of absolutely no consequence whatsoever.

"Well, you see, my dear," said the Speaker, putting his arm on her shoulders as they walked toward his waiting limousine, "Omaha used to be the slaughterhouse to the nation. But then all that changed when the great city of Chicago took over that dubious distinction." His voice drifted off as he led Sarah away.

Jake just shook his head in frustration and followed them. Once again, he had been outmatched by his father. It was par for the course, but that didn't make it any more palatable.

MARY LOU PRITCHARD and Harry Erickson were deep in conversation as the limo crawled across the Arlington Memorial Bridge in bumper-to-bumper traffic. Erickson gave the string of taillights ahead of them a frustrated glance and said, "If this traffic gets any worse, we'll have to move the capital back to Philadelphia."

"They wouldn't take it," said Pritchard with a smile.

"You're probably right."

Getting back to business, Pritchard asked, "What were you able to find out about Coriagra?"

"Nothing."

"That's not a lot," she replied, trying to make the best of a bad situation with humor. It was something she used to do with her former boss. But he wasn't there to smile. And his absence was even more powerful than had been his presence.

"But I did discover something that will interest you."

"Go ahead," said Pritchard, leaning forward slightly.

"DHS ran a cross-tab on all sudden deaths in the District during the past twelve months and guess what?"

"They found another case of SADS?" she replied.

"Two of them."

"Two!"

"Yes. That brings the total to five. According to the Bureau of Disease Control, that's far beyond what would normally be expected. You already know about the first three, but just to refresh your memory: number one was last September near the Supreme Court; number two occurred in January in front of the White House, both of which directly involved Sarah McGill;

and the most recent one, which as it turns out, is number five, involved the Speaker outside the Watergate."

She nodded.

"Number three in chronological order was our agent who died in Potomac Park in January. If you remember, at first we thought he was murdered, because a Japanese couple claimed they saw a strange, hooded man kneeling over his body."

"But he wasn't."

"No. We exhumed his body and a forensics expert redid the autopsy. He concluded it was a case of SADS."

"Who was number four?"

"He was the guy they found near the Vietnam Memorial."

"The one who shot those two Secret Service Agents at Walter Reed Hospital?"

"Exactly. And get this—just like with two of the first three SADS deaths, Sarah McGill can be linked to this one."

"How?"

Erickson recounted how the limo driver, who took McGill and Thomas Porter to the airport following the attempted assassination of the President at Walter Reed Hospital, testified that they passed by the Memorial at the exact time that the fourth victim died.

Pritchard sat there, silently digesting what she had heard.

"What do you think?" he probed.

"Five people die from an extremely rare cause, and three of them are linked to a television news reporter named Sarah McGill."

"It's an interesting coincidence, isn't it?"

"Yes. Of course, you know what Arnold would say if he were here?" she smiled sadly. "Coincidence is a distant cousin to the truth."

He nodded. "Do you want me to dig any deeper on this?"

She thought about it for a minute and then shook her head. "No."

Her answer surprised him. "Are you sure?"

"Yes."

"May I ask why?"

"Because coincidence is a distant cousin to the truth, that's why."

He shrugged and let the matter drop. "You're right. Accusing a woman of witchcraft went out of fashion four hundred years ago, and far be it from me to reinstate it. Especially not with someone as beautiful and charming as Sarah McGill."

"Who said it had to be witchcraft? Maybe she has a guardian angel," mused Pritchard.

"I hadn't thought of that."

Neither said anything for a few moments and then Pritchard asked. "Are you sure she had no link to the other two deaths?"

"Other than the fact that she has interviewed both Jeremiah Kincaid and his youngest son, T.J., and was seen driving his other son, Jake, home from the hospital after the shooting, there is no apparent connection between her and the death of the man who shot the Speaker. And as far as I can tell, she had no link whatsoever to the death of the agent in Potomac Park."

She nodded but said nothing.

He added, "But, going along with your guardian angel theory, that was the only SADS death in which the victim was a good guy. All the rest were what you might characterize as evil doers."

She shook her head. "Somehow I doubt that if Arnold were here he would want us chasing angels."

"You're right. Especially since he probably is one now."

She smiled sadly. "Did you find any connection between Coriagra and Gordon?"

"No. We came up blank. Quite frankly, I don't think we're ever going to be able to get anything on him. He's too slippery."

"Exactly what *do* we have on the madman in the White House?" she asked.

"Which one?"

She flashed him an angry look. "On Maddun Gordon."

"Sorry." He mixed the words with an apologetic smile. "All we have is just that low-quality satellite photo from Potomac Park."

"Keep digging."

He sighed and said, "Okay, boss. But the Bureau and DHS don't think there's anything there."

"I hear you, Harry. But trust me on this one. Maddun Gordon's an evil man. I know it; I just can't prove it. As long as he sits ten steps away from the President, our country's in danger." Pritchard looked out the car window. At that moment, they were passing by the South side of the White House.

She looked back at him and said, "Maybe I should take the photo to the President?"

Erickson was obviously startled. "Is that wise?"

She stared at him. "You said we're not having any luck getting something on Gordon. Why not smoke him out? What have we got to lose?"

"Everything," he replied.

"Other than that," she said with a wry smile that quickly melted into a determined look. "If I'm right about him, he's got to be stopped."

"And if you're wrong, you'll do what every American leader does—throw my ass to the wolves and plead ignorance."

"Not every leader. Some still have character. At least those who have not confused happiness with materiality."

Erickson shrugged. "Character is destiny."

She gave him a quizzical look. "I've heard that before. Where is it from?"

"Heraclitus said it—he was a Greek philosopher who predated Aristotle."

Pritchard thought about it for a moment and added, "Your right. Character is destiny—for both a man and a nation."

The limousine reached the Department of Justice Building. He looked at his boss and asked. "So what are you going to do?"

"I don't know. I guess I'll give it a little more time."

"Good. I'll turn up the heat on our investigation of Gordon."

"Let's hope it's not a lost cause," said Pritchard.

"It can't be. We're on the side of the angels, remember?"

She smiled but didn't reply. She knew he was right, but sometimes it just didn't feel that way. And this was one of those times.

46

Allistair Blevis sat with his usual guests, Cresswell Peabody and Jarlene Martisse. Ever since they started covering the gun-control story, their show's ratings had skyrocketed, and the producers were thrilled. So, too, had their mail, much of it angry due to the show's two polarizing guest commentators and highly opinionated moderator. Together they had achieved the distinction of creating a television show that millions of Americans loved to hate, and they were watching it in increasingly large numbers—a fact which made its personalities behave in ways which were even more unbearable to the opposing factions in households all across the country.

"What can we make of the Jeremiah Kincaid's trip last week to Boise? Somehow I doubt that he was there to talk about putting Wisconsin cheese on Idaho potatoes," said Blevis.

"It's very simple," began Martisse. To her everything in life could be explained in black and white. Her world knew no shades of gray. "Two white men sat behind closed doors and talked about the future of a country that is increasingly non-white."

"For Heaven's sake, Jarlene," interrupted Peabody, "They were talking about gun control, not ways to keep women and minorities oppressed."

"It's the same thing," she replied.

It was now Blevis' turn to jump in. "Could you run that one by me again, Jarlene? What do guns have to do with racial disparity?"

"The gun is the white man's way of keeping minorities and women under control."

Peabody rolled his eyes and raised his hands in frustration. "Oh, please."

She ignored him and kept going. "Despite all the rhetoric coming out of Washington these days, the white man has done nothing to rid the streets of the Saturday night specials that take the lives of people of color each day. Instead of spending money on educating the citizens of our inner cities, the white population has created a protective wall of police cruisers that patrol the edges of center city, ready to pounce on any man whose skin color doesn't match the three shades of white they keep on a color chart taped to dashboard of their cars."

"Three shades of white?" mused a puzzled Peabody.

"Yes," answered Martisse. "White. Whiter. Whitest."

"Sounds like a soap commercial to me," said Blevis.

Peabody pressed her, "What have guns got to do with the oppression of women, pray tell?"

Martisse was ready for him, "You know as well as I do that the gun is nothing more than a phallic symbol—one that spits lead instead of sperm. Do you realize that every year, thousands of women are murdered in this country by their husbands or boyfriends? And in three quarters of those cases, the weapon used was a gun."

Peabody looked at her, which he normally did not do, at least while the cameras were rolling, and said, in a more understanding tone, "Jarlene, I feel deeply for the families of those murdered women, and especially for their children, who face life with one parent dead and the other behind bars. Believe me I do. However, I fail to understand how the President's legislation will do anything to help battered and abused women or the impoverished people in the inner cities of America? The Saturday night specials, as you call them, are already banned, but that doesn't stop anyone from making or selling them. And my guess is that for the most part, the weapons used by husbands and boyfriends to kill their women would not be banned under the terms of the President's bill."

It was apparent that Martisse appreciated her counterpart's gentler tone and manner; but that did not stop her from reacting forcefully, "Cresswell, the issue here is not which guns will or will not be banned. Laws, in and of themselves, rarely change behavior. Emotion is the antonym of reason. Yes, I want all guns to be registered, and of course, I want the police to become an integral part of the community, where every child of color knows the patrolman on his block and can walk to school without fear or harm. But it is much deeper than that; I want us to stop glamorizing guns on television and in the movies. I want us to teach our children, whether they are black or white or red or yellow, that death is a final destination, and that a gun is a one-way ticket to get there.

"I want us to change the way we as a people feel about each other. I want a middle-aged white woman from the suburbs to look upon the face of a young black man from the inner city and not see the devil. Equally, I want our young black men to be brought up knowing what the devil looks like, so that they will turn away from him when he comes calling. I desperately want children to stop killing children with the weapons of their fathers. Perhaps I am being naïve, but I believe in my heart that we have the potential to see all these things in our lifetime, and I will not surrender my dream. Ever."

Peabody was obviously moved. He looked at her through private eyes, not the ones he saved for being in front of the camera, and said softly, "Jarlene, you are not alone. All across this land, there are many who share your dream, and share your journey—myself included. Moreover, Jeremiah Kincaid is one of us, and just like pilgrims through a barren land, we must not lose faith in America. If we do, all is lost."

The studio fell silent. Even the hard-nosed producer was temporarily taken aback by the emotion of the moment, but he soon snapped back to the present and sent a zinger through Blevis' earpiece, who then turned to the camera and said, "Well, there you have it, ladies and gentlemen. Some words from the heart. Now we're going to break for a few words from our sponsors, and then we'll take some calls. Give us a call and let us know what you think. Can we as a nation lay down our guns and walk together into the future, unarmed and unafraid? Or are the weapons of personal destruction so ingrained in our collective psyche that we will never give them up? Call us and tell us what you think. Our number this evening is 1-777-GUNS-4-US."

47

Streets of Washington, D.C.

Jeremiah Kincaid and George Ross rode in the Speaker's limousine towards the White House. The cherry blossoms were in full bloom and the city looked absolutely beautiful. The resplendent scenery plus the fact that the sling on the Speaker's arm was gone had put the Speaker in an upbeat mood.

"The way you handled Mr. Potatohead will rewrite the book on statesmanship," said Ross with a self-satisfied smirk. Ross had a habit of categorizing everyone inside politics by virtue of their "toy-type." Senators were wobble-head dolls, while congressmen were Beanie Babies. Supreme court justices were Jacks-in-the-Box, and the White House press corps were the Muppets. Only the President was spared from Ross' toy-typing, and that was because he only did it with people for whom he had a least a modicum of respect.

"I wish I could have been there to watch you in action, sir."

"It was more due to him than me."

"Regardless, you got the sale and that's what counts. Did you bring up the New Sons of Liberty?"

"I didn't have to. He did," replied the Speaker.

"What did he say?"

"He described the Western Freedom Party and their growing militia Army as a grizzly, and he said that the New Sons of Liberty would be its roar."

"I didn't know that a bear could roar," said Ross.

Kincaid smiled, "Apparently, he's read Winston Churchill. Although he took liberty with the metaphor."

"I don't understand?"

"When Churchill commented on the role he played in winning World War Two, he said that the people of Britain had been a lion and all that he had done was to provide the roar. But he was talking about winning a war, and Morrissey is threatening to start one."

Ross mused out loud, "I can see Morrissey as a bear, but I'm afraid Webster is neither a lion nor a bear, and according to Tanner Spence, the New Sons of Liberty would agree with me. At least the ones who he tracks on the Internet every day."

"What do they call Webster?" asked the Speaker.

"The Raven."

"The Raven?" asked the Speaker. He paused and considered the imagery. "That's an interesting image. He's certainly big and powerful, but obviously not black."

"Perhaps it's his heart that's black—you know, like the harbinger of death."

"That's a bit harsh. I don't think evil lurks behind the façade—just a misguided, if self-serving, desire to do good."

Ross smiled but didn't say anything.

"What?" asked the Speaker, noticing the grin.

"You haven't asked me what they call you."

"They have a name for me?"

"Yes." Ross chucked.

"Well?"

"They call you the Eagle."

"Really?" The thought pleased the Speaker.

"The Raven and the Eagle. Rather untamed imagery, isn't it? You and the President soaring and diving in aerial combat, while down below, clawing at the dirt and gnashing his teeth, is old Morrissey the Bear," Ross found the mental image quite amusing and chuckled to himself.

"If you could come back down to earth for just one second, Mr. National Geographic, we still have a long way to go before we do any victory rolls. And this next meeting will make or break everything we have done up until this point."

Ross nodded. "You're ready, Mr. Speaker. After all, what's a raven when you've already tamed a bear? Oh, and I almost forgot. There are two other people who have asked to see you. It's a father and his daughter, Nathaniel and Jamie Bardham."

"Nathaniel Bardham. What does he want?"

"You may remember that his grandson was shot and killed by a classmate, who had found his father's gun lying around."

"Yes, I remember. That was very sad but why does he want to see me?"

"Not just him but his daughter as well. They've started a Political Action Committee in support of a sensible approach to gun control. And they want to express their support for you and what you are trying to accomplish."

The Speaker thought about it for a minute and then said, "Very well, I'll meet with them. Let's see what Mr. Bardham can do for his country after all that it has done for him."

"And *to* him," added Ross somberly.

"I suppose that's true. Losing a grandchild to a bullet gives a depth of credibility to an advocate on either side of the issue."

"I'll set the meeting up."

The limousine arrived at the gates to the White House, and after a thorough check of the car's occupants and their identification, the uniformed guards allowed them to pass. Within another minute it pulled up under the front portico and stopped.

"Here I go, George," said the Speaker.

"Good luck, sir."

The Speaker nodded solemnly. "I'll need more than luck on this one, George."

Ross added in a reverent tone. "You're right, Mr. Speaker. I'll say a prayer that God will be on your side."

The Speaker thought about it for a moment and said, "Thank-you, but remember, God made both the eagle *and* the raven."

PRESIDENT ALEXANDER WEBSTER, poised, handsome, and dressed immaculately, stood behind his desk in the Oval Office, staring out the window. He wore a hand-tailored charcoal suit with a pale, mist-gray shirt, French cuffs with onyx cufflinks; a black, silk tie with tiny, white polka dots; and wing-tipped black shoes. In total, his outfit cost twice as much as the average American wage earner brought home in a month. The diamond-encrusted Rolex watch he was also wearing pushed it to a full year.

There was a knock on the door, and his executive secretary stepped in. "Excuse me, Mr. President; the Speaker of the House is here."

Webster spun around gracefully. "Please send him in, Marva."

She disappeared out the door and was instantly replaced by Jeremiah Kincaid. "Good morning, Mr. President," he said, as he walked several steps into the room and stopped.

"Mr. Speaker," the President said, as he glided across the room with hand warmly outstretched. "Please come in and join me, won't you?"

In contrast to the President's fashion magazine appearance, the Speaker's clothes looked slightly less sartorial. His navy blue suit was Brooks Brothers, but he had bought it off the rack several years earlier. His shirt was light blue and crisply starched, but it had button cuffs; and his red- and blue-striped tie, although silk, was a half inch out of style in width. In a room of executives from Fortune 100 companies, Kincaid could have held his own, but in that room with that man, he looked underdressed and overmatched. It was not by chance. Nothing that President Webster ever did was by chance. The two men closed on each other and exchanged what would have appeared to any impartial observer as the warmest of greetings.

"Thank-you for coming, Jeremiah," said the President, turning on his charm.

"Thank-you for inviting me, Mr. President.

The President gestured toward the door to the Rose garden. "Shall we walk outside? It's a glorious day."

The Speaker nodded. "Yes. I'd like that."

As they stepped outside, the President motioned with his head toward the Speaker's shoulder and said, "How's your wound?"

"It's healing well, thank-you."

The President shook his head. "Disgraceful. Simply disgraceful."

The Speaker nodded but didn't respond.

"You know if my bill passes, evil men like the one who shot you won't be able to get a gun."

"The operative word there, Mr. President, is *if*. And even if it does pass, I'm not sure you're assumption is valid. Evil men will always find a way to get a gun, no matter how many laws we enact."

"Perhaps, but that seems a poor excuse for not trying." He paused and then said, "Let's walk, shall we?"

The two men began to stroll slowly across the lawn and through a garden that was resplendent with spring flowers and budding greenery.

"Mr. Speaker, I know that you tolerate long-windedness poorly, so I will come right to the point. What can I say to convince you to support my bill?"

"As it is currently written, Mr. President, nothing."

The President nodded as if he was expecting that answer. "You know, Jeremiah, with that attempt on your life, I think I may have picked up just enough votes on your side to win, even without your endorsement."

The Speaker smiled patiently. "With all due respect, Mr. President, I wouldn't count on it."

The President looked at the older and taller man and said, "Perhaps not. But we'll soon find out, won't we?"

They continued their winding journey under the watchful eyes of Secret Service snipers on the roof and heavily armed agents walking a discreet distance behind them. Neither man said anything, although there was no apparent tension. Just the cagey and mutual respect normally displayed by two worthy and equal opponents.

"What changes would you require to support it?" asked the President, not wanting to press too hard. He knew that there was an iron will under the outwardly calm exterior of this son of the American Heartland. He also knew there was a streak of stubbornness that ran through the man like an unseen current in the Mississippi River that washed the Western shores of his home state; stubbornness that, if provoked, could rear up like floodwaters and wash away everything in its downstream path.

"I would support your bill with the changes contained in my amendment. I want to grandfather gun ownership of legal guns, create an amnesty period during which illegal guns may be turned in to authorities for an appropriate cash payment, provide for the continued sale of most handguns and all sporting rifles and shotguns…"

The President gently interrupted. "Come now, Jeremiah, what is sporting about a rifle?"

"You asked me what I would support, Mr. President."

"I'm sorry for interrupting. Please continue." The President had made a career out of interrupting people. Generally, it was because his mind worked twice as fast as that of the average man, and his tongue worked even faster. In this instance, only the latter applied.

"I also want you to rescind your Executive order forbidding Federal employees to own a gun for private use and establish a Federally funded weapon-safety program for our secondary schools."

"Is that all?"

"No, but that's the essence of it. I also believe that it would be helpful for you to reach out to the ever-growing segment of the population who look upon you as the enemy."

"In what way?"

"I leave that up to you and your advisers, and I certainly would not presume to tell you, Mr. President, how to act. But I must also report to you that I have just returned from a meeting with the Governor of Idaho, and he alerted me to a significantly increasing level of resentment for your administration across the high plains and in the foothills of the Rocky Mountains."

The President smiled a knowing smile and said, "Did he also tell you about the militias that he and the Western Freedom Party are funding?"

"Yes, sir. However, while the Governor's new party may be responsible for the use of those funds, its sources come from a broad cross-segment of society, both within the private sector and from ordinary citizens alike."

"I am well aware that Governor Morrissey's private army is well-funded and equipped."

"Mr. President, whether or not you believe this to be the governor's private army, or just a group of passionate, if misguided citizens, the fact is that they exist. And neither we in the Congress nor you in the Executive Branch can afford to ignore them."

Gradually the men completed a wide circle of the gardens and returned to the portico outside the Oval Office. They stopped and stood near the spot where so many great men had pondered issues of national import. Few of which, however, had risen to the level of gravity that these two men now faced.

"I have no intentions of ignoring them, Mr. Speaker. They are a growing cancer upon the land. There are only a few ways to deal with cancer, and talking to it isn't one of them."

"With all due respect, Mr. President, I disagree. My discussions with the Governor were quite productive, and he agreed to meet you on common ground."

"And if I do not?" asked the President curtly.

"Then, Mr. President, I fear that it will lead to bloodshed."

"So be it."

The Speaker looked the President directly in the eyes and said, "Mr. President, may I speak freely?"

Webster gave the Speaker a sly smile and said, "I have never known you to do anything but, Jeremiah."

The Speaker nodded and began to speak in a measured and respectful tone. "Mr. President, whether you choose to believe it or not, I admire and respect you. I admit that I don't approve of some of your personal behavior, and I sincerely wish you were a religious man, for I believe that many of our nation's troubles today would be healed by a reaffirmation of our belief in God. And it is my impression, Mr. President, that there are times when you could use a patron of a higher power." He paused to let his words sink in. Then he said softly, "However, I did not come here to preach to you."

The look on the President's face spoke volumes, even though for the moment at least, this normally loquacious man was absolutely silent.

The Speaker continued, "I know you to be one of the most intelligent men, if not the most intelligent man, who has ever served as the leader of this nation. This is a great gift that we as a people, and especially we in the Congress, don't fully appreciate. And I truly believe in my heart that you want to do what is right for us as a people on this particular matter."

The President nodded but remained quiet. So far the Speaker had said nothing to arouse his fighting response, but that was about to change.

"Mr. President, you are opinionated, but you have a tremendous natural gift for facts and figures upon which to base your opinions. You are self-centered, but no man who has ever held this office could do anything but be tempted to become so. And you have immense personal magnetism that can shape the hearts and minds of anyone upon whom you so direct it. Finally, while you have perhaps not yet achieved what will be your place in history, you are close to doing so. You have before you the opportunity to bring together a sharply divided people and meld them into one mind, one heart, and one soul.

"It is a task no less imposing than that, which was faced by men like George Washington and Abraham Lincoln. They, like you, were tested by seemingly insurmountable forces, and they were not found wanting. And now I say with the deepest respect and recognition for what you confront, that you have it within your power to leave a legacy that will stand for all time. A legacy not born out of weakness but out of strength. The strength that has always united us as a people when threatened with destruction. I assure you, Mr. President, that now is another of those times. I plead with you, as someone who desperately wants to help you achieve your greatest glory, to listen, learn, and lead us out of harm's way."

The Speaker winced as he finished speaking. The emotional and physical strain of the long days and nights that had led up to that moment had taken a their toll upon him. And now, there he stood alone with the most powerful man on the face of the earth, having placed his own heart and soul where they could be either gratefully enjoined, or harshly rejected. He had nothing more to give. But would it be enough?

The President did not respond directly. Instead he said softly, "Let us go inside, Mr. Speaker, and sit down, for I worry that you are weary from the events of these past few weeks."

"Not just from these past few weeks, Mr. President, but also from these past few months." As he spoke, it was evident that the meaning was far deeper and the message was more painful than the matter of guns and bullets.

The two men re-entered the Oval Office, and the President motioned for the Speaker to sit down on one of the two yellow sofas. The Speaker did so, and the President sat down in his high-backed chair immediately adjacent to the pastel yellow loveseat onto which the Speaker had now settled.

It was clear that the Speaker's words had moved the President. And Kincaid's reference to the President's impending place in history had had a visceral impact upon him. The President settled back into his chair and said, "Mr. Speaker, I want to thank-you for what you have just said." He then smiled wryly. "While I obviously do not share some of your views about my personal style and beliefs, I have never felt so honored and—" he paused, as if considering the implications of what he was about to say, "so drawn to anyone in my political career."

The President's comment caught the Speaker by surprise, but it was clearly a pleasant surprise. He choose not to interrupt the President.

"Quite frankly, your candor and forthrightness has shamed me, Jeremiah, for I must confess that I carried far less noble baggage with me into this meeting than did you. I sought only to show you the error of your ways or to allow you the opportunity to vent before I continued on with what I had always intended." The President paused, as if reaching out for words and thoughts that would be born of the future rather than dying with the past. "I must tell you that you have touched me in ways that even I cannot fully comprehend, and I will share with you something that I have told no other soul. I desperately want to be loved by the people. I do care what they think about me, and my whole life has been a never-ending crusade to find acceptance." Again he paused. "Does that sound foolish?"

The Speaker could feel the goosebumps rise on his forearms and down the back of his neck. He sensed that he was witnessing a crucial moment in the life of another human being. And what was all the more frightening was that he knew how fragile and fleeting such moments can be. "No, Mr. President. It sounds Presidential."

Webster nodded appreciatively. In the horror and desolation of the days to come, the Speaker would often reflect on the moment, the place, and the man. He would wonder and wish and weep for what might have been. Not just for a nation that searched for greatness but for a man who wanted so profoundly to be great. But even the deepest faith can only provide the fortitude to withstand the triumphs and the tragedies of fortune, rather than to change them.

The President continued. "Thank-you. Now before I lapse any further into the depths of sentimentality, let us turn back to the issue at hand, shall we?"

The Speaker nodded. He knew they must, but he was reluctant to let go of the emotion of the moment. It had been almost magical, and one he knew would never come again. "Yes. Of course, Mr. President."

"The ownership of rifles and shotguns would have to be strictly controlled and Federally licensed, with no exceptions," said Webster.

"Yes," replied Kincaid. His pulse began to pound at the President's words. He couldn't believe what he was hearing. The President was actually talking of compromise.

"Grandfathering would not apply to automatic nor assault weapons."

"Agreed, but I assume they would be covered by the amnesty program?" added the Speaker.

"Yes. The ability to own a handgun would be severely cut back, with very few exceptions."

"That will be a difficult sale."

"It's non-negotiable, Jeremiah."

"I understand."

"Gun manufacturers and retailers would be held liable for any weapons that they knowingly allowed to fall into unlicensed hands, and there would be strict new regulations on the sale and distribution of all firearms."

There was a long pause after which the Speaker asked, "With those changes, will you agree to the proposal?"

The President hesitated before answering. Finally he said, "Yes, I will, Jeremiah, but quite frankly, I am not sure that the people who support me will."

The Speaker nodded. He had heard that same sentiment a day earlier and two thousand miles away. "The mark of a great leader, Mr. President, is to be able to bring two opposing forces together and make each of them think that their views have prevailed."

The President looked the Speaker directly in the eye and asked, "I'm not sure that I can meet that standard."

"I'm not sure I can, either. But that would be a poor excuse for us not to try," answered Kincaid, using the President's own words from earlier in their conversation.

The President smiled and nodded. "I am willing if you are, Mr. Speaker."

"Yes. I am."

Outside, the President's staff was beginning to wonder what was happening. They had never known the President to meet alone with a political leader, or anyone else, for that long, with the exception, of course, of his female friends and admirers.

"Mr. President, there is one more thing that I must tell you. I am afraid that you will not like it."

Webster's eyebrows raised slightly. "Yes?"

The Speaker hesitated for a moment and then said, "There are a large number of people, important people in all areas of the government, both elected and appointed, who seek your removal from office."

All expression faded from the President's face. "Is that so?"

"They call themselves the New Sons of Liberty."

Without hesitating, the President observed, "After old Sam Adams and his band of ruffians, I presume?"

"Exactly." The Speaker was not surprised that the President instantly recognized the parallel.

"How quaint," the President mused.

That brought a smile to the Speaker's face. "First, let me assure you that I am not one of them."

"I'm pleased to hear that. Thank-you."

"You're welcome. The point is that, regardless of whether or not you and I seek to find common ground, I doubt that they will back off."

"Then neither must we."

"Of course not, Mr. President. But I'm afraid that the country will be the loser in this confrontation."

The President digested the issue. "Do you know who they are?"

"Only by inference. I have no hard evidence. As a result, I don't think it appropriate to name them."

"I see."

"However, if you and I quickly and forcefully pursue what we have discussed here today, I believe we can defuse their power base, for it would be very difficult for them to justify continued opposition in the face of such high-level, bi-partisan unanimity."

"Can you deliver your party, Jeremiah?"

"Yes, sir. Can you?"

The President momentarily directed his thoughts inward. "Yes. I believe that I can."

"Good," said the Speaker. It was his second victory in two days and his head was spinning, although he worked very hard to not let it show.

The President stood up, thrust out his hand and said, "Mr. Speaker, let's begin."

Kincaid also got up. It would not have been an easy task for such a tall man sitting in so deep a loveseat, even without the shoulder wound. But the Speaker was on a roll and he made it look easy. "Yes, Mr. President. Let us begin together to reunite our nation."

The two men stood there and then, to the surprise of the Speaker, the President stepped over and embraced him. As he stepped back, he asked, "What church do you belong to, Jeremiah?"

412

The question caught the Speaker off guard and for a moment he couldn't remember, a fact which his wife would later never let him forget. "First Presbyterian, Mr. President. Why do you ask?"

"Perhaps I could join you some Sunday. If that would be all right."

The President's request sent a tingling feeling down the Speaker's spine. "Yes, Mr. President. I would be honored."

The President smiled, but it quickly faded. Then he said, "Jeremiah, there is one other matter for which I think we need to clear the air."

"Yes, Mr. President?"

"It is the matter of your son, T.J."

The Speaker's shoulders seemed to sag under the weight of sadness that suddenly filled the room. "Mr. President, I am truly sorry that my family's own personal tragedy has spilled over into the nation's business. I assure you that I didn't want it to be so."

The President put his hand on the Speaker's shoulder and said, "I know that, Jeremiah. I would like to make you an offer. If you can get T.J. to turn himself in to Federal authorities and disavow any support for the militia movement, I will grant him an absolute pardon."

The Speaker was taken aback by the President's generous offer. A Presidential pardon would wipe his son's record clean. "That is very kind of you, Mr. President, but I am afraid that my youngest son would never accept it. Moreover, I doubt that he would even listen to me if I tried to reach out to him to offer it."

The President shook his head sadly and then said, "That's too bad. But I will keep the offer open in case you and he are somehow reunited."

"Thank-you, Mr. President. You are very kind."

The two men shook hands again and then Jeremiah Kincaid walked out of the Oval Office. The President's reaching out to him had truly been a magnanimous gesture, and Kincaid was certain now that fate was finally turning in their favor. But fate is a fickle friend. It favors neither the weak nor the strong. Only the lucky. And unfortunately for the Speaker and the nation, luck is a bad thing to rely upon when dealing with guns.

THE PRESIDENT was standing, staring out the bulletproof window directly behind his desk, when there was a knock on the door and Maddun Gordon stepped in. "How did it go, Mr. President?"

"Very well," answered Webster tersely, as he sat down behind his desk.

Gordon waited for his boss to elaborate, but he didn't. It troubled him. "Did he agree to support us?"

The President looked at his chief of staff and said coldly, "You mean support me?"

The little hairs on the back of Gordon's neck bristled. He hesitated and then said, "Yes. Of course. Did he agree to support you?"

"No."

There was a pregnant pause. Gordon didn't like what he was sensing. Something had happened in that room that he had not been a part of. Something bad. At least as far as he was concerned. "May I ask what happened?"

"No," said the President for a second time.

Gordon just stood there. The tension in the room was palpable. He stared at the President, but the President's stare was fixed on the photograph of John Kennedy.

"Do you know what the mark of great leadership is?" he asked Gordon without looking at him.

"What?" asked Gordon knowing full well what it meant to him, but not yet understanding where the President's question was leading.

"It is the ability to bring two strongly opposing forces together and make each of them think that their views have prevailed."

Gordon suddenly got what had just happened, and it sent a chill through his entire being. "Did you agree to a compromise, Mr. President?" he asked, not wanting to hear the answer.

The President nodded. "Yes, I did."

Gordon's shoulders sagged. He slowly sat down on one of the yellow sofas and looked around the room. At first he didn't respond, as his brain considered and rejected several possible exit strategies, the way it always did when he felt cornered. His first impulse was to attack, figuratively, of course. Although there were certainly times with this President that Gordon wished he could grab the man and shake the living shit out of him.

Finally, he decided that retreat and regroup was his best course of action. "I'm sure you know what's best for the nation, Mr. President." Of course, he didn't mean it, and the President knew it. But at that moment in that room, neither man had the will nor the way to deal with the other. Gordon stood up and said, "Perhaps we should discuss this at another time?"

"Yes. Why don't we?"

With that, Gordon walked out of the room. He knew what he had to do, and time was against him.

MADDUN GORDON walked back into his office and sat down at his BTC console. He typed several keystrokes and instantly, the voice of Chadrian came over the speakers. "What do you want?" Chadrian was sitting behind the wheel of a forty-nine foot ketch, the Red Dragon, holding his PTC in his left hand.

"I've been trying to reach you all day."

"I do not appreciate an emergency call when there isn't one."

"We need to talk."

"Not like this."

"We're on a clear channel with the highest level of encryption that money can buy, remember?"

"I do not care. I am not going to talk with you over the airwaves. Meet me tomorrow morning at 7:00 a.m. at Tracy's Landing, and I will take you out on this new toy of mine, and you can talk business until you are blue in the face."

"Where is that?"

"You will find it."

"Wait," said Gordon, but Chadrian was gone. He signed off and shut down the computer. Then he sat there in the stillness of the room and said to himself. *No, Mr. President. The mark of great leadership is power. And as Bertrand Russell said, power is the ability to achieve the intended effect. And we will achieve that effect, even if I have to do it for you.*

JEREMIAH KINCAID was ebullient as he and George stepped back into their waiting limo. The look on the chief of staff's face was one of excitement and awe. Although he would never admit it to anyone, least of all to the Speaker himself, he didn't think his boss had any chance whatsoever to get the President to agree to compromise. Even the Speaker's victory in Boise had only served to raise Ross's expectations slightly. But he had been wrong. His boss had pulled it off, and he could barely contain himself.

"Congratulations, Mr. Speaker," said Ross, as he literally launched himself into the other side of the stretch automobile. Then he added with a smile, "Or should I say Mr. Eagle?" In his enthusiasm, he completely forgot about the shooting, and he patted the Speaker on the back of his shoulder, just above where he had been shot. In horror, he remembered a millisecond before the blow landed, causing the Speaker to wince.

"I'm so sorry, sir. That was thoughtless of me."

"I'll be fine, George. But it's lucky for you that I'm not an eagle. Otherwise I'd never fly again," he said, as he rubbed his shoulder.

"Sorry, Mr. Speaker, but my emotions have gotten the better of me. I'm not sure that you have grasped the full significance of what you have accomplished."

The Speaker smiled and said patiently, "George, we're not there yet."

"Yes, sir. But we're getting dangerously close."

The Speaker reached down and hit the button that raised the partition between the driver and the back seat. "No offense, Payton," he called out to his driver as he did so.

"None taken, Mr. Speaker," replied Payton, glancing in the rear-view mirror.

It was a little ritual that they went through every time the Speaker needed to discuss confidential matters with someone riding along with him or on his PTC. It was completely unnecessary, of course, but the Speaker always did it. It was one of the things that differentiated him from other powerful men, and it endeared him to all those who worked for him. Ross had seen him do it a hundred times and yet every time he did it, he could not help but notice that as gentle and caring a touch that the Speaker had with his staff, he was an unrelenting taskmaster with his family.

"Now, here's what I want you to do," said Kincaid, as soon as the partition was closed. "When we get back to the office, put out a call to the party leaders. We need a special caucus right away. The vote on the President's bill is ten days away, and I need to solidify the party behind the compromise. So tell them that it's urgent, but don't tell them why."

"They'll think that you're going to resign—again."

"Good. That ought to guarantee a big turnout," said Kincaid. "Nothing like the prospect of moving up in the line of seniority of power to make a politician's nose twitch."

There was a long pause and then Ross said, "You aren't going to, are you?"

"No. At least not until we pass this amended bill."

The Speaker's reply was like a warm glass of milk on a hot day, but Ross chose not to pursue it. He was worried that the mental and emotional stress of managing the debate of the highly charged gun bill in the House, combined with the physical stress caused by the shooting had placed too heavy a burden on his boss. He knew the Speaker would not slow down until the amended bill passed, but after that, he was afraid that the country would lose the man whom he believed was its last great hope.

"And one more thing," the Speaker added.

"Yes, sir?"

"I mentioned the New Sons of Liberty to the President."

Ross's thick eyebrows arched like two woolly caterpillars getting ready to rumble. "You did! What did he say?"

Kincaid paused before answering. "He acted like he had never heard of them."

"Do you think he had?"

"Absolutely. His reaction was measured and I don't know…"

Ross completed the Speaker's thought the way he often did. "Too controlled for a man who had just learned that there was a conspiracy in the Congress?"

"Exactly," replied the Speaker.

They were jostled a bit as the limousine navigated the zigzag pattern between the concrete security barriers in front of the entrance to the underground parking in the Rayburn Building. Then their conversation was briefly interrupted as Ross electronically lowered the window so that the heavily armed guards could see their faces. After they had been cleared to enter, Ross turned back to his boss and said, "If the White House knows about the NSOL, do you think they know who the members are?"

"No. If they did, I think the President would have admitted it."

"So, he was hoping that you would tell him?"

"Yes. He asked me if I knew. I told him we couldn't confirm their identities and that until then I wasn't prepared to accuse anyone."

"What did he say to that?"

"What could he say?"

Again they paused, as the car came to a stop in front of the elevator doors; Payton got out and held the door open for them. The Speaker winced slightly as he got out, and both his chief and his driver noticed. The two of them walked over to the elevator, waited until the doors opened, and got inside. They were alone in it.

Ross nodded. "So what do we do now?"

"Call Sarah McGill and leak it to her that we now have secondary confirmation on the New Sons of Liberty. Tell her she can run with it but not to name the men and women whose computers are linked into the site."

Ross was puzzled, "Yes, sir. But may I ask why?"

"I think it's time to bring the New Sons of Liberty out of the shadows and into the light of public scrutiny."

"To put them on the defensive?"

"Exactly. If I can get the compromise bill through the Congress, it will largely defuse their issue, and hopefully avoid any further conflict."

Ross smiled and said, "You'll steal their roar."

The Speaker now smiled, "Something like that."

A grin spread across Ross's face, "And all they'll have left is a big bear wandering in the Idaho wilderness, while high overhead the eagle and the raven will soar on the wind."

The doors opened, and they quickly walked down the busy hall filled with people, which caused them to be more circumspect in what they said to each other. The Speaker shook his head and with a loving zinger said, "You are definitely working too hard, George. I think you need to get out more."

Ross feigned hurt and said, "I get out a lot, I'll have you know."

Kincaid was quick with his comeback, "I'm talking about somewhere other than the National Zoo."

"At least in the zoo there are bars between each member of the food chain. In Congress, you never know who is about to eat whom."

They reached the door to the Speaker's outer office and paused. The Speaker patted his chief on the back with his good arm and said, "Well, at least for the time being, George, no one is going to eat anyone else."

They both laughed. Then the chief of staff pushed open the door, and they went inside.

<u>48</u>

The Chesapeake Bay, Maryland

The forty-nine foot ketch, Red Dragon, was moored in one of the countless coves that dot the four thousand miles of shoreline on the estuary known as Chesepiooc by Native Americans, or the Chesapeake to everyone else. Maddun Gordon was sitting on the deck with his feet dangling in the water when Chadrian came up from below with two drinks in his hands. He was dressed impeccably in a black Polo shirt, tan summer weight wool slacks, black loafers, and a black belt with an unusual buckle that Gordon noticed right away.

"What is that?" asked Gordon.

"What?"

"On your belt buckle," replied Gordon, pointing to it.

Chadrian looked down at it. "Oh that. That is a raven."

"A raven?"

"Yes."

"Where did you get it?"

"Do not ask."

"Why?"

Chadrian didn't answer the question. Instead he looked at the shoreline and then back out toward the bay. "I think this is where I drowned that congressman. You should have seen him squirm when I held him under water. You would think I was trying to kill him or something." Chadrian was amused by his own joke. Gordon was not. He quickly pulled his feet out of the water and placed them inside the cockpit. Chadrian handed him his drink and said, "So what was so urgent that you had to track me down on this boat the White House just bought me?"

"I need your help."

"To do what?"

"To stop the President from doing something stupid."

"You mean like keeping you?"

Gordon ignored the jab. "I mean like him going along with Kincaid's amendments to his gun bill. That would turn everything that he and I have worked on for the past six years into simply a footnote in Jeremiah Kincaid's biography."

"You are the one who did not want the Speaker dead."

"He very nearly could have been."

"But he was not killed, so I fail to see what your problem is."

"My problem is that you said you would put him out of commission for weeks."

"And if it had not been for the driver killing my man, he would have been. That was one piece of due diligence you neglected to tell me about. And that kid who died was one of my best apprentices, I might add."

"Kincaid's driver didn't kill the kid," said Gordon.

"Of course he did."

"No. He didn't."

"What do you mean?"

"Exactly what I said. The Speaker's driver didn't kill your man. The police report was sealed, but I know the coroner, and he said your man didn't die from a gunshot wound."

"What killed him?"

"They don't know. Apparently he just suddenly stopped living. I think they called it SADS—Sudden Adult Death Syndrome."

Chadrian said something sharp and short in a language Gordon didn't recognize. For a moment he grew silent and stared out across the water.

"What was that? Russian?"

"No."

"Then what?"

Chadrian looked back at him. "It was Aramaic."

"Where the fuck did you learn that?"

"From my Father."

"Jesus Christ, how old are you, two thousand years?" Gordon said with a belly laugh, but almost immediately his smile vanished. "Oh shit. I said it again. I'm sorry." But it was too late.

Chadrian reached over and grabbed Gordon by the throat.

Barely able to breathe, Gordon choked out, "I'm sorry."

A growl rose in Chadrian's gorge, and he choked Gordon almost into oblivion. Just before it was too late, he released him.

Gordon doubled over, grabbed his throat and moaned. "Stupid. Stupid. Stupid."

"Yes, you are," said Chadrian, without pity. "You knew never to say that name again in my presence."

Gordon nodded and rubbed his neck, but said nothing.

Chadrian pressed a button that electrically retracted the anchor and another to start the engine. "Our cruise is over." He put the sleek boat in gear, pushed the throttle forward, and slowly headed it out into the bay.

Gordon gave a furtive glance at Chadrian. "What possible difference does it make how your man died, anyway?"

"None to you."

Gordon fell silent for a long while. Finally he looked back at Chadrian and said, "I need your help, Stefan. I really do."

Chadrian stared at him for what seemed like an eternity and then said, "Very well. What can I do to help you, you poor, pathetic little man?"

Gordon's expression drooped and he shook his head. "Please help me stop the President from making a terrible mistake."

"By accepting the compromise proposed by the Speaker?"

"Yes."

Chadrian thought about it for a moment and then said very matter-of-factly, "Very well, I will kill the President."

Gordon flinched. He started to say "Jesus Christ" but caught himself at the last second. "Don't even joke about something like that."

"I was not joking. I never joke about anything. Killing President Webster would be very good for a sympathy vote. He would be dead, of course, but at least he would have his precious legacy."

Gordon, still trying to regain his voice, shook his head. "I don't want you to kill anyone, especially not the President. We've got to get the public's attention and support without anyone dying."

Chadrian replied, "In case you had not noticed, Maddun, the highest-rated television shows are all about death."

"I know. I find that pathetic."

"No, it is not. It is reality in the purest form. Death by gunfire is the new American way. Or actually it is the old American way. It has always been, is now, and will forever be."

"What exactly do you propose to do?"

"I will show death by gunfire to be what it is. Brutal. Bloody. Barbarous. Live on national television. Recorded as it happens in all its visceral horror."

"I don't understand—"

"Do not worry. Leave it to me." Chadrian adjusted the wheel slightly and steered the boat carefully past a buoy. "And no more questions. It is better that you do not know. Just stay away from the front lawn of the White House for a few days."

Gordon, for all his vulgarity and self-indulgence, was troubled by what he had just heard. Somehow, in the back of his mind, he knew it would eventually come down to this: an agonizing choice where a few must die so that the rest can survive. But now, there it was in all it's harshness, and he felt compelled to go along with it. "This must not be traceable back to me nor the White House."

"You think?"

"Just be careful."

"I always am."

"Not always."

"What are you talking about?"

"Potomac Park."

"What about it?"

"The acting Attorney General has a photograph of the two of us."

"That is impossible. I destroyed that disk."

"It wasn't from the camera. There was a UAV overhead that day, taking photos of the Park."

Chadrian pounded his fist against the gunwale and said something again that Gordon could not understand.

"Don't sweat it. The print is so blurry that even the FBI photo lab couldn't be absolutely certain that it was us. They can't prove anything."

"How do you know all this?

Gordon grinned. "I have my sources."

Chadrian's eyes narrowed to slits. "I will have to eliminate that threat."

Gordon's face went pale. "If you mean terminate Pritchard, the answer is no."

"Do not worry, this one is, how do you say, on the house."

Gordon leaned forward. "Listen to me. You are not to harm that woman."

"Why not?" Chadrian asked matter-of-factly, like they were debating whether or not to step on a bug.

"Because if you harm her, I won't pay you another dime."

Chadrian shrugged. "So be it. The woman lives. She is more of a threat to you than me."

"Perhaps. But I think my boss is in love with her, and if you kill her, it will make my life a living hell."

"What makes you think it is not so, already?"

Gordon didn't acknowledge the comment. Instead he asked, "So how much will this next event cost me?"

"Twice what the last one cost."

"Four million!"

"Yes."

Gordon started to complain but thought better of it. "All right. But someday, I won't be able to meet your demands."

"Then that is the day you will die," replied Chadrian coldly.

"My money supply isn't unlimited, you know."

"Mr. Gordon. The committee to reelect the President collected over two hundred million dollars in soft campaign money when he won his second term. Your opponents were in such disarray that you only spent half, which means there is plenty more funding available for your *special projects*."

Gordon looked out across the water. Chadrian was right. The fact that it was getting harder and harder to cover up his withdrawals was his problem, and not one for which Chadrian would have any sympathy.

The boat neared the public dock at Tracy's Landing on the western shore of the Chesapeake. Chadrian had already electronically furled the mainsail, and now he did the same with the jib. Switching to diesel power, he expertly guided it in. Gordon went to the bow, and at the last moment, he jumped onto the dock, pushed the bow aside, and carefully guided the hull up to the rubber bumper on the dock.

Chadrian stood in the cockpit and said, "I will help you and after I have done so, we will talk about how you can repay me."

"We already discussed the money."

Chadrian gave him a look that sent a cold chill up his spine. "I said we would talk about it later. Now push me off."

Gordon did what he was told, and Chadrian eased the yacht away from the slip under power. Then he pointed it out toward the open water and motored away without looking back.

May, 2018

G Day - 120

The Death Of Innocence

Let me die the death of the righteous
and let my last end be like his!

Numbers 23:10

49

River Of No Return Wilderness, Idaho

Ursus arctos horribilis, or the grizzly as he is commonly known, is not the biggest species of bear. That dubious distinction goes to the polar bear. However, the adult male grizzly that ambled slowly across the meadow a mile downriver from the southern perimeter of Camp Freedom was large—very large. At his peak during the previous Fall, he weighed over nine hundred pounds, which was near the highest weight that had ever been recorded for a male of his species in the wild. But this was early spring in the high country, and he was thin and hungry, with a disposition to match. The lightly colored or grizzled fur on his head and shoulders, set above his dark brown body and even darker legs, made it appear that this king of the wilderness walked in permanent sunlight.

The bear's extremely long front claws, huge canine teeth, and massive foreleg muscles, which gave him his characteristic hump, made him one of the most lethal, live killing machines on earth. However, contrary to popular belief, this bear, like all the others of his species, sourced over eighty percent of his nutrition from the world of botany rather than zoology. And on that bright May morning, only a few hours after waking from a long but fitful winter's sleep, all the big animal wanted to do was finish his meal of legume roots and be left alone. It was not to be. As he finished tearing up a particular area of sod, a strange and intriguing new smell suddenly caught his attention, as the wind shifted to the south. He immediately stopped what he was doing, stood up, and turned his huge, dish-shaped forehead into the wind. After sniffing and snorting for a few minutes, he dropped back down onto all fours and started to follow the scent trail. With that simple move, his fate was sealed.

If a scientist had ever tranquilized this bear and counted the rings of cement holding his teeth in place, he would have recorded twelve—one for every year of this bear's life. Even though this animal was approaching middle age, he had never had direct contact with humans. His home range had for the most part existed inside the boundaries of the Bitterroot National Forest, and as such, he hadn't been subject to hunting pressures or the inexorable encroachment of human habitation. But the previous summer had been particularly dry in the West, and forest fires in his home range had forced the animal outside the park boundaries. That brought him at that particular moment to within a gunshot of the large military training camp that, like the bear, sought safety and succor in the silence of the wilderness.

Fifteen hundred yards away, the private backed his small, but powerful all-terrain vehicle, painted in dull camouflage colors, into the dark, damp glen, deep in the pinewoods. He got off, climbed up onto the back bed, and began dumping drums of kitchen grease and fatty scraps onto the ground. The private knew that it was forbidden to do this, as the kitchen staff had standing orders to take the trash, including these drums of fat, to the incinerator at the north end of camp, over two miles away. But this soldier was too lazy to follow orders. He'd been given a week of KP duty for mouthing off at an officer, and his attitude hadn't gotten any better during his punishment. So after making sure that no one had followed him up the brushy trail through the thick pines, he dumped the greasy liquid and scraps onto the ground, leaned back against the vehicle, and lit up a cigarette. It would be the last defiant act of a foolish man.

Two factors conspired against the soldier that morning and led to his untimely and grisly death. The first was the nature of the garbage that he had dumped. Had it not contained a large amount of bacon grease scraped off trays used to feed an army of young soldiers, the scent of the private himself would have likely been enough to keep the bear away. But as the magnificent beast ambled slowly through the pines toward the smell, he either did not notice, or did not care about, the traces of human scent mixed in with fried pig. The second factor was that the man had spent his entire twenty-four years of life in Tampa, and before joining the militia, he had never been outside of Florida, let alone in a rugged mountain wilderness. He had responded to an ad for the militia that he had seen on the internet without fully comprehending what military life entailed. This left him totally unprepared for what he found at the training camp. Nothing could have prepared him for what was about to happen next.

The bear broke out of the heavy brush twenty-five yards from where the soldier stood smoking. It was unclear who was more startled by the sudden encounter—man or beast. Regardless, the soldier did the worst thing that he could have done. Instead of calmly getting back onto the Gator and driving off, he panicked and ran. An Olympic athlete can run fifteen miles an hour. An ordinary man who was a non-smoker and in good shape, maybe half that fast. The soldier was neither. On the other hand, a grizzly, despite its enormous size and weight, can sprint in bursts of nearly forty miles an hour. It was no contest. The sight of the man racing away in panic brought out the predatory instinct in the bear, and in a matter of seconds, the animal caught up to the man and bowled him over. Before the private could scream, the bear grabbed his skull in his powerful jaws and shook it violently, cracking it like an eggshell. The soldier's body convulsed twice and then hung limply. The bear chewed the dead man's head for a few more minutes, tearing off half the scalp and a large flap of bone. It was a taste that he did not particularly find appealing. So he dropped the body and ambled over to the bacon fat and food scraps, where he began to scoop up great, greasy mouthfuls.

He had only gulped down ten pounds of the smelly mixture when the Humvee with two military policemen rounded the corner and came face to face with the gruesome scene. They had been called by the man's sergeant who had had enough of his lip. It hadn't taken long for the MPs to follow the Gator's tire tracks into the woods and now, in one horrifying instant, they found their man, or at least what was left of him. After giving the MPs a perfunctory glance, the bear went back to his fatty feast. The MPs, realizing that the subject of their search was beyond military justice, and that their sidearms were woefully inadequate, put their vehicle in reverse and backed quickly away from the scene. The bear didn't notice them depart. Nor did he stop what he was doing. Unfortunately for this magnificent beast, not leaving the area immediately would be his second and final mistake of the morning. The first had been to kill the human.

THOMAS PORTER walked across the parade ground in front of the large pre-fab building that served as the Wolf River Militia's command post. Beyond it were many more buildings, both large and small but all made out of the same prefabricated panels of pressed, pre-treated wood. There were also storage sheds, oil tanks, and numerous military vehicles of all types and sizes spread across the valley floor. However, there were very few men or women to be seen, for it was early on Sunday morning and the base was quiet. Kincaid had been on his way over to the officer's mess tent when he saw the Humvee coming down the dirt road at break-neck speed. It raced up to the front of the building nearest to him and lurched to a stop. Out jumped the MPs, neither one of whom had any color in his face. Spotting Kincaid, the man nearest him started to babble in a barely understandable stream of consciousness.

Kincaid had arrived in the camp a week earlier, and after watching the live fire exercises on the first day, he had spent the rest of his time getting to know Lieutenant Colonel Snow Eagle and his men. He had also been practicing his marksmanship and was quite pleased with his ability to hit small targets at great distances. But those targets were made of plywood and paper, not flesh and blood, and there was a world of difference between the two as Kincaid was about to discover. After an enjoyable dinner the night before with General Latrobe, who had arrived that afternoon at the base, and a good night's sleep in the cool mountain air, Kincaid was feeling well-rested, self-confident, and calm. It helped him quiet down the two MPs, neither of whom was as yet able to clearly state the problem.

"Calm down, soldier, and tell me what the problem is," Kincaid said in a loud and firm voice.

"Bear, sir. A monster bear," said one of the soldiers, pointing somewhere vaguely down the road toward the south.

"A grizzly?" asked Kincaid.

"Yes, sir. I think so," said the other soldier frantically, "And it's eating someone."

"What?"

"Yes, sir. Half his head is gone," added the other MP.

By that point, several other soldiers who had been passing by walked over to see what the commotion was. One of them was Lieutenant Colonel Joseph Snow Eagle and another was Command Sergeant Major Jones.

"Are you telling me that there's a bear eating a man near the camp?" asked Kincaid incredulously.

"Yes. Yes. Yes," answered the first MP.

"Where?" asked Snow Eagle, joining the conversation.

"Down beside where the creek meets the river," the MP said, barely able to get a breath. The two policemen had served in WWT and had seen many dead bodies. But the sight of that dead soldier had completely unnerved them. They thought, incorrectly, that their colleague was the bear's main meal and nothing so discomforts a human as the concept of not being at the top of the food chain.

Snow Eagle turned to Jones and said, "Sergeant Major, I think you'd better find General Latrobe. And tell him we'll need a rifle."

"Yes, sir," said Jones, as he headed off toward the general's quarters.

"Better make it a fifty caliber," shouted one of the MPs after him.

"And maybe a grenade launcher," added the other.

"Did you understand where the soldier said the bear was, Colonel?" Kincaid asked Snow Eagle.

"Yes," said Snow Eagle in a calm voice. "I know exactly where he means."

"Good. Then let's go," said Kincaid.

Snow Eagle nodded, and the two of them climbed into the Humvee and drove off.

BY THE TIME the general and a squad of heavily armed soldiers reached Kincaid, Snow Eagle, and the two MPs, the bear was gone. The noisy arrival of Kincaid's Humvee had chased him off. Latrobe climbed out of his shiny, black SUV, with its four-star pennant laying quietly against the thin pole on its front bumper. The vehicle wasn't military issue, but no one was going to tell the general that he had to ride around in a vehicle that looked like a jeep on steroids. Latrobe walked briskly over to Kincaid, who was kneeling beside the fallen soldier while Snow Eagle looked on. The two MPs stood with their weapons drawn, nervously facing the woods. Each man quickly switched the sidearm into his left hand and smartly saluted the general with the right, as he walked up and stopped near Kincaid.

"Put those away!" snapped the general. He was dressed in starched utilities and wore a chrome-plated, .44 magnum revolver, with an eight-inch barrel on his belt. "If that grizzly comes back, he'll kill both of you twice. Once for the minor annoyance that you'd cause him with those pea shooters and once more for just being stupid."

The MPs did what they were told.

The general looked down at Kincaid, who was examining the dead man's badly mauled head. A huge flap of skin was folded down across his face, exposing the back of the eyeballs where the optic nerve enters the skull. Gray brain matter oozed out of a long, ragged gouge in the skull itself. One of his ears lay on the ground connected to the skull by only a thin strip of skin. The other one was missing entirely. Great quantities of blood had turned the soil a shade of deep purple.

"At least it was quick," said the general.

Kincaid stood up and nodded somberly. "Yes, sir."

The general stepped carefully over to a patch of ground where no one had disturbed the bear's tracks and knelt down to study them. "A male. And a big one," he said. He placed his hand with fingers open wide inside the bear print. He was a big man with big hands, but it looked tiny in the soft indentation of the bear's front paw. Then he stood up and turned to his driver, who was standing behind him, and said, "Get me my rifle, son." The soldier ran back to the SUV and returned with a long black case which he held while the general opened it. Inside was a custom .458 magnum bolt action rifle with open sights. It was clear to everyone that this long gun was meant to kill animals far larger and more dangerous than the two-legged kind. It was also clear that the general knew how to use it. Quickly and effortlessly, he loaded four shells into its magazine and put a handful more into his jacket pocket. Then the general said to his driver, "Get a stretcher and take this man's body to the infirmary." The soldier, who by now was as white as a ghost, replied in the affirmative and walked away.

The general looked at Snow Eagle and said, "I'm told that you used to be a pretty good tracker in your younger days, Joseph, isn't that so?"

"Yes, General, and I still am. In fact, ever since my brother died up on that mountain over there, I am the best in the West."

"Good. Get a radio from your platoon and let's go," said Latrobe. Then almost as an afterthought, Latrobe looked at Kincaid and said, "We're going on a bear hunt. Care to join us?"

Without hesitating Kincaid said, "Yes, General."

The general smiled. Then he walked over to a soldier and asked him for his military rifle. The soldier gave it to him and he then handed it to Kincaid and said, "Let's go. He couldn't have gone very far."

The thought of the general heading out after a giant man killer didn't please his executive officer. "Are you sure this is a good idea, General?"

432

The general smiled and said, "I've stalked enemies more dangerous and less innocent. And at least with him, I know exactly what to expect."

"Yes, sir," answered the exec. But it was obvious that he wasn't happy.

"After the bear is dead, we'll radio base and you can send a chopper for us."

"Why don't you let me call one in for you now, sir, and you can follow the bear by air."

The general smiled and said patiently, "Because it's kind of difficult to sneak up on a bear with two thousand horsepower twin turbines screaming."

"Understood, sir." He saluted smartly and left.

"You men ready?" Latrobe asked Kincaid and Snow Eagle.

"Yes, sir," answered Snow Eagle, who headed off in the direction of the bear tracks.

"Absolutely," chimed in Kincaid having a hard time controlling the adrenaline pumping through his body.

"Good. Let's go. I don't want to be out there after dark."

Kincaid didn't answer. He didn't have to. The look on his face clearly said that the thought didn't appeal to him either.

With that, they headed off into the deep woods.

"WHY ARE YOU HERE, Captain Porter?" asked the general, as they reached the top of a rise overlooking the river and stopped to reconnoiter. Snow Eagle was nowhere to be seen. Before them lay a vast panorama of mountains that stood shoulder to shoulder as if forming a protective barrier to keep civilization out of the wilderness.

"To watch your back," replied Kincaid.

The general looked over at the younger man and said, "I didn't mean on this bear hunt."

"Neither did I," said Kincaid with a sly smile.

Kincaid's answer surprised the general. He looked at him for a long moment and then stared out across the vista that lay before them.

"To watch out for whom?"

"Everyone," said Kincaid with a straight face.

The general turned back toward Kincaid but didn't say anything. Nor did his expression give any indication as to what he was thinking. Slowly a big smile spread across his ruddy face, and he laughed as he said, "I like you, Thomas."

Kincaid smiled and said, "The feeling is mutual."

The general looked back out across the river valley and added, "I didn't at first. I thought you were a self-serving, pig-headed, vainglorious dilettante."

Kincaid nodded and said, "Ditto. Except, of course, for the dilettante part."

The general snapped his head back toward Kincaid and laughed again. Then he said, "Come on. Let's go kill that bear before he decides that the taste of human flesh wasn't so bad after all."

"Yes, sir."

At the bottom of the rise, Snow Eagle appeared out of the shadows of the forest. He motioned for the other two men to come down and join him. The general and Kincaid headed down across the sunlit meadow, while all around them, wild flowers danced on the wind.

As they reached the colonel, the general said calmly, "Do you have him, Joseph?"

Snow Eagle nodded and replied in a matter-of-fact tone, "Yes. He's starting to circle back on us. By now he should be lying in ambush just off the trail fifty yards ahead."

"You mean he knows that we're following him?" asked Kincaid.

"Yes. He probably picked up our scent ten minutes after we started the chase," said the colonel. "They can smell dead animals from miles away."

Kincaid smiled lamely and said, "I wish you could have used another example."

The general chuckled and added, "And now that he knows we're closing on him, he's decided to give us a welcoming party. Complete with munchies. Except that *we're* it."

"Why would he do that?" asked Kincaid. "I mean why wouldn't he just keep going deeper and deeper into the wilderness?"

It was the question of a man who had not grown up near wild animals, at least not big ones. The general said patiently, "Because grizzlies have a keen sense of personal space, and we're trespassing in his."

The colonel pointed off to their right and said to the general, "If we head in that direction we'll make our approach from downwind."

The general nodded and said, "You are good."

"Yes, sir. I am," answered Snow Eagle with a proud smile.

"Let's go," said Latrobe.

Within minutes they were at the edge of a thick wall of elderberry bushes and young aspen trees. The general said to Kincaid, "Climb back up the hillside, and stay there."

Kincaid reacted to the order with mixed emotions. But he nodded and did what he was told. Snow Eagle and Latrobe headed noiselessly into the brush, and Kincaid soon found himself all alone on a hillside staring at the dark, threatening forest. He looked down at his weapon and checked to make sure that the safety was off. He thought he heard what sounded like a deep growl coming from the brush, and he quickly climbed another fifty yards up the side of the meadow. He wanted to give himself enough distance to be able to see if it was man or beast that came back out of the brush to meet him. He waited but didn't have to wait long.

The sound of thunder filled the air, but it wasn't the thunder of gunfire. Instead it was the earsplitting noise of a jet helicopter, as it swooped down the hillside behind Kincaid and roared over his head not fifty feet off the ground. It then climbed up and away from him until it was barely visible against the backdrop of the mountains. As it did, the sound of its powerful turbine engines rumbled down the valley like rolling thunder. There was a brief respite as the thumping of the rotor blades diminished, until the chopper spun its tail around and zoomed back down directly at Kincaid. At first he stood there frozen and then turned and started to run, but the sound of gunfire over the returning thunder and the sight of dirt flying up in front of him brought him to an abrupt stop.

"Federal agents. Stay where you are," said a man's voice booming out over a loud speaker as the helicopter slowed and began to hover overhead.

Kincaid froze.

"Throw away your weapon, and lie down on the ground," the voice barked.

Kincaid glanced toward the treeline where Latrobe and Snow Eagle had disappeared, but there was no sight of them.

"Do as I say, or you will die," came the order.

Kincaid did as he was told. He threw the rifle off to one side and knelt down. As he got onto his knees, he thought he caught a glimpse of movement in the alder thickets. *It's probably the other two men,* he thought, *but they're waiting for their chance to save me.*

Then in a crescendo of flying brush and blinding dirt, the helicopter settled onto the hillside on the opposite side of Kincaid from the treeline. As the turbines began to wind down, two armed men dressed in black fatigues with FBI printed in bright yellow letters on their backs jumped out of the passenger compartment and started to head toward the prostrate Kincaid.

Kincaid let out a deep sigh as he wiped dirt from his eyes. *Oh well, this was bound to happen sooner or later,* he thought. *Maybe it's just as well.*

What happened next was little more than a blur to Kincaid. The two agents had only taken ten paces toward him when they froze.

"Holy shit!" one of them exclaimed, and they both looked as if they had just seen the devil. They hadn't. It was something just as dangerous, perhaps even more so. Racing across the ground toward them was the grizzly. Its eyes were filled with fury, and froth lathered its jaws, which were open, revealing enormous incisor fangs. And it was closing on them at the rate of forty miles an hour.

Seeing their expression, Kincaid turned his head and saw what they saw, except that unlike them, he was unarmed and too far away from the helicopter to have any chance of making it.

The pilots had also seen the bear and they started to power up the engines, but there was nothing they could do to speed up the process. The heavy rotors began to swing, slowly picking up speed with each rotation. And the bear was getting closer by the second. One agent ran like hell for the safety of the helicopter, while the other raised his weapon and began firing. It was a mistake. Had he joined his buddy, they might have lived, but without realizing it, he had just sealed their fate. The first shot hit the bear high on his shoulder and didn't have any physical effect, whatsoever. It only served to enrage him further. The second and third shots missed the bear completely. Before he could get off a fourth shot, the bear raced past the prone Kincaid, who had now placed his hands over the back of his neck and was lying as still as possible in the face of such fury. In two more strides, it reached the hapless special agent, knocked him down, and grabbed his throat in his jaws. With one violent bite, the bear bit the man's head off, and his body went limp. As soon as it did, the bear dropped him and turned his attention to the helicopter, which by now had just reached lift-off power. The bear raced the last few meters across the distance, separating it from the aircraft and its terrified occupants.

"Get us up. Get us up!" the agent who had climbed back into the aircraft screamed, as he pulled up on the open door handle with all his might as if to lift the aircraft himself. With a dip of its nose, the helicopter gradually began to lift off the grass and it almost made it into the sky. Almost.

At the last second, the bear stood up on its haunches, reached up with one of its powerful arms and swatted at the left landing gear. He hit it with such enormous force that it destabilized the heavy aircraft at a critical moment before it achieved full lift. The helicopter shuddered and rocked violently, first to one side and then to the other. The bear hit it again, and that was all it took. Despite the pilot's best efforts, it gained only a little more altitude and then began to pitch and roll wildly. As it did, it slipped sideways up the hill rather than down and away from it. Then in what seemed to Kincaid to be slow motion, the tip of one of its enormous main rotors caught the dirt on the uphill side. And that was that. The rotors literally exploded, throwing lethal shrapnel everywhere, and the big mechanical bird turned on its side and crashed heavily into the mountainside. For just an instant it lay there like a gigantic broken toy; and then it exploded. The force of the explosion bowled the giant bear off his feet, and he rolled to within a few meters of Kincaid.

As soon as the shock wave from the crash passed over him, Kincaid struggled to his feet, holding out his hand to shield his face from the searing heat of the burning aircraft. Dazed and overwhelmed by it all, he hesitated for a moment, and while he did, the giant bear also got to its feet, facing Kincaid. They both stood there, eyeing each other, feeling the heat of the fire, neither man nor beast quite certain of what to do. Kincaid felt the hairs on the back of his neck rise up, and his heart was pounding so hard, he couldn't catch his breath. Later, he would tell everyone that he was certain the bear and he somehow made a connection with each other on some primal level. But no one would listen. They would just smile and say, *Yes. Yes. You were very lucky.* But it wasn't luck. He was convinced of it. He knew somewhere deep inside that the bear intentionally spared him. Although for what purpose, he couldn't possibly know. Finally, the beast dropped down onto all fours and ambled off toward the brush. After a few yards, it stopped and looked back. Kincaid tensed, but then it looked away and bounded off towards the deep brush.

Kincaid watched it go. Inside he felt a mixture of relief and yet sadness, for he knew the beast was doomed. At that moment, out of the brush stepped

Latrobe and Snow Eagle. The general immediately raised his rifle and pointed it at the oncoming bear.

"No!" screamed Kincaid. But it was too late. Two shots rang out followed by a third. Instantly, the giant beast that only moments ago had stood in judgment of Kincaid and let him live, collapsed into the soft prairie grass and wildflowers, groaned once, and became still.

Kincaid raced down the hill to the fallen beast. He reached it moments before the other two men did. Lying on its stomach in the soft grass, with sad, sightless eyes wide open, was the once proud and mighty king of that wild domain, never again to roam freely across the golden hillsides beneath the majestic purple peaks or to splash in the clear, cold rivers that ran wild through forests of cinnamon and green. Reduced now to a silent hump of fur and flesh and matted blood. It was a sight that Kincaid would never forget. Never once in the aftermath of the massacre up on that mountain, nor during the long months since, had he ever felt the profound sense of loss or grief as he did at that moment. Then he had only felt anger. Now, he only felt sorrow. And that dichotomy of feeling bothered him even more than the death of the bear itself.

Snow Eagle and Latrobe arrived at the spot where the animal lay. After checking to make sure that it was dead, the general stepped around the bear and stood there staring up the hillside at the still burning wreckage. "Poor bastards."

But Snow Eagle was more concerned about the living rather than the dead. "Are you all right, Captain?" he asked, as he noticed that Porter was unsteady on his feet.

At first Kincaid didn't answer. He just stared at the dead animal. Then he looked over at Latrobe and muttered, "You killed him."

"Yes. That was the idea, after all," said Latrobe.

"But he could have killed me and he didn't. We should have let him go."

Snow Eagle patted Kincaid on his back and said softly, "We could not. He would have killed again."

Kincaid looked at Snow Eagle but said nothing. Instead, he laid his gun down on the ground and swore a promise to himself that he would never hold one again as long as he lived.

Snow Eagle picked up the weapon and headed up the hill toward the wreckage.

"I could understand you being upset about the men that died in that chopper, Captain, but quite frankly, I can't see getting all worked up about the death of a bear."

Kincaid gave the general a cold stare. "This wasn't the death of a killer here today, General. It was the death of innocence." Then he turned and walked away.

Latrobe shrugged his shoulders. He looked up the hill toward the burning wreckage and muttered to himself, "Damnedest thing I ever saw. That bear literally knocked it right out of the sky."

Snow Eagle returned. "They were FBI."

Latrobe grunted, "That's what I figured." He pulled out a long knife and squatted beside the dead animal.

"What were they doing here?" asked the colonel.

"I expect it had to do with our reluctant hunting companion," said the general. "Now, while we wait for our helicopter to arrive, I think I'm going to cut some bear claws. Do you want any?"

Snow Eagle shook his head no.

"Suit yourself."

Snow Eagle followed Kincaid down the hillside, leaving the dead monarch of the forest lying in a hump on that grassy knoll with the long hairs on the back of his enormous shoulders dancing on the breeze. He found Kincaid sitting on a fallen log at the edge of the forest. His face was flushed and he had opened the collar of his shirt wide.

"Do you mind if I sit down, T.J.?" he asked Kincaid, who appeared to be lost somewhere in another wilderness—the one that exists deep inside all men as a tiny primal vestige of our beginnings.

"What? Oh, no, not at all," he said, snapping out of his trance.

"Good."

Snow Eagle didn't say anything for a long moment, and then finally he asked, "Are you sure you're all right?"

Kincaid looked over at him and shook his head in deep frustration. "I honestly don't know."

Snow Eagle sat down, picked up a slender stalk of prairie grass from beside the log, and placed it in his mouth. Without looking at Kincaid, he said softly, "That bear had tasted human flesh and would have killed again had we not done this."

Kincaid nodded but said nothing.

Snow Eagle continued, "It's not the bear's death that weighs heavily upon your spirit, is it?"

Kincaid started to say that it was, but then he caught himself. "No. I guess not. At least not completely."

"Do you want to talk about it? I'm a better listener than I am a tracker."

Kincaid smiled and asked, "Is there anything that you're not good at Joseph?"

"Give me a week and I'll think of something."

Kincaid stared out across the field toward Mount Freedom, which towered above the lesser peaks in the distance. "Before the hunt, you said that your brother died up on that mountain."

The smile faded from Snow Eagle's face. "Yes."

"How? If you don't mind me asking."

Snow Eagle gave him a knowing smile. "He was one of the Army Rangers who retook the club from you and your men."

"Oh God. I'm sorry. I didn't know," said Kincaid.

"I know you didn't. It's all right. It wasn't your fault," said Snow Eagle gently.

Kincaid's shoulders sagged. "Yes, it was, but there is nothing I can do to change it."

Snow Eagle didn't push the matter. He had followed Kincaid to help him, not to reopen old wounds. "How long has it been since you saw *your* brother?"

"Too long," answered Kincaid softly. "I doubt that I ever will again."

"It's too late for me, T.J., but it isn't too late for you."

Kincaid nodded but said nothing.

Snow Eagle hesitated. "I'm sorry if I intruded."

Kincaid shook his head. "The truth is never an intrusion, but it's a long story. Perhaps another time."

"Of course." Snow Eagle stood up. "The helicopter is coming."

Kincaid couldn't hear anything, but like Snow Eagle, he stood up.

As he did, the eagle amulet that he was wearing around his neck swung out of the collar of his shirt. Instantly, Snow Eagle froze, his eyes fixed upon the small silver charm.

"What is it?" asked Kincaid.

"Where did you get that?" asked Snow Eagle, examining it closely with his sharp eyes.

Kincaid pointed at the mountain. "Up there. Inside a cave." He then told Snow Eagle the story of how he ran down the mountain and slept in a cave; how he was awakened in the morning by a large gray wolf; and how he immediately afterwards discovered the tiny eagle in the dirt.

The story confirmed what Snow Eagle's eyes had already told him. It was *the* eagle amulet—the one his grandfather had lost over a hundred years earlier. He thought it had been lost forever, but now there it was, hanging around the neck of T.J. Kincaid.

"You obviously recognize this. Please tell me—why?" said Kincaid.

Snow Eagle told Kincaid the story of Gray Wolf and his grandson, who was Snow Eagle's grandfather, and the day they had climbed the mountain known to his people as the Kingdom of the Wind Spirit. He finished by saying that Gray Wolf died before he was able to make another one for his grandson, but that the legend of the lost eagle amulet had been passed down through the years as vividly as if it was still a part of their family.

When Joseph finished, it was obvious that Kincaid was deeply moved. "Here," he said, starting to unclasp it. "You must have it back."

"No," said Snow Eagle firmly.

Kincaid stopped what he was doing. "But why?"

"Because the eagle carries with it great power and magic. And the Great Spirit must have had a reason in having you find it."

"What reason?"

"I don't know. But he has a reason for everything that he does."

"What shall I do with it?"

"In the same way that he guided you to it, the Great Spirit will guide you in what he wants you to do with it and when."

Kincaid nodded and carefully tucked it back into his shirt.

Just then, the whumping sound of the general's helicopter broke the stillness of the wilderness, and soon the aircraft flew into sight and landed high on the side of the hill well away from the carnage below.

Nothing more was said between the two men, either about the bear or their brothers or the eagle amulet. At least not that day. But out of that moment a friendship was born. One that would affect the course of all that was yet to come.

<u>50</u>

The White House, Washington, D.C.

In an effort to enhance his relationship with the military, which could be characterized as constrained at best and caustic at worst, the President decided to hold a dance during the week before the Memorial Day weekend. His staff recommended against it, fearing it might appear inappropriate to hold a festive event during a time when the nation remembered its fallen warriors. However, the President disagreed, and the party was on. As the full-length portrait of the nation's first President looked down upon the crowd in the East Room, the current President, looking debonair in his tuxedo, entertained his guests in his usual charming style. He mingled freely with the crowd, made up of the Chairman and the Joint Chiefs of Staff, senior Pentagon officers and their key staff, as well as Cabinet members and other top aides. He had also been especially friendly to newly promoted Brigadier General Mitchell Pritchard and his wife, the acting Attorney General, who looked ravishing in a dress with a plunging neckline that her husband had argued with her about before the dance. She had won out but now, as she noticed the wandering eyes of all the men in the room, even she was beginning to regret her decision.

Also present at the ball were Lieutenant Colonel Jake Kincaid and Sarah McGill. He was wearing his dress uniform, she was in a stunning dress, and together they looked like they had just stepped out of a storybook. Following lunch with his father a few weeks earlier, Jake had asked Sarah McGill to be his date at the ball, and she had gracefully accepted. She could tell by his manner that he was interested in her, but her feelings at that point were simply platonic. Or at least that was what she kept telling herself; but as they danced around the floor in that magnificent building, thoughts of the Speaker's youngest son, the daring rebel who she had first met on that mountain far to the west, began to fade deeper into her subconscious.

As the Pritchards danced near Jake and Sarah, they both caught the President's eye again. "Shit," said Mitchell. "Here comes your boss. Again. Can't he find some other boobs to stare at?" He squared his shoulders and gave a slight nod of his head toward the on-coming commander in chief. "Try not to push them too much in his face, will you?"

Mary Lou looked up angrily at her husband and said, "That's not fair, and you know it."

"You're the one who's wearing that dress."

"You never said I shouldn't," she retorted. She would have continued the conversation but just then, Webster arrived.

"Hello again, General and Mary Lou," said the President.

They stopped dancing and faced him. "Hello, Mr. President," said Mary Lou, as her husband visibly stiffened.

"Stand easy, soldier," said the President with a friendly grin. "By the way, General, I forgot to congratulate you earlier on your promotion. It was well-deserved." His voice lacked sincerity but the new general didn't notice.

"Thank-you, Mr. President," said Pritchard, as his cold demeanor softened. "And I forgot to tell you about the excellent progress that we're making with the M1A3 battle tank."

"Yes, yes," replied Webster, but his eyes had already looked away over the general's shoulder. It was clear to Mary Lou that the President had no interest in what her husband was saying but that he hadn't picked it up.

"Colonel Jeremiah S. Kincaid, Jr. and Ms. Sarah McGill," said the President, as the young couple danced nearby. Dutifully, they stopped and joined the Pritchards and the President. General Pritchard was clearly displeased at being ignored. There were very few people who could insult an Army General and not worry about it. The President was one of them.

"Sarah, you look lovely tonight," said the President, oozing charm.

"Thank-you, Mr. President," she replied, unmoved by the compliment.

"Good evening, Colonel Kincaid," said the President with a forced smile.

"Good evening, Mr. President."

The President looked at Sarah McGill and Mary Lou and said, "Ladies, I think I feel a dance coming on. Which one of you two beautiful women would like to dance with the leader of the free world?"

It was clear by her expression and body language that Mary Lou was eager to accept the offer, but before she could, her husband interjected, "Actually we were just about to go outside for a breath of air, Mr. President." Mary Lou's eyes showed her regret.

"Very well, then I guess the honor falls to the lovely Ms. McGill," said Webster. She looked at Jake, who smiled and said, "He's the commander in chief."

The President patted the colonel on the shoulder and said, "Good answer. You'll go far, my boy."

As the Pritchards started to walk away, the President said, "Mary Lou, I need to see you in my office later." Then he looked at the general and added with a twinkle in his eye, "Sorry, General, but I need to meet with my staff. I assure you it won't take long."

The general nodded but did not smile.

"What time would you like me there, Mr. President?"

"At ten." Then he looked at McGill and extended his arm. "Shall we dance, my lady?"

She smiled at Jake, then took the President's arm, and walked off with him.

"You'd better be careful, Colonel, or he'll steal your woman away from you," said General Pritchard. Then he and Mary Lou walked away, leaving the colonel standing all alone in the crowded room. A white-coated steward walked up with a tray of champagne.

"Champagne, Colonel?"

Kincaid started to reach for it and then caught himself. "No, thank-you."

The steward nodded and walked away.

Kincaid took a deep breath and headed off to find a soft drink. As he did, a pair of eyes saw what he had done. They were Sarah McGill's, looking over the shoulder of the President as they danced across the floor. A smile spread across her pretty lips. The President assumed it was for him. But it was not.

"COME IN, MARY LOU," said the President, as a uniformed Secret Service Agent held the door to the Oval Office open and then closed it firmly behind her. "Make yourself comfortable. I just have to pop into my private study for a moment."

"Where are the others?" she asked, glancing around the office and seeing that they were alone.

"What others?"

"You told my husband that you wanted to meet with your staff."

He looked deeply into her eyes and replied, "Did I? Humm. I don't remember saying that. Well, anyway, it's just you and me. I'll be right back." With that, he left her there alone.

Mary Lou Pritchard stood nervously in front of one of the yellow sofas. Not realizing that there were several peepholes through which the Secret Service could keep an eye on the room, she tugged at her bodice, trying unsuccessfully to reduce the cleavage. Had she known that the most powerful man on the face of the earth was watching her through the peephole in the door that led into his study, she would have been mortified. Or perhaps not. For as much as she tried to ignore it, the instant he told her they would be alone, down deep inside she found herself strangely excited at the thought. But she quickly dismissed it and tried to focus on what it might be that he wanted.

Then it came to her. He had probably brought her there to discuss the top-secret report that she had sent him the previous day. In it, she had outlined allegations about his chief of staff and had included photographs, which she believed were damning. She had wanted to present them in person, but Maddun Gordon insisted that she send them over before the meeting. Given the contents of the material she had been reluctant to do so; however, she doubted that even Gordon would have the audacity to open an envelope marked "For The President's Eyes Only." But as she stood there waiting for the President, trying to keep her mind on the matter contained in the envelope, Mary Lou Pritchard could not ignore the hard reality—that she was unmistakably excited. And not in an innocent way.

"SSSSH!" said Sarah McGill, as she and Jake walked down the corridor in the West Wing toward the press corps lounge. The recessed overhead lights and expensive lamps sitting on antique tables had all been slightly dimmed given the late hour. They would stay that way until dawn brought in

445

the flood of people who worked there. The West Wing of the people's house never went completely dark. At least not literally, although several times in its recent history it had done so figuratively.

"Why are we whispering?" asked Jake, with a bemused grin on his face.

"Because I'm not supposed to bring you here."

"Then why are we doing this?"

"I want to show you where I work." As they rounded a corner, they came face to face with the head of the President's Secret Service detail. "Hello, Agent Wiseman!" said McGill, with as much poise and dignity as she could muster.

"Good evening, Ms. McGill. A little late to be filing a report, isn't it?"

"I forgot something in the lounge," she replied with a twinkle in her eyes.

He smiled patiently. "I suggest you make it quick."

"We will. By the way Agent Wiseman, this is Colonel Jake Kincaid,"

"Yes, I know. How do you do, Colonel?" He eyed the ribbons and medals that hung on Jake's uniform; one in particular caught his eye. It was a five-pointed star that signified the nation's highest military honor. "It is a privilege, Colonel."

"No, the privilege is mine, Agent Wiseman."

"Thank-you, sir." Then the agent turned to McGill and said, "Don't stay too long."

"We won't." With that, Sarah gently guided Jake down the hall. As they walked, she asked him, "What does the 'S' stand for in your name?"

"Sinclair."

She stopped abruptly and looked at him. "Really! As in the Scottish clan Sinclair?"

Her reaction surprised him. "Yes. The Kincaids were part of the Sinclair clan, from the Orkney Islands off Scotland. Why?"

She stared at him for a few seconds, then started walking again. "No reason."

He pulled her hand to stop her. "Sarah. Why did you ask?"

She looked deeply into his eyes. "Have you ever heard the theory that Jesus Christ had a child?"

"No."

446

"Well, there are some who believe he did—a daughter, by Mary Magdalene. And supposedly, her descendants ended up in Scotland—in the Sinclair clan."

"No kidding. What a beautiful thought."

"Yes, it is."

"What was his daughter's name?"

With a radiant smile, she replied softly, "Sarah."

He nodded. "Of course."

Then hand-in-hand, they headed down the hall toward the East Room.

"SORRY to keep you waiting, Mary Lou," said the President, as he powered through the door from his study, holding an envelope in his hand.

"No need to apologize, Mr. President," she said eyeing the envelope. She had obviously been correct in what he wanted, and she couldn't help but feel a tinge of disappointment.

"By the way, I want to say that you look spectacular. Is that dress a Vera Wang?" he asked, as he walked over and placed the envelope on his desk. His compliment only served to disarm and unnerve her further. Now, she was completely tongue-tied. He smiled and said gently, "You know, Mary Lou, when the President of the United States of America asks a question, he generally gets an answer.

Finally her brain regained control of her body and she said, "Yes, sir. It is."

"I thought so," he said, opening the humidor. He took out a large cigar and smelled it slowly, moving its full length along his lips just under his nose. Then he looked at her and said, "Don't be afraid." There was a distinct glint in his eyes as he said it, and she could feel the tiny hairs on the back of her neck rise.

"I beg your pardon, sir?"

He laughed, "Surely, Mary Lou, you haven't done anything that warrants a Presidential pardon. Now have you?" Standing there in his perfectly tailored tuxedo, he was Hollywood's ultimate vision of a President. Ever since he had first met Pritchard nearly six months earlier, Webster had been working out daily in the White House gym, and it showed. He was buffed and tanned and irresistible. And the aura of power that surrounded him only served to accentuate the magic of the moment. He walked over to the door to the Rose Garden and opened it a tiny bit. "I hope you don't mind me opening the door, but it's a beautiful evening outside, and my secretary doesn't like the smell of my cigar."

"Not at all," she replied. "I actually like the smell of cigar smoke."

"Really—does your husband smoke them?"

"No."

He smiled and said, "I see." He paused and lit the cigar. Then he looked back at her and said, "The reason I said that you needn't be afraid is that the cigar is from the Dominican Republic, not Cuba. After all, I wouldn't want you to have to arrest me in our first private meeting, now, would I?"

At that moment, all of Pritchard's mensa level intellect, all her years of outstanding academic and professional achievement, along with her sense of decorum, were like a beautiful little butterfly that spread its delicate wings, fluttered out the door, and disappeared into the night. With uncanny charm and poise and charisma, the President had completely disarmed her. What would happen next was now entirely up to him. And they both knew it.

"Now, about the matter of the envelope, let's discuss it, shall we?" he said, motioning for her to sit down on one of the yellow loveseats, which she did, managing to do so as ladylike as possible, given her outfit.

He sat down in an adjacent wing-backed chair and pulled out the contents of the envelope.

"I've read this report thoroughly, Mary Lou, and naturally, I would be extremely concerned with its contents were they true. However, I'm afraid I can't agree with the experts in the FBI photo lab. If this is a photograph of Maddun Gordon with that other man—what is his name again?"

"Stefan Chadrian," she replied. "He and Maddun served in the CIA in Central America together."

"I was aware of Maddun's service in the CIA, but quite frankly, Mary Lou, if that is him in this picture, then I'm the devil incarnate." He handed them back to her with a gentle, if somewhat patronizing smile.

"I admit that it's not conclusive, Mr. President, but I still believe it is Maddun Gordon in that photograph."

"I'm sorry, Mary Lou, but you haven't convinced me."

"I understand. But what about the other evidence in the document concerning Mr. Gordon's purported involvement with the break-in at the offices of the National Rifle Association?"

For just the briefest instant, the President's smile faded, and he sat silently looking right through her. Then like the sunrise after a stormy night, his smile returned. "Mary, Mary, Mary. What is in this envelope wouldn't persuade a grand jury to even open an investigation, let alone bring formal charges. And you know it. Which makes me wonder." He paused.

"Makes you wonder what?"

"It makes me wonder why someone with your brains and talent, and with all the legitimate issues facing your office, would be wasting even one second of your valuable time on such a wild goose chase."

Now, it was Pritchard's turn to lose her smile. "With all due respect, Mr. President, I think recent history provides a telling precedent regarding the seriousness of the involvement of the West Wing in illegal activities. Especially those in which a man died."

The President studied Pritchard the way a python studies a parrot that it is about to pounce upon. He nodded and said to her, "All right. I'm sorry. I will give consideration to appointing an independent prosecutor to investigate any and all charges related to that break-in, regardless of where the investigation may lead."

His answer caught Pritchard off guard. She had won, and the flush of victory made her skin tingle. "Thank-you, Mr. President." She glanced down at her watch nervously. "Perhaps we should get back to the dance?"

"Yes. Perhaps we should," he said.

There was a pregnant pause and finally she said, "Is there something else, Mr. President?"

He smiled, "I just want you to know that I have been carefully watching you since Arnold's untimely death to determine whether or not you would make a worthy Attorney General."

"What have you concluded?" she asked, somewhat hesitantly. She desperately wanted the job, but deep down inside, she longed for something else from him. Something darker and more basic. And it frightened her.

"I have decided that you will make an outstanding leader of the nation's law enforcement branch."

His answer thrilled her, but she tried not to lose her poise. "That's wonderful, sir. I assure you that I won't let you down."

"I'm sure you won't, Mary Lou," he replied. Again, he paused. She wondered if he was doing it on purpose to fluster her. If so, it was working.

"We really should be going." She stood up, trying to keep her bodice up as she did. But she couldn't help but notice that the President's eyes were fixed on her cleavage as she rose.

He stood up, too, and stepped closer to her. "One more thing."

"Yes?" she answered, with a quiver in her voice.

"I want you to know that I personally asked the chairman of the joint chiefs of staff to review your husband's records for promotion. Obviously, he found Mitchell worthy of receiving his star, and I hope you are as pleased with his promotion as he apparently is."

The President's admission of his involvement with her husband's promotion surprised her, and she could feel every pore on her body start to tingle. The feeling both disgusted her and titillated her at the same time. Inside her, there was a raging battle going on, between her sense of loyalty to her husband and her deep and insecure feelings of self-worth and repressed sexual desire.

They stood there for a few moments locked in each other's gaze. Then softly and unhurriedly, he said, "Have you ever seen the President's private study?"

"No."

"Would you like to?"

No! A little voice inside her screamed. *Please, God, get me out of here before I do something I will regret.* She thought to herself. But God doesn't help those who don't truly want to be helped. And so with willful premeditation, she took a deep breath and said, "Yes. I'd like that, Mr. President." That was that. The deal was done. All that remained was for them to consummate it.

After they were inside the dimly lit passageway, he closed the door behind them and turned to her. They stood there. Face to face. She was trembling, and he could see it. Softly he said, "It's all right, Mary Lou. This has been coming from the very moment that we first met, and you have known it all along."

Her quivering lips parted as if she was about to say something, but she didn't. Instead, her eyes told him that he was right. And in that last fleeting second before her Superego surrendered to her Id, the words her former boss had spoken in the limousine after her first meeting with the President came rushing back into her head. She had been protesting too much that night about the President's blatant flirting with her. It did please her, despite her protests to the contrary. Arnold had been right all along. *Thank God* she thought, *that Heaven has already taken him.* She would not have been able to bear having her mentor see his precious protégé surrender to the dark side.

The President made the first move. It was a gentle one. An almost innocent brushing of his hand against her breast. Almost innocent, but not quite. For in another instant, he had leaned forward and gently placed his lips over hers.

"No, please." She started to pull back but then surrendered to both his and her own desire.

"I know you want me," he murmured. He reached around her back and unzipped the top of her dress, dropping the bodice and exposing her firm breasts.

She moaned softly and expectantly, as he cupped a breast in his hand, whispering, "You are so beautiful." He lowered his head and gently took her nipple in his mouth. She placed her hands on the sides of his head and lifted it back up. They kissed again, this time more passionately.

"Oh God, Mary Lou, I want you so badly."

There was still time to stop what was about to happen. Still time to prevent the ultimate act from which there could be no turning back. But she didn't stop him. She couldn't. From that point on, the evil of unbridled lust took over while reason and decency stepped outside for a breath of fresh air. And even as the lovers consummated their immoral act, a greater evil lurked nearby. For as they stood there in that dark hallway consumed by their passion, they didn't notice that the door on the other side of the President's study was open just a crack, and standing there watching them was the chief of staff of the President of the United States of America.

MY GOD, SHE'S BEAUTIFUL, thought Jake, as he dutifully followed Sarah on the tour of the White House press corps lounge and the briefing room. When they were finished, they walked back down the hallway of the West Wing toward the dance.

"I wish I could show you the Oval Office," said Sarah, but I'm not authorized to go in there unescorted."

"Good thing," Kincaid replied with a sly smile.

At first she didn't get his meaning. "Why?"

"Let's just say that many young women have gone in there unescorted and regretted it afterwards."

A faint blush brushed across her cheeks. "Oh. Yes. Well, not this young woman, I can assure you."

It was his turn to be embarrassed. "I'm sorry. I never meant to imply…"

She stopped to face him and put her finger up to his lips. "I know." To lessen his discomfort, she addressed the subject head on, which was one of the traits that made her so good at what she did. "I wonder how many people have made love in the West Wing?"

Still feeling somewhat foolish, he replied, "I have no idea."

With a mischievous smile, she persisted. "Well, let's see. The West Wing wasn't added to the White House until 1902 and since then, there have been twenty Presidents, including the incumbent, all of whom were married, and many of whom were notorious naughty boys. So, I would guess, conservatively—around one hundred. Wait a minute. The President is here tonight, and the building is filled with pretty women." She added with a sly smile. "You had better make that one hundred and one."

He shook his head in mock consternation, "Sarah McGill. You are too much."

She poked him gently in his side. "And don't you forget it."

For a moment they stood there, facing each other under the subdued lighting in the world's most powerful building—a building that had a way of overwhelming the senses and distancing all who tread there from the proprieties and realities of the world outside. Caught up in the emotion of the moment and the nearness of such beauty, Jake started to lean forward, as if he was going to kiss her on the lips. She made no move to avoid it. But suddenly he stopped, and the moment passed. They smiled at each other, he took her hand in his, and they rejoined the festivities.

Of course they couldn't know it, but Sarah was absolutely right. Another woman had joined that list of dubious distinction that night. And like many of those who had gone before her, she was a married woman and the sex had not been with her husband. Mrs. Mary Lou Pritchard, the acting Attorney General of the United States of America had been overwhelmed by self-indulgent, adulterated lust. And her partner in passion had been her boss, the President. Among the gossipmongers inside the Webster White House, the act would soon become just another footnote to his enigmatic legacy. But in the bedroom of the cuckolded man, it would be a very different story, and it would change the lives of the general and his wife forever.

TWO HOURS LATER, in the bedroom of the Pritchards' home, Mary Lou Pritchard told her husband what she had done to him and to their marriage. She had already broken one sacred vow that night, and in the interminable ride home following the dance, she had been tormented by whether or not she would break another. Could she, would she, lie to him? It seemed a rather paltry additional sin, given the act she had just performed with another man only hours earlier. But somehow, in the convoluted dissonance that preoccupied her thoughts, she agonized about telling him a lie. They had never lied to each other. Ever. And the torment that was going on inside her head was almost too much to bear.

"What did you just say!" exclaimed Mary Lou's husband. "Are you telling me that you fucked Webster in the Oval Office? While I stood waiting for you?"

Mary Lou Pritchard sat on their king-sized bed. Her eyes were swollen with tears and she nodded. "It was in his private study and not the Oval Office," she said, making the kind of totally irrelevant statement that people often do when faced with an overpowering situation.

He smashed his fist into the door to their walk-in closet, breaking the door off its hinges. "Damn it all, Mary Lou, do you think that makes it any better?"

"No," she sobbed under her breath.

He paced back and forth like a caged tiger. "How could you do this to me? Cuckolded by the most powerful man on earth. My God, I'll be the laughing stock of the entire Army."

She looked up at him and cried, "Mitchell, I am so sorry."

He stopped and looked at her incredulously. "You're sorry!" He shouted it again. "You're sorry! For God's sake, Mary Lou, why didn't you think of that before you did it?"

"Please forgive me, Mitchell. I swear I will never do it again."

He looked at her. His hands were trembling, and the veins on the side of his forehead were bulging. "Do you have any idea what you have done to me? To my career?"

"No one will know," she sobbed.

"No one will know!" he shouted. "You are the acting Attorney General of the United States of America and you fucked the goddamned President. The whole world is going to know."

"Please, Mitchell. Forgive me," she pleaded, but it was too late.

"You unfaithful bitch. You want forgiveness? I'll give you forgiveness."

Before she knew what was happening, he walked over and hit her full force with the back of his hand across her cheek, stunning her and throwing her back onto the bed. Then he tore open her dress, pulled down his pants, and raped her. Harshly. Cruelly. As if the selfish act could expunge the sin rather than make it worse. When he was done, he climbed off her, pulled his pants on, and stormed out of the bedroom. As she lay there in a dazed state, with blood trickling out of her nose and her eye swelling shut, she heard him slam the front door, get into his car, and drive away into the night.

After he was gone, she got up off the bed and dragged herself into the bathroom. She stood there staring through her good eye at her bloodied and bedraggled image in the mirror. In her torn dress, with tangled hair, bloody and bruised face, she looked like a refugee from a war crime rather than the most powerful law enforcement officer in the land. It was the final indignity. She began to sob uncontrollably, until she could take it no more. She left the bathroom and went to her husband's side of the bed, where she opened the top drawer in his nightstand. Inside lay a .38 caliber snub-nosed revolver. She stared down at it for a long while without moving. Finally, she reached in and picked it up. She neither hated nor loved guns, and she often questioned the maturity and mental stability of people who felt either of such powerful emotions about a weapon. But equally, she wasn't afraid of them either. During her years at the Justice Department, she had taken an FBI weapons training course at the insistence of her husband. She held the gun in her right hand and with an expert movement, flipped open the cylinder. It was loaded. She sat there for a moment, contemplating using it as a final solution to her sadness. But reason prevailed over emotion, and she carefully placed it back in the drawer. She sat there for another few minutes, feeling more alone than she had ever been in her life. Then she closed the drawer, and as she did, her eyes fell upon the telcom sitting above it. She quickly looked over at the clock radio, the face of which read 1:30 a.m. She hesitated for an instant, and then like the mythical Phoenix rising from its ashes, Mary Lou Pritchard dialed 411. She waited until the operator came on the line, and then she said purposefully and clearly, "Washington, D.C.—Representative Jeremiah Kincaid."

AN HOUR LATER, Jeremiah Kincaid sat in one of his deep leather chairs, sipping a cup of coffee. He was dressed in loose-fitting blue jeans, with a perfectly faded navy and maroon rugby shirt, which fashion hounds, might have thought he purchased specially for that look. The truth was that he had simply owned it for a long time, and it had faded naturally. Kincaid hated to throw away anything, and his wife would use his long periods of absence from their home in Wisconsin to get rid of the flotsam and jetsam that her pack rat husband accumulated as he sailed through life. He didn't mind. It was their little game and they played it perfectly, the way that people who deeply love each other always seem to do. But at that moment, the pain and sadness of another marriage preoccupied him rather than the joy and security of his own.

Standing silently near his window, staring blankly out toward the Capitol through one good eye and one swollen nearly completely shut, was Mary Lou Pritchard. Her coffee cup sat behind her on Kincaid's desk, but she had not touched it. She had told him everything that had happened that night, absolutely everything. She left nothing out, except the details of the actual lovemaking.

"Are you sure that you shouldn't see a doctor, Mary Lou?" Kincaid said tenderly. "Please let me take you to the emergency room now."

"No! I will be fine."

"All right."

She looked back out across the lights of the Capitol. "Have you ever cheated on your spouse, Jeremiah?"

"No."

"Neither had I before tonight," she said with a deep sigh. She turned around and even in the soft light of the desk lamp, her black eye was painfully evident. "But I sure set one hell of a precedent my first time out, didn't I?" She walked over and eased herself into the matching chair beside his.

He smiled gently and said, "Mary Lou, I am not going to insult your intelligence by saying that I condone what you did. However, if I may be permitted to talk like a father rather than a colleague, you are a human being. Intelligent, highly educated, professionally competent, and yet no more or less vulnerable to the temptations and frailties of life than any other person. Trust me when I say that for better or for worse, we are all God's children, the good, the bad, and the ugly. Tonight, both you and the two men who played leading roles in this one-act tragedy have proven once again that good and evil are two sides of the same coin."

She nodded sadly but said nothing.

"In every good person there is a dark side, and while it may be difficult to see, the opposite also holds true. Each day is a coin toss. Some days we win and our good side shines. Other days we lose and the worst in us shows. The measure of our character, Mary Lou, is not which side shows but how we deal with it, both the good and the bad. And how we react to the coin toss of those whom we care about. Unfortunately, some are more able to deal with this than others."

"Mitchell proved that theory," she said.

"While I disapprove of what he did, I honestly don't know how I would have reacted under similar circumstances. Therefore, I will not presume to judge him. However, I do feel empowered to judge the President. Not for how he acted as a human being, but for how he acted as the leader of our nation. As a man, he indulged both his, and your lust. Only the two of you can—and must—deal with it in whatever way you choose. However, as the north star in the night sky of our existence as a people, he has failed you, me, and every other citizen of this Republic."

"It takes two people to sin in that way, Jeremiah, and I am equally to blame," she said, with tears welling up in her pretty eyes.

"Yes, you are, Mary Lou. However, by virtue of the oath he took, the President must be held to a higher standard. It is no secret that Alex Webster has bedded many women in the White House during his tenure there. But up until tonight, I let myself believe that they were single, consenting adults. This may have been a delusion that I chose to sustain due to my own admittedly prudish morals. However, with your painful personal confession to me tonight, I am now faced with the reality that we have an immoral and reckless leader. And given the magnitude of the decision on gun control that he is about to make on behalf of us as a people, I must tell you that I am deeply distressed."

The room fell silent, except for the steady ticking of the Speaker's grandfather clock. Each of them was lost in their own thoughts. Each wrestled with their own private worries. Hers concerned a failing marriage that the regrettable acts of the evening may have finally destroyed. While his centered on a country that he was now afraid was about to be destroyed by forces over which he had no control.

Finally she broke the silence, "Jeremiah, do you think I should resign?"

"Absolutely not," he replied. "This nation needs you."

"Then what should I do?"

He looked at her through caring and understanding eyes and said, "Shakespeare probably said it best. 'To thine own self be true. Then it must follow as the day the night thou canst not then be false to any man.'" He paused then added, "First trust yourself, Mary Lou. And in that trusting, you will know what to do and when to do it."

She smiled and said, "My father died several years ago, but if he were here, Jeremiah, I think that is the kind of advice he would have given me. He was a great human being and a wonderful father."

The Speaker nodded, "Yes, I had the privilege of meeting him once when I spoke with a group of his fellow Federal judges. I am quite familiar with his long and distinguished record. You should be very proud of his memory."

A look of sadness flashed across her face and she said, "I am. But I doubt that he would be very proud of me this night." The look of loneliness that she felt inside was etched deeply on her pretty face. "Jeremiah, I have made such a fool of myself,"

"Listen to me, Ms. Mary Lou Pritchard, and listen well. Tonight you have sinned in the eyes of God. But if you ask him to, He will forgive you. Whether or not your husband will is up to him. Regardless of how difficult your personal situation may or may not be, you have a duty to perform to the people of this nation and you are eminently qualified to perform that duty. And you will, because you are your father's daughter. Do you hear me?"

She nodded. His words had a markedly calming and reassuring effect upon her. She had turned to this great man in her hour of crisis, and he had not failed her. He had soothed her pain and restored her hope. And he had guided her back from the brink. What neither of them could know at that moment was that it had been a metaphor for what was about to happen with America.

"Thank-you, Jeremiah. No matter what happens now with my marriage, I know that I can handle it. And some day, perhaps I can even find redemption."

She glanced at the clock. "I had better go. I have imposed on you too much already." They both stood up.

He smiled and said, "Mary Lou, if you will indulge me for one more piece of advice. Before you give up on your marriage, make sure that it is what you want. You know I speak from personal experience when I say that losing someone you love not to death but to a life apart, is more than any man or woman should ever have to bear."

She nodded and then walked over to him, stood up on her toes, and kissed him gently on his cheek. "God bless you, Jeremiah Kincaid."

"Thank-you, Mary Lou. And may He guide you through the dark days ahead."

She turned and left. Neither of them had any idea of how prescient his wish would for her turn out to be.

<u>51</u>

GNBC Studios, Washington, D.C.

Sarah McGill was in a good mood. In fact, she was in a very good mood as she walked down the hall toward her office. Later that evening, she would break the news story about the New Sons of Liberty on the national newscast, a story she had written and produced herself, and for which she was certain she would be nominated for an Emmy; although that thought did not obsess her as it did many of her colleagues. On top of that, she had had a wonderful time on her date with Jake Kincaid. Her feelings toward him were growing, and she tried not to dwell on how much of the attraction was due to the uncanny similarities to his younger brother, and how much was truly due to Jake himself. McGill had a way of compartmentalizing the emotional vectors affecting her life; it was something she had learned to do when her mother left her and again later, when her father died. It had served her well up until that point, and she assumed nothing would happen to change that; so within limits, she let her feelings go where they needed to go, like a river that could be channeled but never dammed.

"Well, don't you look like the cat who swallowed the canary," said a familiar voice. She greeted her boss, Keene Lange. The video disk he held in his hand and the smile on his face told her that he had watched her story and was pleased with it. He handed the disk back to her and said, "Break a leg, kiddo."

She smiled and said, "Thank-you, boss." The sparkle in her eyes caught his attention.

"Is that expression on your face a result of your story or something else?" he asked, already knowing the answer.

She demurred. "No comment."

He sighed. "I thought so. Look Sarah. You know that I love you, and I would never want to stand in the way of your happiness."

"Go on," she said, as her smile froze.

"I know Colonel Kincaid is a war hero and all that, but the word on the street is that he has a hair-trigger temper, and..."

"And what?"

He sighed. "And that he drinks—too much."

She stared blankly at her boss long enough to make sure he knew that he was treading on thin ice, then said, "First of all, he's just a friend—a good friend but nothing more. And second, I'm a big girl, Keene. I can handle myself."

"You're right," he said, wishing he had kept his mouth shut.

"And finally, he hasn't had a drink since he met me. I doubt that he ever will again." As she finished her sentence, Tanner Spence approached them. He didn't look like his usually cheerful self.

"Okay, okay. I'm sorry I meddled," said Lange.

"Hey, Keene," said Tanner as he approached them. "Sarah—"

His tone and manner distracted McGill from her own defensiveness and set off her innate alarm system. "What's the matter?"

"I found another computer system that is linked into the NSOL extranet. One that I didn't know about before."

"Where was it?" asked McGill.

Tanner looked troubled. It was obvious that he wasn't happy about his discovery. "This one was connected to the site through a separate server with its own complex security system. It utilizes twenty forty-eight bit encryption technology, the kind that only Granite Shield is capable of running, and a sophisticated Internet passport that makes it virtually invisible to the network itself. I had to surreptitiously use quibitware again to get through to the other side of the firewall. I doubt that the boys in the Internal Affairs at DHS even noticed, because most of them were students of mine at MIT."

"Tanner if you don't tell me where this new computer is located in the next ten seconds, I will personally hack into your quantum computer myself," said McGill.

He stared at her and then Lange, and then back at her. "Sixteen Hundred Pennsylvania Avenue."

"The White House!" she exclaimed.

He nodded.

"Do you know in whose office in the White House?" asked Lange.

"Yes. The computer is in the chief of staff's office."

"Maddun Gordon?" said a disbelieving Lange.

"Yes, sir."

McGill asked, "Could Gordon possibly be part of the conspiracy to undermine his own President?"

Lange had a different take on it. "Or could Gordon have been monitoring the group, just like Tanner has been?"

"Perhaps with a more sinister purpose," added Spence.

They stood there quietly for a few moments, each lost in thought. Finally, McGill said, "I've got to tell the Speaker!"

Lange nodded and added, "Yes. And right away. Before your story runs tonight."

"I'll go see him right now." She looked at Spence. "You're incredible, and no matter what DHS is paying you, it isn't enough."

Spence gave her a melancholy smile but said nothing. His faith in the American way, which had already been sorely strained by the seemingly endless stream of corrupt politicians, self-serving CEOs, and litigious common folk, was now teetering on the edge of a complete meltdown. The fact that someone in the White House might be involved with the ever-widening circle of conspiracy distressed him greatly. To his brilliant but naive mind, he liked to think of the world in comic book terms: everyone was either on the side of right or wrong; either they were heroes or villains; and the dividing line between good and evil was as distinctive as that between black and white. Unfortunately for the talented and yet fragile young genius, the real world was painted in seven shades of gray.

Sarah sensed exactly what was going on in his mind, but she could not find any words of wisdom to help at that moment. Instead she patted him lovingly on the shoulder. "Let's go, little brother."

The tenderness of her comment brought a little smile back to his lips. He said, "Did you ever hear that story about the woman who fell in love with a man who she found out was her brother? But then it turned out that he really wasn't, and they lived happily ever after."

"No," she laughed, "And I don't care to."

They headed down the hall leaving Lange standing there by himself. *Where will this story end?* He thought to himself. *Where will it end?* But

461

R.A.R. Clouston

had he known the answer, it would have shaken the veteran newsman to his very soul.

52

The Capitol, Washington, D.C.

The Republican members of the House sat in a closed-door session on the House floor. The visitor's gallery was closed, and the seats of the Democratic members were vacant. Speaker Jeremiah Kincaid, looking weary, stood in front of the podium he usually occupied. He was wearing a lavaliere microphone, and as he finished his speech, his voice filled the chamber with its resonant, if somewhat strained tones.

"*That*, ladies and gentlemen, is the essence of what I discussed with Governor Morrissey and the President." He started to walk slowly up the center aisle. "Before I open up the floor to questions, there is another related matter that I feel duty bound to discuss." He stopped after several rows and looked out across the men and women seated before him.

"It has recently come to my attention that some of you are members of what I will generously call a discussion group, with the issue of gun control as its principal focus. The group calls itself the New Sons of Liberty, and for those of you who don't know what I'm talking about, the name should give you a sense of the broader intentions of the group." He paused and looked at several members who squirmed uncomfortably in their seats.

He moved on. "My comments are directed at this group, although it would serve the other members well to hear what I have to say. I will not presume to question the judgment of those of you who have aligned yourselves with these so-called patriots. Nor will I challenge your patriotism. All I ask is that you give serious consideration to the amended bill for which I have secured the support of both the governor and the President. Moreover, I implore you not to do anything that will jeopardize the chances of this compromise becoming law. To do so will threaten the very existence and future security of our Republic."

He returned to the front of the chamber. A hand was raised in a row near the back.

"Mr. Speaker, what if the President reneges on his promise?" asked one of the junior members.

"There are numerous pressure points in this fragile alliance. That is just one of them. All we can do is to go forward in good faith, and trust that we are dealing with others who care more about the common good of the country than their own personal opinions."

Another representative sitting in the front row raised his hand. "Mr. Speaker, all of us in this room know that you could charm the hair off a hog." The laughter of respect and affection filled the room. "But I am just a simple country boy from Georgia, and I need you to explain to me why the President has suddenly become so accommodating, because I for one don't trust the man one wit."

The Speaker walked over to where the representative sat. He smiled at him and said, "Gus Teeter, you are about as simple as I am the King of France." More laughter rippled through the hallowed hall. "However, as usual, your question is right on the mark."

Representative Teeter sat up a little straighter and smiled a little deeper.

"It is a question that I have asked myself." Kincaid said, as he climbed up to the Speaker's podium. All eyes were glued on him as he went. He reached his chair and turned to face the audience, which put him directly in front of the large Stars and Stripes that hung proudly behind the podium.

"I honestly don't know whether the man we have elected to lead us has the strength of character, the moral courage, and the wisdom to guide us through these dangerous times. After my recent meeting with him in the Oval Office, I believed that he did. Since then, something has happened which has given me cause to question this, but it will serve no purpose to discuss the matter here and now. Suffice to say that it was an act of personal misbehavior that does not threaten the agreement that he and I have reached."

The Speaker paused as if rethinking the events of the other evening and the advice he gave to Mary Lou Pritchard: *To thine own self be true....* The words rang out inside his head. He continued, "There is no question that

President Webster is a man with multiple flaws of character. However, I would remind this esteemed body that it was not so long ago that I admitted my own failings to you. I told you that I had kept something from you and from the American people. In so doing, I behaved in a manner unbecoming a leader and a gentleman. But you rejected my letter of resignation, and you forgave me my transgressions."

He paused and took a long sip of water from a leaded crystal glass that sparkled in the bright lights that had been installed when televising the House many years before. He put the glass down and looked around the House chamber, as if to take in its majesty. The room fell silent, then Jeremiah Kincaid took a deep breath and uttered words that those present in the room would reflect back upon during the difficult days to come. "My fellow sojourners in this hallowed hall, regardless of what you may think of Alexander Webster as a man, he is still the President of the United States of America. And while some of us disapprove of his personal behavior, and many of us reject his policies, all of us must accept his right to act as he sees fit within the Constitutional limits of his power." He paused again. No one moved.

Then with the conviction of a man for whom failure was not an option, he continued, "In all such defining moments in our history, we have had to put our faith in our leaders: great men—like George Washington, Abraham Lincoln, Franklin Delano Roosevelt, and Ronald Reagan—and sometimes the not-so great, who have still accomplished great things. Obviously such faith, in and of itself, is not sufficient to see us through the storm. It also takes vision, courage, and an iron will to protect Lady Liberty with all her frailties and foibles. But without faith, all is certainly lost. So tomorrow, I intend to put the amendments to the President's bill to a vote; and I intend to take a strong stand behind this compromise legislation. I ask each and every one of you to stand with the President; to stand with the governor; and to stand with me. Help us succeed in our mission of compromise and conciliation. For the consequences of failure are dire and irrevocable."

When he finished, the room fell absolutely silent. Then one representative clapped. And another. And soon the chamber thundered with the cheers and support of virtually all the two hundred and twenty representatives in the room. But what the Speaker sensed was that some of the applause was tentative and uncertain—as uncertain as the outcome of the bill upon which the entire future of a nation depended.

THE SOUND OF APPLAUSE inside the House chamber echoed into the hallway outside. Standing in the hall waiting for the Speaker were George Ross, Sarah McGill, and Tanner Spence.

"I had a page pass the Speaker a note," said Ross. "He told her he would be right out."

Just then the doors opened and Jeremiah Kincaid exited, surrounded by members who seemed to just want to be near him. He patiently shook their hands and politely acknowledged their compliments. Then he spotted Ross, and he excused himself from the group and walked over to greet McGill and Spence.

"Mr. Speaker, this is Tanner Spence, the young man from DHS I told you about."

"You mean, the young genius you told me about?" He shook Tanner's hand. "How do you do, son?"

"It's nice to meet you, sir."

"The pleasure is all mine. From what Sarah tells me, you are doing your country a great service."

Spence blushed. "Thank-you, Mr. Speaker."

The Speaker looked back at McGill. "What have you got, Sarah?"

"We have something to tell you about the New Sons of Liberty. Something important."

The expression on his face became serious and he said, "Not here." Then he escorted them to a private meeting room nearby.

THE FOUR OF THEM sat around a large wooden table in the private room. The room was silent as the Speaker digested what he had just heard. He turned to Spence and said, "You have done good work son. To be forewarned is to be forearmed."

"Mr. Speaker, you said you were fairly certain that the President knew about the New Sons of Liberty when you mentioned it to him in the Oval Office," said Ross.

The Speaker nodded.

"This may be how he found out," added Ross.

"Possibly," said the Speaker.

"So you believe that Gordon was just monitoring the activity of the group, rather than being a part of it?" asked McGill.

"Yes," said the Speaker.

"But wouldn't that be risky on his part?" asked Ross.

Kincaid said to Spence. "Would it have been possible for any of the people who were connected to the extranet to be able to detect Gordon if he were just monitoring them?"

"No."

"I think that's your answer, Sarah."

She said to Spence, "Then Gordon, or whoever it is in the White House, wouldn't know that you had tracked them?"

"No." He answered her in a calm and self-confident tone. "But just in case, I placed what in layman's terms would best be described as a booby trap on my digital trail. Had they circled back on me, it would have triggered and sent them to another intranet site."

"Where?" asked Ross.

"To Beijing," he said with a big grin. "Inside the Communist Party's headquarters."

The Speaker laughed, "I'd like to see the look on the President's face if the CIA informed him that the Chinese had hacked into the White House."

Spence shrugged and said matter-of-factly, "They already have. Several times."

"What should we do with the story about the New Sons of Liberty extranet, Mr. Speaker?" asked McGill.

"When are you planning to run it?" asked Kincaid.

"Tonight in prime time," said McGill.

The Speaker thought about it for a moment and then said, "Go ahead with it. But don't mention the locations of any of the computers. Especially not the last one."

"We weren't planning to." She was glad he didn't ask her to kill the story. That would have put the network in a difficult spot, one she did not to want to have to deal with.

Ross asked, "Should we bring the Justice department in on this, Mr. Speaker?"

"No."

"Do you think Pritchard might be involved?" continued Ross.

"No. But as Tanner has already told us, he thinks someone at DHS might be, and if we tell the Attorney General now, she may inadvertently tip them. Besides, we still have no proof of who is actually involved in this conspiracy, or even if it really is a legitimate threat to the government."

Everyone nodded their agreement.

The Speaker looked at his watch and then at Ross. "Don't I have that meeting with Nate Bardham now?"

"Yes, sir. Sorry. I'm afraid I got distracted."

"That's our fault, Mr. Speaker," said McGill, her mind already racing ahead to why Nathaniel Boone Bardham might be meeting with the Speaker.

"It's not a problem, Sarah. I'm glad you came," said Kincaid.

She smiled at him, and without even the slightest trace of embarrassment asked, "So what does one of the biggest hawks in America want with the Eagle?"

Jeremiah Kincaid looked at the beautiful but brazen young blonde reporter standing before him and said with a sly smile, "Don't quote me Sarah, but I think it has something to do with our mutual foe, the Raven."

She returned the smile and said, "I see. Well, good luck, Mr. Speaker, and if the two of you want to make a statement after your meeting, I'd be glad to take it."

George Ross just shook his head, more out of admiration than anger. "You never stop, do you, Sarah?"

"A reporter who stands still is as dead as last year's fashions, George. You know that as well as I do."

He shrugged, "I guess I can't blame you for trying."

"Good luck with your story, Sarah," said the Speaker. "Now if you will excuse me, I've got to go." With that, the Speaker and George Ross got up and left the room.

After they had gone, Tanner said, "What do you suppose that crusty old bastard Bardham wants with the Speaker?"

"I don't know, but it's probably to do with the gun bill. Ever since his grandson was killed, the hawk has turned into a dove."

"Hawk, dove, either way in a confrontation with the Eagle, he'll come off second best."

She looked at her young colleague and added softly. "So will the Raven."

He smiled knowingly. "Feathers will fly and birds will die."

With a far-away look in her eyes, she nodded and said softly, "Very poetic, Tanner, and very sad."

THE SPEAKER OF THE HOUSE sat in one of the high-backed leather chairs in his office. Standing discreetly off to one side was George Ross, while Nate Bardham and his daughter Jamie sat directly across from the Speaker. Jamie Bardham gave none of the outward appearance of self-confidence bordering on smugness that had characterized her life up until that horrible day her child died. Instead, she sat quietly, patiently, willing to let her father do the speaking.

The Speaker was obviously considering something that Bardham had said. "I sincerely appreciate your offer to help, Mr. Bardham, but quite frankly, I'm not sure exactly what you can do right now."

"Rumor has it, Mr. Speaker, that you are holding together a very fragile compromise between the President and Governor Morrissey. A compromise that may or may not survive when it comes to a vote on the House floor," said Bardham.

"You're right about the compromise, but I think you underestimate it's strength," said Kincaid.

Bardham looked at Kincaid with the calculated respect that he had always given to those with whom he negotiated over his career. "Mr. Speaker, if I may, I would like to speak plainly."

"Your reputation for such is well known."

Bardham acknowledged the compliment with a nod and said, "Mr. Speaker, I know that you know about the New Sons of Liberty, and if you are as smart as I think you are, you know that they count me among their members."

"Yes, Mr. Bardham, I'm aware of that fact. I also know that you are their largest single benefactor."

"Quite right," said Bardham with a simple nod. He continued, "Up until recently, I was about as far right on the issue of gun control as Webster is on the left."

Again, the Speaker said nothing. It was a trait that he had learned through his years on the Hill, which was to let the other person fill in the gaps of silence in a conversation. In so doing, they often said more than they would have, had he probed them with questions. It was a very successful

469

tool and one that few people could manage, given that the average person loves nothing more than the sound of his or her own voice.

"But when my grandson was shot to death, everything changed. Forever," said Bardham, with heartbreak in his words.

The old man and his daughter did not look like two of the crème de la crème of American society. Death has a way of humbling even the richest and most powerful. It is the one thing that neither money nor influence can defy.

"Mr. Bardham, my heart goes out to you two. I have one grandchild myself; however, I would not presume to know what you are going through right now. But with the deepest of respect, sir, I'm not sure why you have come to me today."

The old man's eyes were deep, dark pools, into which love had dived and never returned. He slumped back into his chair and could not reply. His daughter finally spoke up. "Mr. Speaker, my father and I represent, or at least we did up until three months ago, the two poles in the terrible debate that is tearing our nation apart. He was ready to die for his right to own guns, and I was ready to let him." She paused and dabbed her eyes with a tissue. "But in the end, it wasn't my father who died. It was my son. And just like my son, there are thousands of other sons and daughters who will die if men like President Webster and Governor Morrissey are allowed to continue on the paths they have chosen. You, Mr. Speaker, are our only hope. You are the savior of this nation, because only you among our leaders seem to have grasped what is happening right now. You understand that America's strength lies in our ability to put aside our personal differences when confronted by a common enemy. Just like we did when terrorists tried to defeat us and we wiped them from the face of the earth. And now, once more, we are faced with an enemy who threatens to destroy us. But this time, unlike any other time in our history but one, the enemy we face is far more dangerous, and more frightening, than any we have faced in over one hundred years—for it is us." She paused and looked down at her hands.

George Ross took a step forward and asked softly, "May I get you a glass of water, Ms. Bardham?"

She looked up at him and said gently, "No thank-you, I'm fine. Mr. Speaker, my father and I plan to launch a national advertising campaign in support of the President's bill, with your amendments attached to it, of course. It will feature thought leaders and nationally known personalities who will speak out eloquently against the slaughter occurring daily on our streets, and I can assure you it will touch the hearts of all Americans, especially those with children of their own."

The Speaker nodded sympathetically, but it was clear from his expression that he doubted the campaign would have any impact upon those who opposed the President's bill.

At this point, the father reentered the discussion. "I can see that you have reservations about the effectiveness of such an effort, Mr. Speaker, and quite frankly, I do as well. However, the advertising does not constitute the sum total of our efforts. Far from it. In addition, I wish to make a large donation in support of your efforts. Specifically, I am talking nine figures, Mr. Speaker, over one hundred million dollars. Money that will be given to you to do so as you see fit in your efforts to make Americans see the stupidity of their ways. To make them understand that if both sides persist in their unilateral efforts to win, we will all lose. Money that will buy the depth and breadth of political and public support that you need to sell your story to everyone before it's too late. Money that can perhaps play a vital role in saving a nation."

The room fell silent as Kincaid digested the magnanimous offer that had just been put forth. He glanced at Ross who flashed his eyebrows in amazement, then he looked back at the father and daughter.

"Your offer speaks for itself. Rightly or wrongly, in our society, such a large sum of money can often sway public opinion regardless of the complexity or propriety of the issue."

"Why do I feel a *but* coming on, Mr. Speaker?" the daughter asked.

Kincaid smiled gently, "Please don't take this wrong, Ms. Bardham, but your father was quite correct when he said that the alliance that I have been able to create between the two opposing sides in this issue is fragile. I pray that it will hold together during the vote in the House and withstand the scrutiny of the Senate and the state legislatures thereafter. However, I am afraid that no amount of money, no matter how generous and well-intended, can affect the outcome at this late date. Perhaps months or even years ago, we could have used your wealth to build a more powerful and lasting allegiance to a common cause of sanity, but at this late hour, I sincerely doubt that our fate will be determined by anything short of the will of God."

"There is no God, Mr. Speaker. If there were, then my grandson would not lie cold in his grave. The only god this nation has, and has ever had,

471

is the greenback. And if you won't join us in our efforts to buy America's hearts and minds, then we will do it on our own."

The harsh tone of the senior Bardham caused Ross to lean forward, as if to defend his boss. "With all due respect, Mr. Bardham, the Speaker has been fighting this battle long before you—"

The Speaker raised his hand, instantly silencing his chief of staff. "Mr. Bardham. My heart tells me that yours is broken, and your words are understandably born of pain, not anger. You are most certainly entitled to your opinion on God, or whatever else you chose to discuss. That is one of the inalienable rights that the Constitution guarantees you. But at present, my entire focus is upon the Second Amendment, not the First. Having said this, I may have been too quick to assume that your money cannot help the cause of compromise, and I will take the matter under advisement, pending the vote in the House. Given the imminence of that vote, there simply isn't anything we can do with or without your money to change it. Assuming we succeed in our efforts to get the amended bill passed in the House, I commit to you that I will find a way to leverage your financial resources to help us though the hurdles we will still face beyond the walls of the House chamber."

The elder Bardham's demeanor softened, "Thank-you, Mr. Speaker. I'm sorry that I spoke out of turn."

"No need to apologize, sir. I know that your heart is heavy," said Kincaid.

"Yes, sir, it is. And with all due respect, Mr. Speaker, you're wrong about the House vote. There is something that I can do even at this late date."

"What is that?" asked Kincaid.

"I can put out the word to the New Sons of Liberty that I have changed my mind regarding compromise legislation. That I now believe such a compromise is in the best interests of the nation. And I can strongly suggest to them that my support for their organization, monetary and otherwise, depends upon their willingness to stand with you, Mr. Speaker."

The Speaker seemed to suddenly get a second wind in his sprint to the finish of the race for victory. "Thank-you, Mr. Bardham. I suspect that the members of my party in the New Sons of Liberty will listen to your words more diligently than to my own."

Bardham smiled and added, "Perhaps, sir. But those who do are not in your league, nor will they ever be."

"Thank-you," said the Speaker, standing up and extending his hand.

Bardham and his daughter also stood. "You're most welcome, Mr. Speaker."

"May God bless you, Mr. Speaker," added his daughter.

Her father looked at his daughter and then back at the Speaker and said softly, "And may God bless America."

"Amen," said Ross.

"Amen," added the Speaker.

The meeting was over and a powerful new alliance had been formed. The only issue was time, for it is the one commodity that money cannot buy.

53

The Pentagon, Arlington, Virginia

A group of senior Army officers and several men in civilian clothes sat around a long table in a no-nonsense conference room deep inside the Pentagon. At the head of the table sat General William McWilliams, Chief of Staff of the Army, and on his immediate right was General Bradford Curtiss, Deputy Chief of Staff For Operations & Plans. Beside Curtiss was Colonel Jake Kincaid, and seated across from Kincaid on General McWilliams' left, was newly promoted Brigadier General Mitchell Pritchard. The rest of the places at the table were occupied by other staff officers. At the other end of the table, Garrison Dodge, a squirrelly man in civilian clothes was standing in front of a screen on which there were so many numbers that it was hard for anyone, including the man himself, to read them.

"I'm afraid that this next slide is an eye chart," said the man. "But…"

"But you chose to inflict it upon us, anyway," said General McWilliams with a slight smile.

The general's comment flustered the already harried man. He stopped what he was doing and dove into the electronic notebook that sat on a small podium off to one side of the table. The computer was connected to a port on the podium, and the man immediately started to type something on the keyboard, "Perhaps if I just change the font." He typed a few more characters and hit the Enter key. Instantly the numbers on the screen appeared larger. Unfortunately he also lost the totals on each column of numbers. As he stared at the screen through his thick glasses, he said, "Oh dear, I've lost some data." He looked up at the small projector that hung overhead and from which the image on the screen was being projected. Then he looked below the screen as if the numbers that he lost were somewhere down there, which of course they weren't. As he fiddled around, the silence in the room grew louder.

"Mr. Dodge, we can dispense with the figures. We all know them as well as you do. Please continue with your report," said McWilliams, who was still maintaining the calm and poise characteristic of a man who had spent his whole career in harm's way.

Garrison Dodge was far more competent than the image he was conveying to the men in that room. As a civilian analyst working for the inspector general's office, he was an expert in mechanized warfare weapons systems. He had asked for a meeting with the general and his staff to present a report on the unexpected and significant cost increases for the M1A3 development program. Given the subject and his ongoing concerns with the military's historical pattern of buying weapons that didn't meet expectations, he had anticipated receiving a cold reception. The fact that he was having difficulty presenting his data only made the situation worse.

"Yes, General. I'm sorry, sir," said Dodge. "I'm afraid that I have placed too many figures on this spreadsheet."

Mr. Dodge, please get on with your presentation." The tone and inflection of the general's statement, while courteous, made it clear that it was an order and not a request.

Dodge was a nervous man, but he was also technically brilliant, and he knew when to cut his losses and move on. He hit a key on his laptop, and the image disappeared from the screen. Then he looked at the general and said, "General, with all due respect, my point is this. The problems with the M1A3 development program are due to subtle glitches in its secure targeting and recognition system, and its interface with Granite Fist. I do not have to tell you or the men seated around this table that the consequences of systems failure in a combat situation are grave." He winced after he said it, realizing the rather unfortunate pun, but he ignored it. Thankfully, so did the general. "The latest report by the General Accounting Office has listed this program as a high-profile, big-budget and seriously flawed project that should not be allowed to go into full production."

"I have been briefed on the GAO director's recommendation to Congress that full production and force deployment of the M1A3 Main Battle Tank be delayed," said McWilliams.

"I assume that the General also knows that the Secretary of Defense intends to try to kill the program entirely," added Dodge hesitantly.

The expression on the general's face clouded over at the mention of the secretary. "Yes, I am acutely aware of this administration's views on this program," he answered in a slow, deliberate voice. "Thankfully, the majority of the members of the Senate Committee on Armed Services under the leadership of Chairman Lamar Wacker do not share the Secretary's views. They, like the senior officers on my staff, know that the M1A3 main battle tank is an essential component of our new Granite-Fist-based armored force, and that the benefits it will provide to our national defense far outweigh its cost."

Dodge replied, "Yes, sir, I agree." Despite outward appearances, he was actually a strong supporter of the M1A3 program, and his purpose there that day was only to identify what the general and his staff were up against. As was often the case in such situations, the career military officers seated around the table wanted to shoot the messenger. However, any such display of hostility would not be permitted under the general's stewardship, and they knew it.

"Mr. Dodge, I appreciate your taking the time to brief us on the latest cost situation with this program. Now, if you will excuse us, I would like to meet with my staff," said McWilliams.

"Of course, General." Dodge quickly disconnected his laptop from the port on the podium, gathered it and his papers up, and left the room. The general looked at Pritchard and said, "General Pritchard, General Curtiss has fully briefed me on your unbridled support for the M1A3, and I respect your opinion." McWilliams was a man of few words and even fewer adjectives, and his use of the term *unbridled* did not go unnoticed by those in the room. It was his way of warning Pritchard not to let his emotion overshadow his judgment. In case there might be any doubt on Pritchard's part, the general continued, "However, and hear me loud and clear on this point, General, I do not want another Griffin. Do you understand?" The general was referring to one of the most technologically sophisticated and costly aircraft that the military had ever developed. And one of its greatest failures.

"General, I assure you that the deficiencies we have encountered with the M1A3 are no worse than should be expected in any such high-tech weapons program. Moreover, we anticipate limited waivers of deficiency, and I strongly recommend that we approve full-production of the tank."

The general didn't say anything. He turned to Kincaid. "Jake, as the only soldier in this room who has actually ridden this tank into battle, albeit a simulated one, I would like to hear your opinion. Do you think the M1A3 is ready for active service?"

Kincaid looked at Pritchard, whose cold stare had an unmistakable message behind it. Then he looked back at the general and said, "No, sir. I do not."

Silence fell upon the room as loudly as if the walls were made of lead. The other officers could already feel the wrath of Pritchard building, and they knew it was about to be unleashed. But General Curtiss intervened. "Go ahead, Jake. Tell General McWilliams why."

Despite the glare that he was getting from Pritchard, Kincaid did not back down. One of his father's traits that he had inherited was courage under fire, and Jake Kincaid had faced far more lethal foes than Brigadier General Mitchell Pritchard. During the short time that he had been working at the Pentagon, he had been singularly unimpressed with the new general who seemed more concerned with what the Army brass thought of him than whether the M1A3 was truly battle-worthy. On several occasions, Kincaid had expressed his reservations about the readiness of the tank to Pritchard, only to have them rebuffed. Had Kincaid been aware of the emotional trauma that Pritchard had suffered recently, he would have displayed more empathy for the man who sat across from him. But he wasn't, and he didn't.

"Yes, General, thank-you." Kincaid directed his gaze toward General McWilliams. "The improvements in the electronic subsystems, and in particular the command independent thermal viewer and integrated display systems is outstanding. And the integration of the killing power of this new lighter and faster platform with the Granite Fist secure tracking and response system is the most significant development in land warfare since the invention of the tank itself."

"But?" McWilliams queried.

"But there is a glitch somewhere in the downlink from Granite Fist. Specifically, I believe there is a flaw in the new fire control electronics unit, which under certain conditions delays the IFF targeting and firing response by a few seconds."

"What kind of conditions are you referring to, Colonel?" asked McWilliams.

"I think it might be related to atmospheric or meteorological conditions, but I am not an expert in either of these two fields."

"And those who are disagree with you, Colonel," Pritchard interjected.

"Yes, sir, I understand that."

"Even one second is long enough to have lethal consequences for the crew," added McWilliams, ignoring Pritchard's comment.

"Yes, sir," replied Kincaid, without adding drama to the ominous conversation.

McWilliams turned to Pritchard, "Obviously you don't agree, General?"

"No, sir, I do not."

"Why not?" asked McWilliams.

"Because, sir, the flaw which the Colonel speaks of hasn't shown up in any of the combat-readiness reports filed by experts who have spent the last eighteen months exhaustively checking and rechecking every system on the tank, and running computer simulations of all types of conditions under which the tank will operate."

"I don't know about you, General, but the last time I sat in a simulator, no one was trying to kill me," said McWilliams. Pritchard didn't dare take the bait. McWilliams then looked at Kincaid and asked, "Can you explain why no one else has experienced this problem, Colonel?"

"No, sir. I can not," replied Kincaid.

"In your testing of the tank under simulated battle conditions, have any of the other men in your squadron experienced any such delays?" probed McWilliams.

Kincaid hesitated before responding, flashing a chilly glance over at Pritchard. Finally he looked up at the general and said in a calm and deliberate voice, "Yes, sir. One of my tank commanders noted the same problem."

Before Kincaid could continue, Pritchard interjected. "But isn't it true that neither you nor this man formally reported any such difficulties?" asked the general, already knowing the answer.

Kincaid shrugged his shoulders slightly and answered, "Yes, sir."

The discussion clearly troubled McWilliams. He asked Kincaid, "Why not?"

"I discussed it with my regimental commander, but I decided not to file a formal report," replied Kincaid.

"Go on, Colonel," said McWilliams.

"The delay only occurred once for each of us, and we were subsequently unable to replicate it. However, based on my concerns, my CO recommended that I be temporarily assigned to General Curtiss's staff so that I could help identify and correct the problem."

"I see," said McWilliams, digesting what he had heard. He looked at Pritchard and asked, "And you were aware of Colonel Kincaid's feelings on this matter, Colonel?"

"I was aware of his opinion, sir, one which is overwhelmingly refuted by the body of evidence we have accumulated to date," replied Pritchard.

"Have you seen this evidence that the General is referring to, Colonel Kincaid?" asked the general.

"Yes, sir, I have," Kincaid replied.

"And after reviewing it, you still believe that a fatal flaw exists?" the general asked.

"Yes, sir."

"May I ask then, other than the two isolated instances which you yourself have been unable to replicate, upon what exactly do your base your concerns?"

"A feeling in my gut, sir," replied Kincaid.

There was a soft but perceptible gasp from the other officers in the room. Each of them believed they were watching the career of a senior officer crash and burn. The only question in their minds was—whose?

"Gentlemen, will you please excuse us?" he said, looking around the room. "I would like to discuss this matter with Generals Curtiss and Pritchard in private."

"Certainly, sir," said Kincaid, quickly getting up on his feet. Then he, along with the others, left the room.

After they had closed the door behind them, McWilliams looked at Pritchard and said, "Let's hear it, Mitchell. I can tell that you have your deficiency waiver pad all ready to go."

The general was furious with what had just happened, and he was at that very moment plotting how he could get Kincaid out of his hair. But he knew McWilliams was singularly unimpressed by emotional arguments, so he calmed himself down and said in a controlled tone, "I don't think the Colonel's gut is sufficient reason to delay full production and deployment of the most technologically advanced main battle tank that the world has ever known."

"That young man's guts won him the Medal of Honor, General," said Curtiss curtly.

Curtiss' comment cut Pritchard to the quick, because unlike Kincaid, he had never been in combat, and everyone in the military knew that this was a roadblock to any officer who hoped to attain a general's rank. The fact that it had obviously not stopped Pritchard's promotion to general was a puzzle to everyone. "Understood, General. But with all due respect, that doesn't change the facts."

McWilliams interjected, "Would you be willing to bet your life on it?"

The question was a loaded one, and Pritchard knew it. But he also knew that he had no choice but to take the bait. "Of course."

"But you won't ever have to, now, will you, Colonel? asked McWilliams.

The colonel did not reply. The general had made his point, and there was nothing that he could add that would make the situation any better. He knew that based on the pressures McWilliams was getting from the joint chiefs and the Congress, following the disastrous failures of the then-preferred lighter and faster armored vehicles at the end of WWT in the liberation of North Korea, he had no choice but to approve going forward with the M1A3. And he was right.

McWilliams looked at Curtiss, "What do you think, Brad?"

Curtiss was in a difficult position. He had the highest respect and admiration for the young Colonel, and he was extremely uncomfortable ignoring the gut feel of a battle-tested soldier. However, based on the facts, he had no choice but to agree with Pritchard. "General, I must conclude that the problem Jake described was an aberration. Therefore, I support General Pritchard's recommendation." His words spoke of his support for Pritchard's views, but the body language left no doubt that Curtiss was not a fan of the general.

That was that. Curtiss' words sealed it. He would later come to regret them.

General McWilliams said, "Very well, General Pritchard. I will recommend to Chairman Pace and the Joint Chiefs that we approve the M1A3 for full production." He paused and then added ominously, "I pray to God that you and your technical *experts* are right." His emphasis on the word experts made it clear that he was using the term loosely.

Pritchard was not bothered by the general's veiled warning at all. He believed that the M1A3 was going to be his ticket to glory, and he wasn't going to say or do anything that would risk this chance. This included allowing his present marital difficulties to become public. He also believed that he could get Mary Lou back whenever he chose to forgive her. He was wrong on both counts.

<u>54</u>

GNBC Studios, Washington, D.C.

A television studio is proof that what you see is not always what you get. Each evening across America, sometime between 5:30 and 7:00 p.m., over a hundred million households welcome complete strangers into their living rooms, family rooms, kitchens and dens, although the men and women who anchor the nightly news broadcasts seem more like family than strangers. Regardless, the chances of the average American ever actually meeting a news personality, let alone having one physically present in their homes, is about as likely as the government rescinding the sixteenth amendment to the Constitution. That's the one, which created income tax.

To the television viewer who sits and stares at his or her favorite news anchor as they dispense the network's interpretation of what is important, the boundaries of the newsroom are circumscribed and reassuringly familiar. They consist of the obligatory crescent-shaped desk, an eye-catching backdrop upon which photographic images magically appear and disappear in time with the carefully modulated tones of the anchor's voice, and a screen on which the talking heads of field reporters pop up like targets at a shooting gallery, each one hoping that his or her story has that certain something that will get them noticed by the head of another network who is looking for fresh meat, even though one network's fresh meat is another's leftovers.

However, if the viewer could gain access to the television studio from where the nightly news is broadcast in orchestrated pieces of contrived sound bites, they would discover that the gap between perception and reality is immense. That's because just out of camera range, unlike the image on their

482

BTC screen at home, the studio is big and cluttered, with all the glamour, drama, and charm of a plumbing-supply warehouse. Moreover, unlike the unblemished and carefully coifed image that news anchors present on the small screen, in person they appear disappointingly human.

GNBC's Washington studio was no exception. But on that particular night, there was something different about the studio and the people in it. It seemed somehow brighter, fresher, and more inviting. And the difference traced to one person—Sarah McGill. Instead of being at her usual place on the lawn of the White House, giving her nightly update on the activities of the President, she had come to the studio to introduce her report on the New Sons of Liberty. She would give the introduction live on the air and would also do the lead-ins after each commercial break. The rest of her report had been pre-recorded and in total, her exposé on the New Sons of Liberty would fill an entire hour, or actually an entire forty-eight minutes after allowing for commercials. If ever she looked radiant and poised, it was on that evening, in that studio, before millions and millions of Americans, who were as enchanted by her image as they were soon to be engrossed in her story.

"GOOD EVENING, ladies and gentlemen, my name is Sarah McGill," she began with a steady cadence. "Tonight I will share with you a story about unbridled power and misguided purpose; about raw ambition and rank acrimony; and about dark secrets and simmering discord at the highest levels of government. No, this is not a spy novel or a made-for-television movie. It is, rather, an unfolding tragedy that threatens to destroy our nation." She paused to let her words sink in. "When we return from the break, I will tell you about a group of men and women who occupy some of the most important political and public offices in our land. They have come together with the stated purpose of defending what they believe to be a Constitutionally guaranteed right, namely, the right to keep and bear arms. And they intend to do this through whatever means necessary, including violence. They call themselves the New Sons of Liberty. But as we shall see, one man's liberty is another man's treason."

AT THE SAME time that GNBC cut away to a commercial break, a plain white tradesman van turned east on Nelson Boulevard off Highway 115 and approached the main gate of Fort Carson Army Base in Colorado

Springs, Colorado. With a neatly lettered logo that read Pike's Peak Florists on its sides and an enormous bunch of brightly colored balloons that filled the passenger seat, it appeared innocent. It was anything but. The van slowed to a stop when it reached the main gate, designated as Gate 1. Since it did not have a temporary pass, one of the military police guards on duty stepped over to the driver's side of the van and said, "Please state your business, sir."

The driver, a fair-skinned young man with blonde hair and wearing a starched white shirt with the Pike's Peak Florist logo on his breast pocket gave the MP a big friendly smile. "I have a delivery of a dozen red roses for the wife of the commander of the 7th Infantry." He held out a delivery slip, which had the general's name on it as well as the florist's logo. "It's their twenty-fifth anniversary," he added with another big smile.

As the driver spoke with the guard, several more cars and another truck, all without passes, pulled up behind it. At the same, time a black sports sedan made a slow and deliberate U-turn twenty-five yards away from the gate on Nelson Avenue. Meanwhile a steady stream of cars with post-registration stickers flowed freely past the guard station in both directions.

The guard examined the flower delivery slip. At first glance, it appeared in order; however, all commercial vehicles without long-term temporary passes had to be checked before entry onto the base, and any that were not easily searched visually were required to drive through the pulsed fast neutron scanner that sat off to the side of the guard station. It was large enough to accommodate even the biggest of vehicles, and it could instantly identify explosives or any other man-made threats. In point of fact, it would not have detected the lethal danger lurking in the back of the van, even if the guard had directed the driver to pass through the PFN scanner. But it was a moot point. He wouldn't get that chance. "I will need you to open the back, please," said the guard in a firm, but polite tone.

"Of course," replied the driver. He opened the door and walked toward the back of the vehicle. However, when he reached the rear bumper, instead of turning and opening the door, he broke into a dead run.

The suddenness of his action momentarily caught the MP by surprise, "Hey!" he shouted, as he watched the man reach the black sedan and jump inside. With tires squealing, the car drove away. It was at that moment that the MP realized what was happening.

"Code red!" he screamed to the other MP, who immediately pressed a button which raised heavy metal barricades up out of the road, blocking all egress and ingress. But it was too little too late.

The first MP reached for the truck's door handle and yanked the door open. Inside the back of the truck were twenty large arrangements of flowers in big white porcelain vases. Although it seemed rather strange for there to be so many vases all exactly alike, other than that there was nothing particularly unusual about what he saw. Puzzled but still troubled by the driver's behavior, he closed the door and turned back toward the road. The last image that his eyes conveyed to his brain was that of a young second lieutenant, his wife, and their three children as they sat in a van at the front of the line that was now stopped, waiting to get back onto the base. It was at that instant that the bomb detonated.

Military explosive experts later that night would be completely baffled by the lack of residues from any known high-tech explosive. It would be another few days before the National Security Agency and the CIA took senior military officers into their confidence about the deadly new explosive that had first shown its horrible face in the U.S. at Walter Reed Hospital several months earlier. The effect of the detonation was catastrophic. The florist van and the guard post literally disappeared. Tiny bits and pieces of them would later be found spread over an area the size of a football field. However, no trace would ever be found of the two military policemen and three other people walking near the van, all of whom were instantly vaporized by the initial blast. In one sense, they were the lucky ones.

The occupants of the vehicles near the guard post suffered more protracted and gruesome fates. Three vehicles, including the van carrying the second lieutenant and his family, were thrown high into the air, where they did slow-motion cartwheels, spewing body parts and flaming gasoline over the entire scene. Five other vehicles were also destroyed by either the initial shock wave or the conflagration that followed, including a brand new Harley Davidson motorcycle and its rider, a young infantry captain who was to have been married two days later. One witness, a seasoned master sergeant, said he hadn't seen anything like it since WWT, and the image would haunt him in all the dark days to come.

In all, the lives of nineteen human beings were snuffed out by the explosion. Five more would die later of their injuries. As the sound of sirens filled the air, the two men who had visited the death and destruction upon the unsuspecting Army base had already abandoned their stolen sedan and were heading in a silver SUV towards the Colorado Springs airport, where a chartered jet was waiting for them. By the time the first of the wounded reached the hospital, the two men were sitting in a luxurious cabin of the jet that was climbing out of Colorado Springs and heading northwest across the Rocky Mountains.

THE U.S. FOREST SERVICE field office in Missoula, Montana was located in a three-story red brick building that had once been the head office of the Whitefish and Kalispell Railway, a local branch line that, in its heyday, used to carry affluent vacationers from Missoula to Glacier National Park. But the rail line had gone bankrupt during the Great Depression, and all that remained of it now was the building on East Broadway, plus a few boarded-up passenger stations along the right of way, which stood as silent reminders of a kinder and gentler time in America.

But kinder and gentler was the antithesis of what was about to happen on that unusually hot spring day in Missoula. The building had none of the security screening devices that were standard issue at most government buildings in big cities. Despite the acts of terrorism back East, and the subsequent World War on Terrorism, the Forest Service's budget would not permit the kind of expense that was necessary to install security systems in its regional offices. Besides, the local head of the service refused to believe that terrorism would ever rear its ugly head out there in God's country. He was wrong.

On the first floor at the front of the building in a large conference room with rickety floorboards and pale green walls, a group of twenty-five smokejumpers were being briefed on the numerous forest fires that were burning in the region. It had been a dry spring, following a snowless winter, and every person in the room knew that the fires they had fought over the past month were only the beginning of the fury that was to come.

As the smokejumpers' meeting went on inside, a tradesman van pulled up in front of the building. On its sides, in neat letters were the words Lolo Hills Florists, and a large bunch of brightly colored balloons filled the passenger seat. The van stopped in a handicapped parking space directly in front of the building, and the blonde-haired driver opened the door and got out.

A man who was the forest health monitoring coordinator exited the building and shouted to him, "Hey, buddy. You can't park there."

The van driver smiled but said nothing.

The coordinator started to say something else, but before he could, a sports coupe pulled up alongside the van, and the van's driver quickly opened the car door and jumped inside. Then the car roared away, leaving the coordinator staring at the now-empty van. Empty except for the twenty white porcelain vases in the back, filled with pretty flowers. The coordinator shook his head angrily and walked over to the back of the van, where he opened the door and looked inside. As he did, it exploded in a fireball that ripped open the building, killing him instantly, along with all but two of the smokejumpers, plus ten other people either inside the building or on the nearby street. The casualties included a Native American woman and her seven-year-old daughter. They had been on their way to buy the little girl a confirmation dress. Now the mother was dead, and the little girl was grievously wounded. It would take police two hours to locate the girl's father and get him to the hospital. During that time, the little girl had been a small, lonely, and terrified bundle on a stretcher in an emergency room, while a team of doctors and nurses with focused minds and aching hearts tried desperately to save her.

As the medical team worked on the little girl and the other wounded, the two killers strolled into the corporate air terminal at the Missoula International Airport. They chuckled as they passed the airport sign and guessed correctly that the designation referred to the daily flight to Canada. But they could care less about the regularly scheduled flights out of the airport, for they were traveling in style. A ground attendant ushered them across the tarmac to the chartered jet that sat waiting for them. On board were the two men who had made the delivery to Fort Carson, and before long the four of them would be settling back into deep leather seats as the plane headed eastward into the growing darkness that covered the land.

A pretty flight attendant served the passengers a meal of lamb and rice with a fine wine but except for a polite few words to her in broken English, they spoke in a tongue that was strange to her ears. Mercifully for her, she could not understand anything they said, because the men were proudly recounting what they had accomplished that day and the pathetic Americans that they had killed. They were foreign-born killers who had done what they had been paid to do, and now all they wanted was to get back to Washington and collect their fee from the man who had hired them—the man who lived on the estate in Tysons Corner, Virginia.

After their meal, three of the men settled back to watch a movie, while the fourth stretched out on his fully reclinable chair and closed his eyes. The flight attendant covered him with a heated blanket, and he drifted off to sleep, wondering what it would be like to rape her in the plane's tiny bathroom. It was the last thought he would ever have.

It would have taken the FAA and the FBI only a matter of hours to cross-check the flight plans for all the aircraft flying in and out of Colorado Springs and Missoula that afternoon, and to discover that this particular jet had made stops at both airports shortly after the bombings. The two innocent pilots would also have quickly reported the coincidence to the authorities after they learned of the bombings. The professional killers realized that fact, but they had been assured by the stocky man with a thick British accent who had hired them that by the time any of this would happen, they would have already landed in Washington and disappeared into the shadows from where they came. It had been a lie.

The man was Major Smythe, and what none of the killers knew was that he never left any loose ends after a job. This time would be no exception. At the instant that the altimeter in the cockpit indicated that the jet had reached it's transcontinental cruising altitude, the third and final bomb of the day, this one cleverly disguised as a large service of white china in the plane's galley, exploded, tearing the jet apart, and sending it plummeting straight down into the rugged, snow-covered mountains of the Swan Range. It would take search crews several weeks to locate the crash site, since the main wreckage was buried deeply in the snow on the side of Mount Scarface. Meanwhile, a terror of ravens would dine heartily on the bits of flesh that lay intermingled among charred pieces of metal spread out across the snow.

AS REPORTS of the two bombings began pouring in, the activity level in GNBC's Washington newsroom, like its counterparts at a thousand other newsrooms around the country, suddenly increased tenfold. The producer of McGill's New Sons of Liberty report debated whether or not to interrupt her report with the breaking news of the two bombings. Keene Lange made that decision for him.

"We're going to cut in," he said, as he barged into the control room and grabbed the microphone from the producer.

"Sarah, this is Keene," he spoke into her ear, as she was about to introduce the third segment of her expose. "We've got breaking news and we're going to cut in on you." Unruffled, McGill handled the situation with the poise and grace that had become her trademark.

Holding one hand up to her ear to give the audience a visual cue that something important was happening, McGill looked at the camera and said, "Ladies and gentlemen, we're going to interrupt this report to bring you late-breaking news from our newsroom in New York." With that, the feed switched to GNBC's New York studios, where the network's lead news anchor was already standing by with his reports. As soon as she was off the air, McGill got up from behind her desk and walked quickly into the control room.

"What's going on, Keene?" she asked, knowing that it would have to be big—real big—for him to cut away from her report.

"There have been two bombings out West," he said. "The first was at Fort Carson Army base in Colorado, and the second happened outside the U.S. Forest Service field office in Missoula, Montana."

"How bad is it?"

"We're not sure of the exact count yet, but I think there have been at least twenty fatalities, maybe more," he answered.

"In total?" she asked.

"No. At each location," he replied with a dead-serious face.

A look of realization flashed across her face. "Keene!"

"What?"

"The Army troops who took back the Bitterroot Rod and Gun Club were stationed at Fort Carson."

Lange's expression instantly showed that he knew where his star pupil was going.

"And the Missoula office of the Forest Service was the one that closed the club to begin with," she added.

"You're right," he said, as the full implications of the fact sunk in.

As they stood there in the crowded studio, watching the first pictures coming in of victims lying covered by white sheets, row on row upon the ground, the curtain was about to go up on the final act in the three-part tragedy. Except that the location had just been switched from the Rocky Mountains to Sixteen Hundred Pennsylvania Avenue. And this one had absolutely nothing to do with the bombs or the man who built them.

A BLONDE-HAIRED man with pale skin walked slowly along Pennsylvania Avenue in front of the White House. The avenue had long ago been closed to vehicular traffic, and during the war on terrorism, pedestrian traffic had been forbidden as well; but one of President Webster's election promises had been to reopen the people's house to the people, and he had kept it. Public tours of the White House had been reinstated and pedestrians were once again allowed to stroll in front of it along Pennsylvania Avenue. However, every person who did was under constant and vigilant surveillance by the battery of long-range scanning devices and cameras. The Secret Service had also wanted each person who walked anywhere within one hundred yards of the White House to have to submit to backscatter x-rays, but Congress had put an end to that after they had seen a demonstration of the device which literally disrobed the subject electronically. However, use of the device had become standard operating procedure at the hundreds of social affairs that took place every year in Washington, and on more than one occasion, a senior politician had secretly been allowed to view the monitor when attractive female guests had been scanned.

Thanks to the relaxed public access and Congress' objection to backscatter scanning, no one could know that the blonde-haired man hunched over against the rain with the collar of his trenchcoat turned up was carrying an automatic rifle on a shoulder strap under his coat. In fact, to the casual observer, he offered no indication of the evil that lurked within. In one hand he carried an umbrella and in the other a briefcase, and he looked like just another Washington bureaucrat on his way home to dinner.

One hundred yards away from him, the White House correspondents for the various television networks were standing under umbrellas on the lawn, taping their reports that would shortly be used on their respective evening newscasts. None of them, including Latrel Elwood, a reporter from GNBC's Washington bureau who was filling in for Sarah McGill, had yet heard about the bombings. It wouldn't have made any difference, because no one would have linked the two bombings two thousand miles away with what was about to happen on the very doorstep of the presidency.

The blonde-haired man reached his predetermined position. With a slow, deliberate movement, he put down his briefcase and umbrella and opened his coat. The drizzling rain had driven away the tourists that usually populated that stretch of the avenue, causing the police to later say that at least they could be thankful for small blessings. Unfortunately for the reporters, they were well within the range of the weapon that the man pulled out from under his coat. Knowing that he would instantly be on camera, he wasted no time; he assumed a firing stance and began shooting. Elwood was the first to die. The bullet hit him in his chest with a loud whack, knocking him down, but it took another few seconds for him to lose consciousness, during which time the fact of his own death registered unmistakably in his brain, and those who were near him heard him clearly and calmly say, "Tell Ellie I love her."

His death was immediately followed by that of his cameraman, a reporter from another network and a uniformed Secret Service agent. Seven others were wounded, two of whom would be pronounced dead when they reached George Washington Hospital. Before the other Secret Service agents or the guards at the front gates could react, the man calmly laid the rifle down, walked across the avenue to Jackson Place and disappeared among the crowd of people who had gathered to see the blood and gore.

KEENE LANGE and Sarah McGill were sitting in his office with Tanner Spence, watching the network feeds from Fort Carson and Missoula, when Lange's administrative assistant interrupted them.

Lange looked up from the BTC and said, "What's wrong?"

She looked over at McGill, and then back at Lange and said, "There's been a shooting at the White House."

"What!" exclaimed Lange.

"Latrel Elwood's dead," she said, with tears welling up in her eyes.

McGill jumped to her feet. "Oh, no!"

"Latrel's dead?" blurted out Lange.

The assistant nodded as tears filled her eyes, "Yes, along with five or six others."

By now, both Lange and Spence were also on their feet.

"Who did it?" said Lange.

"It was a lone gunman with a rifle. He got away," she replied.

McGill said, "I'm going over there now."

Before Lange could stop her, she was on her way out of his office as he spoke. Her mind was spinning with the image of Latrel Elwood's face. He had been her friend and confidant. Now he was dead. There would be time for grieving later, but for now her reporter's instincts told her she had to get the story. And her mind was already spinning with the images of the Army base in Colorado, the field office in Montana, and the Rod and Gun Club in Idaho, all interwoven against the backdrop of the red, white, and blue of the New Sons of Liberty web site.

After McGill left, Spence turned to Lange and said, "I think I'd better get back to DHS," and then he too, quickly exited the office.

Lange looked at his assistant and asked softly, "Do you know whether the police have notified Ellie?" He was referring to Latrel's wife.

She nodded and said, "No. They asked if you wanted to do it."

Lange sighed, "Tell them yes. Get me a driver."

"He's waiting for you downstairs," she said.

He grabbed his jacket off the back of his chair. "What's the name of his little girl?"

"Charisse," answered his assistant. She paused and added, "Today was her birthday. She's ten years old."

He nodded and headed toward the door, "Let's pray that no one broadcasts the names of the victims until I get to his house."

It was a futile wish. While none of the television stations covering the shooting had released any names pending notification of next of kin, an Internet reporter had already sent an e-mail to Elwood's house, and Ellie would learn of her husband's death online, ten minutes before Keene Lange got there.

It was only one of the heartbreaking repercussions of the multiple tragedies that had occurred on that dreadful afternoon in late May. But that didn't make it any less painful for the man's wife and daughter. And the dying had only just begun.

55

The White House, Washington, D.C.

It had been three hours since the bombs and bullets had taken their deadly toll. All across the nation, shock, fear, and bewilderment prevailed, while in the White House Situation Room, the members of the National Security Council sat waiting for the President. The mood was somber and in hushed tones, they discussed what had happened and debated the possibility that these attacks were the reappearance of foreign terrorism upon American soil.

Suddenly, the President entered the room, and everyone jumped up to attention. "Be seated, gentlemen and Mary Lou," said the President, scanning the room and quickly spotting something that displeased him. "Where's Maurice Bouchard?" he asked, referring to the Secretary of Homeland Security.

"He has been on vacation with his family in New Hampshire, sir," said Gordon. "He's on his way back here now."

"Who in the hell said he could take a vacation?" snapped the President. But before Gordon could tell him that *he* did, Webster turned to the others and said," Now then, who is ready to tell me what the hell is going on?"

No one said anything. They had learned from long experience that it didn't pay to be the first one up when the President started his rapid-fire verbal attack. The group gathered around the table included the members of the National Security Council, both those who served by statute and those who were statutory advisers. The former included White House Chief of Staff Maddun Gordon, National Security Adviser Patrick Fitzgerald, Vice President Richard Knox, Harlan Caruthers and Poland Snetzinger, the Secretaries of Defense and State respectively. Among the latter group were Chairman Halston Pace of the Joint Chiefs of Staff, Springer White, Director of the CIA and last, but certainly not least, Mary Lou Pritchard, the acting Attorney General. Her makeup hid the last traces of her black eye, and she looked her usual beautiful self. Only one other person in the room had any idea of the depth of the hurt she still felt deep inside and publicly, at least, he could do nothing to help her.

"What's the body count?" the President asked Fitzgerald.

"Fifty-two dead and fifteen wounded out west, Mr. President, some of them seriously," replied Fitzgerald.

"So many?" the Vice President said, slowly shaking his head.

"The gate they hit at Fort Carson was the main access point to the base, and there was quite a bit of traffic at the time the bomb went off. In Missoula, a training session for twenty-two young smokejumpers was being held on the first floor at the front of the building. All but two died," said Fitzgerald.

The President continued, "How about here?"

"Five dead, sir," replied Fitzgerald.

The President thought about what he had just been told for a few moments without saying anything. No one in the room could gauge what he was feeling as he was maintaining tight control over his emotions. For all his arrogance and vanity, President Alex Webster was not a man without feelings. He knew that what the country needed at that moment was a leader with a cool head and a tough hand. And he was determined to give them just that. He looked at Caruthers and said, "Harlan, have you put our military bases on highest alert?"

"Yes, Mr. President," replied Caruthers, an aging ex-warrior with drooping earlobes and wire-rimmed glasses, who many believed had stayed around for one war too many.

"We're prepared for the worst, sir," added General Pace.

"Right," answered the President, smiling politely at the general. *He doesn't like me and probably doesn't respect me. But you'd never know it. That man is a class act regardless of what Maddun says,* he thought as he carefully studied the general's steady demeanor. He next looked at Pritchard. "Has the Bureau got anything, Mary Lou?"

"No, Mr. President. Not yet," she answered crisply.

"Why am I not surprised?" he replied. His relationship with the FBI during his tenure in the White House had been tense at best. Their inconsistent performance during his first term in office, and more recently, in the months since the Bitterroots incident, had made him deeply skeptical about their abilities. In particular, the recent botched attempt to snatch T.J. Kincaid off a hillside in Idaho had created a public relations nightmare for both the Bureau and the White House. What he didn't realize was that in the case of any type of armed force, and the FBI was certainly that, a leader gets the army he deserves. And under his administration, the FBI had been constantly second-guessed, underfunded, and generally unappreciated. Mary Lou planned to change all that, but it would be a Herculean task.

"What about you, Springer?"

"Mr. President, we haven't picked up anything from our global network. No one has taken any credit for what happened."

General Pace added, "Given what we accomplished during WWT, I'm not surprised. Any terrorist who would stick his head out from under a rock and take credit for such acts now knows he'll have it immediately blown off."

Webster looked at his Secretary of State, Poland Snetzinger, a tall and bony man with dark circles under his eyes that wouldn't go away no matter how much sleep he got, which was usually very little. "What do you think, Poland?"

"I have spoken with the leaders of the Arab nations as well as the heads of the new democratic governments in the former terrorist nations, and they have all assured me that these attacks did not have their roots in their lands."

"Do you believe them?" asked the President.

"Yes, sir. I do. If for no other reason that they know what happened to their predecessors in office during WWT."

The President nodded and said, "Thank-you, Poland."

"Excuse me, Mr. President," interjected Gordon. "I think we all know who was behind these attacks. And it isn't some new fanatical religious group from a foreign land."

"Please enlighten us, Maddun," said the President.

"These terrorists are the worst kind, Mr. President, because they are parasites who seek to destroy the very land that harbors them. They are traitors and cowards and hypocrites. Their base is in a remote valley in the Bitterroot Mountains of Idaho, and their leader is Governor Edward Morrissey."

Everyone, including the President, was taken aback with the bluntness of Gordon's accusation. Even though many of them secretly shared his opinion, to state it so unequivocally in such a high-level forum pushed well beyond the limits of propriety.

The President looked at his chief of staff and paused before answering. Finally, he said, "You may be right, Maddun, but before we accuse a governor of treason, we need facts, not emotion."

"Mr. President, we have circumstantial evidence by the direct link between the sites they attacked and the closing of that gun club," Gordon replied. "Who else but the militia would have any reason to attack Fort Carson or the Forest Service?"

"But why shoot the reporters here at the White House?" questioned the Vice President. "What has that got to do with the gun club? If anything, the national media showed sympathy for the group up on that mountain. Especially GNBC, whose news team took the full brunt of the fusillade."

The question annoyed Gordon for reasons known only to himself. "With all due respect, Mr. Vice President," said Gordon without meaning it, "I have no idea what goes on in the minds of madmen. I leave it to the intelligentsia to practice psychiatry without a license. For all I know, they were trying to send the President a message and the GNBC news crew was simply in the wrong place at the wrong time."

There had never been any love lost between the Vice President and Maddun Gordon, but Knox was too smart and too classy to indulge in a tit-for-tat zinger match with Gordon, so he ignored him. "Mr. President, I urge you to proceed with extreme caution before jumping to any conclusions."

"The Vice President is right," added Pritchard. "This is an extremely delicate situation."

There's a blinding flash of the obvious, thought Gordon. "I never assumed that it wasn't, Madam Acting Attorney General," he said, emphasizing the word "acting."

Pritchard ignored Gordon and continued. "Not only with respect to what actions we take, but also from the perspective of how the American people will react. If these attacks were the work of some new, foreign-based terrorist group, then our war on terrorism will be viewed as a failure, and the thousands of casualties that our military has sustained will be seen as lives lost in vain. If on the other hand, they were the result of attacks by Americans on their fellow citizens, and we unilaterally take action against one faction in this derisive debate, we risk having the country deteriorate into an armed camp."

"It is already an armed camp," snapped Gordon. "There are more guns among our general population than there are in all the rest of the free world combined. That's why the President introduced his gun legislation in the first place."

"That may be true, but it is also irrelevant to the issue at hand," Patrick Fitzgerald interjected. "I agree with Mary Lou and the Vice President; we need to get more facts before we take action against any foe, foreign or domestic. Especially before we accuse one of the most powerful governors in the Union of a crime. Whoever was behind the shootings here at the White House may have intended to provoke you into taking precipitous action. Action that you might later regret."

Knox added, "If we declare war on the militia without sufficient cause, we may wake up a sleeping tiger."

Gordon rolled his eyes. *Oh shit. What the fuck is this, a circle jerk?* "A paper tiger," Gordon grumbled under his breath.

The President did not respond. He had tuned out of the discussion—something that he had increasingly been doing during the past few months. Only a few of his closest aides had noticed, but at that moment it was quite apparent to everyone that he hadn't been paying attention to the feud going on between Gordon, the national security adviser, and the Vice President. Finally the President asked, "What did you say about GNBC, Richard?"

Like everyone else in the room, the Vice President was troubled by the fact that the President had not been paying attention. He thought about the question for a moment and then said, "I said that their news team had taken the full brunt of the opening volley from the gunman."

"Was Sarah McGill one of the victims?"

"No, Mr. President," replied the Vice President.

Only by the grace of God, thought Gordon. On the long and growing list of people he viewed as FOPs, or Foes of the President, Sarah McGill was near the top of the list. He hadn't liked her from the minute she started covering the White House. Her brains intimidated him, and her looks tantalized him. And now that she was dating one of the Kincaid clan, her rating on the FOP list had gone sky high. To him, the Kincaids were the royal family of FOPs.

"Where was she?" asked the President.

"She was in the studio doing a special on the New Sons of Liberty," said Fitzgerald. "We discussed that it was going to be aired this evening, if you remember, sir."

The President nodded absentmindedly. "Ah, yes. The New Sons of Liberty—John Adams' misbegotten descendants in bloodlust, if not blood." He turned to Gordon, "There's another potential group of suspects for these attacks, Maddun. What did Adams call them?"

"Saucy boys," replied Fitzgerald.

"Ah, yes. I like that expression. Saucy boys. You naughty little saucy boys," mused the President while his puzzled staff looked on. An air of discomfort permeated the room.

Gordon tried to get his boss focused back on the issue at hand. "I doubt that the New Sons of Liberty had anything to do with the bombings or shootings, sir."

"Why?" challenged the Vice President.

"Because they are nothing but a bunch of old farts and has-beens from the other side of the aisle, who sit in smoke-filled rooms and talk of glory days, while their bellies grow soft and their arteries grow hard. They haven't got the guts to stand and face you in the open." He made no effort to hide his contempt for them and for the Vice-President.

"I wouldn't be so sure, Maddun. For all we know, the militia and the saucy little New Sons of Liberty may have joined forces against us," said the President.

Jesus Christ, the man is flipping out right in front of us, thought Gordon. "That may well be, Mr. President, but whether or not the militia have any affiliation with the New Sons of Liberty, they are a real and present danger to the security of the Union. And that is all the more reason to take immediate and decisive action against the militia camps in the West," added Gordon.

"What do you think, Harlan?" asked the President of his Secretary of Defense, who up until that moment had been relatively silent.

The old man, nicknamed Longears by his detractors, many of whom wore military uniforms covered in ribbons and braids, squinted at the President through his glasses and said with a smile, "The militia are like snowflakes, Mr. President. They put on a good show, but they'll melt in the heat of battle."

The corners of the President's mouth scrunched up, but he didn't blast Carruthers. He already had enough trouble with the Pentagon, and the last thing he needed was to take on its leader, at least in public. However, had he done so, he would have found more support in that five-sided building than he realized. He asked General Pace the same question.

Without looking at his boss, the general replied, "I'm in agreement with Mr. Gordon," replied Pace, looking like it surprised him to say it. "I believe that the militia units are growing stronger every day, not only in Idaho but in many of the other western states, and they represent a significant threat to our national security."

Carruthers frowned but withheld comment. However, he made a mental note to write a nasty memo to the general later. It was his weapon of choice. So much so that the media loved to get hold of them.

"What action would you suggest, General?" queried the President.

"I would first place the National Guard units in those states that are part of the Group of Seven, or G7, under your direct command."

"That would mean enacting the War Powers Act," interjected the Vice President. "I don't think—"

"Go on, General," said Webster, cutting off Knox.

"Then I would demand the governors of those seven states to immediately disband the militia units."

"If they refuse?" asked the President.

Pace thought about it for a long moment, then said, "Then, Mr. President, I would send in the Army to disband the units, and arrest their leaders."

Maddun Gordon was obviously surprised by the general's statement. "I seem to recall, General, that you had rather strident views regarding sending the Special Forces up onto that mountain in the Bitterroots. I believe the words you used were 'a strategic blunder of colossal proportions.'"

The general stared at Gordon without any expression. "Sending the Army into the Bitterroots was a bad decision, and I don't deny that I recommended strongly against it at the time. I also believe that if we had not done so, we would not be in the situation we are in today. Having said that, to allow the Western militia groups to grow unchecked is to make a bad situation even worse." When he was finished speaking, the general looked at the President. To his dismay, the President wasn't listening. Instead, he seemed lost in thought.

"Mr. President?" said the general.

The President didn't answer, which caused all eyes in the room to focus upon him.

The general looked at Gordon and then back at the President, who was still lost in thought.

Come on, Alex. For Christ's sake, stay with us. You're the fucking leader of the free world, thought Gordon. "Mr. President," he said more sharply and forcefully than had the general.

Gordon's words brought the President back to the then and now. "Yes, Maddun?"

"The issue before us is whether or not we should nationalize the Guard and move to disband the militia camps, sir."

"Once again, Mr. President, I strongly recommend against taking such action," said the Vice President.

The President looked at Mary Lou. "What do you think, Mary Lou?"

"I agree with the Vice President, sir."

"I do as well," added Fitzgerald.

The President absorbed the three statements without comment, but they seemed to be having their desired effect.

Gordon didn't like the way the meeting was going. He knew that he commanded very little respect from the people around the table—from all except the President himself. Accordingly, he was careful not to say anything that would place the President in an awkward position and thereby jeopardize his position. "Mr. President, I agree with Secretary Carruthers." The truth was that he thought Longears was a flaming idiot, but it served his purpose to agree with him at that moment. "We are dealing with cowards who will run away and hide at the first sign of bold and decisive action on your part. Therefore, I recommend that you send a Marine Expeditionary Force into the militia bases out West now, before they have time to strengthen their forces."

Gordon's comment alarmed the Vice President. "Mr. President, that would be a grave mistake."

Without looking at Knox, Gordon added, "To do nothing is to dig America's grave."

Mary Lou Pritchard had heard enough of Gordon's paranoid rantings. She could not hold back any longer. "Mr. President, may I say something, sir?"

All eyes shifted to the other end of the table. As far as she could tell, no one knew about her escapade with the President. Had she been aware that

Gordon knew all about it, she might have held back on what she was about to say. But she wasn't, and she didn't.

"Of course, Mary Lou," said the President.

She flashed a contemptuous look at Gordon. "I think Mr. Gordon does you, and the rest of us, a disservice by trying to turn this discussion into a witch hunt." Her opening salvo created a bevy of flashing eyebrows. "The FBI, in cooperation with the military and other law enforcement agencies, are investigating these incidents as we speak. As soon as they have hard evidence of who is responsible, we will brief you, sir, and you can take the appropriate action. Until then, I strongly recommend that we follow the advice that the Vice President and Mr. Fitzgerald have given you."

The President smiled at her. "What if Maddun's theory proves to be right?"

"If the western militia groups turn out to be responsible for these terrorist acts, then they will feel the full might of the forces you have at your command, Mr. President. But if they are not, you risk giving them an excuse to start something that could lead to a holocaust." She paused and added somberly, "Only you have the power to choose."

The room fell silent as many waited to see who would sway the most powerful man on earth, his chief of staff or his acting Attorney General. Most presumed that Pritchard would prevail, both because she was right and also because she deftly played to the President's Achilles heel—his ego. Gordon, too, suspected that she had won this battle, but for another reason—one that only he knew. After all, she could give the President the one and only thing that he could not—a great piece of ass.

"Thank-you, Mary Lou." He looked around the table. "Gentlemen, we will await the outcome of the investigation before we take any definitive action." He looked back at her. "However, Mary Lou, I want to know what is going on in those militia bases out West. I want to know how many troops they have, what kind of weapons, and what their capabilities are. If General Latrobe even takes a shit in the woods, I want to know about it."

"Understood, Mr. President," said Pritchard.

"And one more thing."

"Yes, Mr. President?"

"No more screw-ups by the FBI."

"No, Mr. President," she replied with a frown.

501

The President, ever an astute observer of human nature and body language, caught a hint of something in her response. "Did you want to add something, Mary Lou?"

She hesitated and then said, "Yes, sir. Actually, I do. But perhaps we should discuss it in private."

"I'd like to hear it now, please."

She took a deep breath and said, "Mr. President, I think you should allow me to suspend our efforts to bring T.J. Kincaid into custody. Instead, I believe you should offer him a pardon if he will turn himself in."

To Gordon's dismay and the surprise of everyone in the room, the President didn't dismiss the idea outright. That was because he had already proposed it to Jeremiah Kincaid, but he kept that fact to himself. "And what do you think that would accomplish?"

"I think it would take the public's attention off the Bitterroots and its tragic legacy and refocus national attention on the real issue here, which is the future safety and security of America. What's more, Mr. President, it would remind the public of your softer side—a side that they haven't seen very much of lately, sir."

The Vice President's eyebrows arched in admiration, and Fitzgerald cheered to himself under his breath. Even Gordon was impressed at how well Mary Lou had learned to play the President. Of course, unlike the others, he also knew that she had had sex with him, and that's a trump card in any boss-and-employee relationship.

The President didn't say anything at first. Then, gradually, a smile spread across his lips. "Of course, the positive reaction that such an act might receive in the Speaker's family would be another potential benefit?"

She smiled back at him, "Of course."

"I'll give it my full consideration, Madam Attorney General," he added with a smile.

Of course, everyone knew that she was only the acting Attorney General, but the way she had just handled the President added considerably to the likelihood that she would get his nomination.

Finally, thought the President. *I have an Attorney General with balls.* The little repartee that he had shared with her seemed to boost his spirits.

Gordon knew that whenever the President shifted back to manic from depressive mode, he suddenly would become very charitable, and the very fact that he would even consider pardoning the little bastard who had eluded

502

him for so long was a clear sign that the manic light had just been switched on. He hunkered down and hoped that the President wouldn't get too warm and fuzzy. But it was not to be.

Webster turned to the Chairman of the Joint Chiefs and said, "General, I am well aware of your views regarding the use of the military in domestic matters. I have been remiss in not apologizing to you personally for the challenges that you have had to deal with as a result of my orders to retake that gun club. Moreover, I have never publicly thanked you for the steadfast leadership you displayed through those long years of battle against terrorism abroad. But I hope you would agree that late is better than never. Therefore—" he paused, while everyone in the room held their breath, "I hereby apologize to you in front of your peers."

The general didn't know what to say. He smiled awkwardly. "No apology is necessary, sir."

"Yes, General. It most certainly is. I hope that you will accept it and pass it along to the joint chiefs.

The battle-hardened general was clearly touched. "Thank-you, sir. I will."

The President smiled and then said, "Good. Now I must ask you, as your commander in chief, to take on another difficult task."

"Yes, sir. Of course," said the general with just a trace of hesitancy in his voice.

"I want you to prepare a contingency plan, and I emphasize the word contingency. The objective of the plan is to provide for the safety and security of this nation, and its mission will be to take massive and decisive military action against the militia, or any other internal force, that might threaten the government of the United States."

"Are you saying that you want the military to be prepared to go to war, Mr. President?" asked Carruthers. "A civil war?"

"Yes, Mr. Secretary, that is exactly what I am saying."

The room fell silent once again. The fact that the President of the United States of America would discuss the possibility of an armed force rising up against the land that nurtured it was alarming. That he would ready the nation for war was staggering.

The general looked the President directly in the eyes and said, "Yes, sir. It will be done."

"Thank-you, General." Webster then looked slowly around the table, making eye contact with everyone. "Gentlemen and Mary Lou, these are difficult times. Although I will await Poland's further assessment of the situation overseas, at this point I am of the opinion that the attacks which we have witnessed over the past twenty-four hours were the work of traitors among us; traitors and cowards who would seek to prevent the legally prescribed process of government. We now face the very real possibility that an evil force is rising up inside our nation. A force that threatens to destroy everything that we have built over nearly two and a half centuries."

Atta boy, Prez, it's nice to finally see you flex muscles other than the one between your legs, thought Gordon.

Webster shifted his gaze to Gordon so suddenly, that for an instant, Gordon thought that he might have said his thought out loud.

"I share your concern about the militia, Maddun, and as you have just heard, I do not intend to allow our nation to be attacked in its vulnerable underbelly. However, as Mary Lou has proposed, at this point we will take no action; we will attack no enemy, real or perceived; and we will make no public statements until I have decided where and when to make them. To do so prematurely and with lack of evidence would create a crisis of confidence in this administration among the American people. Is that understood?"

"I understand, sir," said Gordon. "You know that you have my full and complete support." But that wasn't what he was thinking. *Shit, I should have known. Here, you have been handed the fucking Western Freedom Party, the chicken-shit militia, and even the New Sons of Liberty on a silver platter, and you are being led by your dick instead of your balls.* "What about the compromise with the Speaker of the House, sir?" asked Gordon, knowing what would surely be the answer.

"Regardless of who was behind these killings, that deal died with those fifty-seven people," replied the President with a look of deeply felt sadness that was a stranger to his face.

"Shall I get the Speaker on the telcom, Mr. President, so that you can tell him?" asked Gordon almost gleefully.

"If he is as smart as I think he is, he already knows." Of course, he was right. "Okay, that's it. I'll see you all at seven tomorrow morning." With that, the President stood up, prompting the others to do the same. As he headed out the door, he looked back and barked, "And it might be nice if the Secretary of Homeland Security was here to discuss our goddamned national insecurity." With that, he was gone.

IT WAS PAST TWO in the morning and the directives that the President had given to his staff several hours earlier were now being diligently acted upon by somber-faced personnel at the Pentagon, the J. Edgar Hoover building, and CIA headquarters. The President had retired to his private quarters, and the only person still in the West Wing was Maddun Gordon. But he wasn't in his own office.

Instead, he was standing in the Oval Office, looking out the window toward the Washington monument. That brazen act, in and of itself was highly unusual, but what completed the bizarre scene was that he was also talking heatedly to another person on the President's BTC console. Like the one in his own office and the others located throughout the building, this one had its video call capability disabled. The Secret Service had done this for security reasons. They did not think it wise to allow those with whom the President was speaking to see him or the Oval Office.

Beyond the President himself, Maddun Gordon was one of only three other people who were authorized to use the President's BTC. The others were the Vice President and the Secretary of Homeland Security. However, it was highly inappropriate for him to be doing so without the President present. Some might have taken this behavior to be the final act of an insane man; however, Gordon was confident that the Secret Service would never presume to think that he was acting without the President's permission and prior knowledge. And finally, he wasn't worried about anyone else seeing him in there, since there was only one person who would be allowed to walk these halls at two in the morning. And he was upstairs fast asleep. Or so Gordon thought.

"I told you never to call me," said Chadrian on the other end of the line.

"Don't worry, I'm using a clear channel," said Gordon, referring to one of the hard lines that were only available to the President and his chief of staff. They were protected by a complex security system that had been installed after the amorous late-night conversations of an earlier President had been intercepted and recorded. It was almost impossible for anyone to tap one of these clear channels. Almost but not completely.

"Make it quick."

"I want to know if you had anything to do with the bombings."

"I already told you that I did not."

"If you weren't behind the bombings, who was?" Gordon said into the telcom.

"I do not know," said Chadrian on the other end of the line.

"Don't give me that bullshit, Chadrian. I thought you were going to shoot a few reporters in front of the White House. I never agreed to filling a gymnasium with body bags."

"Do not lecture me, you pompous little sycophant, or I will cut your heart out while you sleep," replied Chadrian.

The thought of having his chest ripped open toned down the stridency of Gordon's words. "All right, all right. Relax. But if you didn't blow up half the West, who did? And why, for fuck sake?"

There was a pause before Chadrian replied. Then he said, "I told you, I do not know, and I do not care. And all that you should be worried about is getting me the rest of my money."

"You'll get your money, Chadrian. Have I ever not come through with it?"

"The first time will be your last. And that goes for the man you work for."

"I'll bring it down to you tomorrow," said Gordon.

"Good. Be there before noon. I have got to go pick up a new Rotweiler puppy from an old lady who breeds them."

"I don't want to hear about it," said Gordon, figuring correctly that it had something to do with his perverted implementation of pro bono work.

Chadrian continued anyway. "I made a delivery for her to a stockbroker who stole her life savings."

"I don't get you. You are as cold-blooded and evil a man as I have ever known, and yet you do these good deeds. If they can be called that."

"I do not do it for the happiness of the people I help, you stupid little man. I do it for the eternal pain of the people I kill."

"Whatever turns you on. Now I'd better get off the President's telcom. I don't want to press my luck," said Gordon, beginning to get nervous about where he was and what he was doing.

There was a long pause and then Chadrian said in a measured tone, "Do you mean to tell me that you are calling me from the Oval Office?"

"Yeah. So what?"

Chadrian laughed again, this time louder. "You have big balls, Gordon. Unfortunately, the size of your brain is inversely related to the size of your balls."

"You just worry about your sorry ass, and I'll worry about mine. I'll see you before noon tomorrow, and you better make sure that you didn't leave any loose ends from today's events."

"It is well past midnight and 'the events,' as you call them, occurred yesterday. And I have cleaned up the loose ends. All but one, that is."

Gordon hesitated, "What does that mean?" He was clearly troubled by the implications of Chadrian's last comment.

"It is nothing that you need be concerned about," replied Chadrian. It was a lie and a big one, like everything else he had said on the call. But Gordon didn't pursue it. He knew that sometimes it was better to not ask a question if you can't handle the answer, and something deep inside told Gordon that this was one of those times. With that, he reached over and terminated the call. He stood there for a long moment, struggling to overcome the anxiety attack that every contact with Chadrian provoked. Then, still with his back to the door, he opened the President's humidor and took out a cigar. It was Cuban like all the others. He was just about to light it when the President's voice pierced the silence.

"Need a light?"

Gordon spun around. What he saw made his heart skip a beat. The two most basic of human instincts, fight or flight, took over his brain, as their silent but equally powerful chemical partner, adrenaline, flooded his body. However, in this case, neither was an option. Fight would have brought swift and deadly retribution from the Secret Service, and flight was now no longer possible. Standing in the doorway between the private study and the Oval Office was President Alex Webster. And by the look on his face, he had heard every word. "Mr. President!" exclaimed Gordon.

"Tell me that wasn't what I think it was," said Webster.

"I can explain," Gordon started to say, but the President interrupted him.

"You can explain! Explain what? Murder?"

"I had nothing to do with those bombings. I swear."

The President was incredulous. "Oh, well, that makes everything all right then, doesn't it? The chief of staff of the President of the United States is involved in murder and conspiracy—but only by bullets not bombs. Are you out of your fucking mind?"

At first, Gordon stood there like a deer frozen in headlights. Then he did what was probably the only thing that he could have done to prevent the President from calling out to the Secret Service. He collapsed onto his hands and knees on the floor and started to weep. Not with little tears of shame or guilt, but giant sobbing tears that poured down onto the carpet and spread out across it like the evil that he had knowingly unleashed upon the land.

His reaction caught the President by surprise. "Maddun, get up."

But Gordon didn't, and as Webster watched in stunned disbelief, he began to crawl across the carpet on all fours toward the President like some pathetic animal that was in terror for its very life. For the first time in his life, President Alex Webster didn't know what to do. One shout of alarm would have brought a detail of heavily armed men bursting through the doors. And for the briefest instant, that was exactly what the President thought about doing. But then he heard one coherent expression being repeated over and over again among all the blubbering gibberish that was emanating from the beast on the floor. "I did it for you. I did it for you." Then in an act of outrageous contrition that would later be debated by historians and political pundits ad nauseum, as they reconstructed this extraordinary scene and speculated about what might have been, Gordon reached up, took the President's hand, and began to kiss it. Webster tried to pull it away, but Gordon held on tightly. "Please Alex, forgive me," sobbed Gordon. "Please. In the name of all that is good and Holy," he begged, invoking religion as most evil men do when caught.

"Let go!" exclaimed the President.

"Please, Alex. Please," groveled Gordon.

Repulsed by what was happening, the President swung his other hand down harshly and slapped Gordon hard across his cheek, momentarily stunning him and causing him to release the President's hand. Gordon fell back on his haunches and looked up in shock and disbelief. Slowly, he raised his hand to the welt that was rising on his cheek, and he began to whimper softly like a child. At that moment, the entire history of the nation reached a crucial fork in the road. One path led to doom for the few and deliverance for the many, while the other led to just the opposite. Tragically, for reasons that had their roots deep within a psyche scarred long ago by love withheld and praise not given, the President chose the latter. He would not turn in Gordon. Instead, he would cover up his murderous acts. And that, as Robert Frost once wrote, would make all the difference.

<u>56</u>

Watergate Hotel, Washington, D.C.

For all the cool and calm that Colonel Jake Kincaid had demonstrated time and again under fire, on the night of the bombings, he was a deeply conflicted man. When he first heard about the shootings at the White House, his body went completely numb. He momentarily forgot that someone else was filling in for Sarah McGill while she gave her report on the New Sons of Liberty. And now that person was dead. As soon as he realized that Sarah hadn't been there, he was filled with an overpowering anger, bordering on rage. That there were people who would do such cowardly acts was bad enough; that he could do nothing to stop them was quite another. He could deal with an enemy who faced him across a field of battle. But the evil that lurked in the shadows of secrecy and struck out at the innocent in the name of a cause was a plague upon the earth that deserved no mercy, and would get none from him.

During the hours immediately following the acts of terrorism, while the President and his staff were meeting in the White House, Sarah McGill was there as well, pushing and probing the press secretary as she gathered the facts, and recorded the video report that would be given on the network. Jake had also been busy as a result of the military being placed on the highest level of alert. They both had tried to reach each other by telcom without success, and by the time he arrived back at his father's apartment of the Watergate complex, he was worried and weary from a day of frustration and failure. During his stay in Washington, he had moved into the spare bedroom of his father's spacious penthouse suite. Living with his father wasn't an ideal situation, but given the temporary nature of his assignment in the capital and his soldier's pay, it was a comfortable and an economical choice.

The only thing waiting for him at the apartment was the bottle of non-alcoholic champagne that stood forlornly in a bucket of water. He had ordered it from the concierge to celebrate two things: McGill's story on the New Sons of Liberty and what he hoped would have been his success at the M1A3 readiness hearing. It was alcohol-free for obvious reasons, but it was the idea that counted. However, champagne or not, there would be no celebration that night. Her report had been pre-empted and despite his objections, General McWilliams had approved the M1A3 tank for full production. As he mulled over these frustrations, he knew they were minor in the context of the murders of over fifty innocent people that day. All this was going through his mind as he picked up the bottle and stared at the tiny droplets that slid down its sides and fell back into the icy water below. He placed it back in the bucket and then picked up the present that he had bought her. He wondered now whether it was an appropriate gift, but before he could decide, the doorbell rang. He put the present down, hurried over to the door, and opened it. Standing there, with big, sad eyes and a down turned mouth, was Sarah. For a long moment, the two of them just stared at each other.

Finally, McGill said softly, "My friend is dead." As she said it, a large tear welled up in the corner of one eye and rolled down across her cheek.

He nodded gently and said, "I know."

"Five of the wounded, including a precious little dark-eyed, Native American girl in Missoula, have died since the bombing."

Again, he nodded sympathetically.

With a deep sigh, she said, "Do you think anyone noticed?" She paused. "Do you think they even care?"

"I care, Sarah." Tenderly, he reached out and wrapped his arms around her, guided her inside, and shut the door.

AN HOUR LATER, Sarah and Jake sat silently at the dining table in the spacious L-shaped dining and living room of the apartment.

"This really isn't bad," she said, as she took another sip of the champagne.

"It sucks," he replied.

"Yes. I suppose it does," she replied with a smile. "What's that?"

He followed her gaze and saw that she was looking at the present. "It's a present."

"For who?"

"For you."

"May I have it?"

"Of course." He stood up, walked over, and got it for her. "It's kind of silly, actually."

"I'm sure it's wonderful," she said as she tore it open, making no attempt to save the paper or bow.

Kincaid smiled, because he hated people who opened presents as if that was the last piece of wrapping paper on earth. Inside the paper was a box, and despite her obvious delight at receiving a present, she wasn't quite prepared for what she found. It was an exact 1/32nd scale model of an M1A2 main battle tank, perfect in every detail. When he bought it, it had seemed like a good idea, but now that he saw it in McGill's hands, he suddenly felt foolish. He reached out as if to take it back from her. "You probably think this is dumb."

She yanked her hands back to keep the model out of his reach and said firmly, "I do not. I love it!" Then she pointed to the various parts on the tanks exterior. "There's the Commander's Hatch and his Independent Thermal Viewer. Here's the 7.62 mm Coaxial Machine Gun and there's the 120 mm Smooth Bore Cannon."

Kincaid was surprised and absolutely delighted. "You are too much."

"I am, aren't I?" she said with a gentle grin.

"Where did you learn all that?"

"On the Internet. Where else? Tanner showed me where to go. You'd be surprised how much information about our military hardware is out there in cyberspace for all the world to see."

His smile dimmed, "Yes. That's another matter entirely. But I'm truly impressed."

She stood up, stepped over to him, and kissed him on the cheek. "Thank-you."

McGill's PTC rang. She answered it. "Hello, Keene." She listened for a few moments and then looked at her watch. "He's on now? It's past prime time here on the east coast." She listened again and then said, "Okay, thanks," Then she added, "Yes, I'm fine. How is Ellie?" She listened and nodded silently. Then she added, "Tell her she's in my prayers." She hung up the telcom.

"Do you have to leave?"

"No," she replied, looking quickly around the room and seeing what she was looking for—his video monitor. She headed over to it "The Governor of Idaho is giving a news conference. May I?"

"Of course," he answered and the two of them sat down in front of the screen. McGill picked up the remote, turned it on, and quickly switched to GNBC. Immediately, the image of Governor Morrissey filled the screen. He was standing behind a podium at the state house, and off to one side stood Jesse Latrobe dressed in civilian clothes. Neither man was smiling.

"FOR THE RECORD, I want to state it again. Neither the Western Freedom Party nor the Wolf River Militia had anything to do with the tragic events of this day. We deplore these heinous acts, and we will cooperate fully with the Federal authorities in their efforts to apprehend those who are responsible."

The camera pulled back slightly to reveal a room full of reporters. Numerous hands shot up and the governor pointed at a tall woman near the front.

"Governor, isn't it true that each day for weeks now the militia has been dramatically growing in number and acquiring more sophisticated armaments?" asked the woman.

"The size of the militia and its military capabilities are irrelevant to why we are here tonight. General Latrobe and I simply wish to express our outrage at the murderous acts perpetrated against the Federal Government today, and to convey our most sincere condolences to the families of the victims."

The woman persisted, "Governor, now that you have mobilized the state's National Guard, do you intend to place them under the direct command of General Latrobe?"

"I have no plans to do so at this time," he responded in the usual calculating way of a master politician leaving the door wide open for him to do so later. "Now perhaps we can go back to the subject at hand, which are the reprehensible acts of terrorism that occurred in our sister states and on the front lawn of the White House."

Again, a sea of hands waved before him. He pointed at a man.

"Governor, you said these acts were taken against the Federal Government, and yet in Washington, it was only members of the media who were shot."

"I believe the target was the White House, and those unfortunate members of the media were simply at the wrong place at the wrong time," replied the governor.

"Then I take it that you believe this was done in protest against the President's handling of the Bitterroots Rod and Gun Club?" continued the man.

The governor nodded, "That is one possible explanation. I have made no secret of my opinion that the President made a grievous error when he ordered the Army to take that club." He looked out across the crowd, and pointed at an older woman with a grandmotherly look about her.

"Governor Morrissey, I would never presume to give someone of your political stature a lecture on civics. But the President's bill will not become the law of the land unless it is approved by the Congress and a majority of the state legislatures," she said with a gentle and respectful tone.

The governor smiled politely, "Yes, ma'am, that is true. And I intend to do everything within my power to see that the rights of the people are not trampled by well-meaning, but grossly misinformed politicians."

The woman nodded and then went for the kill. "Then, governor, I think my readers would be interested to know what you plan to do if the bill passes both Houses of Congress and is put to a vote in all state legislatures, including yours?"

Without batting an eye, the governor said, "Let's cross that bridge when we get to it, shall we?" He looked at the group and said, "I'll take one more question." The governor pointed to another reporter, a thin man with wiry red hair.

"Governor, why won't you hand over T. J. Kincaid to Federal authorities?"

The governor's eyes narrowed. "Because I believe Mr. Kincaid is no less a patriot and no more a traitor than is his father, the distinguished Speaker of the House, Jeremiah Kincaid. That is why I pardoned him. That the President chooses not to do likewise is both his prerogative and his blunder. However, the recent deaths of two FBI agents and their pilots, while trying to arrest Mr. Kincaid, is but a small taste of the risks the Federal Government is taking by trying to inflict its will upon the people of Idaho and the six other states who have publicly announced their support for my views."

The red-haired reporter pushed his luck, "That sounds like a threat against the President, sir."

The governor stared at the reporter for a moment without answering. The tension in the room was palpable. Off to the side, two State Police officers wearing black T-shirts under their shirts looked at Chief Swale, who was standing on the stage near the governor. He held them off with a subtle shake of his head.

"Be careful, sir. Be very careful," replied the governor.

The reporter instantly backed down, "Forgive me, Governor, I meant no offense."

The governor nodded and gave the reporter a smile. "Apology accepted. I understand how it might have appeared that way; however, I assure you that it was not my intent to threaten the President. I only stated the facts for his consideration before he takes any further action. It is no secret that a large and growing percentage of the American population is appalled by his plan to deny them their Constitutionally guaranteed rights. And it is my intention, as it is that of the Western Freedom Party, to do whatever we can within the limits of the law to stop this egregious assault on the Constitution. In the case of the bombings in Montana and Colorado, and the shooting at the White House, we cannot be held responsible for the irresponsible acts of others, including those of the President."

"Then you blame the President for what happened today?" asked the red-haired reporter, who seemed to his colleagues to be pushing for a Pulitzer or a beating by the Black Shirts, or both.

"It is not for me to apportion blame. The American people and our justice system can do that. However, I would suggest that if the President persists in his present course of action, then he and only he must be held accountable for the outcome."

An attractive young female reporter raised her hand. The governor acknowledged her with a nod.

"Governor, how is Mr. Kincaid?"

The governor's answer surprised everyone. "Why don't you ask him yourself?" With that, he looked over their heads to the back of the room. As the reporters turned and the television cameras spun around, there, standing in the shadows at the back was T.J. Kincaid, dressed in a dark suit, white

515

shirt, and pinpoint tie. He looked more like the corporate CEO that he had once been than the fugitive from Federal justice that he now was. He slowly walked up to the front with every eye and lens focused tightly upon him. When he reached the podium, the governor gave him a warm embrace. Kincaid's response was polite but noticeably restrained. He looked at the reporter who asked the question. "I am fine. Thank-you for asking," he said with a big smile. "How are you?"

The woman hesitated and then replied, "I'm well."

Many hands flew up, but Kincaid continued to look at the woman. "Did you have another question?"

Slightly flustered, she nodded and replied, "Yes, Mr. Kincaid—or should I call you Captain Thomas Porter?"

"You can call me anything you like," he replied, obviously flirting with her.

She blushed, and then regaining her composure, she asked, "What do you think of the tragic events at the White House and here in the West?"

His smile changed to a look of genuine concern and compassion. "First, my heart goes out to the loved ones of all those who were killed. Such acts of terror are devoid of any justification, and those who perpetrated them must, and I'm certain, will be brought to justice. Second, I want to reiterate what the governor said. I am confident that no one who is in any way associated with the Western Freedom Party or the Wolf River Militia had anything to do with these cowardly acts." He paused and looked directly into the cameras. "If I had any doubt whatsoever about that fact, I would not be standing here before you. Ever since the President illegally sent Federal troops up onto Mount Freedom, causing the deaths of so many fine young men, this nation has been spinning wildly out of control. Through President Webster's actions, and his alone, the country has become polarized; a black cloud of disharmony and distrust darkens our skies; ordinary citizens all across the land have been turned against their neighbors; and at this moment, we risk falling into a state of anarchy. The burden of saving our once great nation now rests squarely on the shoulders of men like Governor Morrissey, my father, and all men of good conscience, to calm the troubled waters and restore peace and tranquility. And with the help of the citizens of the West and people of good will who live throughout this great land, we will prevail, and America will survive."

When he finished, the governor stepped up to the microphone and said, "Thank-you, ladies and gentlemen. And may God bless America." As he stepped down off the stage, the governor leaned over and said a few words to Kincaid. Those who saw it assumed that he was thanking him. They were only partly right. His exact words were, "Nice job, son, but next time go a little easier on the national unity thing."

JAKE KINCAID muted the BTC and leaned back with a deep sigh. "Oh, T.J. What in the hell are you doing there?" His choice of words was more apt than he realized.

"Your brother certainly knows how to command an audience. Do you still think there is a chance for your father's compromise?" McGill asked.

"You tell me."

"What do you mean?"

"I mean you have a sixth sense."

She frowned. "Do we have to go there again tonight?"

"Sorry I brought it up." On more than one occasion, Sarah McGill had predicted things to him that later turned out to be true—things that she couldn't possibly have known at the time she had said it. And that wasn't the only thing she did that puzzled him. She often flipped books open to the exact page she wanted—big books—without even looking at them before she opened them. And wherever they went, street lights had a habit of burning out as she walked under them. It had happened more than once and much too often to be the simple coincidence that she claimed it to be. But as much as he knew that there was something different about her, something special, he also knew that it embarrassed her to speak about it. It also angered her when someone questioned it, as if it was something she could turn on and off like a light switch. And the one thing he didn't want to do was upset her that night. "No. I don't think there is any chance for my father's compromise."

"Why not?"

"For one reason, trying to explain the benefits of compromise to Morrissey is like trying to teach a 'live-and-let-live' policy to a tiger. And second, even if he had been once amenable to it, the bullets and bombs put an end to that today."

McGill nodded thoughtfully. She stared down at the tank model in her hands and then asked, "How thick is the armor on one of these?"

He smiled a knowing smile, "Very. But I don't ride in a tank, Sarah. I'm in an armored mobile command vehicle."

She looked up at him with sad eyes and asked hopefully, "Far behind the tanks?"

"Let's talk about something else."

"Yes, let's." She paused and then asked, "How about your brother?"

It was his turn to grimace. "Is this payback for me bringing up the sixth sense thing?"

"No," she said snuggling closer to him and gently caressing his cheek with her finger.

"What about him?"

"Do you think he'll ever come back into the family?"

"No."

"Why—because he's a fugitive?" she asked.

Kincaid shook his head no. "My father told me the President offered to pardon him if he would turn himself in. So for the time being at least, the President has called off the FBI hunt. But that won't change anything."

"Why not?"

"I don't know. Perhaps because the things that drove him away haven't changed. Regardless of the reason, T.J. told my mother he wasn't interested in the pardon." After he finished speaking, he just sat there staring at the video monitor. Then he raised the remote and flicked it off.

Slowly, McGill leaned into him. "Tell me what happened to your family, Jake."

"I can't."

"Talking about it might lessen the pain."

He fell silent for a long while and then, finally, he shook his head yes and began to talk. At first the words came slowly, but then they gathered momentum as he poured out the story about the night a family died. As he spoke, she closed her eyes and pictured the scene as if it were from a movie.

THE FARMHOUSE was decorated for Christmas, including the kitchen which was big and warm and inviting. Adjacent to the kitchen was an enormous great room with a roaring fire in a fieldstone fireplace. In between was an eating area, where the Kincaid family was gathered around a large harvest table. Jeremiah was sitting at the head of the table while Kathleen sat at the opposite end. Joanna and Jake were sitting to their father's right, while directly across from them sat T.J. The table was covered with the trappings of an American family Christmas, but the tone and manner was strained and distant.

"So, T.J., how is school going?" Jake asked.

"As if you care?" he replied.

"There's no need to get defensive. I wouldn't have asked if I didn't care."

A look of dismay spread across Kathleen's face, and she tried to intervene. "Have some sweet potato, T.J. It's your favorite."

"I dropped out, if you really want to know," T.J. replied, looking at his mother and shaking his head no.

"You did what?" said Jake. "How many schools does that make since West Point? Three or is it four?"

"I've lost count, but evidently you haven't."

"Let it go, boys," said Jeremiah, trying to head off the crisis that everyone knew was coming.

But Jake wouldn't or couldn't. "Why?" he asked.

"Maybe I'm just not as smart as you?"

"Oh please, T.J., modesty doesn't suit you. Your SAT's were higher than mine, and your grades were better. At least when you were still bothering to take exams."

"That's enough, boys," said Jeremiah firmly.

"Joanna, have you seen that quilt Mrs. Wilkensen made for us?" asked Kathleen, trying desperately to change the subject.

"Maybe I'm just not cut out for college," T.J. said, lowering his voice.

"How would you know? Have you ever actually attended a class?"

"Go to hell!"

"T.J. Please!" exclaimed Kathleen.

"That's enough!" said Jeremiah louder than before. But it was no use. The situation had reached critical mass, and all that was left at that point was for it to explode.

"I'm sorry, dad," said Jake. "I give up trying to be his brother."

"Funny. I can't remember a time when you ever were."

"Then your memory is even shorter than your attention span."

"T.J. Your brother has always been your biggest supporter," said Kathleen plaintively.

"Yeah. Just like Brutus was to Caesar."

"Spare us the melodrama, will you?" replied Jake. He stood up and threw his napkin on the table and headed into the great room.

T.J. jumped up and followed him, "What's the matter, Jake, does the truth hurt? You know, I don't know which is more pathetic, the fact that you were never a brother to me or that you think you were."

"Jeremiah," Kathleen pleaded, with tears gathering in her eyes. "Make them stop. Please!"

Jeremiah got up and walked over to the boys. "All right, that's enough out of both of you." He was trembling as he said it.

Joanna burst into tears, got up and ran out of the room.

Jake took a step toward T.J. and pointed his finger at him. "Before you lay any blame, go look in the mirror, you spoiled little brat."

"Get out of my face!"

"Or what?"

He pushed Jake back and they began to grapple. It only lasted a few seconds before their father stepped in and tried to separate them. "Stop it! When you're under my roof you will act like adults!"

But they ignored him and continued to shove each other back and forth. Seeing that they weren't listening to him, Jeremiah stepped between them. And then it happened—it wasn't clear who swung first. It didn't really matter. They both went to hit each other, hard. Jake's swing missed both his brother and his father, but T.J.'s didn't. Before he could stop himself, his fist landed a punishing blow on the side of his father's head. Instinctively, without thinking, Jeremiah swung the back of his hand hard and caught T.J. full force in the face, knocking him down onto the floor and momentarily stunning him. He lay there for a long, terrible moment, not moving, as blood began to gush out of his nose.

Kathleen screamed, "Oh no!"

Jeremiah gasped and bent down to help T.J. while Jake just stood there over them, not knowing what to do.

Kathleen ran over and knelt down beside T.J., trying to stop the blood that was by now pouring down across his face. But he regained his senses and pushed her away. He got up and stood there for a moment, as blood and tears mixed together on his cheeks, and cascaded down onto his sweater. Then without saying anything, he turned and walked down the hall and out the front door.

WHEN HE WAS FINISHED telling the story, Jake's body seemed to sag, as if in the recounting of it, the pain and suffering was even more acute than it had been when he actually lived through it. He looked so alone, so sad, and so vulnerable, that it made her heart ache. She was filled with conflicting emotions. Part of her wanted to mother him, to push back the darkness and protect him from the demons that roamed inside his soul; while another part of her wanted to hold him and make love to him. But before either of these urges could prevail, the matter was taken out of her hands because he drifted off into a deep and troubled sleep in her arms. For a moment she sat there holding him; then she carefully extricated herself and covered him with a quilt. She wrote him a note saying good night and explaining that she had an important interview in the morning, which was true; and that she had to go back to her apartment because she needed to get an early start, which was not true. As she drove home, all she could think about was that farmhouse and the two brothers who had so completely taken over her life—and the profound sadness that had taken over theirs.

June, 2018

G Day - 90

The Valley Of The Shadow

Yea, though I walk through the
valley of the shadow of death,
I will fear no evil.

Psalm 23

57

Camp David, Maryland

President Webster, wearing a navy blue fleece jacket with the Presidential Seal on the left breast, sat at the center of the large table in the conference room of the main building at the mountain retreat. With him were the members of the National Security Council. Outside, the warm sun bathed Camp David in its reassuring glow. However, inside the room, the talk was somber and provided a stark counterpoint to the promise of hope and new life that bloomed upon the gentle hills. Since the bombings, the President had spent every weekend away from Washington. He said the mountain air helped clear his head, but the real reason was that the Secret Service was still very uneasy about the possibility of additional attacks upon the White House, and the more that they could keep him away from there, the better they liked it.

Sitting to the President's right was Patrick Fitzgerald. It was a spot usually reserved for Maddun Gordon, but for some reason he sat on the other side of Fitzgerald that morning. To Gordon's left were Poland Snetzinger and Harlan Caruthers. Directly across from the President was Mary Lou Pritchard and beside her was Maurice Bouchard, the Secretary of Homeland Security. The President was in a foul mood, which was understandable given recent events, and there were few people around the table who had not felt his wrath that morning, with two exceptions being Pritchard and Bouchard. Everyone in the West Wing suspected why he was gentle with Pritchard and they were right, but few could figure out why the President never raised his voice to Bouchard. There were two reasons which the President kept to himself: the first was that he was in awe of Bouchard's overwhelming

525

intellect; and the second was, quite simply, that he liked the man. This latter fact was the reason that Gordon despised him, but it didn't bother Bouchard at all, which in turn made Gordon dislike him all the more.

Bouchard was originally from a small town in Northern Maine where his parents had immigrated from Quebec. By the time he was twenty-three, he had earned undergraduate degrees in both political science and economics from Princeton, and a law degree from Harvard. After graduation from law school, he went to Europe, where he earned a doctorate in international criminal law from the Sorbonne, and studied German and Russian to add to his native English and French. Maurice was truly a renaissance man in the giant economy package. Everyone, knew not to debate with him on any matter or they would face certain humiliation. Everyone, that is, except Maddun Gordon, who referred to him as Fatty the Frog, behind his back of course.

Like the President, everyone was dressed in business casual, which in Mary Lou's case included a loose cotton sweater over wool slacks. She thought it would hide her figure, but in fact the soft folds only served to make it even more alluring. Ever since that one night of lust in the West Wing, she and the President he had behaved strictly within the boundaries of propriety and professionalism, and even more so since her appointment as Attorney General had been approved by the Congress. She had insisted upon this or she said she would resign. He knew that she meant it, and he had reluctantly gone along with it. However, it was apparent from the way that he looked at her that the memory of that night would not leave him, and he couldn't stop trying to win her love or, at least, rekindle her desire.

At that moment the President was reading a report which he finished, and he looked up. "Explain it to me in layman's terms, Maurice."

"It is a chemical analysis of trace amounts of the residue from the bombs that were used at Fort Carson and in Missoula. It shows conclusively that it was Cepox, the same kind of extremely powerful, explosive agent that was used in the cast that young Mr. Kincaid wore at Walter Reed Hospital."

The President nodded and thought about the connection for a moment. Then he said, "That links the two incidents, but it doesn't tell me who was behind it."

"No, sir. But with the help of Interpol, we have uncovered the source of this new explosive," said Bouchard.

"Don't tell me. Another clandestine chemical plant has popped up somewhere in the Middle East," said Webster.

"No, sir." As Bouchard said it, the expression on Snetzinger's face was grave.

"Then where?" asked the President with knitted eyebrows.

"China," interjected Snetzinger. After he said it, the word hung in the silence of the room.

Webster didn't move at first, nor did his expression change, but the tone of his voice said it all. "China!"

"Yes, Mr. President. We now have irrefutable proof that this new explosive was developed by the Army of the People's Republic of China."

The President looked perplexed. "But surely, you're not going to tell me the Chinese were behind these bombings?"

"No, Mr. President. We are confident that the Chinese government had nothing to do with these incidents," said Snetzinger.

"What makes you believe that?" asked the President.

Snetzinger passed the question to Bouchard. "Because, sir, according to Springer White, our deep cover agents in Asia have reported to us that a large quantity of the compound was stolen last year from the top security facility where it was manufactured six hundred miles northeast of Beijing in a city called Harbin."

"You mean a not-so-top security facility?"

Bouchard nodded. "Yes, Mr. President. Those who stole the material apparently had help from the plant's director of chemical engineering. After the loss was discovered, he, along with his entire staff, were publicly executed when they reported for work the next morning."

"That'll ruin the rest of your day," snorted Gordon.

"Unfortunately, Mr. President, the Chinese government chose not to advise any foreign governments about the loss," added Snetzinger.

The President nodded thoughtfully. "How did it end up in those two flower delivery trucks?"

Bouchard looked over at the Attorney General. Despite the potential for inter-agency rivalry, he and Mary Lou got along very well, and as a result, so did their respective organizations. Pritchard pulled a photograph out of an envelope on the table in front of her. She handed it to the President. It had obviously been taken from a UAV at altitude, but it still showed a group of men standing at an outdoor shooting range. "One of our surveillance aircraft took this a few days ago." Then she handed the President an enlargement which focused more tightly on the two men at the center of the group. "The man on the right goes by several aliases, but Interpol knows him as Kahil Bin Aladir, a Saudi national with a dubious background but no criminal record. His government has disavowed him and canceled his passport, but his current whereabouts are unknown."

The President studied the dark-eyed man's face carefully. Then he looked at the other man who was wearing what appeared to be a military-issue sweater, the kind that British officers like to wear, even on hot days. "Who's the other man?"

"His name is Anthony Conlan Gardener Smythe, Mr. President," said Pritchard.

"He has two middle names?" asked the President.

"Yes, sir. That's not uncommon in the U.K.," added Bouchard.

"Why not? Their royalty put on names like jewelry," muttered Gordon.

Pritchard ignored him and continued, "He was a major in the British SAS and was decorated for bravery early in the First Gulf War. He suffered severe wounds and spent seven months in hospital. After recovering from his injuries, he received an honorable discharge from the service and then apparently joined the dark side. He now resides in an estate in Tysons Corner, Virginia, which is where that photograph was taken." Pritchard paused to catch her breath. It was apparent that what she was saying was alarming even for a seasoned criminal prosecutor. She continued, "Smythe has been on the FBI and the CIA's watch list for several years now. Although he is in this country legally—he has a green card—we believe that he is the kingpin of an enormous gun-running operation; but unfortunately, we have never been able to get any hard proof."

"Well, he certainly didn't get that estate from his British Army pension," said Gordon.

"No, that's obvious," she said, glancing at Gordon. She looked back at the President. "He derives his income primarily from a record and television production company that he started in London after retiring from the Army, and he also owns an airline and a fleet of cruise ships. But at least as far as we can tell, it is all legitimate. His tax returns are clean."

"I know that you must be heading somewhere with this saga, Mary Lou, so why don't you get to it," said Webster with an air of restrained impatience.

"Yes, sir. It has recently come to our attention that the major is linked to the New Sons of Liberty. According to our informants, he heads a militant wing of the group, and he was on the verge of breaking away from it over some serious disagreements that he had with the group's founder, Senator Harridan Niles."

As she said the group's name, she recaptured the President's full attention. "The late Senator Niles," said the President.

"Yes, sir. Evidently whatever issues had existed between Major Smythe and the NSOL cleared up after the senator's sudden death. A death originally determined to be of natural causes but which we are now reinvestigating based on this new information."

Bouchard fidgeted uncomfortably as Pritchard spoke, but no one took particular notice. It was not unusual for a big man to be uncomfortable in a chair designed for narrower bottoms.

The President thought about the matter for a few moments and then said, "So you think that the New Sons of Liberty were behind the recent attacks?" asked the President.

"That is one possibility we are investigating, Mr. President. At least as far as the bombings are concerned. We're still not sure about the shooting at the White House. It doesn't seem to fit."

"Of course we can't confirm any of this at present, Mr. President," added Bouchard.

The President nodded and continued probing. "You said that this explosive was the same one that was used in the cast that was found in the basement of Walter Reed?"

"Yes, sir. Exactly the same," said Pritchard. "And there's one more thing. Ballistics testing has confirmed that the gun used to kill the two Secret Service agents at the hospital shortly after the attack on you was the same one found on the body of the man who was killed near the Vietnam War Memorial later that day. His name was Heiki Suitola, a Finnish national who was on the Interpol's most wanted list. He had been linked to several assassinations of key government officials both in his own country and in several other European countries. And what's more, in another photograph taken several months ago by a UAV in northern Virginia, Major Smythe can be seen driving his Bentley convertible with the top down, and with him is Mr. Suitola."

At first the President didn't say anything. He didn't need to. Everyone in the room shuddered at the thought that the New Sons of Liberty, through their affiliation with the mysterious British major, had been behind the assassination attempt on the President. An attempt that would have succeeded but for a last-minute change of heart by the youngest son of the Speaker of the House. Up until now they had viewed the group as nothing more than an annoyance. Suddenly the stakes had changed. But what was even more unsettling was the thought that it might not be the NSOL. And if not, then who? Finally the President asked, "What do we do next?"

Bouchard looked at Pritchard, who answered. "We have obtained a search warrant for Major Smythe's estate, but before we execute it, we thought that you should be consulted. Not just because of the possible links to the incidents out west, but also because of the obvious implications for our relationships with Great Britain."

Snetzinger chimed in, "The major is a very high-profile British figure, Mr. President. He is extremely well-liked by the common people, and he has many well-placed friends in parliament and among the British upper class. He is also a third or fourth cousin to the royal family."

"So are half of England," snorted Gordon. "And the other half claim to be."

The President looked at Carruthers and Snetzinger and said, "Do you gentlemen share Mary Lou's hypothesis that Smythe is somehow involved in the bombings?"

"Yes, Mr. President. I do," said Snetzinger. Caruthers nodded his agreement.

"Patrick?"

"I think we have no choice but to search Smythe's estate, Mr. President," he replied.

Then, in what seemed almost an afterthought, the President looked over at his chief of staff and asked, "Maddun?"

"If you will excuse my French, Mr. President, screw the British upper class. If the son of a bitch was behind the bombings and the assassination attempt on you, I think we should give him a fair trial, and then hang the bastard." No one picked up that Gordon said bombings not killings, as his subconscious overpowered caution.

The President nodded and looked over at Pritchard. "Do it."

"Yes, Mr. President."

The President looked around the room and said, "Thank-you, gentlemen."

They all stood up, including Pritchard. She hadn't missed the President's use of the word gentlemen, but she didn't think anything of it. As she started to leave, the President looked at her and said, "Mary Lou. I'd like a word with you, please."

His comment froze her in her tracks. She glanced at Gordon, who had a disgusting grin on his face.

"Yes, of course, Mr. President," Pritchard replied hesitantly, as she sat back down.

The President smiled as he waited for the others to leave. Gordon was the last one out, and he pulled the door firmly closed behind him. Webster looked over at her in the way that he did to women he desired. "Mary Lou..."

"Please don't, Mr. President," she said, thinking he was going to talk about them and what they had done together.

Her comment apparently surprised him. "Don't what?" he asked rather brusquely.

The tone of his reply suddenly made her think that her assumption had been wrong and she flushed with embarrassment. "I'm sorry, Mr. President. I thought you were going to..."

"Going to talk about us?" he replied with a gentle smile that made him look more like a friend than a lover.

"Yes. I'm sorry. It was inappropriate of me to even think that."

At first he didn't respond. He just sat there with a soft smile on his handsome face. "No. You were right the first time, Mary Lou. That was exactly what I was going to talk about—us."

She got up and said, "I'm sorry, Mr. President. There is no us," and with that, she started for the door.

He sprang to his feet and glided over to her, intercepting her just as she reached the door. Gently but firmly, he reached out and prevented her from opening the door, turning her body to face his and pressing her against its hard wood surface. For an instant they stood there, unmoving, while inside each of them hormones raced around at the speed of their pounding hearts.

"Mary Lou. I'm in love with you."

She didn't believe him, because Alex Webster was a man who had never learned what the word really meant. "No, Mr. President. You're in love with the idea of being in love. There's a difference."

"Mary Lou. Please listen to me. This time it's different."

She brought her right hand up from her side and placed her forefinger over his lips. "Mr. President, please let me go." She stood there paralyzed with emotions, including fear, anger, and perhaps the most frightening of all, desire. Inside her tormented mind, one little voice kept screaming to submit to him. While another begged for her to leave. And for the briefest of moments, the former almost won.

He backed away and saved her the need to make any decision at all. He smiled and said softly, "You're right, Mary Lou. You should go." The look in his eyes was more that of a little boy who had been chastised by his mother rather than a lover whose advances had been rejected.

"Mr. President. I'm sorry, but…"

He held up his hand and shook his head.

She stopped. She knew he was right. There was nothing more to say. Instead, she nodded quietly. Then she turned her back to him, opened the door, and walked out the room. After she had gone, he stood there alone. The most powerful man on the face of the earth. A man who could have any one of the hundreds of stunningly beautiful women who decorate the boardrooms and ballrooms of power. But he no longer wanted them. Instead, he wanted a woman who didn't want him. And it filled him with an ache unlike any he had ever known.

<u>58</u>

River of No Return Wilderness, Idaho

The Idaho National Guard helicopter with Lieutenant Kelly Wright at the controls performed a perfect flair and settled onto the helipad in front of the Wolf River Club. As the whine of the twin turbines wound down, Kelly got out of the left side of the aircraft, opened the rear passenger door, and helped Sarah McGill out into the glaring sunlight of a high mountain summer day. Her cameraman and sound technician followed her out into the daylight.

"Thank-you, Lieutenant," said McGill, "for getting me here in one piece," she added with a smile. During the flight over the mountains, Kelly had talked Sarah through some of the rough air.

"You're welcome, Ms. McGill. It was the least I could do. And thank-you for the autograph. My parents are huge fans of yours, and they will be excited to know I flew you up here today," said Wright.

"Will you be flying us back to Boise later, Lieutenant?"

"No ma'am," she answered. "But I know the crew who will, and don't worry, they'll take equally good care of you."

McGill was obviously disappointed. "Thanks again, Lieutenant." With that, Sarah McGill and her crew headed across the helipad to where the governor's chief of staff stood waiting for them. By her expression and gait, it was clear that Sarah was excited to be there. When she had approached Keene Lange with her idea for this interview, he had been non-supportive, but she had worn him down. Convincing him of an interview with the Governor of Idaho had been a relatively easy sell given what was going on in the nation. Convincing him that she should be the one to do it had been much more difficult. But eventually, he agreed with her reasons, at least as much of them as she was willing to share.

Jake Kincaid had been another matter entirely, however. He didn't want her to go, and he made it very clear. However, their relationship, although still relatively new, was strong and trusting. Besides, he quickly learned what Lange had known for a long time, which was that once Sarah McGill made her mind up to do something, only God could stop her; and at least as far as this trip was concerned, the Supreme Being seemed to be preoccupied elsewhere. So Jake had dutifully accompanied Sarah to Reagan airport and wished her well. The primary purpose of her trip was to interview Governor Morrissey. However, although neither of them raised the subject, both knew that there was a possibility of her seeing T.J. as well. Sarah was relieved that Jake hadn't mentioned it, because as hard as she tried to think of T.J. strictly in the context of his relationship to the pro-gun cause, there was more to it than that. Something that she would not and could not admit, even to herself. Something that drew her closer to him, even as she fought to keep him away. As she walked toward the governor's chief of staff, she couldn't get Jake's little brother out of her mind. And the fact that he might be nearby sent shivers through her body and made it almost impossible to keep her mind focused on why she had come in the first place.

"Did you have a nice trip, Ms. McGill?" the governor's chief of staff said, warmly extending his hand.

"The flight from D.C. to Boise was excellent, but I'm afraid the helicopter ride was a bit tense," she replied.

He smiled. "Flying over the mountains in the late spring can be a little rough. There is a lot of clear air turbulence at this time of year."

"Now you tell me," she said, flashing one of her prettiest smiles. "But the crew was wonderful, especially the co-pilot."

"Yes, Lieutenant Wright is one of the governor's favorites. In fact I think he's recommended that she be promoted to Captain."

The thought pleased Sarah. "Great. I like to see good people succeed."

"I could say the same thing about you, Ms. McGill," said the chief of staff. His compliment rang a little hollow, and McGill's crew picked it up, smirking at each other. Sarah also noticed, but she was too polite to let on. He continued, "Please, follow me, and I'll show you where you can set up your camera. The governor is in a meeting upstairs in the club, but he will be with you shortly."

As they walked along the pathway bordered by a profusion of bright wild flowers that led up to the large log building, McGill couldn't help but feel invigorated by the sights and smells around her. She loved the Rocky Mountains in the awestruck way that flatlanders often did. "God, this is beautiful country," she exclaimed to no one in particular.

"Yes, it is," said the chief of staff as they reached the large covered verandah.

Just before McGill stepped up onto it, she paused and looked over her shoulder at one mountain in particular that stood out from all the others around it. "What mountain is that?" she asked, obviously impressed by its sweeping lower reaches covered in dense, dark greenery; its jagged shoulders of granite; and its magnificent purple peak still covered in snow.

"The Lewis and Clark expedition named it Mount Freedom in honor of President Jefferson and his role in the Revolution, but I prefer its Indian name, or I suppose I should say, its Native American name. It's a name that very few people outside the Nez Perce tribe know. They call it the Kingdom of the Wind Spirit, due to the steady winds that constantly swirl around its peak and pour down onto the wild river down there at its base."

She immediately recognized the name and the place. "Oh yes, of course," she said with a trace of sadness. She knew it well. It had been on the side of that mountain that she had first met T.J. Kincaid, or Thomas Porter, as he was known at the time—Captain Thomas Porter of the Wolf River Militia.

"Have you been on Mount Freedom before?" he asked.

McGill nodded. "Yes. Twice last year."

"Oh, that's right. You interviewed Captain Porter at the Bitterroot Rod & Gun Club."

"Yes. And then I came back with the President. But I bet even President Jefferson would agree that the Kingdom of the Wind Spirit is a more appropriate name." She stood there staring up at it for another few moments with a faraway look in her eyes.

Her cameraman cleared his throat, "We need to get set up, Sarah."

That brought her back down to the valley floor. "Sorry about that. I'm afraid I just got caught up in the beauty of the mountain."

The chief of staff smiled patiently and said, "Perhaps someday you might come back here and climb it again, under less tense circumstances."

Without taking her eyes off it, she nodded. "Yes, I will climb that mountain again." Throughout her life, there were things that she just knew would happen to her. And these feelings had started at a very early age. After her mother left them, she knew that she would lose her father before his time. And she had. She knew she would go to the University of Michigan at Ann Arbor and graduate at the top of her class. And she did. She knew she would be a successful journalist, and one day cover the White House. And she was. Now, as she stood there staring up at the most beautiful landscape that she had ever seen in her life, she knew that the Kingdom of the Wind Spirit would forever be a part of her life. And it would.

Her words and the assuredness in her voice startled the chief of staff. But before he could comment, Sarah turned away from the mountain and walked through the door to the club. As her cameraman passed by him, he winked at the chief of staff and said, "If Sarah McGill says she will do something, it's as good as done. Trust me."

McGILL AND THE GOVERNOR sat facing each other in the great room of the Wolf River Club. It was obvious that the governor had already fallen under Sarah's spell. "I want to formally welcome you back to our beautiful state, Ms. McGill. I hope that you enjoy your visit."

"Thank-you, Governor. I'm sure I will. Judging by our surroundings here today, I think Idaho is as close to heaven as I have seen anywhere in America."

He smiled. "I obviously agree. But as delighted as I am to have you here, Ms. McGill, one thing does puzzle me."

"What is that, Governor?"

"Unless you have just joined the National Geographic Channel, I don't understand the reason for your trip. You are the Chief White House correspondent for your network, and I'm not sure what the White House and Idaho have in common. In fact, most would say that we have very little in common," he added with a wry smile.

"Governor, the President of the United States is my beat, and right now, nothing figures more prominently in the President's world than you."

Her candor caught him off guard. He smiled politely and then said softly, "Well said. Okay, Ms. McGill, what would you like to know?"

McGill then spent the better part of thirty minutes patiently but persistently probing the governor's attitude toward guns; his views on the rights of gun owners; the history of gun ownership in America, on which he was quite an expert; statistics on gun-related violence; and the Western

Freedom Party's platform. She had carefully avoided any sensitive questions until she had softened him with her charm, and finally, she felt that he was ready for a few tougher questions.

"Governor, now I'd like to address the subject of the President's proposed legislation directly."

"Shoot," he said with a sly smile.

She ignored the obvious pun. "Would you be willing to reopen talks with the White House regarding a possible compromise bill?"

"If you are referring to the amendments to the President's bill proposed by Speaker Kincaid, my answer is a conditional yes."

"And what would the conditions be?"

"I would do so on condition that the President agrees to delay the vote on the House floor."

"For how long?"

"At least until the furor over last week's tragic incidents die down."

"Is that because you feel they may have swung public opinion in favor of the bill?"

The governor realized that he had set himself up, but it was too late to avoid it gracefully. "Yes."

"But doesn't that make it all the more likely, then, that the President will press for closure as soon as possible?"

The governor stiffened and sat up straighter in his chair. "Ms. McGill, I represent literally millions of Americans who will not tolerate the abrogation of a right that was guaranteed by the Constitution. I am not going to insult your intelligence by repeating all the same old rhetoric. Suffice to say that if the President chooses to proceed with his bill, then the Western Freedom Party will be forced to reconsider its options."

It was McGill's turn to sit up straighter in her chair. Unless she was dreaming, which the lingering helicopter-induced nausea in her stomach told her she was not, the Governor of the State of Idaho had just delivered a veiled threat to the President of the United States of America. "What options might those be, Governor?"

"Our actions will hinge on those of the President, Ms. McGill, and it will serve no purpose to hypothesize what they might be. Let's just say that we are keeping all options open."

"Is one of them secession?"

A sly smile crossed his lips. "You said it, not I."

"Is it not true, Governor, that Ms. Sheila Landsdowne, the Chief Justice of the State Supreme Court is opposed to your strident position and that, as we speak, she is diligently gathering support among the state's legislators to impeach you?"

The governor's jaw muscles tensed. McGill noticed it and realized she had touched a nerve. One reason Sarah McGill was such an successful interviewer was that she could ask tough questions without making the interviewee feel like she was doing it to aggrandize herself. Of course it didn't hurt that she possessed what one envious competitor described as a pure and unassuming beauty with a magnetic smile and an outrageous figure.

"I have the highest respect for Ms. Landsdowne. She has the same right to free expression that we all do under the Constitution. Other than that, I have no comment."

"But then you don't deny it?"

"I think I have already said too much, Ms. McGill." Turning on the charm, he added, "Do you have this same effect on everyone you interview?"

With a smile that could melt blue ice, she replied, "What effect, Governor?"

They both shared a tension-relieving chuckle. But McGill was not through with the governor yet. "Governor, does the Western Freedom Party have any ties to the New Sons of Liberty?"

Morrissey remained calm and cool despite the fact that off-camera, his chief of staff was becoming highly agitated. "The answer to your question is an unequivocal no. Other than sharing the same deep-seated concerns with the President's attempt to deny law abiding citizens their rights, we have no connection with the New Sons of Liberty organization."

"Have you ever met with any of their members?" she persisted.

"Not that I am aware of. In fact, as I understand it, few if any of them have actually met with each other. Apparently the NSOL exists primarily via the auspices of an extranet. In effect, I guess you would have to call them a 'virtual group,' which I find rather bizarre. But then again, I am from another generation where you stood side-by-side, with your brothers-in-arms, facing your common enemy. Not as disembodied digital pen pals sending nastygrams over cyberspace." As he finished speaking, he flashed a look at his chief of staff.

McGill saw it too, and she knew that the interview was coming to an end. She decided to go for one more big one. "Governor, I know that you are pressed for time, but I wonder if I might ask you one final question?"

"You mean in addition to that one?" he smiled.

"Yes," she replied.

"Fire away," he said, with a twinkle in his eye.

For the second time, she chose to ignore the pun, but his slightly impudent cowboy charm did make her smile. "I wonder if you would tell my viewers exactly what role T.J.—," she caught herself, "I mean, Mr. Kincaid plays within your administration?"

The governor paused for a moment and then said, "Thomas Porter is a charter member of the Western Freedom Party and a trusted adviser to my office. He is also a close personal friend whom I view as a son. And while I obviously cannot condone the methods by which he chose to demonstrate his opposition to gun control, his intellect and wise counsel is of great value to me—far greater value, I might add, than the name he was born with."

She was delighted that he added the last sentence, and she closed in on the subject that many people had at the back of their minds. "Do you foresee the possibility of Mr. Kincaid—I'm sorry—Mr. Porter acting as an intermediary between your administration and the Congress over this matter?" Taking her cue from the governor, she switched to Kincaid's alias despite the fact that it bothered her. Aliases were usually reserved for criminals, and she just couldn't think of him in that way.

He smiled patiently. "Is this your final, final question?"

"Yes," she replied with a soft and irresistible smile.

"President Lincoln abolished slavery in 1863, and Thomas is free to do whatever he chooses." He looked over at his chief of staff, who discreetly pointed at his wristwatch. "Now, Ms. McGill, as much as it disappoints me to say so, I'm afraid our time together is up."

"Thank-you, Governor. You have been most generous with your time." She turned and spoke her few brief closing remarks into the camera, after which her cameraman flicked off the camera. With it off, McGill looked back at the governor as the tiny microphone was being extricated from his shirt and asked "Do you think it would be possible to meet with Mr. Porter before we return to Washington?" she asked, with a hint of excitement in her voice that even the governor noticed.

The governor looked over at his chief of staff, who nodded, then back at McGill and said, "Yes. That might be arranged."

"Is he in Boise?"

"No, Ms. McGill," replied Morrissey with a bemused smile. "My staff and I had a meeting here at the club just before you arrived. It's my office away from the office, if you know what I mean. And Thomas is here at the club. Right now, I think he's upstairs."

McGill's heart skipped a beat. *Oh my God,* she thought. *He's here.* Ever since she had seen Kincaid disappear into the crowd at Dulles International Airport, he had been there, lingering at the back of her mind. She tried to refocus her thoughts on the journalistic reasons why she should see him, including the degree of his involvement with the pro-gun, anti-Washington movement. Given his wealth, charm, power, and his notoriety among the population, it was completely understandable that she would want to interview him. But there was another reason, far less obvious. Despite the sincere feelings of affection that she now had for Jake Kincaid, something inside her told her she cared even more deeply for his younger brother, and, as much as she tried to deny it, the feeling would not go away. The truth was that Sarah McGill was in love with two men, which was made all the more difficult by them being brothers. This had created an enormous cognitive dissonance within her, but as she wrestled with this inner turmoil, she was determined not to let it get in the way of her job. Steadying herself, she asked, "Do you think he would be willing to meet with me right now?"

"Yes, but not on the record. Those are my conditions, not his, by the way. However, with that caveat, I would be glad to ask him to meet with you. Do you agree to my terms?"

"Yes, Governor," she replied, with obvious disappointment in her voice. An off-the-record interview would be of little or no use to her story. But it was certainly better than nothing. And besides, there was still the other reason that she wanted to see him.

"Good. Wait here, and I'll have my chief of staff go upstairs and get him." His assistant left, and the governor stood up and stepped over to shake McGill's hand. "As you prepare your report, I hope that you will present our views in a balanced light."

"Yes, Governor. I will."

He already knew that she would, or her request for an interview wouldn't have been granted in the first place, and she knew it, too. But they went through the motions of political correctness, anyway. "Excellent," he shook her hand warmly. Then his chief of staff returned and said, "Ms. McGill. Mr. Porter will meet with you—alone. But I'm afraid that we must keep it brief, because your helicopter will be returning here in fifteen minutes, and it's on a very tight schedule today."

He didn't say why and she didn't ask. Instead, she nodded and turned to her crew. "Give me a few minutes, guys."

"No problem, Sarah, we'll wait for you in the bar." They had been told by Kelly Wright that the club's bar was the most well-stocked in the state, and they were not disappointed at the prospect of having to kill some time drinking fine old scotch on the tab of the people of Idaho.

McGill followed the governor and his top aide out of the room. In the back of her mind, she assumed that the helicopter was busy ferrying people up to the club, but who? she wondered, and why?

The governor's chief of staff took her back outside onto the broad verandah that smelled of cedar and pine, where he motioned for her to sit down in one of the sturdy old wooden rockers. She did so and soon found herself staring up at the Kingdom of the Wind Spirit once again. A feathery stream of white cirrus clouds hung above its jagged peak, frozen against the stark blue sky, like the ghostly tail of some gigantic bird of paradise. Just below the peak, a bib of snow with a sawtooth fringe lay draped across the granite ridges and crags, impervious to the pull of gravity that otherwise ruled the precipices and sheer walled canyons of solid stone and slippery shale. Still further down the mountainside, below the layer of cumulus clouds that sat like yesterday's porridge upon the belly of the mountain beast, a carpet of green and brown corduroy lay bunched up against the valley floor. Entranced by this profusion of natural beauty, Sarah didn't hear Kincaid coming until his voice greeted her ears with familiar words from a poem she had once learned, and loved, but left behind long ago.

> *She walks in beauty, like the night*
> *Of cloudless climes and starry skies;*
> *And all that's best of dark and bright*
> *Meet in her aspect and her eyes.*

She turned her head quickly, and their eyes locked. She felt a quickening in her soul, and blood rushed to her cheeks. Suddenly the normally loquacious young woman was completely tongue-tied.

"I doubt Byron was thinking of a mountain when he wrote those words, but they apply, don't you think?" T.J. said, with a flirtatious smile.

Her voice returned. "Yes. They certainly do," she replied, standing up to greet him. *He's even more handsome than I remembered,* she thought. Then a little voice deep inside whispered to her, *Just like his brother.* But his brother wasn't there, and he was. She walked over and extended her hand. "Hello, T.J."

He took her hand and squeezed it gently. "Hello, Sarah. It's good to see you again." Before she could reply, he leaned forward and kissed her on the cheek, catching her off guard. The touch of his lips sent an electric shock through her body, and for an instant, she stood there with her eyes closed and her heart pounding, like a schoolgirl kissed by a movie star. He stepped back and gallantly gave her a moment to recover.

"What was that for?" she asked.

"Does a man need a reason to kiss a beautiful woman?" he replied with an amused grin.

"No. Of course not. But I thought we were talking about the mountain?"

"I'll get back to the mountain in a moment, but actually, that kiss was for not turning our little limo ride into a national tabloid feeding frenzy."

"In that case, you're welcome."

"Now, with respect to that beautiful mountain over there, did you know that the Nez Perce tribe believes that it's magic? That it possesses special powers, which, in turn, it grants to those in whom the Great Spirit finds favor."

She looked back up at it and nodded. "Yes. So you told me last September when we first met. I can see why."

He smiled and extended his arm. "Why don't we take a walk?"

She took it and soon they were strolling along a path that wound its way across a field of wild flowers and down through the shadows of the tall pines toward the river. "On most days the wind pouring off the mountain turns the river's surface into a white chop, but as you can see, today it is quiet and well-behaved. Apparently it's on its best behavior for you," he said with a smile. As they walked down the trail toward the river, a cool breeze caressed her, and she shivered.

He noticed and took off his leather bomber jacket, wrapping it around her. "Gives you goose bumps, doesn't it?"

"Yes. Yes, it does," she said, pulling it tightly around her, not solely for its warmth. They came to the river bank where the trail paralleled the fast flowing water. He guided her along it to a rough-hewn wooden bench facing the river and the mountain beyond, and they sat down together.

She gazed at the magnificent vista before them. "It's so beautiful. Just like…"

He finished her sentence. "The doorstep to paradise."

"Yes, exactly," she said, turning and looking deeply into his eyes. For a moment their eyes locked. Then she turned away and drew in a deep breath of the clean, cool mountain air and gazed out on the incredible panorama that lay before them. Across the river was a rolling green field covered with bright yellow flowers. As the sun shone down warmly upon her face, she couldn't remember a time in her life when she ever felt more comfortable, more at ease with the world, and more at home. "I feel like John Denver must have felt when he wrote about coming home to a place that he'd never been before."

"The Rockies will do that to you."

"I wish I never had to leave," she said, with melancholy in her voice.

"Then don't."

She looked at him. "I have to."

"No, Sarah, you don't. You control your destiny."

She sighed. "I suppose you're right, but then again, the things in my life that have affected me the most are those over which I have had no control."

"Like being kidnapped?" he asked with a teasing smile.

She laughed in her charming little way and gave him a look that was anything but that of a kidnap victim. "It was hardly that."

His smile faded, and he looked up toward the mountain. "The FBI doesn't agree with you."

She paused before answering, studying him closely, seeking to know him better. "For what it's worth, I didn't press charges, but they didn't care."

"What's one more felony charge to someone who's on the ten most-wanted list?"

"I'm sorry for whatever part I played in that."

"You have nothing to apologize for, Sarah. You handled yourself with class, and I truly admire you for it."

"Thank-you."

"You're welcome," he said, peering so intently into her eyes that it was as if he was trying to get inside her heart, while she tried desperately to find a way to let him. There was an awkward silence as they sat there staring at each other. Then without taking his eyes off her, he asked, "What if I were to kidnap you again and take you up on that magic mountain, where we could live happily ever after?"

She smiled sadly, "Many a true word is spoken in jest."

"Ah, yes. One of my favorite proverbs, and one that I am often guilty of."

"Is that all it was?"

"It's whatever you wish it to be."

She blushed and looked away. "You're making this very difficult."

"Good. I'm working on that lack of control thing." His cheeky flirting and irresistible charm were at once both reassuring and unsettling. However, as uncomfortable as she felt, it was T.J. who was more affected by her presence that she his. He knew that Sarah and his brother were an item on the Washington scene. But that didn't stop him from feeling the way he did. If anything, it made her even more attractive to him, and he refused to listen to the tiny voice inside that questioned his motives.

"As much as I appreciate the offer to run away with you, I think that I had better get back to why I asked for this meeting."

"If we must," he said, giving an over-the-top sigh.

"I have two reasons, one professional and one personal."

"How intriguing. Let's start with the second one and forget about the first altogether."

She laughed. "No."

"Very well, then. Press on."

"The governor insisted that this be off the record."

"To hell with the governor. Ask me anything. On the record. Off the record. From your mind or your heart."

She laughed a nervous little laugh. "All right. Tell me how it was that you became involved in the militia and the pro-gun movement. It's not exactly a role that I would have expected from a CEO of a multi-billion dollar company."

For a moment he didn't say anything. Then he looked out across the river and began to speak, slowly and with passion. "You use the word militia like it's evil. I can assure you that the boys that I led to their deaths on that mountain over there were anything but evil."

"I'm sorry. I didn't mean it that way."

"It's all right. Perhaps some militia groups deserve that label, at least in the past, but not mine. They were simply impetuous young men with wild spirits and untamed hearts. Men like the native warriors who once roamed that mountain, and who gave it its name. Men to whom freedom is life, and life is freedom. Pure and uncomplicated, without all the baggage and bullshit that politicians have attached to the word." He paused and looked back at her. "That's why I led those men up that mountain. That's why I support what Governor Morrissey is trying to do. And I'd do it again in a heartbeat. Except..."

"Except what?"

"Except this time—I wouldn't come back."

It was a powerful statement. One that would have smacked of false bravado and cheap showmanship, if spoken by another man. But not this man. She could tell he meant it, and it filled her with sadness. She hesitated before asking the next question, but her reporter instincts made her ask it. "Then you don't believe banning guns will reduce deaths by gunfire?"

"The way that prohibition eliminated drinking?"

She nodded thoughtfully. "Point taken, but aren't the consequences for society in this case far more deadly?"

"Are drunk drivers any less deadly than criminals with a gun?"

She shook her head no. "Then what would you propose?"

"Congress should provide more funding to put more police officers on the streets to enforce the laws that already exist. They should allow the courts to administer those laws, without interference from hypocrites, left-wing lawyers, and other sunshine liberals—people who care more about the rights of criminals than those of the victim, that is, until they find themselves alone on some dark street, listening to footsteps behind them and cursing the police for not being there."

"I understand."

He nodded patiently. "You understand, but you don't agree?"

She smiled and dodged the question gracefully. "Whether I agree or not is irrelevant."

He paused and then asked, "Let me take this from the global to the personal. Do you think that taking away my gun, right here in Idaho, would have prevented that man with a gun from trying to rape you beside the Supreme Court or the other one who wanted to shoot you in front of the White House?"

The memory of both incidents flashed through her mind, accompanied by the fleeting image of the giant white horse and its dark rider. "I don't know."

"I think you do, Sarah. You know in your heart that it wouldn't have changed anything. Taking away my gun, or those of any other law-abiding gun owners, would not have prevented either of those occurrences, because in both cases the weapons they carried were brought into this country illegally, and they were sold illegally and used illegally."

"How do you know that?"

"Because I make it my business to know these things. It's one of the privileges of money and the power it brings. The law that President Webster intends to impose on America would not have stopped either of those guns from appearing on the street, nor either of those men from trying to kill you and being killed in the process. Laws don't stop criminals from having guns. Laws won't stop them from killing people with them. If they did, our death rows would be empty, and the death chambers would be broom closets."

She could see why he had been able to hold the nation captive for two months. And why the President had acted so harshly to get the cameras off him.

He continued, "We don't need more laws that restrict the rights of good and decent people. We simply need to enforce the ones we already have. We need to stop pandering to criminals and the civil libertarians, who force their continued presence upon us. We need to walk toward the light of freedom, not hide in the darkness of fear. We need to accept the fact that some people are evil and focus our energies on getting rid of *them*, and not the guns they carry. Because they got them illegally in the first place, and making weapons illegal won't change that reality, no matter what the liberals would have you believe."

He spoke with such passion that she could not help but be swayed. "You missed your calling, T.J. You should have been a politician."

546

"God forbid."

"Or a preacher," she said, with a twinkle in her eyes.

"God really would forbid that one," he laughed.

"Or perhaps a writer," she laughed, keeping it rolling.

"Nope. Too lonely. And too hard."

"What, then?"

"How about a television journalist? You get to ask all the questions, and you never have to give any answers."

"Perfect. Then you could be the one doing this interview."

His smile faded and a light went out somewhere behind his eyes. "Is that all this is?"

It was at that moment she realized he really didn't want a political platform. He just wanted someone to listen to him. Someone to laugh with and cry with. Someone to be his friend. "I'm sorry, T.J. No, it's more than that. Much more."

His smile returned but with less intensity than before. "Now, let's get to the good part, shall we? What was your personal reason for coming?"

She sensed that she had hurt him, and set about righting the wrong, no matter that it had been a small hurt and quite unintended. She took a deep breath, sat up a little straighter, and said, "It was to tell you that your brother loves you. And that he misses you—more than he even realizes himself."

He looked away, out across the river. "Did he tell you to say that?"

Her plan to make amends was off to a bad start. "No. It was my idea, but I know that's how he feels."

For a long moment, he sat there staring toward the mountain. Without looking back at her, he asked, "How is he doing?"

"Physically, he's fine. Psychologically and emotionally, he's having a hard time with life," she said.

Her candor surprised him, but it also seemed to bring him back from the river. He looked into her eyes and said, "It goes with the territory."

"You mean being a soldier?"

"No. Being Jeremiah Kincaid's son." There was a hint of melancholy in the way he said it—a yearning for what might have been.

She didn't reply. She knew that there was nothing she could say that would help. It was clear that both Jake and T.J. carried with them the burden that often accompanies being the sons of a great man. And it was a heavy burden, indeed. One that crushed some men and made others rise to greatness, or spend their entire lives trying to.

They sat there quietly for a few more moments until he broke the silence. "So tell me, Sarah McGill. Are you in love with my brother?"

The question caught her off guard, and she answered it clumsily, "I—I don't know. I'm not sure I can answer that."

"You just did," he said with a penetrating stare.

She looked away, embarrassed.

"But he loves you, doesn't he?"

She sighed, hating herself for being so transparent. "Yes. I think so."

"Good. Life without love is lonely, Sarah. Believe me, I know."

She looked back at him. "T.J., why won't you reconcile with your family? They miss you more than you can possibly know."

He didn't answer her for a long time. Finally, just when she was beginning to feel that she had gone too far, he said, "Perhaps someday. When this is all over."

"Why not now?"

His expression turned serious, "Sarah, if the President's bill passes, Idaho will secede from the Union, and at least six other states will follow. You know what that will mean."

She nodded. "War."

"Yes. A civil war in which my brother and I will be on opposite sides."

His words sent a cold shiver through her. "That's so sad, T.J., so very sad."

"War is always sad, Sarah. At least for the survivors. The dead don't seem to care too much; perhaps that's why there are so many of them."

She sat there not knowing what to say, staring at the river and the mountain beyond. Then she asked softly, "Are you afraid of dying, T.J.?"

"Yes, of course I am. Anyone who says he isn't is either a liar or a fool."

He shifted in his seat and as he did, the collar of his shirt fell open, revealing the small metal amulet in the shape of an eagle with its wings outspread hanging around his neck.

It caught her eye immediately. "What's that?"

He unclasped it and handed it to her. "It's an Nez Perce charm. I found it in a cave up on that mountain. It's over a hundred years old, and it's supposed to possess special powers."

"How do you know?"

"I met a man who knew. He's a Nez Perce chief."

She held it carefully and seemed to draw strength from it. "There's something very special about it," she said. "I can feel it." She handed it back to him.

"So he said." He carefully put it on and placed it back inside his shirt. Her eyes followed it all the way. "What about you?"

"What about me?" she asked.

"Are you afraid of dying?"

She nodded. "Yes. When I was a little girl, my father taught me to say 'Angels Nine' whenever I was frightened. He said that there are nine orders of angels in Heaven, and when I said that, it would be like calling out the cavalry. They would all come to save me."

"Did it work?"

She looked up at him with a warm smile. "I don't know if the angels came, but my father always did."

T.J. smiled and said gently, "Who do you think brought him?"

There was so much more that she wanted to say to him, but just then, a helicopter raced across the river toward them, swooped down, and landed noisily a hundred yards back up the hill, disturbing a terror of ravens that were sitting in the tall pines nearby. They exploded into the air and flew directly over T.J. and Sarah.

She watched them go. "Those are big crows."

"They're not crows. They're ravens."

"So that's what they look like."

"Yes. Why?"

"It's nothing. Just something a friend of mine once told me."

"About ravens?"

"Yes, and eagles."

He nodded. "Eternal enemies."

She nodded sadly and looked down at her watch. "I guess I'd better go or I'll miss my helicopter ride back to Boise."

He nodded, and they both stood up.

"You don't want to do that. It's a long bumpy ride by car, complete with a few roadside cliffs that drop straight down for a thousand feet."

They started up the path, but just before they reached the club, he stopped abruptly. He looked into her eyes, deeply, longingly, as if probing her soul. "My brother is a good man, Sarah."

It was not what she had expected. She was disappointed and angry at herself for being so. "Yes. He is."

"Will you tell him that I miss him?"

She smiled. "Of course! He'll be glad that you said that."

"And tell my father…" he started to say, but then he caught himself.

"Yes?"

The roar of the helicopter's engines grew louder. She could also see the governor's chief of staff beckoning to them as her camera crew climbed into the aircraft.

"Nothing. You'd better go."

She stood there for a moment looking up at him, and then she rose up on her toes and softly kissed him on the cheek. "Goodbye, T.J. Please take care of yourself."

"Goodbye, Sarah."

She started to walk away but stopped. For a moment she just stood there with her back to him. Then she spun around and walked back to him purposefully. "No. This is stupid," she said out loud as she reached him. She looked him directly in the eyes and said, "T.J., come back to Washington with me. Now. Don't think about it, don't get your bag, don't talk to the governor. Just come with me. Please."

"No."

"Why not?"

"Because I can't."

"Yes, you can. The President is willing to grant you a pardon. Your father told me so."

He stared at her for a long moment and then he said, "It's too late, Sarah."

The shouting of the chief of staff could be heard over the whine of the turbines, and the backwash of the rotors blew Sarah's hair into her eyes. She brushed it away and pleaded, "No. It's not. Not as long as you are alive. Come back with me, T.J., and make a new start."

"No, Sarah."

"Why not? she pleaded. "Everybody loves you, T.J."

"I don't!" he shouted.

"What?" she asked with a startled look. "Why?"

"Because, Sarah, I'm a loser. I've been one all my life." He paused and added, "And I hate losers."

Her delicate eyebrows knitted in disbelief. "Oh, T.J. How can you say that? You are one of the richest men in the world. You built a multi-billion dollar corporation from nothing. You have worked with hourly workers and CEOs, and were respected and admired by both. You held a nation's attention for two months with your wit and charm and bravery, while you and a band of boys paralyzed the mightiest government on earth. And now you have the ear of one of the most influential political leaders of our time." She paused and brushed the hair out of her eyes again. She knew the governor's chief of staff was becoming annoyed, but she also knew that he wouldn't dare say anything to T.J. "I don't know what dictionary you've been reading lately, but in mine, you wouldn't come close to meeting the definition of a loser."

He smiled gently and patiently, the way someone does to a loved one when they don't understand something. Then he began to speak with a resonance that came from deep within. "The success I have had, Sarah, has been nothing but a veneer. I have spent my whole life chasing the expectations of others rather than my own, and in the process I have not lived up to either. I went to the best prep school in the nation, just as my grandfather, father, and brother did before me. But unlike them, valedictorians all, I was a B student, and even then, the grades were a courtesy to a legacy that I could not fulfill. I made the football team but warmed the bench—the same bench that my brother, the first string quarterback, had only sat upon when the defense took the field, which was hardly ever. Like my brother, father, and grandfather, I obtained an appointment to West Point. But the long gray line in the Kincaid clan ended with me. I dropped out, and it was only because of the Kincaid name that I was quietly excused from having to serve as an enlisted man. The records were then expunged, as if I had never been there in the first place. I subsequently dropped out of three more colleges in rapid succession, and with each successive failure, the distance between my father and me widened.

"Finally, one Thanksgiving night in a fit of anger and self-pity, I abandoned the only people whose approval I had ever sought, and I ran away. I took a dying man's name, and through pure luck I joined two other men who let me tag along on their rocket ride to riches. Later we sold the company to a competitor, walking away with billions. The buyer then gutted it, leaving thousands of our employees with nothing to show for their loyalty and hard work except pink slips. And then, in what a psychiatrist would say was an ill-fated attempt at redemption, I led a group of naive innocents up the other side of that mountain over there in the name of freedom. I assured them they would find honor and glory, and instead they found only fear and pain and eternal rest. And now, I walk alone among a crowd of men who neither trust nor respect me, but simply want me around because of what they thought my birth name might be able to get for them, which as it has turned out, is nothing." He paused and looked her directly in the eyes. "America loves a winner, Sarah, and over many generations, the Kincaid family has had more than its fair share of them. Unfortunately, our allotment ran out one son short."

They stood there in silence for a few moments as she absorbed the depth of feeling that she had just heard. Finally, she said, "Regardless of what the world may say, I am certain in my heart that neither your brother nor your father think of you as a loser. And neither do I. So don't expect me to stand here and willingly let you accept the prospect of spending the rest of your life alone, when there are five people who love you; and if you don't come back to them right now, you may never get another chance."

The passion in her voice and the forcefulness of her words reached deep inside him, and for a moment, just one moment, he almost gave in. "Five people?"

She looked at him, and with a trembling voice, she said, "Yes, T.J., I love you too."

He eyed her cautiously, like a fox before a trap—one that he knew would hurt him and yet one that he could not resist. "Like a sister?"

She hesitated and then lied to him, and to herself. It was a lie that she would regret for the rest of her life. "Yes."

He looked over at the helicopter and then back at the Kingdom of the Wind Spirit. For one brief moment, Sarah McGill felt that she had won. He was going to leave with her, and the Kincaid family would be reunited and live happily ever after. But it was not to be. The governor's chief of staff shouted at them again, more loudly than before. T.J. looked over and gave him a perfunctory wave. Then he turned back to her, and with resignation in his voice, he said, "Thank-you, Sarah. Your words mean a lot to me. More than you will ever know. But neither you nor my family can be my judge.

Only I can be that. And I have judged myself to be beyond forgiveness and beyond mercy."

She was crushed. She wanted to pursue it, but the far-away look in his eyes told her it would be of no use. Instead, they stood there facing each other, each locked in their separate worlds; each somehow desperately wanting to reach out to the other, but not knowing how; each feeling the presence of another man standing there between them—a man they both loved so much, that neither was prepared to break his heart. And so, instead, they broke their own hearts. Slowly, Sarah stepped closer to him, placed her arms around him, and pulled him to her. He didn't resist. They stood there for a long tender moment, and then she kissed him gently on the lips. And all that was and might have been for them drifted away slowly on the wind.

Without saying another word, he turned and walked away. She watched him go all the way down the trail, until he disappeared into the shadows of the forest. After he was gone, she stood there with her hair blowing in her eyes, taking one last lingering look up at the mountain they call the Kingdom of the Wind Spirit. Then she walked slowly toward the waiting helicopter. As she did, tears streamed freely down her cheeks. They caught the attention of the pilots and the others waiting inside the helicopter. But she didn't care. It was the first time that a Kincaid brother had made her cry. It would not be the last. And one day soon, the entire nation would cry with her.

<u>59</u>

Smythe Estate, Tysons Corner, Virginia

The faint sounds of morning rush-hour traffic could be heard in the distance on the western half of route 495, a highway that looped around the city. Washington insiders called it the Beltway. On the eastern horizon, pastel shades of pink and orange were spread like watercolors on a pale canvas sky, as Major Smythe, wearing baggy shorts and a tight T-shirt was halfway around the two-mile jogging path that he had built on his estate. In one ear he wore a digitally encrypted micro-cell telcom, and he was deep in conversation and completely oblivious to black unmarked cars and SUVs as they closed in upon the estate. An assistant was telling him that ever since the recent resurgence of terrorism on Homeland soil, gun sales in America had once again taken off. The World War on Terrorism had given Smythe's gun-running business a tremendous lift, and now his illicit business was benefiting from the national hysteria over the coming of gun control. No one wanted to be left unarmed when the last gun store closed. And inside the beltway, the running joke was that a pacifist was the guy who bought his gun last week."

"That's fabulous. Are you sure that we can keep up with the demand?" he said between breaths. Again the news on the other end of the telcom was positive. "Wonderful. We'll let's keep it going, shall we?"

It was at that moment, as he traversed the path near the front gates of the estate, that the world closed in on him. A black, unmarked SUV with a heavy wooden front bumper smashed through the gates and raced up the driveway. Simultaneously, a sleek helicopter suddenly appeared in the sky overhead. Due to the new noise-dampening technology and the use of a jet thruster in place of a tail rotor, Smythe didn't hear the aircraft until its dark shadow blocked out the sun and raced across the ground toward the house, like the angel of death on the hunt. Reaching the courtyard, the helicopter slowed and went into a hover mode. Instantly, a team of black-uniformed, heavily armed men rappelled out of it and took up defensive positions on the ground. At first, the major panicked as he thought someone was coming to kidnap him, or worse. But he soon realized that this was a government operation, and he relaxed slightly. The major was many things, but stupid wasn't one of them. After all, this was America and the authorities had to play by rules that bad guys could ignore.

Initially, not one of the police or Federal agents saw the major standing there, watching the parade of vehicles race by. As he would later tell his phalanx of lawyers, he was amused by the fact that he could have simply walked out the gate, while the legions of heavily armed men roared right by him. But he didn't. Instead, he simply followed the vehicles up the long driveway. When he got to the courtyard, he walked over to a man, who by his manner appeared to be a leader. He wore a navy windbreaker with the FBI's logo on his back in bright yellow letters that made a perfect target, Smythe mused to himself. The special agent was giving directions to the other agents and police, as they took up their positions around the mansion. However, it was quite evident to the trained eye of the major that this diverse group of heavily armed men was a many-headed monster with poor coordination and a complete lack of inter-agency cooperation.

No one stopped Smythe as he walked over to the man, tapped him on the shoulder, and said, "Excuse me. I'm the owner of this house. Can I help you?" He had to keep from laughing at the ineptitude of it all. If this was any measure of the capabilities of American law enforcement, then the world of criminals and terrorists had little to fear.

The agent was startled and obviously taken aback by the effrontery of Smythe, but he hid it well. "Are you Mister Smythe?" he asked harshly.

"Major Smythe, if you please. I earned every bit of that rank in the First Gulf War, and I should like it very much if you would address me as such."

The special agent eyed the major closely. He would have liked to have driven the butt of his pistol into the major's smiling face, but he maintained his cool. "Very well, Major. I am Special Agent In Charge Snaks of the Federal Bureau of Investigation, and I have a search warrant. Now, if you will be so good as to open the front door of your house and step aside, we will do our job."

The major took the piece of paper and gave it only a perfunctory glance. He handed it back to the agent, walked over, and opened the ten-foot high, solid-oak doors, and stepped aside. "Help yourself, Special Agent Snaks, but if you don't mind, I think I shall call my lawyer."

"Suit yourself, Major," the agent replied with obvious disdain.

The major calmly reached up and touched the tiny pad on the outside of the headset's one earphone, said his lawyer's name, and waited for the call to go through. When it did, he began to speak softly into the tiny microphone that made him look more like a rock star on stage than the dangerous felon that they supposed him to be.

The agent looked to his men and said, "Go." Immediately, a large group of agents poured into the house. Another group headed around the side of the house toward the seven-car garage and adjacent riding stables. Snaks turned back to the major and said, "Please stay here, Major. We wouldn't want you to be accidentally hurt, now, would we?"

A smirk spread across the major's face. "My, we are a cheeky little devil, aren't we, Agent Snaks? Of course I'll stay here, but do try to be careful not to damage anything, would you?" he said with the haughtiness of a man who thinks he has nothing to fear. After all, he had paid over two million dollars to a contractor and his specially trained construction crew that he had flown in from Montreal to build his secret command center deep underground, outside the footprint of the mansion. He knew the FBI would never find it, and there was absolutely nothing in any of the other fifty rooms that was in the slightest bit incriminating. Unfortunately, he was wrong.

Snaks said to one of his men, "Stay here with the Major. And see that he doesn't go anywhere." Then he disappeared into the house.

As Smythe stood there on the front step, smirking at the flurry of activity all around him, suddenly two large men with biceps of steel appeared. They were carrying sledge hammers.

"My word," he said to the man guarding him, "We're not going to knock the house down, now, are we?" Smythe's words were still wise-ass, but his tone and manner had changed. The sight of the sledge hammers worried him.

He had reason to worry because after only ten minutes, Snaks reappeared and said, "Major Smythe, you are under arrest. You have the right to remain silent. Anything that you say can and will be used against you in a court of law—"

"What! On what charge?" interrupted Smythe.

The agent ignored the question and finished reading him his rights. Then with a smile, he said, "You are being charged with possession of restricted weapons and the trafficking of those weapons. And if the white powder we just found along with the weapons in your secret vault is what I think it is, we'll add conspiracy to commit murder, as well as murder, to a long list of charges that we haven't even begun to prepare."

"My secret vault? I don't know what you're talking about," Smythe said, still not believing that they had found it.

"Please, Major. Let's cut the bullshit, shall we? Do I really need to take you downstairs and walk you through it? I'm sure that there are enough of your fingerprints in those three rooms and on those crates of weapons to put you away until your guns have turned to rust."

The major stared at the agent. They had obviously found his vault and penetrated it. He decided that he had better shut his mouth and not say anything further. Which is exactly what he did. Suddenly, the sound of a muffled gun shot echoed from the side of the house, followed by complete silence.

"What the hell was that?" Snaks barked at the men standing nearby.

"Sounded like a gunshot," said one of them in a blinding flash of the obvious.

"Go check it out!" shouted Snaks, and two agents sprinted off in the direction of the garage and stables. Snaks asked Smythe. "Are any of your people armed?"

A fine fucking time to be asking me that, isn't it? thought Smythe, but he kept the thought to himself. "Yes. All of my men are licensed to carry in this state and in the District."

After an interminably long wait, one of the agents reappeared at the side of the house. He did not look good. He walked sheepishly over to Saks, and one said, "You'd better go back there, sir. Right away."

"What is it?" said Snaks.

"I think we should discuss it in private, sir," the other man replied.

"Goddamn it, what happened?" shouted Snaks.

"I'm afraid we've shot one of the horses."

"We did what!" exclaimed Snaks.

Smythe's face went pale. "Which horse?"

The agent looked at Snaks and then back at Smythe. "It was the black one, sir. The big stallion."

"Oh my God!" exclaimed Smythe. He took off at a run toward the stables.

Snaks turned to the agent and asked, "Did you call a vet?"

The agent, whose face was pale white, nodded his head in the affirmative and added, "But it won't do any good. The horse is dead."

"How did it happen?"

"They were searching the horse's stall when he reared up and tried to hit them with his front hooves."

"So they just fucking shot him?"

The agent nodded glumly.

"Shit. Shit. Shit!" said Snaks, shaking his head angrily. "There's going to be hell to pay now."

It was an understatement of colossal proportion.

60

The Capitol, Washington, D.C.

Jeremiah Kincaid walked briskly down the hall of the Capitol toward the House chamber. George Ross was with him. The hallway was crowded with representatives, their aides, and other hangers-on; no one wanted to miss the day's historic vote on the President's gun bill. Upstairs, the visitor's gallery was filled to capacity, and there would be many who would grumble when the ushers asked them to leave after their allotted time.

"Why am I not surprised that the President didn't return your call, sir?" said Ross.

"The victor doesn't seek out the vanquished," replied Kincaid.

"A victor with character would," said Ross.

"He's preoccupied with destiny."

"Whose? His or ours?"

"This isn't helping, George."

"Sorry, sir."

A group of reporters plus a television news crew approached the Speaker. The light on the top of the camera cast a large shadow of the Speaker on the wall behind him.

"Excuse me, Mr. Speaker. May we have a word with you?" asked one of the reporters.

Ross stepped between the group and the Speaker and said, "Not now, gentlemen."

The reporters wouldn't take no for an answer, and they walked along beside Kincaid and Ross. The Speaker smiled politely but kept walking.

They had only taken a few steps when another reporter asked, "Our polls show that the bill will get more than the two-thirds majority it needs. How does that tie with your expectations, Mr. Speaker?"

"The Speaker isn't going to speculate on this vote," replied Ross.

They reached the door of the House and stopped. The Speaker glanced at the reporters. "I'm sorry, gentlemen, but I will have nothing to say until after the vote. Now, if you will excuse us."

One reporter blurted out one last question. "Do you think the New Sons of Liberty will concede graciously, sir?"

The Speaker thought about the question for a moment and then replied, "I trust that they will act with the best interests of the nation in mind."

Ross looked at the reporters and said firmly, "That's all, gentlemen." He emphasized the word "all," and they knew that he meant it. Over his years working for Kincaid, Ross had earned a reputation of being tough but fair with the media. They could see that the first of these two traits was about to show itself. They departed, leaving the Speaker and his chief of staff alone.

"There is no shame in this defeat, George," said the Speaker.

"He might still not get the 290 votes he needs, sir," said Ross hopefully.

The Speaker smiled and said, "No, my brilliant young friend. It's all over except for the counting."

"Yes, sir."

Kincaid patted his assistant on the back. Then he took a deep breath, squared his shoulders, and entered the House chamber.

AT THE SAME moment, another chief of staff and his boss were also talking to each other. But whereas Kincaid and Ross spoke out of respect, trust, and affection, this conversation knew no such traits. In fact, it was exactly the opposite. President Alex Webster was pacing to and fro in the Oval Office. Sitting on one of the yellow sofas in the office was Maddun Gordon.

"As I said I would, Maddun, over the past few days I have given your transgressions the deepest of deliberation. And here are my terms. They are non-negotiable. After my bill becomes law, that is, after it has been fully ratified by the state governments and we have finally ended the national nightmare created by the Second Amendment, then you will resign. The

560

reason that you will give is your health, which ironically is the truth. I have made arrangements for you to be committed into the Beverly Hills Clinic, where you will stay until the doctors and I are satisfied that you are no longer a threat to yourself or to society."

"That's a hospital for the rich and insane," said Gordon sheepishly.

"Yes, that's exactly what it is. And the thousand dollars a day charge guarantees your privacy."

"Mr. President, you know I can't afford that. I'm still paying alimony to three wives and child support to seven children."

"The costs will be covered from the same funds that you were using to run roughshod over the law. At least now the people's money will be put to saving a life, even though there are many who would say that yours isn't worth the effort."

"Do the doctors know what I have done?"

"Of course not. If they did, they would be compelled to call the FBI regardless of what I said. However, they have been told that you are a sociopath, which you are."

"I did it for you, Mr. President, and for the good of the country."

"Oh please, spare me. You can't bullshit a bullshitter, Maddun. I know that everything you did was for your own gain."

It was apparent that Gordon was having great difficulty constraining himself. But he did so, if for no other reason than that he knew the Beverly Hills Clinic was far better than an eight-by-six cell just a short walk away from the gurney ride to hell. "Yes, sir. You're right. I'm sure the doctors will make me a better person again."

"I'm sure they will," said the President, but it was clear that he didn't believe it any more than Gordon did. At least having him committed would allow the President to put time and distance between him and the acts that Gordon had perpetrated. Eventually, that distance would allow the President to disavow any knowledge of the crimes. But for now, the last thing that the President needed was a scandal in the White House. "Do you understand and accept these terms, Maddun?"

"Yes, Mr. President. Thank-you for giving me another chance, sir."

Just like you gave another chance to those people on the White House lawn, thought the President. "Right." He looked at his watch and added, "Now, go tell the others to join us to watch this historic vote."

"Yes, sir. But before I do, there is one more issue that I'm afraid I must raise," said Gordon.

"What?" asked the President brusquely.

"There's the matter of the money that I still owe Stefan Chadrian."

The President's face clouded over. "Good God, Maddun, haven't you heard a word that I've said? Your evil past is over. You will not give that killer one more dime. Do I make myself clear?"

"Yes, sir, but—"

"No buts. Not one fucking but. Period!" said the President.

Gordon shook his head affirmatively and then asked softly, "I am going to have to meet with him and give him the bad news personally."

"Do whatever you have to do."

"He won't take the news well, Mr. President."

The President was losing his patience. The veins on the side of his neck began to bulge. He raised his right hand and pointed his index finger directly at Gordon's face and said, "You tell that cold-blooded slimeball that if he doesn't climb back under the rock where he came from, I will bring the full power of the law crashing down upon his skull."

Gordon gave a grudging nod. He knew that the subject was closed. What he didn't know was how on earth he would keep Chadrian from retaliating. "Yes, sir."

"Now, let the others in," said the President as he calmed himself down. After all this was his moment in the sun, and he wasn't going to let any creatures of the night spoil it, including the man in the room with him. "Are we finished?"

Gordon nodded his head and said, "Yes, Mr. President. We are finished." *More than you'll ever know,* thought Gordon, *More than you'll ever know.* He walked over to the door and opened it. He said a few words to the President's assistant, and soon several others joined them, including the Vice President, Patrick Fitzgerald, and Mary Lou Pritchard.

The President settled down onto his favorite chair and motioned for the others to sit down on the yellow sofas. "Lady and gentlemen, we are about to watch one of the most significant votes in the long and mostly distinguished history of the House of Representatives," said the President with obvious pride.

As Gordon watched the President welcome the others, he couldn't help but admire the man's seemingly bottomless capacity to compartmentalize the good and the evil in his world. Gordon knew that the President believed passionately in the need to remove guns from the American landscape. But it infuriated him that now everyone would give all the credit to the President, while in reality, without him, the President's bill would have been watered down to the point of insignificance, and the Second Amendment would live on. *That son of a bitch is going to reap the harvest of my efforts and send me off to a funny farm for Hollywood coke heads and perverts,* he thought to himself as he watched the President weave his magic charm over the others in the Oval Office, just like he would over the entire nation after the bill passed. *But what choice do I have?* he asked himself. And at that moment, he didn't have an answer.

Everyone smiled as they took their places in front of the large HDTV screen that appeared from behind a panel in the wall. When the Websters first took over the White House, his wife had advised him not to have the Oval Office wall cut to put in the screen. He did what he always did with every other recommendation of hers—he ignored it. He had even swung the first blow of the hammer himself.

"Congratulations, Mr. President," said the Vice President, but there was tenseness in his voice. Both he and Fitzgerald were worried about the New Sons of Liberty and the potential repercussions of a positive vote, in Washington and Boise. They knew that Governor Morrissey and the Western Freedom Party were unlikely to accept defeat gracefully. But during the past few days since the bombings, the President had been unwilling to listen to either the Vice President or his national security adviser, as they pleaded with him to stick with the compromise put forth by the Speaker of the House. It was to no avail.

"Thank-you, Richard, but let's wait until the votes are in," Webster said. He turned to Gordon and said, "Maddun. Put on C-Span." In the past he would have had his administrative assistant come in and turn on the BTC, but not today. Ever since the bombings, there had been a noticeable cooling of the relationship between the President and his chief of staff, and it had not gone unnoticed by the others in the inner circle.

Gordon did what he was told, and soon the image of the House floor filled the big screen in front of them. The vote was just about to begin, and the usher read the opening few words of the bill: "Be it enacted by the Senate and House of Representatives of the United States of America in Congress assembled, that all...."

IN THE GREAT room of the Kincaid home in Kettle Moraine, Wisconsin, another BTC was being watched in rapt attention by Kathleen, her daughter Joanna, and a large gathering of their friends. The polite verbal banter in the room belied the seriousness of the event that everyone was watching.

"Don't worry, mother. Everything will be all right," said Joanna, holding her mother's hand.

"Yes, dear, I'm sure you're right. I'm just worried that your father won't," answered Kathleen. "It has torn him up inside almost as much as losing T.J."

The mention of the prodigal son's name quieted everyone down. An elderly gentleman looked around the room in a slightly confused manner and then turned toward Kathleen and asked, "Is T.J. here?"

Kathleen looked over at him and said, "No dad, T.J. isn't here."

The man's bushy white eyebrows rose up in alarm, and he said, "Where did he go?"

"He's in Idaho, dad," answered Kathleen, obviously wishing that she hadn't mentioned his name in the first place.

"Will he be back in time for supper?" continued the old man.

Kathleen couldn't deal with it. She got up and walked out of the room. Another woman immediately followed her. Joanna looked at the old man and sighed, "No, grandpa, T.J. won't be coming to supper."

The old man digested what he had just been told and then looked down and said softly, "My little T.J. is never coming back. Is he?"

Joanna didn't answer. She just picked up the remote and turned up the volume on the video monitor. The gun vote was underway.

T.J. KINCAID and Colonel Joseph Snow Eagle sat in the officer's club at the Wolf River militia camp in the River Of No Return Wilderness. Also present were several other officers including two women. Actually, the club was nothing more than a big tent on a raised wooden platform, but it did have a few comfortable, if slightly battered, armchairs, a pool table and a bar, plus a large-screen video monitor that was hooked up to a satellite dish. The table and the BTC were gifts from Kincaid, since General Latrobe would never have allowed any of the militia's money to be squandered on such a frivolous use of funds.

The BTC was tuned to C-SPAN and the Group of Seven officers watched in silence as the vote was electronically tallied on the screen.

Ayes 135   *Nays 66*

"The President's going to win," said Snow Eagle, shaking his head.

"There are still over two hundred votes to go, Joseph," said Kincaid.

"If you don't mind me asking, have you asked your father what he'll do next if the bill passes?" asked Snow Eagle.

"No," said Kincaid.

"Well, no matter what happens, T.J., your father is a hero in my book. If it hadn't been for those bombings, I think he would have succeeded," said Snow Eagle, shaking his head.

"Thank-you," said Kincaid.

There was a pregnant pause in the conversation until one of the women officers, a first lieutenant, asked Kincaid, "Have they made any progress on their investigation of the bombings?"

"No. But I'd be willing to bet a million bucks that the blood trail leads right up to the Oval Office."

The woman shook her head and looked back at the screen. The count kept slowly ticking away.

Ayes 174   *Nays 93*

Another lieutenant asked, "What do you think it means for us, sir, if the bill passes?"

"Well, first it still has to go to the Senate, where it has to win sixty-seven votes. As you know, the Senate is controlled by the Republicans, but by only two votes, and my guess is that a dozen of them are in favor of gun control, maybe more."

"So the President only needs to convince another six Republicans?"

"Only is a long way from certainty," said Snow Eagle. "Especially when the future of a country depends on it."

"Actually, he probably needs a few more than that to offset the Democrats, who will vote against it. And the Colonel is right that it is far from a sure thing. Even if it does pass both Houses, it still must be ratified by at least thirty-eight states. So we are still a long ways off from the bill becoming the law of the land."

The lieutenant smiled a knowing smile and looked back at the screen. The gap was narrowing, but only slightly.

Ayes 196   *Nays 121*

"I hear you, sir, but what if after all that, it does become law? Are we going to surrender our weapons?"

Kincaid thought about it for a minute and then said, "No, Lieutenant, we must never allow that to happen, because to do so would mark the beginning of the end of America as we know it. And for me, personally, to do so would mean that forty-two militiamen will have died up on a mountain for nothing."

IN GNBC'S New York studios, Allistair Blevis, Cresswell Peabody, and Jarlene Martisse sat in front of a screen on which their network was keeping a running tally of the vote. As they watched, the yes vote approached the deciding number of 290.

Ayes 256   *Nays 135*

Blevis looked at Peabody and asked, "Looks like your side's going to pull it off, Jarlene."

Martisse said without any expression, "Just barely."

Peabody nodded and added, "As much as I hate to admit it, it's all over."

"It would appear that the President picked up enough Republican votes to offset the centrists in his own party," said Blevis.

"Yes," said Peabody. "Any chance that the Speaker had to gain a compromise died with those poor people last week."

Blevis said looking back at the screen. "Watch now, here it comes."

Ayes 287   *Nays 140*

And then, as the three of them sat in silence, the *Ayes* column clicked past 290. It was over. The President and his party had won. Now all that remained was to see how big the margin of victory would be. The answer was soon apparent as the final tally filled the screen.

Ayes 292 Nays 143

Underneath the tally, a large crawl slowly moved across the screen. In big letters it proclaimed, *Gun bill passes the House. President victorious!*

Blevis placed his hand up to his ear and listened intently. Then he said, "I have the party count for you, now. It appears that the President picked up a total of eighty-one Republicans, which, after netting out the four Democrats who voted against the party line, gave the President his total of 292 votes in a House where his party only had 215 seats." He hesitated and looked down at his note pad. "Did I get that right? These vote shifts are very confusing."

"Yes, Allistair, you got it right," said Martisse.

"You got it right, but the House of Representatives just got it wrong. In a big way," added Peabody with an ominous tone in his voice.

"Oh, come on, Cresswell, don't be a sore loser," said Martisse. Her words were negative, but her tone and the way she looked at him were clearly not.

He looked at her, which is something that he rarely did, and he said, "Not *me,* my dear. The only losers here are the American people. And they will see what they have lost soon enough."

Blevis waited for Martisse to respond, but she said nothing. Lately, both he and the show's producers had noticed that the close personal relationship that existed between the two commentators off-camera was beginning to affect their on-air contentiousness. It was becoming a problem and unbeknownst to the two of them, the producers had begun a search for their replacements. Trying to re-ignite some controversy, Blevis looked back at Peabody and asked, "Cresswell, tell me what you think the implications of this vote will be for the New Sons of Liberty. Do you think this vote might just get their juices boiling?"

Peabody studied the host with cautious eyes. "What do you mean?"

"What I mean is this. Take a group of secretive congressmen and women, throw in a handful of governors, sprinkle on a helping of state and local elected officials, mix in a batch of senior military officers with perhaps a dash of a supreme court justice, stir briskly, and bake in the oven at high temperatures for several months. Doesn't that add up to a recipe for disaster?"

Peabody stared at Blevis for a minute and then said in a dead-serious tone, "I hope your culinary skills outweigh your literary ones, Allistair. Whoever the members of this group are, and whatever their views may be regarding the President and his anti-gun legislation, they are patriotic Americans first, last and always, and they will follow the rule of law."

Blevis' plan worked. Martisse jumped in, continuing the metaphor. "Come now, Cresswell, let's call a spatula a spatula, shall we? The New Sons of Liberty is a cowardly group of government employees and elected public officials, who hide in electronic anonymity. Instead of coming out into the open and declaring themselves, they skulk around the dark corners of cyberspace, feeding off each other's distaste for the present administration and beating the war drums, albeit softly, at least for now. Dissidents certainly, rebels most likely, and potentially traitors, but hardly patriots by any sense of the term."

Peabody paused before replying. Then, very softly he said, "A patriot, Jarlene, is someone who loyally supports his country. That does not necessarily mean that he supports the men who are running it. At one point or another, in our oftentimes inglorious history, the government of this nation supported the annihilation of Native American people, the slavery of men of color, the suppression of women's rights, unrestricted child labor, and isolationism in the face of the Holocaust." He paused to let his words sink in. Then he continued with a cold stare that made even the normally unflappable Blevis squirm. "Would you call the brave men and women who disagreed with those policies traitors? I think not. One of the traits that makes America great is our stubborn refusal to accept blindly that which we know in our hearts to be wrong, regardless of who would have us believe otherwise, be he a king or a prophet or a President. And God help us should we do otherwise."

The studio fell silent. Finally, just before the producer was about to panic, Blevis turned to the camera and said, "Well, there you have it, ladies and gentlemen, the most important issue facing the American people since the war on terrorism—the war on guns. And despite the deeply held views of many citizens to the contrary, the President today in a historic vote successfully passed the first hurdle in his attempt to overturn the Second Amendment to the Constitution. After a few words from our sponsors, we'll open up the telcom lines to hear your thoughts. So don't touch that remote. We'll be right back."

An assistant producer signaled to Blevis that they had cut away to a commercial. Blevis looked back at Peabody and said, "Nicely spoken, Cresswell. For a moment, I was afraid that you had lost your acerbic tongue, like some others I know." He didn't look at Martisse as he said it.

Martisse didn't say anything. Instead, she stood up and began undoing the clasp of the tiny microphone on the collar of her blouse.

"Where are you going?" asked Blevis.

"Anywhere but here," she replied, and it was obvious that she meant it.

"Come, Jarlene, you know I love you, babe. I was just trying to get your dander up."

"Well, *babe*, it worked." She took a few steps over to Peabody, leaned over, and kissed him on the cheek. Then she straightened up and looked at Blevis. "Take care, Allistair. It's been real." With that, she walked off the set.

Blevis cast pleading eyes at Peabody and said, "Cresswell, tell her to come back."

But Peabody just smiled and said, "Would that I could."

Exasperated, Blevis turned toward the production booth and said, "Now what the hell do I do?"

"What you always do, Allistair," came the deep voice over the speakers, "Just talk."

Allistair thought about it for a moment. Suddenly he got an idea. One that obviously pleased him immensely. He got up from behind his desk and ran around to the door of the control room. He conferred with his producer, and then he quickly returned to his seat. He sat down and an assistant helped him with his microphone. Then he looked over at Peabody and said, "Once again, old boy, you have nailed it."

"I don't understand," replied Peabody.

Blevis grinned, "You'll see. By the way, did you realize that the words patriot and traitor have exactly the same letters, except for one, the letters 'p' and 'r'. If you exchange the 'p' in patriot for an 'r,' you can spell traitor, and if you swap an 'r' in traitor—"

"I get it, Allistair," interjected Peabody.

Blevis smiled as he enjoyed his own little piece of trivia. "Hey. PR. Get it? Public Relations. The only difference between traitor and patriot is PR, or as we otherwise know it, spin."

Peabody stared at Blevis and slowly shook his head. He couldn't believe that this vacuous and self-absorbed ninny was one of the most-watched men on television. But then again, the show's ratings had certainly done a lot to advance his own career and bank account, so he quietly accepted the hypocrisy of his own actions and smiled politely.

The assistant producer began his countdown, "We're back in five, four, three…" He counted out two and one in the air with his hand and then pointed at Blevis.

"Welcome back, ladies and gentlemen. This is *Speak Up America* on GNBC, and I'm your host, Allistair Blevis. With me tonight is Cresswell Peabody, noted author and historian. If you were with us just before the break, Cresswell made what I thought was a particularly salient argument that patriotism is loyalty to our nation, but not necessarily to the people who we have elected to run it. Now we would like to hear your thoughts on this highly provocative and timely issue. So what do you think, America? Are the members of the New Sons of Liberty, and all those who support their views, traitors or patriots? We're going to take a vote. If you feel that they are traitors, call 1-900-TRAITOR. Or conversely, if you believe they are patriots, call us on 1-900-PATRIOT. The call will cost you one dollar, which I think you will agree is a small price to pay to stand up and be counted on this weighty matter. And we'll select several of you from each side to talk with us on air. So go ahead and make the calls now."

As he finished speaking, the telcom panel in the control room lit up like a Christmas tree.

61

The White House, Washington, D.C.

The White House press corps was sitting in the press room listening to President Alex Webster make his triumphant victory speech following the passage of his bill in the House of Representatives. Despite the concerns of his staff, he had begun the press conference immediately after the yes votes hit two hundred and ninety while the House was still in session. It would prove to be an embarrassing mistake.

"In conclusion, ladies and gentlemen, the courageous vote taken by the House of Representatives today was far more than just a vote for the elimination of the specter of death that has darkened this land for so long; it was a vote for all that's good and decent about us as a people. It was a vote of faith in the future. And while it will not bring back Meagan Brooks, or any of the thousands of precious children who have been killed by guns, it will put a stop to this carnage once and forever, and it will restore us as a people to the position of honor and nobility, which we have lost since it became acceptable to keep an instrument of death in bedrooms of fear and closets of hate."

The President looked up from his text. "That concludes my prepared remarks, and I would now like to take a few questions." Overall, his remarks had been an eclectic mixture of pride of achievement, concern for a nation under siege, and a rather unfortunate amount of pure and shameless gloating. It was classic Webster, and from the looks on the faces of Patrick Fitzgerald and Jane Kimberly, his press secretary, it had reared its ugly head at a moment when grace and compassion were so desperately needed. Maddun Gordon, however, was delighted. A victorious President was a happy President. And a happy President would be a forgiving one, or so he hoped. As he stood near to the President, his mind was already spinning with ways he could redeem himself and escape the President's edict to resign. He was the embodiment of evil reinventing itself in the face of its own dark destiny.

As usual, the President gave the first question to Mrs. Nancy Moriarity, the grand dame of the press corps. "Yes, Nancy?" He smiled as he prepared to listen patiently to her question, which from long experience would be an ordeal in itself.

"Mr. President, it is apparent that you are pleased with the result of today's vote," she began.

The President interrupted her, which under ordinary circumstances might have appeared rude, a trait Webster often displayed to men but rarely, if ever, to women. But this was certainly not an ordinary day. Besides, Webster had on his very best lovable rogue's smile. "Aren't you pleased with it, Nancy? After all, it will make the streets safer for those wonderful grandchildren of yours."

Mrs. Moriarity was too savvy to be drawn into the trap. She answered using the third person to refer to herself. It was something that she had learned from watching royalty and had adopted as her own. "What we think is irrelevant, Mr. President, but we do thank-you for thinking about our grandchildren's safety." She quickly got back on point. "As you know, the vote in the House of Representatives is only the first step in a long and complicated process of amending the Constitution. Ahead lies the need for a similar ratification by two thirds of the Senate and three fourths of the state legislatures. However, judging by your remarks, it would seem that you feel the final outcome is all but assured?"

Gordon winced and rolled his eyes. But the President was nonplused. His smile didn't even flicker. Instead, his eyes sparkled, and his demeanor radiated calm. "Nothing is certain, Nancy, save death. Even taxes are vulnerable, that is, if you would believe my opponents." He smiled coyly and then quickly put back on his serious face. "As long as there is one ounce of breath in my body, I will not stop until death by gunfire vanishes from the face of this great land of ours." Clearly pleased with himself, he looked directly at the television cameras in the back of the room. "Today, my fellow Americans, in the aftermath of this great victory for good over evil, I make this pledge to every mother and father and child across this great land. With all my strength, with all my heart, and with every ounce of power that is vested in this office, I will continue my fight to draw back the shades of darkness that threaten to destroy our land." He paused again and looked back at Mrs. Moriarity. "As you so rightly have pointed out, Nancy, the passage of this bill by the House of Representatives is only the first step in a long process. But today, the Congress has sent a clear signal to those who would oppose our efforts: that we will not rest, we will not be deterred, and we will not stop from pursuing our goal until it is the law of the land."

Mrs. Moriarity gave the President a polite smile. She couldn't stand the man's policies or pontificating, but had she been thirty years younger, she damn sure would have loved to jump his bones. It was a common feeling in almost every female in America, and it engendered penis envy in nearly every man.

Just as the President was getting ready to take another question, a PTC rang somewhere in the room. But for the ringing, the room fell deathly silent, as everyone knew full well how intensely the President disliked having to compete with such interruptions. Instinctively, every reporter and even several of the President's staff members reached for their PTCs to make sure that the sound wasn't emanating from them. It soon became evident whose it was, as Sarah McGill stood up and excused herself. She hurried towards the door, but whatever it was that she heard on the other end of the line stopped her dead in her tracks.

"Would you like to share what is so important with the rest of us, Ms. McGill?" the President asked in a stern but not ill-humored tone.

McGill closed the small communication device that had carried an enormous message and looked directly at the President. It was apparent from the expression on her face that what she was about to say was consequential, and that fact made all the President's men uncomfortable, especially Maddun Gordon.

"I am truly sorry, Mr. President. I accidentally left my PTC on. I apologize to you and my colleagues."

"Apology accepted," said Webster. He was obviously in a forgiving mood, and Gordon felt more confident about his own future with each passing minute. "Perhaps, Sarah, you could share with us what it was that you felt was more important than the subject of this press conference?" said the President, leaning forward slightly.

She looked at Gordon and then back at the President. "I have already disturbed you enough, Mr. President."

Her look and comment made Gordon's blood run cold. For an instant, he was afraid that the authorities had discovered his connection to the shootings on the White House lawn. He flashed a panicked look at the President, who ignored him.

The President continued, "Sarah, if it was important enough for you to interrupt this conference, then it is certainly important enough to tell us all what it is. So go ahead, disturb us some more." He had no idea how ironic his comment was about to appear.

McGill nodded her head reluctantly and said in a clear and chilling voice, "Mr. President, I have just learned that fifty-four members of the House of Representatives have announced their intent to resign from the Congress in protest to your bill's passage." Her words cut through the pretentious stillness of the room like a scalpel through blubber. Her fellow reporters were stunned, not only by her words, but by her incredible brazenness in speaking them. They were certain that they were witnessing the death of a supernova, as bright as the heavens had ever known, but one now clearly destined to become a black hole in the broadcasting universe.

Even the normally unflappable President was momentarily silenced. Then he slowly replied, "What?" as his brain struggled to process the enormity of the few simple words in her sentence.

"I said—" she began.

"Never mind, I heard what you said," he interrupted, as his mind began functioning once again at its normal light speed. "Who is your source for such a preposterous statement, Ms. McGill?"

"I'm sorry, Mr. President. I cannot tell you."

Another audible gasp washed across the room like the aftershock of an earthquake.

The President looked over at Kimberly, who immediately stepped up to the microphone and said in a firm voice, "Ladies and gentlemen, this press conference is over."

The President stepped away from the podium and spoke a few words to Kimberly, who hurried to where McGill was standing and said, "Ms. McGill, the President would like to have a few words with you."

Sarah felt her insides do a double flip, but it was too late to turn back now. "Of course," she replied.

Kimberly returned to the front of the room and gave the message to the President. He nodded, looked at Gordon and Fitzgerald, and said, "Gentlemen. The Oval Office. Now!"

He didn't need to ask twice.

IN THE NINE MONTHS since Sarah McGill had been senior White House correspondent for GNBC, she had only been in the Oval Office once before, and that was for a no-question photo opportunity, or photo op, with the President and the President of Mexico. It was a source of frustration to her and ironically, only a few days earlier she had been pushing Jane Kimberly to get her an interview with the President, but to no avail. But at that moment, Sarah McGill was filled with mixed emotions. On the one hand, she felt extremely uncomfortable and wished she was anywhere else but in the Oval Office. On the other, she was excited to be the only member of the press present in the room on such a momentous occasion. While these two opposing forces played havoc with her emotions, she sat quietly on one of the President's two yellow sofas. Directly across from her on the other sofa sat Patrick Fitzgerald, and the Vice President sat in the high-backed chair that the President normally occupied. Maddun Gordon was nowhere to be seen. While McGill and Fitzgerald listened attentively, the President paced back and forth and ranted out loud, like a caged lion just before feeding time.

"Would you please explain to me, Patrick, how it is that GNBC was able to discover this before the White House did?"

Fitzgerald quietly responded with a simple, "I don't know." It was the same straightforward way he always answered questions when he didn't know the answer. No excuses, no lame explanations—just a simple "I don't know."

Webster looked at McGill and said, "Sarah, you know that I can call Mary Lou Pritchard and get a court order to make you reveal your sources." It was an idle threat, because the President knew she would go to jail before she would violate the confidentiality of any source.

McGill sensed how frustrating it had to be for the President not to be able to determine whether or not her warning was accurate, and if so, when it would occur. However, she was now certain of one thing; by his silence immediately following the news conference, it was clear that either Maddun Gordon was not the person in the West Wing who had penetrated the New

575

Sons of Liberty extranet, or that for whatever reason, he was keeping it a secret. For if he had checked the site following the House vote, like Tanner Spence had, he too would have learned that the House of Representatives was on the verge of spinning out of control. But if he was keeping it a secret, a secret from whom? From them, or from the President himself? What Sarah McGill didn't realize was that, in the flurry of activity following the vote, Gordon had not had time to go to the extranet site and to witness the looming revolution for himself. At that moment there was a knock on the door and in walked Maddun Gordon.

"Well?" asked the President.

Gordon glanced over at McGill and then looked back at his boss. Then he said, "Ms. McGill is right. Fifty-four representatives, all but four of them Republicans, and virtually all of them from the Heartland, plan to submit their letters of resignation to the Speaker of the House effective at midnight tomorrow night."

I hope that Tanner has briefed the Speaker of the House by now as I told him to do, thought Sarah.

Gordon continued, "They plan to return to their home states, and to seek support from the legislatures of their respective state governments to block any Federal actions regarding guns."

"Why midnight tomorrow night?" asked the Vice President.

"Probably so that they can get home before their congressional travel privileges are revoked," said Fitzgerald.

"Why fly in coach on your own money if you can fly first class on a congressional credit card?" said Gordon with a bemused grin.

The President unleashed an angry glare at him.

The smile vanished from his face. "Sorry, Mr. President." But as soon as the President looked away, the grin returned to his face, and he made a point of flashing it at McGill.

The room fell silent as Webster paced back and forth across the dark blue carpeting, with its seal of the President of the United States of America, making Sarah McGill very uncomfortable. To her, Gordon looked like the Cheshire cat, sitting in the tree looking down on Alice In Wonderland, while the Queen of Hearts stormed around the room wanting to take off someone's head. It was an apt comparison, she thought, because as she sat there watching the most powerful man on earth fuming over an out-of-control government—one that he himself had knocked off its course by overloading the gyroscope of reason with an unbalanced burden of ego—she truly felt as if she had stepped through the looking glass herself.

"Is what they're doing legal, Patrick?" the President asked.

"I'm not a Constitutional scholar, Mr. President, but I doubt that there is anything in the Constitution to prevent them from resigning en masse. Then the executive branch of each state can appoint an interim representative until the time elections can be held."

"But if the governors sympathize with their representatives, they may choose not to do so," said Knox. "And that would create a Constitutional crisis."

Fitzgerald looked at the Vice President and added, "I'm not sure I would agree that it would be a crisis, but it would certainly be a matter for Constitutional experts to assess."

Everyone digested the thought, but none so aggressively as Webster himself.

"There's more, Mr. President," said Gordon almost sheepishly.

His recent behavior change from arrogance to obsequiousness had not gone unnoticed by those who walked the hallways of the West Wing, including McGill. This was another thing that made her feel that she was living in a world gone mad.

"Spit it out, Maddun!" snapped the President, without any trace of the respect and caring that he had once displayed his ally of ten plus years.

Gordon took a deep breath and said, "At least twelve senators plus one supreme court justice intend to resign in support of the representatives."

"What!"

"Now that would a Constitutional crisis," added Knox.

"Has the whole fucking government gone mad?" exclaimed Webster. With that, he picked up a porcelain vase that had been one of Eleanor Roosevelt's favorites and hurled it against the fireplace, smashing it into a hundred pieces. At the sound of it breaking, the doors to the room flew open and Randy Wiseman, the head of the President's Secret Service detail, burst into the room with his weapon held at the ready, pointing toward the ceiling. He was followed close behind by two other agents, one of whom was in uniform. Their sudden entrance changed the situation entirely. Gone was the smile on Maddun Gordon's face. Gone was the atmosphere of controlled anger and disciplined probing. And gone, long gone, was any desire on the part of Sarah McGill to be there. Instead, she was now certain that she was present at the Mad Hatter's Tea party.

The President regained his composure and said calmly to the agents, "It's all right, boys. I'm afraid that I just got a little riled up."

Wiseman studied the President's face and then quickly scanned the room. Satisfied that all was secure, he excused himself, and along with his colleagues he exited the room. No one said anything. What was there to say? The President had in one day experienced the greatest legislative victory of his political life and now, only a few hours later, he was on the verge of suffering the most humiliating repudiation that any President had ever known. And in the biggest irony of all, sex had nothing to do with it.

"Are you absolutely sure?" asked the President.

"Yes, sir," answered Gordon without hesitation.

"Where did you learn all this?" probed the President.

Gordon looked over at McGill and without taking his eyes off her said, "I expect from the same place that Ms. McGill did. Off the Internet, or to be more precise, off the New Sons of Liberty extranet."

All eyes in the room focused on Sarah McGill. *Now what do I say? What do I do?* For just the most fleeting of moments, she actually wondered if she might be in danger. In fact, she was in danger, as were all her fellow citizens. But not from the men in that room. They were in danger from a far greater evil that stalked the land.

"Ms. McGill, is there anything that you want to tell me? Anything that will shed some light on this group that calls itself the New Sons of Liberty?" asked Webster.

"I'm sorry, Mr. President, but—"

He interrupted her. "Before you answer, I want to remind you how grave the circumstances are which now face our nation." He paused and then added one word that unnerved McGill and startled the other men. "Please."

Sarah stared at the President and took a deep sigh. "Mr. President, judging by Mr. Gordon's comments, you know as much as I do about the New Sons of Liberty."

"Why don't you let me be the judge of that and tell me all that you know? Starting with who your source is."

It was a tense moment. There she was, sitting in the Oval Office, staring into the eyes of the most powerful man on earth, who had just asked her a question that she did not want to answer. On top of everything else, he was as handsome as he was forceful. Had it been another reporter, it might have been different. But it wasn't, and despite the pressure, Sarah McGill stood her ground. "I'm afraid I can't do that, Mr. President."

He stared at her for what seemed to her like an eternity, and then he said, "Very well, Ms. McGill, you can go."

She did. Quickly.

THREE HOURS LATER, Sarah sat on the sofa in her apartment with Jake sound asleep beside her. The BTC was on and she was watching the end of *Casablanca*. As Ilsa and Rick said their painful goodbye, tears streamed down Sarah's cheeks. That scene made her cry every time she watched it, but it wasn't up until that very moment that she knew what Ilsa was going through. When Humphrey Bogart and Claude Raines walked off into the fog together, she got up, walked over to the window, and looked out across the city. As she stood there, a rain drop hit the glass in front of her. Then another and another after that. Soon the window was awash with summer shower.

Please God, don't let me break his heart, she thought as she stood there listening to the theme song from the movie and watching the rain come down. Upon her return from Idaho, she and Jake had talked at length about his brother; what he had said, and what he had not said. She managed to recount the story without exposing what she had really felt when she stood in front of that magic mountain, holding his little brother in her arms. She knew he would never understand. She didn't herself. Every minute on the long plane ride home, and every second since, she had spent avoiding the impossible reality that she was in love with two men at the same time. And in her running away from it, she only drew it closer and closer, until it finally had begun to consume her.

"What's the matter?" he said, waking up and looking at her face.

"Nothing."

"You've been crying."

"I always cry when I watch Casablanca."

He nodded, rubbed his eyes, and said in a sleepy tone, "If I was Rick, I wouldn't have given up so easily."

"Then don't."

"What?" he said, sitting up.

579

She walked across the room and sat down beside him. "Resign from the Army, and let's go away."

"Go away where?" he asked, with a bemused chuckle.

"Anywhere. Anywhere but here."

"Sarah. You're not making any sense."

She sighed. "I know, and I don't care. It's just that I don't want you to go to war."

"First of all, we're not at war yet. And second, if war is the final solution to this national crisis, then I'll have to go. That's what a soldier does."

She looked at him through reddened eyes and whispered, "Please call your brother." It was the wrong thing to say, and she knew it as soon as she said it. He pushed her away gently but firmly, got up, and walked into the kitchen, where he opened the refrigerator and pulled out a bottle of alcohol-free beer.

She followed him. "Jake. Talk to me."

"You said you weren't going to bring him up anymore."

"I can't help it."

He looked at her with a sharp stare. For a moment she was afraid that he was going to say something about her feelings for his brother. Feelings that she knew he must sense. But he didn't. "Sarah. I told you that there is nothing that I, or my brother, can do to change what is going to happen."

"How do you know that if you won't even try?"

He let out a huff and put the bottle down hard on the counter. Then he walked back into the living room, where he picked up his jacket.

"Where are you going?"

"Anywhere but here," he snapped. And with that, he was gone.

She stood there staring at the door for a long, lonely moment; then she sat down, pressed the play button on the remote for her DVD, and the opening credits of Casablanca filled the screen. Quickly she scrolled to the scene where Rick said to Ilsa that they would always have Paris, and then she sat back and watched the rest of the movie for the umpteenth time.

62

Bluewater Wildlife Refuge, Maryland

The black eastern sky was just beginning to turn pinkish gray as the sedan slowly drove the last few hundred feet along the dirt road that led to the cottage beside the wildlife refuge. The lone occupant of the car, Maddun Gordon, looked nervously from side to side as he steered the car into the grassy parking area and put it in Park. He sat for a few moments and muttered to himself, "Maybe he's not here." It was more of a plaintive wish than a statement of belief. He was motionless except for his eyes, which scanned the cottage and the surrounding area. In the dim glow of the lone light at the end of the dock, he could see that a sleek power boat was moored behind Chadrian's ketch, the Red Dragon. But both were dark, and there was no one to be seen. Finally, he reached over, grabbed the door handle, and slowly swung it open. Immediately, the smell of the brackish water and marsh grass filled his nostrils. The light breeze off the bay cooled his perspiration-soaked forehead, but it did little to calm his pounding heart. Cautiously, he got out of the car and closed the door.

"Chadrian," he shouted tentatively.

There was no reply, only the plaintive clanging of a buoy somewhere out on the dark water. He walked up the path, peering nervously into the shadows all about him, and climbed up the two wooden stairs, wincing as they creaked under his weight. Finally, he reached the front door and stopped. "Chadrian," he said once again, only this time softer and without the conviction of someone who wants an answer.

Thhhwaack!

581

"Aaah!" Gordon exhaled loudly in more of a groan than a scream, and he jumped back two feet, as the razor-headed arrow smacked into the door. It had come from somewhere behind him and to his left, and the long thin metal shaft vibrated noisily.

Terrified, Gordon looked behind him just as Chadrian stepped up onto the porch carrying his bow and quiver of arrows. "Sorry about that," he said with a grin on his face. "I did not know it was loaded," he added with an even broader smile.

Struggling to catch his breath, Gordon exclaimed, "You crazy bastard. You could have killed me!"

Chadrian tossed him his stringer with three Striped Bass on it. "If I had wanted to kill you, you would be dead," he said, reaching for the doorknob and pushing the door wide open. "Did you come to whine or dine?" And with a smirk he added, "No pun intended."

"Neither." Still visibly upset, Gordon stood on the porch as if hesitant to go inside.

"Suit yourself." Chadrian took the fish back from Gordon and stepped inside.

"Whose boat is that behind yours?" Gordon called after him.

"None of your business."

Gordon took a deep breath and followed Chadrian into the cabin.

"We will talk after we eat," said Chadrian.

Gordon grimaced, "You mean eat those fish? For breakfast?"

"Yes. It is my favorite way to start the day," he smirked. "There is nothing more pleasing to me than the smell of fish in the morning."

"No thanks. I think I'll pass. I just came to talk."

"Very well. But before we do, I trust you brought the rest of my money, or you will be trading places with these fish."

Regaining a modicum of his composure, Gordon snarled, "I brought your damn money."

"Good," said Chadrian. "Now clean these while I start the fire." With that, he tossed the fish back to Gordon.

"Clean them with what?"

Chadrian opened a drawer, took out a wooden-handled knife with a long, thin blade, and without looking back at Gordon, threw it in his direction with a sharp flick of his wrist. It flew through the air, passing Gordon only inches from head, and stuck solidly into the open door.

"Stop fooling around."

Chadrian snorted. "I assure you Gordon, I never fool around."

Gordon stared at the other man but said nothing.

Chadrian smirked. "Now clean the fish in the sink and grind their guts down the disposal. It is a job for which you are perfectly suited." With that, he disappeared into the bedroom.

Gordon pulled the knife out of the door, walked over to the sink, and started cleaning the fish.

THE TWO MEN were seated at a small round table. In front of them were fine china plates with sterling silver cutlery and partially empty, coffee cups. Gordon had not touched his fish, while Chadrian's plate had only a few long, white bones. Chadrian pushed his trim body back from the table, got up, and picked up a partially smoked cigar laying in an ashtray beside the fireplace. He took a long match out of the brass holder beside the fire-screen, snapped it across the stones, and lit the cigar.

Gordon didn't look happy.

"What is troubling you? Your boss got his bill passed by the House, and although the Senate vote will be close, I think he will get the necessary cross-over votes."

"It's not that simple."

"Life rarely is," he replied, blowing out the match.

"We're concerned that we may not have a quorum in the Senate since some senators supposedly plan to join the House walkout."

"You have just got to hand it to those New Sons of Liberty boys. They really have ruined your little party."

"I'm not worried about them. They can't do squat. It's those stupid militia fuckheads in Boise I'm concerned about. They must have been out of their minds to think those two bombings would help their cause."

"Quite a coincidence, were they not?"

Gordon lifted one eyebrow. "Yeah. If I didn't know you better, I'd say it was too much of a coincidence."

"Meaning?"

"Meaning nothing," said Gordon backing down. "I know you don't do anything for free."

"It depends on your definition of the word free," he said with a smirk. "So now what?"

"I don't know. Governor Morrissey and his fucking Western Freedom Party has got us by the balls, and they know it."

"Well, if someone has you by the balls, you can only do one of two things: either start a fight or make love. I assure you that the latter course of action is far less painful."

"What does that mean?"

"It means perhaps you should offer to join them."

Gordon snapped a look at him. "Are you nuts? They stand for everything the President has been trying to eliminate."

"I do not mean that you actually should, only that you give the appearance of doing so."

Gordon's eyes widened. "You mean, spy on them?"

"Yes. That is a rather pedestrian way of looking at it."

"Go on."

"I will establish contact with them through an associate who will tell them he has a mole in the White House. Of course, he will actually be a double agent acting on your behalf."

Gordon thought about it, and the more he did, the more he liked it. "It might work. But how do I know that you won't double-cross me?"

"You do not. But have I done so up until now?"

"No."

"Right. That is because our relationship is built on the one fundamental principle that drives your entire society: greed. Money always buys loyalty—the only issue is, how much?"

"How much does your loyalty go for these days?"

"Seven million dollars."

Gordon's face contorted, "What! Are you out of your mind!"

"Do not whine, Gordon. It does not become you. Besides, what is seven million dollars compared to what your average CEO makes these days? Or even compared to what you will make when you write your tell-all book after you leave the White House?"

"There's no way that I can afford that."

"It is not your money, remember?"

Gordon toyed with his fork. "You don't understand. It's getting harder to siphon off these funds. Especially now that—" he caught himself.

"Now that what?" asked Chadrian.

"Never mind. You don't need to know."

Chadrian didn't like secrets. Especially when they involved him. He stood up and said, "This meeting is over."

Gordon shrugged and said, "Wait. Sit down, and I'll tell you." He proceeded to tell Chadrian the truth, which was not something that came easily to him.

Chadrian looked away and sat there for a few moments. Then he looked back at Gordon and said, "It will now cost you ten million."

"No! That's impossible. I can't," said Gordon.

"Please. Save the drama. And do not tell me that your boss would not want to have a direct pipeline into Governor Morrissey's inner circle."

"I can't take that much. Ten million dollars is more than a rounding error, even in Washington."

Chadrian stood up and said, "Good night, Mr. Gordon."

Gordon agonized over it for a few moments longer, then with a look of resignation, he said, "Okay. Ten million, but half now and half later."

"No."

"Why not? That's been our standard arrangement," said Gordon.

Chadrian looked at him and said coldly, "Because Maddun, now that the President is onto you, you have a half life of a fruit fly."

Gordon didn't respond. His mind was racing ahead. Even though the President had told him to sever all ties with Chadrian, he was sure that he hadn't really meant it. Or at least even if he had, Gordon felt he would change his mind if he knew how he planned to use Chadrian now.

"Do we have a deal?" asked Chadrian.

Gordon looked him directly in the eye and said, "Yes, Mr. Chadrian, we have a deal. But that's too much money for me to handle in cash."

"No problem. Wire the money to my Swiss account tomorrow morning."

Gordon nodded. He knew he was taking a gamble. But what did he have to lose? Absolutely nothing. Unfortunately for him, a man who acts on the premise that he has nothing to lose, already has. "How soon can your associate be in Boise?"

"As soon as you get me the money."

"You'll have it tomorrow," said Gordon.

"Excellent. Good night, Mr. Gordon. Do not worry. Your problems are as good as over."

Gordon got up and started for the door. Then he stopped and turned back.

"Is there something else?" asked Chadrian.

Gordon nodded, "Yeah."

"Was is it?"

"There is something that I have been meaning to ask you."

"Go on."

"Why the don't you ever use contractions? I mean, you say 'it is' instead of 'it's' and 'do not' instead of 'don't'. Do you get paid by the word, or what?"

"It is because that is the way we all speak where I come from."

"You mean in the Soviet Republic, where you were born?"

Chadrian's eyes narrowed, and a sinister smile spread across his bluish lips. "No. Before that."

"I don't understand."

"You will find that out soon enough. Do not rush it."

A chill ran down Gordon's back, and suddenly the killer's grammar didn't seem so interesting anymore. "Whatever," he said with an uneasy shrug.

"Now leave, before I raise my fees," said Chadrian.

Gordon didn't say anything more. Chadrian followed him out onto the porch and watched him get into his car and drive away, as the first rays of the sun began to paint the underbelly of the low-lying cloudbank in shades of hot pink and flame orange. After it had disappeared around the bend, he slowly walked down to the dock. As he neared the motor yacht, rocking gently at the dock behind his ketch, the figure of a man stepped out onto the deck. It was Major Smythe.

"Did he go for it?" asked Smythe, as Chadrian climbed aboard.

"Of course. But it is a little more complicated than we thought. The President knows about me." The two men sat down in the sleek boat's open cockpit. Chadrian continued, "He told his little sycophant to cut me off."

"Will he?"

"Of course not. Governor Morrissey has got the White House by the testicles, and the President is obsessed with beating him."

Smythe nodded and then added. "Quite honestly, old chap, I trust Gordon as far as I can hurl him."

Chadrian snickered. "It is throw."

"Beg pardon?"

"The expression is, 'As far as I can throw him.'"

"Throw, hurl, what's the difference?"

"To Americans there is a big difference. They use the word hurl to describe vomiting."

Smythe's face wrinkled. "Really? How disgusting. But now that I think of it, my comment stands. What I was going to say was that I'm not sure why we need to risk using Gordon for anything at all, other than target practice."

Chadrian glared at the other man. "We will use Gordon, because I always hedge my bets, Major. And since it is in my best interests to play both sides against each other, and your best interests to play along with me, the more players we keep on the field, the better."

"Very good. I'm with you."

Chadrian smiled. "That is a good thing."

"What do you mean?"

"Dealing with me is a permanent arrangement. There is no going back."

Smythe tried to ignore the chills running down his spine. "Tell me, old chap, do you ever enjoy it?"

"What?"

"Killing people."

"Yes. But not for the reason you think."

"What then?"

Chadrian smiled but didn't answer. Instead, he just sat there staring at the other man with a self-satisfied grin on his thin, blue lips.

"Never mind. I'm sorry I asked."

"No. I will tell you. I enjoy the exquisite symmetry of people getting what they deserve. It is the one thing that my arch rival and I agree upon. Life always comes full circle, Major; never forget it. Ever. The only difference is that with Him, the circle always ends in light, and with me in darkness." He paused and then added, "I will particularly enjoy bringing Maddun Gordon's life full circle."

"I don't understand."

"*Honi soit qui mal y pense.*"

"I've heard that, but I can't remember what it means."

587

"Evil to him who evil thinks. It is the Motto of the Garter, spoken by King Edward the Third."

Smythe shrugged. "Shakespeare never particularly interested me."

"Not Shakespeare—the *real* King Edward III, in the fourteenth century, during his reign that the Hundred Years War started."

"Ah, yes. Now that was a war for you."

Chadrian shrugged and replied matter-of-factly. "Man is stupid, and then he dies."

Smythe studied the killer for a moment and then said, "You are the embodiment of all that is evil, Mr. Chadrian."

"Thank-you. That is the nicest thing you have ever said to me, Major."

"You must have had a very harsh upbringing."

"Yes—I did. My father cast me out when I was very young, and I have been trying to pay him back ever since."

"Your father is still alive?"

"In a manner of speaking. I see his face on every man that I kill."

Smythe paused as if debating whether to ask the next question. He decided to do so. "How is it that you became a professional killer?"

"Why do you ask?"

"I don't know. I'm just curious."

"Be careful, Major. Be very careful."

Smythe flinched. "What did I say?"

Chadrian looked out across the bay toward the open waters of the Chesapeake. And he slowly began to recite a poem:

> *Once upon a midnight dreary, while I pondered weak and weary,*
> *Over many a quaint and curious volume of forgotten lore,*
> *While I nodded, nearly napping suddenly there came a tapping,*
> *As of someone gently rapping, rapping at my chamber door.*

Smythe recognized it immediately. "'The Raven,' by Edgar Allen Poe."

"Exactly."

"But I don't understand…"

Chadrian recited another verse from the poem—the last:

> *And the Raven, never flitting, still is sitting, still is sitting*

On the pallid bust of Pallas just above my chamber door;
And his eyes have all the seeming of a demon's that is dreaming,
And the lamp-light o'er him streaming throws his shadow on the floor;
And my soul from out that shadow that lies floating on the floor
Shall be lifted - nevermore!

"What does it have to do with my question?"

Chadrian smiled. "Nothing. Everything."

He didn't understand, and he wasn't sure that he cared to. "Perhaps I should be going. I've got an early flight to Boise in the morning."

"Perhaps you had better."

"Help me cast off, will you?" said Smythe as he turned the ignition key and the throaty roar of the twin diesels filled the brisk morning air.

"Certainly." Chadrian stepped back onto the dock and picked up the bow line. He cast it onto the boat's foredeck and then did the same with the stern line.

Smythe carefully guided the boat away from the dock. Putting the throttle in idle, he looked at Chadrian and said, "Good luck with Gordon."

"Luck is the last hope of losers, Major."

The two men eyed each other the way a snake and a scorpion would—a very large snake and a very small scorpion.

"I suppose you're right," said Smythe. He nodded at Chadrian, then he pushed the throttles forward, and the big boat surged ahead. He guided it in a perfectly symmetrical circle, and then when the bow was pointed toward open water, he punched it and in a blast of noise and spray, it roared away.

Chadrian stood on the dock watching him go. He looked up at the burning sky, and scoffed to himself, "Red sky in the morning, sailors take warning." It was a common paraphrase of an ancient proverb, in which the warning was given to shepherds. As he watched Smythe's boat head out into the choppy waters of the Chesapeake, silhouetted against the glowing eastern sky, the maritime version was clearly more appropriate. But for the land that was awakening all around him, and the President who might easily be considered the shepherd to the people who had elected him, the original proverb still applied.

63

River of No Return Wilderness, Idaho

Night falls quickly in the mountains. It does so with an air of finality that is vaguely discomforting. The sun doesn't linger in its journey across the sky, the way it does over the Great Plains, or above the concrete canyons in the East. Instead it simply hesitates for an instant above the tallest peak, as if uncertain of its course, then abruptly drops down behind the ridgeline, and is gone. And after it has disappeared, the chill of the high mountain darkness reclaims the wilderness once more. On that unusually chilly night in late June, Governor Edward Morrissey's helicopter swooped in low over the treetops at the edge of the dark forest that sheltered the Wolf River Club from the rest of the world. The sleek aircraft lacked a tail rotor, and in its place was a jet thruster that, along with the noise-dampened rotors, made the craft sound like a giant dragonfly. The landing lights on the helipad cast an eerie glow on the sleek aircraft as it flared for landing. At the same moment, a second helicopter exactly like the first took off and headed back to Boise to pick up another group of special guests of the governor. Taken as a whole, the scene was more reminiscent of a lazy summer night on a farm pond rather than the gathering place for a council of war.

In the days since the passage of the President's gun bill by the House of Representatives and the subsequent walkout of over fifty of its members, the temperature of the country's political scene had reached the boiling point. Everyone both inside and outside the Beltway could sense that something was about to happen. Something bad. Everyone was acutely aware that the Governor of Idaho and the Western Freedom Party had publicly stated that they would never accept the President's bill as the law of the land. Equally, everyone knew that the President would have no choice but to force the issue. But no one knew exactly what was going to happen or when. No one, that is, except the governor himself, along with several senior political and military advisers, his fellow governors from the Group of Seven states, and the Executive Committee of the New Sons of Liberty. It was a somber group that had gathered at the isolated mountain retreat over the past twenty-four hours. To the outside world, they said they had come to find ways to preserve the Union, but their words of peace and the calm expressions on their faces belied the war paint on their souls.

As the inevitability of the confrontation between the governor and the President became apparent, Morrissey had made the rustic club his office away from the office. It wasn't that he and his staff were particularly concerned about his safety in Boise—at least not yet. It was simply that the club offered a sanctuary from the prying eyes of Federal spies, whom the governor believed were everywhere in the state capital. And he was right. A joint taskforce involving the DHS, FBI, and the CIA had been pressed into action by President Webster, based on his obsessive belief that the governor and his new party were conspiring against the Republic. At that point, few among the President's staff shared his views. Most simply could not bring themselves to believe that the blustering and bravado of a cowboy governor would ever, or could ever, amount to much. They were about to be proven wrong.

It had been less than two weeks since Sarah McGill and her film crew had interviewed the governor at the club, following which she had met with T.J. Kincaid. In her subsequent televised news report, she had been thorough, and yet fair in her presentation of the issue from the Western Freedom Party's perspective. That fact had angered the President and had caused him to threaten to lift her White House press privileges. However, he had not done so, and the Washington wags speculated that it was because he would then not be able to ogle her firm body anymore. As agreed, McGill had said nothing about her meeting with T.J. Kincaid, at least not publicly.

On the day that McGill flew back to Boise on the governor's helicopter, she had plied her charm and guile on the pilots in an attempt to find out who it was they would be flying back to the Club after dropping her and her crew off. She failed, not because her reportorial skills had been lacking, rather because they simply didn't know. Up until that time, the men and women being ferried back and forth to the mountains for meetings with the governor had traveled under assumed names. It was a tactic that the governor had insisted upon because they were drawn from the highest circles of prestige, power, and position in society. Among them were corporate CEOs, judges, politicians, senior law enforcement officials, mostly from the western states who had formed the alliance known as the Group of Seven. However, following the successful vote on the President's gun bill in the House of Representatives, the governor had dropped any pretext of secrecy, and the scope and frequency of the VIP visits to his mountain hideaway had increased dramatically, as had their national scrutiny.

Had she been there on that particular night, Sarah would have had no problem identifying the governor's guest. That was because the man who stepped out of the aircraft into the dull glow of the landing lights was none other than Major Anthony Smythe. Smythe had gained instant notoriety through his very public arrest a few days earlier on the grounds of his sprawling Virginia estate. A botched affair in which the FBI had accidentally shot and killed Smythe's prize Arabian stallion. The story received wide national coverage, and the American public could not help but be intrigued by the mysterious, dark-eyed Brit. And what drew even more attention to it was the embarrassment that his arrest and subsequent speedy release had caused the White House. It had been an easy victory for Smythe's high-priced Washington lawyers and a painful defeat for the President and his Attorney General. It was only the first round of the fight between the White House and the part-time nobleman and full-time gun-runner; the final round would not go nearly as well.

But all that was yet to come, and as Smythe ducked instinctively below the slowing rotor blades and headed over toward a waiting state trooper, he was a smiling and self-satisfied man. After all, the Governor of Idaho had sent his private jet to Washington to pick him up, followed by a helicopter ride over the mountains. Since the Wolf River Militia was currently the biggest customer for Smythe's arms importation business, it wasn't surprising that the governor had agreed to meet with him. Smythe was also a senior member of the New Sons of Liberty, a group whose leader, Senator Lamar Wacker, wanted to establish a pact between his group and the Western Freedom Party. However, it wasn't the sale of munitions that Smythe wanted to talk about, nor the NSOL. There was another reason for Smythe's request for a meeting with the governor, which was to offer the services of Chadrian to the Western Freedom Party, and in so doing, ensure that the wildfires of rebellion that were burning across the West would be fanned into a national conflagration.

The state trooper greeted the major and said, "Please follow me, sir."

"Right you are," replied Smythe, and the two of them walked up the pathway toward the club, as darkness rolled down the mountainside and enveloped the club, the helicopter pad, and everything in between.

ONE OF THE CLUB'S waiters carefully placed a leaded crystal glass containing single malt scotch on the rough-hewn pine table in front of the major. He then quickly exited the large room with its yellow pine log walls and eclectic mixture of bearskins; mounted heads of various members of the deer family; Native American artifacts; and a large wooden propeller from a World War One biplane, complete with several German bullet holes. The room was lit by a huge chandelier made from elk horns, and it cast a strange shadow about the room, giving a vaguely sinister feel. There were two other persons in the room with the major. Sitting directly across the table from Smythe was Governor Morrissey, and to his immediate right was General Jesse Latrobe in his crisp, militia uniform with five stars on its collar, one of which was new.

"I would love to have seen the look on the President's face when the Attorney General told him that they had to release you. He must have shit in his tight-assed pants," laughed the governor out loud.

"I've never actually met the man, but from what I gather, he doesn't take defeat lightly," said the major.

"He doesn't, and if I were you, Major, I'd watch my back," said Morrissey.

"I'm not afraid of the White House. They have to play by rules that I ignore. The events of the past few days bear strong evidence of that," said the major in a matter-of-fact tone of voice, as if he were talking about beating a parking ticket rather than a felony—one that could have sent him to prison for the rest of his life.

General Latrobe said, "I don't understand, Major. They found a large inventory of weapons and illegal explosives, along with enough incriminating evidence to lock you away until your country abolishes the monarchy."

The major chuckled but without any animation. "That's what makes this so bloody ironic. The FBI had me dead to rights, but they blew it."

"How did they do that?" asked Latrobe.

"They outsmarted themselves. The way they had discovered my secret underground bunker was by using satellite infrared technology. It's one of the Homeland defense subsystems of Granite Fist."

"So they knew about your hidden underground vault even before they entered your house?" asked the governor.

"Yes. The FBI had detected subterranean heat outside the footprint of my house. So when they arrived that morning with the search warrant, they knew exactly where to go to find the vault. I knew that they hadn't discovered it by chance, because it took a team of craftsmen seven months to build the vault and hide it behind the footings of a massive stone fireplace. However, I'm pleased to report that my lawyers were able to convince a Federal judge that their tactics violated my civil rights. Isn't that paradoxical? They know I'm as guilty as sin, but they can't do a thing about it. God, I love this country. You're so bloody civilized. It makes it a joy to be a criminal here."

He turned back to Latrobe and added, "As a point of clarification, I could care less about the longevity of the British monarchy. I'm an American now. My naturalization papers came through while I was being held in jail. My lawyers arranged for me to be sworn in as a U.S. citizen in the same Federal courthouse where I had been arraigned the day before."

"That's rubbing it in," said the governor with a gleeful grin.

"It couldn't happen to a more deserving man," said Smythe.

"I'd still be careful if I were you," said Latrobe. "The White House is a formidable enemy." It was obvious that the general didn't think much of the Brit. But the major hadn't made his mind up yet about the general. Any man who accomplished what he had in combat was all right in the major's book. Most men who have looked death squarely in the eye on a field of battle and lived to talk about it feel a certain kinship with others like them.

"I appreciate your warning, General, but I rather think that the President has more to fear from me than I him," said Smythe.

"Go on, Major," said the governor.

With a sly smile, Smythe replied, "Actually, I'd better not. I've probably said too much already."

The governor nodded appreciatively. "Yes, I expect that you have, and I find it all damn interesting."

There was a long pause during which no one spoke. Finally, Smythe said, "Well now, if it's all the same to you, Governor, I'd like to discuss the reason that I asked for this audience with you."

The governor's expression grew serious as he replied, "In due course, Major. But first there is something that I would like to discuss with you."

Smythe had been a little suspicious when the governor had readily agreed to meet with him, and now his suspicions proved accurate. In reality, it had been the governor's meeting all along; Smythe had just made it easy for him. "Go ahead, Governor, I'm listening."

With a serious look on his well-weathered face, the governor said, "First, I must warn you, Major, that what I am about to tell you is to be kept in the strictest confidence. Any violation of this trust will have the most severe of consequences for you." He paused and then added, "Do you understand?"

The major chuckled and said, "Death doesn't frighten me, Governor. You forget that I'm in the business of dealing death, and I'm very good at it. But if it's my silence you want, you'll have it. Without need of a threat."

Latrobe interjected harshly, "The governor wasn't joking, Major."

The smile vanished from the major's face. He looked at Latrobe with a steely gaze and answered, "Neither was I."

A pregnant silence filled the room. Finally, the governor broke it. "Very good, Major. I think we understand each other. Let's get down to business, shall we? You are a gun runner, and I am in need of guns. Lots of guns. Big guns."

"I'm already supplying you with guns right now, Governor. Everyday, truckloads of weapons come down from Canada into your state."

"I'm not talking about trucks, Major. I'm talking about planes and trains."

"Sounds like a movie title."

The governor smiled. Latrobe did not.

"Sorry," said Smythe. "Just my British sense of humor."

The governor continued, "Up until now you have been supplying us mostly with small arms and light armor. I'm talking now about heavy artillery, main battle tanks, and attack helicopters."

The major's eyebrows arched. "That won't be easy. I mean, I can get them, of course, but transporting them here will be problematic."

"How you get them into Idaho is your problem. But money is no object."

Smythe nodded, "Time and money, Governor, solve all matters."

"Does that mean you can you do it?" asked Latrobe impatiently.

The major's mind raced over the possibilities. *Ships to Vancouver, trains to Idaho, planes over the North Pole.* "Yes, gentlemen, I can. I'll bring you the best that the global armory has to offer, and then some. I'll even bring you some tanks and helicopters that the United States Army currently owns. You'd be surprised how poorly they keep track of what the tax payer has bought them."

With that, the governor brought one more conspirator into the fold. However, unlike the others who had already lent their moral and monetary support to the cause, the major could provide the governor with more sinister assistance—namely the weapons and hardware that Idaho and its Western allies would need should bluster turn into battle. And Smythe could also serve as a liaison with certain Middle Eastern countries who could provide another essential ingredient of war—namely oil. After the governor finished describing his plans for the declaration of independence of Idaho, and all that it entailed, Smythe sat back and took a deep breath. "My word, Governor, I'm really quite impressed. And I am truly honored to be of service to your cause."

"With all due respect, Major, the governor was not seeking to impress you nor honor you. We simply need you to provide the materiel that we need and soon," said the general.

The major's expression darkened. He was not used to such boiler plate negotiations. He stared at the general without replying, for a long awkward moment, and just when Morrissey was about to step in, he said, "General, within a matter of weeks, I can bring you trainloads of artillery and tanks, and jet freighters filled with Humvees and helicopters. I might even be able to get some of the new British Challenger, and French Leclerc tanks, if you'd like. They're of the same class as the Army's new M1A3 main battle tanks but without the Granite Fist technology, of course."

The comment piqued the general's interest. "Can you get us any M1A3s?"

The major's smile disappeared. "No. I doubt it. Those haven't gone into full production yet, and they are in short supply. While the Challenger and Leclerc microelectronics are not quite up to the level of sophistication of the M1A3, I assure you they are still quite lethal. Certainly better than the old M1A2s that your Army Guard units are still using."

The governor was clearly pleased. "Major, I want you to supply the Idaho Guard and militia with everything that you have to offer. As I said, money is no object. The superb fundraising of Thomas Porter has seen to that. Just work out the details with General Latrobe and his staff."

Major Smythe looked at Latrobe and then looked back at Morrissey. "No disrespect to General Latrobe, Governor, but wouldn't it be more appropriate for me to meet with the adjutant general of the Idaho Guard?"

Morrissey was quick to reply. "Today I promoted General Latrobe and placed the Idaho National Guard under his command. He will now oversee a combined force comprised of the Wolf River Militia and the Idaho Army and Air National Guard. As you know, the Idaho adjutant general commands what is referred to as an enhanced brigade comprised of infantry, field artillery, and armored units both here in Idaho and in Utah and Montana, and I'm pleased to say that governors Taylor and Sanderson have graciously approved this change."

Smythe asked, "Doesn't that brigade have units in Oregon as well?"

"It did," replied Morrissey curtly. "But it doesn't anymore. Based on the position that the governor of Oregon has taken with respect to the President's bill, I have decided that it would be in everyone's best interests if the Oregon Guard units no longer were part of the enhanced brigade."

"I see," said Smythe, whose mind was already racing ahead over the possibility of gaining additional sales of weapons in Oregon. "If I may, Governor, I have a question for the General."

"Of course."

"General Latrobe, how have the commanders of the various Guard units reacted to your appointment?"

"I know most of them by having served with them in Vietnam, Desert Storm, and most recently in WWT. Those whom I haven't met I know by reputation and they me. I don't anticipate that we will have any difficulty working together. As a matter of fact, Major, this afternoon all of my new command officers have been flown to Camp Freedom where I will be joining them after we are through here."

"Do you think it would be possible for me to join you, General?"

The general thought about it for a few moments and then said, "No. I'm afraid not. Perhaps another time."

"I understand," said Smythe, who actually didn't expect that the general would agree but thought it was worth a try.

"Now, Major, you have a helicopter to catch, and I have a speech to prepare. We have arranged for you to stay overnight in Boise, and in the morning, my jet will fly you back East."

The governor stood up. He was through with the major, but the major wasn't through with him. "Excuse me, sir, I don't mean to appear impertinent, but I believe that I was the one who originally requested to meet with you."

The major's strident tone did not sit well with Latrobe, but the governor motioned to him to stay calm. "You're absolutely right, Major. I apologize." He sat back down. "Now what can I do for you?"

"Actually, Governor, a better question might be what I can do for you, beyond selling you weapons, that is."

"Go on. I'm listening."

"I have a friend. Well, let's just say he is a business associate who has a contact inside the White House. A very senior level contact who talks too much and because of this, I believe he might be of some assistance to your cause."

"What sort of assistance?" asked the governor.

"The kind that might make the difference between victory and defeat."

"You've got my attention. When can we meet your friend?"

"Business associate," Smythe added quickly.

"Whatever. When can we meet him?"

"You can't. He will only deal through me."

The governor frowned. "Very well. What can he do for us?"

Smythe proceeded to tell the governor that through his associate, he would be able to provide them with something far more valuable than the most sophisticated of killing machines, which was information. Information from the very heart of the presidency. And all it would take was money. Big money. But as Smythe would remind the governor, what price could anyone put on freedom? The governor readily agreed. And so another cobblestone was laid on the road leading to war, a road over which tanks would soon roll and blood would soon flow.

THE GOVERNOR sat in a straight-backed chair beside a river rock fireplace, in which a log fire could be seen blazing away. In front of him was a television camera with a through-the-lens teleprompter. To his right was the Stars and Stripes, and on his other side was the flag of the state of

Idaho. The governor was dressed in freshly pressed, gray flannel slacks, with a cashmere, navy-blue sweater which had the seal of the governor embroidered in gold on its left breast. Underneath the sweater, he wore a pin-striped blue button-down shirt. On his feet were black-dress cowboy boots, and beside him lay a very large, wolf-like Alaskan Malamute Husky. Everything had been perfectly choreographed to make him look Presidential. Standing behind the camera were a few key aides plus the camera crew, one of whom was counting down. "Five, four, three…" After the word three, he motioned silently with two fingers, and then one. Then he pointed at the governor and nodded.

The governor took a deep breath and began to speak in a measured cadence with restrained power and deep conviction. "Good evening, my fellow citizens. I am speaking to you tonight from the lodge at the foot of Mount Freedom in the Bitterroot Range. It is wholly appropriate that I address you from this location, near the mountain known to the Nez Perce as the Kingdom of the Wind Spirit, for it is the place where seven months ago, forty-nine American boys died needlessly as a direct result of the careless and cavalier actions of the President of the United States. As it says in Ecclesiastes, there is a time to be born and a time to die. But, my fellow citizens, it was most certainly not the time to die for those brave, young men. There is a time to kill and a time to heal, but our President chose the former, even as many of us were pursuing the latter. As a result, young men who fell on that nearby mountaintop now lie silently in their graves, not just in Idaho or elsewhere in the West, but in Indiana, Virginia, and New York." The governor paused for effect. As if right on cue, the dog looked up at the governor with melancholy eyes.

"Beyond the human tragedy that the President's actions created for the loved ones of those brave, young men, there is a deeper Constitutional issue here that must be addressed. By ordering Federal troops into the sovereign State of Idaho, the President violated our State Constitution in that Article Fourteen, Section Six precludes the importation of any armed body of men into the state for the suppression of domestic violence without the express approval of the legislature or the state executive branch. The President sought no such approval. And now, by virtue of the passage of the President's gun-control bill by the United States House of Representatives, and its likely support in the United States Senate, the Federal Government has set a collision course with the most fundamental of our rights as citizens of this state, as guaranteed us under Article One, Section One, which states that we have the right to enjoy and defend life and liberty; and Section Eleven which guarantees that you, the people of this state have the right to keep and bear arms which shall not be abridged."

The governor continued, "And so, my fellow citizens, the tragic events on that mountain were but a shadow of the darkness to come. A darkness that has enveloped the land, stifling the human spirit, and stomping out the voice of freedom. A darkness that has set our system of justice back three hundred years to the days of the Salem witch trials." Again, he paused. "Then, two days ago, in an action that served to punctuate the darkness, not with the dawn, but with the threat of eternal night, the Government of the United States of America ceased being a government of all the people."

The governor paused and picked up a sheet of paper that was lying on a table beside him, and he began to read from it. "Whenever any form of government becomes destructive of these ends, namely life, liberty, and the pursuit of happiness, it is the right of the people to alter it or abolish it, and to institute new government, laying its foundation on such principles as to them shall seem most likely to effect their safety and happiness." He paused and laid the paper down carefully on the table, looking directly into the camera.

"Those words are not mine. They were taken from one of the mightiest pieces of paper on which man ever put pen and ink—the Declaration of Independence. But sadly, they were no more true and necessary over two hundred years ago than they are today. And so, it is with a heavy heart, but an iron will, that I have called a special joint session of the state legislature for the day after tomorrow, July 3rd. It is appropriate that these brave and noble citizens of our state be called to duty on that day, the day when in 1890 Idaho became the forty-third state to join the Union. And now it shall be the day on which we decide whether or not we shall leave it." He paused again. Then with a look of deep conviction and fervent concern, he began again. "My fellow citizens of this great state and of all our neighboring states, who share our passion for liberty, we now find ourselves faced with the heavy burden of defending our lands against tyranny. It is a burden that we did not seek, but from which we will not shrink. It is a challenge fraught with danger, but one in which we must not fail." He paused to set the stage for what he was about to say. Then, with great deliberation and power, he said, "Accordingly, during the special session, I intend to introduce a bill for the secession of the state of Idaho from the Union."

There was absolute silence in the room, and in every room, in every house across the nation. It was as if the collective being of a nation had been stopped in mid heartbeat. Frozen in time and place, unable or unwilling to accept what was happening. And then with one massive sigh, the air rushed back into the lungs of every American at exactly the same instant, making a giant sucking sound that could be heard from sea to stormy sea. So it was that the die had been cast. From that point on, there would be no turning back. Now there could be but one outcome, and one ending to the story that would be written in blood, not ink. The governor finished his address with a promise to live by the vote of the state's legislature, whatever the outcome might be; however, there wasn't anyone within electronic earshot of his words who doubted what that outcome would be.

THE GOVERNOR'S IMAGE faded to black on the giant screen BTC in the officer's mess at the Wolf River Militia Camp. While the governor had been polishing his address, General Latrobe had hopped over to the camp by helicopter where he watched the speech alone, in his private quarters, while the Guard company commanders viewed it in the officers' mess at the camp. All of them had responded immediately to the governor's directive to travel to Camp Freedom posthaste, and they now sat or stood around the large room, waiting expectantly for their new commander to address them. They didn't have to wait long.

"Ten hut!" shouted a major, who snapped to attention and saluted as the general walked into the room. The others did the same.

"At ease, men," said the general as he strode to the front of the room. "Take your seats." In his right hand he carried a Bible, which he placed on the counter. They all sat down in the leather chairs that looked like they had been taken from the fighter pilots' ready room on an aircraft carrier. Which is exactly what they were. During WWT, General Latrobe had been an admiral's guest on board the U.S.S. George Bush, CVN-77, and after he saw the chairs used by the fighter jocks, he made a mental note to get some should the appropriate occasion ever arise, which it had when Camp Freedom had been built.

The general looked at the men for a minute without speaking. Then in a move that instantly commanded their admiration and respect, he walked slowly around the room and shook the hands of each one of them. Moreover, to add to the positive first impression, he called them each by their name without once looking down at the name badges on their chests. After he shook every hand, he walked back to the front of the room and said, "Men. I have served my country through three wars, over forty years, and never once during all those years have I ever done anything to dishonor the uniform I so proudly wore. And I damn well am not going to start now."

There was a murmur in the room, and then it fell quiet again.

"Let it be known to friend and foe alike that I have not abandoned my country. My country has abandoned me." As he spoke he paced slowly and purposefully, like a lion stalking his prey, unhurried and unquestioning of the outcome. His eyes scanned the room, stopping every now and then to stare directly into the very souls of the men who sat spellbound before him. "When the President of the United States of America placed his gun-control bill before the Congress, it was intended for one purpose, and one purpose alone, which was to secure for himself a legacy. It mattered not to him that the bill would revoke a sacred promise that our founding fathers made to you, and to me, and to all those who came before us, and all those who will follow. It mattered not to him that in the history of our nation, over a million men and women have given their lives to preserve the very freedom which he now chooses to plunder. It mattered not to him that half of all Americans do not support his action. And now, with the backing of a misguided Congress, he is moving to solidify his stranglehold on liberty. Gentlemen, I say to you with all humility that I am not a politician nor a Constitutional expert. But I do know right from wrong. And I know that the government of the people, by the people, and for the people will cease to exist if we allow the few to usurp the freedoms of the many. This is a cause worth fighting for. This is a cause worth dying for. This is the cause of liberty."

He stopped pacing and said softly but firmly, "Each of you came here today because you were ordered to by the governor. But I am certain that some, if not all of you, came here with a troubled mind, and a heavy heart. I am equally certain that the events that are unfolding all about us have given you pause and have made you question where your allegiance lies. Gentlemen, you are the last best hope of liberty. You are the living legacy of all those who have gone before you. Brave men and women, who when called to duty, came, fought, and died without ever asking once what was in it for themselves. Because each of them knew that beyond friends and family and work and play, there is a far greater calling that mankind must heed. A noble calling that is as old as time. A calling that is more precious than any one life. It is the call to defend the freedom for us all." He paused again. A few of the officers cleared their throats.

Then he looked around the room one last time and said, "I am going to walk out of that door in a minute, and return to my quarters. After I do, each one of you must make a choice. There are three helicopters warming up on the landing pad as we speak. You may chose to resign your commission in the Idaho Guard, walk out of here, and get on one of those aircraft that will fly you back to Boise. Or you can choose to stay and sign your names in this Bible. I have carried it with me through three wars, and I will carry it forward through whatever God has in store for me. If you leave, I will not think less of you. There will be no dishonor in it. However, if you choose to stay, and I deeply hope that you will, then we will stand shoulder to shoulder, and together we will form once more the Army of Freedom. Regardless of what choice you make, may God bless you and keep you through the coming storm." With that, he walked out of the room.

The room fell stone-cold silent. Those who were there said later that they could hear each other heart's beating. Then one by one, each of them stood up, walked to the front of the room, and signed their names in the general's Bible. For all of them it would stand as the roll call of honor; for many it would also be their epitaph.

AT THAT MOMENT, as the officers of the Idaho National Guard committed themselves to the cause of freedom, a lonely figure stood staring out a window in a penthouse apartment in downtown Boise, less than two hundred miles away. It was T.J. Kincaid. The haunting melody and lyrics of the song "Danny Boy" drifted throughout the apartment, and while those other men found comfort in a shared commitment, Kincaid could find no solace from the loneliness that haunted him. Ever since he had returned to Boise and been welcomed into the governor's inner circle, he had desperately tried to fit in. At first it seemed that he would. When Jeremiah Kincaid flew to Boise a month after that to plead his case for a compromise with the governor, T.J.'s stock climbed with the governor and his staff. But then, things started to sour.

The incident with the grizzly had been a sore point between the increasingly militant Morrissey and the progressively pacific Kincaid.

Seeing that magnificent beast lying dead by gunfire had caused Kincaid to turn away from the gun. It would be inconsequential in its effect on the governor's cause, but it annoyed him, nevertheless. Finally, when the bombs went off in Colorado and Montana, the governor felt betrayed by Jeremiah Kincaid. Neither he nor Latrobe believed that the Speaker of the House had anything to do with the bombings or the shootings at the White House, but they were disheartened that the elder Kincaid had not come out more strongly in support of the Western Freedom Party in their aftermath. This only served to deepen the growing rift between Kincaid and the governor.

As a result, the governor had not asked Kincaid to join him at the Wolf River Club during the past few days of war planning. In particular, he did not let anyone on his staff tell Kincaid about Major Smythe's visit, since the governor was well aware of Kincaid's distrust of the major. Morrissey didn't know the reason for this animosity, but he knew that it was real and deeply felt. The net effect of all of this had been the ostracism of T.J. Kincaid by the inner circle of the Western Freedom Party in general, and by the Governor of Idaho in particular. This came to a head on the day that Sarah McGill met with Kincaid at the club, and after she left, the governor had advised him that it would be better if they put some time and distance between them.

And so, as Governor Morrissey made his monumental announcement, one that would mobilize hearts and minds on both sides in the conflict, if not yet the armies, Kincaid stood all alone in his penthouse. A solitary and sad figure silhouetted against the soaring windows of his two-story penthouse apartment, physically within the territory of one side in the coming war and linked forever by blood to the other, and yet belonging now to neither. As the governor's face filled the giant screen on one wall of the room, T.J. recited to himself the words that had comforted him as a child when he was alone in the dark: "Yea, though I walk through the valley of the shadow of death, I will fear no evil." But on that night, he found no comfort in the words, even as the dark clouds of war came rolling across the high desert skies and bore down on Idaho.

64

Camp David, Maryland

As silently as a shadow, the graceful animal slipped through the mixed hardwood forest that was bathed in the fading glow of the early summer twilight. He came so gently, so silently, and yet with such purposeful movement, that it was as if he had been charged by God with pulling the cloak of evening over the well-worn mountains that man called Catochin. He was large for his species, standing forty inches at the shoulder and weighing over three hundred pounds. His coat was sleek and full, with a reddish hue on his sides and back, while the pure whiteness of his belly, buttocks, and the bottom of his tail stood out in stark contrast to the onrushing darkness. Under its hairy covering of velvet, a bulbous growth belied the magnificent antler rack that would soon appear in all its glory when summer ceded the forest to its autumnal sister.

This full-grown, white-tailed deer buck was, in a word, a truly magnificent creation, with a thick store of fat beginning to show under his sleek coat, one that would carry him through the long winter months ahead. He had lived for fifteen years, longer than most of his kind, especially in the over-hunted woods of the Eastern United States. He had done so through cunning and caution, and it was with that same sense of caution that the large buck approached the eight-foot-high chain link fence that formed the outer perimeter of the multiple lines of defense around the Camp David Presidential retreat. Had it been a normal fence surrounding a farm or cottage, the deer would have gone unnoticed as he stood there sniffing the night wind. However, this was no ordinary compound, and the deer had been tracked by heat sensors and motion detectors from the minute that he got within one hundred yards of the fence. Had it not been immediately determined that the intruder was four-footed and represented no threat whatsoever to the President, he would have been summarily dispatched. And so the magnificent animal was allowed to turn and disappear into the forest without ever knowing that he had been in the crosshairs of a Marine sniper's scope.

"He was a real beauty," whispered one of the Marines sitting in a guard tower, as he lowered his infrared binoculars. "In another month or two, he'll be carrying eight points on that rack. Maybe ten."

His fellow Marine lowered his sniper rifle with its infrared scope and smiled. "Yeah. Maybe he'll come back during deer season."

"I doubt it," said the first. "He hasn't lived this long by being stupid."

His buddy smiled, "You're probably right. Besides, the way things are going, we won't be back here for a long time."

"What do you mean?" asked the other soldier.

"I think the White House is getting a little nervous about having POTUS come out here to the boonies, given what's going on in Idaho."

"Yeah. I guess you're right. You never know, if they're crazy enough to try to break away from the Union, they just might be crazy enough to try to assassinate the President. He'd probably be safer in the White House."

"Or at the fortress," added his buddy, referring to the secret bunker hidden deep under a mountain in Virginia.

"If it comes to that, we'll all be in a world of hurt."

"Yeah. And it won't be a deer in the crosshairs of this scope."

"Do you think we'll really be going to war against Idaho?"

The other Marine stared at him and said, "If they secede, what choice will the President have?"

His buddy sighed, picked up his night-vision binoculars, and peered back out into the night. The big buck had reappeared near the perimeter of the compound, when suddenly there was a loud gunshot, and the deer dropped like a stone.

"Holy shit, what was that?" shouted one of the guards.

The other man ignored the comment and grabbed his radio. "Gunfire. Sector Six." Then he hit a switch and floodlights lit up the entire area as if it were day. Both Marines trained their rifles in the direction from which the shot had come. Within less than a minute, two Humvees roared into view on both the inside and the outside of the fence, and instantly more Marines and

Secret Service Agents wearing body armor and carrying automatic weapons dispersed into the woods.

It only took ten minutes for them to find the shooter and bring him back to the Humvee. It was an eighteen-year-old boy along with his thirteen-year-old brother. They lived several miles from Camp David, and they had taken their father's hunting rifle out without him knowing it. The boys had seen the deer go into the woods from a nearby road just before nightfall and decided to go after it. They had gotten lost in the darkness, and as they walked toward the guard post, the older boy spotted the deer again and fired. Neither he nor his brother had any idea how close they had come to being killed. Later, when the boys' embarrassed father arrived, the Secret Service told him they would not press charges against the boys or him. He thanked the agents and promised them that it would be a long time before either of his boys would ever touch a weapon again. He was wrong. A week later his oldest boy ran away and joined the Army. He would be among the first to die in the war that the Marine guard had predicted.

AT THE SAME MOMENT that the two boys had been sighting in on the deer, over a mile away inside the main lodge, President Webster was meeting with a select group of his staff. They included Maddun Gordon, Patrick Fitzgerald, Maurice Bouchard, and Mary Lou Pritchard. They were watching the televised coverage of the Governor of Idaho's address. The Vice President had remained at the White House. As the national situation grew increasingly tense, the Secret Service had prevailed upon the President to minimize the number of times that he and the Vice President were together. Webster had immediately agreed. The tension between him and Knox had only deepened during this crisis, and he was delighted to have an excuse to distance himself from the Vice President.

At the sound of the gunshot, everyone in the room jumped up, except the President, who continued to stare angrily at the video monitor. Suddenly, Randy Wiseman and two other Secret Service agents burst into the room with their weapons drawn, which only served to put an exclamation point on the already disconcerting situation.

The President smiled at Wiseman. "Getting a little jumpy lately, Randy?"

Wiseman didn't know how to answer it. "Sorry about that, Mr. President." Seeing that the President was in no danger, he and the others holstered theirs.

"Please stay inside the room." Then leaving two of his men there, he turned and left. The President quickly lost interest in the excitement around him, and he got up and started pacing. "A time to kill and a time to heal. That son of a bitch. Quoting the Bible and courting the devil all at the same time."

"I don't think you should take this personally, Mr. President," said Fitzgerald.

"Thank-you for your sage counsel, Patrick," the President replied facetiously. It was unnecessary, but then again, so too had been Fitzgerald's comment.

Within a few minutes Wiseman returned and explained what had happened. Then he and the other two agents left the President and his team alone again.

"I wonder what the Secret Service will do with the venison," said Gordon.

Before anyone could answer, a harsh look by the President at Gordon told them that he didn't care. "Let's focus on the situation at hand and forget about the goddamned deer, shall we?"

"Yes, Mr. President," said Gordon. "Sorry, sir."

"Thank-you," said the President sternly. He sat back down. The others followed.

Pritchard said, "While he was quoting those articles from their state Constitution, he conveniently forgot Article One, Section Three, which states that the State of Idaho is an inseparable part of the American Union, and the Constitution of the United States is the supreme law of the land."

"The governor has put a whole new meaning to the term *spin*," said Fitzgerald.

Gordon piped in, "You have no other choice than to declare martial law in Idaho and place the Idaho National Guard and militia under your immediate control."

"That would mean invoking the War Powers Act, Mr. President," interjected Bouchard. "Any such action would only serve to exacerbate an already tense situation."

"I agree with Maurice, Mr. President," said Fitzgerald.

"So do I," added Pritchard.

There's a surprise. Hot lips and egghead agree with fat, old froggy. What a team, thought Gordon, as he let out a contrary grunt and shook his head. Then, controlling his sarcasm as much as it was possible for him to do, he said, "With all due respect to my learned colleagues, Mr. President, we cannot let this go without taking action."

"Exactly what would you propose that the President do?" asked Pritchard, displaying a complete lack of fear of the chief of staff. As embarrassed as she had initially been following her dalliance with the President, it had given her a certain self-confidence around him and his top aides. A girlfriend of hers had once lamented under similar circumstances, "Once you've screwed the boss, screw your fellow workers!"

Gordon flashed an angry glance at her and said snidely, "Well, I sure as hell wouldn't send in the FBI after that fiasco at Smythe's castle."

Pritchard was about to defend the Bureau, which was something she had had to do a lot recently, but before she could say anything, the President stepped in. "What do you recommend, Maddun?"

Without hesitating, Gordon replied, "Call the governor immediately, sir, give him twenty-four hours to cancel the vote, and tell him if he does not, you will declare martial law, send in the Army, and throw his sorry ass in jail."

The President considered Gordon's proposal. Then he looked at Pritchard. "How about you, Mary Lou?"

"I disagree," she replied.

"Why?" he asked.

"Morrissey sees himself as the last great defender of freedom, and as such, I think his emotions have overtaken his powers of reason."

The President nodded. "Go on."

She hesitated. "Mr. President, I think we are well past the time for making threats. Any such ultimatum by you will be used by Morrissey to inflame the rebellion that is already spreading across the entire West."

The President listened attentively.

"Moreover, it has even moved north across the border," said Bouchard.

"What do you mean?" asked the President.

"Several groups in the Canadian Prairie Provinces who have been promoting western separation from the rest of Canada have been emboldened by Morrissey's move. Apparently the Premiers of Alberta and Saskatchewan called the governor yesterday to express their support, and they have offered to form an alliance with Idaho," said Bouchard.

"How do we know this?" asked the President.

Bouchard and Fitzgerald exchanged glances.

Then Fitzgerald answered the question. "From the Canadian Ambassador. He came to the White House this morning before we left to come here," replied Fitzgerald. "He asked to meet with you, but obviously that didn't happen."

"Why didn't I know this?" asked Webster, looking around the room.

Fitzgerald looked at Gordon but said nothing.

Finally, Gordon spoke up, "I didn't think you needed to waste your time with him, sir. Their whole country is smaller in population than California, and you have more important things to do than worry about a few frustrated farmers from Moose Jaw, so I sent him over to the State Department. I think he met with some deputy assistant secretary for Pan American Affairs."

"That must have played well in Ottawa," murmured Fitzgerald.

The President was obviously not pleased. "Damn it, Maddun, all we need right now is to have Western Canada join with the State of Idaho in this madness."

"I wouldn't worry, Mr. President, the Canadian Army probably has only a dozen tanks that they bought online at surplus armor dot com."

Bouchard looked at Gordon and asked, "You never served in uniform, did you, Maddun?"

Gordon started to respond but the President cut him off. "There is nothing funny about tanks, Maddun, especially not when you're looking down the wrong end of the barrel. Now, I'd like us to return to the matter of how in the hell we are going to keep this from involving even a single soldier, let alone tanks."

It was a futile wish, but none of them could know it at the time. And Maddun's tasteless joke would later come back to haunt him when the latest versions of British main battle tanks, "liberated" from the Canadian Army by the Government of Alberta, rolled on railroad flat cars across the 49th parallel to join Morrissey's militia.

Pritchard was extremely frustrated by the President's seeming insensitivity to the danger that Gordon represented, and his unwillingness to deal with it. But there was nothing she could do except sit tight and wait for the chance to get the man who to her was the very embodiment of evil. She was determined to uncover his treachery if it was the last thing she did as Attorney General. She looked at the President and said, "I hate to bring up a sore subject, sir, but I should make you aware of another development with Major Smythe."

"The gun runner?" asked the President.

"Yes," she replied. "We've been tracking him following his release from custody."

"How?" asked Gordon.

Pritchard looked at the chief of staff and with a straight face said, "You don't need to know." She looked back at the President, who was having trouble hiding his smile. "Smythe was flown today on the governor's private jet to Boise, and then by helicopter to the Wolf River mountain retreat to meet with Governor Morrissey."

The President's eyes narrowed. "Really?"

"Yes, sir," she continued. "He is there now."

"Do you mean to say that the terrorist who you let slip through your fingers is now conspiring with that traitor in the Idaho state house?" said Gordon angrily.

Pritchard shot back, "The only charges we could support against the major were for illegal trafficking in firearms, not terrorism," she retorted.

"But thanks to the ineptitude of the Bureau, even those didn't stick, did they?" snapped Gordon.

Bouchard jumped in, "We had no hard evidence that Smythe was involved in conspiracy with the governor or anyone else for that matter."

"And guns don't kill people, people do," muttered the exasperated Gordon.

"Why do you think he's out there, Mary Lou?" the President asked.

"I don't know, Mr. President, but as we speak, agents from the joint services task force are trying to find that out. However, in the absence of any further evidence, and notwithstanding Mr. Gordon's more extreme theories, I think the very fact of Major Smythe's presence at the governor's retreat is certainly troubling. It only strengthens my opinion that the governor has likely gone past the point of listening to reason."

The President thought about it for a few moments and then asked, "What do you propose that I do?"

Pritchard looked at Fitzgerald. He answered, "There are a small but very powerful group of moderates within the state's legislature, Mr. President, who just might listen to you if you were to reach out to them. They are led by the Chief Justice of the State Supreme Court, a woman named Sheila Landsdowne, who happens to be a former classmate of mine from college. I haven't spoken with her in years, but I am certain she will remember me.

She is clearly not in Morrissey's inner circle, and with your support, she may be willing to take a public stand against secession, and possibly even prevent the governor from getting the three quarter majority that he needs. She has also recruited the former adjutant general of the Idaho guard to her cause, and apparently he has told her that many senior officers in the Guard will mutiny against Morrissey if it comes to war."

"Do you have any evidence that she will accept our help?" asked Webster. "Or are you just hoping that she might?"

"Until I speak with her, of course, it's the latter, Mr. President," Pritchard replied.

"Mr. President, it has also recently come to our attention that there is a growing rift between the governor and the youngest son of Jeremiah Kincaid," added Fitzgerald.

The President's expression darkened. "Ah yes, T.J. Kincaid. The black sheep of the Kincaid clan who started this mess on that godforsaken mountain in the Bitterroots."

"And then flaunted your authority and the rule of law in public, sir," Gordon added.

Fitzgerald continued, "Be that as it may, we've learned that the moderates in the Idaho state house led by Landsdowne recently approached Kincaid and asked him to join them in a move to impeach the governor."

"Why Kincaid?" asked the President.

Pritchard joined in. "Because, Mr. President, regardless of what we in this room might think about him, T.J. Kincaid is an articulate and charismatic leader with a magnetic personality. As a result of the way he handled himself up on that mountain, he's become a hero in the eyes of the people of Idaho, and most of the Western States."

"Apparently, the moderates see him as the perfect replacement for Morrissey," said Fitzgerald. "He shares their independent spirit but not to the radical extremes of the governor."

"What did Kincaid say to all this?" asked the President.

Fitzgerald looked over at Pritchard and then back at the President. "He rebuffed them. But we think if you reach out to him that his answer might be different."

A look of alarm flashed across Gordon's face. "No, no, no! Mr. President, you should not contact that smart-ass kid."

Mary Lou quickly said, "Anyone who has accomplished all that he has and been through what he has at the age of thirty-four is hardly a kid."

"I shouldn't have to remind the Attorney General that Kincaid is still a fugitive from justice on felony charges issued by her department," said Gordon.

The atmosphere in the room was growing increasingly tense, and the President had had enough. "I'm only going to say this once. We are on the verge of having Idaho secede from the Union, and I need all the brainpower residing in this room to work together to find the best solution. Now knock off the posturing, and give me the benefit of your collective IQs and all those years of post-graduate education."

The room fell silent until Pritchard spoke. "Mr. President, we should get a message through to T.J. Kincaid that you are willing to reopen discussions regarding the compromise proposed by his father, if he will publicly take a stand against secession and simultaneously join the effort to impeach Morrissey."

Gordon waited for the President to rebuke this ridiculous proposal. When he didn't immediately do so, he spoke up. "Mr. President. I understand the logic behind their position, and if it works, our troubles with Morrissey would finally be behind us. And we would be able to avoid a confrontation with Idaho that can only lead to war."

"But?" asked the President.

"But even if it worked, it would mean that you would have to accept the compromise bill authored by Jeremiah Kincaid, and it would annul the victory of your original proposal in the House. I know you were willing to live with that compromise, Mr. President, but I also know that you passionately believe that your bill, which we have succeeded in getting through the first stage of the Constitutional amendment process, is still the best plan for America."

Webster considered what his chief of staff said. When he wanted to, Maddun Gordon could be an intelligent and convincing speaker. He hadn't risen to become the alter ego of the most powerful man on earth through blind luck.

"What do you think, Maurice?" asked the President, noticing Bouchard's silence.

"Mr. President, I find myself in the rather unusual position of agreeing with Mr. Gordon."

The others present were startled at his reply, but no more so than Gordon himself.

"Why?"

"Quite frankly, sir, because I don't trust Governor Morrissey or anyone associated with his cause, including the young Mr. Kincaid."

Gordon was delighted and sat back with a smug look on his face. He was certain that with Bouchard's endorsement, the President would follow his advice. He was wrong.

"Thank-you, Maurice." The President looked over at his chief of staff and said, "Of course I believe my bill is the best possible outcome for America. However, unless we find a way to defuse the situation, that cowboy will start a fire that neither he nor I can extinguish. Therefore, I agree with Mary Lou and Patrick that Morrissey has gone too far down the road to hell to turn back now. And quite frankly, I don't see a way to give him a graceful exit. We'll pursue the plan proposed by Mary Lou and Patrick. As much as it bothers me to admit it, I need to ask the Kincaid family for help."

Fitzgerald smiled, while Gordon flopped back in his chair.

Pritchard and the President exchanged a look that carried with it a shadow of what had happened between them. "Mr. President," she said softly. "If I may say so, sir, that is a very Presidential decision."

Gordon was obviously unhappy with the President's plan. But he was too smart to push the matter further. He believed that the chances of T.J. Kincaid being willing to even accept a call from the White House were slim, let alone agreeing to work together.

Bouchard sat silently with no outward show of emotion.

"I will place the call for you to T.J. Kincaid immediately, sir," said Fitzgerald.

The President then added, "No, Patrick. I think we need to speak to his father first."

"Of course, you're right, sir. Will you call him?" asked Fitzgerald. There was a high degree of risk in the White House trying to reach out to the younger Kincaid directly, and they would have a better chance through the father.

"No. Not me," said the President. Then he looked at Pritchard. "I want you to call him, Mary Lou." As he said it, the President gave Mary Lou a knowing smile. He was well aware that she had turned to the Speaker for help after their tryst. And he suspected that if there was anyone in his administration that the Speaker would listen to, it was Mary Lou. Of course, he was right. Much could be said about this President's flaws and foibles, but understanding the complexities of human interaction wasn't one of them.

Pritchard nodded and said, "Thank-you for your trust, Mr. President. I'll call the Speaker as soon as I get back to my room and ask to meet with him first thing in the morning." She got up.

"What if this plan fails? What then?" asked Gordon.

"You tell me?" asked the President.

"Then we send in the troops."

"And start the second Civil War?" asked Webster.

"There won't be any war, sir, if we hit them hard and fast."

Pritchard said nothing. She was weary of arguing with Gordon.

Fitzgerald stepped in. "If your attempt to defuse the situation through the Kincaid family connection should fail, Mr. President, I think you should go on national television and make an appeal to the entire country to remain calm. You need to explain your position once more, but in a conciliatory manner that doesn't paint Morrissey into a corner. You need to ask the people, all the people, for more time. Time for men of reason to talk. Time for tempers to cool." He paused and glanced over at Mary Lou with an almost apologetic expression. "And time, Mr. President, for the Army to prepare itself for the worst."

"Are you saying, Patrick, that if the Kincaid initiative fails, you support military action against Idaho?"

"Yes, Mr. President. I am."

The President glanced at Bouchard. "What about you, Maurice?"

Bouchard slowly shook his head and said softly, "You would have no choice, Mr. President."

Webster looked at Pritchard. "Mary Lou?"

She sighed and then said softly, "I agree."

Gordon was delighted.

Fitzgerald continued, "If it comes to such drastic action, we must limit its scope and duration. Military action against one state can be handled with the precision of a scalpel, with limited trauma to the nation as a whole. But if we let the situation get away from us and it escalates into military action against seven states or more, it will be as gruesome as an amputation with a dull ax."

Everyone sat quietly absorbing the imagery.

"Do you really think an address to the nation can buy us such time, Patrick?"

"Yes, sir. If you speak from the heart."

Gordon coughed derisively, but the President ignored him.

"Very well, Patrick. Work with my writers and prepare my speech." He paused. "And make it from the heart, as you suggest—but not a bleeding heart."

"Yes, sir. I hear you."

The President looked at Gordon. "Maddun, please see to it that Marine One is ready to fly us back at 0600 hours."

"Yes, Mr. President," replied Gordon. Outwardly he was putting on his best team-player façade, while his mind was already racing ahead with the implications of these last-minute peace initiatives. He realized all too well that his only hope of staying on the President's staff, and near the seat of power, was through the continuation of the struggle between the governor and the President. If and when a peaceful compromise was reached, the President would likely carry through with his pledge to banish him from the kingdom. Then he would be on his own. Outside in the real world. In a mental hospital. Where there would be no one to protect or serve him. No legions of high-priced attorneys, no squad of Secret Service agents, no West Wing groupies. No one. And most frightening of all, it would be where Stefan Chadrian could be hiding around any corner.

Regardless of the consequences for the nation and the young men and women who would be placed in harm's way, the only life Maddun Gordon cared about was his own. And it was right then and there that everything changed. Maddun Gordon's entire reason for being was transformed—from need for achievement to the need for survival. It was the oldest and most primal of mankind's needs. Like all wild animals, when cornered, Gordon would attack anyone and anything that threatened him. Even the President. From that moment on, nothing would ever be the same again for Gordon or the man he served—and the die was cast for their ultimate showdown.

The President stood up and said, "Okay. That's it. We have a busy day ahead of us tomorrow."

Everyone stood up and headed for the door. The President said, "Maurice. May I have a word with you?"

Bouchard looked surprised, as did Gordon. "Of course, Mr. President," he replied, as the others started filing out.

"Good. Let's talk, Maurice," he said, gesturing for the other man to sit back down.

"Yes, sir. What about?"

"About Homeland Security, of course."

"Of course," replied Bouchard.

With that, the President smiled at the others and then closed the door behind them.

PATRICK FITZGERALD, Mary Lou Pritchard and Maddun Gordon walked down the hallway of the main staff quarters at the Presidential retreat, and the first room they came to was that of Fitzgerald. He said goodnight to the other two, and they headed down the hall together. They next came to Mary Lou's room, and she placed the key card in the reader and listened to the soft click, followed by the green light indicating that her door lock had released. She looked back, expecting Gordon to already be several steps down the hall. Instead, he was standing right behind her. So close that when she turned, their bodies almost touched.

It startled her, and she let out a small gasp. "I have to call the Speaker of the House right away. So if you'll excuse me—" she said, growing alarmed and glancing down the hall to see if there was a Secret Service agent there. There wasn't.

"I saw you that night. With the President in his study," said Gordon, with a guttural growl.

His comment caught her off guard, and at first she couldn't seem to get any words to come out of her mouth. "I beg your pardon?" she finally responded.

"Does your husband know you had sex with the President while he stood waiting for you down the hall?"

Her mind was now racing with what she should do. Instinct told her to scream, but reason said he hadn't done anything, and if she did, she would appear a fool when the agents came storming up the stairs. Pride told her to stay calm and stand up to him. In her years as a district attorney, she had seen many a bully back off when confronted by their intended victims. "What happened between me and the President is none of your business. Nor is it any of your business what I discuss with my husband. Now I suggest that you get to your own room before—"

She didn't get to finish her sentence. He reached behind her with his right hand and twisted the door knob, throwing the door wide open. "Here, let me help you," he said, as he pushed the door wide open.

"I'll scream," she blurted out as she braced herself against the door frame.

"Listen to me, you stuck-up bitch. We both know you screwed the President's brains out, so don't try to play the innocent victim here. Now, why don't we just go inside so I can show you what it's like to do it with a real man. Not one who uses the Oval Office to get laid, or that limp-dick soldier boy who only got promoted by being cuckolded."

He took a step toward her. Simultaneously, she stepped back into the room and grabbed the door. She swung it hard, trying to close it, but he jammed his foot in the way and pushed it back hard with his left hand. "If you don't stop, I swear to God I will scream."

He leaned on the door and said, "Oh, please. The entire Secret Service detail knows what you did. Do you really think they will believe that you didn't want this?"

She was beginning to feel sick. She realized that he wasn't going to back off and that there wasn't much she could do to stop it. Mixed in with the raging emotions of fear and anger was an overwhelming sense of guilt that she had brought this upon herself.

Then his tone changed to be more of a bedroom rather than a backroom voice. "Come on, Mary Lou. I promise I won't tell anyone if you don't. Just think of it this way: you can be the first Attorney General to sleep your way though the entire Cabinet." He laughed and took another step forward and cupped one of her breasts in his hand. She instantly grabbed his hand and pushed it away. He chuckled and said, "Then again, maybe not."

"Mary Lou. Are you all right?" Both Gordon and Pritchard looked down the hall. Walking purposefully toward them was Patrick Fitzgerald. The cavalry in an unlikely form, but the cavalry nonetheless.

"Patrick!" she exclaimed.

Fitzgerald reached them. His fragile frame looked woefully ill-equipped to take on the stocky, big man. Yet by the look on his face, it was clear that he sensed exactly what was going on, and his body language made it equally clear he had not come to chat. Before he could say or do anything, Gordon said, "Mary Lou and I were just getting to know each other a little better, Paddy my boy." Then he looked at her and said, "I'm afraid we'll have to take this up at a later time, Mary Lou. But thanks for the offer, anyway." He stepped past Fitzgerald and tossed a "Good night, kiddies" at them as he left.

Fitzgerald started to go after him, but Mary Lou caught him by the arm and said, "Let it go, Patrick."

"But—"

She interrupted him. "I'm fine."

"Mary Lou. You can't let this go."

She smiled and said gently, "Please Patrick. I'm all right, now."

The tone of her voice told him to do what she asked. He relaxed but said, "It's none of my business, but you really should tell the President, Mary Lou. That man is dangerous in more ways than one, and he should be stopped."

"I know. I will handle it. I promise."

"Okay, if you're sure you're all right."

"I am. Thank-you. I owe you one." As she said it, she stepped over and kissed him gently on the cheek. "You are a classy guy, Patrick Fitzgerald."

"Yes, I am, aren't I?" he said with a grin. Then he stepped back out into the hallway and was gone. She closed the door, bolted it, and fell back against it. Her experience with Maddun Gordon, although repugnant, was hardly what an impartial observer would have characterized as a contributing factor to the troubles that were facing America. And yet, the very fact that a man such as Maddun Gordon occupied the office next door to the Oval Office was one more vector in the confluence of forces that was driving the country into the valley of the shadow. Each, in and of itself, was insufficient to awaken the gods of war, but when taken as a whole, they would achieve critical mass. And so, as Mary Lou sat down on her bed and reached for the telcom to call the Speaker of the House of Representatives, the clock kept running down toward the dawn, and with it, the nation took one step closer to the brink.

65

Rayburn Congressional Office Building, Washington, D.C.

The sun was barely above the horizon when Jeremiah Kincaid opened the door to his inner office, walked over to his desk, and sat down. As was his normal practice, he would have been at his desk that early anyway, but the urgent telcom call that he received from Mary Lou Pritchard seven hours earlier served to guarantee that he would not be late that morning. She said that Marine One would be bringing her back to the White House by six thirty, and she expected to be at the Speaker's office by seven. She didn't say what it was that she wanted to discuss, except that it related to the gun bill and that she was acting at the President's request.

For obvious reasons, this piqued the Speaker's interest, but there was something more about her tone and manner on the telcom that worried him. He couldn't put his finger on it, but she sounded more like the vulnerable woman that he had consoled a month earlier than the tough Attorney General. The purpose of her visit was obviously professional rather than personal, but he couldn't help but wonder if something else had happened at Camp David to upset her. Kincaid was working his way through some papers when there was a knock at his door and George Ross walked in. "Good morning, Mr. Speaker," he said in the unmistakable fog of someone who is not a morning person.

"Morning, George," said the Speaker with a smile. "You know, after all the years of working with me, I would have thought your inner clock would have reset itself by now."

"Not a chance, sir. After you and I finish our time together, and let me add that I hope it isn't for a long while, I intend to never get up before noon again."

"I bet your eyes will pop open at 5:00 a.m. no matter what you try to do to stop them."

"You're probably right, and every time they do, I shall lie there in bed cursing you."

They laughed and quickly got back to business. "What time will the Attorney General be here, sir?" asked Ross.

The Speaker glanced over at the grandfather clock quietly ticking in the corner. "Anytime now," he replied.

Ross looked at his watch and then said, "Good."

The telcom buzzed on the Speaker's desk. He picked it up, listened, and then said, "Very well. Send her in." He hung it up. "Mary Lou's here."

Ross nodded and asked, "Do you need anything right now, sir?"

"No thank-you, George."

"Do you think Morrissey will really go ahead with the vote tomorrow?"

"I don't know anyone who can stop him at this point. Not even the President."

There was a knock at the door, and in stepped Mary Lou Pritchard. Despite the obvious fatigue and worry on her face, she still looked beautiful in the dawn's early light that streamed in through the Speaker's office windows.

"Mary Lou," said the Speaker, standing up.

"Mr. Speaker," she replied.

"You look terrific, but I guess I'm not supposed to say that, am I? What with political correctness and all."

"Mr. Speaker, you can say that to me anytime you want," she added with a smile. She greeted George Ross, who then excused himself and pulled the Speaker's door shut on his way out.

The Speaker motioned for her to sit down on one of the two overstuffed leather chairs in the far corner of his office nearest the grandfather clock. "Ever since you called me, I've been eager to hear what you want to discuss. It sounded important."

They both sat down and she said, "Yes, Jeremiah. It is." She began to lay out the plan that she, the President, and Patrick Fitzgerald had developed.

She had no difficulty in outlining their assessment of the situation and the unacceptability of trying to reopen discussions with the governor. On that point, the Speaker strongly agreed. He was supportive and keenly interested in what she was saying until she got to the part where she brought up the Speaker's son. At the mention of T.J.'s name, and the role that the President wanted him to play, the Speaker's expression changed markedly. It was at that point that Mary Lou felt, for an instant, that she had lost him. But she was wrong.

The Speaker thought about what she had just asked him to do, for only a brief moment, and then he looked at her and said, "All right, we'll do it; but I need to bring someone else into this to help us."

At first, Pritchard looked puzzled; then she realized what he meant.

The Speaker continued, "I'm not sure that T.J. will listen to me, but despite all that has gone on between them, I think he will talk with his older brother. Is that okay with you, Mary Lou?"

"Yes, of course." She knew that they had to do everything they could to stop the vote, and if the Speaker thought Jake could help, so be it.

With that, he reached over and punched the speed-dial number for his apartment onto his BTC keyboard. Jake's voice came over the speakers, but there was no picture on the screen. The Speaker caught him as he was getting ready to go to the Pentagon. Throughout his courtship of Sarah McGill, he had never moved in with her. In fact, they hadn't even slept together. After he stormed out of her apartment a week earlier, he wasn't sure they would ever see each other again.

"Jake," said the senior Kincaid.

"What's wrong, dad?"

"I need your help.

"My help? To do what?"

"To call T.J."

There was a momentary silence on the other end of the line.

"Jake, are you still there?"

"He won't listen to me."

"You have a better chance than I."

"I don't think he'll listen to either one of us—but I know someone he will listen to."

"Who?"

"Sarah."

Jake's answer surprised the Speaker. "Really?"

"Trust me, dad. She's the best hope we have. I'll tell her it's off the record, and she'll honor it."

The Speaker looked at Mary Lou Pritchard. She agreed immediately. "Okay. Do you know where she is?"

"Yes. She's at her apartment."

"How can you be sure?"

"I just am." He wasn't about to tell his father that he had had a friend at DHS track her NIS card each night to see if she was going home alone. Which she was. He was certain that she would not have been happy had she known about it. But he didn't care. He justified it to himself that it was for her own safety. The irony of it all was that she had asked Tanner to do the exact same thing for him.

"Okay. Call her. We'll send a car to pick you both up." The Speaker hit the call disconnect key and looked at Pritchard. "I hope this works."

"It has to, Mr. Speaker. Hiram Johnson once said on the floor of the Senate that truth is the first victim of war. If that's true, then surely hope is the last bastion of peace."

The Speaker nodded sadly as she called her office and ordered a car to pick up the colonel and Sarah McGill.

THE UNMARKED SEDAN, with its siren blaring and red strobe light on the dashboard flashing, raced through the city toward Capitol Hill. Before WWT and the terrorist attacks in Washington and other American cities, cars often refused to get out of the way of police cars or other emergency vehicles, despite their sirens and lights. Not anymore, however, because a new law had been passed giving police the right to arrest and imprison violators for ninety days without exception. As a result, on that morning, the car carrying Colonel Kincaid and Sarah McGill, who were sitting on opposite sides of the back seat, had no difficulty cutting a neat swath through the heavy morning traffic of the capital.

"Are you sure I should be involved in this?" asked McGill. "This is a family matter."

Both McGill and the colonel knew better than to say anything that they didn't want the driver to overhear.

"No, Sarah, it's not." He reached over and took her hand. "But even if it were, you are family as far as I'm concerned."

623

In the mirror, she saw the driver glance back at them and smile. She knew he would love to know what was going on, but she also knew that he wouldn't dare ask. She hoped she could help and that this last-minute effort would succeed. But somewhere deep inside her subconscious, a little voice told her it would fail. Although she wouldn't say it to Jake, that little voice was never wrong.

FORTY MINUTES after the Speaker's call, Jake and Sarah sat with the Attorney General of the United States of America and the Speaker of the House of Representatives in his office. They quickly planned their strategy and agreed that they would do two things simultaneously. First, the Speaker would call Tanner and have him run a covert personal tracker through Granite Shield, using T.J.'s NIS card codes. And Sarah would place a call to T.J.'s apartment in Boise. Meanwhile, the Attorney General would call Sheila Landsdowne and reach out to her and her supporters. As the rest of the nation woke up to a beautiful morning in early summer, oblivious to the fact that the dark clouds of evil loomed on the western horizon, four patriots made one last grasp at peace.

TWO THOUSAND miles away, directly under those looming dark clouds, the youngest son of the Speaker of the House of Representatives, kid brother of the decorated Army Colonel, and secret admirer of the most popular female news personality in America, would have gladly accepted a call from any of them had he been in his apartment. Unfortunately for them, and for the nation as a whole, he wasn't. Given how lonely and isolated he felt at that moment in his life, he very likely would have jumped at the chance for a reconciliation with his father and family. And he certainly would have talked to Sarah McGill, whom he had not been able to get out of his mind since their meeting at the Wolf River Camp. But it was not to be. T.J. was not there. Once more, fate intervened, as the progression of events fell into each other like dominoes, beginning on a mountain in Idaho and tumbling rapidly across America, until they crashed headlong into the White House itself. At that moment, T.J. was alone in his car, driving up the winding, gravel road that led to the Bitterroot Rod and Gun Club. A road that he had climbed ten months earlier with a group of men whose faces still haunted him.

He left Boise in the middle of a fitful night and now, three hours later, the gates of the club, which had been strongly rebuilt and securely locked by the Federal Government, came into view. He pulled his car up to the gates and stepped out into the cool morning air. He walked over, picked up the heavy padlock, and examined it. After a few seconds he dropped it and walked back to his car. He reached inside and switched off the headlights and ignition. Now the early morning scene was only lit by the soft glow of a three-quarter moon. He cocked his head and listened to the silence of the forest. All was still except the gentle rustle of the wind through the tall pines. Satisfied that he was alone, he walked back over to the gate and placed his hands as high up in the chain link as he could reach. Then with a powerful motion, he pulled himself up the fence and didn't stop climbing until he reached the top of the eight-foot-high barricade. He swung himself over, hesitated on the top edge for a few moments, then dropped to the ground, his landing cushioned by the soft carpet of pine needles below. As he did, a heavy revolver fell out of his jacket pocket and landed on the earth beside him with a soft thud. He stood there, looking at its shiny chrome exterior as it reflected the moonlight. Then he reached down, picked it up, tucked it back into his pocket, and headed up the road toward the club. Over a month earlier, he had promised himself that he would never again hold a gun, but promises were meant to be broken, and this gun wasn't meant for hunting a bear.

T.J. didn't notice the five pair of eyes that followed his every movement from the safety of dense branches near the top of the tallest of the surrounding pines. They were the eyes of a terror of ravens, and they watched him intently all the way, until he disappeared around the bend in the dirt road that led to the killing ground where so many young men had fallen in what seemed to T.J. as an eternity ago.

IT WASN'T the raucous croaking of the ravens that woke him from his deep sleep, nor was it the mid-morning sun that shone brightly through the broken window of the burned-out building that had once housed the Bitterroot Rod & Gun Club. Despite the bitter cold, he had slept for five hours on a damp, dirty mattress that did nothing to soften the sharpness of the rusting springs underneath. It had not been his intent to sleep in that place so full of bitter memories. Instead, T.J. Kincaid had come back up onto that mountain to do one thing, which was to kill himself. He had come very close to doing just that, even going so far as to place the barrel of the weapon in his mouth three times. But each time, the face of Sarah McGill had appeared in his mind's eye at the exact moment that his thumb had begun to squeeze the trigger, causing him to stop cold. Finally, after the third try, his wrist began to cramp from being held in its backward position, and he had placed the gun down on the dirty floorboards and fallen over on his side, emotionally drained and physically exhausted. Alone, dejected, and feeling abandoned by the world, he lay there until he drifted off into a dreamless sleep, unaware that while he slept, his father and brother and the woman he loved were trying desperately to find him.

So it was that the little boy named T.J. Kincaid, who had once been lost inside the man named Thomas Porter, slept soundly despite the croaking of the ravens and the slender shafts of sunlight that sliced through the swirling dust in the shadows of the bullet-riddled building—and oblivious to the fruitless efforts of his father and three others who were on a mission from the President of the United States of America.

It was very likely that T.J. would have slept on for five more hours, had it not been for the loud thumping of the rotor blades that filled the morning air and scattered the ravens. As the noise grew louder, his eyes suddenly opened and he jumped up, reflexively grabbing his weapon from the floor and shouting out loud, "LT... LT, wake the men. They're attacking us!" But, of course, there was no lieutenant to hear his cries, and most of the men with whom he had climbed the mountain would never wake again. Finally, as the dust thrown up by the helicopter swirled in under the door, he regained his senses, and the reality of time and place returned to him. Cautiously he got up and walked over to the door, still clutching his gun. He pried it open and stared out into the blinding light of day. At first, all he could make out were the shapes of two men approaching the building. They were bathed in a glow that gave them an other-worldly appearance, and had he not now been fully conscious, he might have thought that they were the ghosts of his dead soldiers come to take him home. Then one of them spoke.

"Thomas, are you all right?" Through his grogginess, he recognized the voice as being that of Governor Morrissey.

Slowly he stepped out into the bright light, weapon still in hand. As he did, he felt another hand reach down and remove the weapon from his. It was the hand of Jesse Latrobe, who then placed a thick wool blanket around his shoulders and said softly, "You're going to be fine, son."

Then the governor put his arm around his back and said, "Come on, Thomas. I think it's time for you to come home. This is going to be a big day for us, and your are an important part of it. We can't have you looking like a mountain man, now, can we?"

As they shepherded him over toward the waiting helicopter, Kincaid turned his head toward the governor with a slightly bewildered look on his face and asked, "How did you know where to find me?" He had left his NIS card back in the apartment so that no one could find him.

The governor glanced at Jesse, and then he looked back at Kincaid and said gently, "I'm the governor of this state, Thomas. Nothing escapes my reach."

Standing beside the open passenger door of the helicopter was newly promoted Captain Kelly Wright, the aircraft's commander. As her co-pilot helped the governor and Latrobe ease Kincaid into the back of the aircraft, it was obvious from the look on her face that Wright was deeply disturbed by Kincaid's disheveled appearance.

Kincaid obviously didn't understand what was happening. He didn't know that the governor had anticipated that he would not be carrying his NIS card and had a global satellite tracking device placed in his car. Nor did he know that his father had been reaching out to him. And he would never know because the governor's aides had erased the digital record on his BTC in his apartment. As a result, the efforts of a father to reach out to his son, and the President of the United States of America to reach out to the enemy within, were thwarted.

The vote in the state legislature would now proceed as planned. Father and unsuspecting son had come close to playing a part in the salvation of the Republic. So close and yet so far. Separated not by the thousands of miles that lay between them, but by all the years that they had missed spending together during T.J.'s childhood. Time that could never be recaptured. Time that might have been sufficient to save a nation.

NIGHT HAD FALLEN on the nation's capital by the time that Jeremiah, Jake, Sarah, and Mary Lou finally admitted defeat in their quest to locate T.J., after fourteen hours of searching, a process which involved countless confidential telcom calls and the top-secret national satellite scantrack using Granite Shield, which Tanner Spence had run for them.

Pritchard excused herself and went to call the President to inform him about the bad news.

"I'm sorry, dad," said Jake. "Is there any thing else you want us to do?"

"No. We're done," replied the weary congressman.

"At least we established contact with Ms. Landsdowne," said McGill.

"I was quite impressed with her, and I understand her reluctance to take on Morrissey directly." It was unusual for the Speaker to use the governor's surname alone, and it did not go unnoticed by the others in the room. It was clear that any friendship or respect that may have once existed between the two men had vanished.

Jake stood up and said, "If it's okay with you, dad, I've got to go."

Sarah did the same. "I do too. My boss is probably wondering whether or not I fell off the face of the earth."

The Speaker stood up just as Pritchard returned. All eyes fell upon her.

"How did it go?" asked the Speaker.

"As you would expect."

They all stood there, quietly contemplating the future.

Pritchard added, "The President asked me to convey his sincere appreciation to all of you."

The Speaker nodded and looked back at Jake and Sarah. "I guess you two had better go." But it was obvious by his tone that he really didn't want them to. He walked over and gave Sarah a big hug, and then he faced Jake. There was an awkward moment, and then the Speaker reached out, grabbed him, and pulled him close. They stood there—father and son—holding tightly on to each other as tears welled up in the eyes of Sarah McGill and Mary Lou Pritchard. Tears not for the nation that was about to be torn apart, but for a father and son who were finally being drawn together. Then the fleeting moment of tenderness passed, and Jake and Sarah left.

Pritchard looked at the Speaker and said, "It looks like the vote in the Idaho state assembly is unstoppable now."

The Speaker walked over to the window of his office. He stood there staring at the clear night sky. At length he said, "A star for every state and a state for every star."

Mary Lou didn't understand. "I'm sorry?"

He looked at her. "Robert Charles Winthrop in his address on the Boston Common in 1862." He looked back up out the window into the moonless night that sat like a giant black umbrella over the city punctured by a million tiny points of light. Then with a sigh, he said, "However painful my personal problems are, they pale by comparison to those facing the President tonight. I have lost a son, but the President has lost a nation."

"And there is nothing anyone can do about it," she added.

"You know, Mary Lou, every time I'm troubled by a particularly spiteful debate on the House floor or by the self-serving partisanship in Congress, I go up on the roof and lose myself in the sky."

Pritchard was puzzled. "Do you mean the roof here in this building?"

He spun around, and with the zeal of a school boy about to do something deliciously naughty, he said, "Yes. Exactly. Would you like to join me?"

She stared at him for a moment. And then, with an equally mischievous smile on her face, she replied, "Why not?"

He took her by the hand and led her out of his office, past his staff who were still hard at work, and down the hall, followed dutifully by William Murray and several other Secret Service agents, who had not left his side since the shooting. Then they continued on up a stairwell that smelled of old marble and new floor wax to a door on which an officious sign read, "Alarm will sound if opened." Before Pritchard could say a word, the Speaker turned back to the agents, gave them a wink, and said, "We'll be just a few minutes, boys. I promise."

They smiled and took up stations on either side of the door. They knew there was no way an intruder with evil intentions could make it to the top of the Congressional office building, as it was protected from aerial attack by the same defense system that guarded the White House. Then Jeremiah Kincaid, Speaker of the House of Representatives, third in line for the presidency, and Mary Lou Pritchard, Attorney General of the United States of America stepped through the door, out onto the roof, and back through all the years to their childhood, when they had gazed up at the heavens and wondered why it was there.

THE GOVERNMENT SEDAN sat waiting at the curb for Jake as he walked Sarah to the door of her apartment building. They looked weary from the long, frustrating day of failure—failure on both a public interest and personal level. With respect to the former, they had failed to locate T.J. and thereby failed to prevent Governor Morrissey from his plan to secede from the Union; while on a personal level, they had failed to find common ground in their on-again, off-again relationship. Jake was in love with Sarah; neither had any doubts about that. However, as much as Sarah had been drawn to Jake emotionally and physically, she did have doubts about whether or not she loved him—and that made all the difference.

They reached the door. The uniformed doorman stood waiting at a discreet distance inside the lobby, in case the couple wanted privacy. But there would be no need for that; Jake was in no mood for tenderness. "Good night, Sarah," he said in the detached way of a friend.

Sensing correctly that his frustration was deeper than simply the result of failing to find his brother, she looked up, probing his eyes. "Jake?"

"Yes."

She hesitated, not knowing what to say, or how to say it. A mixture of emotions seethed inside her; one part of her wanted to reach out, hold him, and tell him that she loved him, while another wanted only to turn and walk away. "I'm sorry."

"Sorry for what?" he asked, a tiny ray of hope ghosting through his gaze.

She hesitated before answering. Then she said softly, "I'm sorry that we didn't find your brother."

He shrugged her answer off. "Yeah, me too." He hadn't really expected anything more in her words, but that didn't stop him from wanting it.

They stood there for another moment in awkward silence. Finally, Sarah stepped over to him, kissed him on the cheek, then entered the building. He watched her go all the way across the lobby and into the elevator. She never looked back. He stood there alone, in the cold and darkness, with his eyes glistening and his heart broken. The woman he loved was in love with another man; and what made it unbearable was that the man was his brother, whom he, too, loved and had lost so long ago.

THE SPEAKER HAD NOT ONLY BROKEN the rules about going onto the roof of a Federal building, a building in Washington no less, but he had also lied to Murray. Not a malicious lie, just a simple one, because they hadn't gone out onto the roof for just a few minutes. They had been out there for over an hour, during which time they had sat on two lawn chairs that the Speaker had "appropriated" several years earlier at a Fourth of July concert on the Mall.

"God, it's beautiful up here," said Mary Lou.

"Yes, it is," he answered, equally lost in space. "When there's no moon, like tonight, you can see forever, despite the fact that we are in the heart of a metropolis."

"I suppose that's because we don't have the skyscrapers of most big cities," she said.

"Exactly."

Her eyes were wide with wonder as she scanned the sky. "Do you think Abraham Lincoln ever used to go up on the roof of the White House and stare at the sky?"

"I don't know, but one thing I do know is that if he did, it would have looked exactly the same way it does tonight, with a little bit less ground glow, of course."

She marveled at the thought. "I hadn't thought about that, but you're right. As much as our nation has grown and changed, the night sky has been a constant. Up there somewhere, looking down on us and frowning right now is the face of God."

The Speaker nodded solemnly. "Had I but served my God with half the zeal I served my king, he would not in mine age have left me naked to mine enemies," whispered the Speaker with a certain palpable sadness in his voice.

Pritchard looked over at the Speaker and said quietly, "King Henry the Eighth."

He flashed a big smile her way and said, "Yes. That's right. Are you a Shakespeare fan?"

"Yes. I majored in English Lit."

He looked back up at the sky and said wistfully, "In my case, the king I have served has been this city, and all its kings and courtiers and jesters, while I have neglected my family, and through them, my God."

She kept staring at him and said, "You're wrong, Jeremiah. As far as *you* are concerned, a more appropriate quote from that play is, 'He was a scholar, and a ripe and good one; Exceeding wise, fair-spoken, and persuading; Lofty and sour to them that loved him not; But, to those men that sought him sweet as summer.'"

He looked back at her, and with one eyebrow raised in mock seductiveness, he said, "I'm not sure we can stay up here together if you're going to describe me in terms of being ripe and sweet, my dear."

631

They both laughed. It was a good laugh, from deep within. A laugh without the cagey falseness that accompanies most titters around that city; a laugh that at least for an instant served to push back the darkness.

Finally, after the last little giggle had slipped away from them into space, Pritchard sat up and said, "Well, Mr. Speaker, as much as I have enjoyed this time together under God's great sky, I had better get back to the White House. The President is holding an emergency Cabinet meeting tonight."

The Speaker looked at his watch, but no matter how hard he squinted at it, nor how many times he tapped it, he couldn't make out the time. "Kathleen got this for me last Christmas. It's supposed to light up in the dark and be waterproof down to three hundred feet of pressure. Personally, I'd prefer it if they would just make the damn numbers bigger."

She chuckled again and said, "It's ten thirty."

"The President is holding a Cabinet meeting this late?"

"Yes. He often holds Cabinet meetings late at night. Sometimes they last until two or three in the morning. I don't know when he ever sleeps."

"Poor lonely man."

Pritchard's expression changed. There was something very sad about the notion of a man who could have anything he wanted being so alone. But she knew that the Speaker was right. "Well, lonely or not, I must be off. At least tonight he has a good reason. We have to go over the content of the speech he plans to give to the nation tomorrow night."

"Do you need me to explain to him that I kept you?" the Speaker asked as they both got up.

"No, that won't be necessary. But thank-you, anyway."

They walked back over to the door and stepped through it. Murray and the other agents were still standing there. They greeted the Speaker and the Attorney General with courteous nods and then followed them back down the stairs.

As they reached the corridor that led to the Speaker's office, Kincaid looked at Pritchard with the loving concern of a father and asked, "It's none of my business, Mary Lou, but is everything all right with you and the President? I mean—"

She interrupted, "I know what you mean, Jeremiah. And it is very much your business. I made it so that night when you saved me from myself. Since then, his behavior has been strictly professional." She didn't bother to tell the Speaker about the President's recent expression of love. It would serve no purpose. He had not tried to seduce her again, and that was enough.

"Good," he said, visibly relieved.

For just an instant, her expression clouded over. She forced herself to think of something else. But it was too late; the Speaker noticed, and he called her on it. "What is it, Mary Lou? I can tell by your expression that something is bothering you."

They came to his office and entered. As they passed though the outer office, George Ross greeted them. The Attorney General then followed Kincaid into his office, where he motioned for her to sit down. He closed the door and did the same.

She hesitated, "I really shouldn't involve you in this, Jeremiah."

"It's all right. You can tell me. And then, if you have to, you can kill me," he added with a grin.

The humor broke the tension. With a pained smile, she said, "You're very perceptive, as usual. I am having trouble in the White House, but it isn't with the President. It's with his chief of staff."

"Maddun Gordon," said the Speaker with narrowing eyes.

"Yes."

"I've never trusted him, and it troubles me greatly to know that someone like him is ten steps away from the seat of power."

"Your distrust is well-placed." She glanced down at her watch and said, "I still have a few more minutes."

"Go on," he said.

She took a deep breath and then started talking, slowly at first, as she recounted Gordon's association with a former government assassin by the name of Stefan Chadrian. She described the death of the FBI agent in Potomac Park and the suspected role Gordon might have played in the shootings on the East Lawn of the White House; and then finally, she told him about the incident from the night before at Camp David. After she finished, she appeared exhausted. Not the physical kind of exhaustion, but the more wearing, deeply draining, and mental kind.

He thought about everything she had said for a few minutes, and then he said softly but firmly, "You keep doing what the people are paying you to do, Mary Lou. Follow the leads, look for any and every bit of evidence that you can get on him. We need to isolate the cancer cells that infect the West Wing and then cut them out cleanly and permanently. In the meantime, with your approval, I will take steps to ensure that he never threatens you again."

The seriousness of his tone startled her. She didn't answer.

Sensing this, he said, "Don't worry, Madam Attorney General, I won't do anything that will jeopardize either my position or our friendship. Trust me."

She smiled at him and said, "I'd trust you with my life, Mr. Speaker."

He looked back at her with love in his eyes. Not the kind of love that is based on a physical attraction, like that of the President, but the kind of love that is based on the deep bond a man has for someone he wants and needs to protect, like a wife or a daughter, or even the people of an entire country.

They both stood up. Just before she turned to leave, she stepped over and kissed him lightly on the cheek.

He smiled and said, "It's great to be ripe and sweet."

She laughed and left.

After she was gone, George Ross entered the room.

"George, call Maddun Gordon. Tell him I want to meet with him first thing tomorrow. Alone."

Ross looked puzzled, "Yes, sir. What shall I tell him is the subject?"

The Speaker thought about it for a moment and said, "Tell him that it is a matter of life and death."

The tone in his voice was one that Ross understood well. It was one the Speaker used whenever he wielded his enormous political clout. Ross would have probed further, but it was obvious that it was a personal matter. And on matters of that nature, the Speaker could be more a tyrant than a king. Unbeknownst to the Speaker, this same trait would soon be called upon to save another lady-in-distress, and her name was Liberty.

66

Washington, D.C.

There were many days in 1861 which could be considered the first day of the First Civil War, including January 2nd, when South Carolina, which had become the first state to secede from the Union several weeks earlier, seized Fort Johnson in Charleston harbor; or April 14th, when they bombarded Fort Sumter; or May 18th, when the Union launched its first offensive against rebel forces at Sewell's Point, Virginia; and of course July 21st, when the First Battle of Bull Run showed a disbelieving and totally unprepared public the horror that lurks a heartbeat away from the glory that is war.

Similarly, there were many days and many events that history would record as pivotal to the start of hostilities in the Second Civil War, but none perhaps so notable and so dismal as July 3rd, the day that Idaho would secede from the Union. It dawned damp and dark in the nation's capital, as an unusually cold air mass rolled in off the North Atlantic during the early hours of the morning and formed a thick fog bank over the warm, shallow waters of the Chesapeake. Gradually, it drifted up the Potomac River, and settled itself squarely over the Tidal Basin, where it would stubbornly lay siege to the city until it was chased away by the searing shafts of a D.C. summer sun, but not before the storm clouds of war had formed on the western horizon.

Early on that ominous morning, there were few pedestrians and even fewer cars evident in Potomac Park, save for two of the long, black variety. Washington has more stretch limousines per capita than any other city in America or in the world, for that matter. And what makes this fact so ironic is that virtually none of the city's permanent residents have ever been inside one, except, of course, for the uniformed few who drive them. However, the sleek, black hulls of these four-wheeled U-boats were so common in the streets of the city, that the over-priced and over-built German touring sedans, which the elite of cities like New York and Los Angeles so desperately craved, seemed, at least in that town, to be lesser ships on the crowded vehicular sea.

The Speaker of the House's limousine rolled to a stop within shouting distance of the Roosevelt Memorial. The heavy vehicle had barely stopped moving when another, just like it, approached from the opposite direction and pulled up nose to nose with it; and their headlights beamed directly into each other's halogen lenses, creating an eerie, blue glow in the swirling morning mist. For a moment both limos sat there quietly, with only the tinny creaking of their cooling exhaust pipes to break the silence. Finally, the driver of the Speaker's car got out and opened the back door. The first man out was William Murray, who scanned the surroundings before turning and nodding to the Speaker, who then unfolded his tall frame out of the back seat. Another agent got out of the front passenger's seat, and the two of them took defensive positions to the side and slightly behind the Speaker. It was clear that they were not pleased with either the location or the conditions.

After a pause that was long on attitude and short on courtesy, the driver of the other limo got out and opened the back door, out of which stepped Maddun Gordon. As his eyes fell upon the Speaker, he started to say something, but a low-flying jet on its final approach to Reagan Airport drowned out his words. By the time the plane had passed, the Speaker had closed the gap between them and seized the verbal initiative.

"Good morning, Mr. Gordon," said the Speaker, with as much warmth as the cold, damp morning air. "Thank-you for coming."

"Can we dispense with the formalities and get to the reason why you called me out here? I've got a hell of a lot of work to do before those cowboys and tractor jockeys in Idaho vote."

"You don't have much faith in the democratic process, Mr. Gordon, do you?"

"Quite the contrary, Mr. Speaker. I have every faith that this President who was elected by a majority of the people—twice I might add—will deal with these traitors in exactly the way that the democratic process proscribes."

"Which is?"

"Which is that he will listen to their shrill speeches and tolerate this charade for just so long, and then he will wield the full power of his office to crush the little shits and bring potatoland back into the Federal fold."

"You've never been elected to any office, have you?"

Gordon eyed the older man cautiously. "No."

"But you were considering running for Congress in California before President Webster asked you to run his first Presidential campaign. Isn't that right?"

Gordon was surprised the Speaker knew about that. His decision to abandon his plans to enter the congressional race in his home district eight years earlier had barely received any national attention, despite his high profile in California power circles. "Yes. That's true. But that was before I realized that being in Congress was nothing but a fool's game for hypocrites and narcissists." He smiled slyly and added, "Present company excepted, of course."

The Speaker sighed and then added softly, "He jests at scars who never felt a wound."

"I beg your pardon?" said Gordon.

"Nothing. Just a little bit of Shakespeare in the park," mused Kincaid.

Gordon didn't get it.

"Let's walk, shall we?" replied the Speaker. He doubted that Gordon knew much Shakespeare, and he certainly was not the type who would have ever read Romeo and Juliet.

The two men headed down the walk toward the Roosevelt Memorial, which loomed like a gray shadow in the fog. The Speaker's Secret Service protection followed at a discreet, but actionable distance.

Gordon took note of the agents. "Pity that you have to be saddled with armed protection."

The Speaker looked over at Gordon and said, "I don't mind, really. It's less of an inconvenience than being shot, wouldn't you agree?"

"I suppose," Gordon shrugged. "Have you recovered from that unfortunate incident?"

"Completely."

"Do the D.C. police have any idea who your assailant was or why he shot you?"

"They know his name but nothing else."

"I'm not surprised," Gordon said without any trace of the relief he felt.

They walked a short distance, and then the Speaker began to talk. "You know, when my daughter, Joanna, was a senior at Simmons college in Boston, there was a Harvard student who became infatuated with her. The feeling wasn't mutual, and my daughter politely tried to deflect his amorous attention."

"Mr. Speaker. I really don't have time for a replay of *Love Story*."

"I said my daughter went to Simmons, not Radcliff."

Gordon shook his head in frustration but kept in stride.

"Despite her concerted efforts, his words and actions became increasingly hostile, until finally, one day, he stepped over the line." The Speaker stopped and faced Gordon. Whether or not Gordon realized it, they now stood at approximately the same spot where the FBI agent had been murdered.

"What did he do?" asked the chief of staff in a tone that had more than a hint of libido.

Kincaid stared knowingly at the other man. "He threatened her and put his hand on her breast. Unfortunately, there were no witnesses to the incident, but he left no doubt in my daughter's mind that he intended to harm her if she didn't acquiesce to his sexual overtures." The Speaker shook his head. "You know, Maddun, despite the power and perquisites of my position as a United States congressman, the police were helpless to do anything." The Speaker's intentional switching to Gordon's Christian name was a deceptively innocent backdrop to the increasingly harsh tone of his voice and coldness of his manner.

Gordon feigned concern and said, "Mr. Speaker, I'm sorry that your daughter had to go through that experience, but judging from the fact that she is alive and well today, she obviously survived it. And quite frankly, I have no idea why you are telling this to me."

The Speaker's eyes narrowed. "She survived it because the man's increasingly threatening behavior finally forced me to take action. Action of which I am less than proud."

The chief of staff's curiosity now aroused. "If you are going to confess something to me, Mr. Speaker, I recommend that you have your attorney present." He tossed off a perfunctory laugh.

The Speaker didn't smile. "No. I didn't do anything to the man. I simply made a call to a friend of mine. I won't tell you his real name but his enemies know him as Jimmy D., and the 'D' stands for doom—if you catch my drift. Jimmy D. is a seafood trader from Boston and a business associate of my father-in-law. He also happens to be the godfather of my wife, Kathleen. Ironically, his office is located down by the harbor on Northern Boulevard right above the Gloucesterman restaurant where you dined recently."

"Yeah. I was there. So what?" Gordon loved seafood, and he had eaten there with the President and the senior senator from Massachusetts during their last visit to Boston, only a few months earlier. It was beginning to trouble Gordon that the Speaker seemed to know so much about his background and activities. Moreover, at first he had thought the Speaker's choice of a location for the morning's meeting was purely coincidental with his meeting six months earlier with Chadrian, but now he wasn't so sure.

The Speaker continued, "Anyway, after my telcom call to Jimmy D., this young man suddenly found himself on a fishing boat one morning that took him out beyond the Boston Light. And on that ride, he was placed inside a large wire-mesh cage, sort of like a giant lobster pot. The cage was then lowered over the side until the young man's face was barely above the waves. Occasionally, a wave would catch him full in the face, choking him and making him struggle and claw his way up higher in the cage. Now, he was naturally a little bit uncomfortable with this fish-eye view of the world, and over his screams, Jimmy D. shouted to him that if he ever went within a mile of Joanna again, or if he did anything even to upset her, much less harm her, then he would be brought back out to sea, placed in that same cage, and dropped over the side in fifty fathoms of cold, black water to the rocky bottom, where the lobsters would feed on his rotting corpse." Then with a gaze that drilled right through Gordon's head, he added, "Mr. Gordon, I want you to know that I care about Mary Lou Pritchard as if she was my daughter."

Gordon's face flushed bright red, the way it always did when he was on the verge of a blow-up. But this time, he managed to control his rage, and he said in a stiff monotone, "Mr. Speaker, are you threatening me?"

The Speaker didn't bat an eyelash. "Oh it's much more than a threat, Mr. Gordon. It's a promise. From this point on, your behavior toward the Attorney General had better be wholly in keeping with the level of respect and professional courtesy that her position demands. And lest there be any doubt in your mind whatsoever, should you in either word or deed ever deviate from this, for even an instant, I will ask my friend Jimmy D. to take you out to sea and feed your sorry body to the lobsters." He paused for effect. "Do I make myself clear?"

The President's chief of staff stood there in the fog trying to gauge the risk. "You wouldn't dare."

The Speaker stepped closer to Gordon, intruding on his personal space; he then looked him dead in the eyes and said clearly and with unmistakable intent, "Try me."

Gordon grew stone-cold silent. Then very slowly, he replied, "Very well. Have it your way."

"Excellent. Now why don't we get back to doing what the people pay us to do?" The Speaker took a step in the direction from which they had come.

But Gordon didn't move. "I want to get something in return."

The Speaker stopped and looked back at Gordon. "You will. It's called breathing."

Gordon studied Kincaid's face carefully, as if trying to decide exactly how to word what he was about to say. "No, Mr. Speaker. I want something else, because if I don't get it, then death will be a welcome relief."

"I'm listening."

"I want Pritchard to close the investigation of my purported ties to a certain former CIA paramilitary operative, who may or may not have been involved with the killing of the FBI agent on this very spot."

The Speaker held his response long enough for the other man to twist in the breeze that was building off the river, and then very deliberately, he replied, "Mr. Gordon, if you are innocent, then you have nothing to fear from the Department of Justice." He paused and added, "Are you? Innocent, that is?"

Gordon remained expressionless. "Of course, I am. But I doubt that Pritchard will believe me, and I want some reassurance that she will back off."

"Sorry, I don't make deals. You'll have to take that up with the devil." The Speaker turned and headed back toward his limousine. As he passed his Secret Service detail, he looked back at Gordon and shouted, "Be sure to give my best regards to the President, will you?"

Gordon didn't reply.

Then Kincaid and his Secret Service agents disappeared into the mist.

SARAH McGILL was late, as usual, and by the time she reached the Washington studios of GNBC, the fog had lifted, and it was a perfectly beautiful summer day in the nation's capital. However, her mood matched the gloomy political climate rather than the weather. With the exception of the day that she had helped Jake and his father try to find T.J., they hadn't seen each other since he stormed out of her apartment, and her heart was heavy with conflicting emotions. She knew that Jake was in love with her, and part of her wanted to love him in return, but she could not, because there was another part of her that wanted someone else; someone who didn't want her. That person was, of course, Jake's younger brother, and the turmoil inside her was tearing her apart.

"Good afternoon, Sarah. Nice of you to join us," said Lange teasingly. But she didn't smile.

"It's still morning," said a confused Tanner Spence as he joined them, glancing up at a wall clock.

"Are you okay, Sarah?" asked Lange.

"I'm fine," she replied curtly, clearly signaling him that she did not want to pursue the matter.

He shrugged and looked at Tanner. "Don't you ever report for work at DHS?"

"My boss lets me keep my own hours," said Spence with a mischievous smile.

"And we wonder where our tax dollars go," said Lange. "However, unlike the Federal Government, here at GNBC we work for our salaries." He looked back at Sarah, "Speaking of which, Ms. McGill, I think it's time for you to get over to the White House and cover their reaction to the vote in Idaho and the President's address to the nation tonight."

"I'm going," said McGill. "See you two later." She started to leave.

"Don't forget we've got you on the network feed tonight right after the President's speech, so make sure you get the story," added Lange.

"Have I ever let you down?"

"No."

"Well then," she said and then walked out the door.

"This would be a very bad time to start!" he shouted feebly after her.

"Boy, you really told her," said Spence.

Lange scowled and said, "Now as for you, don't you think you'd better get back to the DHS before someone realizes that they pay you for never being there?"

"Yes, sir," Spence replied. As he turned to go, his expression darkened. He looked at the older man and said, "All kidding aside, do you really think they are going to go through with it?"

"I don't know, Tanner. But I can tell you this: if they do, the President will have no choice but to send in the tanks."

"But I thought Sarah said the President was going to try to reach out to them one more time for a peaceful resolution, tonight, in his address to the nation."

"That's the official White House position, but the cynic inside me tells me that it is simply a stalling tactic to buy them more time to prepare for military action against Idaho."

Spence thought about it for a moment and then said, "I just can't imagine Americans shooting Americans."

"It happens every day."

"You know what I meant. On a battlefield. Not after all we've been though during the past few years."

Lange nodded sadly, "Yes, son. I know. What terrorists were unable to do, we will do to ourselves."

The two men stood there in silence.

Finally, Lange put his hand on Spence's shoulders and said, "Let's take it one day at a time."

"Yes, sir. But somehow, I have a feeling that this will be a very long day."

IT WAS AFTER NOON when President Alex Webster walked at a brisk pace under the portico outside the Oval Office, and stepped smartly through the door being held open by one of his Secret Service agents. Ever since the equivocal victory in the war on terrorism several years earlier, there had been a constant war of wills between the Secret Service and the President's staff regarding his accessibility and visibility to the public. His key aides reasoned that this was a man for whom the highest number of Americans in history had voted, and they deserved to be able to see him in public, at least occasionally. But the on-going threat of assassination shifted the argument in favor of extreme caution, an outcome made all the more certain following the incident at Walter Reed Army hospital.

Normally, Webster would have been behind his desk in the Oval Office by 7:00 a.m. But on that day, he had spent the entire morning alone in his private quarters working on his speech. As Webster entered, Maddun Gordon, Patrick Fitzgerald, and the Vice President all greeted him. "Good morning, Mr. President," Fitzgerald said.

"What the hell is so good about it?" snapped Webster.

"Nothing, sir," replied Fitzgerald.

The Vice President smiled benevolently at Fitzgerald. "Well, let's hope it will be a better day than yesterday, and not quite as good as tomorrow," said Knox.

"Hope is for losers, Richard. There's only one thing that will make this a good day, which is for the people of Idaho to overthrow the madman in the state house. But I don't think that's going to happen, now, do you?" The Vice President shook his head and gave a barely perceptible shrug.

Webster glanced at his chief of staff. "Do you have the vote projections?"

"Yes, Mr. President," he replied, handing him a slim folder.

The President quickly opened it and scanned down the first page, then the next one, and the next. "Damn it!" he exclaimed.

"Yes, sir. The bastard might actually pull this off," said Gordon. "That is, unless the pork we offered to the state Democratic Party prevails."

The President looked up from the folder. "No. Idaho is lost. Now we have to turn our attention to the other six states." He looked at Fitzgerald. "What do we know?"

His national security adviser shook his head. "It's not good, Mr. President. None of the G7 governors have the courage to do this unilaterally. But if Morrissey gets Idaho to secede, we think at least four of them will follow."

"Who?" asked the President.

"Wyoming, Montana, Utah, and Arizona for sure. Possibly New Mexico. For now, the only member of that group who is leaning our way is McCabe of Colorado."

"Why?" asked Knox.

"Because McCabe's ego is even bigger than Morrissey's, if that's possible," replied Fitzgerald.

"What time's the vote?" asked Webster.

"At 1:00 p.m. our time, Mr. President, thirty minutes from now," answered Fitzgerald.

"Will you watch the vote in here, Mr. President?" asked Gordon.

"No," was the President's terse reply.

"Where do you want to watch it, sir?" asked Gordon.

"I'm not going to watch it anywhere."

The three other men in the room looked surprised.

"May I ask why not, sir?" asked Fitzgerald.

"Because I am the President of the United States of America, and I don't intend to watch a man with cow shit on his boots trample the flag." He paused and added, "I want to rehearse my speech once more." The President paused again, but no one said a word. Then he looked at Gordon. "I do not want to be disturbed this afternoon. Understood?"

"Yes, Mr. President," replied Gordon dutifully, but even he was startled by this request. For a President to spend such a momentous occasion alone was unusual, to say the least. And in particular, for this President to now turn his back on those who sought to provide counsel was unsettling.

Webster looked at Fitzgerald. "Are we all set for tonight?"

"Yes, sir, the networks will carry your speech live at 9:00 p.m. Eastern."

"Good. Now, gentlemen, I would like a moment alone with Maddun."

"Of course, Mr. President," replied Fitzgerald, and he and the Vice President left the Oval Office.

Webster waited until they closed the door behind them, and then he asked Gordon, "What was that about this morning?"

"What was what about, Mr. President?"

The President frowned and said, "Don't make me ask you again."

The chief of staff swallowed hard and lowered his head slightly. "It was nothing, sir. The Speaker wanted to say he was sorry that he had been unable to broker a last-minute deal through his son."

The President stared at his chief of staff. He suspected he was lying, because despite the major differences of opinion that he had with the Speaker, he felt that there was a bond, of sorts, between them. One that had been forged in their meeting weeks earlier, and one that would certainly have been conducive to the Speaker calling him directly. Moreover, Mary Lou Pritchard had already done a thorough job debriefing the President following her meeting with Kincaid, a fact that Gordon was unaware of, because the President had not invited Gordon to the meeting at the Attorney General's request. But then again, Webster didn't care. Whatever game his chief of staff was playing, it was inconsequential now in light of what was happening to the nation. Ever since he had decided not to have Gordon arrested for his role in the shootings on the East Lawn, the conspiracy meter had been steadily ticking away right there in the Oval Office, like some apocalyptic metronome, which, once started, could never be stopped. And its ticking grew louder and louder with each passing minute. Deep inside, the President knew that eventually, someone else besides he and Gordon would hear it.

Ironically, the President's fall from the moral high ground had been the direct result of his obsessive desire to impose his own sense of morality upon the nation, at least as far as it applied to guns. Up until his decision to look the other way regarding the shootings on the White House lawn, the President's moral failings had consisted exclusively of acts banned by God rather than by man: lust, lechery, and adultery, all apparently mere pimples on the face of morality, judging by the public's seemingly boundless supply of forgiveness. Now, however, the pimples had become a melanoma, wrapping its mottled, black tentacles of death around the cover-up of murder by gun.

In perhaps the greatest irony of all, the President was now a prisoner of his own making, trapped by his inability to cut out the cancer that was growing in his White House, for fear that by winning the battle against the disease that threatened to destroy his presidency, he would lose the war against that which threatened to destroy the body of the nation. It was a no-win situation. And Webster knew it. Faced with this Draconian choice, he chose to act in what he believed was the country's best interests. Not only did he trust that this would ensure a victory against the evil of guns, but in the filtered light of history, he hoped his acts would be seen as understandable, and possibly even noble, even if clearly illegal.

SARAH McGILL could feel the tension in the West Wing as she entered the press room. Everywhere she looked, she could see glum faces and anxious glances. Any organization formed for any purpose beyond its own existence draws heavily upon its leader not only for vision but for tone and manner. The White House was no exception. *As goes the President, so goes the White House*, she thought, and this old adage was never more true than now, in the second term of President Alex Webster's presidency, as both he and the entire nation faced their most serious domestic challenge since the Civil War—the first one, but now not likely to be the last.

"Hey, Sarah," said a reporter from another network, as she entered the room and took her place near the front in one of the seats reserved for reporters with special privileges.

"Hi." Then she rubbed her arms through her jacket and said, "It's freezing in here." She could feel her nipples hardening, and she was glad she had worn a jacket. She hated it when that happened to her in the silk blouses that she liked to wear. Her male colleagues never complained.

"Yes. It is a little cold," he responded, trying to be subtle as he glanced at her chest.

She noticed and ignored it. She didn't mind when men stared at her figure. But she was never a tease, either. "They must have the air conditioning cranked way up again." Several of McGill's colleagues regularly complained to Jane Kimberly, the White House press secretary, that they kept the room too cold. In the summer, that is. In the winter, they had exactly the opposite complaint.

"It's frigid. And not just the temperature," he said, motioning with his head toward the assistant press secretary, a prim woman with an expression that could freeze fire.

McGill nodded, "The vote's got them all a little jumpy."

"I heard that the President has refused to watch it," said the other reporter.

"He doesn't have to. He's the President. He has people who will watch it for him."

"Yeah, he has someone to do everything for him, including taking a bullet. The only thing he has to do alone is take the heat."

"And the heat is always on in the Oval Office," added McGill.

Her colleagues nodded and wondered how they could steal the line without her noticing.

At that moment, Jane Kimberly entered the room, and everyone quieted down. "Ladies and gentlemen. If you could please take your seats. We're going to pipe in the feed from Boise, so that you can all watch the vote together." She glanced at one of the wall clocks in the room and then said, "The vote is expected to take place in ten minutes. Following the vote, I will return with the White House's official position. Are there any questions at this point?" Several hands shot up. She motioned with her head to the most senior reporter, Mrs. Moriarity, "Yes, Nancy?"

"We've heard that the President doesn't intend to watch the vote. Would you care to comment on this?" As usual, Moriarity spoke in the third person. Some were amused by it. Others just found it pompous.

"Nancy, you know better than anybody else in this room how hectic the President's daily schedule is, especially today, as he prepares for his address to the nation tonight."

It was obvious that Nancy wasn't satisfied with the answer. "We understand how busy the President is, but quite frankly, we find it difficult to believe that there could be anything more important to the President on this day than a vote which threatens to destroy the Union."

The room fell silent. After six years in the West Wing, Jane Kimberly was a seasoned veteran of the press room, and she could give and take it with the best of them. But one thing that she didn't appreciate was to be lectured to. Many in the room expected Jane to ignore Nancy's position of privilege and let her have it right between her eyes. But she didn't. Instead she just stood there, saying nothing. And her silence spoke far louder than any words could have. Finally, Kimberly said, "I have no further comment on that subject. Now, if you will excuse me." She motioned with her head to her assistant, who switched on the BTC monitors positioned at several strategic points around the room. Instantly the legislative chamber in the Idaho state house filled the screen.

TWO THOUSAND MILES separate Washington, D.C., and Boise, Idaho. A distance that once took more than six months to cross in a canvas-covered wagon pulled by a team of oxen. Months filled with privation, toil, and mortal danger. It was a trip that now Air Force One could make in less four hours. Four hours sealed safely inside a cylinder of shiny metal, surrounded by deep pile carpeting, rich leather, and hand-rubbed walnut. Four hours of being protected, pampered, and presented with literally any piece of information ever known to man.

It was a trip that President Alex Webster had never made during his five and a half years in office, nor once during the two years of campaigning before that. But even had he done so, he would have never known the people, places, and differing perspectives that populated each one of those two thousand miles. It was the price of progress, and it was a heavy one indeed, for to become a President of all the people, time and distance necessitated that the President could only meet with some of the people, and could never get to really know any of the people. As such, to most of those whom he governed, he was nothing more than an electronic image, made up of a million pixels on a BTC screen, or a tiny bit of flesh, tucked deep within a silver cylinder seven miles overhead and a million miles away.

Now as history slipped silently on padded feet into the Idaho State House and took its place at the back of the room to watch along with mortal men the beginning of the end of the American play, the only way that Alex Webster might have avoided that moment and saved the Union would have been to have taken that ancient oxen team and wagon and walked every mile between D.C. and Boise; for in that walk, he might have realized that the danger from which he so desperately sought to protect the nation was in fact one of his own creation.

GOVERNOR EDWARD MORRISSEY stood at the front of the room, which was filled to overflowing. It was not normal procedure that the governor would lead the process of taking a vote on the House floor, but it was to be no ordinary vote, and Morrissey was no ordinary governor. He had single-handedly outmaneuvered the President of the United States, the United States Congress, and his detractors, who were legion. And now, there he stood, on the verge of becoming only the second governor in history to cast the first vote for the dissolution of the Republic.

"Honorable members, we will now take a voice vote on Joint Resolution 76, a mooting for the secession of the State of Idaho from the United States of America." A roar went up in the chamber, leaving no doubt in anyone's mind, either among those present, or among the millions watching across the nation, as to what the outcome would be. The governor waited until the noise began to subside, and then he smacked the gavel down sharply. "As many as are in favor, say Aye."

Instantly, all but a few of the state's representatives jumped to their feet and shouted Aye in unison. Again cheers and whistles broke out, not only on the chamber floor but in the visitor's galleries.

The governor pounded the gavel several times and motioned with his other hand for the floor to quiet down. He was literally seconds away from achieving his greatest glory and ironically, his fanatical supporters wouldn't quiet down long enough for him to finish the vote and declare victory. Again and again he pounded, until finally, the audience began to quiet down.

"As many as are opposed, say Nay.

A hush fell upon the room. It was a hush that could be heard all the way across the universe.

Then slowly, a small and obviously brave group of state legislators raised their hands and said Nay. As they did, some in the visitor's gallery began to boo, but they were quickly silenced by their peers who, like the governor, wanted to get to the climax.

IN A DISCOUNT DEPARTMENT store in Boston, Massachusetts, hundreds of women put down the towels, dresses, and blouses, and they watched the video monitors in the nearby appliance department.

IN TIMES SQUARE, New York, normally aloof New Yorkers stopped dead in their tracks and stared silently up at the giant video screen on the side of the GNBC building.

IN THE STREETS OF ATLANTA, Georgia, sanitation workers huddled around a co-worker, who held a small BTC in his palm and squinted at the tiny screen.

IN A RUN-DOWN CLUB HOUSE on a public golf course in Tampa, Florida, elderly men dressed in polyester pants and matching shirts put their glory days on hold and fixed their stares on the small video monitor over the bar.

IN OMAHA, Nebraska, in the classroom that was Meagan Brooks' home room, her former classmates and her teacher watched a wall-mounted video monitor in somber silence, as her pretty face smiled at them from a black-ribbon-draped photograph on the wall.

IN A PRIVATE MEN'S CLUB in Dallas, Texas, masters of the universe put down their martinis and scrutinized a large plasma screen built into the cherry paneling in a room that smelled of fine cigars and old leather.

IN A PARKING LOT in Newport, California, a woman sitting in her Jaguar turned up the radio, and sat silently, staring at the dial.

IN A COFFEE SHOP in Seattle, Washington, yuppies watched any one of ten video monitors around the room and gripped their designer coffee cups a little tighter.

IN SOUTH DAKOTA, at the Mt. Rushmore National Memorial, a Park Service maintenance worker perched precariously on the forehead of George Washington's likeness and pressed his small transistor radio to his ear, trying to hear the words over the sound of distant thunder from an approaching storm.

IN THE WHITE HOUSE press room, Sarah McGill whispered to herself, "My God, these people have no idea what they are doing."

FINALLY, IN BOISE, Idaho, Governor Edward Morrissey looked around the room and said with a clear and purposeful voice, "The Ayes have it." Then he took a deep breath, sucked in his stomach, puffed out his chest, looked out across the assembly with a forced air of self-importance, and uttered the words that would reverberate around the world at the speed of light on the Internet; every television station, radio station, and short-wave radio band; and even high above the earth inside the space station, where American and Chinese astronauts sat in awkward silence beside their Russian colleagues. "The Union now subsisting between Idaho and the United States of America," he paused, and millions of hearts skipped a beat, "is hereby dissolved!" He slammed the gavel down, sealing the finality of what they had just done. He hit it so hard that the gavel broke, and the head of it tumbled down across the podium and onto the chamber floor. But no one noticed. Pandemonium had taken over.

BACK ON MT. RUSHMORE, the first few drops of the sudden thunderstorm began to patter against the dry stone faces of the Presidents. As the storm gained in volume and momentum, the beads of water became droplets, and the droplets became puddles, and soon, one of them spilled down across the cheek of George Washington, followed by another, and another. And before long, rivulets of water slipped down over the cheeks of the other three Presidents, looking for all the world like giant tears. It would have been a poignant television moment for all those who had just watched the Governor of Idaho take the first step in the dissolution of a nation. But there was no one there to see it. The Park Service maintenance worker had already scrambled back up to safety, and far below, where broken and crumbled pieces of granite bore silent testimony to the once proud and unblemished face of a mountain, all the tourists had run for cover. All that remained was the stone and the tears and the silence. A silence that would soon deafen the world.

AT EXACTLY 9:00 P.M. Eastern Daylight Savings time, the President of the United States of America sat down behind the Theodore Roosevelt desk in the Oval office and prepared to speak to a stunned nation. Standing off-camera were Maddun Gordon and Patrick Fitzgerald. Slowly, the director counted down. Then he pointed at the President and nodded his head.

President Alex Webster took a deep breath, looked directly into the camera, and began speaking. What followed would be long discussed and parsed ad nauseum in political science and American history classes for decades to come. For not since Abraham Lincoln had stood tall and proud in the White House had any President ever faced the imminent destruction of the Republic. Other Presidents since Lincoln had certainly had to deal with war, but it had always been a war on distant soil. Even WWT, the World War on Terrorism, had quickly shifted offshore after the initial savage attacks on the American Homeland. In none of the wars since the first Civil War had Americans ever intentionally killed Americans on the field of battle.

As he began to speak, everyone on his staff, including Maddun Gordon, expected the President to reach out to a torn and divided nation to try to calm the savage breast that had been beat upon earlier that day by Governor Morrissey; to tame the wild beast that now paced to and fro in the dark pine forests of Idaho; and to rise above the fray and lead the people, all the people, back from the edge of the abyss. It was President Alexander Webster's moment in the sun, a golden opportunity to carve out an enduring legacy of greatness, and his last chance to choose good over evil. But it was not to be. Instead of giving the speech that had been written for him, he allowed his ego to get the better of him, and he began to ad lib. Where the audiences, both near and far, desperately looked for signs of empathy and humanity, they saw only aloofness and unyielding hubris; where they needed to hear words of warmth from the heart, they got only the cold semantics of a distant intellect; and where they sought diplomacy and tact, they were offered only veiled threats and dogma. It was in a word, an unmitigated disaster. The worst possible outcome for a nation teetering on the brink of war, and a clear victory for evil. The greatest irony of all was that Webster had not sought evil. His ego had been an unguided missile, and its target had been his sense of reason. In his blind search for happiness, he had single-handedly destroyed any chance that he had ever had of finding it. And the worst was yet to come.

SARAH McGILL stood on the lawn of the White House in front of her news crew, finishing her summary of the day's events, live before a national television audience. She expertly synthesized the complexity and enormity of the vote that had taken place earlier that afternoon in Idaho, parsing it into digestible pieces that the viewing public had come to expect from her. Then she dispassionately analyzed the President's speech, placing it carefully in context and skillfully unraveling its complexity and import. When she was through, she paused and then began what was for her an act completely out of character. She started to close her piece with an editorial. "Ladies and gentlemen, on this the eve of the celebration of the Declaration of Independence, the Union whose birth we are about to celebrate has been broken in two. No matter what will now follow, great statesmanship or great carnage, nothing we ever say or do will erase this ugly entry in the journal of the American saga. For that, we are a lesser people in a lesser land."

Her cameraman momentarily took his eye off the eyepiece and looked directly at her. Their eyes met, and for the briefest of moments, they simply stared at each other. Then he nodded ever so slightly and looked back through the lens.

The same level of understanding was not present back at the studio. "What the hell is she doing?" said her producer, watching the feed from the White House lawn. Instantly, he was on the telcom to Keene Lange, to whom he repeated the question.

"I don't know," said Lange. "But go with it," he ordered.

"Go where?" asked the producer.

"Wherever she takes it," came the reply.

With a shrug and a nervous cough, he did just that.

Sarah McGill looked straight into the camera lens and spoke with the same degree of poise, presence, and polish that were her trademark. And yet, to inveterate McGill watchers, on that night, in that broadcast, something was unmistakably different. She spoke with a conviction that was palpable, and there was something else—a certain sadness and sense of aloneness that reached out across time and space and touched the human spirit. "Whereas up until this act, we could pretend otherwise, we must now come face to face with the stark reality that we are no longer one nation with a shared sense of purpose and a common set of values. Instead, we have become a land of two unequal opposites, with each side seeing its cause as just; with each side refusing to come at least part way across the no man's land of rhetoric and emotion that now divides us, a gap that grows wider with each passing hour; and most tragic of all, with each side seeking to win, even if it means the country as a whole loses. But make no mistake, ladies and gentlemen, regardless of who is the victor and who is the vanquished, it will be a Pyrrhic victory. There will be no winners—only losers. There will be no right—only varying degrees of wrong. And their will be no joy—only sadness."

The producer lowered his head into his hands. He was certain he was watching a rising star stop in mid-trajectory and self-destruct into broken bits of wreckage, streaking across the night sky. Sarah McGill could not see him, but even if she could, it wouldn't have mattered. The words that poured from her pouting lips at that moment came in a straight line from her heart, and nothing could stop them from coming.

"As Americans, we have always loved a winner. Among those of us for whom winning has only ever been a vicarious experience, we spend our lives seeking to be on the winning side, even if it is only an allegiance in our minds. This obsession with winning has its origins deep in our history. We are a nation that was carved out of a hostile and unforgiving wilderness by people who refused to bow before birthright, by people tired of the terror of tyranny, and more to the point, by people longing to be free. In those early years, as the roots of our society dug deeply into a once savage soil, the foundation of our love affair with winners was firmly laid. Our forefathers quickly learned that either you were strong and survived, or you weren't and you didn't. But time and progress inexorably tamed the frontier, eliminating this harsh bipolarity of survival, making safe the experience of a hunter-gatherer society, whereby the hunters no longer had to kill to eat, and the gatherers no longer had to fear being eaten. As such, we have been lulled into a false sense of security. Our society now rests on a featherbed of mediocrity, where none are threatened, few are challenged, and all are the weaker for it."

Despite himself, the producer was being inexorably drawn into her words and into the passion that underscored them. He was not alone. At that moment, Sarah McGill was being watched by more people on the face of the earth than any single human being in history. And if there was any doubt in anyone's mind about the depth of the torment that America was experiencing, the anguish on McGill's face and the pain in her eyes gave immediate rest to the doubt.

"We are now at a moment in our history, where two rapidly diverging, and equally strident champions have drawn a line in the sand, and we find ourselves desperately trying to decide who among the two will be the winner, and on which side of the line to make our stand. Both the Governor of the State of Idaho and the President of the United States of America have prevailed upon us to hear their call and join their calling. To either rise up in support of guns, or perhaps in what would be the most tragic irony of all, to take up arms against them. And so it is, that today we have taken that first fateful step out onto a playing field, where the time clock will be forever, and where no matter what the score, all will lose, save evil.

"What remains to be seen now is whether others with calmer hearts and clearer minds will step in and put an end to this cursed game before the first man falls. Others who perhaps do not see themselves as winners or heroes, but upon whose shoulders now rests the burden of a nation's salvation. Men and women, as President Kennedy once said, 'to whom much has been given and from whom much is required.' We would be well-served to pray that these men and women will heed this clarion call before it is too late; before the last man standing is knocked down; before the final score is chiseled on the granite slab of history; and before the lights in the national stadium are extinguished forever." She paused and stared directly into the camera. "For GNBC, this is Sarah McGill, at what once was the people's house, in what once was, and perhaps will never be again, the United States of America. Good night, and God bless us all."

GNBC cut away to a commercial, while all across America, and far beyond its borders, hundreds of millions of viewers and listeners sat in stunned silence. It was as if she had been standing on the top of Mount Freedom in far-off Idaho, with a giant megaphone, powered by the infinite energy of the human heart. Sarah McGill had just given the most significant performance of her professional life; her words and the manner in which she had delivered them would echo across the land and around the world for years to come. Many would say that she had put the period at the end of the last sentence in the American story; others would say that it had only been the opening paragraph. Either way, it had devastated her; and as she stood there, in the glow of the lights that cast a pale wash on the front of the White House, she was all alone among the crowd of television crews and correspondents.

Out of the shadows, a tall, dark figure appeared and slowly approached her. For the briefest of moments, she thought that it might be Michael Falconer, coming to save her from the gloom that had overtaken her soul. But it was not Falconer. Instead she saw that it was Jake Kincaid, dressed in his uniform, looking every bit the American hero that he was. But as he stepped up to her, it was not the uniform that caught her attention, nor was it the single red rose he held in his hand; instead, it was the tears that gathered in the corners of his deep, blue eyes, and which, as he drew nearer to her, rolled slowly across his cheeks and tumbled down, disappearing among the ribbons on his chest. He closed the distance separating them, and stopped. Neither said a word, but the emotional tension in the air built a bridge between them more powerful than any words ever could.

Taking a deep breath, he said, "Sarah. I have tried to stop loving you." He glanced down at the rose, then back into her eyes. "But I can't do it."

She saw that he was trembling, and she felt her own knees start to shake. Her heart began to pound so loudly that she wondered if he could hear it.

"You must decide for both of us. Tell me to go, and I will, and I will never come back. Or ask me to stay, and I will, forever and after. Either way. It's your decision."

Suddenly, it was as if they were standing alone on the edge of the universe, a trillion light years away from the rest of mankind, safe from its savagery and sorrow, its willfulness and wantonness, its agony and ecstasy. She reached out and took the rose and stepped close to him. She buried her head on his shoulder, and began to cry softly, and held onto him with a power and purpose that transcended all that had been, or would ever be, in their lives together. Hesitantly, he reached out and comforted her, still unsure what her answer would be. Finally, pulling back, she looked him in the eyes and whispered, "Don't go Jake—I love you."

That was that. From that moment on, they would be together in spirit if not in body. And whether America or Jake and Sarah would survive the coming war was now in the hands of God, and God alone.

About the Author

R. A. R. Clouston, or Bob as he is known to his family and friends, is a Canadian-born American citizen who has been writing all his life, both as a result of his profession and his passion. From his early days as an MBA student in Canada, to his role as the President and CEO of several nationally-known consumer products companies in the United States, his professional life has involved extensive business writing; while in his spare time he has written numerous screenplays and poems. Where Freedom Reigns is his first novel. He and his wife live in Wisconsin. They have four grown children.

Printed in the United States
20995LVS00003B/25-42